DREAMS OF GLORY

DREAMS OF GLORY

FIELDS OF FIRE

R. M. COOK BARELA

To order additional copies of this book, contact:
Xlibris Corporation
1-888-795-4274
www.Xlibris.com
Orders@Xlibris.com
45538

CONTENTS

For
Ronald Allen Moore
And the Marines of India Company

Then I heard the voice of the Lord saying,
"Whom shall I send? And who will go for us?"
And I said, "Here am I. Send me!"
—Isaiah 6:8

First Marine Division
Third Battalion
Seventh Marines
India Company

India Company's Commanding Officers

Captain Clark, Read M.	December 1966-July 19, 1967
Captain Baggette, John C.	July 19-January 19, 1968
Captain J.R. Reeder	January 20-April 14, 1968
Captain Charles S. Rob	April 15-August 17, 1968

First Platoon Lieutenants

Lieutenant Cortazze, Joseph D.	February-July 15, 1967
Lieutenant Wilson, Lawrence E.	July 16-December 16, 1967
Lieutenant Nowicki, Henry K.	December 18, 1967-June 1968

PROLOGUE

On the morning of April 12, 1968, I woke up with a stiff neck. I ached from having slept for the last two hours on the hard Vietnamese ground. During my early morning watch, a heavy fog had covered the jungle's floor and was now being quickly dispersed by the rising sun. An hour later, India Company, Third Battalion Seventh Marines moved out, and I was walking point.

We moved out cautiously through thick overhanging vines and heavy underbrush. Within minutes, we were all drenched in sweat from the hot, humid air. We were patrolling in Dodge City on a search and destroy mission. The area was known for its many booby traps, ambushes, heavy enemy engagements, and fierce firefights. As we moved out, I was looking for trip wires hooked to booby traps and smelling the air for the odor of the enemy. In the thick underbrush, I knew we would smell them before we could see them. Behind me in a long stretched-out column, the rest of the company followed.

My trousers were torn on the first day we entered the thick jungle by sharp needlelike leaves, which cut with razor-sharp edges. We were out on patrol, dirty, hot, hungry, and miserable. It was the beginning of another day in Vietnam.

My eyes began to sting from the sweat that was steadily flowing from my helmet's wide web band. As I reached up to wipe the sweat away, I stepped out of the thick underbrush into a small clearing. At about the same time, forty feet away, an enemy soldier broke into the clearing.

I stopped, and the company stopped behind me. The NVA Communist soldier was looking down. He had been carrying his AK-47 rifle parallel to his right leg. The protruding vines had entangled themselves in his rifle's front sight housing and its bayonet attachment. As he jerked it free, he turned, looked up, and saw me. He froze, and the promise of sudden death filled the air.

All my thoughts, vision, hearing, combat training focused on the enemy soldier before me. An adrenalin surge rushed strength and courage to my fingertips and I tightened the grip on my weapon.

We stood there silent, staring at each other—two, three, five long seconds passed. My mind, completely alert, was taking it all in: the stillness in the air, his eyes opening wide, his mouth opening halfway, his lungs taking in what might be his last breath. His hair wasn't combed. One side stood stiff from having been slept on. Sleep wrinkles were still clearly visible on his light-skinned, unwashed face. His uniform was dirty, tattered, and torn like mine. A thin, limp bedroll was draped over his shoulder, and he wore no hat.

I could see in his face, months of pain and sorrow. He was young, but aged by the turmoil of war. His rifle was pointed downward, mine was at port arms, and we both knew I had the advantage. Behind us, others didn't know what was happening.

In the next few seconds we were going to be engaged in a fierce firefight. There was going to be a lot of spattering of blood, guts, and pain. We would be firing blindly and violently at each other. The bullets, noise, and the clamor of war would soon wreak havoc, death, and destruction. He knew it, and I knew it. The NVA soldier slowly took one small step backward and waited for me to react.

Life, death, and eternity flashed before us. Then I heard his stomach growl, loud and empty. Instead of raising my rifle, I lowered it slightly and also took a small step backward.

Life returned between us with its promises of tomorrow. His eyes grew wide, and he released a deep sigh. He took another small step backward, and I followed suit. Our eyes never moved, never blinked. He turned to his left and quickly disappeared into the tall elephant grass. I turned to my right to get out of the clearing, and behind me the company started moving again.

I never told anyone about that encounter, and to this day, I wonder if that enemy soldier is still alive.

I kept a diary in Vietnam. I did it out of curiosity more than anything else. I jotted down notes on what occurred and listed the names of friends and acquaintances I knew mostly by nicknames. During my tour of duty my world revolved around the lives and actions of the forty-seven men in a Marine infantry platoon. We were young, naïve, and lived on borrowed time.

Over the years the diary sat like a silent soldier awaiting its call to service. It gathered dust, and I never talked to others about my war experiences. I had no desire to see a Vietnam War movie nor had I read any books about the war. Then one day as I began to read a book on the history of the Marine Corps, I realized that in the diary which I had written so many years ago, there was a story that needed to be told: a story about Marines in battle, about earned honor and glory, comradeship, love, pain, and sorrow. It was another side of the Vietnam War that had never been shared, and the diary's silence begged to be broken.

I found my diary and sat down to write. I wrote for three months. I wrote what I remembered and what the pages of the diary brought to remembrance: the loud, angry sound of the Vietnamese language; the beauty of the country; the military slang unique to Vietnam. The diary stained with mud and grime from the rice paddy fields of Southeast Asia brought to my memory the smell of spilled, hot blood lingering in the air long after a firefight. I recalled the days of pain, sorrow, glory, joy, laughter, and friendship; it all returned, fresh and real. When I finished writing the book, the thirty-five years of silence was broken when I read the last page to my wife, and cried.

The book written from the heart would lay still for yet another number of years before I found the courage to revisit its pages. When I did, I realized that over the years I had forgotten many of the words, phrases, and military jargon as well as the nomenclature of the weapons we used in war. I wanted the reader to know what we knew; to see and hear what we saw and heard, what we felt, what we experienced; to understand the weapons and military training of our time, to sense the fear, strength, and courage that we found in each other as Americans, as warriors, and as Marines; to see how friendship forged in the battle zone remains forever; and to understand what we added to life and to the history of war.

I wanted to dispel the Hollywood hype found in Vietnam movies; I finally sat down to watch. I researched government documents and obtained copies of the Marine Corps command chronologies, the after-action combat reports, unit diaries, journals, and other forms of documentation that would help to depict our time, what we did, and what occurred. I wanted to be as historically accurate as possible in reporting the events that transpired according to my diary, other personal accounts, and Marine Corps' records. I checked the dates and events, facts, and figures—both of the enemy's dead and of the Marines that were wounded or killed.

I searched the Internet made hundreds of telephone calls, and found some of the Marines I had served with, in Vietnam. Marines that had been there at my side mingled their recollections with my accounts of what had transpired so many years ago. Many of those events were still fresh in our minds. These were incidents we would not, could not, allow ourselves to forget.

I found out some of the events we witnessed were not reported and that others were in conflict with what was narrated in Marine Corps records. Many Marines I thought had been killed were listed only as wounded in action (WIA). Later, I found those same names inscribed on a black granite wall at the Vietnam War Memorial in Washington, DC. Others I thought only wounded, I found listed as killed in action (KIA). I don't know which account is correct. With the passage of time, it no longer matters except to those who were there, their relatives, and those who cherish the value of history.[1]

I have tried to be as accurate as possible and have given fictitious names to only a couple of Marines whom I could not identify by name or records. I wrote what I saw, what we experienced, and what happened to a platoon of Marines fighting the war in Vietnam. I also wrote about my personal life and how it changed while I was away from the States. I wrote about how life back home would never be the same because I had come of age and now saw things differently with new insights, values, and needs.

There are Marines alive today because I volunteered to serve in Vietnam and because I fought alongside them against a well-trained enemy force. There are others that died when I should have been the one killed. Some died near me because of the M-60 machine-gun I carried. They died believing in each other and that other people of the world had the right to experience the freedom and the liberty Americans enjoy. We believed that liberty and justice should be experienced by others who hunger to taste its flavors and embrace its values.

Many of us during that time in history were unaware of the protests and demonstrations being waged against the war at home. We were fighting because our country called us to battle, because we believed in our country—in America—and that made the difference in the way we fought and in the way we died. We were Marines and Americans, and that is the reason this book is written. It is not a war story, but a story of war written to give due respect to all that served with honor and with the hope that we never again make the mistake of not supporting the American military men in battle.

History shows us that the vast majority of Vietnam War veterans went on to live productive lives but have remained silent about their war experiences. It is hoped that this book will help end that silence so that others will share their experiences and thereby we can more fully understand what it means to fight for freedom and the value of life.

It was our country that sent us to war; we went there to kill Communist soldiers. That is what we were trained to do, what a Marine does. I went there to kill and to come back alive; I did both. I don't know if I ever killed a Vietcong guerrilla. I do know that I killed many North Vietnamese Communist soldiers. These were individuals that were trained and supplied by the Soviet Union and Communist China. They invaded South Vietnam and many of them, without hesitation, killed innocent civilians, old men, women, and children; and we, as Marines, sought them out and destroyed them when we could.

There are words I use in this book that some may find offensive. In today's society, they are not politically correct. I use them here because they are the words of war, words of that time and era. They are words we used in a Marine rifle squad that was made up of individuals from all across America. Blacks, Mexicans, and whites—in the Marine Corps, we all enjoyed a common bond, a unity and relationship, held together by the Marine Corps green we all wore. We used words to describe the enemy, ourselves, and a culture we didn't understand. That's the way it was then, and it was our way of life.

Civilizations may never again fight battles as we did in the rice paddy fields of Southeast Asia. Very few fighting men will ever experience war as we did. With today's weapons, satellite and laser-guided missiles, as well as mass communications in the field and at home, the type of war we fought may very well have been fought by America's last ground warriors.

I don't regret having fought in the Vietnam War; I wouldn't give up that experience for anything in the world. We fought for democracy and for a dream that was obtainable by the people of Vietnam. We felt honored to have served our country, to have been given the opportunity in life to be more than a witness to history.

If we failed, it was not because we did not do our duty; it was because others entrusted with higher responsibilities failed to do theirs.

COOK BARELA
Riverside, California
June 13, 2009
1300 hours

ACKNOWLEDGMENT

During the battle for Belleau Wood on May 27, 1918, U.S. Marine Gunnery Sergeant Dan Daly yelled at his men, "Come on, you sons of bitches! Do you want to live forever?"

At times while writing *Dreams of Glory*, I felt the book would take forever, mostly because there were times I did not want to visit what I now share with you here. But it was individuals like those I have listed below that urged me on to complete the task and to them I am truly grateful.

First, my wife, Marylu, and our daughters: Rebekah, Serah, Deborah, Joannah, and Elizabeth. My daughters gave up time with their dad so that I could spend hundreds of hours listening to Marines as they shared from their recollections the events that are found in this book. My two sons, Troy and Jeromy, in reading this book, I hope they, like other sons of war veterans, will find the father's heart they never knew. Then there is Larry Wilson, our lieutenant in Vietnam. I spoke to him more in five minutes after an absence of thirty-three years than I had in the six months when he was my platoon commander. I also want to acknowledge the help of Stan Villareal who compiled India Company's rosters, which helped locate the Marines who shared their recollections of the events found in this book. I am grateful to Ralph Keenan for the hours we spent in phone conversations; Ed Stiteler, who without reservation, supplied me with his own copy of Captain Baggette's photo narrative; and Captain Baggette, who supplied me with over one thousand photos of our time, which helped my recollection of those events. Larry Callahan, who taped for me his recollections of certain days of battle; both he and Steve Wilhelmsen shared their remarkable recollections of the first battle scene duplicated in this book. I owe special thanks to Ira Bruce Rahm, a Marine's Marine, and Monte Gennai, who supplied personal recollections of events I had forgotten about. Their photos and Marine Corps documents, led me on a quest to find other documents and military reports. Steven Paul Aguilar, who, when I contacted him over the phone after thirty-five years of silence, answered with "My old friend!"

I thank Dennis "Marty" Martinez, who, like other Marines, encouraged me to finish the book. A special thanks to Victor Vilionis, his valuable research and his Seventh Marines Web site, for his compilation of valuable information that helped me, and others, find much of the information we have sought about our time in history. I wish to thank all those Marines that called, e-mailed and shared with me their recollections of a war fought years ago yet still so very fresh and near to us; all those other Marines, their parents, spouses, children, so many who took the time to talk with me and helped in the accumulation of information now shared here as history. To Marine Moms on line, for their encouragement. I haven't listed everyone's name, but please know that all those of you that contributed have my gratitude and appreciation for helping me bring to others the truth of what we experienced that would otherwise have been lost in time.

I especially want to thank those Marines of the First Platoon who were there at my side, in war and who remain my friends, for a friendship forged in war remains forever. Semper Fidelis! My brothers.

I am grateful for Claremont McKenna College, Professor Cathy Decker's help in editing the first text. My daughter Rebekah who spent days working on my manuscript and of course my chief editor and initial critic, my daughter Joannah, whose expertise in the editorial field laid the foundation for its content and delivery. John Lewis, her husband who designed the book's cover. In addition, I am grateful to my good friend Becky Martin, who spent hours reading my handwritten notes and witnessed the first pains of remembrance. I want to thank her for her time for typing the words I shared from the heart into what you now hold in your hands.

CHAPTER ONE

Sentimental Journey
El Toro Marine Corps Air Base
El Toro, California
June 13, 1967, 1300 hours

We are lined up alphabetically against a tin metal hangar at the Marine Corps Air Facility Station in El Toro, California. The headquarters of the Third Marine Aircraft Wing is located here.[2] The morning sun has scattered the heavy fog layer which earlier covered most of the Santa Ana Mountains and the San Joaquin Hills surrounding the airbase. The air is cool, crisp, fresh, and clean.

There is no military or combat troop transport plane before us. Instead, on the runway directly in front of the hangar, a Continental Airlines Golden Bird is being fueled up. The plane would be ready for our departure at 1300 hours.[3]

In the three years I spent in the corps, I never understood its fondness for starting everything at 1300 hours. The daily marching on the parade field at Marine Corps Recruiting Depot (MCRD) in San Diego always started at 1300 hours. It was at that same hour that we received our orders for Vietnam; and now, six months after the date of my enlistment, my classmates and I assigned to combat duty in Vietnam, would be boarding the 707 airliner at 1300 hours.

Most of us standing in line were assigned to the First Marine Division.[4] All of us had gone through ten weeks of basic recruit training at MCRD, in San Diego, California, or Parris Island, South Carolina. All of us had completed an additional three months or more of combat or military specialty training in our MOS (Military Occupational Specialty). Some of us had gone through training together at Infantry Training Regiment (ITR) at Camp Pendleton, where we were trained as grunts (0311's). My MOS was 0331 a machine-gunner.

"Atten-chun!," the duty noncommissioned officer (NCO) in charge of the flight shouted, and we snapped to. We marched around the hangar in cadence until we were about fifty feet from the plane.

"DETAIL, halt!" the corporal shouted and we stopped. "Left face! At ease," and some of us went into parade rest while others relaxed in place.

"Hey, Barela, take a deep breath," said Baracki in his hard Texas accent while he took in a deep breath through his wide nostrils. I sniffed the air but didn't smell anything.

"What do you smell?" I asked.

"America," he answered. "Sure, wish I could put this smell in a bottle and take it with me," Baracki said. "I hear gooks[5] smell like fish and mothballs and the air like acid and piss."

Bennett, who was standing behind Benevedo and me, turned his back toward us and passed gas. The sound was loud and long.

"Smell that," he said, and we all moved away from him.

A short time later, Good Samaritans started to walk up and down our formation offering us Dixie cups filled with ice and cold, raspberry-flavored Kool-Aid, cookies, and a small, pocket-size New Testament Bible. Everyone took the miniature Bibles. No doubt on everyone's mind was the question of whether or not they would return from the war in Vietnam.

For some reason, I knew I would return. I just knew it. I might get wounded, but I knew I would return alive. It's always "the other guy" that gets killed or seriously wounded in battle. It's always someone else who returns from war in a body bag, a dull, gray casket, or as a disabled veteran. It's always someone else, someone like Baracki, who was standing in front of me; or Balisher, in front of him; or Benevedo, behind me; or Bennett, Blain, Brian, Cervantes, Cincenerros, Cordavan, Douglas, and Duran. It was always people like them, and it was them.

Sometimes the difference was pure luck; at other times, it was experience and our training that made the difference. During recruit training, long hours of rigorous physical exercise was coupled with tedious mental exercises; and in the classrooms, recruits would often nod off during long lectures. Sergeant Nelson, our drill instructor at MCRD, would then come up behind those recruits that were beginning to fall asleep and slap them upside the head while yelling at them.

"Recruit, you're dead and you just killed other Marines. You don't need to sleep. Not until you get back from Vietnam," he would shout. "I've been south; I spent my thirteen months in hell. I ain't goin' there. You are. That's the land of no postage stamps. The only bennies you'll receive in Vietnam is that you'll be able to write home for free. You don't have to put a stamp on the envelope to send a letter home. You just write 'free' on the envelope where the stamp goes, and Uncle Sam sends it home free for you. It's the same if you get killed in Vietnam; the Marine Corps send your body back home in a plastic body bag for free. They just write on it 'Dead Marine' and ship it home; it won't cost your parents one cent."

Sergeant Nelson warned us often to stay awake and to pay close attention in class. He made sure we were above average in our hand-to-hand combat training classes, and that we knew how to clean and properly care for our weapons. He made sure we understood our training was based on the understanding that it was all part of our duty to shoot and kill the enemy and not get killed.

"If the enemy shoots you, you don't stop fighting. You don't stop shooting. You will not drop dead and die. If you are killed, you will not die until you kill the bastard that killed you. Do you understand that?"

"*Yes sir!*" we always shouted back loudly.

"Recruit, if you want to stay alive, if you want to make it home alive, pay close attention in class. If you fall asleep in combat, you're Dead! Dead! Dead! Dead!" he would yell into the face of the shaken recruit sitting in class. While his words varied, Sergeant Nelson would often then deliver one of his usual lectures.

"You're going to Vietnam to kill, not to be killed. Marines won't win this war by dying in Vietnam. The Vietnamese people don't want you to die for them. Uncle Sam doesn't want you to die for him. I don't want you to die in Vietnam. All Uncle Sam wants you to do in Vietnam is to kill VC (Vietcong). Your job is to kill the enemy. You will not win the war by getting laid by the local village whore. If you do that, you'll get the black syph and the black syph will eat away at your pecker and you'll die, and Jody back home will end up with your girl. If you die in Vietnam, the Marine Corps Commandant will bust me to buck private; I'll be just like you maggots because he'll say I didn't train you right. You better not die in battle because you did not pay attention in my boot camp and didn't learn how to stay alive. If you die in Vietnam for some dumb reason, I'll find you when I get to heaven and I'll kick your ass for making me look bad in front of the Marine Corps commandant. I don't want to look bad in front of the Marine Corps Commandant. Do you hear me, recruits?"

"*Yes sir!*" the platoon always responded.

Sergeant Nelson was a short, black Marine, hyper, fidgety, and always looked guilty as if he had just gotten away with something. We knew he wasn't telling us everything he knew about the war in Vietnam. He told us how he felt; he had cheated death in the jungles of Southeast Asia a number of times. His number had been up, he said, but somehow he had made it back. Sheer luck had crowned him with the honor of belonging to the survivors' choir that sang of the perils of war. When he spoke from personal war experience, he displayed a particular type of fear that both scared and made us hunger to know more. It was a fear we knew we would have to face. It was a fear we would have to accept, the type of fear that can only be understood by those who have been to war, who have had to fight for life. It was a fear accepted by those who feared the fear of failing more than death.

One of our other drill instructors was Staff Sergeant Conrad. He was a different breed of Marine. He was tall, intelligent-looking, and a white male who reflected Marine Corps professionalism. His likeness has decorated Marine Corps recruiting posters for decades: rugged, dedicated, decorated, and committed to the Corps' moral values. He wore his Vietnam service ribbons with confidence and pride. He spoke little about his military war exploits or experiences, so we figured he might have served more in a logistical supportive role while in Vietnam than in actual combat. He was, in our eyes, administrative material and probably belonged to that family of individuals who often come close but never quite got involved in actual combat. They were rear echelon personnel we called pogues.

The pogues were administrative personnel, support Marines, trained like the rest of us who may or may not face the same risk of direct enemy fire, as most grunts, but were still awarded the same ribbons and medals as those who did. I didn't know which would be worse: to face the enemy up front and personal or to do a tour of duty in a combat zone and not have the opportunity to do what all Marines are trained to do.

Staff Sergeant Conrad was a levelheaded Marine who commanded respect as well as a listening ear from us. By him, we knew we could gain a broader prospective about the overall combat situation we might face in war. While he was more of a spit-and-polished Marine, Conrad stressed familiarization with our weapons as being of the utmost importance. "It's more important than chow or sleep. Neglect your weapon and you're dead," he would tell us.

Still, it was Sergeant Nelson who depicted the common warrior's sense of reality and loyalty. Nelson belonged to the brotherhood of combat Marines who were familiar with fear and courage, death and the value of life, love and war, brotherhood and honor, the esprit de corps that reflected responsibility, faithfulness, honor, dedication, courage, and commitment in the face of battle. Nelson depicted the glory of the Corps as well as the shame of war.

Sergeant Nelson had gone through drill-instructor training at Parris Island. Over the entrance to the drill instructor's hut was a wooden plaque with these words inscribed: "Let's be damned sure that no man's ghost will ever say: if your training program had only done its job." Now five months after graduating from Marine Corps boot camp, we would be putting into action what we learned.

I flipped a coin. Benevedo called it, and I won the window seat. We boarded the plane, and at precisely 1300 hours, the front doors were shut tight and the plane began to taxi.

Our stewardess was Susan Cagey, an attractive twenty-two-year-old brunette with a slender body and foxy light brown eyes. As the plane began to taxi, she welcomed us aboard over the intercom. She spoke with a Southern flat drawl that accentuated her femininity. It wasn't long before she was being propositioned by dozens of Marines on board. She promised a date to the first Marine who would call her upon completion of our thirteen-month tour of duty, and for that she got an *ooh rah*.

I pocketed the small Bible I had been given by an elderly gentleman. Besides the cookies, Bibles, and Kool-Aid, the Good Samaritans had uttered words of encouragement and had quoted scriptures from the little Bible we had been given.[6] I wished I could remember what the old man had said or where to find the words he had recited in the little book.

An hour later with nothing but the deep blue sea below us, we began to doze off or to listen to the stereo music coming through our headsets.

The captain of the plane, having welcomed us aboard, announced we would be cruising at an altitude of twenty-two thousand and traveling in a southwesterly direction. I took out my pen and made my first entry in the spiral notebook that would become a daily journal of my tour of duty. As the plane made a slight left turning movement and leveled off, I closed the notebook, switched the music control knob on the armrest to the number one listening position, and sat back. Over the headset, Barry Manilow was beginning to sing "Sentimental Journey."[7]

CHAPTER TWO

Thoughts Of Another World
Naha International Airport, Naha, Okinawa
June 14, 1967, 1700 hours

Including the plane transfer in Honolulu, Hawaii, fourteen hours after our departure, we were setting down at Naha International Airport in Okinawa, Japan.

As a Marine, you are trained to obey orders. It's drilled into you from the time your feet hit the yellow footprints on the deck at the Marine Corps Recruiting Depot. You're trained not to ask why, but to do as you're ordered. That's what makes the Green Machine work, why it doesn't break down.

Raised in a small town, at eighteen years of age, I was naive not only about life but also about military structure, political and world affairs. I found it strange that we had flown by commercial plane and not by military transport and that we were scheduled to land in Okinawa and not Vietnam.

When we boarded the plane, I wasn't wondering about combat gear, a rifle, or a helmet. I knew that if we needed them, they would have been issued. As Sergeant Conrad would say, "If you need it, the Marine Corps will issue it to you. If you don't have it, you don't need it. If the Marine Corps wanted you to have a wife, it would have issued you one."

The plane landed and as we taxied along the runway, it was bright and sunny, five in the afternoon, Okinawa time. [8] My watch read 0300 hours, California time, and I wondered if Dorothy was sleeping and what she was dreaming about.

In the year we had been married, we had spent less than two months together. We spent my last weekend together, and then I left for El Toro by way of the Greyhound bus. She could have driven down to see me off. Her sister Cathy had volunteered to drive us, but she showed no interest in doing so.

I met my wife Dorothy in the summer of 1965 when I was fifteen; I went from Casa Grande, Arizona, to Farmersville, California, with my sister Dominga and her husband, Phillip Minjarez, to pick fruits and vegetables in the labor fields of the San Joaquin Valley. All summer we worked and the last month I spent in a town called Sanger with my half sister, Connie her husband Joe Sanchez and their family.

Across the street from them lived the Cedillo family who had six daughters and one son.

Every evening, the Sanchez group, the Cedillo girls, their cousin Cora, and I would take long walks down McDonald Road. Both sides of the road were filled with groves of nectarine and peach trees, and a spicy fragrance always lingered in the evening air. Dorothy was oldest of the Cedillo girls, followed by Josie and Cecilia or Cece as everyone called her.

Cece was my age, slender with long brown hair, a light complexion, and inviting, light-colored eyes. Dorothy was short with dark black hair; she had a small frame with dimples and dark brown eyes and was older than I was and was working full time in the Sanger canneries. Cece was the one I was attracted to, and her cousin Cora and sister Dorothy knew this as well as the Sanchez girls.

One evening, as we were about to go on one of our walks, Dorothy asked me to follow her. She had something she wanted to show me. The others went on, and I followed her to a small storage shed in the back of their house. Once inside the shed, she asked, "Have you ever played 'spin the bottle'?"

"No," I replied, and she spun the bottle. When the bottle stopped spinning, it was pointing toward her. "You lost," she said. "Now you have to kiss me," and we kissed.

For the next three times, the bottle stopped spinning in between; and when it was her turn again, she spun the bottle and it landed on me and she said she lost and would now have to kiss me. Dorothy had already graduated from high school so I figured she knew what she was doing.

That evening, Dorothy told Cora about our kissing and a couple of days later while Cora and I were talking, standing across the road in front of their grocery store in between large wooden crates that were used for the picked peaches then sent off to the packinghouses in Sanger, we kissed. Kissing Cora felt strange because she had two front teeth that were false. She told me about them only after we kissed, but they were noticeable during the kiss.

The following day, Cora arranged for her, Cece, and me to go swimming in their family swimming pool behind the store and Cora conveniently disappeared. When I had gotten out of the pool, Cece called me over to where she was at the edge of the swimming pool.

I moved to the edge. "Closer," she said, urging me forward with an inviting curve at the corner of her mouth. Her eyes sparkled, and I wondered what she was up to.

I leaned in, to get closer to where she was and she took a rubber inner tube, held it up, and said, "Closer," inviting me to place my head through the tube and kiss her.

As I moved in closer, she closed her eyes and parted her lips. Counting Dorothy and Cora, I had only kissed two other girls before kissing Cece, and for the first time I wanted to keep kissing her. We kissed and it felt good, and I wanted more.

Perhaps the feeling was because it was something I had desired and wanted to do from the first time I saw her or because Cece seemed just as interested in me and not just a kiss, at least her inviting eyes seemed to indicate that. When Cece went home that afternoon, she told Dorothy about our kissing and there was a fight at their house that evening. From then on, their mother wouldn't allow Cece to go on our walks.

When I left to return home at the end of the summer, I only got a chance to say good-bye to Dorothy who promised to write. We wrote for a month, then the letters stopped coming and I stopped writing.

A year later, I returned during the summer to help care for my sister Connie who was dying of leukemia. While I was there, Dorothy and I spent some time together, but she was also seeing a lot of her high school boyfriend Roger.

After my sister died, Dorothy said she wanted to get married. I knew she had had a fight with her boyfriend, shortly before that, so when I showed no interest in getting married she threatened to commit suicide and showed me an empty bottle of aspirins she had swallowed to prove to me that she was serious. Being naïve and afraid she would succeed, I agreed to marry her.

I didn't love her—not the way a man is supposed to be in love with a woman he wants to marry, and she knew it.

The juvenile court judge in Sanger, who was authorized to issue wedding licenses to those under eighteen, when the two of us showed up to apply for one may have seen through all that and was hesitant to issue us a license.

He questioned my youth and maturity and refused to marry us unless I obtained my mother's signature.

My mother wouldn't sign until Dorothy told her she was pregnant, which wasn't true as we had not been sexually together before marriage. I didn't know she had told my mother this, until after we were married, but my mother believed her at that time, and she signed the court document, approving the marriage.

"Do you think, our marriage will last," Dorothy asked, as we left the court house.

When, she asked that, I recalled what I had read in a book my high school art teacher, Karen Kuyendell, had given me.

It was the first book I had read for pleasure and had really enjoyed. In the book, *The Illusionless Man* by Allen Wheelis. The main character Henry cites why he did not believe his marriage would last.

"For our age and economy bracket, we have a 47.3 percent chance of staying together," I added, "for two weeks."

On our way to my sister's house, where I was staying, Dorothy said she hadn't told her father we were getting married and felt it best if we just waited until the next day to get together.

We had made no plans so; it really didn't make that much difference and I agreed. When we got home, I went back to my sister's house to spend the night there and she went home to be with her folks.

That evening, my brother Ernie and his wife Norma came to visit. When he found out that I had been married that day and wasn't planning to be with her that night, he insisted I go over and tell her father.

"After all," he said, "she is your wife."

We didn't have a place to live, so my brother and his wife offered to let us stay with them. When he had gotten married, he said, he didn't have a place to stay and our aunt, Alice Medina, had given up her home to them for two weeks.

I crossed over the road and jumped over the small irrigation ditch that separated the two houses. Before I got to their door, Dorothy came out and was visibly upset at me for being there.

"We're married, and I need to talk to your father," I told her. Just for her to come out of the house to speak with me required explanation, she said. Now, she didn't know how her father would react.

I insisted she tell him or I would.

She went back in and told him I wanted to speak to him. When he came out, I said, "Mr. Cedillo, your daughter and I were married this morning."

"I don't like that you did it that way," he said. "But you're married, so take her."

With those words, he turned around and went back into his house. Those were the only words he had spoken to me until the day before I left for Vietnam.

"I won't say good-bye," he said to me. "But be careful."

Dorothy and I lasted exactly two weeks before our first separation. We tried again a week later but continued to argue back and forth and finally agreed she should stay with her family while I went to live with my brother who was moving to San Jose.

In San Jose, I found a job as a kitchen helper, washing dishes at Joe's Cafe near the Greyhound bus depot. About a month later, when I got off work, Dorothy was waiting outside the cafe. We tried to live together again and again, but it was always one argument after another mostly because she was very controlling. This lasted for four months until I turned eighteen. When, I no longer needed to obtain my mother or wife's signature, I enlisted in the U.S. Marines.

I chose the U.S. Marines because I knew more than likely I would be going to Vietnam, and I wanted to get the best training possible.

On New Year's Eve, at midnight, December 1966, I arrived at the Marine Corps Recruit Depot in San Diego, California. As my feet touched the yellow footprints at boot camp, my wife was spending that night celebrating the New Year with her old boyfriend. I wouldn't find out until months afterward when I received my orders for Vietnam and one of her sisters told me.

Okinawa, Kamikaze Style
Naha International Airport, Naha, Okinawa
June 14, 1967, 1710 hours

We disembarked and were told to grab a seabag.[9] We were mustered into formation and marched in the direction of the air terminal where four olive-drab military buses were parked near a side entrance. "Kadena Air Force Base" was stenciled on their sides. We loaded the bags on board and within minutes were *en route* to the air base and the Marine Corps transit facility located there.

The roadway we were traveling on was narrow and crowded. Two vehicles could barely pass each other at the same time. Clear fields, rocky and hilly terrain lined both sides of the road. Off in the distance, little dark-skinned people were busy working the sugarcane, pineapple, and rice fields. We passed numerous villages with small shops cluttered with colorful advertising signs of all sizes and shapes. Almost every shop had a bright-colored, red, white, and blue sign advertising Pepsi or Coca-Cola.

The houses, bamboo shacks, they used for homes varied in color and shape. The better ones were made of wood with rusty-colored tile roofs. The people wore kimonos or black silk pants with loose-fitting black or white jackets. The people looked in some way frail, deprived, defeated.

For the most part, the Okinawans kept their heads down as they zigzagged in and out of the crowded traffic lanes. They rode on bicycles, small cars, and lopsided, overcrowded buses. Large straw hats covered their Asian facial features. Many walked briskly alongside the road, carrying long wooden shoulder poles with wicker baskets tied to each end. Some carried large wire cages filled with skinny white chickens or big brown roosters. Others had large straw baskets strapped to their backs filled with fresh fruits, vegetables, ducks, or small pigs.

I didn't know why, but I didn't trust them. Less than one hour in their country and I disliked them. I couldn't understand why, and that bothered me. Perhaps it was because the people of Okinawa represented a culture and a way of life so vastly different than my own. Perhaps it was the effects of a high school class or a Marine Corps history lesson taught during recruit training that brought back repressed resentment. In the back of my mind, I was wondering how many American lives had been sacrificed for this island, yet it remained heavily crowded by hundreds of little Japanese-looking people. They represented part of the Japanese empire that had attacked us at Pearl Harbor. "We won the war; why aren't Americans living here?" I asked myself.

I knew that on the island of Okinawa, one of the bloodiest campaigns of World War II had been fought. It was here that a bitter air, sea, and land battle had taken place where Japanese kamikaze pilots gained notoriety by wreaking devastation on our U.S. naval and military armed forces. That was the way Japanese pilots were taught to die for their emperor god and for Japan's honor[10] by killing themselves in the process.

We heard that the highest honor a Vietcong soldier could obtain in war was to die for his country.[11] The NVA/VC soldiers dying in the fields of battle were immortalized as national heroes by their local villages.[12] But such suicidal guerrilla assaults, mostly directed at civilians or government officials in Vietnam, were nothing less than terrorist acts.[13]

While each kamikaze incident may have been counted as a mini-battle won by the Japanese, there was something wrong about it. It seemed to me it was a wrong way to fight a war, a wrong way to die. We were trained to fight, to protect life, and win battles by killing our enemy while retaining the honor of survival.

During our ITR training, we had learned that the North Vietnamese Army (NVA)[14] and the Communist Pathet Lao terrorist organization[15] were operating out of Laos and Cambodia. They trained and sent troops as well as Communist-supplied arms into South Vietnam. They were responsible for training and supplying the VC with military supplies and weapons made in Communist countries.[16] The specially trained NVA terrorists could be expected to make suicidal assaults on our forces and base camps. Such attacks would be fierce, destructive, and unrelenting. We should not expect them to hit, break contact, and run as the VC were known to do. Firefights with the Communist-trained NVA soldier would last, and they would fight with the intention of wiping out any target they chose to attack.

Seeing all those foreign-looking people, in their hurried lifestyle while looking out the bus window, I began to accept the fact that I was a long way from home. As soon as I realized this, the chain link fence running alongside the U.S. Air Force base came into view.

The bus slowed down to turn into the base. On the right side of the road, four skinny young Okinawa girls in tight white short shorts were standing near the front gate talking to Marines and Air Force personnel.

"Hey, maybe we'll get liberty tonight," Bennett said as he stood up inside the bus. He stretched out his long neck and opened wide his bubble-shaped eyes to get a better look at the girls. As he rushed toward an open window, he placed his right hand to his mouth, pulled on his lower lip, and let out an earsplitting long whistle. The girls turned quickly to look at the bus and waved blindly at the busload of Marines. Bennett gave out a loud shout, "Yeah, babe!"

The bus made a left turn, and Bennett scrambled to regain his balance. The MP at the booth on guard duty snapped to attention and smartly waved us through.

We entered the military compound, and I breathed a sigh of relief.

"Welcome to Camp Henson," the sign at the entrance read, and I was grateful to be back on a U.S. military base.

We disembarked, obtained our own seabags, and were assigned to a barrack for the night.[17]

The barracks filled up along the transit rows daily as new Marines came in and were shipped out. Everyone was processed for duty in Vietnam in the order of arrival unless there was a delay with an individual for medical reasons. Usually everyone that came in together, left together, and most were in and out in less than forty-eight hours. Every day, the process began all over again.

CHAPTER THREE

Powdered Eggs and Mush
Camp Henson, Kadena Air Force Base
Naha, Okinawa
June 15, 1967, 0600 hours

Reveille sounded at 0600 hours the following morning, and we mustered for chow. The air felt sticky, moist, and hot. The chow line wound around the rear of an old converted World War II hangar transformed to serve as a large mess hall. While being in formation we slowly made our way toward the entrance and passed by a double row of garbage cans. The smell of burned bacon, boiled eggs, and the foul odor of old coffee grounds was nauseating.

Once inside, I was surprised to see Okinawa civilians working behind the skillets serving our food. They looked small and dirty and chattered incessantly in their native language while serving us minute portions of cold, watery scrambled, powdered eggs; burned bacon; and dry hashed brown potatoes. When we cleared the chow line, I was glad to see six small aluminum milk containers sitting on top of one of the counters.

I touched the container near the white rubbery spout. It felt cold, so I poured myself a tall glass of cold milk and took a long, deep swallow. Immediately, I spit it out. It was weak powdered milk. I hated powdered milk.

When I was three years of age, my father was returning from selling scrap metal in Phoenix, Arizona, when a drunk driver ran his truck off the road, killing him instantly.

My brothers and sisters and I were raised on welfare; under a government food surplus program, our family was provided with World War II government—issued food rations which included navy beans, powdered eggs, and powdered milk.

My father, Felix Lucero Barela, had been commissioned by the city council of Casa Grande, Arizona, to be the caretaker of the city's dump. We lived there in the city's waste disposal site among the garbage and refuse of life. From discarded plastic, cardboard and lumber he found, my father built a home for his children. There were thirteen of us in the family, two half brothers, two half sisters from his first marriage, and nine of us that were born during my parents' twenty years of marriage. I was my father's seventh son. My father's first wife had died of cancer. When he met my mother, he was thirty-two, she was seventeen.

My mother often told us as we were growing up that we never went hungry while my father was alive. Friends and relatives would often drop by our cardboard shelter amidst the city's refuse; and there in our little home, they would find warm tortillas, beans, potatoes, freshly made chili, or sweet Mexican bread my father shared with them. Every day, before he went to work early in the morning, those of us lucky enough to be up would find ourselves being picked up by his strong arms and placed on his lap. He would dip a warm tortilla in his coffee, then in the sugar bowl, and give us a taste.

I don't remember the funeral or how long afterward we moved into the city. We were raised with the help of government assistance. Every month the welfare lady would come by to make sure we were okay and to check on my mother. She also came by to make sure my mother wasn't making too much money in the odd jobs she took to supplement our income by cleaning houses or ironing clothes for other people. In time, the welfare lady became one of my mother's clients and my mother cleaned her house as well, and we somehow managed to get by.

At the beginning of each month, we were given food substance from the government's surplus food supply: rice, cheese, navy beans, powdered milk, and powdered eggs. That was what we ate and lived on for many years. To this day, I hate navy beans, powdered milk, and powdered eggs.

I sat down and ate what I could, then quickly got up and left the foul-smelling mess hall. "I'm gonna starve in Vietnam," I muttered to myself.

At 0800 hours, a mass formation was called and Marines who had arrived two days earlier received their final orders. The rest of us began our final processing phase for overseas combat assignment. We marched in formation to the dispensary where we went through a complete physical examination: X-rays and inoculations for cholera, yellow fever, typhoid, typhus, and tetanus shots were given to those needing them. It was a thorough physical examination. Later that day, we were issued large yellow-colored malaria tablets and were told we were to take them weekly for the next thirteen months.

They gave us new seabags to store our dress greens and other unneeded military or personal equipment in. They would be kept in storage lockers there until the end of our tour of duty. Our khaki shirts, trousers, dress, shoes, boots, and combat utilities we kept in our old seabag. We were to take them with us.

That evening, I ran into Marines from the old 101 recruit series at MCRD. Some had left the States a couple of days before and were now assigned to a barrack close by. We visited and compared what tidbits of scuttlebutt we had heard about the war in Vietnam.

"Dustin and Borgman left yesterday," Benevedo told Baracki, Bennett, and I at the barracks where we were bunked for the night. The six of us had become friends during machine-gun training school.

Just before we finished our ITR training, we ended up at a Naval watering hole near Long Beach, California. About midnight, Benevedo, the "Wop," was drunk enough to start an argument with a swabbie; and before long, he yelled, "MARINE" and a full-blown donnybrook ensued. We spent the rest of that night in the brig at the Naval base.

Early the next morning, all of us were transported to Camp Pendleton and marched in to see our commanding officer.

We didn't know how the bar fight would affect our overseas assignments, but we knew that we were destined for some charges and possibly some brig time.

While we stood at attention, still reeking of alcohol from the night before, a tall, gray-haired, bulldog-looking lieutenant colonel came into the room. His pug nose resembled that of the Marine Corps mascot. His stern, squinting eyes and heavy eyebrows showed his displeasure. He seemed like the type that would be more comfortable behind field glasses than the granny glasses he picked up to look over the MP's report.

Immediately, he began to ream us up and down, shouting and telling us how embarrassing it was for him to receive a phone call from a junior Naval officer concerning our misbehavior. He was angry about the damage and the injuries we caused to Naval property and personnel.

Somehow, the way he told it, the damage we caused had been quite extensive; yet it didn't seem like it had been such a big deal at the time. When he finished, he asked for our response. The lieutenant colonel was wearing a short-sleeved khaki uniform shirt that was smartly tailored and neatly pressed. The Marine Corps eagle, globe and anchor were tattooed under his left forearm; and he wore five rows of combat and other honorable military ribbons on his chest.

The colonel paused. He was about to start yelling at us again but asked, "Why?" Without thinking, I blurted out loudly what naturally came to mind, what the five months of Marine Corps training had produced.

"Tradition, sir!"

With that remark, the colonel tightened his lips, turned away from us, and brought a hand to his mouth to hide and suppress his laughter. He quickly regained his composure, turned toward us, and reamed us again. But his eyes had already betrayed him, so he quickly dismissed us while admonishing us at the same time that it was our duty to kick ass in Vietnam and we had better not get in trouble again or we would answer to him personally.

"Yes, sir," we answered and were glad to have gotten off without being charged with anything. At that moment, we all feared him more than being shipped to war.

During our ITR training, out of 120 Marines, I came third in the class among machine-gunners training for overseas duty.[18] Dustin and Borgman had come first and second. I had done lousy in firing the Colt .45 caliber pistol, which was a machine-gunner's secondary weapon, earning only a pistol sharpshooter's badge.

"There are two reasons the gooks in Nam will try to shoot you first," the training sergeant at ITR had said. "The first reason is because you carry the M-60 machine-gun[19] and secondly because you carry the .45 caliber pistol. With the machine-gun, you can put out a wall of lead, so Charlie wants to knock you out first. The second reason is that if he sees you walking around in the field with the .45 strapped to your hip, Charlie may believe you're an officer. Charlie likes to kill machine-gunners, radiomen, and officers, usually in that order."

Slimy Yellow Mud
Kadena Air Force Base
Naha, Okinawa
June 16, 1967, 0900 hours

A warm summer breeze from the East China Sea bathed the Air Force base with dampness and gloom. As we stood in formation on the morning of June 16, the low clouds held down the humid air, and in minutes we were soaked with perspiration. Little beads of moisture formed quickly and clung to our foreheads as we waited listening for our name, flight ticket, and boarding number to be called.

Anticipation and anxious minds were in conflict with having to stand still while standing in formation, patiently awaiting our orders to war. After a while, impatience overruled my anxiety and I just wanted my name called. I wanted to get my orders, get on the plane, and leave. When our names were finally called, we were given a flight number and told to board the bus.

It started to rain shortly before our base departure and what had been ordinary brown dirt turned into slippery, slimy, yellow mud. At the airport, we were lined up alphabetically and I was among the first lined up in formation. As we were about to board the plane, the NCO in charge of the flight assigned five others and myself the task of loading all of our seabags aboard.

The rain started to fall in torrents, as we loaded the seabags into the rear of the plane. In a matter of minutes, our heavy cotton utilities were dripping wet and our shiny black leather boots were covered with fine, gooey yellow mud. When we finished, I was the last one to board the plane. As I walked through the door, the stewardess reached behind me and closed it tight. It was exactly 1300 hours, and immediately the plane began to taxi along the runway.

Phantom Escorts
Da Nang Air Base
Da Nang, South Vietnam
June 16, 1967, 1300 hours

This time, there were no in-flight movies, no stereo headphones, and the stewardesses were older and grouchier. Like a dispirited soul, a cloud of gloom walked up and down the airplane's aisles and a solemn silence echoed throughout the plane. We sat in secret wonderings, staring at each other and at nothing in particular. No one spoke. Some lit a cigarette to calm their nerves. We were on our way to Vietnam, and war, and there was no turning back.

Two hours later, two camouflaged Marine phantom jets appeared at our wing tips, and I realized they were our escorts as we entered South Vietnam's air space. Seconds later, the pilot turned on the no smoking light and announced that we were beginning our descent into Da Nang.

Far below us the Vietnam coastline with hundreds of small- and medium-size sampans listing offshore came into view. Small craft could be seen traveling into or coming out of the mouth of a number of large rivers. Off in the distance, a huge mountain range flowed in cradling, descending levels toward the coast where its massive strength was silently swallowed by the waves of the South China Sea.

As we began our circled descent into Da Nang, I could see the area's flat terrain below us. Well-cultivated, checkered, fertile fields were outlined by hundreds of tall trees. It was beautiful, a multicolored quilt and patchwork of rare beauty.

Off in the far distance, twenty, thirty miles away, the mountain range with its thick green forest provided a beautiful and spectacular contrast to the clear blue sky that served as its background.

As I enjoyed the country's beauty, our phantom escorts accelerated, banked left, and disappeared. The noise from their afterburners brought my mind back to our destination.

Our plane banked right, dropped suddenly, and quickly leveled off before touching down smoothly.[20] The plane taxied to the other side of the airport and stopped near a long wooden barrack. Portable metal stairs were rolled out to the plane's forward door. We disembarked and our utilities still soaking wet from the Okinawa rain, dried instantly once we stepped into the hot Vietnamese sun.

The air was hot and dry with the smell of dead fish, burning incense, and rotting vegetables. The acrid smell lingering in the air made it hard to breathe. I felt it burning the lining of my nose; its toxic sulfuric odor working its way deep into my lungs. It was the smell of human waste, jet fuel, and expended ordnance. It was the smell of death and fear mixed with confusion, lost hope, and forgotten dreams.

Since those of us who had loaded the seabags on board were seated up front, we were the first to disembark and were assigned to unload seabags. When we finished, we were reassigned to load the seabags of the Marines going home. Noticeable was the heaviness of our seabags compared to those of the homeward-bound Marines. Our olive-drab canvas seabags were large, bulky, crispy, and clean. Those we loaded on board were light, scrawny, faded, dirty, dusty, and torn. I wondered if mine would be just as faded and worn after my tour of duty or if the seabag would be sent back home alone.

Before us was a large wooden hangar with a thin metal roof and a wide-open entrance. The front doors were missing; the facility was always open. We found our seabags, fell into formation and together we walked through the hangar's wide entrance. As we entered, a squeaky loudspeaker greeted us.

"Welcome to the Republic of South Vietnam. Please report to the front of the depot and convert all U.S. currency into Military Payment Certificates (MPC)."

The MPC we received in exchange looked like Monopoly money, but printed on both sides. We were further instructed to stay near the transit barrack and await further orders.

Two aisles of long wooden benches filled the hangar. Marines in various stages of transit lounged around. Some were sitting, waiting, drinking sodas, or playing cards. Many of the wooden benches held a number of seabags and Marines who were sound asleep on them. A hand-painted sign on the wall read No Loitering, and another read, "You're here because you want the real thing."[21]

The wooden benches reminded me of the ones outside the train station in Casa Grande, Arizona. It was there a dark, red-faced old Native American Indian with puffy cheeks and long, thick black hair first offered my brothers and me a shot of whiskey. Trainloads of cantaloupes, lettuce, tomatoes, and other produce made their seasonal pilgrimage to the cannery in Casa Grande; and every year, my brothers and I would make our way there to have our annual cantaloupe fight. We played "king of the hill" on top of the rail boxcars containing cracked and spoiled cantaloupes. We usually made quite a mess and the Indian that was supposed to be on guard duty just sat watching us and laughing. Sometimes he would join in our fights and then offer us a shot of whiskey in the form of a peace treaty. The old Indian was a World War II veteran, and my brothers and I recognized him as our warrior chief.

The entrance of the city I grew up in had a large red, white, and blue road sign proudly announcing, "Welcome to Casa Grande, Arizona, an all-American city"; and it was. The city, with a population of about seven thousand, had a strong patriotic spirit that was found in the city's hard workers, ranchers, farmers, engineers, children, businessman, and grocery clerks alike. It was a friendly city of shared respect, regardless of color or social standing. At the local coffee shop, the men folk gathered to discuss politics, world events, and the weather that was always hot.

At the center of the town was Pearl Park, but no one knew who Pearl was, or why the park was named after him. On one end of the park was the library, at another side the public swimming pool where one of the Blackburn kids had drowned, on Main Street, City Hall, the county building and the fire department were all housed in a large white stucco-covered building. Florence Boulevard ran along the north side of the park, across the street was the biggest and tallest building in the city: the two-story Casa Grande Union High School building, home of the CG Cougars.

Two of my favorite teachers in high school were my English and Art teachers. Karen Kuykendall, my art teacher, was a rough looking woman, with dark blue eyes, and a twitch in the corner of her mouth. She rarely smiled, but made one smile by what she did and how she gave us instructions. She had a way of drawing out our creative abilities. She once told me what ever I would want to be or do in life I was capable of doing, if I set my goals and did something every day to achieve those goals. She had me paint a mural of an angel for Christmas on a large window of the Bank of America building in downtown Casa Grande. She took a picture of it and it was printed in our high school newspaper.

My English teacher was a beautiful woman, with blue eyes, long blond hair, long legs and she always wore short mini skirts. I sat up front in her class and almost failed her class. But, I can't remember her name.

Beyond the south end of the city and the railroad, the Casa Grande Mountains looked barren from a distance but once you hiked it's hidden trails, its colorful, full blooming desert cacti held both beauty and pain in its hidden landscape. A large canal ran along its base, and often while on a hike, it was not unusual to stop and go skinny-dipping and no one thought it strange or weird; we just stripped and jumped in and were later dried by the warmth of the sun.

In the late 1800s, desert temperatures had caused the Southern Pacific Railroad construction crew building a rail line from Yuma across Arizona to stop and rest because of the area's hot temperatures. It was called the end of the line or "terminus" for several months until rail construction resumed, but by then, the area was stacked with materials and supplies that had accumulated and the area became known as *Casa Grande* (Spanish for "big house"), named after the four-story adobe building located not far from there that had been built by the Hohokam Indians some centuries ago.

The city, located almost midpoint between Tucson and Phoenix, had a mixed population of Chinese, Mexicans, Native Americans, Anglo-Americans, and blacks; all contributed to a community spirit of pride and openness that attracted others to come and stay in its dry and warm climate.

Two main roads intersected the city. Trekell Road ran north and south and Florence Boulevard east and west. Where Florence Boulevard ended at the edge of town, near where the historical society had its large stone building, the Gila Bend Highway began. That highway ran west, and a few miles out was the Francisco Grande Hotel with its large baseball playing field where the San Francisco Giants trained in the spring. Willie Mays supposedly hit a home run so far out of the field there, legend has it the ball disappeared into the desert sun, and was to be forever lost. In the background was Table Top Mountain and beyond, the dry desert for over a 300 miles to San Diego, California.

Late in the afternoon, I was standing next to a water buffalo[22] with Baracki, Benevedo, and Bennett, who had just met and made friends with a Marine from Camp Lejeune, South Carolina. The Marine had just received his orders and was assigned to the Third Marine Division. We were talking about what he could expect and where he was going when a Marine came up and handed me a handful of MPC and some funny-looking currency. [23]

He was a lance corporal wearing a wrinkled and faded khaki uniform. His cover was missing its Marine Corps eagle, globe and anchor emblem. His shoes were old, scuffed, unpolished, and missing their shoelaces. He was unshaven, tanned, and his eyes looked tired.

"Keep ya ass down, keep ya mouth shut, lissen to the old-timers, don't volunteer for nuthin', an' in thirteen months you'll leave here in one piece," he said to me, with a Southern drawl.

Looking at me straight in the eyes, and with a satisfied grin on his face, he said; "Ahm on mah way home, an' I ain't got no time ta change this." He turned and walked agilely away. He had a slight limp, and this added to the admiration he was receiving from all of us. The Marine disappeared as he turned the corner and walked toward the departure area.

He made it through Nam and is now going home. I can make it too, I said to myself. The Marine had a satisfied look in his eyes. He was a proud Marine with an arrogance of strength about him that was appealing, but also present was a very lonely side the Marine couldn't hide. He was taking back something that was deep inside of him, and I wondered what it was.

I spent the rest of the day lying around waiting for my military orders to be processed. Marines who had been with the Third Marine Division before assignment to Vietnam were being processed quickly and were sent out to their military units within a few short hours of their arrival. The Third Marine Division[24] was operating near the demilitarized zone (DMZ)[25] while the First Marine Division was located near Da Nang.[26]

The majority of us had come from the West Coast. We were supposed to be assigned to the First Marine Division, but I noticed, orders were being cut both ways. It was a toss-up as to where you would be assigned. It all depended on who needed your MOS the most.

Throughout the day and into the early evening, I watched as many of the Marines that had come in on our plane were processed and dispatched to their units. When darkness fell, about eighty of us remained in the transit barracks. We would not be getting our orders until the following day, we were told, and were to sleep in the depot wherever possible, on the floor or on the hard wooden benches.

The most inviting spot I could find was in a remote corner of the depot, away from the lights and bustling commotion. I pounded on one end of my seabag until it flattened out to use as a pillow, I curled into a ball and fell asleep.

All night long, names were called and military orders were received and processed. Outside the depot, the roar of combat jets taking off and landing constantly shook the building, causing the walls to vibrate. I don't think anyone slept that night. I would soon find out, no one really slept in Vietnam; you just took short naps and were grateful for that.

Scuttlebutt
Marine Transit Barracks
Da Nang, South Vietnam
June 17, 1967, 0600 hours

June 17, 1967,[27] when sunrise came, the almost empty depot had an eerie silence hanging in the air. The NCO in charge of the transit barracks announced we were all confined to the immediate area until further notice. Two hours later, he was back on the intercom.

"You people that have been here since yesterday, the Seabees have a mess hall behind the depot, four barracks down.[28] You can chow down there but you must be back here no later than 1000 hours."

Sitting in the chow hall, we heard that the Marines who were sent out to the Third Marine Division the day before had been involved in a fierce firefight when NVA soldiers ambushed their convoy near Phu Bai. Some Marines had been killed and many wounded. Phu Bai was located only thirty-five miles north of Da Nang, almost halfway to the DMZ. I realized some of the Marines killed or wounded might have been from the old 101 platoon series at MCRD. They may have been Marines I trained with in boot camp; Baracki, Benevedo, Bennett, and the new Marine we had just met received their orders to the Third Marine Division and had left in the same truck convoy. I wondered if they were among yesterdays dead and wounded.

I returned early from chow, anxious to hear any information on the ambushed truck convoy, but all was quiet. A short time later, another planeload of Marines arrived, and the loudspeaker once again squeaked and cracked, then buzzed loudly as the same voice that had welcomed us the day before announced the same message to the new arrivals.

"Welcome to the Republic of South Vietnam, please report to the front of the depot and convert all U.S. currency into MPC," and the process began all over again. By late afternoon, much like the day before, most of those who had arrived had been processed and dispatched to their units.

Rumors soon began to circulate that some of the new Marines that had arrived on our plane had cracked during the convoy attack. Some had gone berserk and were found crying alongside the road while the battle raged on. Could that have happened to my former classmates? We had graduated from boot camp and had gone through infantry training schools together. I couldn't and didn't want to believe it. We heard Marines had jumped off the trucks to seek cover alongside the road and had stepped on booby traps, which either killed or wounded them and others.

"They were all scared, stiff and crying like a bunch of babies," I overheard one of the Third Marine Division's truck convoy drivers say. He was describing what had happened the day before to the new Marines he was picking up. He might have been trying to encourage them but I could see that it was causing the opposite effect, especially since they, like the others sent out the day before, weren't armed. I wanted to ask him if Baracki, Benevedo, or Bennett were among those killed; but at the same time I didn't want to know. Less than twenty-four hours in country and for some of them, their seabags would be shipped back home, just as clean and new as when they arrived.

That evening, we were allowed to go to the NCO (noncommissioned officer) club. Inside, the air was heavy, with the silence and the loneliness often found in war. I decided to go outside and stood near some old-timers sharing their stories of war. Most of them were on a five-day R&R leave.[29] Other Marines standing alone, silently drinking their beer, were on their way home.

Watching the veterans, the way they spoke, how they moved, their overall presence, I began to question myself, *Do I have what it takes? Would I freeze or fight in combat? Would I be killed or seriously wounded? How would I react under fire?* There was no way to know until that moment.

I now realized more than ever that I was in Vietnam and in a combat zone; soon, by the luck of the draw, I would receive my military orders and would be assigned to a Marine division and perhaps just as soon meet with a fate that some of my classmates may have already faced. I was thousands of miles from home, and all of a sudden I felt lonely. A feeling of total helplessness came over me. There was no one I could turn to. The Marines I had known since boot camp or ITR training were gone. I shrugged the feelings off and went back into the club for another beer. Budweiser, Pabst, Schlitz, and Coors were the brands of beer available. They were ice cold and taken from a tub filled with ice. The twenty cents paid for the can of cold Budweiser was small consolation for the empty feeling I was experiencing. I was eighteen years old, and my life was in the hands of those who pulled the strings and flipped through personnel files and made decisions of life and death by simple numerical needs. I was only a serial number followed by a military occupational status. Sometime ago, a unit had requested a machine-gunner with a 0331 MOS and I was destined to fill that slot. A machine-gunner replacement was needed because someone had been killed, wounded, or had miraculously completed his tour of duty and gone back to the States.

It's amazing; the transformation one goes through in the military, from civilian life to military discipline spit and polish in just a few short weeks. The rigid physical conditioning and combat training I had endured for six months had drained, changed, and given me confidence. Now it was all going to be put to test in a war zone.[30]

I went back outside the NCO club and listened to war stories and rumors of what lay ahead. The more I listened, the more intrigued I was with what I was hearing. Listening and hearing to what I did, made me realize military spit and polish didn't matter in Vietnam, certainly not under combat conditions. I was learning that combat military training alone was not going to keep me safe. Survival was going to be determined more by my instincts and what I learned from veterans than by relying on what we had been taught.

I sat there in my fresh starched green utilities listening to veteran jarheads that, for the most part, were out of uniform. They seemed to have a total disregard for military uniform compliance, and I wondered what Staff Sargent, Conrad would say to them. Sergeant Nelson used to tell us "there was no pogie bait (candy) in Vietnam." From combat Marines, I was finding out that the Corps were also not supplying other more important items. Marine units in the field were undermanned. Weapons, uniforms, and weapon cleaning equipment weren't being provided as needed.[31]

While the Marine Corps' sharp dress blue uniforms and rugged recruiting posters were attractive reasons to join the Corps, I had joined the Marine Corps instead of the other branches of the Armed Services because I figured I was going to end up in Vietnam and I reasoned the Marine Corps would give me the best combat training possible. From what I was hearing, I began to wonder if my chances for survival would have been better in the Army. They were better equipped and ran reinforced units while the Marine Corps was often going into combat situations undermanned and ill equipped.

One thing for sure, in Vietnam, following the Corps' tough military uniform regulations was not going to be a priority and this slackness in the Corps was hard to believe. I looked down at my soiled boots and realized I had only brushed off the yellow mud from the day before and hadn't bothered to polish them.

Special Orders
Marine Transit Barracks
Da Nang, South Vietnam
June 18, 1967, 0900 hours

Sunday morning,[32] I was among the last Marines left over from the planeload of Marines who had arrived on Friday. Military orders continued to be cut, and the majority of assignments continued to be to the Third Marine Division. I had come to believe I would be sent to that division and eventually to the DMZ. The DMZ was known as "No Man's Land" where Marines were catching hell on a daily basis. They were engaging regular NVA Communist forces there, fighting well-trained and disciplined military soldiers.[33]

At 1300 hours, the NCO in charge called for all of us to muster at the front of the barracks. He cleared his throat and spoke over the squeaky intercom.

"Today, all personnel will be assigned to a division and a military unit. Arrangements have been made for you to be picked up by runners from the battalion you have been assigned to. Listen up for your name, division, and battalion assignments. Trucks going out to your division or battalion are already here and are waiting. You are to go where I direct you when your name is called. Your division or battalion driver will meet you there."

"Balisher, Brian, Blain, Cordavan, Cortez, Cincenerros, you are assigned to the Third Marine Division, Second Battalion, Ninth Marines. Go out the middle doors to the choppers that are waiting to take you to Dong Ha. Your battalion driver will meet you at Dong Ha.

Barela, Perez, you're assigned to the First Marine Division, Third Battalion, Seventh Marines. Come to the right front of the depot. Your ride to battalion headquarters is waiting for you.

Perez, who I had seen hanging around, picked up his seabag and we both moved toward the left side of the building. Louis P. Perez, was a smart Marine, with a good vocabulary, about 5-8, he was about my height, but with a more solid build and weighted at least 20 lbs more than I did. I weighed 125 lbs when I left the states. We were met by a skinny, light-skinned corporal. He was wearing the new type of lightweight jungle utilities; I had seen other Marines wearing. His long-sleeved, lightweight utility shirt had many pockets and looked like a safari jacket, the type news photographers wore. Since he was wearing this new utility jacket, I figured we would probably be issued them once we got to our unit.

The utilities Perez and I were wearing were made of heavy cotton with button-down shirt pockets, which had the Marine Corps insignia stamped on the left breast pocket. It was the same type Marines had worn since World War II and seen on John Wayne's shirt in the movie, *Sands of Iwo Jima.*

There was no insignia on the lance corporal's left breast pocket. His was a loose-fitting jacket that had two large puffy pockets sewn on the lower part of the loose-fitting shirt that hung low and past his waist. The shirt design did not have that professional sharp dress so characteristic of the Marine Corps uniform appearance.

Our shirts were tucked into our heavy cotton trousers. The corporal's trousers were lightweight with a number of puffy pockets on each leg; his trouser legs were folded up, not bloused. Ours were dressed with a boot band, which held the bottom of the trouser folded in.[34] His fatigues didn't appear to be the type of military uniform the Marine Corps would approve of, much less issue.

"Barela? Perez?" he asked as he looked us over. Reading our stenciled names on our shirts' pockets, he verified the name on the military folders in his hands. We answered and he turned away, motioning with his head for us to follow. We stopped just outside the depot next to a military six-by truck, which he called the mail truck.[35]

"You guys were the only ones assigned to the First Marine Division. Most everyone else will be going to the Third Marine Division," he said.

"Some of the guys that were sent to the Third Marine Division on Friday were ambushed and killed just south of Phu Bai. Four were killed and twenty-three wounded. Its hardcore, NVA soldiers, they're fighting there, Communist soldiers coming straight from Hanoi down the Ho Chi Minh trail. There are mostly VC regulars where you're going." [36]

Third Battalion Seventh Marines, 3/7, is one of the best in the division, and the area we're in isn't that bad.[37] The corporal kept talking while Perez and I listened. He motioned for us to get into the back of the truck and then got into the cab, and we pulled out.

First Marine Division Headquarters
Freedom Hill, Two Miles Northwest of Da Nang
June 18, 1967, 1320 hours

About two miles out, we entered divisional headquarters located on Hill 327, also known as Freedom Hill. It was a large Marine compound, and the truck stopped near a small command post. There we helped load six cases of soda and ten cases of beer on board that were headed for battalion. A short time later, a Marine lance corporal carrying an M-16 rifle and the battalion's red-colored mailbag joined us. He sat up front, riding shotgun.

CHAPTER FOUR

Sharing Pain, Suffering, and Shame
Convoy Road, Route 540
June 18, 1967, 1400 hours

As we were about to leave, two other Marines jumped into the back of the truck. One of the Marines was carrying a loaded M-16 rifle. He was short and a "boot" like us; I could tell by the clean cotton utilities he was wearing and his clean leather boots. The other Marine was a corporal and an old-timer carrying an M-14 rifle. He was wearing the new type of jungle boots and the new type of lightweight utilities but they were already frayed. The Marine was tall and skinny, his light-colored skin covered by a dark tan. We were hot in our heavy cotton utilities. The old salt looked cool and fresh in his. We sat with our backs up against the cab to avoid the dust; he sat near the tail end where he could watch where we were going, his rifle draped across his lap.

I sat silently studying and staring at him. He seemed like someone that had seen a lot of action. His movements were slow with purpose. His face pockmarked with scabs and reddish spots from small cuts and insect bites. I looked at his wrinkled face, his cut and bruised hands and long fingers. I wondered what a story his torn, dirty, and worn-out fatigues could tell.

His eyes were the most fascinating part about him. They were distant as if he was seeing something we couldn't see. He was fully alert and aware of our surroundings, and I felt a sense of protection with his presence on board. His expressionless round eyes revealed much, but seemed to hide a lot more as they constantly skimmed the roadway ahead. Like a vigilant hawk, he barely moved his head, expertly scanning the terrain ahead. His eyes constantly shifted, checking out far tree lines and nearby hedgerows as well as the numerous clusters of thick bushes that grew alongside the roadway.

There were times when the old salt seemed lost in time and space when he focused on a certain spot along the road, up ahead, and it seemed as if those seconds brought back memories of similar settings and enemy encounters. It was then that a blank, distant stare surfaced. It was as if he was viewing images in the back of his mind. For those split seconds, the Marine was gone into memories of his past and he wasn't with us; he wasn't there in the truck either. Then almost immediately, he was back, his light blue eyes once again focused on the terrain before us. Then his eyes would begin again their shifting sequence, scanning and reconnoitering, seeking, and searching the terrain ahead. To him, it was the habit of survival, experience, and war. To me, he was an experienced Marine that had seen combat and survived. I was fascinated by him and sat there watching, studying his movements. Then suddenly, his head shifted. His eyes opened wide, but his hands never moved toward his weapon's trigger guard.

I knew something was up; he was looking up and toward his left, toward my right rear, taking in and analyzing images from something that was happening up ahead in the air above us. I turned slowly to my right to see what he was looking at. The other Marines, unaware of his interest, were lost in their own secret thoughts.

Eighty feet in the air, a hundred feet away, a fierce air battle was being waged between two birds. The larger of the two, a skinny black bird, had something in its beak and the smaller white bird was attacking, squealing, screaming, and pecking away at the larger bird's head. As the smaller bird dive-bombed, the larger black bird turned, twisted, and tried to maneuver out of its way.

As the truck passed by the commotion, another long, white-tailed smaller bird joined in the attack. The skinny black bird dropped its prey, and the small featherless plump baby bird plummeted to its death. The attacking white birds continued their assault, relentlessly pursuing the larger black bird as it frantically tried to get away.

I caught the eyes of the old-timer just then. He knew that I had also witnessed the aerial conflict; and in his eyes, for the first time, I caught a glimpse of the afterimages that were embedded deep within him, images from his heart and mind. I saw what others never see, the pain and suffering associated with the struggles of life that dwells within a fighting man's soul, and I felt a sense of acknowledgment flowing between us.

For a split second I was there, sharing his pain, suffering, guilt, and shame. I shared with him the battles he had witnessed as well as the strength he had found to endure. I learned more about war in that microsecond of life than in all my training. I had heard about war, but now I was beginning to understand the battles I would have to face.

The route to 3/7 headquarters was a dusty one. We were traveling south, away from the DMZ and the city of Da Nang. The narrow dirt road had no markings identifying it; both sides of the road were barren and dry. To the west of the roadway was a large mountain range with slopes that varied in height with small inlet valleys in between. The top of the ridgeline was covered by thick green foliage and the distant dark shadows of another world.

A short time later, we crossed a narrow wooden bridge sandwiched in between two large dirt mounts. On both sides of the bridge were sandbagged security posts manned by Marines. A small hand painted sign read; Cobb Bridge.[38] Such a small compound; I wondered where the Marines ate and slept.

Scattered rice paddies emerged on both sides of the road followed by a series of canals that broke away from a distant river flowing from the foot of the mountains. The water channels crisscrossed the flat terrain numerous times and emptied into dark, rich, green rice paddy fields.[39]

The rice fields, fed by numerous streams, were overflowing with water; some were flooded. Individual green rice plants stood tall, firm, and healthy. It was the first time I had seen rice plants so close, and I was fascinated by how perfectly balanced, each plant appeared. Each plant had five or six stems protruding from a common stalk. The plants were aligned straight, running parallel to the rice paddy dirt dikes that separated each field. They looked like thousands of miniature green soldiers, all standing perfectly still in perfect aligned formation.

Vietnamese farmers and some children were using narrow-raised, hard-pressed dirt dikes to walk around the rice fields. The dikes rose one to two feet above the flooded fields. Some dikes had agricultural channels running alongside them where dirty brown water flowed feeding other fields.

Near a large canal, two young Vietnamese children—a tall girl and a skinny boy with torn, dirty, and baggy trousers—were busy drawing water out of the canal and emptying it into an agricultural channel. They stood facing each other, one lower than the other with their feet spread wide apart. In between them, they were swinging, a large wooden bucket that had four ropes attached to it. Two of the end pieces of the rope were tied to the bottom and two to the top of the bucket.

They slung the bucket in between them back and forth effortlessly. With each forward step and backward swing, they dropped the bucket into a ditch full of running muddy water. The momentum carried it deep into the canal's water, and as the two stepped backward, they pulled on the ends of the ropes and the bucket rose rapidly and shot across between them. They stepped forward and maneuvered the attached ropes in such a way that the bucket overturned and dropped its water load into the agricultural ditch, and then they slung it back for another load. From a distance, it looked as if they were playing with a large rubber slingshot. One, two, step forward, three, four, step back, and the rocking human water pump watered the rice fields. I wondered if they were actually going to eat the rice being fed by the dirty brown water they were withdrawing from the ditch.

We passed a series of squalid small villages that lined both sides of the road. Off in the distance, a dozen or more straw-covered huts were partially hidden in distant tree lines. Clusters of trees met other tree lines with scattered small clearings in between, followed by jungle areas filled with thick underbrush; the terrain seemed to be flowing out from the sides of the mountain like giant plump fingers reaching toward the roadway we were traveling on.

Dark green rice paddy fields lay like soft velvet pieces of clothing within the raised dikes; each field varied in size, color, and shape. Each field was evenly dressed with rice plants perfectly planted in place. The villages, tree lines, jungle, and colorful rice paddy fields—all of it seemed connected to the huge mountain range by sight, design, or purpose. It seemed as if a master gardener had designed the scenic terrain we were passing through. All of it was beautiful and picturesque like the scenes one would read about in fairy-tale books. The country was beautiful.

As we passed the hamlets closer to the road, black-pajama-clad villagers wearing cone-shaped hats walked slowly and listlessly beside the road. They were mostly wrinkled old men and women. Some carried on their shoulders perfectly balanced long bamboo poles with large straw baskets on each end. The baskets barely moved as the villagers made their way alongside the roadway.

Some villagers sat like ducks only a few feet from the road. They sat silently squatting, chewing, and spitting out dark red betel nut juice from black-stained teeth.

As the six-by truck passed, it bathed the villagers with dust, dirt, and filth, spewing chunks of dry, caked mud toward where they sat. They never bothered to move or cover their faces. They seemed indifferent to us and to the world, to time, and to their future. This was their little corner of the world, and it was their way of life. Sitting and spitting was important now and that was what they were doing; nothing else mattered. Not one of them bothered to look our way as we passed.

There were no American advertisements or signs of commercialism posted along the roadway, just walking or squatting villagers indifferent to the world, showing no signs of emotions.

We passed a number of small South Vietnamese military guard posts that looked more like British phone booths without doors than sentry positions. Some posts were nothing more than a small gate with a wooden overhanging cover at the side of the roadway near the entrance to a village. The booths were mostly manned by ARVN (Army of the Republic of Vietnam) or PFs (Popular Force Soldiers).[40] Some had a Combined Action Platoon (CAP) attached to them.[41]

CAC/CAP units near villages were heavily fortified with sandbagged bunkers and barbed wire at the entrance and around an identifiable perimeter. Unlike the villagers, the armed Marines wearing soft covers and no flak jackets looked up and waved, or just gave the mail truck a quick once-over glance as we passed.[42]

The Marines in the back of the truck, the truck driver, and the Marine corporal riding shotgun were armed; yet Perez and I hadn't been issued weapons. Perhaps where we were going wasn't going to be such a dangerous place after all.

We turned left off the main road and traveled east where we came to another but larger wooden bridge also manned by Marines.[43] Once we crossed the bridge we made a slight right turn and began to climb a long, narrow hill. It was the home and headquarters of the Third Battalion, Seventh Marines.

The road before us was freshly oiled; a suffocating sulfuric odor hung in the air, stinging my nostrils and making my eyes water. The hill was ablaze in activity. Men, trucks, jeeps, tanks, ontos, and amtracks[44] were moving about. Two mechanical mules were racing each other alongside a dirt road on the outskirts of the compound.[45]

A sentry on guard duty nodded at us as we drove through the front gate. The old-timer in the back of the truck reached down, took a can of soda from one of the cases, and yelled out, "Hey, Terry! Goody!" The sentry turned to look at the Marine who'd called out his name as the Marine threw him the can of Coke. The sentry, carrying his M-16 slung over his left shoulder, took a quick step forward to try and catch the flying soda can with his right hand but missed. When he stepped forward, he had to reach up with his left hand to grab hold of his rifle swinging down over his left shoulder. Both his rifle and the can of soda struck the ground at the same time. The warm can of soda popped open, squirting its sticky caramel-colored brown spray all over the Marine and his weapon.

"Damn you, Moses!" he yelled back at the old-timer on top of the truck. The Marine flipped him off, and the sentry quickly picked up the can of soda and sucked at the foam oozing from the top of the can.

As we entered the main compound, the road ran through the center of the hill. At the top, clearly silhouetted against the skyline, were several wooden canvas covered barracks. Marines in various states of military uniform were standing around talking in front of the barracks or walking from one place to another. Very few of them were wearing steel pots or flak jackets. Some Marines carrying eating utensils were walking in loose formation toward what appeared to be the mess hall located on the south side of the hill. A helipad was located on the north side next to what appeared to be a large concrete communications bunker.

The truck passed by battalion headquarters and the company barracks of Mike, Lima, and Kilo companies. India Company, to which both Perez and I had been assigned, was at the very end. We stopped and the corporal took our military orders inside the company barracks. From the top of the truck, I could see that the compound was surrounded by a large river that wrapped itself around the hill, and at its south end near the bottom of the hill was a large Vietnamese village.[46]

We disembarked and sat down on wooden steps that led into the battalion's supply barrack. The barrack, like others around it, was built four feet off the ground. A Marine walked up, and Perez and I moved aside to let him by. As he entered the building, a tight spring snapped the screen door shut. In a flash of remembrance, the sound brought back vivid memories of a small neighborhood grocery store in Las Cruces, New Mexico.

The last time I visited the store was when my grandmother died on my tenth birthday. The store was actually a house near where my grandparents lived. On the store's screen door hung a large round red and white aluminum Coca-Cola sign. A small cowbell was attached to the door. When you walked in, the door snapped shut and the bell would ring so the proprietor would know someone had entered.

Large glass containers filled with soft, colorful Mexican made sugar candies lined the top of the counter. A magazine rack nearby always held the latest copy of *Santos*, the white-masked Mexican wrestling champion turned public hero. It was one of the monthly magazines I enjoyed glancing through. I couldn't read Spanish, but I remember scanning the thick paperback-size comic book to see Santos fight evil caricatures. He took on gangsters as well as corrupt Mexican military and police officials. They shot at him with bazookas, Thompson machine-guns, and all types of fire-spitting weapons; but Santos, although weaponless, always prevailed.

Our corporal escort came out, and we followed him around the corner to another row of wooden barracks. The third one down the aisle was unoccupied. One side of the barrack had its thick green-colored canvas covering rolled up. Torn, thick nylon mesh was stretched from the lower wooden plywood section to the top of the hard back's frame. This allowed fresh air and daylight into the otherwise hot and dark barrack.

As we entered, I noticed the discolored, cream-colored canvas bunks looked like they were all leftovers from World War II. Many of them had dirt or dry-caked mud on one end or the other. I looked around to see what choices I had and saw a newer green-colored cot farther back, but the wooden stick that held the canvas secured to the end was broken and sticking out, so the canvas was resting on the wooden floor. Otherwise, the bunk bed looked new, but just a small flaw had rendered it useless. None of the other cots were any better.

I walked all the way back and chose one with a darker green color to it. The cot had been swept clean. I wanted to be as far away as possible from the barrack's front entrance, the noise, and lights. Sleeping at the Da Nang airfield had not been restful; the lights, noise, and night activity had kept me awake and restless. I was tired and craved a solid night's sleep.

When Perez walked in, he chose the first cot nearest the front door and promptly sat down. A red puff of dust billowed up from the canvas bed, bathing him in a cloud of dry filth. He had been sweating from the hot, humid air and the fine powder was drawn to him like a magnet. He got up and beat the canvas, trying to get the loose dirt and caked mud out. Soon the front of the barracks was covered with a dark red cloud of dust.

In front of the barracks, a trench line zigzagged around the battalion's perimeter. In front of that trench line farther down the hill were sandbagged bunkers and another smaller intermittent trench line. Farther down the hill's slope, barbed wire and coils of concertina wire were intermittently stretched so that the wire was crisscrossed to form a wired barrier. Numerous strands of wire were laid out for about 100 feet down the slope, offering some security from enemy attack.

Nearby was an old French-fortified cement tower. The round bunker was thirty feet high and twenty feet in diameter. Long, skinny vertical slants were cut into its sidewalls with horizontal shooting slants on top. On the roof of the building, Marines had erected an open sandbagged bunker. Sentries were standing watch on top of the tower and in some of the bunkers below. I felt powerless. I had been in country going on four days and still had not been issued a weapon; still, I was more interested in getting a quiet night's sleep than I was in obtaining a weapon.

When darkness came, the humid hot air lingered heavily in the back of the barrack. Sleeping was going to be impossible, so I went outside and lifted the rear canvas to let in fresh air. When I returned, I found that with the fresh air came the light and the noise and small flying insects that somehow found a way inside through holes in the nylon screen.

In the barrack next to ours, Marines were sitting around wooden table playing cards. Among them were the old-timer and the man he called Goody. Loud music blared from a radio nearby. I went back outside and dropped the canvas cover back down. Inside, darkness and silence returned as did the hot, humid air and another flood of loud, buzzing, flying insects. I took off my heavy cloth utility jacket, covered my head with it, and fell into a deep sleep.

A Machine-gunner's MOS
Third Battalion, Seventh Marines Headquarters
Republic of South Vietnam
June 19, 1967, 0600 hours

Early the next morning, I was awakened by a Marine corporal who was assigned to supply (H&S).[47]

"Barela, Barela!" I sat up.

"Barela?"

"Yes," I answered.

"Your MOS 0331?"

"Yes, sir," I answered and regretted having used the word "sir" as soon as I'd said it. I had used the word automatically out of respect rather than military rank recognition.

"Sir, my tenth general order is 'to salute all officers, and all colors and standards not cased.'" During recruit training, we memorized all eleven general orders. We learned to recite them in our sleep, to say them on command, and were taught to take them seriously. Respect for officers and those of higher rank had been drilled into us during recruit training and the first word uttered out of our mouths was always "sir." Once we graduated from basic training, corporals and sergeants were no longer called sir, but officers were, and officers were always saluted.[48]

Second Lieutenant Quartz at ITR was fresh out of Officer Candidates School and would make a point every morning to walk past us at a slow pace as our platoon stood in formation. Every day he would begin to salute, hesitate, and wait because enlisted men are supposed to recognize and render a salute to an officer first. When we snapped to attention and saluted, he would sharply return the salute, grin, and walk away with his head held higher, proud of the privilege that officer ranking had given him.

The corporal who had awakened me was the same Marine I had seen in the back of the truck the day before. Realizing I had called him sir, the corporal with a slight downward grin on the right side of his lips said, "Moses, my name is Moses. Go get some chow and then report to the supply barracks. We have some machine-guns that need cleaning." I acknowledged his request, and then Perez and I went to India Company's office to pick up the mess kits and then headed toward the mess hall, falling in line with other Marines headed that way.[49]

On the left side of the small roadway was a gully filled with damaged amtracks, ontos, six-bys, tanks, jeeps, and other military transport vehicles and artillery equipment piled together in a huge scrap mass. It was an armored junkyard, an island full of victims of the enemy's land mines and mortar shells.[50]

Chow consisted of watery powdered eggs, mush, burned bacon, toast, and a cold glass of powdered milk. This time the meal was cooked by military personnel; Vietnamese civilians were not allowed to work in the mess hall. While I saw South Vietnamese soldiers walking around the perimeter, none of them were eating in the mess hall, and they seemed to stay in their own section on the other side of the hill.

In line at the mess hall, I saw the same Marine I had seen on sentry duty when we entered the compound the day before. He came over to where I was sitting.

"You a machine-gunner?" he asked. I nodded yes. The Marine reached out to shake my hand. "Terry Goodman," he said. "But everyone calls me Goody. You might be First Platoon's machine-gunner replacement,". Goody was a tall, thin, blond-haired Marine full of information. I told him after chow I was supposed to clean nine M-60s and he laughed. "Didn't know there were that many in the whole battalion," he said. "Corporal Moses at supplies was with First Platoon; he'll take care of you if you ever need extra gun parts."

After eating, we cleared our mess trays by scraping the remains into a large garbage can. The mess trays with the utensils hooked together was then dipped into a garbage can filled with boiling hot, soapy water. They were then dipped into two other cans until you pulled them out clean. Oil-burning stovepipes attached to the cans kept the water hot.

Walking back, I could see a column of Marines coming up from the bottom of the hill through a break in the perimeter wire. As the Marines zigzagged their way up the hill, I noticed they were all wearing the new lightweight jungle fatigues. Small green sweat towels hung around their necks. They wore flak jackets and cartridge belts that held grenades, ammo pouches, and at least two canteens. All were carrying the M-16 rifle that was new to the Marine Corps. I hadn't been trained nor had I fired or qualified with the M-16 rifle.[51] Marines going on R&R called the weapon, little Mattie Mattel's because of their black plastic stock that made them look more like toy rifles that belong in a toy store than real weapons for combat. A plus for the weapon was that the ammo was of a smaller caliber so Marines could carry more bullets. I had already heard the M-16 was often malfunctioning in combat. It had faulty extractors or extractor springs, and there had been some problem with the quality of the ammunition. The rifle's magazine was designed to hold twenty rounds, but if fully loaded, the spring quickly became weak in the moist tropical climate of Vietnam, so Marines loaded only eighteen or nineteen bullets into the magazines and this kept the spring's tension tight.

The squad of ten Marines looked like a professional hunting party. They were loaded for war; this time it was not a squad, out on a training exercise in the foothills of Camp Pendleton—this time they had gone out on patrol looking for a real enemy. "The deadliest thing in the world," Sergeant Nelson had told us, "is a Marine and his weapon." And the Marines in the column looked it.

Among the column of Marines entering the perimeter was Borgman from the same machine-gun training class I had attended at Camp Pendleton. As soon as they entered the compound, the squad of Marines who had been carrying their weapons at waist level swung their weapons to sling arms, laid them over their shoulders or behind their necks, holding on to them by the rifle's barrel and stock.

Darrel Borgman was tall and thin. His dark blue eyes contrasted sharply with his light skin color and pockmarked, avocado-shaped pink face. He was glowing bright red from the heat of the early morning sun. Borgman was the type of Marine that would get into dangerous situations but somehow always managed to slide by without getting seriously hurt. He was carrying an M-16, two grenades were attached to the right side of his flak jacket, and another one was hooked by its safety lever to his flak jacket's left breast pocket. He wore no undershirt beneath his flak jacket. Two ammo pouches and a canteen were hooked to his cartridge belt. His trouser legs were rolled up high above new jungle boots; he was not wearing boot bands.[52]

The column stopped in front of battalion headquarters, and the squad leader went inside to give his report. The patrol was made up of Marines from various companies assigned to 3/7. All were Marines in transit; most were waiting to rejoin their companies who were out on a major military operation.

I approached Borgman who seemed to be in a trance, his thoughts far away. It wasn't until I stood right in front of him that he recognized me.

"Hey, Cookie," he said. "When did you get here?" We shook hands hurriedly. His hand was warm and wet. Perspiration was flowing steadily from his brow down the side of his face. He took the thick green towel draped around his neck and wiped the sweat off his forehead, flushed face, and neck. The beads of perspiration reappeared as soon as they were wiped away.

"Yesterday," I answered.

"Tex is here," he added. "Both of us are in India Company, Third Platoon."

"I've been assigned to India Company, but no platoon," I said. "They haven't given me a weapon yet."

"Don't worry, you'll be assigned to weapons platoon and then attached to First, Second, or Third Platoon. It's not the way we were told it would be. Things are done differently here. We're assigned to a company and then attached to a platoon, so we're really not in a weapons platoon except on paper.[53] They'll give you a weapon as soon as you're assigned to a platoon. One good thing about you not having a weapon is that you don't stand watch or go on patrol until you are issued one."

"How do you like the M-16?" I asked.

"I don't know; the day after I got here they gave me the M-16 and then sent me out on patrol. The corporal in charge of that patrol showed me how to lock 'n' load, take the safety off and change magazines. But I haven't fired it yet. We were supposed to famfire (practice shooting) the weapon, but no one knows when or where."[54]

The corporal who had been in charge of the patrol came back and dismissed everyone until 1600 hours when they were supposed to report back for night watch assignment.

Borgman had only been in country a couple of days longer than I but had already been on two daylight patrols.

When I had first seen Borgman walking through the perimeter's wire, he blended in so well with the others in formation that he looked like a seasoned old salt. A veteran of months in Vietnam, I had thought, until I recognized him.

"Today we went out about six klicks,"[55] he told me. "We patrolled around the hill, walking through muddy rice paddy fields instead of going around them or walking on the dikes because the area is heavily booby-trapped. The gooks' booby trap places we might be patrolling through. They come down from the mountains and take money or food from the villagers. Patrolling keeps them away from most of the villages. You really don't know who's VC and who isn't unless they shoot at you. It's spooky because when you come to a village, there are only old men, old women, and little kids around. The villagers look away when we come by. Usually, a company is assigned to battalion and they run the daily patrols, but right now, everyone's out on a battalion-size operation, "Operation Arizona,"[56] across the river," he said, looking southwest across the river.

"Right now, whoever is in transit is assigned to go on patrols, go on working parties, or stand night watch."

"Where's Dustin?" I asked.

"This morning he rode shotgun for the mail truck. Probably in Da Nang—that's a good detail to get assigned to."

Dennis "Tex" Dustin was the complete opposite of Borgman. He was shorter with a heavier build, rough, tough, but naïve. He didn't smoke, but drank hard liquor "like a Texas mule," Borgman had once said. Dustin and I had gone through MCRD and machine-gun school together. We were now assigned to India Company 3/7.

When I reported to the supply barracks, Corporal Moses was standing with his back toward the door, fidgeting with a .45 caliber pistol. Without looking up, he pointed to the M-60 machine-guns on the wooden floor to his left. A gallon-size can of cleaning solvent and cleaning equipment lay nearby.

There were nine machine-guns that needed cleaning, so I took each gun apart, poured the cleaning solvent into a five-gallon bucket, and dropped the rear end of each gun's barrel to soak.

The fetid smell of cleaning solvent soon filled the air. Moses took in a deep breath.

"Ah, the smell of Hoppes!" Moses said. "Like the smell of coffee in the morning and a pregnant woman at night, it's what makes life worth living and it's all part of Marine Corps history. It's what helps us make the world safe and secure," he chuckled and then turned around to finish what he was doing.

A short time later, Moses left, saying he would be returning in the afternoon. I took my time scraping off the caked carbon and heavy residue of filth I was finding throughout the guns. Some of the carbon was baked on and hard as nails to remove. Much of it was deeply embedded in between the locking mechanism and the trigger guards. The guns hadn't had a good cleaning in a very long time, and I decided to do the best job I could with the equipment at hand. It wasn't much: a rod and two wire brushes, one of which had seen better days. I realized that the only way I was going to get out the caked-in carbon and grime was by using a lot of elbow grease, and for the next five hours that's all I did: soaked and scrubbed the guns clean.

I had learned the weapon well and was familiar with its nomenclature and overall effective firing power. We had been trained on how to fire: a short controlled volley of bullets or long, powerful, sweeping bursts of fire. I felt comfortable with the gun, but I was in no hurry to carry it into combat.

With the tripod in place, the machine-gun's accuracy was awesome. A traverse and elevating mechanism attached to the tripod allowed the gunner to fix the gun's firepower onto a designated spot. At night, using this method, you could fire at a suspected route the enemy might come from, without actually seeing the target.

I had a great deal of respect for the gun's and my own ability. I knew that if I had to, I could put out a wall of lead with it. We had been trained to load, unload, and take it apart in seconds. It was a skill I knew I possessed; how that would play out while under fire was another question.

Corporal Moses came back late that afternoon just as I was finishing the last of the guns. He picked up one at random and tore it apart in front of me. The way he tore the weapon apart made me wonder if he had a 0331 MOS.

He examined the gun closely and seemed pleased with the overall thoroughness of the job. He double-checked the gas cylinder, turning the gun's barrel upside down. The cylinder slid down smoothly and made a nice-sounding *thunk* when it hit the bottom. If the piston in the gas cylinder moves smoothly back and forth, the gun will operate effectively. I had left a light film of oil on the guns because of the hot, humid air in Vietnam and I was prepared to give that as a reason if Moses asked.

"Put more oil on them," he said. "They're going to be stored for a while."

Moses did not bother to check any of the other guns but simply went back behind the counter. Although he never said so, when he turned and walked away, I knew he was pleased with the job I had done. Praise was not common in the Corps. It was especially not common in Vietnam, and no one really expected it, but I was proud to have done a good job.

Cpl. Russell Moses, according to Goody, had been shot twice on January 30, 1967, at the base of a small hill near Duc Pho in Quang Ngai Province during Operation DeSoto.[57] Due to his injuries, he was finishing his tour of duty at H&S.

Moses had been the point squad leader, that day, Goody said. Sergeant Holloway had called Moses' squad up and as they entered through a gate leading toward a village, NVA soldiers opened fire on them with .50 caliber machine-guns, small arms, and rocket fire. For six hours, Moses, who had been shot twice in the initial attack, lay prone in the mud in what they later called—the gates of hell. Moses used his squad's radio to call in air strikes and keep Captain Clark, India Company's commanding officer, informed of the situation at the point of contact. That evening, after six hours of battle as the enemy was preparing to assault the dying and wounded Marines still alive in Moses' squad, S/Sgt. Spahn led a squad of volunteer Marines to rescue Moses and his squad.[58]

When they returned they discovered a Marine by the name of Richard Garcia, was missing. Capt. Clark then quickly organized another squad of Marine volunteers to go back to the site with him, [59] and recovered Garcia's body where he had been shot and lay dead.[60]

Before I left, Corporal Moses turned to look at me and for the first time, I noticed how tired he looked. Wrinkles seemed to have suddenly appeared around the dark puffy shadows underneath his eyes. His look seemed to acknowledge what we had shared for that brief second behind the six-by truck, yet at the same time, there was an awareness of guilt and fear for my welfare.

"I looked at your record," he said as he turned to look away. "You've been assigned to First Platoon."

I left the supply barracks wondering what First Platoon would be like. According to rumors, First Platoon was the choice platoon to be assigned to. Second and Third Platoons had recently lost men in combat, and grunts measured a platoon's overall effectiveness by its ability to inflict heavy punishment upon the enemy while suffering minimum casualties. Perez, Borgman, and Dustin had been assigned to Third Platoon. The other two Marines I had met, Goody and Moses had both been in First Platoon, and they were old-timers finishing off their tours of duty and were going home.

Vietnam Orientation
Third Battalion Seventh Marines Headquarters
South Vietnam
June 20, 1967, 0800 hours

On the second day at battalion, a group of us were sent to Vietnam orientation classes where we were taught about the Vietnamese culture; the government of South Vietnam (GVN); the Marine Corps pacification program; and how to distinguish between a VC, an NVA, a Popular Force, or an ARVN soldier. While they all looked alike, the Popular Force and the ARVN soldiers were South Vietnam's armed forces and our allies; but just as often, they could be our enemy, the instructor said.

"We're here," the instructor said to us, "to help them win their war." While the main reason was to stop the spread of Communist aggression, the Marine Corps had other objectives that we were to follow.

We were to serve mostly in defensive positions: to guard, watch, wait for the enemy to act, and then respond. Those were to be our standing orders. In addition to this, we were to provide security for a number of air bases.

We were there to help protect the villagers from Communist soldiers that raided the villages and forced young men to join their services and just as often killed the village chiefs and other government officials. Things didn't seem right to me because, as Marines, we were trained to be offensive, to go after the enemy, to seek and destroy them. But we were now set in defensive positions around our compounds.[61]

In the class, I learned, our primary responsibility was to defend the Da Nang Air Base and our own perimeters. We were also responsible for military bases in Phu Bai and Chu Lai. All three of the military bases were located in what was called the I Corps Theater of Operations. This was the area allocated to the First Marine Division. The Third Marine Division was operating north of us in Quang Tri Province. We were in Quan Nam Province. The U.S. Army was responsible for the area south of us. The Da Nang Air Base had been rocketed on several occasions, and we were on standby to respond by helicopter assault wherever the VC might have been sighted or might have launched their rockets against Da Nang. We were told, we were there to support the South Vietnamese Army in their combat missions and to seek out and destroy the Vietcong when they posed an immediate threat to the South Vietnamese government or its civilians. West of us in Thuong Duc was a Green Beret Special Forces camp. It was located close to the Laotian border, and they were always biting off more than they could chew and often, Marines were called in to bail them out of a tight situation.

Most importantly, we were told that we were in Vietnam to establish a working relationship with the local Vietnamese population. It was part of our job to make friends with the local villagers. By doing this, we would deprive the Vietcong of recruits or recruiting. Marine CAC units were assigned to certain villages for this reason.[62]

In the orientation classes, we learned about the history of the Seventh Marine Regiment and that we were located south of Da Nang. The mountains to our west were called the Annamite Mountains with heights up to ten-thousand-five-hundred feet. They were the natural barrier between Vietnam and Laos. One could follow them north into China or south into Saigon. On the other side of the mountains was the Ho Chi Minh trail, which North Vietnam used to resupply their troops fighting in the South. The South China Sea was east of us. The area to our south was known as the An Hoa basin, and it was heavily booby-trapped.

On June 22, I was called to the administrative barrack. The sergeant behind the desk asked some questions and then said, my pay had been fouled up. He handed me paperwork to take into regimental headquarters, so I could get paid. I caught a ride on the mail truck going to the Seventh Marine Regiment headquarters on Hill 55.

Hill 55 was located just a few miles northeast of us. All the Marine passengers in the back of the truck were armed and on alert. I sat in the back of the truck with them without a weapon, going through an area known as Dodge City.

"Do you want to receive full pay while you're here or send it home?" the paymaster asked me. I chose to send it all home keeping only half of the $65.00 combat-pay increase, which I felt was all I would need for razors, laundry, candles, cigarettes and any other small personal needs.

Refugee Dump Detail
Third Battalion Seventh Marines Headquarters
South Vietnam
June 23, 1967, 0800 hours

After breakfast on the morning of June 23, we fell into loose formation in front of the administrative barrack. We were mustered, so we could be assigned to working parties for the day. When the duty NCO came out of the barrack, he didn't bother to call us to attention. Instead, he started reading off our names from a work-detail list.

"Barela, Muszel, Puder, and Dunning, you have the dump truck detail. Dustin and Borgman, you're riding shotgun for the mail trucks. The rest of you men, see Sergeant Shaffer; he's got a special detail that needs to be done."

We fell out of formation, and those of us assigned to the dump detail boarded a waiting flatbed six-by truck. For the rest of the morning, we went around the compound and unloaded trash from trash cans into the back of the truck. The cans had been converted from empty fifty-gallon barrels and were now filled with garbage. Our last stop was at the mess hall where we picked up the drums filled with the garbage we had earlier scraped off our mess trays. As soon as we loaded the barrels on board, a nauseating smell engulfed the truck and hundreds of thumb-size flies buzzed all around us. As we headed toward the dumpsite located at the southeast corner of the compound, the wind billowing behind the truck picked up the smell of the garbage and sent it back toward where we stood behind the truck's cab.

Corporal Dunning, Lance Corporal Muszel, and Lance Corporal Steven Puder had worked the trash truck detail before and pulled out large handkerchiefs to cover their mouths. The rest of us had to make do by placing our hands or Marine Corps' Caps over our nose and mouths.

Steven Puder was a tall and thin Marine with long legs and even longer arms. He had an oval face with round eyes and an air of confidence about him. His utility uniform was always spotlessly clean and looked freshly pressed compared to ours. His boots were polished and his hair cut short Marine Corps' style. He kept mostly to himself and seemed to know what was going on.

"Goddamn, Puder, this is fucking Vietnam! You don't have to spit shine your boots for a working party," Muszel had told Puder when he had jumped on the garbage truck for the day's detail. Puder just took it all in stride as if he hadn't heard a thing.

"We're lucky," Puder said as the truck hurried along the outside road that ran along the perimeter wire. A cloud of dry yellow dust swelled behind us, covering the roadway and obscuring the view to the rear of us. "We could have been sent out with Sergeant Shaffer and ended up burning shitters all day. Try and get that smell out of your utilities, it can't be done."

Every other day, fifty-gallon metal barrels that had been cut in half were pulled out from the back side of the outhouses on base. The barrels full of human waste had kerosene poured over them and lit on fire. Marines assigned to that detail had to stand by until all the waste was consumed and then they would replace the cans back in the outhouses. The foul smell of burning human waste lingered in the air for hours, long after the last of the shitters had been burned.

"It's the shittiest detail the Corps can assign you," Puder added, and both, he and Muszel laughed.

As soon as the truck came within view of the dumpsite, Vietnamese kids began to emerge from a nearby tree line. Dozens of blackbirds of various sizes and shapes were scavenging through the dump site, and as the truck approached, they flew up as cat-sized rats scurried away in all directions.

As soon as the truck was backed up, Dunning cried out, "Hurry up. Push all the shit off the truck, hurry up!"

I realized why the sudden urgency in his voice as a number of skinny Vietnamese kids came rushing toward the truck. The majority of them wore tan shorts, dirty white short-sleeved shirts and all were wearing Marine utility caps. Some were carrying empty sandbags as they ran toward the truck. The children dove for the trash as soon as we threw it out and began to bite, kick, and fight among themselves for whatever pieces of garbage they could scrounge.

They were war orphans contending for whatever tidbits of food they could find. Whatever appeared edible or usable was quickly stuffed into the sandbags. Some were stuffing globs of the garbage we had scraped off our trays that morning into their mouths. Others were clearly seeking the empty and half-empty cans of C-rations. Some were veterans in this war on poverty and hunger, and the garbage was their spoils of war. Darting about, some kids spied out the better morsels of discarded trash and quickly scooped them up. Those prized possessions would later be sold for money or traded for other basic needs. The more desperate kids quickly shoveled as much of the stuff as they could gather into their pockets, then deposited them at the feet of smaller siblings and quickly returned to the trash pile for another load.

As we rushed to push the trash off, some of the kids began to climb onto the back of the truck for better pickings of the trash that was visibly more appealing to them. One small boy had gotten up so close to the back of the truck that he was being buried alive from the piles of trash we were unloading. The small boy was only about six years old and wearing a dirty yellow Mickey Mouse T-shirt. He was missing his left ear, two front teeth, and his long hair was matted and full of lice.

Muszel and I, thinking the same, reached down to help the small boy. About the same time, Corporal Dunning fired a couple of shots from his M-16 into the air and the children scattered, jumping over the sides of the truck and falling over each other as they ran for the safety of the nearby perimeter wire. The young boy emerged from underneath the pile of rubble, and both Muszel and I pulled him up onto the back of the truck.

We moved faster to unload the remaining trash, kicking the last bit of trash off the truck with our feet. When we finished, I gave the young boy the paper Vietnamese currency I had been given by the Marine at Da Nang and helped him off the truck. The boy stood wide-eyed staring at the money and then at us, his mouth half open.

As soon as the truck started up, the kids ran back toward the piles of refuse. As we pulled out, a half dozen of them started kicking and fighting over an unopened can of ham and lima beans. I had never witnessed hunger so profound, and as the truck bounced back over the dusty road heading back toward the compound, Muszel also seemed troubled.

"It's always the same," he said. "I've had this detail for the past week, and it's always the same. Some are little kids without any clothes on, fighting, biting and kicking for garbage. They're tiny rats, human flies. I swear I wouldn't feed pigs, the shit we threw out that they eat." Samuel Muszel and Puder were both assigned to 60mm mortars. Muszel was a tall Marine with a medium build body; he had strong hands and high cheekbones. It was surprising to hear a Marine make a comment like that, but Muszel cared a lot about others and I could tell he had the ability to become mortars section leader.

When we returned to base, Perez and I were told to report to the supply barracks where we would be issued our M-16 rifle. The supply sergeant took the time to show us how to take the weapon apart, lock and load it, and also informed on what proper care and cleaning should be implemented. He showed us a photocopy taken from the FMF PAC Handbook taped to the wall that read, "The M-16 is rust and corrosion resistant and requires little or no maintenance." Unfortunately, the supply sergeant said there was no cleaning gear for the M-16 available.

Riding Shotgun
Da Nang, South Vietnam
June 24, 1967, 0800 hours

On June 24, I was assigned to ride shotgun into Da Nang with the mail truck. This time, it was Lance Corporal Dunning and I who picked up the new arrivals at the air depot. Among those assigned to 3/7 was a skinny lance corporal by the name of Bruce Ira Rahm, and another guy by the name of Keith Pridemore; both assigned to weapons platoon.

"You guys are lucky to get assigned to the First Marine Division," Corporal Dunning said. "Most everyone else left behind will be going to the Third Marine Division." Then he repeated, almost verbatim, what he had told both Perez and me about a week earlier.

We spent the next three days assigned to similar work details that were called working parties. We worked, but it never was a party. Now that we had been issued weapons, we were assigned to stand perimeter watch at night or to go out on patrol during the day.

The following day, as Perez and I were sitting outside our barracks taking pictures, an ARVN soldier was walking by. The soldier worked at the barbershop and we asked him to pose for pictures. Then we had him hold his hands on top of his head while we took turns posing with the M-16 pointing at him to send the pictures back home. We couldn't speak Vietnamese and he spoke very little English. We communicated by pointing to the camera and the M-16, which we pointed out was not loaded. He smiled, nodded, and posed for us.

The Vietnamese people were small compared to us. The soldier had small hands and a silver-capped tooth. While he posed, I began to get an uneasy feeling about him. He smiled, but something wasn't right.

CHAPTER FIVE

Booby Traps and Land Mines
First Engineer Battalion, Basic Combat Demolition
Landmine Welfare and VC Booby Trap School
June 28, 1967, 1300 hours

On June 28, Perez, Rahm, Pridemore and I, with the Marines assigned to mortars—Sam Muszel, Al Homan, and Steven Puder—were sent to Da Nang to the First Marine Division's First Engineer Battalion for three days of mine and demolition school.

Classes were held outdoors where a mock Vietnamese village had been set up. The village was similar to those in our area where the Vietcong operated. We were taught how to detect booby traps and mines and to blow up tunnels using dynamite (TNT) and a new type of plastic high explosive called C-4.

We learned about sappers who were hardcore elite Communist-trained soldiers and experts in demolition. Sappers set up training schools and taught local VC how to use booby traps, we were told. They trained the VC on everything from a simple bow-and-arrow booby trap where the arrow is released when you step on a hidden wire, to setting up the punji stake or the Bouncing Betty, as well as how to recover and redeploy five-hundred-pound bombs that failed to go off when our planes dropped them.

The VC would often go into an area after it had been barraged with mortar or artillery shells and look for unexploded ordinance. They would then refit them with new triggering mechanisms and bury them in roadways, hang them from tree branches, or hide them under the floorboards of a home or near entrance gates and bridges. The booby traps could be found just about anywhere; in village tunnels, heavy underbrush, and out in the open.

We could expect to find them along the sides of rice paddies or on top of the dikes. The corner of the bamboo gate or around the post leading into a village was a favorite spot the enemy planted their explosive devices. They were found under dead NVA or VC soldiers because the enemy knew that we would search the dead for documents or to obtain military souvenirs. If the NVA/VC did not remove a dead soldier's military gear, it was probably because it was booby-trapped, we were told.

The classes were informative and eye-opening. We were fighting a different type of war than what we had been trained for. Military movies and the training we had received had influenced our thoughts on what to expect. But it was not going to be anything like that. We had been taught to deploy on line and to do a frontal attack against known enemy positions. I had expected the enemy to stay and fight until one side or the other won. I knew we would not retreat so I expected the VC to stand and fight, but this was not the type of war that the NVA/VC was waging in Vietnam.

We had been trained to fight a conventional war, but the VC was using guerrilla tactics. They attacked and then disappeared into the villages, hills, jungles, or into tunnels and spider holes. They were the ones who decided when to make contact and when to break it. When we would pursue them, usually a lone sniper or a cell team composed of three enemy soldiers would stay behind to snipe at us to impede our pursuit. In their retreat, they would leave behind well-placed booby traps and often escaped by running through villages, shooting and wounding civilians to slow us down. The VC knew we always stopped after suffering a casualty to call for a medevac chopper or would stop to help wounded civilians, and this helped them escape just as often they would set up an ambush team or shoot at the choppers when they came in to take out our wounded. All this was new, and none of it had been covered in our training stateside.

Samples of the weapons and booby traps that the enemy used were set up throughout the paths that ran through a mock Vietnamese village. During one of our classes, the instructor passed around several punji stakes for us to examine and feel.

"Anything sharp that you may brush up against or that pops up and cuts you, don't take too lightly," he said. "If it doesn't incapacitate you right away, it may do so later. The bamboo sticks that I am passing around are razor-sharp for a purpose. They are designed to pierce the sole of your boot, to draw blood, and later cause an infection to the foot or other parts of the body. We have found that if the injury is not deep, Marines often do not seek medical attention, but the stakes have often been dipped in human waste to cause infection."

After we heard this, the Marines who had been touching the punji stakes to feel their sharpness quickly passed them on. We learned that chances were just as equal, fifty-fifty, that it will be a booby trap or gunshot that would wound or kill us in Vietnam. After the initial classes, as part of our training, we ran a series of routine squad-sized patrols in the village. As we patrolled along a trail in one of the mock villages, a Marine directly in front of me stepped on something buried in the ground and we all heard a loud click and froze.

"Remember," the instructor immediately spoke up, "if you step on a booby trap, don't move. Stand perfectly still and call for an engineer and one will be sent out. If you're walking on a roadway or trail and you hear a sound like the one you just heard, don't move! You might have just triggered a booby trap. If it doesn't explode right away, it will when you remove your foot from the trigger mechanism. When you do, it might be set to kill you, the man next to you, or the main part of the squad down the trail. If you move, you might kill yourself and the Marine next to you, and if you kill him, he's gonna be pissed off. So don't do anything stupid. Don't move! Just stand still. Most Marine companies have an engineer assigned to them and we're also only minutes away by chopper."

An engineer came forward and disarmed the booby trap, the Marine had stepped on. The explosive charge had been removed, but the trigger still went off making a sound that was loud enough for everyone near the Marine to hear and take a few quick steps away from him.[63]

We completed our training by late afternoon of the thirtieth, and as I was packing my gear, Al Homan came by and asked if I wanted to join him up the hill at the Engineer's Club. Homan had arrived at Battalion HQ shortly after I did, a tall red-haired, freckle-faced farm boy from Nebraska, who was always happy and had never seen the ocean. He said, the first time he had left the state he was born in was when he joined the Marine Corps. His chubby callused hands revealed years of toil and hard labor often associated with rural farm life. His demeanor had already revealed a quest for excitement and a hunger for exploration, yet he was a common sense type of person with an air of humility that invited both praise and association.

We had a few beers at the club when a Marine walked in and announced that the Vietnamese girls were out by the wire. Homan sat up. "Come on, finish your beer, let's go!" he said.

"Where?" I asked.

"To where the girls are at the wire," he answered.

"What if we're caught sneaking out?" I asked.

"Don't worry about it, I was out there last night," he said.

"We might catch the black syph," I told him.

"Use a rubber," he said and reached into his pocket and withdrew a handful of small gray packages. When some fell from his hand, he chuckled like a kid who's been caught with a bag full of candy. He handed me one of the little gray packages.

"We'll take a quick shower when we get back to the area. Don't worry about that black ship everyone talks about, it doesn't exist."[64]

"If you catch anything, a shot of penicillin will take care of it. Most of the girls are pretty clean; they have to stay that way if they want to make any money. It'll only cost you five dollars."

"I don't think I have that much on me."

"That's okay," he answered. "I'll spot you the difference."

As soon as we reached the other side of the wire, two girls came out of nowhere. They reached out for our hands and led us around to some bushes nearby. It was dark and I couldn't really see what the girl holding my hand actually looked like. She looked young and pretty from what I could tell.

She asked me in broken English, "You got rubber?"

"Yes!" I said and showed her the package. She reached out and took it from me.

"Five dollars," she said. I gave her three bucks, and Homan handed her two more. "Come," she said and squeezed my hand, urging me to follow her as she turned toward a cluster of bushes only a few feet away. She sat down, unbuckled my trousers, slipped the rubber in place, and lay down. Her movements were quick and matter-of-fact. As young as she was, it seemed like she'd had a lot of practice at doing what she was doing.

"What if something happens?" I asked Homan who was about twenty feet away and was already lying on top of the girl.

"Don't worry about it; the guys on guard know what goes on over here even though they're supposed to turn us in if we're caught."

"What if we're ambushed?"

Homan was preoccupied and didn't answer. Afterward, we snuck back into the compound, running all the way to the barracks and then to the showers where I used a whole bar of soap getting myself cleaned up.

"We'll go back and drink some more beer, that way you'll pee a lot just in case you might have caught something," Homan said.

The following morning, we returned to Battalion HQ and were told, our company had returned from Operation Arizona and we were to join them on Hill 65 the next day.

A Barren Kidney-Shaped Hill
Hill 65, AT 878577
July 2, 1967, 0900 hours

The hills in Vietnam did not usually have names; they were assigned numbers. Hill 65 stood at an elevation of sixty-five feet above sea level, so it was named Hill 65. Sometimes, the hills were also given a name, usually in honor of a fallen Marine. The distance between Battalion Headquarters Hill 37 and Hill 65 where the field command post for India Company was located was about three miles. The Marine Corps called the route we were traveling on as Route 14, but the Army Corps of Engineers called it Route 4. Since they printed more maps than the Corps, maps showing Route 4 were more readily available.[65] Supplies and equipment were scarce in Nam, and I soon found out that if you needed anything, you usually had to go into Da Nang and trade for it with rear echelon personnel from the different branches of service.

There were nine of us on board the six-by truck *en route* to Hill 65. Three men had been assigned to mortars: Alfred Homan, Samuel Muszel, and Steven Puder.

Besides them, and me, five other Marines were on the truck. One was a boot, he sat wide-eyed looking scared. He hadn't been given the opportunity; the other of us had to adjust a little before being sent out to the company. He had arrived the day before and was now *en route* to our company's headquarters with no inkling of what to expect or what lay ahead, and he hadn't been issued a weapon. At least, I felt I had some idea of what was going on.

The other Marines were Perez, Ira Bruce Rahm, Keith Pridemore and a guy by the name of James Keenan. I had already met Rahm who was a small, skinny, dark-red-haired, innocent, but inquisitive Marine always in good spirits. His curly hair, puffed around his ears, stuck out like cotton candy. He had numerous red freckles that seemed to change colors according to his mood.

Pridemore was a little stockier than Rahm, short fluffy straight hair cut short around the ears, in Marine Corps' style. You could tell he was trying to grow a mustache, at least a small puff of one sat on his upper lip. Pridemore talked as we traveled comparing the area we were passing through with Kentucky where he grew up. All his family lived nearby he said, and once he had met a young girl and brought her home to meet his grandpa, and he told Pridemore, that she was his third cousin. Almost everyone in his family had served in the Marine Corps he said, ever since the Corps was originated. That's how they got the land they now lived on, it was granted to them for their service.

Trees and small villages lined both sides of the road, and rich farmland blanketed the flat lands on the right side of the road. Farther away, scattered villages could be seen along distant tree lines. Villages and hamlets could be seen hidden deeper in the dense jungle. They appeared and disappeared much like one would see pictures while flipping through a series of still photographs, just fast enough so that the figures seemed to move with each succeeding frame that was flipped. Some of the huts were so well camouflaged by the thick, tropical jungles surrounding them that they were barely visible. Large and small trees, tall elephant grass, bamboo, and thick bushes surrounded some of the villages. It was easy to imagine the enemy hiding, living in the jungle or high in the mountains, and then coming down into the villages for supplies.

It was in this overall general area that I would spend the greater part of my time in Vietnam. This was India Company's Tactical Area of Responsibility (TAOR) or "theater of operations." I had thought it strange; they would call a war zone as "theater" as I then understood the word. But then I guessed it was a theater and we were all onstage in this play called life. All of us were subject to change and moved according to who held the script and who pulled the strings that called for action. Unlike the theater, no one knew what the outcome would be at the end of each act—at the end of each battle scene. No one knew how many acts there were or when it would end.

We slowed down and turned right, and the truck began to climb a narrow road leading up the hill. Numerous strands of barbed wire surrounded Hill 65. The sentry at the entrance waved us on as we went through the open gate. A large, newly painted red sign was posted near the left side of the road. It read "Camp R. L. Ringler, in memory of Cpl. Robert L. Ringler Jr., Second Plt. 'Suicide' India Third Battalion, Seventh Marines who gave their life yesterday that, others might live tomorrow, December 17, 1966."[66]

The truck stopped in front of a large sandbagged bunker near the top of the barren hill. Unlike the barracks and bunkers at Battalion Headquarters, most of the bunkers on this hill were cut into the sides of the hill and heavily fortified with sandbags. Each had an accompanying fighting position close by. A small trench line, just a short distance from the wired fence, ran the length of the perimeter.

"Wait here," the corporal who served as the company's runner said, as he went inside the command bunker.

I stood on top of the truck, and I could see all around for miles. The hill was kidney shaped, and at the very top near its center were two 105mm artillery batteries. The air was clean, sweet smelling, and moist. The countryside surrounding the hill was filled with dark green rice paddy fields. At the end of the road we had come up on, was a large village by the name of Truong An (1). The village was bordered by the murky brown waters of the Song Vu Gia River that flowed leisurely eastbound toward the sea.[67] As I looked east, I could see where the river split. The branch going north was called the Song Nghia and it wrapped itself around Hill 37, 3/7's headquarters. On the northern top of Hill 37, the Song Ai Nghia split into two other branches. The wider branch going north was called the Song Yen, and this was the river I had seen that ran between convoy road (Route 540) and regiment on its east side. About five miles further away from there, it split again with the branch going west called the Song Tuy Loan and a branch going east; the famous Song Cau Do River ran northeast, which was one of the large rivers I had seen from the air that emptied into the South China Sea. The branch going northeast that broke off the Song Nghia pass battalion was called the Song La Tho, and it ran along the other side of regiment headquarters that was located on Hill 55. From there the river eventually became the Song Vinh Dien River.

The Song Vu Gia, where it split going south near Dai Loc, took on a snakelike appearance before it mingled with the rapid flowing waters of the Song Thu Bon River.

It seemed that all rivers in Vietnam changed names every few miles and just as often held memorable events. Those who fought battles along the banks of those rivers would always remember those encounters, perhaps not the name of the rivers, but those memories would forever be there as a remembrance.

Route 4, at the bottom of the hill, I could see continued west from where we had turned; and a short distance away from there it crossed a small wooden bridge, then passed through a series of small villages before it disappeared between two large mountain ranges in the far distance. The villages, the road, the rivers, the bridge, the fresh air, and the emerald-colored rice paddies below all added a mystical rare beauty to the overall landscape.

Past the small wooden bridge, a yellow and red South Vietnamese flag was flying high over an ARVN compound. The hamlet nearby was called Tam Hoa, and the Marine compound that provided security for that village was known as CAC 2-2-1.

CAC units were made up of an eight to ten Marine rifle squad. They offered local villagers not only a sense of security but also free medical services provided by a Navy Corpsman assigned to Marine companies. This was a service many villagers needed and readily accepted. However, the village chief, officials, schoolteachers, and other educated people in a secured village were often targeted by the enemy as they blamed the village leaders for allowing Marines to remain in their country. CAC Marines along with a platoon of PF's provided a measure of security for the little village and the bridge at the bottom of the hill. [68]

The Marines stationed there had become familiar with the villagers and as often happens in war, friendships were developed. At night while the village slept, the villagers slept secure, knowing CAC Marines stood watch over them.

Northwest of the hill were a number of quaint Vietnamese villages. Clusters of small huts could be seen bulging out of a series of tree lines bordered by a deep forest at the foot of a dense mountain range. Southwest, across the Song Vu Gia River, the dark green mountains of the An Hoa basin stretched for miles. They were the same beautiful mountains I had first seen from the air before we landed. Now, on the ground looking up at them, knowing what lay hidden under their canopy of dense forest, their massive beauty and strength posed a threat. Even the color had changed from the beautiful deep emerald green I had seen from the plane to a sinister-looking dark military green color.

During the day, Marines patrolled the area below Hill 65 and at night, set up listening posts or ambushes near the trails leading into the villages. For the most part, this kept the NVA/VC away from our area, but during rice harvest time, which occurred twice a year in our area, the enemy would venture into villages and try to extort "taxes" from the villagers in the form of a percentage of the newly harvested rice. To counter this, the Marine Corps launched Golden Fleece Operations, an operation where the Marines provided a security force in the field during harvest time to protect the harvesters and thereby deprive the enemy of a source of food, funds, and supplies.

As the pacification program grew with the support of the local villagers, such source of food supplies were denied to the NVA/VC soldiers; and in return, they began to destroy and burn the villages, rape the women, and take their young sons into captivity to serve in the military ranks of the NVA. Often, village chiefs, teachers, religious leaders, and elders were placed on display in public and then killed in retaliation for supporting the South Vietnamese government. Some villagers and their families targeted for assassination by the NVA chose instead, to relocate to refugee settlements, and one of the largest refugee settlements was located in Dai Loc, the district capital of Quang Nam Province.

First Platoon's radioman, a Marine by the name of Art O'Farrell, came out of the large bunker that served as our company's headquarters and called my name from a list he held in his hand.

"Barela."

"Yes," I answered.

"You're in Weapons Platoon. Guns' hooch is at the top of the hill by the mess tent. When you get there, turn to your left toward the battery unit. Gun's bunker is just down a ways from there."

I slung my seabag over my left shoulder, placed the M-16 at sling arms and headed in the direction the radioman had pointed. As I walked up the hill, I felt that my tour of Vietnam was now beginning.

CHAPTER SIX

A Home with a View
Hill 65, AT 878577
July 2, 1967, 1000 hours

Just past the mess hall was an artillery gun emplacement. From there, I could see a well-beaten path leading from the artillery's position down eighty feet to one of the largest sandbagged bunker on the hill. The bunker appeared to be solidly built, its sandbags laid straight and even. The bunker was unlike the other bunkers I had seen on the hill and what I had seen at Battalion HQs where the sandbags protruded unevenly or had sagging walls.

Two blanket-covered canvas cots were laid out on the barrack's roof. Piles of wooden planks from broken-up artillery ammo boxes were stacked neatly just below a window on the right side of the bunker. The area around the bunker was well policed and swept clean. As I approached the bunker, a stocky white male of medium height with short blond hair came out of the hooch's entrance; he wasn't wearing a shirt so I couldn't tell what his name or rank was.

"You're a machine-gunner?" he asked.

I nodded yes, and he reached out to shake my hand. He had small hands with short stubby fingers and a strong, firm grip.

"I'm Ron Moore," he said, a pleasant look in his eyes, making me feel welcome. "The gun team is out on patrol and Jones, your gun team leader, is in Da Nang picking up supplies." I brought down my seabag.

"You can put your stuff anywhere. Jones will get you squared away when he gets back."

Corporal Ronald Allen Moore was from Manhattan Beach, California. About five feet seven inches tall and well built with the typical California clean-cut, blond hair, blue-eyed, surfer look. Light freckles highlighted puffy red cheeks in his full round face. He turned to go back inside the hooch to finish what he was doing. As he entered the hooch, he reached out and took a stack of letters from a wooden shelf sandwiched in between the wall's sandbags.

A similar shelf in the back of the hooch held a portable record player, candles, flashlights, and someone's personal shaving gear. The bunker's inner walls were lined with stacks of large wooden ammo boxes filled with dirt. Smaller ammo boxes with their bottoms taken out had been turned sideways and were being used as window frames on both sides of the hooch and over the entrance. Sandbags bordered the window frames holding them solidly in place. A wooden stick held the hinged ammo box top open, letting light and air into the bunker.

The bunker was roomy with ample room inside for six to eight men. The ceiling was constructed of long wooden beams reinforced by wooden planks taken from ammo boxes. One could stand upright inside the bunker and still have two feet of clearance overhead. An M-16 rifle hung from its strap near the rear of the bunker; a long nail held it fastened to one of the supporting beams. Other nails held other objects off the floor. The bunker was neatly kept and clean. Ron handed me the letters he had taken off the shelf.

"These are yours," he said.

I counted fourteen letters, all from my wife. Moore was in the process of putting in a new wooden floor using the wooden planks from the artillery boxes.

"Do you want some help?" I asked.

"No," he said. "Go ahead and read your mail. If I had that many letters, I'd be reading them myself."

I realized I hadn't missed my wife since my arrival in Vietnam. I hadn't written to her and was surprised to see she had written so many letters.

I walked outside to find a place where I could sit down to read the letters. Two long, skinny bamboo poles were holding up a canvas-covered porch in front of the hooch. The covering was constructed of both canvas and a number of heavy-duty plastic ponchos. A nylon rope held the poles bowstring tight. Under the overhang were three canvas cots like those I had seen on the roof. They were clean as was the well-swept wooden floor underneath them. A neatly tucked green military blanket covered an air mattress on the cot to my left. Another blanket covered the one on the right. The center cot was bare; it too was swept clean. I sat down on the middle cot to read my mail.

The front of our bunker faced west toward a beautiful passage area wedged in between the two mountain ranges called Happy Valley. To the left side of the hill were the An Hoa Mountains (Que Son Mountains) and to the right side, the Dong Lam Mountains, which Marines called Charlie Ridge, the mountain connected to the Annamite mountain range.

At the bottom of the hill were dozens of checkerboard rice paddy fields. There were square- and rectangular-shaped fields. Some were dry, others flooded. Some were white, yellow, and bluish green in color. All were visibly outlined by the raised dikes. A large Buddhist shrine sat in the middle of a large rice paddy not far from the bottom of the hill.

The villages northwest of the hill were partially hidden behind large fences, hedges, and small trees that formed barriers between the homes and the rice paddy fields. Those thatched huts had covered patios and tile roofs. They were built differently than the hooches I had seen in the villages we had passed through where most of the houses were made of straw and bamboo. Their wide doors, lifted up, served also as a large porch covering. The homes below the hill had large and small matted round disks made of shaved bamboo reeds that were used to winnow the rice free of the chaff by tossing the hulls into the air.

Between our hill and the valley passage was Hill 25 and farther away Hill 52, home to Mike Company 3/7. The top of Hill 25 manned by one platoon from Mike Company was clearly visible. I could see there was a lot of military activity going on, on that barren hill.

In front of our hooch was a two-foot wide × four-foot deep trench line that ran along the full front side of our bunker. The trench zigzagged its way around the hill and had reinforced fighting positions every fifty to sixty feet. A double layer of sandbags lined the top of the trench line with small intermittent openings. They were defensive firing positions from which one could easily see strategic points of the perimeter wire and villages below. Numerous strands of barbed wire, trip flares, claymore mines, and heavy rolls of concertina wire were laid down the slope of the hill all the way to its base.

I arranged the letters to read them according to their posted date. She had inserted a stick of gum in each letter. I peeled off the aluminum covering, but the waxy paper stuck to the gum because of the hot, humid air. I peeled off what I could and chewed on what was left of the stick of gum. She had gotten a job in Sanger with a fruit-packing company owned by an Asian businessman. She wrote mostly about her work, her family, and friends. I read a few of the letters and then set the rest aside.

The Gun Team—John and Keeton
Hill 65, AT 878577
July 2, 1967, 1100 hours

I was halfway through reading my letters when the gun team returned. The first Marine I saw was leisurely carrying an M-16 rifle at his side. Two belts of machine-gun ammo were strapped Mexican-bandit style across his chest. He was breathing hard through his open mouth and sweating profusely. The Marine leaned his M-16 up against the hooch and slung off his ammunition belts, dropping them on the ground next to his weapon. Ward S. Keeton, Jr. was from Texas, a medium built Marine with red hair, freckles, light skin and long arms.

A tall, healthy-looking Marine carrying an M-60 machine-gun over his right shoulder followed closely behind. The Marine moved with grace. He eased the M-60 down onto the wooden floor with care, placing the machine-gun next to the entrance so its barrel pointed out toward the valley below. I watched him closely as he knelt on one knee, opened an empty green ammo can, unhooked a link to the 100-round belt draped across his chest, and fan folded the ammo belt into the opened can. The Marine then unlocked the gun's cover, removed the attached 100-round ammo belt and also dropped it into the ammo can just as carefully as he had the first. The green-colored ammo can with its top flipped open looked like a small hungry alligator with its mouth opened wide. When it finished swallowing the ammo, the Marine closed the cover, snapping the clasp shut.

When he stood up, his height struck me anew. His long arms swung easily at his sides. He had wide hands with long, skinny fingers. As he walked by, I noticed the holstered .45 caliber pistol was strapped low, real low, and Wild West style with the bottom of the holster tied with a thin strap of leather to his right leg. He untied the leather strap and took off his cartridge belt, holster, pistol, and all. The belt was wrapped neatly and placed inside the wooden frame of the open front window.

Ward Keeton, the first Marine, went up to the bunk on top of the bunker; and John Niedringhaus, the Marine who had carried the M-60, took a small book from the pocket of his trousers and lay down to read on the bunk that had the rubber lady air mattress.

Niedringhaus was from North Dakota, and he should have been an officer. He wore thick prescription glasses and was tall and handsome with a fair complexion. He was very intelligent and was always reading a book. John had a dry sense of humor that was complex and profound. What others said in long drawn-out sentences, John said in well-chosen words. When he spoke, you wished you had said what he easily put into just the right thought provoking words. When he drank, John used four- and five-syllable college-type words which none of us in guns understood. Other than that, Niedringhaus never spoke much. He never complained about the details he was sent on unless he felt that Jones was taking advantage of him.

Jones, Gun Team Leader
Hill 65, AT 878577
July 2, 1967, 1200 hours

Jones returned from Da Nang a short time later. He was carrying a box full of goodies from the PX.

He placed the box on his cot, took off his helmet and flak jacket, dropping them in a pile next to his bunk. He pulled out his soft cover from his rear pocket, popped it against his leg to get it unfolded, and it slipped easily over his head. He asked John and Keeton for help to bring in the rest of the supplies, and they quickly followed him up the hill. A short time later, Keeton returned carrying two cases of soft drinks, and John was carrying three fifths bottles of a .45 brand of whiskey and a bottle of rum Jones had picked up in Dog Patch.[69]

Moore had also gone up the hill and came back carrying a large block of ice he had gotten from the mess tent. He placed the ice in a large metal box and chipped away at it, breaking it up into smaller chunks. He and Jones then slid the Cokes and the .45 whiskey bottle into the ice and closed the lid. Keeton asked Jones if he had remembered his smokes, and Jones pulled out two cartons of Kool cigarettes from the box and gave them to Keeton.

"Thanks," Keeton muttered and paid him.

Jones reached into his utility jacket and pulled out a plastic bag filled with what seemed like small hand-rolled cigarettes. With a big grin, he held the bag up and shook it lightly.

"Five dollars," he said. "Paid five dollars for four dozen in Dog Patch."

Jones looked at me and Bro introduced me as the new machine-gunner they had been expecting. Jones turned toward me and smiled, his gold-capped front tooth sparkling as a shit-eating grin crossed his face.

"Refu-Refug-Refugio M. Barela," he said.

"Cook," I answered and reached out to shake his hand. His handshake was weak and flimsy. "I go by Cook for short," I said.

"Cookie," said John, as he chipped off a chunk from the block of ice, dropped it into the aluminum cup that came with our canteens. He opened a can of Coke and poured the dark liquid over the ice into the cup.

John reached over and shook my hand.

"Welcome to Guns," he said.

Keeton nodded his head as a welcome sign.

John was the first one to call me by the nickname my older brother Felix had given me in grade school.

"Cook-San," said Jones, as he placed a small chunk of ice in a canteen cup, then poured Coke and a shot of whiskey over it. "That's what we'll call you, Cook-San."

Jones handed me a canteen cup, and John gave me a can of Coke. I chipped off a piece of ice, pulled off the Coke's flip top, and poured the soda over the ice into the tin cup. Drinking a Coke poured over ice in an aluminum canteen cup enhanced the crisp taste of the Coke.

I wondered how many Marines and U.S. soldiers had drank Coke in this same manner in past wars. World War II comic strip characters, such as Sergeant Rock, were sometimes depicted in the comic strips drinking coffee in a combat zone out of similar canteen cups. It was something unique to military life. Not many people in the world have ever enjoyed the peculiar flavor and pleasure found in drinking Coke in an aluminum military canteen cup.

Michael Andre Jones, my gun team leader, was the most likable fellow you would ever want to meet: a skinny, smooth-faced small black Marine who said he was from St. Louis or Tennessee. He kept changing the city and state he was from. Jones loved listening to songs sung by Stevie Wonder and even looked a little like Mr. Wonder, except for being darker and unable to grow a mustache.

Jones, John, and Moore were all wearing the new lightweight jungle utilities while Keeton still wore the old heavy cotton type. If you wanted the new jungle-type utilities, they had to be procured by other than normal military channels and because of this the fatigues obtained did not always fit. The utility jacket, Jones was wearing was extra large, so he had the sleeves, which were extra long, rolled up.

Jones was street smart and sly as a fox. But I soon learned, you had to be constantly on your guard, or he would take advantage of you when it came to patrol or working-party assignments. Yet he was also the type of Marine you wanted at your side in a firefight. On his shirt collar, he wore his lance corporal rank insignia proudly and it was also pinned on the front of his soft cover, something that I had never seen done before. Jones wasn't gung ho; he just used the privilege that his rank gave him. As long as there were privates and PFCs in the Corps below him, Jones was happy as he used his rank to his advantage whenever possible. With a new machine-gunner in the gun team, Jones and Keeton were already figuring out how it would benefit them.

"That means I won't have to carry the gun anymore," Keeton said, smiling.

"No," said Jones. "You'll have to wait till the next gunner."

"But you said," Keeton blurted out, his face quickly turning red.

You could tell that a heated argument was about to erupt, but Moore quickly intervened. "We'll figure it out later," he said. The lieutenant said, "Second Squad was going to loan us a man. Cookie will carry the gun once he's ready." With Moore's assurance, the argument quickly ended.

The Sounds, Smoke, and Banana Rum
Hill 65, AT 878577
July 2, 1967, 1300 hours

Jones went into the hooch, turned on the juice box, and Stevie Wonder's song "A Place in the Sun" slowly flowed outside and increased in volume; as Jones turned the knob, the song picked up its tempo:

> Like an old dusty road
> I get weary from the load
> Movin' on, movin' on
> Like this tired troubled earth
> I've been rollin' since my birth
> Movin' on, movin' on
> There's a place in the sun
> Where there's hope for ev'ryone

Jones came out, took a sip of his drink, sat down on his bunk, and with a contented look on his face, lay back to enjoy the music. This was Guns' time to listen to our songs in our own corner of the world, to have our place in the sun.

Guns' juice box was the only battery-powered portable record player on our side of the hill, and it had become a central point of congregation. Third Squad had the bunker south of us, and a thin plastic-covered black wire someone had confiscated from the communications bunker ran from the portable record player along the zigzagging trench line to a speaker in that bunker. From there, they listened to the sounds whenever Jones turned on the box. The music was also a signal to Corporal Boone, a fire-team leader in Third Squad, that Jones had returned with supplies; and a couple of minutes later, Boone showed up.

James A. Boone was dark black, tall, and slender. He had deep eyes, and thick, short curly hair. He was well educated but tried not to show it. He told us that a Caucasian family had adopted him at an early age, but there were things he mentioned that didn't make sense. He tried hard to act tough and to fit in the street world that Jones talked about, but one could tell that Boone's early life had been kind to him and that Jones' tough world of the streets was a world, Boone couldn't truly relate to.

Boone had a heart of gold and really cared for the men under his command as their fire-team leader. He looked after them like a mother hen, concentrating on training them to survive and to have the courage to kill and the will to live. He tried hard to impress everyone with his military skills and prowess, wearing a ranger's cowboy hat or a green or black beret.

When Jones introduced me to Boone as the new machine-gunner in Guns, Boone immediately took a liking to me. Boone, not having had a kid brother, took to calling me kid, vowing to take care of me as he would his own brother. I resented being called kid. I was, after all, a Jarhead, a Marine assigned to combat duty in Vietnam. I felt that I could take care of myself, but I, like everyone else in weapons and First Platoon, soon grew to like Boone; we respected him and so I overlooked the nickname he chose to call me. With my arrival, there were now five men in guns. Moore and Jones were only field trained, on the M-60, and although they had fired the weapon in combat, I was the only Marine with a 0331 MOS in First Platoon.

Gun's Welcome Wagon
Hill 65, AT 878577
July 2, 1967, 1500 hours

Second Lieutenant Joseph Cortaze, First Platoon's commander, sent word with O'Farrell, the platoon's radioman, for me to come see him at his command bunker. I followed O'Farrell up the hill and into the lieutenant's command bunker.

The bunker wasn't anything like what I expected an officer to be living in. The bunker's sandbags were torn, the insides barren and dark with a moldy smell. Four cots were set up against each of the four sides of the hut. A tall, skinny Corpsman was sitting on the cot nearest the door. The bunk next to him held a number of radios: one was on, and a squad on patrol was calling in their checkpoints. O'Farrell picked up the handset; "First actual, roger," he said into the radio's handset and motioned me toward the back where the lieutenant was sitting. The lieutenant's cot was to the left of the door, and to the left of his bunk were bundles of military gear all stacked on top of each other. The other cot on the right side of the bunker was clean, well kept, and belonged to the platoon's sergeant.

A cluttered table with M-16 ammo, maps, candles, C-ration cans, binoculars, radios, and a compass was set up in the center of the bunker. Under the table, I could see a dozen or more cans of M-60 machine-gun ammo. Three open windows bathed the inside of the bunker with light. A single overhanging light bulb was on but added little light inside the hooch.

Lieutenant Cortaze was husky, round faced and in his mid-twenties. He was sitting on the edge of his bunk using a plastic fork to fish out the last remains of peaches from a C-rations can.

"What's your name?" he asked, washing down the last bite with a swallow from a can of beer.

"Barela, sir!" I answered and then stood waiting, not knowing what else to say or if I should say anything else. He stared at me for a while, looked me up and down, and then simply said, "That's all."

"Yes, sir," I said, turned around and walked out, back down the hill wondering why he had called me into his presence.

Early that evening I met the rest of the members of Weapons Platoon and others from the squads. From Weapons there was Cpl. Jonathan Boyd, a muscular black Marine from Indiana. He was in charge of the platoon's rockets section and carried the bazooka, a 3.5-mm rocket launcher. Ira Rahm had become Boyd's A-gunner. Rahm shared a bunker with a tall, thin Marine by the name of Kenneth Stoker, a first-rate Marine in First Squad, from Alameda, California, who had arrived in-county a month before.

As darkness fell, we stayed up late talking and getting acquainted while sitting out on the "front porch" of Guns' hooch. A number of Marines from different squads in our platoon came around to listen to the sounds and see what the new machine-gunner in Guns looked like. Everyone greeted Moore by calling him Bro, and it was easy to see that he was well respected by everyone in the platoon. As music played in the background, Coke was poured over ice, then a shot or two of banana rum poured in.

Calvin J. Whiteside, or CJ as everyone called him, was the platoon sergeant and he showed up early, smoking a pipe. He was tall, black, and everything about him was skinny including his mustache—skinny arms, skinny legs, skinny hands, and a skinny face. CJ was also well liked by the Marines in the platoon.

Jones offered him one of the small cigarettes, which Jones called a joint. CJ tore it apart, crumbling the contents into his pipe, and smoked it that way. The small hand-rolled cigarettes looked very much like the ones my grandfather used to smoke. I figured they were a special Vietnamese brand of cigarettes.

As the music played, we broke open a whiskey bottle, soon the others came around. Jones passed one of the small cigarettes he had been puffing on to me, and told me to try it. I inhaled in deep, held the smoke in as I had seen Jones and others do, and then passed the cigarette on to others. A burning sensation traveled deep into my lungs, and I let the smoke out slowly like I had seen the others do.

My eyes were open wide and burning. A couple of drinks of rum mixed with Coke later, I noticed that everyone was out of focus. Everything seemed to be moving in slow motion. Everyone's words were slow and slurred. Even the music playing in the background was slow. I didn't like how I was feeling, and of not knowing what was going on. It was as if I was inside a slow-moving cloud, trying as hard as I could, I couldn't move fast. It took an hour for the effects to wear off and for my mind to begin to clear. I realized how that little cigarette had affected my mind and senses. Right there and then, I decided that smoking grass was not for me—not if it affected me as it had, not while I was in "Nam" where I knew I needed a clear head if I wanted to return stateside. I did begin to wonder how I would fit in with all those around me in battle.

After that night, I recall seeing pot smoked only a few more times during my tour of duty. Smoking the funny-looking cigarette was not something practiced in Guns, and among the squads in First Platoon; no one habitually smoked it nor did they use other drugs. Its use was frowned upon and avoided by most Marines, and as enemy activity increased in the area, fewer and fewer individuals smoked it. We did however indulge in drinking beer and hard liquor whenever we could get hold of some. For the hard stuff, someone always seemed to manage to get hold of the locally produced rice wine that when drank hot, produced a kick no American commercially produced hard liquor could equal.

I learned that first night Marines in Guns were well liked by the other squads, not only because we could put out a lot of firepower in firefights but because Guns had also built up reputation as an independent, carefree group that was always partying.

Marines in Guns always seemed to procure certain items that were not readily available via military supply lines. This meant not only military equipment but also other items that made life in Nam a little bit more civilized. We had three machine-guns instead of the two normally assigned to a platoon.

Goody, Terry Goodman, who had been a machine-gunner with First Platoon and wounded during Operation DeSoto, had acquired our third machine-gun, he told me in a poker game, from a member in another branch of the service.

That was one thing I quickly learned about the Crotch (USMC); if you needed or wanted anything, you usually had to scrounge around for it. Trading combat or captured enemy military equipment with other branches of the military service, or with pogues in the rear, was one way. Guns often obtained new supplies or other highly valued equipment, as both Bro and Jones were experts at that.

It always takes time to become accepted into a tight military unit, especially one like Guns. There are several reasons for this. The main reason is that a new man is inexperienced and because of this, he can be a danger to himself and others. The new man is usually somebody's replacement who has either rotated out or was wounded or killed. If the latter, the memories of a lost friend were always present with the replacement, a ghostly reminder of the man before him. Bro mentioned that I was Browers's replacement, but like Goody, he didn't say anything more, and I wondered who Browers was and if he had rotated home or had been killed.

In Guns; however, I was immediately accepted and I knew I belonged.

That night, I asked Art, the radioman, about Browers and he told me that Donald H. Browers was from Neptune, New Jersey, and a good friend of his.

"Browers had an M-60 MOS like you do," he said.

He went on to say that during Operation DeSoto on March 18, Browers was walking in front of him as they left Nui Dang Hill near Duc Pho on a routine patrol when all of a sudden Browers went down.

"They say you never hear the bullet that gets you," Art said. "Browers was right in front of me when it happened, and I never heard the bullet that got him. I don't think he even had time to think about it; he was walking with the gun over his shoulders, and as he took a step forward, he went down. It was a sniper that got him. India Company lost a lot of men during Operation DeSoto. It was just a constant and continuous loss of men with only a few major days of engagement. They would snipe at us and then disappear."

That night before falling asleep, I sat on the edge of my bunk under the covered porch of Guns' bunker. Keeton and John were sleeping on the cots on top of the bunker. I had taken the empty middle cot on the porch. Moore slept on the cot with the rubber lady air mattress, and Jones was in the cot to my right. No one slept inside the bunker.

Off in the distance in Happy Valley, where the mountain ranges came together toward the Laos border, I could see lightning strike the ground. A short time later, I heard the sound of thunder and thought it was going to rain. I tried counting the seconds between the strikes and the sounds, but for some reason it all didn't make sense. Most of the lightning I was seeing was striking the ground at a rapid pace. I looked out from under the porch cover and noticed there wasn't a cloud in the sky. It took a while before I realized that it wasn't lightning and thunder I was seeing and hearing in the far distance that night.

Who's in Charge?
Hill 65, AT 878577
July 3, 1967, 0900 hours

My first full day with Guns began late. The mess tent opened and closed, and no one bothered to get up for breakfast. I found out later that the mess tent didn't always open for breakfast; and when it did, breakfast usually consisted of runny powdered eggs, powdered milk, burned bacon, cereal, and toast.

At noon, lunch usually consisted of cold lunch meat, mostly a thick hand-cut piece of Spam or salami that was served on stale bread and unless someone made a run into battalion for ice, the meal was chased down with a cup of warm watered-down Kool-Aid.

For the most part, dinner fared a little bit better, but in Guns someone usually confiscated a case of C-rations and somehow, someone always seemed to have a package of Kool-Aid received from home or we had sodas that we had purchased from the locals, down in the village, so we were able to get by for another day.

Bro, who had friends in artillery almost always managed to also secure food for us from their mess tent at any hour of the day or night. It was not unusual for us to wind up spending an evening sharing a gallon-sized can of peaches, applesauce, or other canned goods.

I learned that being in Guns had its benefits. For one thing, Guns did not stand watch at night on Hill 65 and most of us came and went as we pleased. We were in a Weapons Platoon assigned to First Platoon, but no one seemed to be directly in charge of us. There was no Weapons Platoon leader. The lieutenant, respecting Bro's ability and commitment to the platoon, left us alone for the most part. Whenever he needed a gun team, one was usually quickly assembled and whoever was available went. A squad-sized patrol usually went on patrol at least three times a week. That meant ten to twelve riflemen and a gun team of two or three. There wasn't much enemy activity in our sector at the time, and a Marine squad with a gun team was sufficient for routine patrols around the local villages that surrounded Hill 65.

In the afternoon, on the third of July, a gun team was needed for a routine patrol; Jones and Keeton saddled up, and Moore kept me back to help him build up the bunker. Late that evening, the artillery unit behind us opened fire and the ground below us shook. All night long, they fired off their heavy guns, and it was then I found out why no one slept inside the bunker. With each round fired, the bunker would rattle and shake; the dirt would arise and spread like a low cloud filling the insides of the hooch with fine yellow dust. When it rained, the guns were usually silent and we would move inside during those times. The guns firing throughout the night surprisingly did not keep anyone awake. Instead, once you got used to the noise and the clamor of a long fire mission, it was easy to sleep at night; it was a secure feeling of knowing someone was up and that the rounds were outgoing.

Green Berets
Thuong Duc, South Vietnam
July 4, 1967, 0900 hours

Word came down on the morning of July 4, for us to saddle up. The platoon and two gun teams would be riding out on amtracks and tanks to resupply a Green

Beret Special Forces camp located fifteen miles away at Thuong Duc toward the Laotian border. Jones was to carry one of the guns, John the other. I saddled up, draping two hundred rounds of machine-gun ammo over my shoulders and chest, crisscrossing them in the same fashion I had seen Keeton and the others do.

I picked up my little Mattie Mattel (M-16), loaded it with a clip of ammo and chambered a round. Bro handed me a worn-out canteen cover and three magazines of ammo for the M-16 rifle.

Bandoliers for the M-16 were as scarce as were M-16 ammo magazines, and he showed me how I could carry the extra magazines in the converted canteen holder which served this purpose well.

In case of a firefight, I was to be Jones' A-gunner, which meant I was responsible for clipping on additional belts of machine-gun ammo to the ammo belt attached to the gun. I was also responsible for making sure the ammo was fed evenly into the gun while it was being fired, securing more ammo for the gun if it was needed and checking for long or short rounds in the ammo belt so that the bullets would flow evenly into the gun's feed well while it was being fired.

Each gun-team member carried two hundred round belts of machine-gun ammo strapped across our chests. A 100-round belt was always loaded in the gun, and the gunner carried an additional belt of ammo across his chest. Bro carried two extra boxes of M-60 ammo that he placed on top of the amtrack we would be riding on.

All together we had over one thousand 400 rounds of ammo distributed between the two machine-gun teams, and a few hundred more rounds of machine-gun ammo belts were spread among the riflemen in some of the squads.

The amtracks started up, making a lot of noise and smelling of crude diesel fuel. We moved out traveling westbound, along Route 4, bouncing along on top while the tracks churned the dust and dirt of the road below us.

We rode past Hill 25, a pimple of a hill held by a platoon from Mike Company. We went past Hill 52, which was much like Hill 65 but located just a little farther north off of Route 4.

Hill 52 had a reputation of always being sniped at from the villages and hamlets below. One was known as No Name Village.[70] A few miles past Hill 52, the roadway was pockmarked with large crater holes where a truck had hit a mine or an air strike has blown the road surface apart.

The Green Beret camp at Thuong Duc[71] housed over 100 Special Forces' soldiers who were military advisors to a reinforced company of some five-hundred ARVN soldiers.

As we neared the entrance to the camp, Bro told us a story about the Green Berets.

"It seemed," he said, "that when the war for independence started in Vietnam, the South Vietnamese Army would run away from the battle scenes, leaving their weapons behind. But once they received military training from the Green Berets, they still ran from a firefight, but now, at least, they took their weapons with them."

As we started to leave the Green Beret camp, Bro began to sing the Marine Corps version of their popular song, "The Ballad of the Green Berets." John and Keeton picked it up, and soon we were all joined in singing the song loud enough for the Green Berets in the compound to hear. The song was sung to the same tune as the original song, but it was a Marine's response to their popular song.

BALLAD OF THE U.S. MARINES

We're the men, U. S. Marines
Dirty, rough and fighting mean.
From the States, we came this way
Couldn't care less about the Green Beret.

We stalk in paddies both night and day
Don't need chutes or a Green Beret.
Have no wings upon our chests
Fighting Marines, our country's best.

With steel pots upon our heads
We fight like mad and eat hot lead.
Keep your cap and silver wings
Take them home with all your things.

We patrol and kill V.C.
Fighting Cong to make men free,
One-hundred men, overrun today
We saved them all, the Green Beret.

I saw Marines who gave their lives
So a Green Beret could live his life
If I die in this far off land
I hope to God, it's for a better man.

While they jump and sing their songs
We search the fields and kill the Cong.
We're the men who fight each day
Since '75 it's been that way.

(SOFTLY)
Back at home, a young wife waits,
Her Marine has met his fate,
He has died so others could live,
For his land that's what he'll give.

(LOUD)
I know this song, won't be a hit
But a good Marine don't give a SHIT!
And when it comes to glory and fame
We'll kick your ASS and take your NAME![72]

CHAPTER SEVEN

Watchers in the Night
Somewhere along Route 4
July 4, 1967, 2200 hours

On our way back, one of the amtrack's tracks disengaged and by the time it was fixed, it was starting to get dark. The amtrack commander wasn't even sure if the track would hold up if we continued on, so Lieutenant Cortaze decided it was safer for the platoon to set up in a defensive position nearby for the night.

Between the road and the tree line was a series of neglected rice paddy fields. Before we reached the tree line we stepped through heavy hedgerows, clusters of bamboo shoots, groups of small banana trees, miniature palm trees, large and small bushes, overgrown weeds, elephant grass of various heights and a small graveyard. We settled in near a well-used trail that ran alongside a thick tree line; the trail forked off a number of times at the tree line and disappeared into the thick jungle beyond. No sooner had we moved off Route 4, settled in, when darkness fell.

It was my first time out in the boonies, and we were to take turns standing watch. Jones, Bro, and I were grouped together while John and Keeton with another man supplied from one of the squads stood watch with their gun on the other side of our jungle perimeter. Watch was to be for two hours on, and then you were off for four. Jones called dibs on first watch, which was usually from 8:00 p.m. to 10:00 p.m. Since most of us never fell asleep before nine, Jones had company during much of his early watch. I fell asleep at 09:15 p.m. and he woke me up promptly at 10:00 p.m. for my watch.

The lieutenant had set up the platoon in an L-shaped ambush formation alongside a long tree line with the command post (CP) group in the middle. The two amtracks were set up to cover our rear. Their field of fire covered open rice paddies. Farther away was thick jungle at the base of Charlie Ridge.

Our gun team was set up at the corner of the L-shape with a fire-team to our left and the rest of the platoon to our right, making up the long leg of the L formation. The amtracks and the CP were to our right rear.

The flooded rice paddies in front of my position sparkled with the reflecting light coming from a sliver of the quarter moon overhead. Scattered dark clouds moving slowly across the sky above caused the tree line on our left to cast long dark shadows in front of our gun's position.

The moving clouds and shadows of the night changed the size, shape and colors of the bushes, trees, and rice paddy dikes in front of us. The moon's narrow gray beams of light often broke through the clouds, and you welcomed the new light or for fear of exposure, wished for it to go away. The darkness of the night changed often from pitch-black to transparent grays. Darkness and light, good or bad, confidence or fear—it all depended upon the moon's light and the ever-changing shapes of the dark clouds above and the shadows below.

I saw trees as men walking, bushes that grew, crawled, or moved if I dared to look away. Every noise had a human origin, and while I didn't see anything, I saw everything. It's funny how we take the world around us for granted. Before that night, I would only look at things, but now I saw them. I would only listen to sounds, but now I heard them. I would only smell, but now I detected the varied scents left behind by small scampering animals, the body odors of humans, or the musky smell of decaying plants.

It's amazing what fear and silence can teach you; how loud and fearsome a large jungle rat's breathing can be or how much noise a buzzing insect can make. Then there are all those unidentifiable "human" noises one imagines in the dark.

I found myself constantly adjusting my hearing and refocusing my night vision. As soon as I was able to identify the bushes and shapes out in front of our position, the light changed and the figures of the night took on different shapes and meanings. Contemplating the ever-changing colors of the night made my watch go by quickly while I held the M-16 out in front of me with its safety off.

I knew there were other Marines to my right and to my left sides. Marines who like me were awake and on watch, and that was reassuring. I knew that I could trust them to remain alert and awake. We were watchers in the night, and when it was my turn to sleep again, sleep came easy.

Our return trip the following morning went without incident, and as we neared "No Name Village," Marines started to throw our extra C-ration cans to the South Vietnamese children calling out for them along the roadway.

An old woman emerged from a tree line and stood idle while her two young children with outstretched arms begged for food. A Marine from one of the squads riding on top of our amtrack was about to pitch full cans of C-rations to her and her children when Jones stopped him.

"Don't throw them any food," Jones said. "Her name is on the blacklist for giving food and money to VC. She lives in No Name Village and has two sons in Hanoi." A Kit Carson Scout[73] had told Jones that her two sons volunteered to go to Hanoi for training and were now officers with the NVA. "Anything you give her will end up in Charlie's belly. The NVA often raises their flag above the village or dropped printed Communist propaganda leaflets on the trails we patrolled to let us know No Name village was under their control," Jones said.

Return to Hill 65
Hill 65, AT 878577
July 5, 1967, 0800 hours

We returned to Hill 65, and word was soon passed that the company had designated First Platoon to run daily patrols. Bro spoke with the lieutenant about Guns being undermanned. He argued that since there were only two gun teams and there were three squads, a gun team was out every other day. Machine-gunners were out on patrol more often than the platoon's riflemen. Bro also said he didn't like sending a two-man machine-gun team out with only one squad. The lieutenant knew that if two squads went out, he would have to go.[74] He agreed with Moore that it was unfair for Guns to be going on more patrols than squad members and allowed Guns to stay behind. However, we would have to stand front-gate guard duty during the day, and we all felt it was a fair trade-off.

On the first day of our front-gate assignment, I stood guard duty during the early part of the day. The gate-duty assignments were rotated daily with Bro relieving us for breaks and chow. The dirt roadway leading down the hill to the main road was bordered on both sides by a series of rice paddies. Midway between the hill and Route 4 was a broad berm that ran parallel to Route 4. The raised berm was similar but larger and higher than the normal earthen rice paddy dike and used by the farmers to move their water buffaloes and small carts between the villages. To the left of the dirt road and past the rice paddy fields were heavy bushes and a thick tree line, followed by scattered huts and a large village. On the right side past the rice paddy fields was the central section of the village of Truong An (1) and farther west the CAC unit manned by a platoon of PFs and a squad of Marines.

Front-gate guard duty was tedious, but standing watch overlooking the area gave me the opportunity to study and become familiar with the terrain and the layout of the land below. An abandoned small concrete building stood at the end of the road at the northeast corner of the T intersection. On the other side of Route 4 was a large village in a short distance beyond the Song Vu Gia River.

Up to this time, it hadn't occurred to me to ask why we didn't stand watch in front of our position at night. Guns' hooch was situated between Third and Second Squad and was laid a little farther back than most bunkers on that side of the hill. Marines from the other squads manned the two positions on both sides of us at night. I knew that gun teams in Second and Third Platoon stood watch at night on their side of the perimeter. Other units such as amtrack and artillery also had their men stand watch over their sections of the hill.

Perhaps it had something to do with the 105-gun-artillery-battery set up directly behind our hooch. Most nights, Marines from Artillery Battery 1, Third Battalion, Eleventh Marines had fire missions, so there was always a beehive of activity going on behind us as they fired their guns. All night and into the early morning hours, they seemed to have targets of opportunity to shoot at or were firing in support of a Marine operation somewhere or in response to spotted enemy activity. Marine recon units in the field would often call in fire missions on enemy activity close to where they had been inserted. At other times the battery units fired harassing fire into areas known to be used by Charlie.

With so much activity going on just a short distance away and the area out in front of us clearly visible to the two squads of Marines that stood watch on both sides of us, perhaps some squad leader in Guns long ago had decided that Guns didn't need to stand watch at night, so we didn't. I never asked why, and no one ever bothered to tell me I went out to the perimeter wire on the other side of the hill where a sharp cliff overlooked a rice paddy far below. It was where we practiced shooting and testing our weapons. I had been issued an M-16 rifle but had not fired it. That day, I fired over 100 rounds through it before experiencing a malfunction in the weapon. The rifle was not very accurate when shooting at distant objects. I had no confidence in its effectiveness; it lacked the power and accuracy found in the M-14. The plus to the weapon was its high rate of fire and light weight, which may have contributed to its acceptance among Marines, but overall I had heard Marines were experiencing a lot of misfeeds and jammed weapons in the field.

A Puppy named Ho Chi
Hill 65, AT 878577
July 7, 1967, 0800 hours

On the second day of gate watch, a couple of South Vietnamese kids were playing with a small puppy near the front gate. I called them over and asked if they wanted to sell the puppy. They willingly sold it to me for a dollar and a pocketful of Kool-Aid packages. The puppy couldn't have been more than a month old. He had soft, fluffy fur and was tan in color and had a light star-shaped mark on his forehead. He was frisky and mean, so we named him Ho Chi after Ho Chi Minh.

On the eighth of July, we were sent out as amtracks security to Hill 52 and returned with two women VC suspects. Mike Company had captured them probing along their perimeter lines the night before. From Hill 65, they were transported by jeep to Battalion HQ for further interrogation.

The next day, Dennis George Dustin stepped on a bear-type booby trap while on patrol in Dai Loi (3) northwest of convoy road (Route 540). The trap Dustin stepped in had been set up by a local villager and both he and his wife were apprehended and taken to Battalion S-3 for questioning.

That afternoon, a Marine Corps chaplain came to Hill 65 and Christian services were held for those wishing to attend. Most of us who were not on duty attended the service. I wasn't religious but I believed in God.

My sister Dominga had taken me to her Pentecostal church on several occasions when I was in high school and I had even made a confession of faith and was baptized in Jesus' name, but my religiousness was based more on what my sister and others told me about God than a personal commitment.

I still carried the miniature Bible I had been given by the Good Samaritans in my flak jacket's pocket, but when I tried to read it, it just didn't make much sense to me. I never got through all the begats in Matthew's Gospel; the only prayer I knew was the Lord's Prayer which I said often, always trying to figure out what the words really meant. I felt the Hail Mary's I had been taught in Catholic school weren't going to help; at least not in Vietnam. I certainly didn't like that part of her praying for us, sinner's at the hour of our death. I figured it would be too late by then, and repeating the same prayer over and over again would be irritating and annoying even to God's patience. Then again, I thought why should I have to go to God's mother when, as my sister had said, I could go directly to God? It made more sense to me, why not skip a step? My religious obligation to God in Vietnam was conditional; I figured that if God got me out of a tight situation where I might have gotten killed or wounded, then I sort of owed Him one, and so in repayment I would go to religious services—but that depended on whether the religious services were provided for us. If not, I would say the Lord's Prayer, which was the only prayer I knew that made sense. Sometimes if I went to Christian services and I hadn't been in a dangerous situation, then I figured God owed me one, and so it went. It was a one-sided agreement I had made with God, and I tried to stick to it religiously.

In the days following, I continued to be assigned to early gate watch, and in the afternoon Bro had me go out to the back perimeter wire and famfire the M-60. There was no lack of old machine-gun ammo and I was able to practice shooting the gun by delivering intense and concentrated firepower on targets I randomly selected in the terrain below. Every fifth round in a 100-round ammo belt is a tracer bullet so that a gunner can zero in on the target he's aiming at. I enjoyed choosing a target to shoot at then watching the burning red tracers streak across the open field as I watched the bullets blazing toward the target. It was a relief to shoot the machine-gun without reservation and without having someone of higher rank standing over me or telling me how or where to shoot. By the end of the week, I had shot and cleaned all three guns.

A Gun for a Machine-gunner
Hill 65, AT 878577
July 11, 1967, 1300 hours

On the morning of the eleventh, Bro came out to the practice area and watched me as I fired one of the guns. He had me shoot at certain targets he selected and saw that my response and aim were right on target.

"You know how to shoot that gun very well, don't you?" Bro asked as we made our way back.

"Your gun has a good response to it," I answered and he smiled, understanding what I was talking about.

Moore gave me some pointers on our way back on how to release my first rounds of response fire in a firefight at the enemy when they called for "guns up." The way he said it, it was obvious that there was no doubt in his mind that I would soon be engaging the enemy.

Firing the M-60's as I had for the past few days had given me more confidence in the gun and in myself. In these practice sessions, I also learned to distinguish the sound of each gun. Each gun's sound was as unique as the voices of the Marines I served with. Jones' gun made a harsh and forceful sound as it fired. Browers's gun firing was smooth, rapid, and made a distinct echoing sound. Bro's gun was very accurate with its own pulsating sound like that of a determined heartbeat hammering out constant destruction.

I especially liked the way Bro's gun felt and fired and after a while, while firing it I began to get lost in the sound it made and I sensed a unity as if the gun and I were one. Together, we would be invincible; together, we could put out a concentrated wall of lead. When we got back to the hooch, Bro told Jones that I would be taking over as machine-gunner. Jones was to take over my M-16 rifle.

At first I was hesitant to let go of my M-16 because we had been told that if we lost the weapon that was issued to us, we would have to pay the $122 the Marine Corps had paid for it. I knew that Guns had a way of exchanging guns, rifles, military equipment, and parts of weapons every which way for one reason or another so that hardly anyone knew who had what or to whom a particular weapon was assigned to. We had three M-60 machine-guns in First Platoon, but only two showed on the books as being assigned to us.

A Brave Encounter in the Night
Hill 65, AT 878577
July 15, 1967, 2200 hours

On the fifteenth, Jones got hold of a bottle of homemade rum from the village below the hill. It rained during much of the day, and as night fell, it was still drizzling.

The big guns behind us were silent, so we were all inside the hooch enjoying a game of black alley, drinking rum, and listening to music. By the time we got halfway through the bottle, we were toasted. "California Dreamin" by the Mamas and the Papas just finished playing. Bro stood up to change the 45 rpm record, and Jones was bringing down his card to call trump when we heard a loud noise outside the bunker.

Jones quickly blew out the candle and reached for one of the M-60s, but the gun's ammo was kept outside; John took hold of one of the .45 pistols and chambered a round. Bro grabbed his M-16, chambered a round, and backed himself up against the rear wall. Toy, a Marine in Second Squad who had joined us earlier that evening for the card game also chambered a round into his M-16 and joined Bro, Keeton, and Jones against the wall as John moved toward the side window and away from the door.

I reached up, grabbed one of the hanging M-16 rifles, and slammed a clip full of ammo into its magazine well. I was the closest to the entrance, so I backed up against the wall near the right side window as I had seen the others do. Everything was silent and pitch-black inside and outside the bunker.

John leaned over to look out the window. I could tell it was him by the tallness of the figure. He whispered, "Nothing." I looked out my window and couldn't see anything. Everything outside was pitch-black. For the first time, I realized how small the bunker actually was.

We all remained quiet, trying not to breathe hard, listening for any sound of movement outside. We could only hear the rain falling steadily on the bunker's sandbagged roof. A sense of fear was present in all of us, but no one dared move. We wondered what had made the noise.

What happened next was not bravery on my part; I knew someone had to go out before it was too late as I began to imagine a grenade being tossed into the bunker and was thinking this, we heard the noise again. It sounded like the rustling of thick cloth in the wind. Someone was definitely out there, and they were standing just to the left of the doorway. I took the rifle's safety off and ran out the door.

I hit the deck and recovered as we had been trained to do. I was ready to open fire on whoever was there. I strained my eyes looking around for any movement, or any sign of the enemy. I was ready to blast them away if I had to, but there was no one there.

As I stayed in the crouch position, the rain continued to come down steadily. I looked down the hill, nothing. Nothing along the trench positions in front of our hooch. A distance away on Hill 25, a lone pop-up flare lit the sky as it slowly descended on the other side of the hill. Behind us was another flare, high in the air, the falling rain glistening as it fell reflecting the flares' distant glow. [75]

The only sound I could hear was the steady rain falling evenly on top of the bunker and onto the canvas that covered the bunker's porch. The rain, accumulating on the top of the bunker, was running down the side of the bunker, filling the canvas tarp in a steady flow. On one end, the thin wooden pole had given way. As soon as the section of the tarp was filled with water, it spilled out, making a big splash on the wooden deck. That was the noise we had heard.

I started to laugh hysterically, and the others came out of the hooch and started to laugh with me. They were laughing because the water had spooked us all, but I was laughing because in my haste to load the weapon, I had forgotten to chamber a round.

The New Looey
Hill 65, AT 878577
July 16, 1967, 2200 hours

The morning of the sixteenth brought in a new officer that was to take over the platoon from Lieutenant Cortaze. Second Lieutenant Lawrence E. Wilson was straight from the States and a recent graduate of Marine Officer's School. He was young and eager, clean-cut, with an air of maturity. He was round faced, stocky, about five feet nine, with blond hair and blue eyes—a beach boy from Topanga Canyon, California; but since no one knew where that was, he said, he was from Malibu.

Wilson had graduated at the top of his class in Officer Candidates School and as such, he could have chosen any choice duty station in the Marine Corps. As he considered what he should apply for, his commanding officer at Quantico mentioned to Wilson that he should serve as a platoon leader of Marines in Vietnam. As he considered it, not sure of what he should do, the officer said to him, "If you don't do it, other less qualified officers will lead those Marines, and they deserve the best there is and you would make a great platoon leader." To command Marines in combat would offer him a great opportunity to serve and use his talents to the best of his abilities and in the process perhaps save Marines' lives; his commanding officer had gone on to say.

Unlike enlisted men, most officers rotated out of the field every six months while Marine grunts stayed out in the field for a full thirteen-month tour of duty. The new looey would be with the platoon for at least the next six months.

That first day, Wilson called the squad leaders to his bunker and listened to what they had to say. He listened closely to his men, and it was evident he was going to earn their respect. In the next few months, we would face a number of major military conflicts together.

A Veteran's Shared Insights
Hill 65, AT 878577
July 17, 1967, 2000 hours

On the seventeenth, as evening came, having been relieved from gate duty, all of us in Guns were sitting around the hooch. Boone, Boyd, and Perry were inside the hooch along with Jones and they were jamming to the sounds. They made quite a sight—little Jones, gold capped tooth glistening in the candlelight; tall and skinny Boone wearing his black beret cap; heavily built Boyd, stumping around in circles; and tall Perry, who just didn't seem to fit in with the group, standing off to one side, bopping his head, smiling, trying to catch the rhythm and happy to have been included in the activities.

Jones had taken the arm off of the top record on the record player so that Stevie Wonder's "I Was Made to Love Her" played over and over again.

Outside the bunker were Bro, John, Keeton, Stoker, Turner, Chief, Rahm, Pridemore, Izzie, and Joe Cervantes. Cervantes was one of the new men assigned to First Squad and he had already been tagged with the name "Lucky" for some reason.[76]

Private Kenneth Stoker was tall, had short blond hair, pretty blue eyes, a pointed nose, and eyes full of compassion. He was a funny and mature Marine with common sense and a laid-back attitude that was respected by others. He always talked about cars and clothes. At times, he wore a silk stocking around his helmet, a gift from his girlfriend I was told.

Turner was a tall black man with rugged facial features and a strong muscular build. He was always working out pumping iron, fearsome and determined. He was someone you would want at your side in battle.

"Chief," Newman Cuch, a Ute Indian from a small Wyoming town, had a broad nose and wide mouth. His teeth were white and perfectly straight, his hair thick and black. He was tall; broad shouldered and dark skinned, and always bare-chested. He drank hard liquor like Kool-Aid and didn't say much unless he had been drinking. Chief always remained silent until just the right opportunity arose for him to speak and then he would say what was on his mind and you would want to know more. You would want him to expound more on what he had said, but he wouldn't. Chief knew the ways of war.

By midnight, Chief had fallen asleep while sitting on Bro's bunk, his head bent over between his legs, his long arms dangling at his side. In his right hand, he held a canteen cup half full of melted ice, Coke, and rum. With the exception of Boone and Chief, Rahm had been the last to leave, staggering up the hill as he walked to his bunker. Boone was passed out spread-eagle inside the hooch, his black beret on the floor.

Bro and I sat talking; he talked about the firefights and operations he had been involved in and I listened.

"Garcia," he said, while reluctantly pausing to collect his emotions, "was a good friend." I sensed a deep compassion and a sense of emotional bond in his voice as he talked about Garcia. I listened and wished I could do or say something; I realized Bro was sharing something with me he had held back for many months and not shared with others.

"Don't volunteer for anything," Bro said, and I knew that there was a deeper reason why he desired for me not to volunteer for anything, but I didn't understand why. I feared to say anything or ask any questions; it was one of those rare moments in life where it's best to stay silent and listen, but Bro sensed my interest.

He began to speak again, more quietly and reflectively about his friend Richard Garcia, a Marine in First Squad who had been killed during Operation DeSoto. He spoke about Garcia as if it was himself that he was talking about.

"We were on Operation DeSoto near Duc Pho, south of Chu Lai. It was January 30, and the company had been pinned down for most of the day. We were low on ammo, we hadn't eaten, were out of water, and the M-14s; both the guns were caked with mud. Battalion didn't have anyone to send out to help us right away. There wasn't much we could do but lay out in the open, hug the dike, and wait. The guys that were wounded near the entrance to a village had been lain out in the open all day, if we tried to get to them, Marines would be shot or killed. The enemy was too close to the squad in front for an air strike or artillery. Some Marines were already dead, others were hanging on, waiting for help but we couldn't get to where they were to bring them back, to medevac them out."

Bro looked away and then continued, "Most of the M-14s and both of the 60s were jammed because of the mud hole we were pinned down in. By late that afternoon, only a few weapons were still able to return fire. Days before the gooks, had flooded the rice paddies; they knew we were coming. We were caught in a U-shaped ambush. First Squad was still out only a few yards from the enemy and it was starting to get dark. We knew that if we didn't get them out, they weren't going to make it.

"Sergeant Spahn started to get guys together to volunteer to go and try and get First Squad out from where they were. Spahn had been trying all afternoon to get out there, but the skipper, Captain Clark wouldn't let him because of all the incoming we were still taking.

"Several Marines volunteered to go and get them out, which meant they had to leave their weapons behind so that they would be able to grab the Marines that were dead or wounded to carry them out. Just before nightfall, they moved out with Sgt. Spahn leading the men. As soon as they crossed the gate, the gooks opened up and Garcia was hit right away. He went down and never came back up." Bro took a long sigh, holding back tears of regret.

"I should have gone with them," he said. "But only my gun was working, and I had to stay and cover for them. Browers had melted the barrel on the other gun, and we didn't have extra barrels. It wasn't until the next morning that H&S came out to help us. We called the area where Richard, Rhodes, and Sergeant Holloway were killed—the Gates of Hell. Third Platoon also lost two men that day, Charles Estes and Robert Posey. You remember guys like them who tried all they could to help others. Others were wounded that day—Moses, Goody."

I realized that no one tried to find out a Marine's full name, until after they were killed. In war, it wasn't important. Most had nicknames they had been tagged with or names they earned.

"A couple of months later, Browers was killed. He never knew what hit him." Bro said, and then he stopped talking, took in a long sigh and released it slowly. His eyes reminded me of Moses, the Marine I had ridden with on the back of the six-by truck when I first arrived at Battalion Headquarters. It seemed like a small world that the first few Marines I had met were from First Platoon finishing their time in the rear getting ready to go home. I was glad they had made it. Bro looked at me; and for that split second, I felt that same sense of awareness, friendship, and understanding that Moses and I had shared, for a split second.

"All that stuff you were taught back Stateside is useless here," Bro said as he shifted his weight and arched his back to straighten up. He took a deep sigh. "Your instincts will tell you more about what you should do and where you should place the gun in a firefight. Sometimes you just don't get a choice.

"You can put out a lot of firepower with it and save a lot of lives; you need to listen to the old-timers in the squads; you can depend on them. They've seen a lot and if you take care of them, they'll take care of you. You protect them, and they will protect you. They won't leave you behind; they will cover for you and will get you out if you're hit or in a tight spot. You're a machine-gunner with a gunner's MOS and they respect that; they know what that gun can do and they believe you know what you're doing, so they'll be depending on you. Almost everyone in the squad carries extra ammo because of that. Some guys at first don't want to carry that extra weight until they see what the gun can do in a firefight. It turns them into believers, and they'll gladly carry that extra ammo."

"When you open fire, always fire low; the gooks get real low to the ground, but they scare easily. Firing right at them may not have the effect you need to gain fire superiority if they have Marines pinned down. So put your first volley of rounds just above the enemy's heads; that will scare them and they'll stop firing for a few seconds, and that's all you'll need. You can then come back at them at ground level. There's nothing like the sound of a round going by just inches above your head to get your head down. Once they go down, then it will take them another few seconds to decide when to put their heads back up and that's to your advantage. From there it's all up to you to keep the gooks' heads down. If you can keep Charlie's head down, the guys that are pinned down will be able to shoot back and get out of the kill zone. The VC will not stick around after that. Most VCs hit and run, but the NVA will stick around to fight. They are the hardcore, but they don't like fighting Marines.

"If you get pinned down, don't worry; someone will come to get you out. Just keep your head down and as close as you can to the gun when you're firing. Don't worry about being scared; we all get scared."

"As a machine-gunner, you can't afford to stay scared; you have to have your wits about you and need to keep a clear head. Don't get sucked into the firefight right away; think and look around before you open fire. Otherwise, Marines will get killed. Once you get incoming, you'll know what to do."

We kept talking for quite a while, and I wished I could recall all of it or had written it down. I wish others had heard what Bro had shared with me. It was as if Bro was sharing the secrets of a warrior and of war, the secrets of life and what it takes to stay alive, things not normally openly shared with others; but he shared and I listened.

I asked Ron about the men in the squads, and he gave me a quick and brief answer. "Each of the squads is different, so you'll need to know who you are with when you go out with them. Ira Hullihen is First Squad's squad leader. He won't take you into trouble if he can avoid it. Stoker and Turner are in his squad, they are new. Chief and Izzie, and most of the other guys in that squad have seen combat, so you can depend on them. When you go out platoon size, try to always have a full squad in front of you."

"In between the CP group and the squad bringing up, the rear is the best place to put the other gun team."

"Jones will teach you all that, but he doesn't talk about it; he just does it. So you'll have to learn by seeing and doing what he does. The squads know what they're doing. If you get in a tight spot, First squad has the most veterans, so they'll figure out a way to get you out. Stick close to that squad if you can."

Chief opened his eyes, looked around, settled his eyes on us, farted and smiled a wide grin that raised the cheekbones on his face. He then crawled under Bro's bunk, turned on his side, closed his eyes and drifted into a deep sleep. A second later, he was snoring loudly.

"Chief's a good man," Bro said as we listened to him snoring. "He was there during DeSoto; he'll fight right alongside of you. There's something about him—brave! Crazy, but clearheaded in firefights, that's what you want to be, clearheaded. Chief takes it all in and keeps his wits while under fire. Watch him. He always walks point and can smell the gooks. If you get hit, he'll be there right beside you. Chief doesn't wait for anyone to tell him what to do. He just does it."

"Most of the guys in First Platoon have been here for a while, but in a few months many of them will be leaving. They're short-timers, and they won't be taking any chances if they don't have to, so the platoon will be changing."

"The squad leader in Second Squad was killed during Operation DeSoto and 'Moose' Doug Harris took over, but I think James Stanley leads that squad today. He's been here for some time and is alert. He knows what he's doing, and thinks things over before doing them, but most of the men in Second Squad are new. Perkins is new in that squad, but he's been here for a while but was assigned somewhere else; I don't know much about him."

"We now have a new lieutenant in the platoon," he continued. "You have to be careful when you get in a new looey, some are ninety-day wonders that try to do things by the book. However, that doesn't work in Vietnam."[77]

Bro talked about a number of other firefights he had been involved in and some of the friends he had lost. The reason a new machine-gunner was needed in First Platoon, he said, was because Browers had been killed and I was his replacement.

"You don't want to get close to anyone," Bro said.

I asked Bro how it felt to lose a close friend in combat.

"Well, one day you're sitting around like this talking, and then the next day they're gone." After answering, he lay back with his eyes opened and went into deep thoughts. I asked him no further questions, laid my head down, and went to sleep.

Saddle Up
Hill 65, AT 878577
July 17, 1967, 0900 hours

On the morning of the seventeenth, the word was passed down for First Platoon to saddle up. Squad leaders reported to the CP where Captain Clark, India Company's commanding officer and our new lieutenant were waiting. While the lieutenant and the captain talked, Art, our platoon's radioman was busy gathering supplies. Bro returned from the CP meeting and told us we would be going on a one- or two-day operation looking for the rockets' sites from where enemy forces had hit the Da Nang Air Base and Marble Mountain, a couple of days before.[78]

At 1300 hours, Keeton picked up Bro's gun, and I had a choice between taking Jones' gun which was newer or Browers's old gun.

We boarded six-by trucks, then headed eastbound on Route 4, and then north on convoy road (Route 540). It was the same stretch of narrow roadway that I had traveled from Da Nang to Battalion HQ. A short time later, the trucks stopped, flipped a U-turn and pulled off on the west side of the road. We got off and moved toward a small hill on the west side of the road. The hill was a pimple of a hill only about ten meters in height, just a few feet higher than the surrounding rice paddy dikes and adjacent roadway. As we disembarked, squad leader Corporal Stanley said, "Welcome to 'Hill' St. Peter."

As we moved toward the perimeter, our new lieutenant stepped forward to take lead, but Cpl. James Stanley stopped him. The lieutenant and Stanley moved aside and spoke silently for a few seconds, and then the lieutenant had us stand down as Corporal Stanley moved his squad in to check out the area for booby traps and mines. After a while, he motioned an all-clear sign and the rest of the platoon moved in.

Dry rice paddy fields surrounded the small hill. Across on the east side of the road about 100 yards away was a small village, Phu Son (3). The village was located near a curve in the roadway, seven miles south of Da Nang.

North of the village, open rice paddy fields ran for about three-hundred meters. There were thickets of dry bamboo stalks with clumps of tall elephant grass and heavy undergrowth just past the open fields. Parallel to the road and on the other side of the rice paddies was a thick jungle with tall trees and waist-high bushes that formed a thick fence barrier from the village that ran all the way to the edge of the Song Yen River. While only four klicks away from regimental headquarters (Hill 55), the river was a barrier between us. To the west, of our side of the road, a huge mountain range loomed over us like a dark shadow watching over us as we set in on the desolate hill.

The hill offered no shade, no protection from the sun, the elements, or the enemy. It was completely barren, free of vegetation. Along its perimeter, we found old sandbagged fighting positions and strands of a deteriorating barbed-wire fence that had been left behind by former tenants.

As Bro helped the other gun team set up, Jones found an area where we could set up the gun at the northeast corner of the hill. Our field of fire would cover much of the roadway to the left of the entrance to the hill. The other gun team was set up to cover the right side so that we could have interlocking fields of fire.

For the rest of the day, we worked in the hot sun clearing the area and setting up our defensive fighting positions around the hill. Late that afternoon, a water buffalo with fresh drinking water was dropped off along with cases of C-rations, ammo, and other supplies; we were going to be here for awhile. The lieutenant sent out two quick squad size patrols, to recon the area and they came back before nightfall.

That evening, First squad provided an odd man to stand watch with Keeton and Niederinghaus' gun team so instead of staying there with his gun, Bro came over to stand watch with Jones and me. Guns were the only ones with three-man sharing night watch duty. The squads spread thin around the hill had dug two-man fighting positions.

Before sunrise the following morning, we were out already on patrol. Our mission was to run day and night patrols in the area, searching for rocket sites and enemy activity in the area. Two squads were sent out in opposite directions while the other squad stayed on the hill as a reactionary force along with M-60 mortars. Jones and I went out with Corporal Stanley's squad, and we patrolled west of the road for a good five-mile radius traveling near the base of Charlie Ridge. We returned before noon, ate C-rations, rested for about an hour, and then saddled up and went out again to patrol in the opposite direction. The village Phu Son (3), we were told, was off limits; so this time we patrolled south of the village along the river. The other gun team with Niedringhaus and Keeton had gone out with First Squad, patrolling along the river's banks in the morning; and this time, they went out toward the base of the mountain. We returned just before nightfall.

Bro had cleaned the area and set up our fighting positions. It wasn't much, the few sandbags he managed to gather were stacked tight giving us a place we could crawl in behind. Still, it made me feel secure, and it was as comfortable as one could be in a fighting hole out in the middle of a barren hill. Bro had set up the tripod behind a sandbag wall he had erected at our gun's position. The wall was a perfect height so that only the barrel of the gun cleared the top of the bags, and the gunner could feel secure in returning fire from that protective position. Before dusk, I cleaned and oiled the gun then placed it on the tripod for the night. If we got hit, all three of us could find cover behind the sandbagged wall, Bro had built.

As evening fell, Bro, Stanley, Hullihen, Wilhelmsen, Calderon and other Marines that had been on Operation DeSoto, along with other old-timers in the platoon, gathered near the water buffalo talking and I stood close by, listening. Turner and Kenneth Stoker joined the group a short time later and Rahm came walking over to where I was. The two of us stood close enough to listen to what they were saying; we didn't dare join the group of combat veterans. At first, we felt out of place as if we were eavesdropping on the exploits of Marines that had proven themselves in battle. As the conversation turned to religion, Turner looked over and asked Rahm if he was a Catholic.

"No," he answered. "Why do you ask?"

"Because you're wearing a cross," Turner said, pointing at a crucifix hanging from Rahm's neck.

"It's a nice cross," he added matter-of-factly, so Rahm wouldn't think there was anything wrong with wearing the cross.

"No, I'm not Catholic," Rahm answered. "My mother gave it to me before I left. I'm a Protestant, Southern Baptist."

"Me too," answered Turner, "Southern Baptist." And with that, the group seemed to have accepted our presence in their midst.

We stood and listened as the conversation turned back to military operations they had participated in, and it was as if they wanted us to hear their stories then perhaps by what we heard, we just might learn something about keeping all of us alive. As they spoke, there was no glorification of exploits and performance done while under fire, no heroes praised, just Marines sharing what they recalled of actions accomplished in the midst of battle.

I listened to their exploits and deeds, to the operations they had been on, and always the talk returned to Operation DeSoto, and the day on the dike. I felt honored to have been accepted among such respectable Marine warriors and was awed by the courage, and bravely they dismissed as normal. In my eyes they merited great honor. I wondered how anyone could ever measure up to such standards.

Pvt. James Turner Jr. was a muscular, healthy-looking Marine with strong facial features. He planned on joining a national basketball team when his enlistment was up. Kenneth Stoker from Alameda, California, was a handsome Marine with caring eyes and a firm grip when he shook your hand. He was engaged to a girl he always talked about and looked forward to seeing again. Cpl. James Stanley was short and thin. He had blond hair and was clever; with over six months in country, he was trusted by all the members of the platoon. He didn't say much, just listened to others as they spoke. Ira Hullihen was tall and thin. A soft-spoken Marine from Baltimore, Maryland, he always wore a cap to hide his bald head. Steve Wilhelmsen was an old-timer, a tall, broad-shouldered Marine with a harsh voice, and a soft spirit. Leonard Calderon was also tall with long strong arms and a sturdy build. A quite, approachable Marine that didn't say much, but when he did, he spoke as one with knowledge of the events and with a good recollection as how they transpired.

As the group, called it a night, and began to disperse, Rahm turned toward Turner, took off his cross, and gave it to him.

"Here," Rahm said. "I feel like you should have this."

Turner thanked him for it, and put it on, tucking it, under his shirt.

"Maybe, he'll protect me," he said to Rahm, as he walked off.

That evening, we were once again spread thin; the squads for the second night were manning two-men fighting positions all around the hill, and the running patrols during the day, so they were getting little sleep. Bro stayed at our gun's position again, John and Keeton once again were supplied an extra man to stand watch with them by one of the squads. That night, Third Squad, which had stayed behind during the day, sent out a fire-team listening post, and the rest of the squad went on an ambush mission. No gun team went with them.

Before coming back to our position, Bro met with Lieutenant Wilson who asked him if he felt confident to take a fire-team out.

Bro answered yes, and when questioned about being able to read a map, Bro showed that he knew how to do that.

"It's going to be a daylight patrol so you probably won't run into anything, but since you're not going out with a full squad, take a gun (gun team) with you," the lieutenant said.

CHAPTER EIGHT

The Warmth of a Marine's Jacket
Hill St. Peter, AT 938642
July 19, 1967, 0450 hours

While the days are hot in Vietnam, the nights can get pretty cold. Since it was warm; when we left Hill 65 I brought only my green undershirt on the operation, not my long sleeve utility shirt or jacket as we called them.

After standing watch, I was laying on the ground, trying to hug the earth for what warmth it could offer. I had covered myself with my flak jacket and was using my rolled-up plastic poncho as a pillow. If you covered yourself with the plastic poncho, you would soon be drenched in sweat. I hadn't been issued a poncho liner like some of the others who were using them to keep warm at night. I was thankful for my backpack as it was cutting off some of the morning breeze blowing at ground level.

I wished I hadn't stayed up so late the evening before listening to the old-timers share their stories. But at the same time, I was glad had.

Jones stood early watch, Bro from midnight till two, and I stood watch from two till four. The moon, almost in full phase, had provided illumination during the first hour of my watch but had set before three that morning. Low-lying clouds then moved in and hid what light the rest of the sky would have provided to help detect any enemy movement in front of our perimeter. During the last hour of my watch, the night was pitch-black. At 4:00 a.m., I awoke Jones to stand last watch before sunrise.

An hour later, I heard movement from out left side where First Squad was located. Then I heard footsteps of someone as they came walking over silently to where Jones was. I opened my eyes to see Jones point toward where Bro was sleeping. I started to fall back into a deep sleep when I heard Bro and Jones disagreeing over a gun team, if a gun should go out with the fire-team reconnaissance patrol; the lieutenant had asked Moore to lead. I heard Bro say that he wasn't going to send me since I had just gotten off watch.

A minute later, Bro came over to where I was and laid his utility jacket over me. I felt its warmth and awoke slightly and saw Bro go over and pick up the M-60.

Realizing what he had done, I felt like thanking him, but I was too tired to open my eyes. Besides, a jarhead doesn't say thanks easily. How do you thank a Marine when he does such a caring deed like that? As it was, I was struggling to keep my eyes open and started to fall into a deep sleep. I forced them open one last time and saw the fire-team of three men along with Bro, with Browers's machine-gun swung over his right shoulder walk out the compound. Their dark silhouettes disappeared into the dense fog covering the road at the edge of the perimeter.

A couple of feet away, Jones sat upright with his M-16 at his side. He was wrapped in a camouflaged poncho liner. He lit a cigarette, cuffing it in his small hands and puffed on it through a small opening between the thumb and forefinger of his right hand. With the secure feeling of knowing Jones was on watch, a listening post and ambush team out and the added warmth of Bro's utility jacket, I fell fast asleep.

All Hell Breaks Loose
Hill St. Peter, AT 938642
July 19, 1967, 0600 hours

Whzzz! Whzzz! The swift beelike buzzing sound awoke me. I heard Jones move quickly as he dropped behind the wall of sandbags. He reached out and grabbed hold of his rifle, then buried his head into the ground as another round of bullets split the air just inches above us. *Whizzz! Phzzz! Phzzzz!* As Jones recovered from where he had hit the ground, he reached out and got a hold of his helmet, then shuffled himself on his back up against the small sandbag wall.

Off in the distance, I could hear the report of small arms fire. I turned on my belly and crawled toward Jones who was slowly peeking over the sandbagged wall looking out in the general direction of where the firefight was taking place.

Two more bullets whizzed overhead, followed by four others that kicked up dust a few feet to the left of our position. The bullets struck the ground where I had been sleeping only seconds before. I picked up Bro's M-16 and chambered a round. A round was ejected from the chamber; Bro had it already loaded.

Off in a distant tree line, the cracking sound of small arms fire followed by automatic rifle fire being discharged could be heard, it sounded like the M-60 opening up; from the distance it was hard to tell. A low, thin layer of clouds sat on the ground, making it hard to see clearly. The majority of the shots didn't sound like M-16's firing. A few seconds later, we heard a series of faint explosions followed by a fierce firefight that lasted for a short time and then silence.

Having crawled up behind the sandbagged wall, close to Jones, I asked him, "Where's Bro?"

"Don't know," he answered as he strained his eyes looking for any movement between our position and where the rounds had been fired from. A few more stray rounds were fired in our direction, and I got farther down and moved in closer to the sandbags.

All we could do was to look over the sandbagged wall and wait. Then a few more rounds zipped overhead and I must have had a puzzled look on my face because Jones turned to me and said, "We can't return fire! I don't know where the fire-team is." Jones spoke angrily, frustrated by the realization he hadn't learned from Bro where the fire-team would be setting up their ambush.

We laid there looking out in silence, listening for any sound, any movement. A minute later, only the stillness of the early morning hour remained. A pervading sense of helplessness passed over us. A chilling breeze slowly sweeping across our barren hill like a disembodied spirit, sent chills up and down our arms and necks.

Where Are They?
Hill St. Peter, AT 938642
July 19, 1967, 0605 hours

Behind us I could hear O'Farrell, the platoon's radioman, frantically trying to raise the fire-team, but he was not having success. Lieutenant Wilson, trying to ascertain the fire-team's location, kept repeating,

"Find out where they are."

"Find out where they are."

"Did they call in their checkpoints?"

O'Farrell answered, "No, Lieutenant." A worried look on his face was the cause for alarm.

By the time the word was passed for us to saddle up, most of the platoon was already assembling near the front of the perimeter.

The night before, Wilson had organized for two early morning patrols to go out. First Squad was to leave first and patrol along the river, counter-clockwise. An hour later a small fire-team was to go out and patrol clockwise toward the foothills and open area to the west of us.

For some reason the assignments were switched and the fire-team got the early river assignment and the squad was assigned to patrol toward the mountain to the west of us.

An hour after Bro's fire-team left, First Squad had geared up to leave on their patrol. When the lieutenant reported to Battalion HQ's by radio where the squad was headed, Wilson was informed by them to have the squad stand fast.

Awhile later the platoon was notified by radio not to send out a patrol toward the foothills as artillery would be registering some firing in that general area.

"Bro's going to be pretty upset that it was switched," Calderon told Ira Hullihen, his squad leader when they heard the news over the radio that their patrol had been cancelled.

"Wait till he gets back and finds out we didn't have to go out," he finished saying as the first incoming rounds were fired.

Already geared up for the patrol that was cancelled, the squad quickly assembled at the perimeter wire anxious to move out toward Bro's position.

When I saw Keeton at the entrance carrying Bro's M-60, I handed him the M-16, and he gladly handed me the gun. He took the extra belt of machine-gun ammo as well and fell in behind me. It was a little past six in the morning; dawn was breaking and we were ready to move out.

At the CP, I could hear the lieutenant telling O'Farrell to call in a spot report of enemy contact to battalion. Wilson was then issued some orders with a relaxed but authoritative voice to our squad leaders. There was a calm urgency in his commands, but the troubled look on his face revealed that the dread of the unknown occupied his mind.

As Wilson got ready to give out orders for us to move out, one of the squad leaders mentioned one of his fire-teams wasn't ready, and the lieutenant became visibly upset.

"We're moving out!" he told the squad leader angrily, as he picked up an M-16 and motioned for his radiomen to fall in behind him.

"Get what men you have and have them fall in behind the CP group," he said to the squad leader that had the unorganized fire-team. "The rest of your squad can catch up later."

By the time Lieutenant Wilson gave the order to move out, Corporal Hullihen had already told First Squad to move out. Chief was walking point.

Hold Your Fire!
Hill St. Peter, AT 938642
July 19, 1967, 0610 hours

As the rest of the platoon fell into formation to move out, we heard an indistinct voice crying out of the dense fog.

"Hold your fire! Hold your fire!"

We could barely make out the outline of a lone figure as it approached the hill from the direction where the firefight had occurred. A lone gray figure appeared on the roadway, materializing out of the shadow world, Bro and the others had disappeared into.

It was McIntosh—a tall, skinny Marine who had been in country since early February. We strained to see if any of the others were with him.

He was alone, walking hurriedly, but limping. He didn't have his boots on nor was he carrying his weapon. Ira Hullihen rushed toward him to find out what had happened, and where the rest of the fire-team was.

McIntosh told him the fire-team had set in by the tree line next to a stone building and as soon as they got that information from him, the squad left in search of the missing Marines.

The lieutenant had McIntosh sit down on the ground inside the compound as the platoon's Corpsman stepped forward and began to examine McIntosh's wounded foot. Blood soon saturated the cardboard he was laid on.

McIntosh began to speak loudly and excitedly answering Wilson's questions but it seemed as if he was speaking to convince himself of what had happened.

"We were ambushed," he said. "We were set up when they hit us from three sides. It was a whole bunch of them coming at us all at once!"

"Where were you," the lieutenant asked.

McIntosh stopped, looked up, his eyes widened, then his eyebrows dropped and he looked down turning his head to the left as in shame.

"Everyone is dead, sir—Bro, Stoker, Turner, everyone; they're all dead! There were too many of them," he cried out with a whining exhausted tone in his voice.

"Where are they," Wilson asked him

"At what checkpoint were you?" McIntosh started to point in the direction of where they had set up, and then with a frustrated sigh, he dropped his hand and head as if confused from where he had come from. When he continued to speak, he spoke more slowly and softly while shaking his head from side to side.

Shot in the foot, McIntosh was not seriously hurt but remained shaken from the ordeal and fear of what happened. It was hard to understand him, but he managed to finally point toward the location where the fire-team had set up.

"It was a whole bunch of them, they just opened up, and they came at us all at once. I didn't see them."

As he finished his sentence, the rest of Second Squad had saddled up, moved into position and were ready to move out with the rest of the platoon.

Lieutenant Wilson, unable to get any further information from the wounded Marine to ascertain more accurately where the rest of the fire-team might be, gave the order to move out.

Stanley directed Corporal Steve Wilhelmsen's fire-team to peel off to protect our right flank, and John decided to join them.

Third Squad who had been at an ambush site all night and the 60s mortar crew stayed behind on the hill. The squad would be ready to respond as a reactionary force if we called upon them.

I didn't want to believe, Bro was dead or Stoker or Turner. Last night, we were standing around talking in the early moonlight. We were all listening to the old timers reminisce about prior firefights and battles they had witnessed, shared, and endured together. I liked Stoker; he was good and kind. Turner had won my respect as well not only for his Christian convictions but also because he was a unique Marine who spoke frankly from the heart. He had a strong and honest quality about him that defined him as a firm and squared-away Marine who had his wits together. He was too strong of a Marine to die so quickly; he couldn't be dead. Weren't they among the seasoned Marines of First Platoon? The old-timers, admired and respected, skilled, battle-savvy Marines. How could they be dead?

They can't be dead. Not Bro, I thought. I couldn't, I wouldn't allow myself to believe they were all dead. Perhaps McIntosh was mistaken. Perhaps, maybe, if we got out there right away, they might still be alive. Perhaps history could be changed if we get to them in time, get there before the firefight, if only they had been better prepared, and if only they had seen the enemy moving into position to attack them. Perhaps when I overheard Jones and Bro arguing about who should go with him I should have volunteered to go. I could have been carrying the gun.

First Squad had moved out quickly using the right edge of the roadway to move to the ambush site as quickly as possible. They moved in toward the edge of the village and searched the general area McIntosh had said the fire-team had set in. Unable to find anything the lieutenant called them back to the edge of the roadway to meet up with the rest of the platoon.

When the platoon got to the edge of the tree line, Hullihen had one of his fire-teams stand fast while the rest of the platoon moved on alongside the roadway. The fire-team was to wait until we moved into the tree line, then they would hook up with Wilhelmsen's fire-team and both fire-teams would move east along the tree line and set up a blocking force for the rest of the platoon to sweep toward them.

Ninety meters out, Lieutenant Wilson had the point man enter the dense jungle going east toward the river.

By the time the last man in the main force entered the tree line, the column of Marines was stretched out a good sixty meters. We continued inward another fifty meters with at least twenty to thirty feet gap in between each Marine, then the lieutenant halted the platoon and had us turn to our right so that we were in a long scrimmage line and we moved forward on line toward the edge of the tree line.

McIntosh had indicated Bro and the fire-team had set up an ambush site near the tree line to cover the trail leading into the village. If the NVA/VC had spent the night in the village, they probably would have used that particular trail to slip back into the jungle and came upon Moore and the fire-team.

We were in waist-high elephant grass, slowly moving forward on line, toward the edge of the tree line at the end of the forested area we were in. In front of us, bushes and bamboo were at times corralled together making a solid wall of bamboo sticks, some as high as small trees. We had to make our way around them, stepping on sharp, skinny bamboo twigs lying on the hard ground. The dry wood cracked loud underfoot when we stepped on them. We couldn't have been quiet if we'd wanted to.

Silence by now was no longer a priority. The enemy, if they were still around, would have heard us coming. I didn't understand how the gooks could have snuck up on Bro and the others without making any noise. With each step we took, the sharp edges of the elephant grass cut and sliced into our skin and clothing. For some reason, I couldn't feel it. I was numb.

James Turner, WIA
Hill St. Peter, AT 938642
July 19, 1967, 0700 hours

As Corporal Wilhelmsen's fire-team approached the tree line, Turner came running out of a heavy cluster of tall elephant grass. He looked strong and calm but was staggering. When Turner saw the Marine fire-team, he waved at them and as they rushed toward him, he collapsed.

Wilhelmsen and Niedringhaus reached him first and could see that Turner's clothing was soaked in blood. He was breathing heavily, but had a firm grip on his empty M-16 rifle. John Niedringhaus bent over to help the wounded Marine.

"Am I shot in the gut?" Turner asked him. John looked him over. He could see blood all over Turner's neck, chest, arms, and legs, but not around his stomach.

"No, you're not," he answered.

"Good, then I'll make it," Turner said, and with that said, he let out a deep sigh and winced with pain.

About this time, a minesweeping detail was on the roadway working their way from battalion toward Da Nang. They had already passed St. Peter; when Wilhelmsen and John spotted the convoy, they both ran toward the trucks and flagged them down.

The lead driver of the first six-by truck in the convoy without hesitation immediately turned his truck into the field and drove toward where Turner lay. He jumped out of his truck and helped load Turner on the flatbed. As the truck sped toward St. Peter, Wilhelmsen called in for a medevac.

A Wounded Friend and the Story told
Hill St. Peter, AT 938642
July 19, 1967, 0705 hours

Cpl. Larry Callahan, returning from R&R had just stepped off one of the six-by trucks in the convoy when the truck carrying Turner arrived on the hill. He rushed over to see his wounded friend.

Callahan, a tall medium built Marine from Mississippi, had a distinct southern accent, and a remarkable memory, for details, when Turner saw him; he wanted to make sure Callahan knew what happened.

Turner had been shot in the ear, once in each arm, three times in the legs, and twice in the chest area. One of those rounds had entered through his back. He had been shot a total of eight times and was missing a left index finger. As they waited for the medevac chopper to arrive, Turner turned toward Callahan.

"I want you to know what happened," he said, in a strong forceful tone. Callahan leaned forward.

He told Callahan, the fire-team had circled around during their patrol and had set up for a break but in an ambush position alongside a tree line near where they could see a trail that led toward the village. The fire-team was not far from the hill and it would be daylight soon, so they took off their helmets and flak jackets to rest while McIntosh was placed on watch facing down the trail. He had a clear view of everything so the rest of the fire-team moved back a little to relax and wait for daybreak.

"McIntosh fell asleep," Turner said.

"He should have seen them coming because all of a sudden we got hit from three sides. They came at us screaming and firing, as soon as the first rounds were fired, we were all hit."

"Bro fired all the rounds from his .45 pistol and seeing we were seeking cover from the incoming rounds and not firing back, he yelled out to us to return fire. McIntosh was at a good position to fire back at them as they were nearer to him, but he never did. He ran off dropping his rifle as he ran.

Bro picked up McIntosh's rifle, and we all opened fire. Moore kept yelling for us to keep firing. When they began to throw grenades at us Stoker got on the radio, and Bro got behind the gun and opened fire. He kept shouting orders, telling us what to do. The gooks kept getting up to assault, and as they did, Bro just kept firing. Then Stoker was hit by a grenade as he was talking on the radio, trying to get help."

Turner stopped talking, he wanted to make sure what he was about to say would be remembered. He looked Callahan in the eyes and said,

"The gooks stopped firing for a second, and we knew they were going to rush us." So Bro turned to me and said, "Only one of us is going to get out alive. You better go."

"Moore had already been shot in one arm and in the leg, so he knew we weren't going to be able to make a run for it.

"Go," he yelled at me and crawled away with the gun as the gooks started their assault.

"Run," he said, as he turned to face them. I saw two of them fall in front of him as they rushed in.

Some of the gooks ran past Ron and were shooting at me, I think I was hit then, so, I turned and ran toward the road. Then a round knocked me down; and I turned and fired at them and they stopped.

I got up and took off again.

I could tell they were chasing after me. I got hit again, I think I got hit again, and turned and fired at them again. They were trying to outflank me, so I took off again. When they were getting close, I ducked into a hooch near the entrance to the village."

"They were NVA, had on uniforms, green utilities, and green pith helmets. For some reason, they ran past the hooch I was in. I ran into the tall grass toward the road until I couldn't hear them anymore. I stopped running and began to crawl low toward the road until I saw Wilhelmsen, and then I stood up."

As he ended his account on what happened, the medevac chopper being escorted by two Huey gunships appeared overhead. Marines went to lift Turner to help him get on the chopper, but he stood up by himself. He wanted to walk to the chopper and he did.

Help From Above
Hill St. Peter, AT 938642
July 19, 1967, 0740 hours

As soon as the medevac chopper lifted off, St. Peter with Turner on board, the Huey gunship that had been escorting the medevac chopper switched missions and began a search for the missing Marines.

As we moved on line through the thick brush, we could hear the Huey gunship overhead crisscrossing the area several times before it stopped and hovered over an area for a few minutes and then dropped a red smoke grenade, marking the area where they could see Marine bodies below.

We set in near where the bodies were and waited for the medevac chopper to come in. A short time later, Wilhelmsen's fire-team rejoined the platoon.

Jones and John went over to look at Bro while Keeton and I stayed with the gun. After a while, I walked over to see Bro. I knew it would be the last time I would be seeing Bro. Both Moore and Stoker were still lying where they had been shot. Chief was standing by, a solemn look on his face.

Stoker's left side was riddled with grenade fragmentation wounds. He was lying to the left of Bro's body, about thirty feet away. Bro had a gunshot wound to his neck and part of his lower utilities was covered in blood. I really didn't want to look at his wounds. He seemed to be fast asleep, a contented look on his face like I had seen many times before when he had secured the large cans of fruit from the mess hall late at night when no one was looking.

As I walked away, I saw Jones crying. It didn't seem right for a Marine to cry, but I was having a difficult time holding back my own tears. I didn't want to cry in front of Marines, so I walked away and sat silent near the gun. I remembered what I had asked Bro just a couple of days before.

"How does it feel to lose a close friend?"

"Well, one day you're sitting around talking and then the next day, they're gone," he had said. John was coming back, and I turned to look away so that he wouldn't see the tears flowing down my cheeks.

After Bro and Stoker were medevaced, we swept through the area looking for dead enemy soldiers and found none. We found only a few AK-47 spent shells and some blood splattered on trees where the enemy had been. A number of blood trails led away from the ambush site, and there was evidence that some of them had been killed or wounded and had been dragged away. As we passed by the village, the area was surprisingly quiet. None of the villagers were visible as they had been for the past few days.

With eight bullet holes in him, Turner had managed to crawl the length of a football field. He had been seriously wounded yet, when the chopper touched down at Da Nang, as he was being rushed into emergency, he locked eyes with McIntosh who had arrived at the hospital on an earlier chopper.

Turner lunged at McIntosh with a clenched fist, striking him hard, knocking the skinny Marine to the floor. The hospital medical personnel rushed Turner and physically restrained him before he could hit McIntosh again. They, then quickly wheeled Turner into the emergency room for surgery.

There was silence throughout the platoon for the rest of the day. The loss fell heavily on the platoon. Bro had made friends with many and was one of the most popular Marines in the company. Both he and Stoker were going to be missed. One of the last things Bro had told me was "Never, volunteer for anything," yet he volunteered in my place and now he was dead. Ron had been chosen to lead the fire-team by the lieutenant because the other squad leaders spoke so highly of him. Bro was Guns' squad leader. He could have taken a gun team with him, but he chose instead to leave us behind and take the machine-gun himself.[79]

The enemy had killed two Marines, wounded two others, taken a PRC-25 radio, an M-16, M-14, a .45 caliber pistol, and captured Browers's M-60 machine-gun.[80]

Late that afternoon, our company CO, Captain Clark, arrived at Hill St. Peter; along with him was our new company commander Capt. John C. Baggette who would be taking over India Company. Baggette was tall, with a good build, he wore starched utilities and spit-shined boots. He broke open a map, and being Recon-trained, he looked over the terrain and immediately knew where the firefight had occurred.

Wilson's Leadership Surfaces
Hill St. Peter, AT 938642
July 20, 1967, 0800 hours

After Moore and Stoker were killed and Turner and McIntosh wounded, Lieutenant Larry Wilson took a tougher leadership role of our platoon. While battalion wanted several patrols going out searching for enemy rocket-site positions during the day, Wilson would not send out a fire-team by itself into the area. When a squad was sent out, it was always reinforced with a gun team and since we now had only one gun left, either Keeton or I and Jones went. The patrols were now shorter, and we took no rest breaks in between radio checks. If we stopped, we were not to take off our helmets or flak jackets. If we were tired, we were told to come in, and another patrol would be sent out. When a squad-size unit went out at night, no gun team went as they were sent out only as an LP (listening post) and the squad stayed close by.

Wilson had requested a tank from battalion to be positioned on the hill, but he was told that there were no tanks available. Instead H&S dropped off a Caterpillar, and Wilson was told that if he ran the Caterpillar's engine in the early morning hours, the enemy would think it was a tank as they both sounded alike. The lieutenant never bothered to start up the Caterpillar's engine while it remained on the hill.

Payback
Hill St. Peter, AT 938642
July 22, 1967, 1300 hours

Before dawn on the morning of July 22, we moved out with two squads. Third Squad was leading followed by the CP. I picked up Bro's gun and fell in after First Squad's first fire-team and their squad leader and Jones. John and Keeton, made up the rest of the gun team, fell in behind me, and we moved out. The remaining two fire-teams from that squad fell in behind the gun-team and brought up the rear. Second Squad was left behind with 60mm mortars for security on the hill.

John was assigned as my A-gunner and Keeton was designated the ammo bearer. Until now, our patrols had been concentrated away from the village; but during the last leg of the patrol, we circled counter-clockwise and headed toward the village. We stopped before the village, and set up at the same location Bro and Stoker had been killed.

I set up the gun on a small dirt grave mound in front of the tree line. It was just to the right of the spot where the fire-team had been ambushed. The rest of the platoon and the CP set in to our left. A fire-team from First Squad and the gun team made up the shorter end of the L-shaped ambush we were set up in. We were facing north toward the village while the lieutenant, the CP, and the rest of the platoon were facing east toward the dense jungle between them and the river beyond. A small trail leading north into the village ran along the line the platoon had set in. Heavy underbrush, tall, skinny bamboo canes, and small tropical trees surrounded us.

The gun was facing down an old trail overgrown with weeds and waist-high bushes. It was the same area that Turner had run through to escape the enemy. The skinny trail used to lead toward the village, and you could tell, once served as a rice paddy dike. The rice paddies on both sides were neglected and overgrown with small bushes, bamboo shoots, and elephant grass.

I sat down on the ground, next to the gun, with my back toward the trail. Jones was standing up while John was kneeling next to him; both facing the trail.

"Watch our backs," Jones said while he and John kept their eyes on the trail behind me. Jones seemed uneasy about something; the jungle behind him was the same thick jungle, which we had swept through when we were searching for the fire-team three days before, but his concentration was on the trail that led into the village. Keeton was seated to my left, facing the same direction I was.

The M-60 machine-gun is an effective, reliable, and accurate weapon. It weighs 23 pounds, slightly more with the 100-round ammo pouch attached. It has two attached front retractable bipod legs, and with them extended, one can easily pick off an enemy 1,000 yards away. With the M-60 resting on its tripod, its effective range is up to 1,900 yards. The gun's effectual rate of fire is from 200 to 550 rounds per minute. However, the gun is capable of firing up to 750 rounds a minute, but at that rate of fire, the gun barrel melts.

Jones lit a cigarette, reached down, and lit mine. John asked for a light as well, and Jones snuffed out the match, moved over to where John was kneeling, and offered him his lit cigarette while keeping his eyes focused on the trail behind me. John lit his cigarette from Jones' cigarette and handed it back.

I leaned back to enjoy the break from all the humping that we had been doing since before daybreak. We had moved out early, first going west away from the village and roadway. Then I noticed that we had moved clockwise in a circle, crossed the road, and were now set up near the village. As I took a long drag from the cigarette, I saw Jones stiffen. He was standing just to my right only a few feet away. His eyes widened, and he reached up and pulled the cigarette he had been smoking from his mouth, quickly throwing it to the ground.

What a waste of a cigarette, I was thinking, as he raised his M-16 rifle to his shoulder, aimed and opened fire over my head.

By the time Jones pulled the trigger, John had already hit the dirt to my left side and immediately bringing up his weapon opened fire with a twenty-round burst from his M-16 in the same direction Jones was firing. Another Marine to his left also opened up.

As I was turning over to get behind the gun, I could see Izzie to my right aiming his M-79 toward the enemy.

Instinctively, I took the gun's safety off, locked my elbows and shoulders in, while bringing the gun up tight against my head, and opened fire. I hadn't seen anyone and was only shooting in the general direction that Jones and the others were firing.

My heart was pounding hard; my cheek was up firm against the gun's frame as my finger pulled back hard on the trigger. As I fired the weapon, and the bullets exited its barrel, I felt as if the gun was responding with its own form of vengeance.

The rounds went out steady, slicing across the rice paddy field, close to the ground. Whoever it was or whatever it was that Jones and John were firing at I wanted to fill full of lead.

I was firing at an enemy I had not seen with machine-gun fire, and the bullets were slicing through the air, ripping apart the grass and shrubbery on both sides of the small trail in front of us.

When you hold back the trigger on an M-60, 100 rounds of machine-gun ammo go pretty fast. As soon as the first belt was expended, I slapped on another belt in a matter of seconds.

Over to my right, I could see John squirming on the ground trying desperately to reach with his hands the small of his back. Finally he was able to reach into the back of his trousers and he took out two burning-hot machine-gun brass cartridges. The machine-gun, while I was firing, had ejected them right on top of him while he laid firing at the enemy.

Suddenly, there was an eerie silence all around us. I held the gun in tight, ready to open fire again. The area was filled with the smell of smoke, burning hot lead, and gunpowder. The gun's barrel was hot; smoke was flowing out its front suppressor, slowly rising into the air.

It was the first time I had opened fire in combat and all I can recall while I was firing at an invisible enemy was the flash, the noise, and the firepower of a gun that seemed to have responded with a will and determination of its own.

I had concentrated the gun's firepower toward the center of the targeted area, and only as the last fifty to sixty rounds left the gun's barrel did I begin to sweep the area just above ground level as training had taught me. My firing was at first a naked response to danger followed by disciplined military training. It was totally unlike any target practice I'd ever done. This time, it was real and dangerous; this time, it was life and death, and I kept expecting bullets to come flying back at us at any moment, but they never came.

As soon as I let up, Chief, who had been firing at the enemy from a kneeling position to the left of us, quickly jumped up and burst through a small opening, running in hot pursuit of the enemy. Others in First Squad followed close behind him, and Jones and Keeton followed after them.

Chief and the others searched the immediate area in front of us but returned without having found any signs of the enemy. A short time later, the lieutenant had us fan out on a scrimmage line to make a more thorough search of the area, and we moved out in this fashion toward the village. About fifty yards from the edge of the village, the platoon found an NVA corpsman's medicine bag and some abandoned VC equipment. The medic bag had four M-60 machine-gun bullet holes through it.[81] Whoever was wearing it or anyone near it should have been dead or at least badly wounded. Jones and John, who had seen the enemy walking toward us in a column, were sure that the M-16 bullets Jones had fired had also struck the gook that had been walking point.

The NVA/VC were masters in the art of camouflage and always did an incredible job of removing their dead and wounded from the battlefield. We had immediately searched the area but found no body or blood trails. The enemy could have been anywhere. The area was heavily covered with deep underbrush, and the enemy disappeared as quickly as they appeared. The NVA/VC had the advantage over us in that they were familiar with the area. This was their backyard, and no doubt, they knew it well. They could easily hide in any number of underground bunkers or the numerous tunnels near the villages. The tunnel complexes were not easily found.

I had been taught during mine and demolition classes that Communist guerrillas had spent years constructing hundreds of miles of deep underground passages in the I-Corps area. Tunnel complexes ran throughout South Vietnam. Marines saw them at Duc Pho, and some were reported to be found near the Cambodian and Laotian border and as far north as the DMZ. The DMZ was 1,800 square miles with nearly a million people living above ground with untold numbers of North Vietnamese and VC Communist guerrillas living among them but hidden in underground tunnels. The tunnels crisscrossed the countryside and connected enemy military units to villages.[82]

When the French began using air units against the VC, the enemy went underground and years later, much of the area north of Saigon was riddled with miles and miles of tunnels. Some of the tunnels ran deep and had several hiding compartments at different levels underground. They served as safe hiding places as well as places to stash military and food supplies. The tunnels housed hospitals, guerrilla training schools, and provided a safe haven and a place from where the VC could hit and run; and avoid retaliation from ground forces, and from artillery bombardment and air strikes.[83]

Marines known as tunnel rats, usually the smaller Marines in a squad were used to search out the tunnels, but it was easier to just blow up a tunnel's entrance when it was discovered. Sometimes, we would throw in a gas or smoke grenade and then wait for the enemy or for smoke to surface from connecting tunnels.

We searched the area but found no more evidence of the enemies' presence. We were fighting an evasive and obscure opponent. As we swept through the village, we felt the villagers knew where the enemy had gone. The villagers, who were mostly old men and women, avoided eye contact; they kept their heads down covered by the cone-shaped hats they wore or they stayed inside their hooches as we searched the village.

The children weren't out. They had come out to the front entrance of the hill's perimeter early in the morning on the first day after our arrival but hadn't been out since the morning of the ambush. Bro had befriended some of them as he always did. As we passed through their village, I was angry—angry with the old men, the old women, and even the children, angry because they knew where the enemy had been on the morning of the ambush and where they were now. The enemy had been in this village before they walked into our ambush.

Chief, who still carried the M-14 rifle instead of the lighter M-16, made quite an impression on everyone that day. Instead of backing off, seeking cover, or waiting for others to do something, he went running after the enemy soldiers as soon as he could. He knew how the enemy operated and was determined to find those who had evaded us for days and who had killed Stoker and Bro.

I realized that I had responded to Jones' firing; I opened up without reservation and shot at the enemy in retaliation. I shot at an enemy I couldn't see, enemy soldiers who had killed Bro and Stoker, wounded Turner and McIntosh and seized U.S. government-issued military weapons. I realized I had opened fire on the enemy not to help the South Vietnamese people or because our government sent us there but to avenge Bro's death.[84]

Securing From Hill St. Peter
Hill St. Peter AT 938642
July 23, 1967, 1000 hours

Other than in the high mountains, the water in Vietnam was undrinkable. Because of this, we were issued halizone tablets to drop into our canteen water for purification. The tablets gave the water a bitter iodine taste that was supposed to prevent diarrhea, but it didn't. Midmorning of the twenty-third, we were once again supplied with fresh water brought in by truck from Da Nang. Shortly after its arrival, word was passed for us to saddle up. We were going out on another platoon-sized patrol.

As a group of us gathered around the water buffalo to fill our canteens with fresh water, the NVA/VC opened up with a burst of automatic rifle fire in our direction. Bullets kicked up dust to the right of where I was standing, and we all hit the deck. A couple more rounds whizzed overhead, and I jumped up and ran, zigzagging my way back to our sandbagged gun position as bullets kicked up dust left and right, following me until I dived for cover. It was the second time the enemy's bullets had come close to where I was. When you're being shot at, you quickly learn to identify the distinct sound an incoming round makes. As much as Marines wanted to return fire, the distance from which the rounds had been fired at us was too far away for the M-16s to be effective.

A Marine to our left with an M-14 rifle shot off a couple of reactionary rounds at the enemy and I got behind the gun, which was resting on the tripod. The gooks fired a couple of more rounds at us, and from the puffs of smoke, I could see where they were coming from. I sighted in and fired a response in their direction. The red tracers fell short. Jones, gunning for me, called out the clicks and I adjusted the gun's elevation and fired again, adjusting the traversing and elevating knobs as Jones called out the fire adjustments until the bullets were hitting the area of incoming fire. Only an additional few rounds were fired at us after that from a different area, but the rounds flew high overhead and then the firing stopped altogether.

We saddled up and searched the area from which we had received incoming fire. It was the same spot where Bro and Stoker had gotten killed and from where I had opened up with the gun the day before. Our search once again was futile.

The next day, we stood down and went on reactionary force standby as Third Platoon from India Company along with Kilo Company were sweeping the base of the mountain behind us, looking for the enemy. That evening, Third Platoon walked upon and captured an NVA/VC who had taken apart his M-14 rifle, and was in the process of cleaning it. They also found three M-14 magazines and two ChiCom grenades. When the captured prisoner was interrogated, he revealed where the rockets and rocket sites were. Meanwhile, a Kilo Company patrol unit engaged the enemy in a brief firefight, killing an NVA/VC unit commander and recovering the commander's journal that recorded the July 19, ambush. An entry read that on July 19, they had ambushed Marines and in the exchange, two VCs were killed and others wounded.[85] The following day, we secured from St. Peter and returned to Hill 65.

Who Knew Our Son, Please Write
Hill 65 AT 878577
July 25, 1967, 1000 hours

We returned to Hill 65 on the twenty-fifth, and Jones gathered Bro's possessions to send them home to his family. There were pictures of him riding on a water buffalo near a Vietnamese village while kids nearby laughed, then there was another photograph of Bro as he jumped rope with children in another village.

A 1966 Christmas picture of him sitting in a bunker with a small Christmas tree surrounded by Christmas cards and pictures, he had received, showed how Bro was loved by those at home.

The photograph revealed his wide smile and eyes glowing with happier times. A picture in front of the makeshift hooch reminded me of what he looked like the first time I met him on Hill 65. His family had written, wanting someone who knew him to write, but what can you say? None of us wrote them.

Find a Can of Slack
Hill 65 AT 878577
July 26, 1967, 1000 hours

On the afternoon of the twenty-sixth, I met a new Marine by the name of "Jerry" Lionel G. Lucero, a short, stocky-framed PFC in First Squad. He had chubby hands and strong arms. A Mexican from Lubbock, Texas, Lucero had a round face and big brown round eyes. His mouth curled up on one side when he talked, and it was always slightly open as if he was about to say something but he rarely spoke. He came to the platoon scared, alone, and without knowing anyone in the company. He was the new kid on the block assigned to First Squad, and that was what Izzie and Chief were also good at—breaking in the new boots.

"Izzie" LaJeunesse, a Shoshone Indian, like Chief, was from Hudson, Wyoming. LaJeunesse was called Izzie because Marines found it hard to pronounce his last name and he would not tell us his first name, but someone found out it was Herman. When we called him Herman, he giggled with uneasy laughter and it was evident he didn't like it.

"Call me Izzie," he would say. Izzie was only a few inches taller than Lucero with the same type of stocky build but with broader shoulders and shorter arms and legs. He was First Squad's M-79 man, and when we were at our compound, he often came around with his guitar and always waited until someone invited him to play a tune, then he would crack a few jokes and play a tune or two.

Izzie and Newman first set up Jerry when they were sent out on a working party together. As they were stringing up concertina wire, Izzie asked Chief if he had a can of "slack." Chief looked at Jerry, smiled, and said no.

"You know, we ran out the last time we were out here," Chief answered.

"Send the new kid to go get one from the CP," Chief added.

"Jerry," Izzie called out and Jerry, knowing they were talking about him and as the new kid wanting to please his new fire-team leader, came running over.

"Go to the CP and ask Sergeant Whiteside for a can of slack." Then Izzie paused. "No, you better first go to the squads to see if they have any because CJ will just send you back to them to see if they have any. That CJ doesn't like giving out extra stuff when he knows other squads may have the stuff we need." With that said, Jerry took off, going from one squad to another all around the perimeter, asking Marines in each bunker for a can of slack, each Marine at those sites sending him off to the next hooch to see if they had one there. Finally, someone told him he should ask Sergeant Whiteside at the CP.

When Jerry arrived at the CP, Sgt. Whiteside and Lieutenant Wilson were standing outside, pitching K-bars at a round wooden target. Wilson threw his K-bar, and it stuck outside the rings, Whiteside threw his and it stuck in the center, there. He smiled, grinning at the lieutenant.

"Hey, Serge," Jerry said, and Whiteside looked at him. "The guys send me over to get a can of slack from you. None of the other squads had one, they said, they were all out." Wilson looked with a questionable expression at Whiteside. CJ asked Jerry, "Who sent you for this can of slack?"

"Izzie did," Jerry answered.

"And why does he need this can of slack?" CJ asked.

"Izzie said it was to take up the slack in the concertina wire," Jerry answered. CJ cracked up laughing, shaking his head. He placed his arm on Jerry's shoulder and said, "concertina wire is supposed to be curled, and then waited to let Jerry figure it out in his head, the joke that was being played on him. But Jerry, looking confused, still didn't understand. CJ shook his head, finally saying, "There is no such a thing as a can of slack; they are messing with you." Jerry curled up his lower lip, looked at the lieutenant, wondering what the officer would now think of him and went back to the work detail.

As he approached the work detail, Izzie nudged Chief to let him know, Jerry was on his way back.

"Where's my can of slack?" Izzie asked, snickering as he said it.

"You fuckers," Jerry said, and everyone laughed.

Shortly after that, somebody gave Jerry the nickname of "TJ," short for *Tijuana,* a dirt-poor town with illiterate residents residing along the Mexican border near the Marine Corps Recruiting Depot in San Diego. Surprisingly, Lucero didn't mind the nickname and because of his small size, "TJ" became his squad's tunnel rat.

Living Among the Villagers
CAP 2-2-1 Ai Dong AT 923567
July 29, 1967, 1300 hours

For the next few days, it rained off and on, so we mostly stood gate watch on Hill 65. Then on the twenty-ninth, while the Marines who normally manned CAC units were called away for in-country training, we were sent out to man their positions. A squad was assigned to CAC 2-1, which was located near the village of Gao Dong about a mile south of Battalion HQ.[86] The CAC unit was on the east side of a small dirt road that led to a new bridge being constructed by the Seabees across the Song Thu Bon River. The river was only a couple of miles south of the CAC unit. Route 540 was the road's official designation, but the road, like other things around us, was called by different names.

We called it Ambush Row, and the leg from Route 4 to An Hoa; Liberty Road was named after the new bridge being built over the Thu Song Bon River by the Seabees.

North of the CAC unit—Liberty Road came to a T-intersection. Traveling west from there on Route 4, you ran past Battalion HQ (Hill 37) across Golden Gate Bridge, past Hill 65, Hill 52, and on toward the Annamite Mountains and the Special Forces Camp at Thuong Duc. To the east of the T-intersection, the road ran east, and three miles away another road ran north off Route 4.

Ambush Alley, was the name given to that dirt road, which led through Dodge City to the Seventh Marines Regiment located on Hill 55. If you continued east on Route 4, you crossed the railroad tracks and eventually Route 1 to Hoi An, and from there you could take Route 1 north into Da Nang or south along the coast all the way to Saigon.

For the next five days, we were told we would be standing watch at night at the CAC unit and living among the Vietnamese people while getting to know them and their way of life.

The first night at the CAC unit was memorable; we felt very much alone in a village of about 400 people with eighty or more homes just across the compound from where we were. We knew any one of them could be a VC or a Communist sympathizer, and some probably were. They would know the layout of the compound and know that the Marines familiar with defending the compound would be gone. Because of the distance between Battalion Headquarters and us, I knew that if we got hit, it would be a while before a reactionary force could reach us. In the back of my mind, I wondered if we would be able to hold on that long.

Marines assigned to CAC units often suffered a greater number of casualties, but they were also the ones that volunteered the most to stay for a second tour in Vietnam as long as they were allowed to stay in a CAC unit. CAC Marines preferred living in isolated village areas where things were not as hectic as they were in large military compounds where discipline was more likely to be enforced. It took a special breed of Marines to volunteer for this type of duty. Volunteering for CAC duty did not get you an assignment there; Marines wanting that assignment were hand selected from among the best the units had to offer. The Marine squad leader in charge of the CAC unit as well as the platoon of PFs from the local villages was usually a corporal. It was an assignment I wasn't interested in volunteering for.

As the hours of darkness fell, the village grew gloomy. Homes extinguished their candles, and kerosene lamps were quenched. An hour after nightfall, only a shadowy dark outline framed the village from the darker shadows of the thick forest in the background. While there should have been a half-moon overhead to provide some night visibility, afternoon thunderclouds shrouded the area with cold darkness and deep desolation. The CAC unit was separated from the village by only the dirt roadway and a thinly laid wired fence. It would not take much for sappers to penetrate the perimeter's wire.

The nights in Vietnam can get pretty dark, especially when the sky is overcast. When a thick tropical forest surrounds you, as it did the village, pitch-black nights can give you a feeling of profound isolation.

We were assigned two men to a fighting position, with only every other position manned. Standing watch that first night in a secluded CAC unit, all I could do was listen. The night's darkness was so black; I couldn't see anything in front of me, and it wasn't until I brought my hand up to my face and felt it that I was able to see the outline of my hand. We were spread thin and unsure if the PFs normally assigned to CAC 2-1 were dedicated or if they would run off if we were hit or, worse, turn against us in a firefight. The wooden tower at the center of the compound gave little comfort of added security because of the absolute blackness. A large bunker at its base served as the CAC's units CP. We couldn't see anything at ground level, couldn't even see the tower; we knew Marines on watch there wouldn't be able to spot the enemy approaching even from their advantageous position. Darkness and silence were our only security companions that night.

Back on Hill 65, there was always some type of activity going on even at night; bunkers or tents almost always had candlelight. Long white candles, some the size of a fifty-cent piece in diameter and about a foot tall, often burned in many bunkers long into the night. Low, soft music could often be heard playing in the background on that hill into the late evening hours; and every once in a while, especially during the early morning hours, someone would pick up American music on the radio. At six in the morning on Hill 65, when we were lucky, we could pick up the Armed Forces Radio Program when it came on the air, and we'd listen to it for a while until the signal faded away. But it wasn't that way here at the CAC unit or in the village across the road. All was quiet and not a sound could be heard. In the village, there were no flickering candles, no friendly sounding voices, or familiar smells. When the full darkness of the night fell, even the village dogs ran, hid, and were reluctant to bark. It was as if silence feared its own solitude.

I realized what a comfort the sound of a cough or the soft tone of a friendly English-speaking voice could be. Here in the CAC unit, there was an uneasy and fearful feeling that comes with standing watch in silence. It was as if someone was watching us. I couldn't see anyone, but somehow I felt the enemy could see our every move. I felt that they knew the layout of the perimeter and knew the exact spot where we each stood watch and where we were. I felt that it was only a matter of time before the enemy would make a mad rush through the compound's wire and we would be engaged in hand-to-hand combat. But perhaps it was this fear of the unknown that helped keep us alert.

Rahm, assigned to the bunker with me, had taken his K-bar, stuck it in the ground next to where he would be sleeping, and fell fast asleep while I took first watch. Off in the distance just a few miles south of us, someone popped off a small flare into the night—it flickered and glowed, but its light was too far away to reveal any danger where we were; our best defense was silence and listening. We took turns standing watch and with first light, I welcomed the stirring of the Vietnamese villagers across the roadway; their foul-smelling morning fires and the harsh sounds of their voices were a welcome relief and a reassurance of the beginning of another day. That morning, we learned that the other CAC unit, the one down from Hill 65, had been hit during the night. That afternoon, they were hit again.[87]

Five days and four nights we were to spend at the CAC unit, a squad of Marines and a squad of PFs in the compound.

Husked Brown Rice and Salted Fish Heads
CAP 2-2-1 Ai Dong AT 923567
July 30, 1967, 1300 hours

Over the next few days, there was nothing for us to do but stand watch at night, and during the day, we were free to walk through the village. While a few Marines stayed on the compound, some of us chose to walk through the village in pairs with our rifles slung over our shoulders. The village people were friendly, shops were open, and they were busy at the marketplace. Armed PFs were walking around or waiting at a bus stop to take a trip to wherever it was they were going. I felt uneasy walking among the villagers, not knowing if the PFs carrying weapons were our allies or the enemy. But the people of the village seemed to be unconcerned about them and that was a relief, a good indication that they were on our side. The VC were known to not only infiltrate the ranks of the PFs but to disguise themselves also as a Popular Force soldier, then attack redevelopment forces, refugee camps, and CAC units. I learned a great deal about the villagers living among them. Not because I could speak their language but because many of the local kids could speak broken English. I learned about their customs, religious practices, their foods, and their fears. Some of the villagers attended a local Seventh-Day Adventist Church; others were Catholic, Buddhist, or had little memorials with incense burning in the center of their homes in ancestral worship.

For the most part, the South Vietnamese people ate husked brown rice and salted fish heads for breakfast. At noon, they ate dry fish and to their rice they added a salty shrimp paste. Their evening meals were similar, but they added a hot fish sauce called *nuoc nam* to their rice and vegetables, which at times included something that looked like nothing more than roots. The sauce they added had a garlic-peppery smell to it, and you could smell it on the villagers' breath for hours afterward. We tried some of their food and spiced our C-rations with the hot sauce, but it didn't improve our meals' flavor.

When I was growing up, my mom would sometimes add red or green chili peppers from New Mexico to the meals she cooked for a bit of flavor or would have chili sauce on the table for us to dip into to spice up our meals. The green chili sauce my sister Piedad made was not too hot, it gave the food a spicy flavor, and was delicious; the red-hot chili peppers the Vietnamese ate were too hot to enjoy their flavor.

It was while assigned to the CAC unit that I began to really look at the Vietnamese people differently, to see them as deprived people seeking the same freedom we enjoy. Some of them sincerely seemed to want us there. The kids, like kids everywhere, just wanted to be kids and they hung around us. Other villagers just wanted to be left alone by both the South Vietnamese government and the Communist forces that often came into the village at night to recruit and to force their young men and women to serve in the North Vietnamese Army. Any kid thirteen years of age or older was often forced to join their ranks.[88] The South Vietnamese Army on the other hand waited until they were seventeen before drafting them.

The villagers were simple people with simple needs. They led a simple way of life. All they wanted was to plant their crops and to eat from their own gardens and rice fields. They wanted to be free of VC dominance, and having Marines around them helped some of them feel secure. Some would look at us and say, "Marine No.1" and show a genuine appreciation that we were around; others were just silent and indifferent.

I began to understand the unresponsive attitudes some displayed and it was easy to make friends with some villagers, especially those that lived close to the compound. Walking around the village and talking to them, it seemed easy to win their hearts and friendship, but I wondered if it was a genuine response on their part or the willingness in ours. I found it very hard to trust a way of life I didn't understand. Still it was easy to read them, to see the fear or the lies in their eyes; they were very transparent people. Sometimes you knew they were hiding something. At the same time, you felt sorry for them because they longed for the freedom we represented, but for some it was too high a price to pay.

Some villagers set up shop close by the CAC unit compound so Marines could buy basic supplies. Pens, pencils, paper, envelopes, watches, candles, radios were all available just outside the fence. Recording tapes could be bought for twenty cents and a pack of American cigarettes for fifteen. A cold twelve-ounce bottle of Coke cost a dollar, and they charged a deposit of five cents for the bottle and were reluctant to give the deposit back.

On the second day at the CAC unit, Marines by the name of Dennis Martinez, Leonard Calderon, and Jerry Souble were walking through the village when they heard a woman groan inside a hooch. They looked in and found a young girl who had just given birth. As the young girl breast-fed her baby, Martinez gave her a can of C-rats and some? pastries? he had in his pocket and from then on, whenever Martinez left the compound to go through the village, the young girl followed him wherever he went. Soon the guys started teasing him that the baby was probably his.

A Visit Home
Hill 65
July 31, 1967, 1300 hours

On the morning of the thirty-first, I jumped on a truck heading to Hill 65 and spent the day at our hooch. It was a welcome break. On the hill, at least you could relax during the day. The Marines from First Platoon assigned to CAC 2-2 had gotten hit every day since they had been there. They had received sniper fire around noon the day before from across the river.[89] CAC 2-2 got hit again while I was on Hill 65 by sniper fire as did the refugee camp at the bottom of the hill.[90] At 1400 hours, I jumped on a six-by truck to return to the CAC 2-2-1.

Early on the morning of the second of August, we were relieved from our duties by CAC unit Marines and we returned to Hill 65. When we got back, John was asked by Sergeant Whiteside to join the CP group. O'Farrell, the platoon's radioman, was now a short-timer and a new radioman was needed to be trained as the platoon's next radioman, so John went over to the CP. With Bro gone and John assigned to the CP, Guns was now two men short, so the lieutenant asked for volunteers to serve in Guns.

Dennis "Marty" Martinez, the same Marine who had been with us at the CAC unit, was the first to volunteer. He was a naïve Mexican from Sacramento, California, who didn't speak Spanish. He had fair skin; short, thick black hair; thick eyebrows; and a short pointed, upturned nose. Marty saw Vietnam through the eyes of a photographer. Marty took hundreds of pictures of the countryside, its deep, dense jungles, the people, their homes and way of life. Wherever Marty was, there was his camera.

A New Home in the Jungle
Hoa Tay, AT 922548
August 3, 1967, 1300 hours

On the third of August, we loaded all of our gear, seabags, and equipment on board, a number of six-by trucks and left Hill 65 for a new location. First and Second Platoons had been reassigned to provide security for the Navy's Seabees MCB4 (U.S. Naval Mobile Construction Battalion Four), which was constructing a quarter-million-dollar bridge over the Song Thu Bon River. Third Platoon remained assigned to "London Bridge" security. That bridge, located in the northwest corner of Hill 37, connected to Highway 540 leading into Da Nang.

We traveled east on Route 4, then south on Liberty Road to about three-fourths of a mile from where the Seabees were constructing Liberty Bridge. Liberty Bridge was to be the largest bridge ever constructed by the U.S. government in South Vietnam, and it would provide a more direct route to An Hoa from Da Nang. Most of the crossing of the Song Thu Bon River, up until now, was done by using pontoon bridges and ferries.

We disembarked and moved in west of the roadway into an area completely surrounded by scrub jungle, thick underbrush, hanging vines, and a thick cluster of tall trees. We were three klicks from Battalion HQ, and our responsibility was to set up a base camp from where we would go out and patrol the area. We were to search for the enemy to keep them away and from attacking the bridge being built. The area we settled in was an abandoned village known as Hoa Tay.[91]

Over the next few days, we filled sandbags and built new bunkers. With machetes, we cleared the perimeter's inner section, especially around the trees, and removed thick bushes. The Seabees helped clear a field of fire in front of the perimeter by using heavy-duty construction equipment to bulldoze the thick underbrush in front of our fighting positions. We laid new perimeter wire and set steel fence poles into the hard ground by hammering on them inch by inch. It was hot, humid, and miserable; but within a few days the area was looking like a defensible base camp.

Our gun team was assigned the position near the front gate that led into the compound, and we built our new bunker there. In front of our position, we laid strips of sharp tangle-foot wire designed to slow down the enemy's advancement; on top of that, we laid thirty feet of security wire, a number of strands of barbed wire and double rolls of concertina wire, which was all laid out among the different strands of wire. If Charlie chose to attack our position, he was going to pay a heavy price. The guns' position covered the newly constructed dirt roadway that had once been an old cart trail. The roadway ran through our compound and continued south about a mile to where the bridge was being constructed.

North of us, Liberty Road connected to Route 4 at the T-intersection near CAC 2-2-1 and the village of Dai Loc where the district's governing headquarters was located. Farther west from there, about four miles away, was Hill 65.

To the east of Dai Loc, also four miles away, was another T-intersection. There, the intersecting road led north through Dodge City and regimental headquarters on Hill 55. Route 4 from that intersection continued east past a set of railroad tracks and a number of small bridges, eventually connecting to Highway 1 and Hoi An, the capital of Quang Nam Province. The seacoast lay beyond that.

The field of fire the Seabees cleared for us, ran for about 100 meters completely around the perimeter. Near the tree line east of the road, a large tanker truck was spraying the area with an herbicide (Agent Orange),[92] which killed the tall elephant grass and large bushes. It was an area, we would use often for going out or coming in from our patrols.

On the west side of Liberty Road, beyond the cleared area in front of our guns' position, was a large tree line. The trees and heavy undergrowth were about fifty meters thick and ran parallel to Liberty Road for about a mile until you came to the village next to the CAC unit and then the village of Dai Loc. On the other side of Liberty Road to the east, a short distance from our compound were, large open rice paddy fields that ran two to three paddies deep with scattered small villages and clusters of trees in between some of the paddies.

The following days were spent reinforcing our bunkers and our fighting positions. We set up trip flares and booby-trapped grenades inside the wire in front of our bunker. At night, we stood watch or went out on night ambushes, and during the day, we ran daily patrols in the immediate area or worked on our bunkers.

Our meals consisted of C-rations. We would save our favorites or trade to eat them together. Beans and franks, peaches, and pound cake were our favorites. Most C-ration boxes contained cans of ham and eggs, chicken and noodles, tuna, beans and franks, or ham and lima beans—full of protein, but not a meal many enjoyed receiving.

Each C-ration box also contained Winston, Lucky, or Camel cigarettes packaged four cigarettes in a small cardboard box. A small tightly wrapped package of toilet paper, small packets of salt and pepper, and packaged instant coffee or chocolate powder made up the rest of the box.

One of the most useful tools in Vietnam was the P-38, a thumb-sized small strip of hard metal with a folding blade. Twelve of them came in each case of C-rats. To use it, you opened the small blade, placed the blade on the inside rim of the can and then twisted down to puncture a slot in the can, repeating the process until the can was opened. The P-38 came wrapped in brown paper with instructions printed on the wrapper on how to use them. Marines attached the small metal P-38 to their dog tags to always have around their necks or slid it behind the wide strip of stretched rubber band many wore around the outside liner of our helmets. The band could also hold in place a small plastic bottle of insect repellent, cigarettes, or the small bundle of tightly wrapped toilet paper. The P-38 came from the military; the rubber strips for our helmets came from discarded tire tubes. There was hardly anything that we weren't able to use in some form or another in Vietnam. In the Corps, if you wanted or needed anything, you had to scrounge for it. Some Marines were good at scavenging for what we needed, much like the refugees outside the dumpsite at 3/7's HQ. We scrounged for boots, uniforms, cleaning equipment, and other small items not readily available through regular supply channels. Marines assigned to supply often did the same at the risk of facing charges in order to secure needed items for the troops.

First Lieutenant Ted Rathbun, 3/7 logistics (S4) officer was known to be good at obtaining supplies for our company that we would not otherwise have obtained. He made almost daily trips to Da Nang picking up, looking for, and at times begging for supplies. On one of those days he and Sgt. Gephardt happened to find a heavy equipment depot on the Da Nang waterfront where reconditioned equipment came back from Okinawa and was waiting to be picked up.

Always on a look out for a good generator, Gephardt spotted one in the yard of the depot that was waiting to be picked up. He also noticed which battalion the generator was headed for. With that information, Rathbun obtain the name of the supply officer in that battalion and they returned to the depot the next day. While Rathbun signed the other officer's name, Sgt. Gephardt hooked up the generator and brought it to Hill 65. The generator powered a lot of light bulbs and music boxes on Hill 65 while we were there.

What we couldn't scrounge, we could buy from Mamasan or other merchants at the base of Hill 65 or near 3/7. Some merchants came by the front gates selling their wares but because of the possibility of terrorist acts, this was not supported. Others got clearances to come to base but only to the outskirts of the perimeter, and there they set up shop. Among the items we bought from those vendors were Ho Chi Minh sandals, which were made from cut-up, worn-out tire treads. Those sandals were favorites to buy and send back home.

The new bunker we constructed off Liberty Road was similar to the one we had lived in on Hill 65 but without the porch. Large wooden ammo boxes that Jones secured from artillery lined the inside walls of the new hooch. Some of the ammo boxes that had hinges on them, we turned into windows.

The Ghost Ship
Hoa Tay, AT 922548
August 4, 1967, 0200 hours

In the early morning hours of August 4, Jones woke me for my watch. An hour later, the sky's gloomy clouds had shrouded the area in intense darkness. The moon desperately tried to break through the varied gray shades of thick clouds that stood overhead for the longest time. The monsoons weren't expected to start until mid-September, but we had already received several inches of rain. The monsoon season in our area was reversed to that of the rest of South Vietnam. The summer months were hot and dry while the winter months were warm and wet, because of the Annamite Mountain range that surrounded us as well as the prevailing winds that swept in from the South China Sea. The days were beginning to get shorter and darkness fell earlier. Often at night, thick clouds moved inland, covering the sky with solid blackness, and now the clouds were unrelenting in their hold over darkness and fear.

After being on watch for a while, the darkness and the silence become overwhelming. The trees and thick undergrowth inside the compound usually absorbed any noise coming from within our camp. Now, they seemed to be making their own noise, and sounds made by individuals standing watch around the compound seemed loud and often sent a wave of disconcerting sounds along the perimeter's edge. The sounds often carried across the opened fields and then quickly bounced back, bringing a troubling echo filling our hearts with the fear of exposure.

I silently moved away from the top of the bunker, lit a cigarette, and came back with the cupped cigarette held tightly in my right hand; so its red glow wouldn't show. I had just settled down when I heard behind me a long mournful cry. The sound was carried throughout the perimeter and traveled on to the far tree line and just kept going. I looked behind me but couldn't see anything.

A moment later I heard the sound again. *Bbbbrrrrrrrrrrrrrrraaaaaaaaapppppppp*, it sounded like a large sick cow with a lion's growl but filled with deep pain. I thought perhaps it was a stray water buffalo from one of the local villages that had somehow become entangled in the perimeter wire on the other side of the compound.

A short time later I heard the sound again, but this time it was louder, longer, and more eerie. It was definitely coming from behind me; I turned and peered into the blackness of the compound to catch a glimpse of what or where the sound was coming from, but there was nothing visible. Then high and out of the middle of the darkened sky, I saw a thick red ray of light. The fiery beam was streaming straight down. It looked as if an invisible stationary spaceship was shooting off a red beam of laser light straight down into the mountains of An Hoa. Seconds later, I heard the mourning cry and I wanted to wake Jones up and ask him about it, but then I thought he would think I was nuts, imagining spaceships and laser beams in Vietnam.

The beam of light triggered a memory in the back of my mind, reminding me of something I had seen years ago when I was in sixth grade. The remembrance came back slowly. It was the same night that my brother Bobby had gotten into a fistfight with a bunch of neighborhood bullies that lived near the Michella Grocery Store on the other side of Trekell Road. I was only twelve or thirteen at the time. Four of the bullies had gone over to the park across the street from where we lived and had gotten into an argument with my brothers Bobby and Felix over the use of the swings.

Instead of getting into a fight, my brothers decided to come home, and as they were leaving the park the bullies jumped them.

Felix was able to break away and came running home to tell us Bobby was getting beaten up by four bullies. When I ran out of the house, I could see a small cloud of dust on the ground where three of the boys had Bobby on the ground, but it was my brother who was doing most of the swinging and kicking.

I ran across the street and jumped on the back of the largest of the three boys and ended up wrestling with him in the dirt and grass for what seemed like forever. Since he was larger than I was, I wouldn't let go and he seemed just as afraid to break it off, so we wrestled and fought without letting go until both of us were too tired to go on, and after a while, we just stopped fighting. No one won and no one lost that battle; all of us were just too tired to keep going. The bullies seemed to have lost the most as the four of them walked away with shiners and busted lips. Bobby and I went home, dirty and tired but proud of what damage we had done.

Later that evening, a group of kids from the neighborhood gathered at our front yard to celebrate the defeat of the neighborhood bullies. Bobby and I were the new neighborhood heroes and were being slapped on our backs and praised for what we had done. Then someone said, "Hey! Look up at the sky!"

We all stood there, silent, looking into a clear, dark Arizona sky and saw two bright lights. Both were traveling across the sky at tremendous speed while making zigzag patterns in the sky.

At first, we thought they were planes flying night exercises and following after each other, but they were moving too fast to be planes. The objects would zoom across the desert sky in seconds and then stop suddenly and stand perfectly stationary overhead. They hung there like that for a while, totally motionless in the sky. Then they repeated the maneuver several more times, crisscrossing over the desert sky with different patterns flying off in separate directions and then coming together again. As we stood there in awe, still trying to figure out what we were seeing, the lights zoomed off only to return to fly different configurations. They finally flew off in opposite directions, disappearing as fast as they had appeared.

To us standing there in our front yard, it had looked like a giant's invisible hand was using the lights from the small objects to scribble in the sky with a set of white penlights. As we were standing, silently staring up at the sky where the strange objects had appeared, my mother called for us to come in and we all went off to our different homes. After that, I don't remember any of us kids ever talking about what we had seen. We just thought it weird, and I had completely forgotten about that strange night until tonight.

The ray of light reappeared followed by the strange sound. I reached over and shook Jones awake who was lying asleep behind me on top of the bunker. "Hey, Jones! Jones, wake up! What's that?" Jones sat up, looked over his left shoulder, just as the last trail of the red beam of light disappeared into the night. The light beam was followed by the loud foghorn sound that I had been hearing on my watch. I was relieved that he had seen it also so that he wouldn't think I was nuts.

"Oh, that's Puff," he said. "He's just working out." With that said, Jones turned around and went back to sleep.

The following morning, I asked Marty, who "Puff" was. Marty lit a cigarette, puffed on it until it was good and lit, cocked his head to one side, raised his right eyebrow, and with his right index finger raised but slightly bent as to make a point, went on to tell me. "It's a C-130 cargo plane with mini-guns," he said. "They're slow-flying aircraft that put out a lot of lead from a pair of Gatling guns. They sometimes airdrop supplies or flares when someone is getting hit and are able to fly in a very tight circle over a very small area. Some smart Air Force guy came up with the idea some time ago to mount six-barrel mini-machine-guns on the side of the C-130s and created Puff.

"When we got overrun by the NVA at the CAC unit in May, it was Puff that came overhead and saved our ass. A three-second burst of fire from the mini-guns can easily put a bullet in every square foot of an area the size of a football field. They're very effective," he said.

"The gooks hate them," he added as a matter-of-fact as he released a puff of smoke; the smoke flowed out of his mouth and drifted sideways along his peach-fuzzed face. "The gooks are very superstitious people. They think the airship is a ghost ship and they call it the night fire-breathing monster or the flying dragon. Wait 'til you see them work out close by. They're awesome. We call them Puff the Magic Dragon."[93]

I asked Marty about the night the CAC unit got overrun.

"That night was weird," he said. "Before we left Hill 65 for the CAC unit, Greg Vandewalle gave me all his stuff to hold and to mail home because he said he knew he wasn't going to make it back. I didn't know at that time, but we had gotten some information that the CAC unit was going to get hit that night; that's why we had an FAO with us, a guy by the name of Toth.[94] Bernard Toth was a tall, husky Marine, who wore thick black-rimmed glasses and had dark, thick hair. A matter-of-fact, Marine that didn't mess around and was serious in all he did.

"It was one of those surreal nights," Marty went on to say. "Nothing was going on and we decided not to sleep in the bunkers since it was so nice out, and we were lying out in the open, in the middle of the perimeter when we got hit early that morning. Before we knew it, the gooks were in the wire. Using sticks, they had propped up the wire to get in the compound. They ran through, throwing hundreds of grenades, but most of them weren't going off. All I remember is Toth yelling at us to get up and get to the bunkers. Greg and I were running toward the bunker where Calderon was when Greg got hit and went down. I kept falling down and each time I did, I swear there was a gook right there shooting at me with a machine-gun, but I kept falling. I didn't understand why I kept falling until I was medevaced; that's when I realized I had slipped on my boots and hadn't tied the shoelaces, so I kept tripping on the boot laces while the gooks were shooting at me, and that saved me a couple of times. A guy we called Baldie, a good friend was also wounded that day, he got shrapnel in the face, neck and chest."

Front Toward Enemy
Hoa Tay, AT 922548
August 5, 1967, 1300 hours

On August 5, we set up illumination trip flares in front of our position and fragmentation grenades in between the concertina wire and just to be on the safe side, Jones decided to set up two claymore mines in the middle of the wire directly in front of our gun's position as added protection. The front of the mine was concave and embossed in large capital letters with the words FRONT TOWARD ENEMY. The embossing was such so that they could be correctly set up in the darkness of night. Four tiny wire legs protruded from its bottom, and with these extended, the mine was pushed into the ground. Two strands of wires connected the claymore mine to a command-detonating trigger-firing mechanism.[95]

We kept the firing mechanism for the claymore mine on top of the sandbags next to the gun near the A-gunner's position. The dangerous thing about the claymore mines is that the enemy could easily turn them around and when detonated, the lethal pellets could be incoming instead of outgoing. To counter this possibility, Jones set a grenade with the pin pulled under the claymores. If Charlie picked up the claymore to turn it around, the spoon would fly off the grenade, it would explode, and the enemy would be killed either by the grenade or the claymore mine if it went off.

Since the gun was located near the front gate in a prime defensive position, the lieutenant thought it wise for us to also keep pop-up flares at our location. The flares were a foot long, encased in light aluminum handheld tubes. To fire the flare, you remove the cap and then insert it into the flare's bottom. The cap held the firing pin in its recessed bottom. Striking the flare's bottom down hard against a fixed object ignited the flare. A loud swoosh would follow the flare's arched flight in the direction it was pointed. The flare would explode high in the air, lighting the sky as it drifted downward on a small parachute. We kept the flares next to the gun on top of the sandbags and arranged them according to their possible use from left to right. The closest to the gun were white flares. They were used to illuminate the sky often if we saw or heard movement. Next were green flares used as a signal to others that friendly forces were in the area or as a signal to cease firing. Sometimes a patrol coming in late at night, wanting to make sure we were alert to their presence would pop off a green flare to signal that they were coming in. Finally, we had red flares that signaled we were being attacked or enemy forces had been spotted in the area.

At night, at least one or two illumination or fragmentation grenades set in the wire would go off, but we never saw anything. We figured the wind, large river rats, badgers, or other small animals living in the jungle or near the river's edge probably set them off.

Jones also threw empty C-ration cans out into the perimeter's wire. He figured that if sappers saw us set up the trip flares during the day they would know where they were; but the scattered empty cans moved by the wind would never be in the same position, so if Charlie tried to crawl through the wire at night, he might touch them, they would make a noise, and we would be able to hear them in the wire.

The C-rat cans however often attracted small animals, especially the large rats that lived near the river. We never saw those critters when they set off the trip flares because they were small, swift, and scurried off as soon as the primer ignited. By the time the actual illumination or fragmentation grenade exploded, the small critters were far gone or had been blown to bits. When grenades went off, we usually fired a white illuminating flare into the air to check out the area.

CHAPTER NINE

Pop a Flare, Pop a Flare!
Hoa Tay, AT 922548
August 6, 1967, 0300 hours

The early morning of August 6 was sheltered in darkness; only a few stars in the night sky were visible. Gray clouds moving across the night's sky added to the dispirited feeling for those on watch. There was something sinister about the shadowy shapes of the trees behind our bunkers on nights like these. To our right front, the hard-pressed dirt road often reflected the glow of the moon or at times that of a distant flare, but not tonight. Sometimes it seems as if there was just enough light to make the closer shadows distinct, but the darkness elsewhere hid unfamiliar shadows and shapes offering perfect concealment for the enemy.

I was about to get off watch at three that morning, when a grenade exploded in the perimeter wire. The explosion occurred to the left front of our bunker, halfway into the wire.

I dove for cover as Marty, who was sleeping near the gun, woke and scrambled to his A-gunner's position just to the left of the gun. As I recovered, I could see that he had grabbed his M-16 and was poking his head over the bunker's protective sandbagged wall. He shouldered his weapon and aimed it in the direction from which the smoke was billowing.

A second later, just a little farther to our left, a trip flare exploded in the wire. The bright light illuminated a small body that was rapidly moving away from the first explosion. Marty opened up with a short burst of automatic rifle fire, and the bullets kicked up dust near where the body was moving. Jones, shaken awake, turned on his belly and crawled toward the gun. Both Marty and I could see there definitely was a body in the wire, and we strained to find others nearby.

Izzie and Chief were manning the bunker to the left of us, and Izzie was on watch when the first grenade exploded. Chief, sleeping on top of the bunker next to Izzie, woke to the sound of the first explosion, the flare, and Marty opening fire. He saw Izzie with his M-79 in hand, straining to pinpoint a target in the wire. Chief grabbed his M-14 and seeing the moving body in the wire, opened fire with a burst of automatic rifle fire at the form. The distinct sound of an M-14 firing has a way of getting the adrenaline flowing.

"Pop a flare, pop a flare!" Marty cried, as he popped off a couple more rounds and then quickly changed magazines, slapping in another twenty-round clip into his M-16. I reached out, grabbed a pop-up flare, pulled the cap off, reinserted the cap into its bottom, and struck the flare's base hard on the top of a solid sandbag. As the primer exploded, igniting the flare's propellant, I feared I might have struck it too hard and worried, the flare may have been pointed toward Marty.

Whoooosh! The streak of burning light shot past Marty's head and went straight up. Seconds later, it exploded high in the sky. It was a perfect shot, exploding directly over the perimeter's wire where we had seen the body. Only then did it occur to me, I had reached out with my left hand and grabbed the closest flare available, the last flare in the row. As the tripped illumination flare in the perimeter wire on the ground was flickering its last sparks of illumination, the bright red flare I had shot off ignited overhead. The red flare's bright glow high overhead cast a bloody shadow over the crawling body that had managed to get entangled deeper within the perimeter's concertina wire. As the body was struggling desperately to break free, Izzie shouldered his M-79 grenade launcher and took careful aim at the struggling body in the wire. Chief opened up with another burst of automatic rifle fire, and both his rounds and Izzie's fired M-79 grenade struck the target at the same time.

Jones, now fully alert, saw the red illumination flare explode overhead and immediately got behind the gun. He could see where Chief's bullets were striking the ground and where smoke was still billowing from where Izzie's fired round had exploded. He took the gun's safety off and cut loose with a fifty round burst of machine-gun fire in the general direction the other Marines had fired.

The gun's red tracers struck the rock-hard ground and split into fiery sparkles, ricocheting every way. From a distance, it was hard to tell who was firing and where the bullets were coming from.

A Marine to the left of Izzie's bunker yelled out, "Incoming, incoming!" And split seconds later, another squad to their left opened up. We hadn't received any incoming on our side of the perimeter, but the west side of the compound exploded with small arms and automatic rifle fire, and I wondered if that was where the main enemy force was trying to break through. On the other side of the perimeter, we heard Keeton's gun open up followed by a white flare exploding high in the air. As soon as the flare popped overhead, new concentrated outgoing firepower was unleashed. Seconds later, another red flare was popped; this time, it burned on the other side of the perimeter wire where Second Platoon was located.

By now some of the grenades and trip flares we had laid out in the perimeter wire were exploding. They were either being hit, ignited, or exploding when hit by ricocheting bullets or by shrapnel being shot out from other exploding grenades in the wire.

Marines in Second Platoon manning the east side of the perimeter began tossing grenades over the perimeter's wire just in case, enemy soldiers were lying prone on the other side. The new explosions added to the intensity and the roar of firepower we were unleashing.

It seemed we were getting hit hard and the firefight was occurring on the other side of our compound. Perhaps the body on our side was a deterrent while the main enemy force was attacking us from the river's edge from where we wouldn't be expecting them. I wondered if they had penetrated the wire on that side and would soon be rushing through from behind us and overrunning our position. Marty had already experienced such an attack, and the look in his eyes was frightening. While Jones kept his eyes on the front of our bunker, I began to wish we had cleared away more of the heavy underbrush inside the compound. No telling where the enemy might be if he got inside our perimeter.

"Second Platoon must be getting hit hard," I said to Marty as we strained to find movement in front and behind us. Still we hadn't received any incoming rounds, none that were directed toward our gun's position. But we expected them to come at us at any moment.

The only target we had seen and fired at was the lone body crawling in the wire. The body we could see was still moving, so Marty reached over and set off the claymore mine nearest the body. The explosion was loud and powerful. Its explosive force lit up the area and shook the perimeter wire and fence posts up and down our side of the perimeter.

Izzie and Chief believing we had been hit by an incoming RPG rocket round, opened up, sweeping the area and the distant tree line in front of the bunker with both automatic rifle fire and M-79 grenade rounds.[96] About that same time, a grenade exploded right where the claymore mine had exploded and Marty cried out, "Incoming," got down, rolled over on his back, reached out, and grabbed the second claymore's firing mechanism. While still on his back, he pulled the plastic trigger toward his chest and pressed down hard on the handle.

The second claymore exploded and Marty popped up, threw his M-16 over the sandbagged edge and opened fire with a twenty-round burst of automatic rifle fire, spraying the area in front of our bunker with high-velocity bullets. Just as quickly, his rounds were expended and once again there was a secondary explosion where the claymore had been. This time, Marty realized, the secondary explosion was the grenade we had rigged under the claymore mine and he slid back down, changed magazines, and slowly peeked over the top of the bunker to see if he could see any movement. Kneeling next to Marty, I held my fire, waiting to see any incoming; and wishing, I was behind the gun. I felt bad that I hadn't opened fire, but I hadn't seen any incoming or another target to fire at.

The new explosions caused an increase in the intensity of the firepower being released all around the perimeter. Every other bunker around the perimeter was now engaged in the firefight.

Jones pulled the gun in tight into his shoulder, focused on the body in the wire, and fired for effect with machine-gun bullets. He riddled the body with a dozen rounds until it lay motionless. The firefight all around the perimeter continued for another five minutes without interruption until an illumination round fired from Hill 65 exploded high overhead.

One, two, three high-altitude illuminating flares exploded perfectly overhead according to the prearranged grid coordinates, the lieutenant's radioman had called in. Three white parachutes held the bright burning flares suspended in the smoke-filled air. The flares bathed the perimeter in bright light and bunkers around the compound became clearly visible. Marines began poking their helmeted heads over the top of their sandbagged bunkers, searching for signs of the enemy. All firing had stopped.

Not a sign of the enemy anywhere.

The threatening shadows of the dark night were now distinctly outlined and exposed to full sight.

The smell of burning sulfur, smoke, and dust from the bullets, the smoking flares, and the powder from both the exploding grenades and claymore mines lingered in the air.

To our left, we could clearly see the bullet-ridden body.

The long, skinny dog was no longer moving.

The Enemy is Ahead
Liberty Bridge, Vietnam
August 7, 1967, 0800 hours

Early the following morning, Captain Baggette had First Platoon saddle up for a long patrol. We didn't know if this was punishment for the needless firefight we had engaged in the night before or perhaps Baggette figured we were too idle and bored and needed to let off some steam. Humping rice paddies in the hot Vietnam sun, while searching for an elusive enemy was a creative way of releasing pent-up energy.

Our platoon moved out, going through the front gate in a staggered formation, heading east. This was our first platoon-sized patrol in the new area. I knew the area was heavily booby-trapped, and was grateful that a Marine was walking in front of me. One step at a time, and keep your distance, I was thinking, if he steps on something, I don't want to be killed or wounded as well. I wondered if Charlie was watching, he would certainly be able to see the direction we were traveling, and from a distance he would be able to keep track of where we were going.

"Actual One, this is Six Actual," the platoon's radio cracked with the sound of the skipper's voice. O'Farrel kept up his pace as he rogered the call. "One Actual, be advised a bird-dog has advised seeing eight enemy soldiers fleeing the area ahead of you." As the radioman acknowledged the message, Lieutenant Wilson halted the platoon to get a map reading. I started to look, to see where I could place the gun, in case we were hit and looked for the bird-dog plane in the air but couldn't see one.

See what the captain wants us to do, Wilson told O'Farrel. As he got on the mike, I could see Wilson, checking out the area ahead. We had been heading southeast along a skinny trail toward the river, and there was a clearing ahead. If the enemy set up on a far tree line we were going to be a target out in the open.

All of a sudden, we could hear a lot of chatter over the radio.

The company CO was calling for Marines to open fire, and I'm looking around to see if I can see any enemy soldiers. On the FO frequency I could hear another voice coming through calling in an artillery mission. The grid coordinates being given were very close to where we were. I brought the machine-gun down off my shoulder, lowered my gun, and Wilson motioned to me and others that we weren't going to set in.

Seconds later, a burst of automatic rifle fire was heard. The sounds came from about 100 yards in front of us.

In the distance to our right, I could hear the increasing volume of artillery rounds heading in our direction. I looked northwest to see if I could see it and see where it was heading toward. I knew more or less where Hill 65 was, from our location so the rounds would be coming from the 11th Marines Battery located there. The artillery rounds exploded over the Song Thu Bon River.

"A squad of NVA are crossing the river in front of us," O'Farrell, cried out to the lieutenant, as he held the handset to his ear. "The CO wants us to stand still."

I breathed a sigh of relief and moved forward to find an advantageous spot to set up the gun. In the distance, the sounds of an artillery barrage being fired could be heard.

"Fire for effect, fire for effect," the voice on the FO radio shouted over the net.

Eight enemy soldiers had been seen crossing the river in boats south of our patrol's location.[97] The fleeing enemy soldiers were taken under fire by Second Platoon Marines at Liberty Bridge and with artillery fired from Hill 65.

A few minutes later, we moved out again and I heard O'Farrel chuckle. What's so funny, Jones asked him. "An artillery short round took out the Seabee's pontoon Bridge," he answered and both he and Wilson shook their heads and we moved out.

Besides some huge bomb craters, the area we were traveling through showed little traces of war or life. No villages or hamlets were visible as we traveled in a northeasterly direction through a desolate, neglected area. There were no signs that civilians nor the enemy might be near or that either had been in the area.

Within an hour, we were soaking wet from the hot, humid air; beads of perspiration were flowing freely down our shirts and trousers, and the trail we were following was filled with mosquitoes and other small flying insects attracted to our sweat. The trail led us through dry creek beds; thick, tall elephant grass;

overgrown bamboo stalks; and low clinging vines that grabbed our boots and sometimes caused us to stumble.

A Village that Once Was
Giao Thuy (2) AT 938548
August 7, 1967, 1250 hours

Two klicks later, we came upon abandoned rice paddies and the outskirts of a destroyed village, Giao Thuy (2). The dry rice paddy fields surrounding the village were pitted with numerous bomb craters from what must have been a mass aerial bombardment. Only a couple of charred bamboo huts, blackened with smoke remained standing. The other buildings had burned to the ground. The remains of discarded bamboo furniture and dry, mud caked clothing littered the ground. Broken clay pots and cracked steel pans were scattered throughout the deserted village.

As we moved in to search the village, I set up the gun on the outskirts of the village facing down the trail from which we had come. In the village, much had been left behind; either everyone had been hurriedly evacuated or they had all been killed. It was evident not even the enemy had passed through the area for a very long time. [98]

I wondered what happened to the villagers, was it our bombs or the enemy that had kept them away. They had left much of their belongings behind. The Vietnamese are superstitious people and they would not normally leave a place so deserted, it was as if we were standing in the middle of the village of the dead.

Marty had asked me to hold on to his personal property, which included his latest photos before we left Liberty Bridge. He had asked this before, fearing he might not make it back. Once again he was dead serious as he looked at me and said, "Cook, keep these." He always paused when he said that, and then would add, "If something happens, make sure my mother gets them."

I always tried to tell Marty, "You're not going to get hurt," but I knew he was serious and felt that this time, like the other times, he just might not be coming back. Of course, I always took his personal belongings, letters, and photos and stuffed them into my seabag for safekeeping. Marty would go through this same ritual each time we went out on a major patrol or operation. He felt that he was living on borrowed time since he had escaped death on May 14 when CAC 2-2-2 got overrun. He was among those who had survived and he felt a tremendous guilt because of that. [99]

I took Marty's pictures because I figured if we got into a firefight, I wasn't going to get hurt. Marty's faith in me in getting those pictures and his personal belongings to his folks back home meant that he didn't think I would get hurt. In Vietnam, you needed all the lucky charms and good fortune or any good-luck piece you could find to survive. Stuff like that didn't make a lot of sense in the normal world, but in war, you learn to hold on to every shred of hope from whatever the source; perhaps with all of it combined, you just might make it back home in one piece.

As I unhooked the hundred round ammo belt I had been carrying across my chest and sat down, Leonard Calderon was setting up to the right of my gun's position. A fire-team to my left was checking the ground for any trip wires before they too set in.

Calderon had been in country for about nine months, he was an old timer.

"Hey, Leonard, can I ask you a question?"

"Sure," he answered, as he took off his helmet, exhaling a deep breath as he sat down.

"You were there the day the CAC unit got hit, what happened?"

"Let's see," he answered as he titled his head back, adjusted himself into a comfortable sitting position on the ground and began to run the scenes of that night through his mind.

"Intelligence had told us, the CAC unit was going to get hit that night, and so besides the CAC Marines normally there, it was reinforced by a put together squad of eleven Marines from India Company.

We got hit at about 2:00 a.m. Three groups of NVA soldiers had penetrated the compound at three separate locations by lifting the perimeter wire.

All of a sudden we were hit with mortar, rocket, and automatic rifle fire. They rushed in and assaulted our positions from inside the wire. It was all over, in a matter of minutes.

A Marine by the name of Greg Vandewalle from First Platoon was killed that day.[100] It was Mother's Day, weird huh; imagine having to tell a mother that her son was killed on Mother's day.

Another CAC Marine was killed, three other Marines were wounded, George Palmer that everyone called, 'Baldie,' Doug Harris 'Moose' and Marty. I think Marty got some shrapnel from a grenade. Four PFs inside the compound were also killed and another four other PFs wounded. Toth the FO was with us at the CAC unit that night.

Toth had already prearranged certain perimeter grid coordinates, with the artillery unit on Hill 65, in case we got hit. They would know where to fire their artillery. Toth should have gotten a medal for that day. He was directing Marines, as to where to go, and directing their firepower, and was busy calling in the artillery mission. Vandewalle was killed as he ran to help out a machine-gunner under heavy enemy fire. Maybe he should have also gotten a medal. Toth, as soon as he had us secured in our bunkers, called in an artillery barrage right on top on the compound. The artillery barrage saved us from being totally overrun and killed, there must have been about a hundred of them; Toth saved many Marine lives that night. Captain Clark was on Hill 65 and he got together a squad of seventeen Marines led by Larry Callahan and they jumped on tanks to come out to us. When they got there, Toth was already calling in the medevac for the dead and wounded Marines. I don't know how many NVA we killed, but ten dead enemy soldiers were seen being carried away when the fighting ended."

What World Is This
Giao Thuy (2) AT 938548
August 7, 1967, 1250 hours

With the burned-out village behind me, I sat in silence, wondering how people's lives are changed by war. I looked at my watch; it was almost 1300 hours. It would be eleven in the evening, the day before in Sanger, where Dorothy was.

By now, I was beginning to feel as if I existed in two parallel worlds. I felt as if I was living two different lives and neither had any relationship with the other. One of the reasons I had joined the Marine Corps was to get away from my wife.

Before we were married, I had spent two summers at my sister's home in Sanger, California, a small town in the middle of the state. It seemed like it had been years since I last saw the place. Vineyards and orchards full of nectarines and peaches surrounded the area. What a difference between the hot and humid world, I was in and her world with the summer peaches and cool nights. In the morning she would be going to work. With her high school diploma, I felt she could have gotten a better job than packing peaches and nectarines into wooden boxes.

We were expecting a baby, due in August, and Dorothy said she would notify me by way of the Red Cross as soon as the baby was born. She wanted to name the baby after me, if it was a boy. I had never liked my given name and told her not to do that. I didn't want to strap a baby down with a name I didn't like. The name was also her brother's.

As I set up the gun, I was thinking how funny it was that I couldn't remember our wedding night. It had been my first time, and I couldn't remember it.

Doc Never Did Give Anything To the Tin Man
Liberty Bridge, Vietnam
August 7, 1967, 1400 hours

After taking a break for chow, the word was passed for us to saddle up, and I picked up the gun and swung it up to sit on my shoulder. Marty stepped out in front of me, and I followed while Jones fell in behind.

Tin Man was walking point followed by Dennis Grewelding, a short, skinny, light-skinned Marine in Second Squad. We crossed a series of open rice paddy fields and then entered an area overgrown with tall elephant grass and found ourselves walking through thick hedgerows and heavy underbrush until we reached a thick tree line.

David Berg had earned his nickname "Tin Man" when he awoke one day with a stiff neck. The platoon's Corpsman placed him on light duty, and while his squad went out on patrol, Berg stayed behind milking his injury for two weeks worth of light duty. Berg had long, skinny arms, a gaunt face, protruding big ears, and eyes which were set so far apart that if you looked at him sideways it looked as if he only had one eye. Two klicks later, we stopped to rest near an open area but stayed on the trail we were traveling on.

In front of us were dry rice paddy fields and to our right, tall scattered bamboo plants ran alongside the trail that connected to a tree line a distance away. I was about to set the gun down near a small opening in between the bushes and a tall tree when I froze. The tail end of a mortar round could be seen stuck in the ground near the trail in front of me.

Marty came up behind me, and I put my arm to hold him back.

"Marty, is that a live round?" Marty motioned for me to back off.

Jones came over and knelt on one knee to look it over.

No visible wires were connected to the device. It was just the buried fins of an exploded mortar round, he said.

Marty took out his camera and took a picture of the protruding mortar fins. "How about taking a picture of the three of us, Doc?" Marty asked the corpsman who was assigned to our platoon.[101]

"Doc" Marren was tall, thin, freckle-faced, and scared, his long, skinny arms pockmarked with numerous pink and brown blotches. His pale-colored skin clashed with the bright-colored red hair he kept short—real short like a lifer would wear. He carried a .45 caliber pistol strapped to his hip and was assigned to the CP. Outside of staying close to the CP; Doc Marren enjoyed hanging around Guns' bunker. In the bush; however, the gun team posed too attractive a target to the enemy so for the most part, he stayed away from us. In patrol formation, he walked behind the CP group, sandwiched in between the squads where it was more secure for the Corpsman to be.

Doc took off his backpack and flak jacket and popped salt tablets into his mouth, washing them down with a swig of warm water from his canteen. The canteen holder he wore was tattered and torn, the snaps long ago broken off. The canteen holder and his web belt were Marine Corps issued. Other than that, he was wearing the new lightweight jungle utilities and a dark green undershirt. Everything the Corpsmen wore was new, crisp and clean, U.S. Navy Department issued. Doc had been issued an old canteen cover, as most of our good canteen covers had been converted over to carry spare M-16 ammo magazines. Our faded green undershirts paled, in comparison with Doc's rich dark green Navy-issued undershirt. I wondered why Navy personnel were issued green-colored T-shirts while we continued to be issued white undershirts in Vietnam.

I hand-dyed some of my undershirts with green dye I had asked Dorothy to send me from home, but the dye turned them into a bright lime green color, which was an attractive, glowing target in the dark. Fortunately, after a while with a few washings, they turned a dull green color.

Most of us going out on operations or patrols no longer wore undershirts or the white boxer shorts the Marine Corps issued. It didn't take a grunt long before he realized that humidity in the jungles of Vietnam and the constant rubbing of underwear caused a painful rash to develop between his legs, so most of us went without underwear. Those who wore T-shirts usually ended up taking them off to use as towels to wipe away the sweat and grime or they, like the boxer shorts, were used as rags to clean our weapons.

Doc came over to where we were waiting. Ten minutes after we had stopped to rest, Doc's hair was still dripping wet. Little beads of perspiration covered his freckled face, and sweat flowed freely from his forehead down his pointed nose. He wiped it away with a thick new dark green hand towel that had "U.S. Navy" stenciled across its center.

Jones, Marty, and I posed sideways so the "Three Aces" emblems on our helmets would show in the picture. I turned to make sure my holstered .45—worn low, much like the gunslingers of the old West, would also be in the picture. Marty had drawn an "ace of spades" on his helmet with a felt-tip pen; Jones, a diamond; and my helmet had a club imposed over the tightly stretched green-camouflaged helmet liner. We posed with the gun at our feet. Then I picked up the gun, and we posed again. Doc clicked away and took three pictures so each of us could have a copy. Arthur Toy, our radioman came over and posed with us for another round of pictures.

Toy, in Second Squad, was a short Mexican from the San Fernando Valley in Southern California. He carried two belts of machine-gun ammo in bandolier style across his chest. He had short arms, small hands, thick eyebrows, and a heavy mustache, which gave him that real Mexican-bandit look. He was a pleasant and good-natured Marine who was always joking and hanging around Guns' hooch. We nicknamed him TiTi, which was a Vietnamese word meaning "small."

Doc took several pictures of us and when our new weapon's squad leader, Corporal Dumont came over, the Corpsman jumped into the picture and Dumont took a picture of the five of us. Dumont took one photo, advanced the film for another shot, and as he pulled the camera up to take a second picture, the quietness of the area was shattered by the distinct sound of a grenade exploding in the thick underbrush to our left.

One thing you pick up quickly in Vietnam is your reaction time. Sometimes, I swear I would hit the deck and assume a defensive fighting position long before I heard whatever it was that triggered my reaction. Maybe it was just being scared or the ever-present danger that quickened our reaction time. In seconds, the platoon was laid flat out, listening, and waiting.

"Doc, Doc, hey, Doc, I think I'm wounded," cried a voice a short distance from us.

Dumont got up quickly from where he had hit the ground and ran toward our left flank where the explosion and the call for help had come from.

"Corpsman, up," Dumont called out and Doc Marren got up and ran toward the wounded Marine.

"Hey, Jones," I half whispered to him. "Who was walking our left flank?"

Jones, without answering got up and signaled for me to follow him with the gun. Because of the mortar fins, we hadn't set up the gun on the trail and we were more or less out in the open. We moved the gun, setting it up in an advantageous firing position, one that would both provide us cover and give me a clear field of fire.

"I don't know," he answered.

"Grewelding and Tin Man were walking left flank," Marty said as he checked the gun's belt for any loose or offset rounds and then attached another 100 rounds to the belt.

One thing about First Platoon was that we didn't bunch up on patrol. If someone tripped a booby trap, only one or, at most, two of us would be hurt. Lieutenant Wilson was adamant about his men keeping their distance, and he always told us we should always keep our flak jackets and helmets on, while out in the field. We didn't always follow this practice, and often when we took breaks, the flak jacket and the helmets were the first to come flying off.

The word was passed to be on full alert as a medevac helicopter would soon be landing. Whoever was hurt, it was serious enough to warrant an emergency medical evacuation by helicopter. Dumont came over to where we had set up.

"It was Grewelding," he said.

"He's not seriously hurt, but this is his third Purple Heart and he'll probably be sent to the rear." The field policy of 3/7 was that if you were wounded in combat three times, you would be sent to the rear or home, depending on the seriousness of your wound.[102]

Corporal Dumont was a small French-speaking Marine with short arms and shorter legs. He looked very much like Woody Allen up to and including his black-framed eyeglasses. Dumont was a lifer and already on his second combat tour in Vietnam. Because of his 0331 MOS, he was assigned to Weapons Platoon as our new section leader; but unlike Bro, Dumont stayed, for the most part, with the CP crew and bunked with them. Dumont had been with the Third Marine Division when they first landed in Da Nang in March 1965. He had been on Operation Prairie and Operation Union and was there at the onset of Hastings, which was a major military operation involving a number of Marine battalions as well as a number of ARVN units. He had been at the Rock Pile at Chu Lai and for a time, near the DMZ. He cared about his men and that was noticeable in all that he tried to do for us, and we appreciated him for that.

The medevac chopper came in, and Grewelding was helilifted out without incident. The lieutenant seemed troubled and disappointed; we hadn't made contact and one of his men was wounded.

"*Come on*, saddle up," he said in a gruff voice. "We're moving on."

Steven Paul Aguilar, Tired Aggie
Hoa Tay
August 10, 1967, 1300 hours

As we were working, reinforcing the top of our bunker, on the afternoon of the tenth, Jones looked up and saw Dumont coming over. He motioned for me to take a look. By his side, taking a longer step to Dumont's two was a tall skinny, dark Marine with a pock-marked face.

Keeton handed me a sandbag, and I handed it to Jones who laid it on top of the bunker aligning it straight with the others.

"Guys, come around here," Dumont called out, and Keeton came around the bunker as Jones and I stepped down.

This is Steven Aguilar he's been assigned to guns.

"Volunteered," Aguilar said, in a positive tone of voice.

"He was in Third Squad," Dumont added.

"Welcome Aggie," Jones said as he reached out and shook his hand. "Yeah," Keeton added. I nodded acceptance.

"Where you from," I asked.

"San Pedro, California," he said.

"East LA?" Keeton asked.

"No, it's in LA, by the beach," he answered.

While we now had more men in Guns, Weapons in First Platoon was still undermanned. In Guns, there was Steven Aguilar, Ward Keeton, Dennis "Marty" Martinez, Michael Jones, and myself. We were still three men short. Ira Rahm, Jonathan Boyd, Keith Pridemore and James Perry made up the rocket section and they were two men short. Usually there were nine men in a gun squad and three men each in two rocket teams.

Most of the squads in First Platoon had eight to ten men in them. There were supposed to be twelve Marines in each squad. At the most, counting the CP group, we had forty-five to forty-seven men in our platoon when we should have had at least sixty. Sometimes we ended up with new men in Weapons, not because Battalion send them to our sections, but because they volunteered or by other circumstances they were transferred to weapons.

As we sat around talking, getting acquainted, Keeton asked, Dumont, if we could expect anymore men in Guns.

"No, that's it for now," he answered.

"How about rockets, are they going to get any more men? We're assigned working parties together since we're in Weapons? I'm just wondering."

"No, unless, someone is transferred in, by Battalion that has a Gun's or Rocket's MOS."

"Like Perry," Jones smartly remarked."

"Yeah, how did Perry get into Weapons?" Keeton asked.

James Perry from Texas, tall, thin with long skinny arms, large hands, and long legs. His eyes bulged out and his hair, cut short along the sides of his head, made his ears stand out. He had a harsh twang in his Texan accent when he talked and was a bit hard at times to get along with. Because he had been busted down, he would argue about assignments and tried to use time in the Corps instead of in rank as the deciding factor in assignment of work detail. Dumont always overrode those arguments yet was sympathetic to Perry. Dumont was always fair in work-detail assignments regardless of rank or time in the Corps, but at times, he had allowed Perry, some slack, and it seemed that was what Keeton was referring to.

Dumont snickered, and then decided that we deserved an explanation.

"Ok, here's what happened," Dumont said.

"Perry was an E4 (corporal) assigned to Administration and isn't due to rotate back Stateside until late December. But, a bright Marine working at Headquarters found a way to change the rotation date by a few weeks and convinced Perry that they could do it for him, and he would be home before Christmas. Another Marine had left just two months earlier by doing the same thing and Perry agreed, but they were caught and Perry was busted to PFC (Private First Class) and then transferred to the field. Since he had a 0351 MOS (rockets), he was sent to our platoon where he was needed."

"Hey, that's what you get for fudging the system," Aggie said.

"I came, here cause, I wanted to," he added.

Who's Turn Is It, To Carry the Gun?
Hoa Tay, 1700 hours
August 10, 1967, 1300 hours

For the past few days, we had been hearing rumors from Marine reconnaissance squads of regiment-sized columns of enemy soldiers moving down from the An Hoa Mountains toward our location. Both Lima and Mike Company also reported uniformed enemy forces moving east toward Liberty Bridge near the northern section of the Arizona area near Football Island, along the Song Vu Gia River.[103]

Dumont came over, to where Jones was with us, at our bunker's position at the northeast side of the perimeter at the entrance to the compound and told him, a gun team was needed to go out on an ambush with First Squad. There had been quite a lot of enemy activity spotted at night and during the day along the river's side of the perimeter recently.[104]

The enemy would often try to cross the river north of our compound because the bend in the river was somewhat hidden from view and the current was not as swift there.

Intelligence had received information that a large enemy force was going to cross the river there that night, so more then likely the ambush squad would be seeing action.

The lieutenant wanted the river side of the compound to be covered by a gun team at all times. Since I had just gone out the night before, it meant we would stand watch at Keeton's bunker.

When Aggie and I got there, to stand watch, I overheard Keeton say to Jones, "It's not my turn to carry the gun; I carried it out the last time out." They argued for a bit, Keeton saying it wasn't even his turn to go out. Then Marty said, he would carry it, but Jones realized he wasn't ready, so he picked up the gun, and Jones and Marty went out.

I stood first watch, then Keeton, and then Aggie. Perry, Rahm, and Boyd manned our position that night near the front gate.

Keeton awoke me shortly after he got on watch. He had heard an M-60 open up, but nothing else.

A short time later the squad returned, neither Jones, nor Marty said anything about what happened and I didn't ask, but something was different between the two, and neither was saying anything.

Roy Mitchell Wheat
Hoa Tay
August 11, 1967, 1300 hours

On the 11th it was our turn for a day long patrol, and we patrolled north along the river's bank, all the way to Route 4. On our way back, we patrolled along the west side of Liberty Road. While we didn't encounter any enemy activity, a short distance away from us, on Route 4, First Platoon from Kilo Company was providing security for a Navy construction crane working there when a fire-team leader, Roy Mitchell Wheat, accidentally triggered a well-concealed Bouncing Betty-type antipersonnel mine.

Wheat yelled for his team members, Vernon Sorenson and Bernard Cannon to run as he flung himself onto the mine.

The mine exploded, and Wheat absorbed most of the impact with his body. For his actions that day, Wheat was awarded the Medal of Honor.[105]

I'll Trade You My Sister, If You'll Let Me Fire Your Gun
Hoa Tay
August 12, 1967, 0800 hours

On the twelfth, with increased enemy activity, we were assigned, along with Marines from Second Squad, to reinforce our perimeter with new fence wire.

"Hey, Cookie," Jerry Lucero said as he came over from where his squad was working. He jumped over a small trench line Marty and I had been digging, his short legs barely cleared the small ditch.

"You know those pictures we took when I first got here?"

"Yeah," I answered.

"I sent the film home to be developed, and my sister wrote back and asked who the handsome Marine with the hazel eyes standing next to me was. She wants to know if she can write to you," Jerry said, smiling, and I knew he was up to something.

"What does she look like?" I asked.

"Well, do you want to write to her or not?" he asked, acting as if he was insulted. He then showed me a picture of a beautiful young Hispanic girl with thick black hair.

"What do you want in trade?" I asked, knowing he wanted something in return.

"Let me shoot your gun," he said.

"You can hold it and take a picture with it," I said and waited for his response. I reached up and took his sister's picture, and the deal was done.

Felix Duran 0331
Hoa Tay
August 12, 1967, 1300 hours

As I sat on the top of our bunker reading my mail, a small Marine walked up to our guns position with a seabag slung over his shoulder that was bigger than he was. He was a skinny guy with a small square face, bulldog nose, small eyes, and small hands and arms, but was solid build.

He had on a stiff, starched utility cap with pointed ends and I could tell he carried a mean disposition. Before, he opened his mouth, I knew, we weren't going to hit it off. The Marine seemed to be mad at the world, but he looked scared and dead serious.

"This Guns hooch?" he asked, as he set his seabag down. I nodded, yes, and waited for him to say more.

He looked around, "Well, I'm supposed to report here," he said.

Hearing, someone outside, Aggie came out of the hooch.

"Are you a machine-gunner?" Aggie asked.

"0331," he answered. "Are you Mexican?" Aggie added.

"Why, you want to know?" he answered.

As he responded, the Marine looked up at me and I'm sure he could see my registered displeasure at his response.

"Just wondering," Aggie answered his voice cowing down a bit.

"Puerto Rican," Felix Duran answered.

With two men in guns with a 0331 MOS, Jones wouldn't have to carry the gun anymore. First Platoon now had two guns teams with machine-gunners behind each gun.

Duran didn't seem to appreciate having been sent to our unit. He had been in country since mid-July and was with another company and then all of a sudden, he was transferred to our unit. Why, he ended up with us, we never found out. Rumor had it that he had been with the Twenty-Sixth Marines and had been transferred to us because he had gotten into a fight with someone. Even with a 0331 MOS, Duran would still have to prove himself where it counted, under fire. Some Marines acted tough because they were scared, unsure of themselves and hadn't been tested.

I wondered about Duran, if his anger could be directed at the enemy.

Mike Boat Ride to Block for Mike Company, Second Battalion, Fifth Marines
Arizona Territory
August 13, 1967, 0700 hours

Early morning First and Second Platoons saddled up and were loaded on board Mike boats and traveled up the Song Thu Bon River.

We disembarked on the north side of the river across from Football Island. This is Charlie's territory; they call it the Arizona Territory for a reason. Before Operation Arizona it was known as the Independence area, and the name will change if we become engaged in a fierce firefight with the enemy. We moved in, and set up a blocking force for Mike Company of the Fifth Marines, that were sweeping toward us.

We set in and waited, soon Mike Company swept past us, having encountered no enemy between us. A short time later we were loaded back on the Mike boats and returned to Liberty Bridge without having engaged the enemy.[106]

Williams WIA
Thuong Phuoc AT 935553
August 14, 1967, 0800 hours

On the morning of August 14, First Platoon went out on a long early morning patrol. We circled around past the dry lakebed to the north of Thuong Phuoc. As we were heading back toward the bridge Jackie Williams stepped into a punji pit.

"Corpsman Up," someone called out, and we all stopped.

Hullihen quickly, set up his squad in a protective perimeter near Williams and the other squads deployed, in a defensive positions. I could see others, quickly scanning the area to make sure, there were no other traps set up for us to trip.

Williams was not seriously hurt and the lieutenant asked the Corpsman if we needed to medevac him. Doc Marren had Williams remove his boot. He cleansed the wound and said, we could continue on our patrol. When we got back to Liberty Bridge, Williams was taken to Battalion for treatment. [107]

What Do You Call Your Gun?
Hoa Kay
August 15, 1967, 1700 hours

As evening fell, Jerry Lucero dropped by.

"What are you up to Jerry," I asked.

"Just wanted, to drop by," he answered.

"Sure you did."

"OK, I heard you firing the gun earlier, but was on guard duty, or I would have come by, so I figured you would be cleaning it, tonight, so I came over to watch."

"You want to help, clean it," I asked.

"Sure, he said, a smile appeared on his smooth round face.

"You got some dirt, or smudge on your upper lip."

"Smart-ass," he answered.

Jerry sat down on the sandbagged wall, as I took the gun and broke it apart, telling him what each part was called and what it did.

"You know, I volunteered to come to Guns, but my squad leader said no. They need me as the squad's tunnel rat, so, that's cool."

I turned the barrel for Jerry to look at the carbon built up. "A lot of guys don't like to fire their weapons because it means they have to clean them. But I figure, the more I fire it, the better I'll be with it if we need it."

"Some Marine gunners name their guns," Lucero said.

"Dustin in, Third Platoon says, he knows you."

"Yeah, we went to machine-gun school together, Dustin, Borgman and I."

"Dustin named his M-60 'The Widow Maker,' I don't know what Borgman named his gun."

"Machine-gunners in Second Platoon have named their guns, 'The Embalmer, and the Undertaker,'" Jerry said.

"I haven't named my gun," I responded.

"She used to belong to Bro, my squad leader, killed shortly after I got here."

"How, do you know it's a she," Jerry asked, seriously wondering, if there was a difference; I chuckled.

I put the gun back together, and was holding it assembled in my hands, as I answered him. "When I first fired this gun, I knew we belonged together, I just knew it was a she. There's something about her, I enjoy cleaning her, enjoy how she smells afterward. I like hearing the sound she makes, when I pull her trigger, the smell that comes together when the oils and the expanded rounds mix. Sometimes, I think she has her own desires and she wants to be fired, wants her own separate war. It's as if she enjoys it, wants it. I feel secured and powerful behind her, if the first round doesn't get me, she'll fire away and keep us protected."

Jerry, by then was sitting there, listening with his mouth open.

"She was Ron Moore's gun. He carried her during DeSoto. She is the first gun I fired in combat. Keeton carries the new gun, but she's giddy, I don't trust her, she'll fire off, when she shouldn't, so I don't trust her. She's a boot, like you," I said.

"Screw you," he answered back. "Well, do I get to help clean her."

"You can help, clean Keeton's gun, she doesn't mind a Mexican touching her." I laughed.

A .45 for 45's
Hoa Kay
August 15, 1967, 1900 hours

At sunset, after we had finished working on the bunker, Marty was inside practicing to load and unload the .45 caliber pistol in case he had to carry the gun.

He pulled back on the slide to take it apart for cleaning. When he did, he had forgotten to clear the chamber.

"*Wham*," we heard the impact, before the sound of the pistol going off. We rushed inside.

Marty's eyes were opened wide, his mouth open, he looked scared. The Pistol was still in his hand.

The bullet had struck a wooden box inside the bunker, ricocheted up, struck the ceiling and bounced back, striking a stack of 45 rpm records belonging to Jones.

On the floor and scattered throughout the insides of the bunker, were hundreds of small black plastic record pieces. Fifteen of the Jones' records had been shattered.

Jones looked at Marty, and I knew he would never forgive him for what he did. And as for Marty, I knew he would forever try to make it up to Jones, even if he could replace them all, it only added to what was already dividing them.

Time To Move
Hoa Tay
August 17, 1967, 0800 hours

For two weeks, we had worked hard on fortifying our positions and running daily patrols in the area. On August 17, as we laid the finishing touches to our new bunker, we all stood back admiring our work. Duran was standing next to Aguilar, both had their shirts off, and Duran was still sweating. While he seemed to complain about everything, once he started to work he wasn't slack in accomplishing the task.

It was one of the best-constructed bunkers in the perimeter, we reasoned, as Dumont came over and told us we were moving to a new position.

"Shit, that's just like the Corps," Duran said. "As soon as you get a decent place to live in, they move you out."

"We're moving up the road to the bridge to provide security for the Navy Seabees," Dumont said. "The lieutenant and I just came back from checking out the area where we'll be moving. There are regular wooden barracks there for us, and they're brand-new, built by the Seabees. Weapons will have our own billet. The barracks all have new screens all the way around, new canvas cots in each barrack. There're some small fighting positions already set up around the perimeter, but we'll have to build our own perimeter fighting bunkers."

"Here we go again," Aggie said.

"Who's going to live out in the bunkers, and who'll get the barracks?" Duran asked, wondering if he would end up in the bunker since he was the new man in Guns

"No one, we won't be living in the bunkers," answered Dumont, a little irritated at having to respond to Duran's negative and suspicious remarks.

"We're only going to be standing watch in the bunkers at night. All our gear and stuff will be kept in the new wooden barracks." Dumont couldn't believe the flak he was getting from us, and with a frustrated look, he continued to tell us more.

"It's going to be a great spot. Probably one of the best assignments we'll ever end up with. It's going to be the best I've ever had."

"What about this place?" Aggie asked.

"It's going to be plowed under," Dumont answered.

A New Home
Liberty Bridge, AT 923535
August 18, 1967, 0900 hours

Early the next day, we loaded our seabags and jumped on board a number of six-by trucks for the short ride to the bridge. As the trucks rolled out, the Seabees' large Caterpillars began to mow down our bunker while Seventh Marine engineers prepared to blow up the grenades and mines we had set up in the wire.

When we arrived, the 2,040 foot bridge was well under construction, Seabees were busy pounding away with hammers and saws. The bridge was supposed to be one of the largest bridges ever built in South Vietnam. Naval Mobile Construction Battalion 4 (MCB-4) was the Naval unit constructing Liberty Bridge over the Song Thu Bon River. As we unloaded, an acidic smell stung our nostrils and a burning taste filled our lungs with a sting; it was the penetrating odor of creosote, a brown wood tar that covered most of the bridge's surface.

At the perimeter's edge, only a layer of sandbags had been laid out along the top of a thin trench line with small intermittent u-shaped fighting positions set up fifty feet apart. They were typical Naval entrenched cutouts that we probably would never use.

For the next three days, we filled sandbags and built up our new fighting positions. The billets were much better than we had expected. They were brand-new and well constructed as Dumont had said. They were framed by two-by-fours and had a solid plywood platform floor. They were built four feet off the ground and were identical to the company barracks back at Battalion Headquarters. New screens covered all sides of the billet. The screens would keep out most of the giant mosquitoes and other bloodsucking insects. The little flying insects were always the first to suck American blood in Vietnam and after a while, you just got used to them being around. Many of the Marines who had been in country for a while had numerous blotches and scabs on their arms, necks, and faces from insect bites.

Fresh water was brought in daily in large water buffaloes, and Navy cooks provided two hot meals a day at our new location. In just a few short weeks, the Seabees had turned the tropical jungle that at one time abutted the river's edge into a nice military complex. They walked around in camouflaged shorts wearing sunglasses and seeming naively ignorant of the reason we were in Vietnam. Their nonchalant behavior added a sense of civilization and security to the base that was contagious. Within a couple of days, we were walking around the perimeter without our helmets and flak jackets.

During the day, we filled sandbags, built up our bunkers, or went out on daily patrols. At night, we stood watch or went out on night ambushes. The bridge was nearing its final phase of completion, and we were told that once it was completed, we would be assigned to guard it on a semipermanent basis. First and Second Platoons' main responsibility was to prevent the bridge from being blown up by the VC. To prevent this, we were instructed to shoot at any suspicious-looking object we would see floating in the river.

First Platoon set up two new gun emplacements; one was facing southeast overlooking the river. That bunker position was shared with Second Platoon and connected to a larger bunker, which also housed a .50 caliber machine-gun. My gun's position was set up at the new fighting position; we were building at the entrance of the compound. The bunker faced north and was near the front gate and just to the west of Liberty Road. It covered the same area we had covered at our former position at Hoa Tay. Second Platoon was assigned the responsibility of covering the east side of the fenced line that ran on the other side and parallel to Liberty Road. To the left of our new gun position, west of us, the rest of First Platoon circled counterclockwise and tied in with Second Platoon on the south side of the perimeter. The other gun team's position was wedged in between Second and Third squads, covering the southwest side of the perimeter, and overlooked the branch of the Song Vu Gia River that flowed into the Song Thu Bon River.

How the Beer Gardens Prevented 'Tired Aggie' From Carrying Out His Mission
Liberty Bridge, AT 923535
August 21, 1967, 0800 hours

On the twenty-first, we went on working parties while Second Platoon was sent on a patrol along the Song Thu Bon River.[108] That same morning, Lieutenant Wilson needed a runner to send to Battalion, and as Dumont went out of the CP in search of one, he saw Aggie who had strayed away from our working party and happened to be walking by.

We had already nicknamed him "Tired Aggie" because he was slow moving and took his time getting any job done. Aggie, soon after he arrived in Vietnam, came down with what we called "battle fatigue Aggie style."

Battle fatigue in Vietnam was caused by long periods of laborious activity under a hot burning sun during which your mind wandered off to the thoughts of home, friends, and loved ones. These slow periods would often be shattered by an incoming round or a quick firefights while on a patrol or the report to "saddle up," all of which brought a quick adrenaline rush that sapped your will and energy while you waited and waited, with nothing else happening.

While there was always something going on that kept us busy, there were days that gave us a quick rush and days that would turn out to be long days of hard work in the hot sun where the humidity drained us physically and mentally. Not only did the temperature drain us, but any chore or task often became a monstrous burden under such conditions. When Charlie's bullets didn't jar us into an alert state, quick two- or three-minute naps during the day were a welcomed relief and you took as many as possible when you could.

Tired Aggie after only a few minutes of work at any job, slowed down succumbing to "battle fatigue Aggie style." If no one else was around, Aggie soon lost interest in his job and just wandered off or he would take a break or a series of long stretched-out breaks. Often, when we left him alone to do a job and returned an hour or two later, we would find him still filling the same sandbag. And so it was that day that Aggie was on one of his breaks that Dumont spotted him.

"Aggie," Dumont called out.

"I was just going to get my canteen; it's hot and you need to drink plenty of water. That's what the Corpsman said. I think I need to find him for salt tablets so I won't dehydrate," Tired Aggie quickly responded.

"The lieutenant wants to see you," Dumont said, and Aggie hesitantly entered the CP; while trying to figure out how the lieutenant found out he had left the working party and, at the same time, trying to come up with a better excuse than the one he had given Dumont.

"Aggie," Lieutenant Wilson said and Aggie stood still, almost at attention. No use giving the lieutenant an excuse he might not be looking for, he was thinking, so he waited and didn't say anything, wondering why he had been summoned to the CP.

"I need you to drop off tonight's patrol routes at Battalion, and then I want you to come back here and tell me you did it. They are very important. Can you do that?"

"Just go to Battalion?" Aggie asked, already trying to figure out how he might benefit somehow from the assignment.

"Yes, take them to Battalion Headquarters, that's all you have to do, then come and report back."

Battalion, with the information received, would supply the Eleventh Marines Artillery Unit on Hill 65 copies with the grid coordinates of the patrols we were running so that if we needed artillery support, while on our patrols they would be registered and ready for us.

Aggie, strapped on a .45 and instead of waiting for the mule run, going into Battalion, he flagged down a six-by truck that was leaving the compound.

"You guys going to Battalion?" he asked them.

"We're going to Regiment," the driver answered.

"Well, I guess it's on the way," Aggie said. "Can I get a ride with you?"

"Sure, get on," the driver said, and Aggie jumped on board.

At the T-intersection, the truck made a right turn to head toward Regiment and Aggie figured that he would just get a ride from Regiment back to Battalion and then back to Liberty Bridge.

While at Regiment, after getting a hot meal and picking up some cigarettes Keeton had asked him to pick up for him, Aggie was on his way back to the gate to catch a ride to Battalion and had every intention of doing that and would have, had his travel not taken him by way of Regiment's "Beer Gardens," which happened to be open.

After a few beers, he knew he needed to get to Battalion before too long and he caught the last ride out. However, that truck was on its way to Hill 65, so Aggie got off at the T-intersection that led to Battalion and waited there to catch another ride going up the hill. He waited and waited, but no one was headed that way. After a while, some kids from Dai Loc began to come around and wanted to know what he was carrying in his bag. Aggie wouldn't tell them, and while one kid kept him busy, another one grabbed the bag and took off, spilling packs of cigarettes on the ground. The other kids then dove for the stuff, grabbing them up faster than Aggie could move. Aggie, who was carrying a holstered .45, took the pistol out and fired a shot into the air and the kids scrambled.

By then, it was beginning to get dark, and Aggie walked to the CAC unit and from there was able to catch the last six-by truck going to Liberty Bridge. When he got to Liberty Bridge, he knew he was in trouble and went to the CP to report that he had not accomplished the mission the lieutenant had given him.

As Aggie walked into the bunker, the lieutenant smelled beer on Aggie's breath, he asked him if he had accomplished his task. Aggie showed him the patrol logs and tried to convince the lieutenant that gooks had tried to kidnap him in Dai Loc and that some had stolen the supplies he had bought for the guys in the platoon. And he had had to fight his way back; otherwise, he would have been a POW.

"I ought to have you court-martialed!" Lieutenant Wilson yelled at him.

"Yes, sir," Aggie answered with a remorseful look on his face.

"I ought to have you shot," Wilson added. "I can have you executed; you know that, don't you?" Wilson told Aggie.

"Yes sir," Aggie answered, with a surprised look on his face. Wilson dismissed him, but not without first telling him he would be assigned all the shit details from then on until Christmas.

A Night to Remember
Hoa Tay
August 21, 1967, 2000 hours

That night, as we saddled up for a night ambush, Aggie asked me if the lieutenant could have ordered him shot.

"Yes, Aggie," I answered. "He's the Lieutenant, he can have you shot."

"But, heck, I was almost taken hostage and I had to fight my way back; that should count for something. I was bringing back some cigarettes for you guys," he said. "They should give me a medal for escaping from all those gooks . . . ," his voice trailed off, as he slipped a hundred round belt of machine-gun ammo across his chest.

Under cover of darkness, we moved out toward the ambush site. First we traveled along the river's bank and stopped near where Second Platoon had made contact earlier that day. We set up a temporary ambush position there at the river's edge and waited. We stayed silent for about an hour, just long enough to find out if the enemy was following. After a while we got up and moved out slowly, circling clockwise to come back toward our old jungle position.

We were out with Third Squad: I was the gun team leader, Duran was carrying the gun, and Aggie was the A-gunner. There was something eerie and frightening about returning to our old former position with only a squad. As we moved toward the ambush site, we passed by several piles of smashed up concertina wire, discarded wooden beams, and torn sandbags. The rubbish was piled high, mingled with uprooted trees and dried up bushes. The bunkers from our old position had been plowed under by the Seabees using large Caterpillars. It had all been pushed into a dozen or so large piles of rubbish. In the shadows of the night, the piles resembled small buildings in a war-torn city. In a short time, hundreds of hours of our hard labor had been all plowed under by the Seabees' tractors. It was hard to believe it had all been a well-fortified compound just a few days before.

We set up on the edge of Hoa Tay village, near the tree line, concealed in the bushes that had once been inside our old perimeter. In front of us was a small trail with clusters of bushes, large plants, and dark trees farther away. The enemy would have expected an ambush team to be concealed there in the far trees away from the trail but not where we were. To our left was a pile of debris near where we had shot the dog.

Local villagers had reported; NVA soldiers had been seen carrying supplies and equipment through that area late at night. We were to set up an ambush on one of the many trails and engage and destroy the enemy. Aggie was supposed to have dropped off at Battalion, the grid coordinates where we were going to be set up so that if we needed cover, artillery would have been preset to cover for us. But no report had been given to Battalion and we were very much on our own.

As we settled into the secondary ambush site, the silence of the night fell over us with harsh reality. While it was a relief to know that two platoons of Marines were close by at Liberty Bridge, I also knew that if we engaged the enemy in heavy fighting, the platoons were still a good distance away and were at a great disadvantage without someone close by to provide cover for us if we had to make a run for our lives.

As we lay in silence, a deep sense of a horror of deep darkness fell on all of us. It was a dreadful night whose foundation was laid by a thick band of black clouds that slowly sealed our presence in great fear, in helplessness and bathed us with the feeling of deep depression.

It was as if the devil himself and his most fierce and evil demons from hell had all been summoned to stand by our side. Their wicked presence was very real, and so we remained silent, as the great horror of darkness that could be felt overshadowed our hearts and minds, trying to steal from us, our strength and power and will to live. There would be no help from above this night. The moonlight was caught in its own fierce battle trying desperately to break through thick clouds.

Just before midnight, a sliver of moonbeam broke through, illuminating the area before us, so we struggled to make sense of the shapes and shadows we could see.

In the distance, we began to hear the faint sound of human voices. At first, we weren't sure if the voices were coming from Marines behind us at Liberty Bridge, from the village a distance away, or if they were coming from the tropical jungle in front of us. We strained to listen to where the voices were coming from. Above us, minute beams of light attempted to force their way through dark clouds, and we welcomed the light but at the same time feared as the slow-moving light cast gray shadows on the trees and bushes surrounding us causing them to take on their old sinister shapes. To our right, the hard-pressed roadway lightly reflected the moon's eerie glow, and the light seemed to dance with death and spiritual darkness while sharing glimpses of light and life, death and darkness, and so we sat in silence not knowing what the night would bring.

In front of us was a small trail, the villagers used to travel toward the river, but most of it was hidden from view. I hated nights like this. Being out in the bush with limited visibility added insecurity and unwelcome fear.

This time, there was no concertina wire out in front of us. No grenades or claymore mines were set up. No other Marines standing watch in nearby bunkers. We were a squad of seven Marines with a three-man gun team lying prone on the jungle floor and very much on our own. This time, Charlie could very well be perfectly concealed and crawling toward us in the shadows of the night.

Off in the far distance, near a distant village, jungle drums began to sound. The sound had a deliberate rhythmic cadence to them. We had heard the drums before, but now we listened. We knew they were a form of communication the NVA/VC often used, and in silence we wondered what the message meant. Before, we didn't pay that much attention to the drumbeats, but now they took on a real meaning. They were a signal the enemy used to coordinate military movements. We wondered if it was a signal telling them where we were.

Soon the voices began to get closer and their numbers increased, and as they neared, deep fear and a feeling of isolation enveloped us and we all sat silent. We feared to whisper or to take in a deep breath. We didn't dare to move our heads, to look to our left or to our right.

We all knew that it was a large, very large, group of enemy soldiers that were moving through the night in front of us, and they kept getting closer. There were too many of them for us to do anything more than watch and listen.

All night long, we sweated heavily and I feared the enemy would smell our fear, would hear the sweat drops as they poured out and fell on the ground. Heavy droplets of perspiration, poured like blood from our foreheads, and trickled down and burned the corners of our eyes with a salty embrace, but we dared not move to wipe the sting of sweat away for fear that any movement might be detected.

We sat there motionless, listening. We listened to the Vietnamese voices whispering in our ears, echoing fear throughout the night. The column of enemy soldiers moved hurriedly and at times slowly through the heavy jungle an arm's reach away.

All night long, we heard their water splashing back and forth in half-empty canteens; we heard the swishing, clinking, and clanking of their equipment, the rustling sound of cloth rubbing together as they moved by and the shuffling, shoving, and short bursts of muffled laughter as they bumped into each other in the dark. They were little men, all dressed alike, little soldiers whose shadows we could see parading in scattered formation before us in the dark. Sometimes their whispers grew loud and were followed by sharp harsh words of condemnation from those in charge. Words spoken quickly to hush them, a warning to be silent, and it served us as well.

All night long, they marched past. We didn't see each other, but we heard them, and at times they must have heard us because they would stop and listen. We could smell them, smelled the spicy nuoc nam fish sauce they had eaten; and they may have smelled us because all too suddenly there would be moments of complete silence in which you could almost hear the enemies' nostrils flare up as they opened them to breathe in the stench of fear that was in the air, and that smell may have frightened them as well because they moved out more quickly.

Sometimes a low whistle would be heard, it's vibrating sound repeated by others as a signal for silence, and the drums would go silent. It seemed the world would stop and every man upon the face of the earth would stand perfectly still. It was as if all of the enemies' movements and evil in the world stopped and turned and listened, and while they hungered for death, great fear fell upon the hearts of men and even in the evil hearts of the green demons from hell.

In those moments of life and death, silence and chaos, the silence of the night carried within its soul all the horror of war and the deep fear of death and destruction.

The smell of grief, agony and pain, all the sorrow and woes in life were dropped at our front door and it was then, that time stood still and we all took notice of our deeds—both good and bad; and wondered about the color of our souls; what tomorrow would taste like; what eternity felt like; what courage, fear, death, and life were really about.

After a time, the voices would start up again, and all through the night, they talked and walked and moved on. They shuffled their feet and laughed as we lay hidden in the dark only a few feet away.

With the morning came a new sunrise and we all lived for another day, because the enemy hadn't wandered into us and because we hadn't tried to kill them in the night. They didn't know where we were or how scared we were. They went off to live that day and do what enemy soldiers do when they are not firing at us, and we went back to the bridge to fill sandbags in the sun.

A Night Patrol in the Rain
Liberty Bridge, AT 923535
August 22, 1967, 1800 hours

We received word late in the evening for the squad leaders to report to the lieutenant's barrack. A short time later, Dumont returned and called for us to huddle around.

"I need a gun team for a squad-size night ambush," he said. "Barela, it's your turn, Marty's turn too. You'll be going out about four klicks with First Squad, Ira's squad. It's a night ambush between our perimeter and Battalion Headquarters.

We've heard from some local villagers that the VC will be running supplies in between our positions and the CAC unit tonight. They might be getting ready to rocket Da Nang again. You'll be going out and setting up an ambush. The rest of the platoon will be on standby ready to respond just in case a reactionary unit is needed," Dumont paused. "It looks like rain, so you might not run into enemy activity."

It had been raining off and on for the past two weeks and that part of Dumont's message, we figured, would happen. While it was still early in the monsoon season, we had already experienced some days and nights of heavy rain—pouring wet, miserable, cold monsoon rain. During the day in Vietnam, you could see the rain coming. It would come in from the South China Sea in a southwest direction. Sometimes it came from the An Hoa mountain range and moved northeast and when that happened, you could visibly see the rain creep over the mountains around its sides and into the valleys. It was like seeing a thin large sheet of cellophane, bluish gray in color, being unrolled slowly over the mountain range until it covered the valley, and you heard its sound and felt its cold wet drops.

Unlike the rest of Vietnam, the monsoon rains in Quan Nam Province came twice a year. It often rained fast or slow, down or sideways, in soft caressing mists or in terrorizing torrents. One moment the rain would be soft and quiet, the next; hard and noisy. The worst rain was wet, cold, and heavy; it had its own sounds and smells and took on various shapes, intensity, and power. The nastiest storms we experienced came from the South China Sea that blew the wind and rain every which way, and there was nowhere we could turn to get away from its strength.

We would be going out near the general area where Grewelding had tripped a wire and set off a booby trap grenade. As we saddled up, the rain started to come down slowly, a steady rain that increased in velocity so that by the time we left the perimeter's wire, we were drenched. The night before us seemed like it was going to be one of those long, dreadful nights; however, rain or no rain, we were going out.

During my tour of duty, I saw rain act like I had never seen it behave before. Sometimes it would pour down on us in torrents, or when the wind controlled it, it sprayed us sideways. It would blast us from behind, sweep past us then a few steps ahead, stop, turn around, and drench us from the front. At times, it came at us from the east, then from the west, and sometimes it came from the south or from the north. There were times when it seemed like it was a living thing thrashing at us from the four corners of the earth or sweeping down from above; there were times when it was all of that at the same time. Tonight; however, it was slow, constant, cold rain falling in mixed patterns.

I now understood why the Seabees had built the barracks so high off the ground. It was a precaution against the monsoon floods. For the past two days it had constantly rained during the day. Everything was soaked inside the barracks and in the bunkers. Most of the nights while we were on watch out in the bunkers, we wore our ponchos, and while out on ambushes, we almost always became soaking-wet.

On our patrols, we stepped into rice paddy fields and the rainwater in the paddies would meet us ankle deep while at other times, we were up to our waists or chests in water. The difference was often only just a few steps in either direction.

Sometimes we swore the rain conspired with the earth and the sucking mud in the middle of the rice paddy fields, and together they held us in place so the rain would pound down hard on our helmets and slowly soak us thoroughly.

Our biggest problem was keeping our feet dry. They remained shriveled and waterlogged for days. The Marine Corps issued us foot powder in little green containers to help keep our feet dry and free of infections, and we sprinkled the white powder on our feet and poured it into our socks. We were never issued enough socks, but there was always plenty of foot powder. We had small cans and big cans of the stuff, but no socks.

We moved on through the night, plodding across flooded rice paddy fields, and were about to reach our objective when the rain, as if to mock us, began to let up. By then we were all soaking wet. We had taken great pains to be as quiet as possible as we moved through the night toward the ambush site. With the rain stopping, the silence of the night vanished so that now with every step and sound we made, it was magnified by the silence the absence of rain had left behind. Two hours after we had left our perimeter, the rain stopped, the sky above began to clear and we were confronted with having to cross a large open clearing.

Help Me, I'm Drowning
Liberty Bridge, AT 923535
August 23, 1967, 0100 hours

Ira passed the word that the ambush site was just across an open rice paddy field on the other side of a tree line some seventy meters away. We were going to have to cross out in the open, and the rice paddy fields in front of us were completely flooded, the tops of the dikes barely visible. Without the sound of rain and the cover the dark clouds had provided, we were going to be exposed while crossing the open area making us prime targets.

Ira came over to my gun team. "I need the gun to cover for the first fire-team," he said. "I'm sending them across the rice paddy fields to that far tree line." He pointed in the direction the fire-team was going to be heading toward.

Ira's eyes held a worried look, and I wondered if we were doing the right thing. He looked away at the dark cluster of trees; the closest point was no less than sixty meters away. "Once they get across, they'll set up and cover for the rest of us to cross over," he said.

Ira, like all small-unit leaders in the corps in Vietnam, rarely looked you in the eyes when he spoke. It was a safe way to keep from getting close to someone who could be there one day and gone the next. Someone who could get killed by the orders each unit leader gave. It was a way of protection from the painful and often all too rapid exits when someone left the squad by having been wounded or killed. Ira, with the majority of his time in country behind him, had lost many good friends. I could understand why he kept his distance and why he didn't say much.

He reminded me of Bro. He was a practical Marine who cared about his men. In turn, they respected and trusted him and they would follow him anywhere. They had already followed him without question two miles away from our base and two hours away from any help. They were there with him leading the way. We all knew the choppers wouldn't be flying in this type of weather and if we encountered a large enemy force, we would have to hold on until daybreak when help might arrive, though we feared not in time.

In Vietnam, everyone joked around with each other and you learned to get along during working parties and while on guard duty, but it was on patrols in the night where you learned to depend heavily on those around you to trust them. This was where true friendship was born. There was a code of comradeship, of support, and of knowing that a fellow Marine would be there to back you up in a firefight but you still didn't get close. Once you lost a close friend in combat, you understood why.

I was now beginning to understand the pains and the sorrows of war, but there was also another side that only those who have shared blood and guts in battle understood.

Many believe that war's appetite is violence and it can only be appeased with death and destruction. But war also gives birth to respect, honor, to glory, and to shame. Those who fight for life can be full of compassion in times of suffering and pain and that often fosters trust, care, and hope amidst death and destruction. War often cultivates friendship and love among those fighting and dying in the midst of chaos and devastation. Although friendships could be ended quickly, I was beginning to realize that one of the most cherished gifts to come out of war was the friendship it produced. War dispenses this gift of friendship and love to those who have shared its pain, sorrow, and joy in times of conflict and in victory. It does this whether we want it or not.

I set up the gun to offer the fire-team as much cover as possible. They started across and I held my breath and scanned the far tree line for movement. If the enemy opened fire, they were going to be hit with a wall of lead.

The fire-team made it across the open rice paddies without incident. They set up and signaled for the rest of us to come across.

"Spread out and cross slowly, walk along the sides of the dikes," Ira whispered, he repeated the same words over and over to everyone leaving the tree line as he sent them across. When the second fire-team reached the halfway point, the silence of the night was shattered.

We heard a loud splash.

Silence.

The sound had come from somewhere in the middle of the flooded rice paddy field, but we couldn't see or hear anything.

We heard another loud splash then another, followed by a loud, screeching cry.

"*Helllllp!*"

The call for help was immediately followed by a gurgling, gasping, struggling sound. The noise came from a point where two of the rice paddy dikes crossed. At that point, we could see water splashing high into the air.

Joe "Lucky" Cervantes had been walking point for his fire-team and had managed to fall into one of the many deep, water-filled bomb craters. Heavily weighted down with grenades, a flak jacket, a helmet, and a hundred rounds of machine-gun ammo, he could not paddle fast enough to keep himself afloat. He was kicking, splashing, and crying out for help each time he surfaced gasping for air.

The night's stillness and all the efforts we had made to be as quiet as possible were overcome with his loud cries for help. Chief and Izzie dropped their gear and jumped in to get Lucky out of the deep hole. Ira passed the word for everyone to rush across the wide rice paddy field, and we ran past the commotion in order to set up the gun on the other side. Somehow, in between our mad rush across and his struggle for breath and to stay afloat, Lucky was fished out of the hole.

Jerry Ezell a husky, medium build square jarred Marine with short curly hair was carrying Lucky's limp body over his shoulder and dropped him next to our gun team. Lucky collapsed, gasping loudly, trying to catch his breath, I set up the gun as fast as I could to cover for the Marines going back out to recover Lucky's gear. If the gooks were around, I was ready.

Ezell, Chief, and a tall Marine by the name of Earl Lergner returned to the site where Lucky had fallen into the deep crater. As others stood guard, Ezell and Chief dove in to recover Lucky's weapon, his flak jacket, and hundred rounds of machine-gun ammo he had been carrying. All were at the bottom of the twelve-foot-deep water-filled crater. By now, we had made so much noise that if Charlie was listening, he would have thought we were a company-sized operation.

They recovered what gear they could, but not the hundred rounds of machine-gun ammo that stayed at the bottom of the hole. As soon as we reassembled at the tree line, it started to rain, slow rain, and Ira abandoned the ambush idea and called in to notify our lieutenant that we were returning to base. As soon as we entered the perimeter's wire, it stopped raining. Ira made his report to the lieutenant, and we returned to the barracks.

Once inside our barracks, we took off our boots and socks to dry our feet. When we told Aggie what happened, he started to laugh. He handed me a large can of foot powder, and when I opened the can, the lid popped off and foot powder flew all over the barracks and us. We stood there looking at each other covered with white powder and we all started to laugh. Ira came in about that time. In his hand was a can of foot powder and that picture added to our laughter.

When he saw us sitting there bathed in white powder and the barracks floor covered with it; and the can of foot powder in his hand, he joined in on our laughter and we all continued to laugh hysterically. We couldn't stop, and when Marty fell on the floor laughing, white powder billowed up, and we laughed harder and uncontrollably with tears flowing. When we started to control ourselves, Aggie farted and it all started again.

Ira didn't have to come by; he knew we probably didn't need a can of foot powder, but it was his way of saying thanks, and I guess that's why he was there to say thanks for being there. We hadn't engaged the enemy that night; but we had shared a unique incident, a near drowning, and a moment in life and time together. We had battled the rain, darkness and fear, the flooded rice paddy fields and had shared a unique moment in time and it is often those things that have a tendency to bind warriors together. It's not just the battles fought in war but those in-between times that built friendship and trust.

Ira got up to leave, and as he opened the door, it started to pour. We started to laugh again. Still laughing as he stepped out, he pulled his poncho's hood over his helmet and disappeared into the downpour. The warmth in his eyes during those few minutes before he left spoke volumes, and from that day forward, I felt as strong a closeness toward Ira as I had for Bro.

We were friends.

Incoming
Liberty Bridge, AT 923535
August 24, 1967, 0300 hours

I woke to the sound of an explosion, early of the morning of August 24. A burst of gunfire followed, then the incoming automatic rifle fire. The bullets tore through the barracks canvas and I hit the wooden floor and grabbed hold of the M-60. The fresh smell of Hoppe's oil was still present on the gun's barrel as I brought it in close and ran half crouch to the bunker.

Aggie and Jones were at our second machine-gun position near the bridge manning the .50 caliber machine-gun. I had cleaned the M-60 after our last patrol and kept it at the bunker, waiting to bring it out when it was my time to stand watch.

As I made my way in their direction, I knew they wished the gun was already there. The explosion sounded close and inside the wire. The night was lit by a full moon that so much of the compound area was visible. I wished I had been at the bunker, but at the same time, I was glad I hadn't just rushed out there. I had no idea where the enemy was or if they had penetrated the wire. Every night, we wondered if this would be the night the NVA would hit us and try to overrun the compound.

As I got near the bunker, the enemy opened up again with a burst of automatic rifle fire. I hit the ground as the rounds snapped overhead. Other Marines, running to their bunkers, also hit the ground.

I could see the firing was coming from a distant tree line across the open rice paddy fields just east of Liberty Road.

"I'm coming in," I cried out, jumped up, and ran for the bunker.

"Come on in," Aggie answered as I rushed in the bunker's door; Jones had slipped on his boots and was tying his laces.

"Sappers," Aggie said, leaning over from the top of the bunker. "There were two of them." Jones looked up at Aggie, half believing what Aggie was saying.

I handed Aggie the gun, and he placed it on the tripod, as I climb onto the top of the bunker.

"I shot at them," Aggie said in a matter-of-fact way, and Jones picked up the night-starlight-scope looking toward the distant tree line, searching for any enemy movement.[109]

There was nothing visible in the wire in front of us. Jones and I didn't believe Aggie about shooting at sappers in the wire. Especially since he had let his imagination run wild with his story about his "escape" from the kids who had tried to steal his cigarettes. But we were taking sporadic incoming gunfire, so something was up.

As I popped open the gun's cover, the enemy opened fire again.

AK-47 bullets cracked overhead, slicing the air, with a high-pitched snap. The bullets were too high for us to need to take cover, but we still ducked our heads and moved closer to the bunker's sandbagged walls. I dropped a 100-round belt into the gun's feed tray and closed the cover. Aggie attached another 100-round belt to the end of the ammo belt.

If the gooks were searching for weak points along our perimeter's edge and had accidentally set off a trip flare, they might still be near.

In the wire about eighty feet in front of the bunker, the tripped illumination grenade was flickering its last sparks of light.

"I threw a grenade at them," Aggie said, referring to the original exchange of fire that had woken up the perimeter. Both Jones and I didn't answer as we searched the wire for movement.

The enemy fired off a few more rounds. This time, the bullets were fired at Second Platoon's positions and it was small carbine fire. The enemy, we knew by the way they were firing, was retreating. There would be no more incoming, and there was none. It was a pattern the enemy followed.

When a sapper unit probing a perimeter's wire for weak spots was spotted, their supporting element located at a distant tree line would open up with a burst of automatic rifle fire. The initial burst was always followed with sniper shots from supporting units with a small arms carbine or a more powerful sniper's rifle, or incoming mortar rounds. They were all designed to keep our heads down, while the penetrating unit made their escape.

After the sappers tripped the flare in the perimeter wire and Aggie had thrown the grenade, the enemy had fired forty or fifty rounds in our direction. Their intention was to keep our heads down while the sappers in the wire made their escape.[110]

Surprisingly, no one in the platoon returned fire. No one called in mortars or artillery or even called for an illumination round.

Perhaps the phantom incident with the dog in the wire was the reason that First Platoon Marines hadn't opened fire. Second Platoon, manning the east perimeter section and nearest to where the enemy had probed, also didn't bother to open fire. Perhaps we were all expecting a bigger attack and everyone was waiting to make sure they had a clear target before firing. Except for Aggie's pitched grenade and a burst of ten rounds by him at the enemy, no one else opened fire. This obvious lack of enthusiasm on our part must have been puzzling and an emotional blow to the enemy. I could imagine how they must have run out of the area seeking the safety of the dense forest and tunnels to sit and await the barrage of artillery that was sure to follow but never came.

Sometimes, events in war were not played out the way one would expect them to be. As I made my way back to the barracks, I was thankful I hadn't been shot. It would have been embarrassing to be wounded or killed and then medevaced wearing only my helmet, my flak jacket, and my skivvies.

He's Asleep, Let Him Sleep
Liberty Bridge, South Vietnam, AT 923535
August 25, 1967, 0300 hours

We had set up at an ambush site and had been there for three hours when the Third Squad's leader tapped me on the shoulder. He held his finger over his mouth for silence and motioned we were moving. I signaled to Aggie, and we picked up the gun and ammo and moved out. Aggie turned to look at the sleeping Marine whom we were sidestepping over and shook his head in disbelief. We moved out while the Marine slept at the ambush site.

One thing about being in the military is that you need to be able to trust others with your life and for them to trust you with theirs. When that trust is broken in war, life is exchanged for death, honor for shame, friendship for hatred, and it can be costly to the whole unit. In life, there is a need to be faithful in love; faithfulness in war is a sacred trust. There is no room for deceit, arrogance, individualism, or selfishness. Not in the Marine Corps. Your brother depends on you; unity and camaraderie in the unit is extremely important. In Vietnam, it was critical.

Something had happened to the platoon. It started the day after the dead-dog in the wire firefight. We had become, perhaps in spite of our own foolishness, unified; and in a few short weeks, we had become closer as a unit, more protective. As a platoon, we shared not only a common enemy but a secret and a new bond; an interconnection existed among the old-timers and new men who had recently rotated in. Camaraderie had emerged, one of unity, mutual trust and respect. Perhaps our new platoon leader had something to do with it, or perhaps it was the old-timers who were rotating back who didn't have bad habits. They were Marines who didn't take drugs or smoke grass, which fought for each other and respected each other; and those in the Corps who did fail to live up to that honor were looked upon with increasing suspicion and mistrust, in a battle zone.

Trust in a fellow Marine was a commodity you could not afford to be without in Vietnam. The word was passed down from squad and fire-team leaders to their men; if anyone went into the bush under the influence of drugs or alcohol or fell asleep on watch, they would be left out there in the boonies.

The uncertainty of life amid the dangers of war dictates that trust be cultivated and that a strong reliance on each other maintained. This was happening within our platoon, but we didn't realize it at the time. It had happened in boot camp and then during ITR training; and it was now happening here in Nam, in India Company, in First Platoon. We were coming together as a team and as a unit.

A Marine is first of all a combatant, a grunt, and his duties and responsibilities are dictated by military regulations and policies that are there to help protect everyone in the Corps. It wasn't *Semper fidelis* (always faithful), the Corps, the government, or a military way of life that built that unity in war, it was our own individual needs for survival combined with the trust we had in each other that called for us to be faithful.

Marines are trained for war and to depend on each other in armed conflicts, but one of the most important of all aspects of our training was often overlooked, which was the reinforcement of love for God and for our country, first learned at home, the emphasis of shared moral beliefs and the value of life. The effect of those sessions added to the camaraderie and oneness found in the Marine Corps that was strongly reinforced in the Corps because we were, after all, Americans who held those beliefs high.

We were Americans fighting Communism, an enemy in conflict with all freedom-loving people, and that gave us a determination to win because we believed in ourselves and loved our God and country. I understood how that unification had instilled in me a readiness to die for my fellow Marines, and I felt assured that they were willing to die for me as well.

Marines have always been the first to land in a hot combat zone and have always been the first to fight in every major war the United States has been engaged in since its creation. These facts add up to the pride and unity a Marine feels, and I sensed in our platoon a growing pride of belonging. I belonged in First

Platoon with men I could trust; Marines I knew would protect me with their lives. Second Platoon was most often at our side; we trusted them to be there as well when we needed them, and we in turn would be there for them. Because of our assignments together, First and Second Platoons were close to each other. Third Platoon, during my tour of duty, was usually assigned elsewhere so we didn't share that same closeness, but we knew we were all one unit, a company of Marines and would be there for each other if the need arose. We were Marines, and that word was special. It meant commitment and trust.

At boot camp, we had gone through ten weeks of intensive training where we learned to obey military orders given by those of a higher rank. Discipline was stressed as was physical conditioning. Marine Corps history was taught. When one Marine violated these standards for personal or selfish reasons, in a war zone such actions endangered the lives of others. Marines had a way of teaching other Marines that such self-centeredness would not be tolerated. That understanding was not covered in basic training but understood by Marine units who over the years had developed their own special history and traditions. India Company had a tradition of not tolerating individual heroism, which could endanger the lives of others. It would not condone those who placed the unit in danger because they put their own selfish desire for recognition above the safety of the unit.

James McClintock, the Marine sleeping on watch, was from New York who had been assigned to Third Squad, First Platoon. He had come from a well-off family, and he tried to circumvent many of his duties and responsibilities. He had been spoiled at home and was not used to taking personal responsibility for his own actions nor had he been held accountable in life for his failure to act. We all knew it wouldn't be long before something would have to be done to straighten him out.

He had a "salty" attitude, a very unfavorable trait for a young Marine, and he had already been caught on two separate occasions sleeping while on guard duty; he had been warned, but not disciplined. Marines usually dealt with such incidents on their own rather than through military channels, and we could see that his day of reckoning was coming fast for him. To add insult to the Corps, one day someone found a letter he had discarded and had been writing home.

> *Dear Mom and Dad:*
>
> *Last night we got hit again. Hundreds of VC tried to come through our perimeter wire and we had to fight them off in hand-to-hand combat. I was shot in the arm and leg, but nothing else happened to me.*
>
> *Last week after I was shot the first time, the Marine Corps promoted me to sergeant and I was given the M-60 machine-gun to carry in combat. I have shot a lot of the enemy with it, and last night the lieutenant said that I'd be awarded the Navy Cross.*

The enemy is not the only one we have to worry about here. The area we are in has a lot of large rats that live near the river by the bridge. Last night a Marine fell asleep while on watch and was being dragged away by a pack of rats into the bush. When I awoke, I had to fight the rats off with my K-bar, and the Captain is now putting me up for another medal.

We realized that this Marine had a real problem. None of the things McClintock had written home about, of course, had occurred. I had seen some pretty big rats in Vietnam, but no pack of them would have been capable of dragging away a sleeping Marine. Finding these and other letters he'd written only added to the contempt Marines already felt toward him. He was always trying to get credit for the simplest task accomplished. His squad leader showed us the letter because McClintock had mentioned he was in our section, and we of course resented someone claiming to be in Guns when they weren't.

The morning of August 25, 1967, would forever make an impression on Pfc. James McClintock. While he slept when he was supposed to be on alert at an ambush site, the squad got up and quietly left him behind.

By midmorning, he had managed to make it back to Liberty Bridge. While he never fell asleep again while on watch, shortly afterward, he was killed in action when he tried to prove he could win the war on his terms. But the saddest part was when his parents wrote asking about the medals he had written home about that he had received, and Lieutenant Wilson had to write his folks telling them that he had never been awarded such medals.

CHAPTER TEN

Boone's Killer Team
Liberty Bridge, South Vietnam, AT 923535
August 26, 1967, 2000 hours

"Hey, kid, you want to go with us?" Boone asked Jones and me at the front bunker where we were standing watch.

"We need two more guys to go with us on a killer team. I'm pretty sure the lieutenant will go for the idea. We're just going out a couple of klicks to search for gooks. When we find them, we'll open fire and then run like hell back here," Boone said. "You're crazy, Boone," I said. "Didn't you and Bro tell me to never volunteer for anything? You're *booku, dinky dou.*"[111]

Boone grinned and went out in search of his killer team. It was not something I wanted to do. It took a special breed of men to volunteer for details like that, especially when you didn't have to.

The enemy came out at night and that was probably the best time to find them, but since they were familiar with the area, the night always favored them. During our infantry training days, we had been told that if we wanted to find and kill Charlie, we would have to do it at night. Tonight, Boone was going out to do just that. I had been on many night ambushes where we would set in and wait, but to go on patrol, travel at night through Charlie's back door searching for him, was inviting trouble.

The NVA/VC had been going into local villages over the past few weeks because of the upcoming elections to intimidate the citizens. They had kidnapped some of them and had shot some local village chiefs. The NVA/VC was doing all they could to prevent the villagers from voting.[112]

We weren't familiar with the politics of Vietnam. We were vaguely aware of the approaching election, but our awareness of it was based more on personal security reasons than political awareness. We set up ambushes trying to catch the enemy when they tried to sneak into the villages. The South Vietnamese government had asked for assistance in opposing Communist aggression. President Kennedy had promised to provide that assistance, and we had responded when our country called. That was all that was of importance to us. We were there because we were

Marines and our country had sent us there to fight Communist aggression. As Marines, we were there to do our duty, to follow orders. We were trained to defend our country's principles, values, and commitments; that was what was important. We would do what was required of us, but that didn't mean taking unnecessary chances.

Marty relieved me from watch at midnight, just about the same time Boone's killer team left the wire. Jones had gone off to sleep in the wooden barrack and would return to take last watch. Two Marines were always stationed at each fighting position during the night. One stayed awake while the other slept nearby.

Marty was on watch, but there was an uneasy feeling in the air. The night was too quiet and I couldn't sleep. Instead of staying near Marty and sleeping on top of the bunker, I went down into the bunker to write a letter by candlelight.

I had just finished writing, Diana, Lucero's sister, and had written "free" on the envelope's top right-hand corner when the night's silence was shattered with distant automatic rifle fire and a number of small explosions.

I blew out the candle, went topside, and joined Marty who was on his belly staring into the darkness from our sandbagged fighting position.

As soon as I heard the shots being fired, I wished I had asked Boone what direction they were going. I crawled up next to Marty, and we both poked our heads over the top of the sandbags. The shots had been fired some distance away. The night was cold and silent with only a slight breeze. We lay there in silence waiting for something to happen.

"Do you know where Boone went?" I asked.

"No, he never said where they were going," Marty answered. "But I think they went out toward the CAC unit. It sounded like the firing was on the right side of the road just past our old position."

The shots and explosions had been fired in quick succession followed by silence. There had been an initial burst of gunfire but no secondary response. The firefight hadn't continued, so either Boone had pulled off a successful ambush or his killer team had been ambushed. Boone should have been coming through the wire soon with the gooks hot on his heels. We would be covering for him so with the gun loaded and ready, we sat silently listening and waiting.

I looked at my watch. Thirty minutes had passed, we continued to strain, searching through the darkness in front of our position. The half-moon above, which had been visible during my watch, was now hidden behind monsoon clouds.

We were listening for any sound looking for any movement. An early morning breeze suddenly flowed by, sending a chill down my back and goose bumps up my arms. I got behind the gun and waited. An hour passed, and the four-man killer team hadn't returned.

Damn Boone anyways, I was thinking. *Why did he have to volunteer? Why couldn't it have been someone else, someone I didn't know?* Never volunteer for anything, that's what

Bro and Boone and the other old salts always preached. Yet I knew if a reactionary squad was needed, I would volunteer to go look for them.

A half hour later, Marty and I were still sitting silent and wide awake. I took over the watch as Marty lay on his back on top of the bunker smoking a cigarette. The lieutenant hadn't called for a reactionary force, so that was a good indication that the ambush team was all right. They would be in contact with them. Two hours after the brief firefight, we heard rapid footsteps coming up behind us.

It was Dumont running toward our bunker. "Coming in, Coming in," he cried out.

"Boone is right outside the gate in the tree line," he said, pointing toward the dark shadows in the distance.

Dumont told us that Boone had radioed Lieutenant Wilson and told him he was directly in front of Guns' bunker in the tree line. The gooks had followed them, and Boone wanted to make sure we didn't open fire on him.

"We told Boone we were going to open the front gate and then they can make a run for it. The lieutenant is going to drop in some arty right behind them when they leave the tree line," Dumont said.

"Are they all right?" I asked.

"Yeah," he answered and jumped down to open the fence. He swung the gate open and ran back to our bunker with his little legs taking quick hops to get back and out of the open area.

"They wasted a couple of gooks, but we don't know how many followed them. As soon as Boone clears the tree line, the lieutenant said to open up on anyone you see behind them."

Marty set up a group of white pop-up flares to fire off once Boone's fire-team got through the wire. The hunters had become the hunted. It was the seesaw pattern of war. One moment you're the hunter, the next you're the prey. One moment you're up high, the next you're down eating dirt. As we strained to locate Boone's team in the darkness of the night, off in the distance, we heard Hill 65 fire a single artillery round.

A moment later, the spotter round exploded in front of us directly over the edge of the far tree line right over where Boone's killer team was hiding. There was no need for adjustment. The round was right on target, exploding right on the prearranged grid coordinate. Within seconds, we heard the sound of a volley of artillery rounds being launched.

As soon as the spotter round exploded overhead, Boone and his killer team emerged from the thick cover of the smoke, the spotter round was providing. As they ran toward us, Boone cried out, "Hold your fire! Hold your fire! We're coming in."

Behind them, the wind was contrary and was quickly dispersing the cover of smoke. I knew they would soon be exposed to enemy fire, and from on top of the bunker, I pulled the machine-gun in tight, up against my cheek.

As they ran across the open field, the enemy opened up with carbines and automatic AK-47 rifle fire. I returned fire with the M-60, firing over the heads of Boone's fire-team as they ran toward us. Marty and the bunker to our left also opened fire with their M-16's, and as we returned fire, the first of high-explosive artillery shells exploded where Boone's fire-team had been seconds before.

Lieutenant Wilson had prearranged for the smoking artillery round to be Boone's signal as well as a point of reference for the barrage that was to follow. When the lieutenant saw how accurate the spotter round had been, he immediately issued the command to fire for effect. Hill 65 responded by unleashing a volley of twenty rounds in rapid succession. By the time the fire-team got to our gun's position, the last of a compact barrage of artillery shells had rained fire and brimstone all along the edge of the tree line. The rounds landed right on top of where the incoming rounds had been fired.

The beehive rounds devastated the edge of the tree line of what used to be the backside of our old compound. The bombardment struck within only a few meters of each exploding round. We saw the initial explosions and then the scattering of thousands of sizzling pieces of burning small arrow shape steel flechettes as the steel shrapnel scattered high into the air and through the thick jungle. There were secondary explosions detonated deep in the grass and thick underbrush, so we knew they had hit something. Other rounds struck farther in behind the tree line. Seconds later, another volley of artillery rounds were on the way. If Charlie hadn't run out of there by now, there wouldn't be much left of him. Once again within a matter of minutes, the tides of war had turned and the hunter had become the target.

Marty popped an illumination flare, but there was nothing to see. In moments, the silence and stillness of the night had returned. Except for the smell of spent bullets, explosives, and burning sulfur that lingered in the air and a few puffs of smoke floating in the air above us, it was as if nothing had happened.

After Boone gave his oral report to the lieutenant, he came back over, jumped onto the top of the Guns' bunker, and was grinning from ear to ear. He was proud of the excitement he had caused.

He sat down on top of the bunker with his back to the sandbagged wall and lit a cigarette. Pride and confidence had replaced the fear he and his fire-team had exhibited when they came running through the gate. I had mixed emotions about his night's adventure, but I was anxious to hear what had happened.

"You should have gone with us," Boone said. "We went out about a mile when Lucky heard someone talking in Vietnamese. We followed the noise and found four gooks. They were all dressed in NVA uniforms sitting in front of a hooch eating rice. No one else was around, so I gave the signal, and Lucky opened up with a twenty-round clip in full automatic while I and the rest of the guys threw grenades.

"We waited for the smoke to clear," continued Boone, "and searched the area. We found only two of them, both dead. The other two had taken off. I don't see how they got out, but we saw blood trails leading toward the river. We were going to follow them, but hiding behind the hooch was this beautiful fifteen-year-old Vietnamese girl. She wasn't from around here; she had no papers. She was a female gook straight from Hanoi. Long black hair and tits; this gook had tits.[113] We were bringing her in when a booby trap went off and she made a run for it. We tried to find her, but we couldn't.

"Right after the girl escaped, we saw a squad of about eight NVA soldiers following us. We ran and then stopped and lay low, and they stopped behind us. We could hear them trying to move around to outflank us. So we moved, and they moved with us.

I wanted to ambush 'em," Boone claimed. "But they kept their distance, moving in toward us a little at a time. We could hear them talking loud, among themselves, and their squad leaders giving out orders, and then we would hear movement as they tried to get around us. When we got close to the edge of the tree line, we radioed the lieutenant and asked him what we should do since the gooks were close behind us. We could hear them talking, getting ready to move in."

Boone let out the smoke from a puff he had taken and went on with his story. "I was hoping that the lieutenant would send out a squad to ambush them, but he said to come all the way to the edge of the tree line and wait. Then he told us when we heard the first artillery round go off on Hill 65, it was our signal to make a run for the front gate. When we took off running, man, was I praying you wouldn't open up on us?"

How the Lieutenant Captured An Enemy Soldier
Liberty Bridge, South Vietnam, AT 923535
August 27, 1967, 0700 hours

When the sun came up, Second and Third Squad and Keeton's gun team went out on an early patrol along the banks of the Song Thu Bon River. Lieutenant Wilson was leading the patrol, and Corporal Dumont decided to go along. A short distance away, near where the platoon knew the enemy liked to cross the river, near a large sandbar, the point man spotted two VCs, dressed in black. One of them was carrying a weapon.

The point man opened fire on the enemy, and one took off running toward the road and the other seemed to have been hit but crawled away.

As the rest of the platoon provided cover, Lieutenant Wilson and Dumont crossed a small part of the river where they had seen the enemy crawl to hide. They found the VC hiding among the weeds and captured him.[114] On their way back, the platoon searched the area for bodies or wounded NVA soldiers where the artillery barrage had occurred the night before, but didn't find anything.

Frog Men In The Fog
Liberty Bridge, South Vietnam AT 923535
August 28, 1967, 0200 hours

Liberty Bridge was the pride of the Navy Seabees MCB-4. It was solidly constructed and capable of withstanding the heavy vehicles that used it daily to cross over the river on Liberty Road. The bridge connected An Hoa, Battalion Headquarters, and Da Nang. It was an important link in moving military and medical supplies from Da Nang to An Hoa and from there to Battalion HQ and on to the Special Forces camp at Thuong Duc.

In the early morning hours of August 28, the area was covered in fog. As Marty stood watch on the bridge just this side of its center, he thought he heard a noise below. As he went to the side of the bridge to explore, there was a loud explosion.

NVA/VC frogmen had swum up the river and set off two satchel charges under the bridge and had blown a large section of the bridge away.

Izzie, Chief, Lergner, Keith Pridemore and Souble having stood bridge watch earlier were sleeping near the center of the bridge when the explosion occurred. When the debris stopped falling, and the cloud of dust settled, they found themselves stranded on the other side of the blown portion of the bridge. A large ninety foot span had been blown away. They and a couple of other Marines from Second Platoon would have to wait till daybreak to cross back over by way of a pontoon bridge, the Seabees would put together the following morning.

Two Marines in Second Platoon that were standing watch on the bridge near where it blew were wounded in the explosion, but neither of them was serious enough to be evacuated.

At midmorning, Dumont, Aggie, Marty, Jones, and I were standing around looking at the damage the explosion had caused the bridge. It seemed like the NVA divers had planted the explosive charges, very near the water level.[115] We found it amusing that such a large hole could be blown so easily in a bridge that was supposedly so well constructed.

As we stood there, I looked down and there next to the bunker, just a few feet from the bridge, Duran was still sleeping.

"Hey, Duran," what happened last night, I asked him.

The sleepy headed Marine looked up, saw us standing there, blinked his eyes to focus on us, then turned to see what we were looking at and said, "What happened."

"Well, you were on watch," Aggie jived him, irritating the half awake Marine.

"Where were you?" Dumont asked.

Duran placed his cap on his head and answered, "Don't blame me, must have happened, after I got off watch."

"You mean, you didn't hear it," Aggie questioned, in a tone of unbelief.

Duran sat up and put on his boots. "What's for breakfast," he asked, knowing the menu was almost always the same at the Seabees mess hall.

"Spam, on mayonnaise-soaked bread, and warm Kool-Aid," Aggie answered.

"I guess, the Seabees are blaming us that their bridge got blown last night by the VC," Jones said.

Since we had recently been getting two hot meals a day, we weren't sure if this meal had been planned or if the Seabees' cook was pissed off because the bridge had been blown up and we had taken it so lightly. The Seabees had planned to leave in a week, but now they would have to stick around until all the necessary repairs were made.

If It Moves In The Water, Shoot It!
Liberty Bridge, South Vietnam AT 923535
August 28, 1967, 1700 hours

With nightfall we received new standing orders regarding bridge security. While we were on watch, if we saw any suspicious-looking object floating in the river, we were to call for an illumination round to check it out more closely to prevent any further damage to the bridge. We were also to not only fire at anything we saw floating that warranted a concern but to periodically fire small arms fire into the river as a precautionary measure. They were preventive measures, to keep the enemy from blowing up the rest of the bridge.

We, of course, took advantage of the new liberty we had to fire our weapons at will. If we became sleepy while on watch, we simply popped off a few rounds or practiced our grenade pitching at whatever object we saw floating in the river. The grenades made little noise when they exploded deep in the water, but the bullets made a loud noise when fired, a soft thud when they struck the water and a zinging ring as the round, traveled underwater.

Sometimes we tried to time the distance and depth so that the grenade would explode just a foot or two below the water, and sometimes, the grenade could be timed to go off just deep enough in the water to cause an eruption and drench the Marines from Second Platoon walking on the catwalk below. We even practiced trying to skip shoot a bullet on top of the water much like you would a flat stone on a lake, but no one was able to accomplish that feat successfully.

On dark nights, instead of lighting a match or using a flashlight to see what time it was during our watch, we found it easier to call Hill 65 and have one of the artillery batteries from the Eleventh Marines who were stationed there fire an illumination round over the bridge. It made the watch go by faster when the round we called in would go up and pop overhead, providing light for us, to check and see what time it was. We enjoyed watching the illumination flare, float down slowly on a little parachute, bathing the river below with light.

For those of us who didn't know how to call in illumination rounds, Steve Wilhelmsen gave us a class on it. "What you do first is put out your right hand out as if you were hitching a ride. Let's say an Army guy in a jeep drives by without stopping. What do you do? You flip him off. Your thumb is the first digit, and it's horizontal; your extended finger that you used to flip off the guy is your second digit finger, and it's vertical. That's how you read a map and call in artillery."

He laid out the map of the area on the mess hall table where he was holding his class. "If you look on this map of the Dai Loc section that is under artillery control from Hill 65, you will notice that there are numbers running horizontal like your thumb, and there are numbers running vertical on the map like your index finger.

"The squares on the map are all one thousand meters in length, they represent one klick. So to put an illumination round over the river and to the east of Liberty Bridge, you would call in a six-digit number starting with the numbers representing your thumb and then your index finger. All numbers are six digits, so for Liberty Bridge, it would normally be 927532 depending on where you want the round dropped. The first two numbers of each three digits represent the grid square. Then you go up seven meters or two meters. The number five is the center of the square. Since the bridge is just to the right of center about 200 meters, it's a seven or farther away, an eight and so on." After our lesson, Steve told us that since many of us hadn't been trained in calling in artillery support, Battalion had made it easier for us by assigning what was called thrust points to a certain area.

"For example," he said, "to call in for an illumination round at a certain location or grid coordinate, Battalion has given us a code word for that location so you won't have to know the grid coordinates, and Charlie won't know where the round is going. It will be, for example, the name of an animal, a baseball team, or movie star that signifies a particular grid-coordinate section. We simply call in with the code words, and the illumination round would be *en route* to that prearranged location. Sometimes you might have to adjust by saying down two points, or up three, etc."

Steve Wilhelmsen was finishing the last month of his tour assigned to mess duty at Liberty Bridge.

During bridge watch, Marty and I developed a game where we would call in for an illumination round and then try to shoot the slow-floating flare out of the air by shooting single rounds at it with the M-60. At times, we would hold the trigger down a bit too long and a burst of four or five bullets would shoot off followed by a red tracer. We usually would shoot the red tracer into the river; but at times, we would accidentally shoot a tracer up at the flare and then it was evident to others what we were doing especially if the tracer happened to be the round that struck the floating flare. This caused the flare to burst up in the sky, and when that happened, we were provided with a white sparkling fireworks show. To avoid firing a tracer, we pulled the tracers out of the ammo belts and gave them to Chief,

Perry or any other Marine who carried the M-14 rifle, which was capable of firing the same ammunition as the M-60.

We also removed the red tracers from some of the belts we carried into our night-ambush sites. We'd put four or five tracers together at the very front of the belt so that following the initial burst of fire upon the enemy, enemy forces at a distance would not be able to easily pinpoint the gun's position. While the sound and volume of the outgoing rounds made it easy to distinguish where the gun was in relation to the other weapons being fired, if every fifth round was a red tracer, we felt that was a bit too much of an advertisement, especially at night, so we took many of the red tracers out. With the tracers removed and firing a burst of four to five rounds at a time, it was hard to distinguish if it was the M-60 firing or M-14 that could also be fired automatically.

The red tracer rounds were inserted every fifth round to help direct the gun's firepower into a concentrated pattern at a selected target. Another reason for the red burning tracer was to help direct friendly firepower toward the enemy's position.

Helicopter and bird-dog pilots could more easily see our red tracers and pinpoint more accurately from the air where the enemy was located by watching where our red tracers were striking. I thought it convenient that the enemy chose to fire mostly green or white burning tracers in their weapons.

One night, while we had the gun out on the bridge popping caps into the water, Chief came over and we loaded his M-14 magazine with twenty red tracers and we also hooked together a small belt of forty tracers. I opened up with the gun and so did Chief, shooting the burning tracers into the water. It looked like the finale of a fireworks show at the end of a July 4, celebration. Afterward, Chief, Perry, and a new Marine by the name of Keene, who also carried the M-14, loaded at least one of their M-14 magazines with only red tracers.

Cpl. James L. Keene was a likeable fellow, smaller than most Marines, with a sense of duty, compassion and awareness about him that showed confidence in his abilities and a courage that made you want him at your side in a firefight.

A Son Is Born, Across the Sea
Liberty Bridge, South Vietnam
August 30, 1967, 1000 hours

On August 30, the lieutenant called for me to come to the CP. The Red Cross had notified the company commander that I had a son. It was a simple message: I had a son that was born on the twenty-fifth, and I should call home. As I turned to leave, I was handed my mail. It was a letter from my sister Lucy, and she had written to tell me the same thing and that Dorothy had named my son after me. When I was walking back to our barracks, I ran into Lucero.

He smiled a satisfied look on his face. "I got a letter from my sister," he said. "Have you written her?"

"Yeah," I answered, not wanting to give him any more information, which was what he was fishing for. I told Jerry the news I had just received. Jerry had already written his sister and told her about the circumstances under which I had gotten married and I also had not withheld anything from his sister, but now I wondered how Diana would react if I wrote and told her that I was a father. I didn't know if our letter writing would develop into anything, but you could never tell. You always heard about how a serviceman would meet someone through their letter writing, but most of that was in the movies; and while I enjoyed writing Diana and looked forward to her letters, I wondered what she was really like. I asked Jerry if I should continue to write to his sister.

"You told me you really don't believe your marriage is going to work out," he answered. "You joined the Crotch (USMC) to get away from your wife. Diana knows that, and remember that letter you got from your wife's cousin?" Lucero reminded me of a letter I had received from one of Dorothy's cousins who had written that my wife was spending a lot of time with her old boyfriend and she believed Dorothy may want to let me know that after the baby was born. The letter I had received from Dorothy's cousin hadn't fazed me one way or the other, except for the betrayal of trust. It was one thing to not love the one you're married to but to be unfaithful by sharing a love or emotional tie with another at the same time was another thing all together.

Her cousin who wrote knew I had had a crush on Cece, Dorothy's sister. That may have been a motive for her writing. When I first met Dorothy, it was her sister Cece for whom I had felt a strong attraction toward and if I had been more alert, things may have ended up differently. I had often wondered what would have happened if I had not married Dorothy and had ended up with Cece instead. I often wished that it were Cece to whom I was writing to from Vietnam. Perhaps then I wouldn't have felt like it was a burden or that I had to write and say things I didn't mean; I wrote in my letters what Dorothy wanted to hear.

My mind took me back to what seemed like years ago to that early summer's day, in the backyard of Cora's family and their swimming pool. Both Cece and her cousin Cora (whose father owned the corner grocery store) were tall, pretty girls. I noticed them when I first went to visit my sister Connie in Sanger, California. Cora was older, attractive, and had a number of boyfriends.

Before Cora, I had kissed only three other girls: Martina, my sister Lucy's best friend, and Martina's best friend Rose. The kisses happened when we were in the sixth grade.

Martina was pretty, dark-skinned, with dark brown eyes and long black hair. She lived just a couple of blocks from us. Her brother, Anthony, was my best friend in grade school; and the day after I kissed Martina, Rose, her best friend, asked me to walk her home. Rose said that Martina had told her we had kissed while walking and she wanted to try it so we kissed while walking, and then we kissed while on the swings at the city park. After the two girls in sixth grade, I hadn't kissed another girl until I kissed Dorothy, Cora, and Cece during the summer following my freshman year.

The kiss with Cece had been slow, long, passionate, and wanted. I remembered her lips were soft, wet, inviting and I longed to kiss her again.

I recalled tilting our heads slightly, moving in closer and kissing again and again. Once, while we kissed, she parted her lips slightly, released her breath, and unconsciously moaned. I instinctively inhaled her breath and immediately felt my heart quicken as I realized her breath was inside of me, and a new excitement ran through me. I wanted to pull her in closer, and I guess she sensed my reaction because she responded readily by pressing her lips firmer against mine, deepening our kiss. That kiss was eager and playful as we innocently explored each other's reaction only to be confronted with like desires and wants, and it left me hungering for more.

I had never felt like that before; and I desired to taste her, to touch every part of her body, to bottle her scent and keep it with me, to hold that moment in time in my heart and in my mind to hold forever that innocent, loving feeling that was rushing through me. I longed for more and didn't want to stop and wondered if there was more. When we broke our embrace, I looked into her eyes and sensed a passionate desire I never knew existed and it scared me. I dared not move away and was glad I was lying on my stomach.

We kissed again and again; and each time it felt so right, so fresh, and new. It was rich, pure, and innocent and I wanted more. I wanted it to be the first time, each time we kissed.

We spent an hour together before Cora returned, but by then, I had told Cece that I was breaking it off with her sister.

The following day, after having kissed Cece, I walked out to the edge of the Cedillo's driveway to where Cece and I had planned to meet at noon while Dorothy was at work, but Cece never showed up.

I waited for two hours, and she never came out of her house. I couldn't wait for that evening to come. But that evening, only Dorothy came out and none of the other Cedillo girls as the group took our usual evening walk together.

The following day, at noon, I went again to the edge of the driveway and waited for about an hour. I was about to leave when I saw Cece near the corner of their house. She motioned for me to walk down the road as she made her way in the same direction along the trees near their home.

When I got a good distance from their house, we both turned toward the grove of peach trees and met.

Cece told me about the fight she and Dorothy had over me the night before and how the following morning she hadn't made matters any better because at breakfast, she joked about the cereal they were eating. Instead of saying, "I'm Cuckoo for Cocoa Puffs (the cereal she was eating and imitating the commercials being aired on TV for that cereal)," Cece had said, "I'm Cuckoo for Cookie Puffs" and Dorothy and she started fighting all over again.

After that, Cece's mother wouldn't allow Cece to come out to meet me or to walk with us during the evening walks.

Cece said she saw me that day from her parents' bedroom window waiting and told her mom, she wanted to come out and tell me that she wasn't allowed out of the house, but her mom wouldn't let her.

"I hoped you would come back today," she said and smiled, her eyes sparkling.

The two of us walked down MacDonough Avenue alongside the peach trees, and after a while, she reached out and grabbed hold of my hand and we walked together, not saying anything.

We spent the afternoon together in the peach orchard talking and kissing. We talked about anything and everything, and time went by fast.

Cece was closer to my age and I told her I didn't want anything to do with her sister, but both of us wondered how that was going to play out. She knew her sister better than I did.

Dorothy's threats of causing physical harm to herself forever ended my relationship with Cece and with it, my youth and freedom.

As we entered the barracks, Jerry sat on the cot next to mine.

"I told Diana that you didn't love your wife when you got married; you didn't marry her because of love," Lucero said. "I told her how it was that you got married. Now that you have a son, has anything changed?"

Lucero pointed to Dorothy's name tattooed on my arm. "You didn't get that tattoo on your arm because you love her."

During Marine Corps training, while Marines were putting Marine Corps tattoos on their arms, Dorothy asked me to tattoo her name on my arm to prove that I loved her. During leave, Dorothy had me show it off to all her family members, including Cece. Whenever I would send a picture home from Vietnam, Dorothy wanted the picture to show the wedding ring on my finger and her name branded on my bare arm in the picture.

"You don't love her," Jerry said. "You regret getting that tattoo. Does having a son now make a difference in how you feel about her?"

"For a Mexican, you sure make a lot of sense," I answered, but Jerry was only saying words I knew were true and words I wanted to hear. "What am I going to tell your sister?" I asked and wondered what kissing Diana would be like.

"Don't worry about it," Jerry said, his round eyes widening as he shook his head in disbelief. "How can you be so naïve? Just forget about your old lady. You said you don't trust her; she's proven that to you already and probably Jody's with her or whatever that other guy's name is.[116] Cookie, you deserve better. My parents would be glad to have you come and stay with us. Diana said she was going to send you more pictures and wants to continue to write to you," Lucero added.

Diana had indeed sent me another picture. She was a pretty girl with short hair and a slim body. She reminded me of Cece, and I thought about her as I loaded the gun to get ready for patrol.

A Call From the MARS Station "Over"
Liberty Bridge, South Vietnam
September 2, 1967, 0800 hours

The afternoon of September 2, the lieutenant called me back to the CP. "Barela, have you written your wife?" he asked, a bit upset with me.

"No, sir," I answered.

"Well, she's upset that you haven't written or contacted her since your son was born. The Red Cross is inquiring to see if you're alive or dead. I want you to go into Da Nang and use the MARS station to call her. The skipper's upset you haven't written because the Red Cross contacted him. This is the second time he's been contacted about you not writing home. I can't order you to write to her, but if Baggette gets any more calls from the Red Cross because of your wife, you'll probably end up getting a lot of shit details. The mule is on its way in. Take it into Battalion and then the mail truck into Da Nang. The mail truck's waiting for you at Battalion."

"Yes, sir," I answered.

The lieutenant seemed disturbed to have to respond to the will of someone half a world away. Evidently, the Red Cross notification carried some weight behind it. Dorothy, I knew, wouldn't hesitate to use any necessary channels to get her way. She had evidently gotten some help from others as she had written to tell me that if I didn't write soon, she would contact the Red Cross. She wrote that they would notify my company commander and I would get in trouble. I had stopped writing her when she wrote and said that she didn't want to hear anything about the war. I really didn't have anything to write to her about after that.

I quickly grabbed a set of old combat boots to take along for trading. Going into Da Nang meant first going into Battalion HQ, then riding the mail truck in. If the truck was available, you could come back the same day; otherwise, it was at least a two-day turn around trip. Time in Da Nang was usually spent waiting for a ride back to HQ, and from there, it was another wait to catch a ride back to India Company at Liberty Bridge. I got on the mule jeep, and the driver sped down Liberty Road. At Battalion, the mail truck was waiting for me and as soon as I climbed on board, we were *en route* to Da Nang.

The mail truck dropped me off at the MARS station where I could make the phone call home. The station was run by Marine ham radio operators and set up on a small hill close to the Da Nang airstrip. It was run by Marines on our end and by civilian volunteer organizations made up of ham radio operators around the world on the other side. They used their radio stations as relay points to relay phone calls home from Vietnam. Because of the delay experienced, once you got hooked up with the other party by ham radio, you had to say "over" when you finished speaking so the person on the other end would know when to speak. After saying "over," there was usually a delay of a few seconds before the person on the other end heard it and replied.

Dorothy had named my son Refugio Troy, adding a second name, and for that I was grateful. Other than receiving that information, seconds after we had said our hello, our conversation was over. We had nothing more to talk about. While I wanted to know more about my son that would have to wait. I left the station wondering if I would ever get to see him.

I did ask Dorothy to stop contacting the Red Cross because she was getting me in trouble. She never answered, and our call was cut short after that. I had learned before I left the platoon that the Red Cross had called about my welfare on another occasion; but the skipper, having ascertained I was okay, chose to ignore it.

Before leaving the air base, I traded the old combat boots to an airman for two large bottles of whiskey and a bottle of Bacardi 151. I possibly could have gotten more, but it would require some time negotiating the deal, and pogues in the rear sometimes did get the same type of combat gear we were issued in the field. A lot depended on where they were assigned. Combat boots worn in the jungle of Vietnam brought a good price in Da Nang, no doubt because of the stories the new owner could tell of how he had humped the bush searching for Charlie in those boots. I stayed overnight and caught the mail truck run to Battalion HQ the following day, then hitched a ride to Liberty Bridge.

On September 5, the platoon went out on a sweep and blocking force for a Marine battalion-size operation, Operation Swift. We were into the Que Son Valley, some twenty-five miles south of Da Nang. Our platoon never made contact, but we heard many Marines from Mike Company Third Battalion, Fifth Marine Regiment had been killed.[117]

Tired Aggie, Ain't Tired Anymore
Que Son Valley, South Vietnam
September 7, 1967, 0800 hours

By September 7, the Seabees, working in between monsoon downpours, had Liberty Bridge fully repaired and we were back standing regular bridge duty. For the next five days, depending on the rain, we went on working parties, stood watch on the bridge, or went on patrol. Things were back to normal.

Tired Aggie's battle fatigue had now turned into plain laziness. He sprained his foot and used that excuse to get out of working party details for more than a week. Every once in a while, we would see him walking about normally until he felt someone maybe watching, then he would begin limping. While Doc had written him off from going on patrols for a while, Dumont wasn't taken in with Aggie's injuries, so he assigned him to sit and fill sandbags while we were out on patrol or on other working parties.

Often, when we returned from our daily patrols or work details, we would sit around shooting the breeze in Guns bunker near the front gate. Our bunker, like Guns' hooch on Hill 65, had become a gathering point not only for Weapons, but for other members of the platoon. It was a time to just sit around, unwind, and enjoy the evening before the assignments for the night would be issued. When we were lucky, the squads going out on patrol forgot us, so a gun team didn't go out with them and of course, we didn't volunteer.

On the evening of the seventh, Aggie was still filling the last of the twelve sandbags he was supposed to have filled since early that morning when Jones turned on the box to Stevie Wonder's "Place in the Sun" and "My Cherie Amour." They were about the only 45 rpm records that had survived Marty's gunplay.

Dumont then asked Aggie to get some claymore mines from the CP; and Aggie, with a frown and a "don't you feel sorry for me" look on his face, slowly limped away. As he walked off, we could hear him complaining about how his foot hurt and Dumont had no sympathy for him.

Dumont, having recently returned from mine and demolition school, was in a rare playful mood and had unscrewed and removed the blasting cap from a fragmentation grenade and had popped the cap; he then screwed the top back on, placed the lever back, reinserting the ring and safety pin. From the outside, the grenade looked and felt real. While the explosive charge was still inside, the missing blasting cap rendered it harmless.

When Aggie returned, he was accentuating his limp for all of us to see. We ignored him while continuing to listen to Dumont as he tossed the grenade back and forth from hand to hand. Aggie sat down, and his eyes grew wide each time the grenade was tossed back and forth. Dumont then went into one of his long-winded war stories and we listened attentively as he fumbled with the grenade, taking the pin out and reinserting it, as he continued to talk as if he had no idea what he was doing.

This, of course, caused Aggie some anxiety; and he told Dumont that he shouldn't be doing that and so Dumont went into a lecture on just how long a grenade, once the lever is released and the spoon flies off, is supposed to take before it explodes. Some of us argued three to four seconds, citing what we had learned by pitching grenades off Liberty Bridge; others felt the delay was more like five or six seconds.

Dumont then, in the process of reinserting the pin back into the grenade, dropped the pin. As he leaned over to pick it up, he allowed his glasses to fall off; and as he quickly reached down to prevent his glasses from hitting the ground, he accidentally let go of the grenade's handle. The lever popped open with the same sound a grenade usually made.

Aggie, who had been paying close attention to all of Dumont's motions, jumped straight up; and with one leap, he was out of the bunker and in a split second had cleared thirty to forty feet running full speed for cover. As we saw him take off, we began laughing so hard that we were rolling on the ground.

That was the fastest we had ever seen Aggie move. Aggie, realizing what had happened, came back cursing at all of us. Then when he more fully realized the trick we had played on him, specifically Dumont, he reached down, picked up a mud ball, and threw it at us.

The mud ball struck Dumont on his neck, and before we could duck, Aggie had thrown another one that splattered on the bunkers wall.

Both Jones and Marty by then had jumped over the small sand bag wall and grabbed a handful of mud to return fire.

Duran and I ran behind the bunker; grabbed two handful globs of thick mud and jumped on top of the bunker.

As Aggie was bending over reloading, we splattered him about the same time, both Jones and Marty fired off their mud ball at Aggie.

Aggie realizing he was out-numbered grabbed an e-tool and was about to fling a shovel full of mud, when Dumont called for a cease fire.

It was just in time as Third Squad needing a gun team for a night patrol came by.

"If you, guys, are all through, horsing around, maybe you'll, can join us, and fight, a real war," Jerry Lucero said, as he swung his little feet over the small sandbagged wall.

Jackie Williams was leading the patrol that night, and he stood silently, shaking his head, while Aggie and I saddled up to go with them. As we settled into the ambush site that night, Aggie, with mud still stuck to his clothing, sat ready to take the A-gunner's position if we got in a firefight, and I was glad he was there at my side.

L/Cpl. Harold E. Reid's War
My Loc (5) AT913526
September 13, 1967, 0500 hours

On September 13, Second Platoon had security watch overlooking the midsection of Liberty Bridge. During his watch, L/Cpl. Harold E. Reid loaded his trouser pockets with grenades, strapped on several bandoliers of ammo across his chest, and with his M-16 at his side, Reid walked across to the south side of the bridge. Weapons in Second Platoon manned the last Marine post on our side of the bridge, and Reid had been assigned to Weapons for the night from one of the squads to fill in a gap in a three-man hole watch. At the end of his watch, he was supposed to have awakened L/Cpl. Ron Patrick to stand watch. Instead, Reid walked silently past the sleeping Marine.

When Reid, a tall-framed Marine with light blond hair, got to the other side of the bridge being guarded by Echo Company 2/7, he was challenged by a Marine on duty there.

"Hey, where are you going?" he was asked.

"I got a friend on the other side; I'm going to visit him," Reid answered.

"Well, okay," the Marine answered. But he felt unsure about the answer Reid had given him and wondered about all the extra ammo, Reid was carrying.

When the Marine on duty wasn't looking, Reid slipped out the perimeter's gate and started to walk along the river's edge toward a small village on the south bank of the Song Thu Bon River. Although the village of My Loc (5) was clearly visible from where Second Platoon stood watch on the bridge, no one saw Reid walk into the village.

VC cadet member Do Ly Tuan and Vo Ca (Vox Car) from the village of Phu Nhuan with about ten other VC guerilla members were on patrol near the village's edge, when the lead men of their patrol saw Reid; he sounded an alarm that signified an American squad on patrol was moving in their direction.

The VC quickly assembled together and set up an ambush waiting for the Americans to approach. Reid was slowly patrolling near the trail leading into their village and they believed Reid was walking point for a squad of Marines, so Tuan and his unit waited. When they realized that Reid was walking alone and that no other Marines were nearby, they opened fire.

Reid was hit immediately but crawled behind a grave mound and returned fire. He threw several grenades and fired his M-16 at the band of VC guerillas.

As the VC circled around to surround the Marine, Reid killed one of the VC members. The enemy then unleashed a volume of heavy automatic rifle fire killing Reid. Tuan and Ca quickly buried Reid in a shallow grave near the village cemetery and reported the incident and the location of Marines' remains to higher guerilla authorities. They then returned and buried their own comrade near a house not far from Reid.[118]

How An ARV Lieutenant Teaches a Machine-Gunner, A Lesson In Proper Protocol
Da Nang, South Vietnam
September 13, 1967, 1000 hours

On the thirteenth, Dumont sent me into Da Nang to pick up supplies. While I was getting ready to go, James Keenan came over and said, his squad leader told him to go with me to get familiarized with making runs for supplies into Da Nang.

As Keenan stood by, I splashed on oily insect repellent, applying it like aftershave lotion, and offered him some. His eyes widened, and he shook his head no.

"Go on, Keenan," I said. "Makes you smell good when we go into Da Nang. The stuff never keeps the bugs away anyways. It just helps, so when they land on the oily stuff, they just slide right off."

In Vietnam, we had limited use of showers. Each platoon usually constructed their own wherever they could, depending how long they were to stay at a certain base. Battalion was supposed to supply them, but it didn't happen, so Marines made do with what they could or what they could find on hand. Guns used the platoon shower, which meant we had to get our own water out of the river and pour it into the fifty-gallon container on top of the small wooden platform. Guns in Second Platoon had constructed their own shower, but we rarely used it. Most of the time, we washed ourselves out of a small washbasin; a helmet full of water and a small towel was all you needed to get clean.

When we arrived in Da Nang, I saw a small group of ARVNs standing near one of their guard posts. In the middle of the group was a well-dressed uniformed ARVN lieutenant giving them a lecture. I decided to play a joke on them and impress Keenan at the same time.

I approached the lieutenant. He was in his mid-twenties and stood tall compared to the others gathered around him. He was doing most of the talking, and as we approached, he turned to greet us. I smiled and half bowed, and he acknowledged this and did likewise. While standing there in front of him, I took the fake grenade hanging from my flak jacket and pulled the pin in front of the ARVNs.

Keenan, standing close by, became wide-eyed. I extended my arm with the grenade in it to within a foot of the lieutenant's chest. Most of the ARVNs began to back off.

The ARVN lieutenant's eyes were hard-set, and he wasn't shaken. He simply reached out and, while not taking his eyes off me, removed a grenade from his cartridge belt. Then he pulled the grenade up to chest level so that I could see it, and he pulled the pin on his grenade and extended his arm out to within a foot of my chest.

Mine was fake; his was real. We stood like that for about two or three of the longest seconds of my life. His eyes were determined, and I could see that he was calling my bluff.

I smiled and then slowly reinserted the safety pin back into the little hole that held down the grenade's lever. I was hoping he wasn't seeing how badly my hand was shaking. I didn't notice if his hand was shaking as he, likewise, replaced the pin in his grenade. Afterward, we stepped back, once again bowed at each other, smiled, and backed off.

As I walked away, my knees became weak and they buckled from the surge of adrenaline, causing me to stumble a bit. I quickly looked down at the road and managed to pretend that I had tripped on something so that Keenan wouldn't know that my knees had buckled out from under me.

That was the last and only time I used that fake grenade. Keenan never knew the grenade was a fake, and I never bothered to tell him. From then on, he just thought I was the craziest machine-gunner in Vietnam.

For the next eight days, we were either sent out on working parties, patrols or we stood watch over the bridge during the night.

On September 15, battalion got mortared, and Louis Perez, who had arrived in Vietnam on the same plane I had, was wounded in the mortar attack, but not seriously.

That night, Art O'Farrell, the platoon's former radioman, and First Platoon's former lieutenant, Joseph Cortaze, went out on ambush with three other Marines.

Since he had been Cortazze's radioman, O'Farrell volunteered to go and it was like old times for the two of them.

They set up under some bamboo covering near a small hill, not far from Hill 65. At daybreak, just before they were to get ready to return to the hill, they heard a loud thump.

The ChiCom grenade struck the bamboo poles covering the ambush team and exploded, showering both the lieutenant and O'Farrell with shrapnel, dust, and dirt. Both were WIA, but not medevaced.

Why Tex Stiteler Wouldn't Smile For the Camera
Football Island Phu Nhuan, AT 895514
September 21, 1967, 1300 hours

With all three of India Company's Platoons now gathered at Liberty Bridge, more and longer patrols were being assigned. On September 21, First Platoon went on working parties; Second Platoon was assigned perimeter guard duty, and Third went on patrols. Each day we rotated duties.

Late afternoon, and Lieutenant James R. Mullen, Third Platoon's commanding officer summoned his Third Squad leader, Cpl. Edgar "Tex" Stiteler, to his CP.

Stiteler, a tall six-foot-two giant from Texas, was scheduled to return Stateside in two weeks. He was introduced to Sgt. Orland L. McClanahan who had just arrived in country and was assigned to take over Stiteler's Third Squad.

Lieutenant Mullen wanted the new sergeant to get to know the men under Stiteler's command before he left, so, he arranged for amtracks to take Third Squad across the river into the Arizona territory on a quick Search and Destroy Mission.

The area was a freefire zone, so anything that moved was fair game. If the squad made contact, the rest of Third Platoon would be ready to assist.

Three amtracks from Second Platoon, Company A, First Amtrack Battalion were assigned to provide transportation across the Song Thu Bon River, to make it look like it was a bigger operation, then just a squad assignment.

The squad task was to cross to the eastern edge of Football Island and search a small nearby village. They were to return in a few hours.

The detail crossed the river without incident and encountered no enemy activity while they carried out their mission.

By 1700 hours, as they were returning, the first amtrack neared the river's southern bank where it forked around the island; Stiteler was sitting on the edge of the middle amtrack next to Corporal Hoffman.

Stiteler was busy giving advice to Sergeant McClanahan when shots rang out, but because of the roar and the noise the amtracks were making, it wasn't until a sniper's round caught Stiteler on the left side of his jaw and threw him backward that the squad realized they were taking incoming.

Stiteler fell facedown on top of the amtrack and was bleeding profusely from his mouth where the bullet had exited.

The lead amtrack stopped at the edge of the river's bank, and as the squad dismounted and sought cover behind some rice paddy dikes, the enemy opened up with about thirty to forty more rounds of small arms and automatic rifle fire from Phu Nhuan (2), a heavily forested village.

With Marines now out in the open, the NVA/VC started to move into killing-zone positions. As they did, someone called out that the enemy was moving across an open rice paddy dike just to the north of them. The squad of Marines opened fire, as did both of Third Platoon's machine-gunners.

Darrell Borgman opened fire with the 300 rounds already linked to his gun. He shot into the tree line the platoon was taking fire from without letting up on the trigger. By the time all 300 rounds had been fired, the barrel was warped. He had melted the barrel.

John W. Hoffman, the other machine-gunner with Third Platoon and a veteran of the Gates of Hell during Operation DeSoto, also opened fire from the prone position on top of the middle amtrack with his M-60.

Hoffman sprayed two hundred rounds of machine-gun bullets into the NVA/VC position on the dike and into the westside of the tree line from where Third Squad was receiving intensive incoming automatic rifle fire.

As he squeezed the trigger, he saw one gook take a direct hit and go down. Two others quickly grabbed hold of their comrade and dragged the wounded enemy soldier into the dense jungle.

As Hoffman adjusted his fire to follow the trio, Stiteler, who was feeling the pain from the bullet that tore his jaw apart, was still lying on the top of the amtrack next to Hoffman as he fired away with his M-60.

With the vibration and clamor of the battle ranging all around him, all Stiteler wanted was for Hoffman to stop firing, as the noise was making his pain feel worse.

As the amtrack and machine-gun continued to draw enemy fire, Pfc. Jandon Landy—a strong black Marine from Savannah, Georgia, who the squad had nicknamed "Swoop Down"—grabbed hold of Stiteler and shielded him from the incoming fire. Landy then dragged the wounded giant inside the amtrack.

By then, a tank with the call sign of "Blackcoat"[119] from First Platoon, Company B, First Tank Battalion stationed on the north bank of the river at Liberty Bridge, opened fire with two 90mm high-explosive rounds into the heart of the enemy's position.

When the smoke cleared away, all the incoming fire had stopped.

Without further incoming being fired in their direction, Third Squad mounted the amtracks and crossed back into India Company's perimeter.[120]

As Stiteler waited to be helilifted out, Gary Brown, one of Stiteler's squad members, took out his camera and called out to Ed to smile. The Marine wounded and in pain, looked up and flipped Brown off as Brown shot the picture.

Operation Patriot
Regiment Hill 42 AT 947597
September 22, 1967, 0800 hours

We received word on the morning of the twenty-second that India Company would be going out on a five-day operation called "Operation Patriot." We would be patrolling along the banks of the Song Vu Gia River near the Seventh Marines Regimental HQ where NVA soldiers had been spotted.

The NVA was reported to be spending nights in friendly villages near the river's edge and in the small villages surrounding the battalion. We saddled up and boarded six-by trucks to HQ. From there, we hopped aboard amtracks and tanks that took us deep into a dense tropical area near the river. We disembarked near an abandoned village where the NVA/VC had reportedly been seen the day before, but we received no incoming fire nor did we make contact.

No sooner had we moved out on patrol than a Marine we called "The Kid," because his first name was Billy, stepped on a trip wire, triggering an explosive device wounding himself and Tin Man.

We stood still, while Billy R. Stoddard and David W. Berg were medevaced. This was the Kid's third wound, so we knew he would be going to the rear and possibly home. Tin Man's injuries were not serious, he was a short-timer so he also would complete his tour of duty assigned to the rear at Battalion HQs.

The following day, we rode amtracks and tanks through the thick jungle until we arrived at the base of our objective, Hill 42. Recon Marines had reported seeing the enemy there the day before, and we were told the NVA were heavily entrenched at the top of the hill.

We were to make an assault up the hill while another company of Marines acted as a blocking force on the other side. If the enemy fled, they would be running into Marines.

We assaulted the hill and encountered no resistance. Kilo Company, also involved in the operation, had been sweeping toward us from a different direction and received small arms and automatic rifle fire; but the brief enemy engagement stopped as quickly as it had started.

India Company, Second Platoon, on the other hand, had taken two WIAs and a PF also killed in a light scrimmage with the enemy.

As soon as we settled in for the night, it started to rain—a pouring-down cold rain showering us with heavy drops of fish-smelling rainwater. Many of us huddled together sitting back-to-back for support and slept that way.

Others sat silent, covered by ponchos as rain poured over us. Dumont refused to sit down in the mud so he stood up for most of the night until early that morning.

About two in the morning, as Aggie and I shifted position to get into a better comforting position, he nudged me to look at Dumont.

While rain poured down on him, Dumont began to sway. His eyes drifting close, and when he finally succumbed to sleep, his body fell straight forward, burying his face deep in the slimy yellow mud. He sat up, sputtering mud out of his mouth, he wiped it off with his poncho and crawled slowly over to a nearby tree, where propped himself up against it, and fell into a state of exhausted sleep.

Something Soft, Moist, Moving, and Covered in Blood?
Operation Patriot
September 24, 1967, 0700 hours

"Aaaarrrrghhhh!" The morning of the twenty-fourth began with a bloodcurdling cry that echoed down from the top of the hill into the valley below. Marines on the hill awakened by the loud outcry reached for their weapons. I scrambled to get to where Aggie was standing watch at the guns position. I slid in behind the gun, Aggie, surprised as everyone else was looking toward where the scream, had come from.

Jones slid in besides us looking down the hill.

I had not heard any incoming fire and all around the hill, Marines were popping up their heads, from behind bushes and small dirt mounts like little Prairie dogs, searching the terrain all around us for any signs of the enemy.

To my far right, I could see Glen Prescott jumping up and down calling out for the Corpsman.

"Corpsman up, Corpsman up!" he kept screaming.

A Marine hurried over, and pulled Prescott down, as one of the company's Corpsman rushed over to where he was.

Glen Prescott—a skinny, blond-haired, thin-faced Marine from Placerville, California had awaken and felt something soft in between his legs, then a stinging, heavy sensation near his groin.

When he reached into his trousers, he felt something soft and moist and moving. Startled, he pulled out his hand. It was covered with blood.

Prescott at first believed he had been shot during the night or had cut himself on a punji stake and was dying. He stood up quickly, dropped his trousers to see where the blood was coming from, and saw a large black leech fall out. Then he saw a second one attached to his left thigh and yet another smaller leech attached to his penis.

Other Marines were soon, standing up, dropping their trousers and finding leeches attached to various parts of their bodies. The only way to safely dislodge them once they attached themselves was by using the tip of a burning cigarette, which forced them to let go; otherwise if we tried to pull them off, their heads would remain embedded under our skin. The insect repellent sometimes caused them to let go, but we believed it was mostly because the surface became so oily that the leech couldn't hold on. The area was infested with leeches. An hour later, we saddled up and moved out.[121]

Little Men Taking Hurried Little Steps
Regiment Hill 42
September 26, 1967, 0800 hours

For two days, we patrolled and searched, receiving reports of enemy forces seen in the area, but made no contact. On the morning of the twenty-sixth, we swept toward Kilo Company's position. They were set in as a blocking force for us.

As we got near the blocking force, thunderclouds moved in, bringing with them the afternoon monsoon rains. At first it was just a light drizzle, but soon became pounding sheets of cold rain. We set up in a small village somewhere near Regimental Headquarters waiting for the rain to subside. By midmorning I was feeling miserable and sluggish, my throat was sore and it was difficult even to swallow water from my canteen.

As soon as the rain let up we moved out again and passed a small clearing in the tree line along the trail we were following. Jones spotted seven NVA soldiers crossing in front of us eight hundred meters away. I had already seen the first two cross the open field in front of us, but it hadn't occurred to me that they were the enemy.

They had been walking in a column, keeping a good distance between each other, and from the distance, they looked like a small ARVN fire-team. Since ARVN were also involved in the operation, I had thought they were friendlies.

They were all small men, taking little hurried steps. I was trying to figure out who they were when Jones mentioned they were NVA. This was the first time I had seen the enemy out in the open.

In Vietnam, there were no marked boundaries, no front forward line, or a rear echelon. The enemy was everywhere and nowhere. Charlie was behind us and in front of us, and at times, he was at our side. Wherever we went, the possibility for enemy engagement was there and then again, it wasn't. The war was fought on Charlie's terms or he did not fight at all. How to tell the difference between friend, and foe required experience in knowing how enemy soldiers acted, the type of weapons they carried, and a lot of common sense.

No sooner had Jones said they were the enemy than I dropped down and was behind the gun in the prone position. I took careful aim, sighting in on the last men in the column.

I opened fire with a short burst of machine-gun fire. The rounds fell twenty meters short, kicking up dust by the last NVA soldier. He turned and started to run.

Jones called out sight corrections and I turned the windage knob two clicks and the elevating knob counterclockwise to lower the sights and raise the strike of the bullet.

I took aim and opened fire. The last soldier in the column fell and then got up limping, calling to the others. Two others turned and came to help him. All three men disappeared into the dense jungle, as my red tracers chased after them.

The enemy soldiers never returned fire. Later that day, amtracks picked us up and we were dropped off at Regiment; from there, we boarded six-bys and were returned to Liberty Bridge. The operation was over.

Operation Bombay
Liberty Bridge, South Vietnam
October 2, 1967, 0800 hours

On October 2, we were called out to participate in "Operation Bombay." Once again, our duty was to sweep an area toward a Marine blocking force. We swept on the north side of Route 4 toward the Dodge City area. Such operations were known as hammer-and-anvil operations, and we were once again supporting another Marine unit involved in the operation. Sometimes we were the hammer and were sweeping, pushing the enemy toward the anvil; another military unit already set in place as a blocking force. Sometimes we were the anvil waiting for the enemy, to be flushed toward us.

Once again it rained, cold miserable rain, and by nightfall, with wet feet and a sore throat, I had a headache and a fever as well.

On the second day of the operation, the Corpsman examined me in the field and said I had a high temperature and a bad case of tonsillitis. Later that day, I was dropped off at our Battalion Aid Station, and I welcomed the rest, and warm billet. Others there had similar troubles, and were coughing and aching with high fevers and chills.

The company stayed out until October 6, and returned without having suffered any casualties. The operation was called off due to a typhoon blowing toward our area. That evening, I was discharged from the Battalion Aid Station and returned to full duty.

On the morning of the seventh, I rejoined the company at Liberty Bridge. The lieutenant called me into his CP, and I was told I had been promoted to Lance Corporal, effective September 1, 1967. That afternoon, it began to rain. Pouring rain, thunder, lightning, and thick darkness.

A Ship In Turbulent Waters
Liberty Bridge
October 7, 1967, 2200 hours

During first watch on the night of the seventh, Rahm strained to get a better view of an object he saw floating in the river. The dark clouds overhead and drizzling rain didn't help his vision. Willing his eyes to focus, he saw a long wooden boat floating down the Song Thu Bon toward the bridge. Rahm had Perry call in for an overhead illumination round and Rahm opened fire. The boat was fifteen feet in length and two hundred meters away. Rahm concentrated on hitting the boat with as many rounds as he could from his M-16, hoping to hit any explosive charge that might be attached to the bottom of the boat.

The NVA/VC had used this type of decoy before to blow up bridges in the area. As Rahm loaded another magazine into his M-16, Boyd was assembling the front and rear barrel of the 3.5 rocket launcher, joining the two pieces together.

The Bazooka,[122] which I had never seen fired in combat, was a leftover weapon from World War II. Two smoothbore tubes, open on each end, were connected together to assemble the five-feet-long rocket launcher. The weapon, equipped with a handgrip and a shoulder rest was fired when the gunner pulled the trigger providing an electrical current that ignited the rocket. The electrical charge that made the weapon discharge was very sensitive, and once loaded, it was unstable as any electrical charge could set it off. The weapon could be fired from the shoulder, sitting, kneeling, or in the prone position. In the prone position, the gunner had to be especially careful to make sure his body was nowhere near the back blast that would exit the other side of the open tube when the weapon was fired. The Bazooka was an effective antitank weapon, but in Vietnam, it was used mainly to fire at entrenched enemy positions, bunkers or to clear an area of a suspected booby trap. Usually carried in the field in two pieces, the weapon required two men to assemble and fire the weapon, the gunner and the A-gunner. The A-gunner loaded the rocket's nineteen-inch, three-and-a-half-pound high-explosive round into the weapon and gave the gunner the all-clear signal to fire, usually by patting him on the head.

Perry loaded a high-explosive round into the tube, and Boyd lifted the rocket launcher to his shoulder. With half the tube protruding behind him, Boyd sighted in on the boat and waited for it to come into range. The rocket's effective range was limited to about 110 meters (120 yards). As Boyd waited, Marines on guard duty on the bridge began to fire their M-16s at the boat. As soon the target was within range, Perry signaled for Boyd to fire.

Boyd fired, and the back blast shot a glowing flame of heat behind him, as the ignited rocket exited the tube. The sizzling rocket shot straight toward the boat, soaring along only a few feet off the surface of the water; its blazing, glowing path was brightly reflected on the dark water of the Song Thu Bon River.

The round struck the end section of the wooden boat, going right through it and into the river. A large hole was left on one side of the boat. The rocket never exploded.

The boat continued to float toward the bridge, and more Marines on the bridge opened fire. Another Marine began to launch M-79 grenades at the boat, but the grenades were going long or dropping short.

On the north side of the river's bank, near the pontoon boat that rested on the soft clay bottom at the river's edge, Blackcoat sat silently sleeping.[123] When the sounds of war awoke the tank from his slumber, he opened his eyes.

His brazen light burned brightly across the dark waters of the Song Thu Bon River, scanning the water's surface, seeking out what foe had dared to awaken him from his dreams. The drizzling drops of rain blown by the wind were now bathed in his bright light as their silvery glow pounded relentlessly on the dark vessel floating defiantly in the river. Blackcoat's eyes focused on the dark floating object, and he let out a harsh roar, spitting out an explosive growl.

The ship floating silently in the night, on the peaceful waters of the Song Thu Bon River, was blown to smithereens. Thousands of splintered wooden pieces fell back to earth sailing off into eternity. There was no secondary explosion. Blackcoat, having defended his turf, shut his eyes and slipped back into a deep slumber.

Standing Last Watch For The Dead Man
Liberty Bridge, South Vietnam
October 8, 1967, 1600 hours

Late on the afternoon of October 8, Izzie and Chief spotted two enemy bodies in the river caught up against one of the bridge's main supporting beams. They along with Pridemore tried for an hour to hook a rope around them and finally managed to lasso the larger of the two and hoisted the dead body onto the bridge. The other body broke free and floated down the river.

The NVA soldier had been dead for a couple of days. His bloated and foul-smelling body was placed next to a wooden box where we kept the flares. As it was getting late, it was decided to leave the dead gook there until morning and then perhaps a Kit Carson Scout could go through his clothing to see if there were any documents on him.

As evening fell, Ron Patrick, Anthony C. Nicorvo (Nasty Nick), and Ralph Keenan—all from Second Platoon heard of the dead gook on the bridge and came over to see the body. Chief and Izzie; however, had left the rope attached to one of the gook's arms; as the three Marines approached the dead body, Chief, delayed them as Izzie walked past the dead enemy soldier and sat down.

Keith Pridemore from Kentucky, with a 0351 MOS (rockets) had been with the platoon since June was sitting close by. He sort-of figured what they were up to, and just sat back to watch.

"Hey, what's going on," Chief asked, and that should have been those Marines early warning sign as Chief never spoke, unless he was spoken to.

"Oh, we heard you hooked a dead gook and pulled him out of the water." Ron said.

"Yeah, he's over there, you ain't gonna shoot him, are you, Chief, chuckled."

"If we do, we're going to get the credit, for the kill," answered Keenan.

As the three Marines drew near the dead man's body, Izzie pulled on the rope they had left attached to the dead man's arm.

The dead gook's hand shot up to make it appear as if he was waving to the approaching Marines. All three Marines jumped back, startled, and then cursed Izzie and Chief when they saw the rope.

"Man, that was a good one," Ron Patrick said, as the three turned to walk away. They in turn went back to their side of the bridge and sent other Marines over, knowing the same trick would be played on them.

That night, Ward Keeton, Jerry Lucero, and another Marine were assigned to stand watch on our side of the bridge. Their watch had been scheduled and Chief was supposed to return to the bridge to relieve Lucero and stand last watch. But Chief told Lucero to wake up the Marine sleeping on the bridge, next to the box of flares, for last watch.

"He's a sound sleeper, like Duran," Izzie added, "so you might have to shake him a bit to wake him up." Then both of them walked off the bridge.

At 0300 hours that morning, when Lucero got off watch, he walked over to the dead enemy soldier and we heard him trying to wake up the dead gook. He tried calling then shouting and shaking the corpse. Finally, Lucero grabbed an arm to jerk him awake and the dead gook's limp arm became detached, rupturing the gook's skin wide open and squirting out water, pus, and small pieces of rotten flesh on Lucero.

Lucero, still not knowing what had happened and unwilling to try to find out in the dark, walked away trembling. Unable to wake up his "relief," Jerry decided to stand last watch, unknowing he was doing so, for a dead man.

At first light, Lucero returned to find that it was a dead gook sitting upright next to the flare box. The enemy soldier was soiled with pus and his skin had turned into an ugly gray color. Lucero's face turned pale, and he rushed over to the side of the bridge and puked his guts out. Then he began to scream, shaking uncontrollably, traumatized by what had happened to him and vowing to shoot Chief and Izzie.

Doc Bernard McNallen and Lieutenant Wilson, hearing the commotion, came running out of the CP to see what the fuss was all about. As they ran toward Lucero to see what was going on, Izzie and Chief ran onto the bridge and threw the dead gook's body back into the river. It took the compassion of a Corpsman like Doc Mac to finally calm Lucero down.

That afternoon, Jerry came out to our main machine-gun position at the front gate where I was standing watch. He sat down and we talked. "It don't mean nothing'," I said to him, using a saying we often used to encourage one another when things didn't go right in Nam. After a while, he finally realized it was just a foolish prank. Lucero and I had hit it off in the beginning, but it wasn't until after the gook incident that we became friends.

When I was relieved of guard duty, we made our way back to our barracks as the wind and drizzling rain began to pick up. A few short minutes later, the whole basin was covered with dark and heavy rain clouds. I sat down to write a letter by candlelight. An hour later hard rain began to fall.

Off in the far distance, bluish white flashes streaked across the sky followed by the sounds of subdued thunder. A fierce wind swept across the perimeter and battered the billet with heavy drops of rain that fell hard against sandbagged bunkers, the barracks, on flak jackets, helmets, and on the faces of Marines on perimeter watch that night.

Monsoon Rains
Liberty Bridge,
October 9, 1967, 0300 hours

Jones, Marty, and I were assigned to stand watch at our secondary gun position near the bridge. At three, the following morning, Marty woke me to stand last watch. As soon as I stepped up onto the top of the bunker, bitter cold drops of rain soaked me through and through. I sat down unable to see four inches in front of me, listening for any movement of the enemy, but it was useless with the winds slamming hard rain against the bunker.[124] Whatever was not nailed down was being blown away.

Somewhere behind the dark clouds, a quarter moon was hiding. It had begun to form a couple of nights before when I was at Battalion Aid Station; now the storm clouds, winds, and rain hid its light.

During my watch in the rain, I thought about home, Casa Grande, my classmates, family. My mind returned to the cold rain and adjusted myself for comfort and warmth. Bitter wet cold drops of rain were striking my poncho and I had to sit on the ponchos edges to keep the winds from lifting it up. I thought about what had happened to Lucero and wondered about his sister, Diana. I had received and read several of her letters. She expressed herself thoughtfully hinting of other things or other thoughts on her mind, and that only made me want to know more about her. I wondered if something could develop over written letters. Her maturity was different than Dorothy's, and while I could tell she had her own troubles in life by what she didn't say, I was grateful to Lucero for making it possible for me to write to her. I began to look forward to her letters in the mail much more than Dorothy's. Diana wrote with insight, asking questions that showed a genuine desire to know both what was going on with me and with her brother, she wanted to know more about the war and what was going on and that was both puzzling and intriguing. Perhaps it was a way of finding out how safe her brother really was. Dorothy never asked about those things, and I had stopped writing about the war because she didn't want to hear about it. Now I rarely wrote her.

Dorothy wrote about her family and work. Her letters were never filled with love or desires of us being together or her missing me. It was just as well. The letters from Lucero's sister made me feel wanted and important, but I didn't dare think that something serious could come of it, certainly not from a few pieces of paper exchanged over the sea. Yet I wanted to know more about her; maybe it was just waiting for her letters and reading them when they arrived helped pass the time. Other than the letters from Diana and Dorothy, my sister Minga had written a few times as had my half sister Piedad. Pie, as we called her, had sent me some of her homemade cinnamon cookies and a pillow, which she said was from mom. The small pillow had a flower print on it, and it was pink in color but comfortable to lay my head on. Lying next to where I kept my machine-gun, no one ever made a comment about its color.

I enjoyed writing, and I realized that there was something unique, free, and special gained in the process of expressing one's true feelings in letters. So I wrote to Diana about my home life, my family, and, in a poetic way, shared my feelings about what I saw, felt, and cared about. I had no fear of the letters being taken in a wrong way; after all, if things didn't work out, I could always just stop writing and that would be the end of it. I wasn't committed and neither was Diana so I told her about how I felt about my marriage, how unfaithful Dorothy had been, how it really hadn't made that much of a difference as I didn't have the feelings for her like a man should have for his wife. I shared my true feelings as I never shared with Dorothy. For the first time, I was beginning to have hope of returning home and envisioned myself going to Texas, meeting her, and perhaps settling down in that part of the world. She had given me a reason to make it out of Vietnam alive.

Dorothy's letters didn't make me feel that way. In each letter I received, there was no genuine feeling of love expressed from her. Perhaps she was only responding to my letters because I didn't express those feelings. I would sign the letters "love and kisses" mostly because I knew she wanted to read that.

"Take special care of you," Diana had written, and those were words my wife had never written. In Vietnam, the unfaithfulness of a wife can tear you apart, so you dismissed those thoughts, and place them in the back of the mind, to visit at a later time. At times, I thought perhaps, Dorothy would have preferred for me to be killed so she could play the grieving widow and collect the G.I. insurance benefits. Sometimes, it seemed I could read those desires in between the lines she wrote, and there were times I didn't want to open her letters so they stayed unopened for days or I opened them only to take out the stick of gum she would send. While I wondered if one day I might receive a Dear John letter from her, I didn't want to receive that type of letter, not while I was in Vietnam in a combat zone. If the letters didn't represent the real world and home, I probably would never have opened them.

The moon is probably bright over Lubbock, Texas, I thought and wished I had met Diana before I'd met Dorothy. Then again, if it wasn't for my marriage, I wouldn't have joined the corps and I wouldn't have met Lucero and I wouldn't be thinking of his sister right now. Life was fascinating, and things happened for a reason, I knew I was where I was supposed to be in life, in war, in Vietnam and that brought some comfort. Everything else didn't matter that much. Who knew what tomorrow might bring?

A thick downpour caused me to bundle up, but I wouldn't cover my head with the poncho; rain striking it made too much noise and hindered any hearing and vision. I wondered about my high school classmates and what they were doing. What if I hadn't gone off to the war? What if I had stayed in school and graduated with them? On the First of June 1967, as my classmates began their Commencement March to graduate, from high school, I was busy packing my seabag for Vietnam. What would have happened if I had stayed in Casa Grande? I wondered about Sandy Erdmann and the girls in high school who flirted with their eyes and giggled and whispered into each other's ears and smiled with a smirk that could have meant all sorts of things. I wondered about my classmates; where were they? Had I stayed behind, would I just now be getting ready to come to Vietnam?

My thoughts returned to Dorothy and my son. Even if a son had been born, he really wasn't a good reason for us to remain together. I felt alone, struggling and wondering of tomorrow as the wind pressed cold bitter rain against my face my thoughts returned to where I was. It had rained for eight straight hours, and listening for any unusual noise while on guard duty was futile. The monsoon's thundering rain and its continuous downpour made it impossible. I sat there awake lost in thoughts of home.

Noah's Ark
Liberty Bridge,
October 9, 1967, 0500 hours

As dawn approached, the area surrounding our compound became visible with the light as it sneaked through the clouds above. The day's dawn slowly began to reveal that our perimeter was completely surrounded by water. Four feet of raging floodwaters was rushing through the center of the compound. Jones and Marty, who had stood watch earlier during the night, were sound asleep inside the bunker. I jumped down, rushed in, and woke them. As soon as they came running out the bunker's entrance gave way and the floodwaters rushed in. Seconds later, the bunker was completely filled with water.

We stood gathered on top of the bunker, and when full daylight came, we could see the surrounding bunkers completely submerged under rising water. Some Marines were standing on sandbags on top of their bunkers with the floodwaters having reached their ankles while a light rain was still falling steadily on all of us. Some Marines looked as if they were standing or sitting in the middle of a lake. When the rain stopped, the floodwaters became idle. At the CP, the water had reached its entrance.

Lieutenant Wilson, Doc Mac, Doc Marren, John Niedringhaus, and CJ were all busy handing out equipment to each other, passing it up the line from inside the CP to the outside and placing it on top of the bunker.

We waded toward our barracks in waist-deep waters and found water was inches from flooding the insides of the barracks. Hurriedly, we took our seabags and personal items off the wooden floor and placed them on top of the cots in hopes that the water would not reach that high. An hour later, the barrack's floor was covered with six inches of water.

Then the rain stopped falling, the sun came out, and the clouds disappeared.

By late afternoon, rays of sunlight produced a beautiful rainbow running the full length of the An Hoa basin. The rainbow's colors arched all the way across the land, covering all of the Arizona territory. The area was completely flooded to An Hoa, and I wondered where the enemy had found shelter. Only patches of high ground were visible, little islands in the middle of the sea. Off in the distance, the An Hoa mountains remained covered in dark clouds. Below the rainbow, the land was covered by dark brown floodwaters as far as we could see.

We moved between the barracks and our bunkers by wading waist deep in brown water. After a while, Marty started gathering loose pieces of wood and tying them together to construct a raft. The raft was, he said seriously, "just in case we need to paddle to Battalion Headquarters." In the back of my mind, I started to wonder if we might have to do just that. Other than a portion of the bridge and the tower, there was no higher ground than our barracks and the top of our bunkers.

At three that afternoon, someone yelled for us to rush to the bridge. As we hurried over, the midsection of Liberty Bridge cracked loudly and broke away. A few minutes later, the rushing muddy waters of the Song Thu Bon River claimed a huge section of the bridge. Small sections quickly followed, and in less than twenty minutes, most of the bridge had been washed away.

As the evening began to fall, the president of South Vietnam declared the Dai Loc district a disaster area. By then we were holding raft races while other Marines from Southern California were jumping on long, skinny wooden boards, trying to surf in the racing water as it moved through the compound.

Skipping Tracers on the Song Thu Bon
Liberty Bridge,
October 10, 1967, 1500 hours

By the afternoon of October 10, the waters began to recede and the water within the compound's perimeter had flowed into the lower rice paddies and flat terrain. Aggie and I were sitting on top of our bunker watching debris float by the river's edge near our secondary bunker position when Corporal Boone came running over from the CP. In his hand he held a pair of binoculars.

"NVA," he said, as he climbed on top of the bunker and pointed toward a small island about eight hundred meters southeast of us. He raised the binoculars to his eyes and tried to locate them. I picked up the gun and set it on its tripod, setting the sliding scale to sight in, according to the distance where Boone said they had been spotted.

Aggie checked the belt of ammo for loose short or long rounds. There weren't any, so he got on his belly and held the ammo up, knowing I would be opening up with the gun shortly.

"They're to the left, just past that cluster of trees," Boone said as he turned to look at us and pointed at a far distant tree line. I looked toward where Boone indicated the enemy soldiers were and saw three NVA soldiers emerging from a distant tree line. I watched as they got into two small boats and began frantically rowing across the wide gap between the tree line and a small island on the other side of what once had been the river's southern bank.

There was a fairly good distance between them and the safety of the island's edge, and I knew I would be able to sight in on them with the gun long before they would reach the other side. If they made it across, they would disappear into the dense jungle. I pulled the gun in tight and opened fire with a short burst. Boone watched the tracers strike the water about twenty yards short and directed my firepower.

I adjusted the gun's rear slide for the needed distance and accuracy. I pulled the gun in tighter. I sighted in on the boat and fired a burst of machine-gun fire. The bullets moved in toward the enemy's position, and some of the red tracers sizzled as they skipped along the top of the water. I zeroed in closer. In the background, I could hear Hill 65 firing off a series of artillery rounds. At about the time my machine-gun's red tracers struck the first boat, the artillery rounds dropped right on top of both boats. A huge geyser erupted where the enemy had been only seconds before. The artillery rounds exploded right on target. There was no need for adjustment, but seconds later, another load of artillery shells were dropped on the very same spot. The Eleventh Marines' battery on Hill 65 had once again done what they did best. Only pieces of the boats remained, and those pieces were scattered all over the river. As the smoke cleared, the larger pieces of the wooden boat were washed up on both sides of the river; the enemy soldiers were gone.

Tonsillitis Again
Liberty Bridge,
October 11, 1967, 1300 hours

On the fourth day after the typhoon, the waters receded enough to allow supply trucks to travel the muddy roadway between our compound and Battalion Headquarters. That morning, I was once again sent to Battalion Aid Station with a high fever and another acute case of tonsillitis. I would be kept there for four days.

Rough Riders to Quang Tri
Liberty Bridge,
October 12, 1967, 0800 hours

On the morning of October 12, First Platoon was assigned a roughrider security detail.[125] They would be riding shotgun security for a truck convoy *en route* to Quang Tri. Only a couple of Marines from First Platoon and Doc Mac were left behind.

Doc McNallen was well liked by the Marines in First Platoon. A tall, heavyset Corpsman with a good vocabulary, he had short bushy red hair, bold round eyes, a heavy, gruff voice, but one of the gentlest Corpsman I ever met. He cared greatly about the Marines he was assigned to, and being a few years older than most, Mac often found himself giving fatherly advice. Doc Mac had been left behind.

Bald Eagle I
Liberty Bridge,
October 14, 1967, 1400 hours

On the afternoon of the fourteenth of October, I caught a ride on the mail truck back to Liberty Bridge. When I arrived, Marines from Second and Third Platoons were saddled up and sitting on the road waiting for choppers to arrive.

War Cloud, a Company C, First Recon Battalion Unit had been inserted into the Hai Van Mountains in 2/7's assigned area at 0850 hours that morning. A short time later two of the scout's handset radios had failed.

As a chopper dropped off a replacement set by parachute, the radios got caught up in a tree. As MSgt. George Moffett retrieved them, the recon unit became engaged in a fierce fire fight with a large enemy force. Soon they were under heavy sniper fire, grenade and automatic weapons fire. For more then an hour, they engaged the enemy in a fierce firefight. Attempts to medevac or get reinforcements to them had been met with M-50 MG fire, and at 1330 hours, having taken three WIAs and two KIAs, the recon unit requested a Bald Eagle response. A company size unit was needed to confront the enemy and get them out.

Captain Baggette, India Company's CO volunteered Second and Third Platoons. A platoon from Mike Company 3/7 was secured and that made up the rest of the company.

As the mail truck pulled off the road inside the compound, CH-46s helicopters began to land on the roadway at the entrance to Liberty Bridge. By the time the mail truck came to a complete stop, India Company Marines and the CP group were already boarding the first chopper, among them was Doc Mac, he was saddled up and was going out with the rest of the company on the "Bald Eagle operation."[126]

By 1515 hours, 158 Marines including a forward observer and forward air-control task force unit had been lifted off Liberty Bridge and were in the air. The deployment required two airlifts and eight Ch-46's helicopters.[127] Everything went off without any problems.[128]

As the last of the choppers disappeared over Charlie Ridge, the compound became dreadfully quiet. All of India Company was gone, only fifteen of us had been left behind to men the lines at Liberty Bridge. What normally required two platoons, some eighty to ninety Marines to stand watch at night was now going to be covered by fifteen of us. Only every other position would be manned and the manned positions would only have two men per hole.

No sooner had the choppers landed at the base of the mountains where the recon team was located when India Company Marines were already moving out, humping up a steep mountain trail. With high temperatures, thick humid air, and a dense tropical jungle impeding their ascent, five Marines quickly succumbed to heat exhaustion as they raced to the top. For seven hours, the recon unit had held their ground. At 1730 hours, India Company made contact with War Cloud at ZC 183984, and the enemy broke contact, disappearing into the thick jungle. For eight straight hours, the Recon patrol leader, Second Lieutenant Klaus Schreiber had positioned his men and participated in keeping a battalion-size enemy force, from over-running his twelve-man reconnaissance squad's positions. [129]

War Cloud's KIAs were Sgt. Robert Charles Rudd from Dallas, Texas, and Cpl. Edward J. Simmons from Bluefield, West Virginia. There were ten WIAs.

Bald Eagle I
Liberty Bridge,
October 15, 1967, 0700 hours

The following morning at 0715 hours India Company and the recon unit moved out, going slowly down a trail, where they found an AK-47 magazine with thirty rounds still in it. That and other enemy gear was found scattered on the trail, revealing the enemy's hasty retreat.

At 1030 hours, the company discovered bunkers that had been dug along the trail they were on. The bunker fighting positions had a vantage view of the valley below. As they took note of this an alert Marine spotted an NVA/VC enemy soldier in a tree some distance away, keeping watch on the Marines examining the bunkers. The Marines took an advantageous position, zeroed in and fired a single shot at the enemy, and he fell from the tree. [130]

Back at the Base
Liberty Bridge,
October 15, 1967, 1945 hours

Back at Liberty Bridge late that afternoon, a Vietnamese body was caught in the piling of the bridge. With some effort, the body was pulled from the water, by the Seabees. It hadn't been in the water long, and it didn't appear as if there were any bullet holes in it. That evening, the body was turned over to Dai Loc District Headquarters officials.

First Platoon on the roughrider convoy were at that time traveling north past Phu Bai, when the convoy stopped for a road-clearing detail. As they did, everyone was instructed to disembark and take a defensive position. A forward air observer assigned to the convoy detail jumped off the back of a six-by, and as he did, his wedding ring got caught on a metal bolt on the truck's rear railing. His wedding ring finger was ripped off his hand. The convoy stood down until he was medevaced.[131]

The Company Returns
Liberty Bridge, Vietnam
October 16, 1967, 1300 hours

By the morning of the sixteenth, the Seabees had completed construction of a temporary pontoon bridge so that traffic and supplies were flowing again across the Song Thu Bon River between An Hoa and Da Nang.

That afternoon, Second and Third Platoons returned and it was a welcome relief to have so many Marines back at the bridge, especially to help stand perimeter watch at night. One disturbing bit of information they brought back with them was that the enemy was increasing the strength of its force throughout our TAOR.[132]

Bald Eagle II
Liberty Bridge, Vietnam
October 17, 1967, 0800 hours

On the fifteenth, an A Company Recon unit by the call sign "Texas Pete" was inserted in the same general area War Cloud had operated; for over twenty-four hours, they were successful in their mission, doing what recon units do best. Late in the evening of the sixteenth; however, an enemy force of over twenty NVA soldiers engaged them; the recon responded, killing two of the enemy soldiers and the enemy broke contact. Having been discovered, the unit knew they had to get out of there and fast. The following morning at 0800 hours, while the recon unit was moving toward their extraction point, they were engaged by forty to sixty hard-core NVA soldiers.[133] Like the recon team War Cloud, Texas Pete requested a Marine company-size Bald Eagle response.

Captain Baggette again volunteered India Company, and the same platoon from Mike 3/7 saddled up. The company was ready to move out by 0900 hours, but CH-46 helicopters needed to transport them to the recon's location were not available. Second and Third Platoon could do nothing but sit and wait on Liberty Road.

At 1100 hours, Texas Pete reported continued contact with a large enemy force was continuing and they had sustained casualties. At 1120 hours, the CH-46s were secured for the Bald Eagle operation and were *en route* to pick up India Company Marines.

Meanwhile, a platoon from Foxtrot 2/7, the closest available Marine unit to the recon unit, had moved overland toward Elephant Valley and Texas Pete's location.

Thirty-five Marines on four amtracks, one equipped with a 106mm recoilless rifle mounted on its top were speeding toward the Recon Marines' position.

As those Marines were *en route*, 5 CH-46s (Bonnie Sue 10) and 3 H-34s (Tar Bush 3-5) began to heli-lift the first wave of 129 Marines from India and Mike Company to the base of the mountains where Texas Pete was located.

At 1255 hours, India Company's first wave touched down. As soon as the first Marine touched ground the point man headed up the mountain, toward a rendezvous point with the recon insert.

Fifteen other Marines on 3 H-34s from Mike 3/7 landed at 1305 hours. Separated from the rest of their platoon and India Company already having disappeared into the thick jungle foliage, they stood by at the bottom of the mountain to wait the remainder of their platoon to be dropped off. At 1345 hours, the rest of the platoon arrived, and they were ordered to stand by and wait for the Foxtrot Marines.

The recon insert, still in heavy contact with the enemy, was continuing to take casualties but kept the enemy from assaulting their position. Meanwhile, the enemy was jamming Texas Pete's radio transmissions.

The Recon Marines continued to fight back and could see NVA soldiers in full battle gear in the thick jungle slowly pushing toward them. The enemy, by then, had been reinforced by other units, and was seeking more advantageous positions to launch an assault on the pinned-down Marines.

As they prepared to hold off the enemy assault that was sure to come, they heard over the net, "Texas Pete, Texas Pete, this is Beechnut 1 (India Company's CO). How do you read?" The radio broadcast was loud enough for the enemy to hear.

Texas Pete responded with relief anticipation in their voice. They knew India Company 3/7's call sign as the unit that had responded to the call for help for War Cloud.

Now the same company of Marines was coming to their rescue.

While radio communications was established, the company was still a great distance from the recon unit.

On the valley floor below, the platoon from F 2/7 had arrived and established a base area position along with the platoon from Mike Company. It would take them at least two hours to get up the steep climb and cut through the thick jungle and to where the Recon Marines were, so battalion advised them to stay where they were.

By 1500 hours, Texas Pete had sustained three KIAs and nine WIAs, and continued to hold off enemy assaults. A half hour later, they made radio and physical contact with Marines from India Company and the enemy broke contact.

India Company moved through the recon unit's position and established a new perimeter before beginning the process of removing the recon unit's casualties to the base area while searching the area for the enemy.

At 1630 hours, India Company, searching the area where Texas Pete had been engaged in battle with the enemy, found four dead NVA bodies. The bodies were riddled with bullets and had been killed by small arms fire. They were the same bodies that Texas Pete earlier had reported having killed when the NVA soldiers first assaulted their positions. Also found at that location were forty rounds of AK-47 ammo, nine AK-47 loaded magazines, seven ChiCom grenades, four cartridge belts, three first aid kits, two ponchos, two black NVA uniforms, and one blue one.[134] After India Company had finished searching out the area, they consolidated nighttime positions from which they and the remaining recon members would run patrols and set up night ambushes. The recon unit's extraction of their dead and wounded would have to wait until they could get them to a clearing.

Recon Insert Petrify
Hai Van Mountains
October 17, 1967, 1730 hours

As India Company searched the area of Texas Pete's contact, a short distance away, "Petrify," a seventeen-man recon insert, became engaged in a heavy firefight with yet another large enemy force.[135] This time, Golf Company 2/7 responded to the Bald Eagle request, commencing a motor march to a point at the base of the mountain and from there, they moved up a trail to link up with Petrify. Meanwhile, choppers had tried to extract Petrify but could not because of heavy enemy fire. The crew chief on one of the CH-46s was wounded in the process; by late that night, Golf 2/7 still had not been able to successfully link up with Petrify, the recon unit.

At 2220 hours, India Company Marines from Second Platoon on a night patrol spotted two NVA/VCs moving up the trail toward them. They opened fire with twenty-five rounds from their M-16s; the enemy returned two to three rounds of small arms fire and broke contact. The platoon moved in to search the area, with negative results. As they continued down the trail at 0100 hours, Second Platoon found two NVA/VC KIAs. Both of the enemy soldiers were dressed in black pj's. Also found was an AK-47 magazine, a ChiCom grenade, two packs with ponchos, and other assorted gear.

Bald Eagle III
Hai Van Mountains
October 18, 1967, 0800 hours

Early the morning of the eighteenth, another helicopter extraction was attempted to get Petrify out. That chopper was downed by heavy enemy fire. By 1100 hours with 100 meters to go to get to the recon unit, Golf 2/7 became pinned down by automatic weapons fire. Air support was called in, and afterward Golf CO did make contact, but with only six of the recon team members.

Vietnamese Children and Their Toys
South Vietnam
October 18, 1967, 1300 hours

As First Platoon continued with their roughrider detail, and the rest of India Company remained committed to supporting recon units. I was standing front-gate watch alone at the guard shack to Liberty Bridge when three young Vietnamese kids came walking up the road. They were carrying a 105mm round.

I yelled for them to stop when they were about thirty yards from the gate, motioning for them to lay the round down and move back. They stopped but held on to the large round, shifting the heavy load back and forth between them. I didn't know the Vietnamese words to tell them to lay the round down. A minute later, they started to walk toward the front gate again and I yelled at them once more, this time motioning for them to put the mortar round down. They stopped and laid the unexploded round on the side of the road.

The U.S. government had begun a program where they paid civilians for turning in any unexploded ordnance they found. Usually, the Vietnamese sent their children to turn in unexploded ordnance for the cash reward. I got on the landline and a Kit Carson Scout Vietnamese interpreter was called to the front gate. They arrived by helicopter from 3/7 headquarters and the scout conversed in Vietnamese with the three young kids who were waiting patiently near the wire.

The interpreter came up to me and said;

"The boys were afraid you might shoot them, and that you didn't know they were here to turn in the round they had found."

"Where did they get it."

"By the river, they said, they found it by the river, where other artillery shells had struck the day before. They know when there is a barrage, some artillery don't explode, so they go looking for them, to turn in for money, before the VC gets them."

"Were they paid," I asked.

"Yes," he answered, "I paid them an amount of what their family will need for six months. They were very happy to turn it in, so VC don't use it."

"Did you, thank them," I asked. The interpreter looked at me, realized what I had said and answered. "Next time, sometime you pay, you no thank. If you thank, you no pay." he said and headed back to the awaiting helicopter.

Bald Eagle III
Hai Van Mountains
October 18, 1967, 1435 hours

At 1435 hours, Golf CP in search of the rest of the recon unit became engaged in a heavy firefight with a large enemy force; they were hit with 60mm mortars, M-79 grenades, and heavy M-60 machine-gun fire.

When the enemy broke contact Golf moved out and discovered that one of their men from Third Platoon was missing. The missing Marine joined the ranks of the other eleven missing Petrify Recon Marines.

At 1600 hours, India Company was finally able to get the Texas Pete recon team extracted.

Texas Pete's KIAs were GySgt. Lemuel Leneol Alewine from Thornton, Texas, L/Cpl. Edward H. Rauch from San Francisco, California, and Pfc. Lawrence Henry Collier from Memphis, Tennessee.

Bald Eagle III
Hai Van Mountains
October 18, 1967, 1630 hours

At 1630 hours, as a Golf Company made their way up a steep trail, NVA/VC soldiers, shouted, "RECON" and threw grenades at the Marines and opened fire with an M-60 machine-gun, carbines, and AK-47 automatic rifle fire. The Marines responded with fifteen M26 grenades, ten rounds of M-79, five hundred rounds of M-60, and 300 rounds from their M-16 rifles.

Minutes later the enemy broke contact. In the brief firefight, one Marine was wounded and one NVA/VC was probably killed, determined by the amount of blood and drag marks that were later found.

At 1720 hours, India Company was reassigned to help locate the missing Petrify recon unit and Captain Baggette changed course, and India Company Marines turned, to climb a steeper mountain, then the one they had just came down from.

A short time later, Golf Company CP was again engaged in a heavy firefight with a large enemy force, resulting in one Marine KIA and four WIAs.

As the medevac chopper was coming in for the medevac, it was struck by heavy enemy fire and went down.

With Golf Company pinned down in a kill zone, taking heavy mortar and automatic rifle fire, India Company Marines once more changed course and were directed to secure the downed chopper. An India Company Platoon did so, while the rest of India Company continued on their mission to locate the missing Recon Marines. Late that evening, contact with the missing recon unit was made and all were united and settled in for the night.

Bald Eagle III
Hai Van Mountains
October 19, 1967, 0900 hours

At first light, choppers appeared to extract Petrify's KIAs and their seriously wounded Marines, but because of the terrain they were unable to land. The choppers had to hoist the dead and wounded Marines on board while they hovered overhead. One of the Marines was so seriously wounded Doc Mac tied himself to the rope with the wounded Marine and both were extracted. At 1445, the rest of Petrify was finally extracted and India Company was choppered out.

Petrify's KIAs were Sgt. Alan Theodore Jenson from Hales Corners, Wisconsin, and L/Cpl. Jerry F. De Gray from Milwaukee, Wisconsin. Golf Company 2/7s KIA (MIA) L/Cpl. Howard Ogden from Omaha; NE[136]

Liberty Bridge Reunion
Liberty Bridge, Dai Loc
October 19, 1967, 1600 hours

On the afternoon of the nineteenth, Second and Third Platoon returned by helicopter; a short time later, First Platoon arrived from their convoy escort by trucks. The company was once again together as a unit, on Liberty Bridge.

A Night Out and a Morning Encounter
Liberty Bridge, Dai Loc
October 20, 1967, 1600 hours

Late afternoon of the twentieth, Stan Villarreal from Second Platoon, standing watch on Liberty Bridge, observed a large Vietnamese boat loaded with supplies land on the north bank of the Song Thu Bon River. He called it in to the CP, and they alerted the unit 106, stationed at the bridge. Stan watched as two VCs in black pj's begin to unload their supplies; the enemy soldiers were carrying no weapons. The ontos leveled their weapon on their target and fired seven 106mm HE rounds at the enemy soldiers; the rounds missed both the VCs and the boat and the VCs fled, leaving the boat on the river's bank. That night, First Platoon was assigned to set up an ambush nearby where we could keep the boat under observation.

Our gun team went out: Jones, Aggie, and I, and Third Squad. We set up near the river by our old jungle base in the tree line near where we had kept our second gun position. We sat and waited for the enemy to cross the river or approach the boat. As we waited in the darkness, off in the far, distant mountains past Charlie Ridge, an enormous light show was going on as B-52s dropped dozens of five-hundred-pound bombs. They were pounding the area the recon units had encountered the enemy for several days.

Before daylight, we left the ambush position and headed in. The tower at Liberty Bridge then took over to keep the boat under observation.

As we approached the front gate; across the river in the Arizona territory, two jets returning from an aborted mission over Hanoi were dropping off their loads of bombs in the free fire zone. As we neared the front gate, a Marine in our squad fired off a flare to alert the Marine on duty that we were coming in.

Instead of popping off a green flare, a bright red flare, exploded high overhead.

Immediately, we saw the two Skyhawks in the air turn in the western sky and head toward us.

I could hear the squad leader telling his radioman to get on the radio and contact the jets, to tell them, we were friendlies.

High overhead, the red flare was burning brightly, a perfect signal of enemy troops approaching Liberty Bridge. It was the type of target that air wingers pray for. Swoop in and destroy the enemy as they approach a friendly force.

I wondered if they were trying to communicate with India Six, at our CO's headquarters at Liberty Bridge.

I looked around for shelter, anything I could dive into, one of those trench lines, a small dug out hole, anything to hide in or jump into for shelter.

The radioman kept trying all types of frequencies to alert the jets that we were friendly troops, but was not being successful.

The Jets flew by overhead, and I thought perhaps the danger had passed, but they had gone by at a lower altitude and all of a sudden both turned high overhead for an approach, toward us.

Unable to contact them, the squad scattered seeking any cover.

"We can make a run for the gate," Aggie said, as we looked around for anything to crawl into.

"You, crazy, Mexican, they have cannons and would shoot you for sure," Lucero answered him.

"Aggie, there's that culvert, on the side of the road we can run there," I said.

Other Marines, had thought of the same thing, and the squad was beginning to run in that direction. The culvert ran under Liberty Road, it was ahead but out in the open, but large enough to hold the whole squad inside.

The distance was close enough for us to run in for cover. If the jets didn't open up on us with their cannons, they could turn back and drop one of their napalm bombs on us I was thinking and I could already imagine being burned alive or suffocating when the bomb sucked the air out of the area.

With the jets approaching rapidly, Jackie Williams dropped to one knee and popped off a green flare. We all stopped stood still and waited.

The flare streaked skyward and popped directly overhead. It's green glow flooding the ground all around us, exposing us out in the open. We dared not move because the jets might still confuse us with the enemy moving toward Liberty Bridge. The jets flew by and were gone.

We Want You Well, By Making You Sick
Liberty Bridge, Dai Loc
October 21, 1967, 1300 hours

That afternoon, we were all lined up and given some new type of flu shots. Immediately, many of us became sick. For the remainder of the day, there was a line in front of the shitter. Marines were laid out in their bunkers, bunks or stretched out on the ground too weak to move away from where they had puked. Jackie Williams got so sick, the Corpsman gave him some type of pill that caused Williams to hallucinate, and that night while at the aid station we could hear him screaming and crying out that jets were going to drop napalm on all of us. Marty and Rahm were both laid out for two days.

Ambushing the Enemy In Their Own Hooch
Liberty Bridge, Dai Loc
October 22, 1967, 0300 hours

Early in the morning of the twenty-second, a night ambush fire-team was sent to locate a VC/NVA group that was supposed to be meeting nearby according to intelligence from information obtained from local villagers. The meeting was to take place near Hoa Dong, a small village north of Hoa Tay, our old jungle position. According to intelligence a small group of NVA/VC soldiers were to meet near a large hooch that had a smaller hooch in the back. The hooches were located just before the village entrance on the left side of Liberty Road.

Izzie, Chief, Lucky, O'Neil, and Taylor located the hooch without a problem. Taylor and O'Neil were tall and thin, and new to the squad. Vaughn O'Neil was from Lincoln Park, Missouri, and Chief and Izzie had already nicknamed him "Stringbeans." Charles Minot Taylor III, a tall blond kid, from Little Rock, Arkansas; was the quiet one in the bunch. A gentle Marine that always did what he was told, and although new, he had already found his place in the squad.

As they approached the target, they could hear what sounded like an argument going on in the rear structure. As Izzie stood by, the rest of the fire-team moved in to secure the first structure. The door was unsecured, open, and they slipped into the hooch to find no one there. Something wasn't right. They could still hear the sound of voices in the back hooch.

"I think they're meeting in the back hooch," Izzie told Chief, and the fire-team moved in on that target. As they drew near to the sounds they were hearing, it was evident some sort of group meeting was taking place and a heated argument was going on. The harsh sounds of the Vietnamese voice can often be confusing, so the fire-team crawled in as close as possible to the hooch. The voices continued, and it sounded as if four or five people were inside. Chief told Lucky to take Taylor and O'Neil and check out the hooch. Civilians slept at night; they did not venture outside their homes at night for fear of being mistaken for the enemy. With the front hooch being vacant, it was a clear indication that the owners had fled.

"Crawl up to the hooch and check it out; if there's VC in there, pitch in grenades then run out of there, Izzie, and I will cover you," Chief told them. Lucky, Taylor, and O'Neil crawled out silently hugging the earth; when they got up alongside the hooch; each took out a grenade and pulled the pin.

Lucky indicated that he would try to see inside and crawled toward a small window to get a look inside. He was halfway there when there was a loud shuffle heard inside and a large object struck the side of the bamboo hut near where Lucky was. Believing they had been discovered and the enemies inside the hooch were scrambling for their weapons, the other Marines pitched in their grenades as did Lucky. All three Marines then opened fire, spraying the hooch with automatic rifle fire, as the grenade exploded, they ran back, hit the dirt near Izzie and Chief, and changed magazines. Izzie and Chief then opened fire, Izzie dropping two M-79 grenades into the center of the hooch, as Chief emptied twenty rounds from his M-14 into the smoking hooch. When the smoke cleared, the hooch was barely standing. They moved in to check it out and found four dead pigs.

CHAPTER ELEVEN

Banana Rum and Fire Water
Liberty Bridge
October 22, 1967, 0800 hours

All day long, the supply mule had been busy running supplies from Battalion Headquarters and unloading them at our company's CP. With all the supplies coming in, we knew a major operation was in the works. Northwest of us, in the Arizona territory area, a jet plane was circling overhead; a short time later, the area thundered as artillery shells exploded at the base of the An Hoa mountains.[137]

Souble, Third Squad's grenadier, decided to take advantage of the mule's availability as it traveled back and forth on Liberty Road, and hopped a ride into Dai Loc. Jerome "Jerry" V. Souble was tall and thin with long, hanging arms. He had a thin oval-shaped face with big round eyes and walked with a determined look wherever he went. When he made up his mind of what he wanted to do, there was no stopping him. The helmet he wore was two sizes too large, so it lay sideways on his head. Souble returned from the village with six canteens full of banana rum.

"Nothing like locally made banana juice from the old village," he said when he jumped off the mule and came to our bunker.

He offered us a drink, and Aggie took a quick swig. As soon as the liquor touched his lips, a spray of the golden liquid spewed out of his mouth and out through his nose. His eyes watered, and when he tried to speak, his voice cracked.

I held the contents to my nose, and smelling the rum made my nostrils burn. I took a small sip of it and my throat filled with a deep burning, stinging sensation. The alcohol quickly warmed my belly, but just as quickly, the hot liquor burned like fire coming back up. My insides were on fire. The liquor was potent and had a higher kick than Bacardi 151.

Souble took a swallow and his eyes watered.

"Hey, Souble," I said, my voice squeaky from the acidy burn. I cleared my throat.

"Take a swig then breath out slowly, while I light a match in front of you, see if it'll ignite." Souble, still unable to speak clenched his lips, and shook his head no.

210

"Man, this stuff, is potent," Aggie said.

When it was apparent the company would be going out on a major operation, Souble began desperately trying to get rid of his canteens full of banana rum. He traded some of them with the Seabees and the 106 Marines, and before long, he had managed to get rid of all of them except for one canteen, attached to his cartridge belt.

Before noon, Dumont was called to the lieutenant's hooch, and he took Aggie and Marty with him. They returned a short time later with supplies. As we sat around the hooch, Dumont stood up. His glasses sat slightly slanted on his face, making it hard to concentrate on what he was saying with them in that position. He told us about the operation we would be going on.

"A Marine recon team has been ambushed in the middle of dense jungle about two thousand feet straight up a steep mountain. The site is where Second and Third Platoon responded to a recon unit's Bald Eagle request," he said. "The recon insert was on their way up the mountain to check out a downed 47D with USAF personnel on board. A puff plane,"[138] he added. The plane had been spraying the Ho Chi Minh trail near the Laos-Cambodia border and was probably hit by antiaircraft fire and came down on our side of the Annamite Mountains."

"The recon team never made it to the plane, and we have not heard from them." With a worried look on his face, he straightened his glasses then took them off to clean the lens. He placed them back on, but they were still slanted on his face. He sat down in front of the cases of C-rats. "Other companies are already looking for the recon team," he said. "Our job will be to locate the plane, recover the mini-guns, and bring back the bodies if we can find them. We don't know if the gooks have gotten to the plane and its mini-guns or even if the gooks know it went down."

Dumont opened one of the cases of C-rations. "Take three C-rat meals with you. It's going to be hard climbing. The CO said the climb is steep and the jungle in the mountains is too thick for us to be resupplied, so take as many canteens as you can, halizone tablets, and ammo. We're going out by truck to 2/7's headquarters, and from there, we'll be helilifted to the base of the mountain at first light. It will probably be a hot LZ, as regiment-size enemy forces have been seen several times in the area and recon units have encountered a number of large enemy units there." Dumont turned the box of C-rats upside down and removed the cardboard box covering.

Not everyone in our company had been issued the new lightweight utilities and boots. Only a few Marines—like Dumont, Jones, Boone, and a few others who'd traded or bargained—wore them. Wearing the thick, heavy stateside utilities in thick underbrush was going to be hot and miserable.

Duran asked Dumont if we were going to be issued the new utilities before the operation. If so, he wanted to know if he would have time to wash them before we went on the operation so they wouldn't be stiff and new in the jungle.

"Not that I know of," Dumont responded.

"Some of the pogues in the rear already have them," Duran added, an angry tone in his voice.

"The lieutenant has been trying to get them, I think some came in with the supply run, but we don't know when they'll be issued. It would be nice for all of us to have them before the op," Aggie added.

Dumont shuffled the eight-by-ten cardboard boxes containing the variety of C-rats around. A C-rat can opener package holding a PR-38 fell out and I picked it up, tore off the brown paper wrapping, and stuck it under the rubber band around my helmet.

We all chose three boxes, short-timers going first. Dumont, to be fair, was the last to pick his meals. Even though he was not an officer, Dumont always carried out the Marine Corps tradition that Marine leaders ate last. He ended up with two boxes of ham and lima beans. The most distasteful meal in each case, but Dumont liked them. He said they gave him lots of energy and were full of protein.

Jones took the meals out of the cardboard boxes and lined them up before him. He then selected what meals he would eat and the sequence he would eat them in. He placed the three large cans of the main meals in a long green tube sock that was tied tightly on each end by shoelaces he had taken off his shoes. He then tied the sock to the top part of his closed knapsack and then tied both to the back of his flak jacket. To the bottom eyelets of his flak jacket, he hooked two canteens and another one to his knapsack. Jones handed me a smaller light tan-colored knapsack. It was Bro's knapsack.

"Bro would have wanted you to have it," he said.

"Thanks," I said and felt a connection with the lightweight knapsack. The knapsack had been through several firefights. Guns had taken it off a dead NVA soldier the gun team had killed on the day of the dike during Operation DeSoto. Bro had worn it when we went to the Thuong Duc Special Forces Camp and when we saddled up to seek the rocket's site near St. Peter. He had left it behind the day he was killed. The knapsack was compact. It did not sit high on the back as others did but low, just above the waist when strapped around the back of the flak jacket; it was perfect for a machine-gunner as it wouldn't interfere with the gun.

I followed Jones' example in packing the knapsack and in placing my meals in socks and tying it all together to the back of my flak jacket. That way, it was easy to take the whole thing off without having to unbuckle the knapsack or having to untie the string of canned food and it made it easier to drape the extra 100 rounds of machine-gun ammo over the whole thing. It would also make carrying the gun easier since it wouldn't be caught on a knapsack's strap as it sometimes did with the others.

Inside the inner lining of our helmets, we placed our personal items wrapped in plastic—cigarettes, matches, letters, pictures, and other things we wanted to keep dry. Marty wrapped his small camera in plastic and placed it inside his pack.

Each gun team member would carry two hundred rounds of machine-gun ammo on the operation. I took off the gun's attachable ammo pouch. I didn't like it, and it was useless in Vietnam. Instead, I loaded a 100-round belt and wrapped it around the gun and set the gun aside; it was clean and ready. I checked the 100-round belt that I would be carrying draped across my chest for long or short rounds and adjusted a couple, making sure they were seated right in the links that connected them together. Then I set that 100-round belt next to the gun: everything was all packed and I was ready to move out. Besides his gear and two hundred rounds of machine-gun ammo, Dumont was also carrying twenty-five feet of rope and a large machete. We were all issued new light weight utilities late that afternoon.

2/7 Headquarters
2/7 Headquarters, South Vietnam
October 23, 1967, 0900 hours

Early the morning of the twenty-third, we saddled up and waited for the sweeping detail to clear Liberty Road. Outside our hooch, with all our gear on, we posed as Earl Lergner a new fire-team leader in First squad took our pictures. As Chief and Izzie posed for their picture, Lergner had their new squad leader, a Marine by the name of Evaristo Morales move into the picture as well as two other Marines. With all the gear and ammo they were all carrying, it seemed they could carry on a battle all their own.

The culvert that ran under the road near the tree line had been blown by the enemy the night before and now in its place was a massive hole in the middle of the road.[139] When the morning road sweeping detail arrived, they were followed by the truck convoy that was to take us to 2/7's headquarters. At the huge crater hole, the sweeping detail checked the side of the road for other mines and when they gave the all clear, the six-by trucks went easily around the damaged road; it did not delay our departure, and by noon, we arrived at 2/7's Battalion Headquarters on the other side of Da Nang.

We were served a hot meal and were able to buy cold sodas and beer. That night 2/7 provide security, so we didn't have to stand watch and it was the first time since I arrived in country that the company as a whole had been given some time off. The following morning, we were going to be helilifted out when Operation Knox would officially be launched.[140]

Operation Knox
LZ Hawk, Hill 1192, South Vietnam
October 24, 1967, 0800 hours

As the early morning sunlight crept over the horizon on the twenty-fourth, twenty UH-34 transport helicopters appeared high overhead. The four-bladed choppers looked like giant green grasshoppers and the pop-pop sound of their blades piercing the air increased as they drew near. As soon as the first helicopter touched ground, First Platoon climbed on board. Twelve to fourteen of us were ushered on board each of the choppers. My gun team was on the first; India Company was leading the initial wave of Operation Knox.[141]

As we lifted off, the helicopter shook and rattled, its tail rose and its nose dropped and the chopper drifted sideways; and I wondered if we would make it to the LZ—the fuselage was paper-thin, not capable of stopping a bullet.

We climbed higher and began to circle around as below us other Marines were boarding other choppers. The higher we went, the more the chopper shook. It seemed as if it was going to fall apart. Once the last of the choppers lifted off the ground, our chopper took the lead. Behind us, three choppers back, was Duran's gun team. Aggie and Keeton were with him. Jones, Marty, and I were on the same chopper. The chopper picked up its pace, and we moved through the air at a good rate of speed. We were not alone; outside the chopper's open door a couple of klicks away, Marine jets flew past us heading in the same direction we were going.

We sat in the helicopters staring at each other with no one saying a word. It was supposed to be a hot LZ, Dumont had told us.

I wondered if we got hit when we landed, how I would react; would I stand and fight while being shot at, or would I freeze?

I looked at Dumont. His mouth was open, he was breathing hard, and he looked scared.

How many will die?

Will I be one of them?

Will I be able to keep my wits while under fire?

I felt a new state of alertness, anxiety, hope, expectancy, and fear; the fear was not of the enemy and the battle we may soon be engaged in, but the fear of not doing my part, of letting others down. I felt helpless and wondered if everyone else was feeling the same way.

Lucero had blessed himself with the sign of the cross as he climbed on board, his small legs outstretched to their limit just to get on. He looked like a little Boy Scout on his way to camp. Others on board seemed to be saying some secret prayers; a Marine held a rosary in his hands.

Before the choppers landed and we were loaded aboard, I heard John Niedringhaus say to a worried Marine the same words he had once told me, "For those who have fought for it, life has a flavor the protected will never know."

I wondered if Niedringhaus had made up the saying or if he had read it somewhere.

John, Lieutenant Wilson, and the First Platoon CP were directly behind our chopper. They were in the second chopper in formation. Dumont could have been with the CP chopper, but he chose to be with us, to be on the first chopper to land.

John was now a short-timer and more than likely; this would be his last operation. He left the gun team at the right time—after Bro was killed. The PRC-25 radio weighed about the same as the M-60, and you could see him struggling, adjusting the straps to get the radio set up to set just right on his back. If he made it back Stateside without getting hurt or killed, he would have accomplished a great feat having served as both a machine-gunner and as a platoon's radioman without getting killed or wounded.

Aggie was sitting across from me as were some of the new men in Second Squad. I wondered if I looked as wide-eyed and scared as they did. As we neared our objective, I noticed through the chopper's open door, off in the distance, a low-flying Bird Dog (aerial observation plane).

The plane banked right and dropped a white phosphorus grenade, marking a target. Two Huey gunships following closely behind started strafing the marked zone. They turned and dived, each releasing a number of rockets into the dense jungle.

The rockets' explosions shot up black and then white smoke high into the air. Seconds later, two jets streaked across the skyline, and they dropped their deadly ordnance into the same area. The jungle's edge was now ablaze, burning with a strange ashen-colored glow.[142]

Behind us, I caught a quick glimpse of the choppers' tight pattern. The choppers and gunships were all lined up in a huge V-like shape formation. We looked like a flock of geese following one another getting ready to land in a swampland; but it was rice paddy fields below us, and a dense dreadful jungle we were to going to be dropped into.

This is a big operation, I thought, and I realized the magnitude of the operation.

They must be expecting a large enemy force to meet us, I was thinking. I silently started saying the Lord's Prayer, slowly, to myself. It was the only thing I knew I should probably be doing. How it was going to help me, I didn't know. I guess it was my attempt to make some kind contact before something happened and I wouldn't have a chance to say a prayer.

Aggie's facial expression had changed, he seemed committed, with a new look of determination of just getting this done. The choppers we were in started to circle in a long wide pattern, and Marines made sure their rifle clips were seated well in their weapons. We were all locked 'n' loaded, waiting to touch ground. As the whining sound of chopper blades changed and we descended at a rapid rate, the old-timers took in a deep breath.

The night before, Jones had warned me about landing in a hot LZ. "Watch your step when we set down. We're going to land out in the open rice paddies. Since we're the first gun team in First Platoon, we'll land first. Run for cover, but don't run too fast or you'll fall. Make sure your feet are planted on the ground before you take off running. A lot of gunners fall the first time they land in a hot LZ. They run out so fast that they fall flat on their faces. Look where everyone's running toward so you don't end up all by yourself out in the open. We'll need to set up the gun right away to cover for everyone else that will be landing behind us. Just follow Dumont watch your step and don't stop."

The loud noise of the chopper's double blades roared louder in our ears as the chopper struck the ground at LZ Hawk, then the chopper bounced back into the air. It seemed like forever before the first Marine exited the chopper.

Immediately, Marines were running out: one, two, three, and it was all a green blur. The ground was dry and soft, the noise deafening. I was the sixth man to hit the ground. To my left front, I could see other choppers landing and Marines running then diving for cover. Some were already lying prone behind a dry rice paddy dike. Their rifles pointed toward the tree line to our left. They had landed only seconds after us; others on my right were rushing forward.

I strained to listen to the sound of incoming fire, expecting to hear bullets whizzing by. At the far tree line, I was looking for the enemies' muzzle flashes, running, everything was happening in seconds, in flashes of light and whirling shadows from the choppers' blades, in green and dark blue colors, in sounds and silence, in fear and in hope.

To the far right, a squad of Marines from another helicopter landed; they landed closer to the tree line and they quickly moved in to secure it, and I felt a sigh of relief. Behind me, I could hear the helicopter's powerful engines roar back to life and reach the speed necessary to lift the chopper off the ground. Like a huge grasshopper, the chopper raised its hind legs, dropped its nose, and lifted its body off the ground. As the chopper flew past, I knew there was no turning back; it was now up to us to live or die.

Surprisingly, I felt calm. Once committed, Marine Corps training kicks in. When my legs hit the ground, the added weight of the gun and ammo shot me forward and I had to take three quick steps to regain my balance.

"Don't trip and fall," Jones had said, and I felt a momentary pride that I hadn't fallen. As I turned to change directions to run to the right toward Dumont and the far tree line, my legs crisscrossed behind me and I fell sideways across a rice paddy dike. Marines two hundred meters to our right near the tree line had popped a green smoke grenade.

Jones, coming up behind me, quickly reached down and grabbed the gun by its handle and ran toward the safety of a large dirt mound some seventy yards in front of us. I got up quickly and followed him. Dumont, Jones, and I dove into the center of a large crater. We looked out and could see other Marines out in front of us; they were no longer running for cover. Some were casually walking toward the tree line; others were beginning to group together. Marines out in the open rice paddy fields that landed after us had stopped running or seeking cover as we had. The tree line in front of us had been secured, and Marines were walking alongside the smothering jungle where the airstrike had prepared the area for us. There had been no incoming.

As I looked at Jones, he displayed a wide shit-eating grin. What he had warned me not to do I had done. He chuckled. "Bro warned me about the same thing, but I also tripped and fell the first time I jumped out of a chopper carrying the gun," he said.

Dumont got up, and Jones and I followed to join the others. The platoon was quickly gathering at the edge of the tree line. Other Marines, with heads raised high, were straining to locate and join their respective platoons and squads.

While no enemy contact had been made, I felt uneasy about gathering so openly the way we were. We were all bunched up, but it also surprised me how tangled up and separated we had all gotten when we landed and how quickly we had become so separated from our own units. Squads from Second and Third Platoons crossed our position, looking to join up with their platoons.

When I looked back to see where we had crawled out from, I realized the giant dirt mound we had found safety in was actually a huge bomb crater. The hole was at least thirty feet across and twenty feet deep. In its center was the displacement remains from a one-thousand-pound bomb dropped by B-52s—and not too long ago, judging by the fresh smell of the upturned dirt. With LZ Hawk secured, two CH-53 helicopters touched down with I 3/7 and 2/7 command personnel and Marines from Hotel 2/7.

Meanwhile, the choppers that had dropped us off were touching down at 2/7's combat base and loading Golf 2/7 Marines on board. From there, they would be landing a short distance from us at LZ Falcon.

Wait-A-Minute Vines, On the Jungle Floor
Hill 1192, South Vietnam
October 24, 1967, 0940 hours

First Platoon maneuvered into position, and we quickly began to move up the mountain as the rest of the company gathered and fell in behind. We moved out, climbing straight up a small, narrow trail into a dense tropical forest. The rest of the platoon and elements from different squads were scrambling to catch up with us.

By the time the last chopper lifted out of the flatlands. We were in deep, heavy underbrush and thick, moist jungle surrounded us.

Bushes with sharp edges and needle-like tips poked at us from all sides. Shrubs, herbs, ferns, and clinging vines, two inches thick and slippery blanketed the jungle floor. Creeping and hanging Wait-A-Minute vines entangled our feet, arms, helmets, canteens, grenades, backpacks, and weapons. Anything that stuck out, the vines grabbed hold of.

Huge spider webs completely covered some plants, and large ferns grew every which way. In one plant, skeletal large shells of disemboweled bugs could be seen embedded deep inside the spider's lair. Other plants seemed to be entangled in their own war, struggling for survival and seeking their own place in the sun.

Minutes later, it was our turn to seek the sun's rays as the jungle's canopy overshadowed us. The sun was no longer visible. The sky above had disappeared. We were completely under a huge cover of dark green grass, plants, and multi-leaved trees like I had seen only in the old Johnny Weissmuller *Tarzan* jungle films. All around us, weird-shaped trees with long, low-hanging, sharp needle leaves reached out to cut and scrape us as we passed through their world. Tall, straight, skinny trees and fat trees with broad dark green leaves encircled us. Some had beautiful yellow and red flowers growing from their branches, but the smell they emitted was disgusting. They smelled like wet sweat or soiled towels that had been left out in the rain for many days. Trees sixty to eighty feet tall formed an intermingled canopy that hung high over us, completely shielding us from the sky so that no one from the air above could see us moving along the narrow trail we were following.

As we climbed, behind me I could hear Dumont breathing hard and uttering choice words as his little legs hurried to catch up. We were taking one step at a time, making sure one foot was firmly pressed down hard against the dead foliage on the ground before we would take another forward step to keep ourselves from slipping or tripping on the low-hanging vines or the decaying plants crawling along the moist ground. The plants held down the heat and it seemed as if we were in a large greenhouse with no ventilation.

Boyd was in front of Second Squad carrying the disassembled rocket launcher struggling to keep upright. He had already slipped once, knocking down the Marine nearest him. As he went to take a forward step, he slipped again.

Both his feet went flying forward, and I could see him effortlessly being lifted off the earth. Mid-way, while he was in the air, all of a sudden he seemed to gain speed and managed to make a complete backward flip.

He landed upright. We stopped looked at him, and laughed.

"Do, that again," Duran said, with a smirk, we were too tired to applaud.

As our climbing progressed, we slowed down to almost a standstill. We soon stopped on the trail as the point man struggled to break free of thick underbrush and wait-a-minute vines that grabbed him.

A Marine with a machete moved in to cut through the half-inch thick creeping plant. The low-hanging creepers seized our boots, hands, and arms as we struggled along the trail.

Dumont took out the machete that he had been carrying strapped across his backpack and from a large plant with a thick stem; he cut off a broad low-hanging leaf with a thick stem. The leaf easily slid off the large plant. He turned the leaf around, and out from its center flowed thick, clear water. He tasted the water and then offered me some. The clear nectar left a bittersweet taste in my mouth, but the water was clear and cold.

"You don't want to drink too much of it," he said. "It'll turn your insides out, but it's cold."

By 1300 hours, we had climbed one thousand feet straight up. Salty sweat stung my eyes, I was exhausted, tired, and my legs ached. It was all hard, slow climbing; and being fully loaded down with gear, helmet, flak jacket, food, ammo, and the machine-gun, all I could do to keep up with the others was to keep my head down and use all my strength to climb one step at a time behind the Marine in front of me.

We climbed sideways then on all fours as we pulled and pushed each other up the steep mountainside. Sometimes, it seemed like we moved only a foot or two at a time. We would take one step forward and then we'd have to take two quick steps backward to keep from falling. There were times when I only saw the heels of the boots of the man in front of me, for the longest time and in this manner, we worked our way up the steep peak.

Heat Causalities
Hill 1192, South Vietnam
October 24, 1967, 1400 hours

The hot, humid air was strangling our throats and lungs, making it difficult to breathe. Marines started to drop out along the trail from heat exhaustion. Some were dehydrated and struggling to breathe. The salt tablets didn't help much, and some Marines were doubled over, heaving, leaving their un-dissolved white salt tablets and food contents on the side of the trail. Some of the men no longer able to keep up, simply stopped moving. They sat alongside the trail pale-faced and wide-eyed.

We passed Doc Mac who was busy talking to the lieutenant while he was taking Jerry Lucero's utility jacket off. Lucero looked dazed, suffering from heat stroke. Besides him was Souble laid flat off the trail, and Doc was visibly angry with Souble as the only full canteen Souble had left with anything in it was the one filled with banana rum. Lucero would have to be medevaced, I heard Doc Mac say to our lieutenant, as Sgt. Whiteside's a few feet ahead of me, took out his K-Bar, hurled it quickly, and it stuck fast into the dirt and dry leaves in-between the two Marines.

When, he picked it up an eight inch long, two inch wide centipede was attached. "You don't want this to bite them," he said, as he showed the Corpsman, the blue legged monster. "What the heck is that," Wilson asked. "Worst stinging bite anyone can suffer from," Whiteside, answered. "Why, you've never seen one with blue legs before," Whiteside chuckled.

"We have a goal to reach, and we're lead platoon, we're not stopping now, the CO will have to figure out how to get Lucero out," he said, as he stepped out to continue moving on, "Let me see that thing," he asked, as Whiteside handed him the knife, with the centipede still attached.

The trail we were following ended, and then it was slower moving as we cut our own way up the mountainside with machetes, small hatchets, and bayonets.

Certainly, no human had trespassed on this ground since creation. Every two hundred feet, the exhausted point man was rotated; after a while, the squad walking point was rotated as well and I found myself encouraging those who were dropping out to keep moving and to fall in behind.

Sit and Wait For the Rest To Catch Up
Hill 1192, South Vietnam
October 24, 1967, 1630 hours

Early afternoon, we began to follow another trail; and we stopped moving, platoons and squads were no longer together. The company was scattered up and down all along the trail we had cut.

First Platoon had done such an outstanding job of getting the company out and up the mountainside that the rest of the company was having trouble keeping up. The word was passed to us to stop and wait for the rest of the company to catch up. As the platoon gathered, we received word that Lucero and two other Marines from our platoon, along with three more from the other platoons, had to be medevaced. The engineers had blown out an opening in the jungle's canopy, and the chopper had landed on the side of the mountain to pick them up.

The lieutenant passed the word for us to "chow down." We had stopped on such a steep angle that it was difficult to sit upright. If you sat down on the jungle foliage, you would find yourself sliding down the mountain. I had to use Bro's machine-gun as a seat in order to be able to sit upright to eat. Others were just eating lying on their sides. We couldn't sit upright without losing our balance.

I could see from my vantage point on the mountain far below us for thirty to forty miles. The lush valley was beautiful. Rich green colors; light emerald greens and deep, royal dark forest greens blended with spots of yellow, tan and brown fields. The area was covered by blue greens and violet greens and every shade of green you could imagine. The greens gave the valley an unimaginable velvety appearance. It was an enormous bluish green mosaic puzzle that some master engineer designed. It seemed impossible that such a beautiful place was located in a world full of chaos.

Streams of water rushed in from every which way to feed the dark brown rivers creating streaks of rare beauty. Only a few villages seemed to be cultivating a few patches of rice in such a vast and fertile land.

Hotel 2/7 Company moved past us on the trail; McClintock, Kates, Perry, and another Marine from Second Squad by the name of Harold Sotzen passed by. None of them were wearing helmets or flak jackets. Perry's green cotton trousers were freshly ripped open from the jungle leaves that had poked at us as we moved along the jungle trails. The bottom of his trouser legs were rolled up and unbloused.

Stream Water With A Price; Sotzen Is Missing
Hill 1192, South Vietnam
October 24, 1967, 1730 hours

"There's a stream close by," Perry, said. I looked up at the tall Marine standing by the trail. Two other Marines were standing next to him. "Lieutenant Wilson said we can send a man from each squad to fill up our canteens."

Marty dropped his gear, swung his M-16 over his shoulder, and volunteered to go on the water run for our gun team. I drank what water I had left in my canteens and poured the last drops that remained into the small fruit cocktail cup that came with my C-rat meal. Marty collected our canteens and left with them on the water run.

As the water detail moved out following the trail ahead of us, they disappeared from view where the trail turned. If it hadn't been for a Marine sitting at the apex of the trail, one couldn't tell where the trail turned. The area around us looked so much alike that if you turned suddenly, you couldn't tell from what direction you had come.

An hour later, about the time the last of the company's stragglers were catching up, Marty returned with our canteens. As we dropped halizone tablets into the canteens, Marty told us that a Marine from First Platoon was missing.

"That new guy, Sotzen, that was with Kates, he's missing," Marty said. As I switched the water back and forth inside the canteens to dissolve the halizone tables, I realized I didn't know the missing man.

"He was with us when we left for the river, but he wasn't with us when we started back," Marty said as he knelt down and dropped a halizone tablet into each of his two canteens.

"No one saw him when we left the stream; we thought that maybe he had come back on his own, but now he's missing. MIA. Second Squad is out looking for him, he never told them he was going with us." Marty added.

An hour later, Second Squad returned. They had not found their missing man and Sotzen's fire-team leader, Earl Lergner was visibly upset.

The trail Second Squad had searched went past Second Platoon's forward position. Second Platoon Marines had warned Sotzen, they told Lergner, telling him First Platoon was behind them, and that Hotel 2/7 was now in lead.

At the forward position where Hotel 2/7 Marines had set in, they too said, they had advised Sotzen that no one was ahead of their forward position. But Sotzen once again insisted he could get to First Platoon by going up a steep slope from where they were set in. Finally, a sergeant with Hotel Company told his Marines to let him go but warning him no one was beyond their forward position.

The Marines, there said, shortly before the squad came looking for their missing Marine they had heard small arms fire, and then silence.

As it was by then starting to get dark, Second Squad searched only a little further, but had to return before nightfall.

Once Second Squad returned to where we were, we were assigned to bring up the rear.

Captain Baggette wasn't pleased with First Platoon because of our missing Marine. We got up and moved further up the hill to hook up with the rest of the company.

Our gun team and the rest of Second Squad were bringing up the rear. First Platoon was now at the tail end of a two-company formation, and we had rear guard security. If the enemy was in the area, they would hit us in the front going up or from the rear; the sides were too steep for anyone to be able to move about without losing their balance.

Night fell quickly and by the time we settled in, it was so dark I couldn't see the man sitting next to me. The last few minutes before settling in, we held onto the person in front of us, fearing to let go because of the darkness and steep terrain. It would be easy to get lost.

I placed the gun facing down a turn in the trail, but if we got hit, it would be impossible to lie prone behind it. To avoid sliding down, I would have to fire it from the side of the trail at an angle or sitting up, holding the gun. Second Squad had peeled off to my left with some squad members setting up to the right side of the gun. The CP was on the other side of them; other Marines set in above us. As soon as they sat down, Marines began to slide down the mountainside.

The mountainside was steep; it seemed to have no plateau. To keep from sliding down, I dug a burrow with my feet into the dense foliage, making flat footholds for my feet. Some of the Marines above us laid back and quickly found themselves sliding down the mountains steep side. When they slid, they tried to grab hold of the plants and small trees to break their fall only to cut themselves on the sharp leaves. Others helped them get back up to where they had been.

I saw Dumont take the rope he was carrying and tie it around his waist and then to a tree above us. Then he sat down, with a big grin on his face.

"Heyyy," we're down here Aggie yelled out at a Marine farther up the mountain who was relieving himself. The yellow piss came rushing down alongside where Aggie had just made himself a comfortable spot to sit in.

Someone farther up, cried out "Shhhhh."

"Well, he should know we're down here," Aggie said angrily, his voice shifting to a softer tone.

A Can of Coke in the Middle of the Jungle
Hill 1192, South Vietnam
October 25, 1967, D+1, 0100 hours

When I was awakened for my watch; I sat surrounded by the quietness of the night. I couldn't tell where anyone was, who was to our left or to our right, in front or behind us. The light from the half-moon above was mostly blocked by thick, overhanging vines and tall trees.

I reached into the top part of my backpack and brought out a can of Coke I had bought at 2/7's headquarters. I placed the damp towel I had worn around my neck during the climb over the flip-top can, and slowly opened it—not a sound.

I took a drink of the Coke and couldn't help but think that here I was in a part of the world that probably very few people had ever been, high in a forested mountain in South Vietnam, enjoying a Coke that had been cooled by the mountain air. A rich, clean, cool breeze filled the night with a sense of freedom and contentment. I took in a deep sigh, and felt-like I had a part of America with me, a little bit of home. As I drank the Coke, I wondered where the Marine from Second Squad was and hoped he was alive and not a prisoner.

Early the next morning as we stood to saddle up, Duran, having slid down the trail during the night, came climbing back up the mountain toward us. With sleep wrinkles on his face, he looked scared.

"I thought you guys had left me behind," he said. "I woke up and no one was around. I looked and couldn't see anyone. I didn't know what I was going to do; I thought I was all alone until you stood up. I guess I must have slid down the hill."

"You didn't wake-up when you slid down," Aggie asked.

"No, Duran, answered back, a bit disturbed, as if Aggie was saying it was his fault that he slid down a steep mountainside.

"I always, wake up if I turn in my sleep, I don't see how you can slide down and not know it."

"Well I did, so what," Duran said as he stopped and peed where Aggie had been sleeping.

"I don't care," Aggie said, as the word was passed for us to move out.

Recon Marines, Riddled With Bullets
Hill 1192, South Vietnam
October 25, 1967, D+1, 0700 hours

India Company once again was to take point. We passed 2/7 Marines along the trail, and were once again climbing straight up using a trail Hotel 2/7 had discovered before nightfall.

Because it would make it easier going and led in the general direction we were heading, the skipper decided to follow it. Using this trail was a dangerous venture as the possibility for an ambush was high, but I was glad for the footing it provided.

It wasn't long before the point man in Third Platoon saw a Marine's body laying on the trail ahead. The company stopped and Captain Baggette called for our lieutenant to come up. Wilson then called for Perry and Lergner to come up the trail. Both positively identified the body as that of Sotzen, the missing man from our platoon.

Sotzen's M-16 rifle was missing as was some of his clothing. An M-14 was found near him. Sotzen had been shot twice in the stomach and it seemed had bled to death where he had fallen.[143] But why did the gooks leave behind the M-14? Had the M-14 belonged to one of the men missing from the recon team?

We sat down to wait as the engineers blew a landing zone for the choppers to pick up Sotzen's body. Before the chopper arrived, Second Platoon discovered the bodies of two of the three missing recon team members. Both bodies were found partly hidden from view under large bushes covered over with cut-up matted vines. The clinging vines seemed to have wrapped themselves around the bodies. The enemy had tried to cover the bodies by throwing a thin layer of dirt over them, but that was what drew the Marines' attention. Marines hacked away at the foliage and got them out.

The Recon Marines' bodies were riddled with bullets, and they had been mutilated. Their bloated faces, still camouflaged with green-and-tan grease paint, were hardly recognizable as those of human beings. They had been dead for about a week.

We all carried the Geneva Convention card, but it was evident that the enemy didn't abide by its terms. They had been shot, then cut up and parts of their body were missing.

As the medevac choppers approached, we were placed on full alert. We knew that often the NVA/VC would leave American bodies as "bait" near strategic ambush sites where they could be found. They would then wait until the medevac chopper was summoned, and as they prepared to land, the enemy would open fire.

The chopper landed without incident. All the dead Marines were loaded on board; fresh medical supplies, food and water were dropped off. Either Charlie wasn't around, or there were only a few of them and they didn't want to engage two companies of Marines. The rest of the day was spent climbing.

Squeeze the Trigger and His Head Is Gone
Operation Knox
October 26, 1967, D+2, 0700 hours

We began climbing at daybreak, if we continued at the pace we were going, we would reach the wrecked plane by early evening. Anthony Virgil, a Marine from Seattle, Washington, was a sniper assigned from HQ to the company for the operation.

Every so often, he would stop and point his scope rifle at enemy soldiers climbing the mountain on the opposite side. The enemy seemed to be racing us to the top. Captain Baggette would not allow the sniper to shoot, so we wouldn't give away our position, he told him.

Anthony sighted in on one soldier sitting by a trail, and showed Lieutenant Wilson. The scope was positioned dead center on the soldier head.

"All I have to do is squeeze the trigger, and his head is gone," he said to Wilson.

Midmorning and Aggie volunteered to carry the gun for a while. I had a sling attached to the gun and had carried it strapped to my back or on my shoulder with my right hand holding on to its barrel. But even with the flak jacket's padding, the gun would bite into my shoulder, and the small towel I had placed on my shoulder to cushion its weight wasn't helping much. I welcomed his help, but it wasn't long before Aggie began to slow down, then he stopped, turned to me, and said, "Man, I didn't think this gun weighed this much."

I took the gun and gave him the 100-round belt of ammo he had been carrying.

"I don't know how you do it," Aggie said with his eyes opened wide, shaking his head as if in disbelief. I could tell he was glad to be relieved of the heavy burden. "It doesn't look that heavy until you carry it for a while," he said. "Maybe if we weren't climbing, it wouldn't be so bad," Aggie theorized, glad to get back his lightweight M-16.

I was glad to have the gun back. I flipped it over my shoulder and began to climb. While I welcomed the relief, I didn't like carrying the M-16 rifle. My gun felt like it belonged on my shoulder. Immediately, a sharp pain shot down my back from the gun's weight, and I shifted it to a comfortable spot and we moved on. In the back of my mind was the thought that the enemy might have already reached the plane and gotten hold of the mini-guns on board, and I wanted the M-60 in my hands if they had.

Fresh Stream Water
Operation Knox
October 26, 1967, D+2, 1400 hours

A short time later, we left the trail and slowed down to a crawl. We found a small mountain stream and followed it up the mountain and then stopped to rest midafternoon.

Ice-cold, clean, fresh water was flowing down the stream. Marines up and down the stream filled their helmets with the cold water then poured it over their heads. It wasn't long before everyone was dumping what remaining water they had in their canteens, rinsing out the sediment remains from the halizone tablets, and filling their canteens with fresh stream water.

We were in an awkward position at the cleft of the mountain. Third Squad was set up a little to our right. They had been walking our right flank as best as they could. On our left side, the mountainside was so steep that we didn't have to worry about the enemy being on that side. The rest of the company was out in front of us, and only a fire-team and my gun guarded our rear position. The fire-team had set up to cover our rear, fifty yards downstream.

There was no place to set up the gun, no clear field of fire if we were ambushed from our right or from our left side. If we got hit, there was no cover except behind some of the smaller rocks in the center of the streambed. I could shoot downstream if I had to, but there was a curve in the streambed about two hundred meters away so that field of fire was limited. Instead, I just sat down near the stream's edge with the gun at my side, not bothering to set it up; if we got hit, I would determine then where to set it up.

"Hey! This is great water," Marty said as he finished capping the second of his canteens, not bothering to drop in a halizone tablet. The clear running water was ice-cold and thick.

"I've never tasted water as clean as this," Marty said.

Rahm, sitting nearby, held up a four-inch long green and yellow spotted leech he had taken from the streambed. He set it on top of the back of his hand and started to stroke it like a pet. We checked ourselves to see if any leeches had attached themselves to us, but found none.

Incoming or Not
Operation Knox
October 26, 1967, D+2, 1430 hours

"Hey, Cook," Marty said, "do you think if we get out of here okay, we could maybe someday come back here to this very spot after the war?" Marty had been taking pictures of the beautiful and picturesque jungle all around us and of the valley below.

"Take a flick," Marty said as he handed me his camera and stood at semi-attention, his pant legs rolled to just below his knees. He was standing in the stream wearing no boots, socks or shirt. He held his helmet over his heart with his left arm and his right arm was held rigidly straight down at his side. He tightened his upper body, leaned back and waited for his picture to be taken. He looked dorky, but it was Marty's favorite comical photo pose.

I raised the camera to my eye and was about to push the shutter down when a single shot rang out from our right side. Everyone scrambled for cover and safety.

"Outgoing, Outgoing!" the sniper assigned to our platoon cried out. He had shot at an enemy soldier trailing us.

Meanwhile, Izzie, carrying the M-79 grenade launcher, had jumped up from where he had been sitting on a rock in the middle of the stream. As he ran for cover, he accidentally took the safety off the grenade launcher, slipped on the stream's slick bottom, and as he fell backward, he grabbed a tighter hold of the M-79 to keep it from falling into the water and pulled the trigger.

Thunk-boom! The M-79 makes a distinct sound, and everyone turned to see the shot go straight up.

"Outgoing, outgoing!" Izzie shouted. Everyone scrunched down or dived for cover because the round had gone straight up, and we knew it would land somewhere near. Eighty yards away, the CP group, who hadn't heard the M-79 go off, was packed and ready to move out. John had just strapped on his radio and was pulling on the straps of his backpack to adjust his load when the grenade landed in the streambed near him and exploded. A geyser of water shot up from the grenade's impact.

Doc Mac, yelled out; "Incoming, incoming!" as he ran for cover.

John started to run in the opposite direction. Stopped turned, and ran the other way. Then stopped, and turned again. The high-wire antenna on his radio was flipping back and forth like a timing needle gone wild, each time he turned.

He finally stopped, when he slipped and fell into the stream but managed to keep the radio out of the water.

Wash It Down and Move Out
Operation Knox
October 26, 1967, D+2, 1500 hours

I washed the halizone sediment out of my canteens and filled them up with stream water. The water had a rich iron taste and like everyone else, I didn't bother adding the halizone tablets.

By late afternoon, we left the streambed and resumed making our own trail straight up the mountain. The rest of the afternoon was hard going. At times, we'd find a trail and follow it and sometimes we had no choice but to cut our own path through the heavy underbrush. Sometimes, the foliage became so thick the point man, and another, Marine used machetes, to cut a path through the jungle.

The weight of the gun, ammo and gear was beginning to wear me down. I had already slipped a couple of times, but managed to regain my balance. I wondered how much farther we had to go, before we could rest.

Jones came up and took the gun, and he carried it for a while and I welcomed the relief. The M-16 felt as light as a feather compared to the M-60, but as soon as I began to enjoy the feel of the M-16's lightness, Jones returned my gun.

I folded the bipod legs down, loosened the carrying strap, which many Marines didn't use, and carried the gun slung over my shoulder in the same manner others carried their rifles at the sling-arms position. Walking in the jungle or in a column with the gun carried this way made the gun less noticeable for what it was. I had marked the sling so that I could easily drop the gun; adjust the carrying strap and the gun would be set for me to fire from the hip in the assault position, John Wayne style.

CHAPTER TWELVE

The Enchanted Forest
Operation Knox, South Vietnam
October 26, 1967, D+2, 2000 hours

By late evening, of the third day we were once again crawling on all fours, inching our way up the mountain. Ezell, climbing above us slipped and a cluster of rocks gave way, and he slid downward. Rocks, crumbled down the steep embankment.

"Look out below," Jerry Ezell cried out.

I pressed myself hard against the slanted ground as rocks, plants, and debris slid over us.

"Goddamn the Marine Corps," Dumont said out loud as he tightened his grip around a boulder and pressed himself hard to the mountainside. The rocks and debris fell over him then picked up momentum on their way down.

"Hey, watch where you're stepping," someone below Dumont yelled up.

We had been climbing for almost ten hours when all of a sudden thick darkness was up on us, and we stopped moving. We mustered together quickly into a tight half circle so we wouldn't lose anyone. We were sitting close to each other, our shoulders almost touching. We were tired and drained. All of us could barely keep our eyes open, as we sat and waited to see what the company commander would do. I knew if I relaxed and let myself doze off to catch a few precious seconds of sleep, my body would relax and I would find myself sliding down the steep mountainside.

We moved again after a few minutes, but only for a short distance. To make sure that everyone was facing in the same direction. We set in next to Ira Hullihen's squad. It was difficult to get comfortable; and if Charlie hadn't seen where we had stopped for the night, they certainly could hear us as we all constantly had to struggle to stop ourselves from sliding down the mountainside.

Where we set up the gun was not as steep as other places, so I welcomed the advantage, but still had to dig a foot-hold for myself. When I stopped fidgeting about and the dust settled, a thick blanket of thick darkness fell on us. Black clouds and tall trees hanging over us hid the light from the moon above. The darkness in the middle of the forest was so solid, I felt both scared and humble. As soon as I got used to the darkness and the silence that came with it, the jungle all around us began to come alive.

Slowly, the jungle floor began to glow. At first, dark grays emerged from the blackness that surrounded us. Then, dark greens followed by a faint lime glow in the moss on the jungle floor. The mixed colors flowed effortlessly along the dark ground, blending magic stones and sparkling leaves together.

I sat silent, mesmerized as the forest floor released little sparkles of light. The light reflected, bounced, and radiated tiny shades of colors, precious colorful gems of unique beauty.

It was the heavy mildew, fungus, and moisture of the deep underbrush revealing a carpet of phosphorescent stones for us to enjoy. It was like standing in the middle of an enchanted forest that would only reveal its rich reflective gems when the world surrounding it became silent and still. The deep, ancient world of the deepest jungle was now unveiling its secrets, sharing its mystery, a world of hidden beauty and colors never seen before by human eyes.

I sat captivated by what I was seeing. No one dared move lest we miss a moment of the beauty of the symphony being played for us.

I opened my eyes wider, taking it all in. Pearlescent shades of greens, fine gold, silver, bright blue sapphires, and fluorescent greens, all reflecting tiny bits of light on the ground around us. The area was no longer dark and sinister but a radiating scene full of light and life, and I sat fascinated by the colorful lights at my feet.

We could see clearly all around us, because of the light, not from above but from the light below at our feet. It was amazing how we were all captivated by the lights and you could almost hear a silent song being sung. A song filled with nature's mysterious colors. It was a world hidden from war, a world set apart to enchant us with its beauty.

Ira Hullihen sitting next to Jerry Ezell reached out to touch a reflective stone;

When he disturbed the ground cover, and held the rock in his hand, the glowing rays of light reflected by the moist, wet moss disappeared, though his fingertips, a puff of dust appeared in its wake. Seconds later, the sparkling lights returned and no one else dared reach out to disturb the glowing ground.

We sat quietly resting, awed by the beauty at our feet, enjoying a mystical world of rich bright colors, a world we had never seen.

Jones took first watch, and when he woke me for my watch, the forest had lost its splendor. A crescent moon hung high overhead, and the moon glow gave off just enough light to offset the colors on the ground.

I stood watch and as my thoughts turned to the Marine bodies we had found the day before; the beauty of the land turned into deep shadows of darkness and the moss now radiated fear, sorrow, and the horror of war. Every shadow moved, every sound carried, and trees transformed themselves and became moving human beings. Bushes and small trees became two-legged animals that smelled of fish, garlic, and death. I felt as if every creature in the forest could see where I was, but I could not see them. They were hiding in the darkness and in the shadows, and I was bathed in the moon's bright light.

I lit a cigarette behind my flak jacket, allowing only a tiny flicker of the match to light the tip before extinguishing it. I puffed hurriedly on the poorly lit cigarette until it glowed red then cupped it tightly so that none of its light was visible. With my hands covering the lit cigarette, I took a long drag and settled in to stand watch.

Soon dark clouds moved in and covered the moon's light. If I tried to sit up straight, I found myself sliding down. We couldn't see each other but could hear others nearby. As they moved while they slept they would begin to slid, then would awaken and grasp frantically for something to grab hold of to break their fall. Others would help them move back up, to regain their spot, and they would settle in again.

Each time they moved, as they breathed, I wondered if they were really there or if the enemy had somehow snuck up, to where I was.

Was it the enemy sitting there in the darkness next to me? Then another Marine would fall asleep, his body would relax, and he would roll down the mountainside, and the noise he made would startle me, but only briefly. The cry and the cussing that followed gave me comfort to know Marines were still there in the darkness and in the shadows. Half asleep or half awake, I knew that even Charlie couldn't tell the difference who was awake and who slept and who was friend and who was foe.

Found Puff Plane
Operation Knox, grid coordinates ZC 133938
October 27, 1967, D+3, 0800 hours

The following morning, we moved out and started to climb straight up and my thoughts turned to the weight I carried as sweat flowed down my forehead and around my eyes as I struggled to keep up with the others.

We found the downed 47D Spooky Gunship, embedded into the sides of the mountain. Trees in the area were ripped apart where the plane had plowed through. The plane was torn in pieces its engines a mangled mess. Military equipment was scattered all over the crash site, and aside from the burned parts of the plane and the damage that had occurred from the crash, nothing seemed to have been moved or ransacked. We had beaten the enemy to the site. The aircraft had been there since October 03, 1967, when the plane went down.

Second and Third Platoon were assigned security and First Platoon began to search for identifiable property or bodies at the crash site. We sought anything that would help identify the crew members of the fallen plane or any significant papers that had survived. I set up the gun and Aggie stood watch over it as I walked throughout the crash site. We found eight different body parts thrown throughout the area. All were U.S. Air Force personnel. None had survived the crash.

All that was left of those on board were charred remains, burned bones, twisted and torn body parts. We gathered all remains as best we could, and were pretty sure all eight men were among the burned body parts and bones the Corpsmen gathered. Doc Marren used his bare hands to lift burned and mangled body parts and handed them to Doc Mac and Doc Gibbs who placed what was found into two small burlap sacks for transportation back down the mountain. Having recovered what we could, we gathered whatever salvageable equipment we could find to carry out and destroyed the rest with thermite grenades or buried what we could not carry.

We tied the burlap body bags to the middle of two long poles so we could carry them down the mountain, gook-style, in the same manner that we had seen the village farmers carry heavy loads for long distances.

In this manner, we began our trip down the mountain with two Marines on each side balancing the long pole they carried on their shoulders. The charred remains of dead airmen were inside the bag tied to the middle of the long pole.

Killed in the aircraft were; Capt Arthur Raymond Coughlin, Maj.William Whit Duck, TSgt James Charles Krouse, LtCol Van Harold Newville, MSgt Charles Joseph Rogiers, A2C William Ward Scoville, A2C Walter Clarence Wright.

We Carry A Heavy Load
Operation Knox, grid coordinates ZC 133938
October 27, 1967, D+3, 1300 hours

As we moved down the trail, the smell of burned human flesh and death clung to our lungs, and lingered in the air we breathed.

Climbing down was not as easy as I thought it would be; and the smell, if not the weight, of our cargo was heavy on our minds.

After going some distance, we settled in for the night in steep terrain. It wasn't a good place to stop, but it had gotten dark on us all of a sudden and so we had no choice. We were all bunched up together.

No sooner had we settled in, we began to hear noises in the bushes, and in the trees overhead, then all around us. We were in no position to effectively defend ourselves. I knew we were surrounded.

I didn't have to wait until the word was passed that the enemy was probing our lines. We were told to hold our fire until we got a clear shot.

I set the gun facing down the tail we had been on. Not knowing where the enemy fire was going to come from made it hard to set up a good defensive position.

Aggie, silently hooked up a two hundred round belt to the gun and we sat and waited.

The night was dark, and I could hear movement behind and all around us. Whoever had been following us wasn't being very quiet about it. I could hear them, but couldn't see the enemy to get a clear shot at them. We were on the side of a mountain struggling to hold on, and if we got hit from above. I knew we would be in deep trouble.

All the enemy would have to do was pitch grenades down on us or open up from above. It would be impossible to turn and engage them. If this happened, I knew many of us returning fire would find ourselves sliding down the mountainside, at the same time while struggling to stay together.

I nudged Aggie and the fire-team next to us, to tell them, I was moving the gun a bit forward. We moved near where Duran and Jones had set up their gun. The fire-team moved up, but hesitantly, as we were moving toward the noises we were hearing, but it gave me a better vantage point to cover for all of us.

"What do we do, if they rush us," Aggie asked.

"They're all around us we're going to be shooting at each other."

"I know," I said.

"Where's your K-Bar?" I asked.

"You think," Aggie said, a thought of terror crossing his mind. He unsnapped the strap holding his knife on his scabbard.

"I wasn't very good at fighting, hand to hand, not even in Boot Camp," he said.

"You, know, that drill instructor, he just passed me, he knew I wasn't good at hand to hand. He just wanted me to pass, to get rid of me."

"Aggie, you're a Mexican," Duran told him. "All Mexicans know how to use a knife."

"I'm not that type," Aggie half answered, a worried look in his eyes.

"If we get hit, just stick together," I told him, and we quieted to listen. While we could hear movement above us, we waited for the attack. All night long we heard movement in the jungle in the trees.

Aggie's Tossing Tournament
Operation Knox
October 28, 1967, D+4, 0600 hours

Before sunrise, Aggie crossed over the trail to relieve himself. As he went to squat down, in the corner of his eye he saw movement on the trail leading to our position. His M-16 was on the other side of the trail, and the only thing he had in his hand was the tightly wrapped roll of toilet paper that came with the C-rats.

Aggie quickly reasoned if he threw the wadded toilet paper at the figure he saw, hiding behind a tree, hoping the enemy might believe it was a grenade and take cover, giving him time to jump across the trail and grab hold of his weapon.

He threw the wad of toilet paper as hard as he could, got up quickly jumping across the trail. His rapid movement awoke me and several others and we scrambled to get our weapons. I saw Aggie grab his weapon and take aim to shoot at the figure that he had seen moving up the trail.

As, I slid under my gun, I cursed the steep slope as I started to slide down hill right away. I scrambled to get a good foot hold, and knew I wasn't going to be able to fire and stay with the gun, at that angle.

I strained to see what Aggie, was about to open fire at. I pointed the gun in that general direction to provide supportive fire, for him.

Something soft struck Aggie's helmet. On the ground, I saw that someone had tossed a wrapped C-rat toilet tissue at him.

Aggie picked up the wad of paper and threw it back at the figure. Again, the toilet paper was tossed back. I sat there with my finger on the trigger, and my elbows pressed hard against the mountain to keep myself from sliding wondering what was going on.

The sound of loud inhuman screeching screams then filled the air.

Marines woke and grabbed their weapons.

All at once, the jungle shook with movement all around us from our right side and in between Second Platoon and us.

Then the noise and screeching sound came from below and above us as well.

I heard the branches of the trees above us snapping, and branches breaking. I saw the movement of large bodies move into positions.

There was also a lot of movement in the underbrush as well, and I figured the enemy had crawled up close to us.

It's going to be a bloody battle, I was thinking, as I tighten my grip, and pulled the gun in closer.

No one opened up. We had our weapons pointed every-which-way, at the sounds all around us.

"Monkeys!" Dumont shouted.

We were surrounded by a large group of rock apes. They were upset with us for moving into their territory. The noise continued for a while and stopped—then more movement followed by silence.

When it came time for us to move out, I called out, "Hey, Aggie."

"What," he answered.

"Good thing, you didn't throw a grenade at that Rock-Ape."

"I know," he said, as we moved out.

The Promise Of Cold Milk & Ice Cream In the Mountains
Operation Knox
October 28, 1967, D+4, 1500 hours

We made good head way on our way down and the word was passed that if we continued at our present rate of descent, there would be enough daylight left at the end of the trail for Navy choppers to drop off fresh supplies, including a hot meal, cold milk, and ice cream from one of the Navy ships offshore.

The possibility of having ice cream in the boonies was exhilarating. We made our way down at a hurried pace, longing for a break and a hot meal.

The Marines carrying the remains of the dead Airmen were switched often, and each time, the smell of the bodies drifted downwind and reminded me of why we had climbed the mountain and the precious cargo we were carrying.

We arrived at the arranged location near a stream bed long before sunset. Soon two Sea Knight choppers began circling overhead and started their descent.

I couldn't believe we were going to get real ice cream, and a hot meal.

We were in a large clearing in the middle of a deep crevice sandwiched in between the sides of two steep mountains. There was a clearing along the stream, a perfect place for both choppers to land.

As the choppers started coming in, we heard the report of gunfire.

The NVA above us were shooting at the choppers with small arms, and automatic rifle fire. I could hear the thump, thump, thump sound of the enemy's 50 caliber being fired at the Navy chopper.

The enemy, hidden above us was set in along the ridgelines. The distance was too far for us to shoot effectively at them from below.

The choppers only had to drop past them to get to us, I was thinking, when all of a sudden the first chopper took off.

In the background, I could hear Captain Beggette on the radio trying to persuade the choppers to come in, drop their load, and we would cover for them as best we could. But by then, our hopes for a hot meal faded as the sound of their blades disappeared.

Then at the last moment, one of the choppers swooped down quickly, and I could see its crew members quickly shoving what food they had on board out their open door. Crates of milk cartons and ice cream tubs were quickly tossed out 400 feet above ground level.

Long-range meals and two-gallon-sized ice cream tubs, exploded on impact with the rocks in the streambed. The food fell about 150 yards in front of us; and by the time we got to where it had been dropped, ice cream, milk, and scattered food items were floating down the stream. Chocolate, strawberry, and vanilla-flavored ice cream was washed downstream.

Ignoring any incoming fire, the enemy might unleash on us, we ran toward the site. Real milk was oozing out of broken half-pint cardboard milk containers into the middle of the stream, turning the pure clear stream into a pale pasty color. Long-range meals were destroyed. Jones waded into the stream and picked up half a dozen split-open milk cartons; some of them still contained milk in them.

They were waxed cardboard milk containers with real homogenized milk in them, not powdered milk.

He drank what milk remained then tossed the busted cartons into the water, and picked up another. I could see other milk cartons floating down stream with the streams current.

I picked up torn packages of long-range meals, and I asked Dumont what they were they.

"Lurps," he said.

"The Army usually has them," Jones answered.

"I've seen them before. We were given them once to eat during Operation DeSoto. They're called long-range meals because you can take them with you on long-range patrols," Dumont added.

"They're light. All you do is add boiling water and presto! An instant hot meal. The problem with Lurps is that you have to carry a lot of extra water with you," Jones said.

"Recon gets them," Dumont said.

The freeze-dried lurp package I found had a precooked dehydrated chili meal packaged in an airtight plastic bag. Others found a pack containing beef stew, crackers, and dried fruit. I opened up the package and tasted the dry powder. If the meals tasted anything like they did in their dry powdered form, they would have been delicious. Compared to the C-rations we ate, long-range meals would have been like eating at a fine restaurant. We set in, for the night and I opened the last can of food I still had with me.

Ham and lima beans, we were out of heat tabs[144] or C-4 to burn so I ate the C-rats cold out of the can.

A Prayer At the End Of the Mission
Operation Knox
October 29, 1967, D+5, 0800 hours

The following morning, we finished our descent into the valley below. Helicopters landed and evacuated the bodies we had carried down the mountain. The smell of the dead bodies lingered in the air, and it was embedded in my clothes, in my mind and in our memories.

We set in at the base of the mountain and waited for the choppers to come to take us back to Liberty Bridge.

Memories and reflections on what I had done and seen crossed my mind. As we waited, Navy choppers brought out hot chow, perhaps to make up for what had happened the day before.

Before we lined up to eat, a Protestant minister called us together for religious services. The services were held out in the open field for the Recon Marines, the plane's crew members that we had brought down the mountain, and for Sotzen, the only casualty our company had taken.

Anyone can really get religious when every day there is a possibility of danger, mutilation, and death, especially when the very next step you take may be your last. You have many chances to wonder about life, eternity, and hope; you desire to have a right relationship with God. Pray that there is a God. One of the men from Second Platoon standing in front of me during the religious service had a slogan written across the back of his helmet, "*Just you and me, Right lord!*"

"Greater love hath no man than this, that he lay down his life for his friends," the Protestant minister said.

I wished I knew how to pray, what to say, or how I should seek or find God. My memories growing up in a Catholic home were not fond memories. For me, it had been meaningless rituals coupled with strict rules and skinny or fat nuns quick to hit me with a ruler at the side of my head or across my knuckles. The mass on Sunday was recited in Latin, and the words had no meaning to me. Even the teaching about Christianity, which my sister Dominga had later tried to explain to me, I had forgotten. I had never taken the time to read the Scriptures for myself, and I wished I had.

Marty still carried the little Bible he had been given, but I no longer did. If there was a prayer I uttered, it was always the Lord's Prayer. Other than that, I only asked of God that if I was to be shot, please not be in the head.

I figured if I got shot anywhere else, with the response that I had seen from medevac choppers, the chances of survival were pretty good, but not if you were shot in the head. I saw what a shot to the head did.

"These men died defending the lives and rights of others to live. They volunteered for duty," The minister said.

"Here, am I, send me, they said, and they answered their country's call to duty," he went on to say.

When we finished eating, brand-new CH-46 Sea Knight helicopters dropped down, and we boarded. A half hour later, they dropped us off at Liberty Bridge. Operation Knox had officially ended;

The Seabees' Contribution
Liberty Bridge
November 1, 1967, 0300 hours

Early on the morning of the thirtieth of October, we received four incoming 81mm mortar rounds. A Marine on guard duty from Second Platoon reported they had come from across the bridge on the other side of Echo Company. The mortar rounds struck near the company's CP area, but no one was hurt.

Our sandbagged positions at Liberty Bridge had weakened and were in desperate need of repair because of the rain. For the next six days we worked on our bunkers, stood watch at night, or went on patrols during the day or ambushes at night, or both.

The Seabees used one of their trench diggers, to dig a trench in front of our bunker near the front gate but also all around the perimeter.

Every day, we filled sandbags and large empty wooden artillery boxes with loose dirt to reinforce the front and walls of our bunkers. We used long wooden beams donated by the Seabees or commandeered by us when they weren't looking. The beams gave us a solid roof capable of supporting heavy loads and withstanding direct hits from enemy mortar fire. Two solid layers of sandbags were laid on top of the bunker.

To protect the bunker from rain, we borrowed a large canvas tarp the Seabees had ordered for one of their billets. By the time they began to look for it to complete their building project, it had long been buried in between the sandbags on our bunker's roof. The tarp kept the bunker dry, and we asked the Seabees to dig a small drainage gutter around the bunker and connect it to the trench line out front, which they willingly did. If they had known their missing tarp was only a few feet away, they wouldn't have been so obliging.

An opening on the top of the bunker made it possible to see all around and the sandbags provided protection from incoming small arms fire. Aside from a direct hit, the bunker's construction offered excellent protection from most incoming weapons fire.

Before long, Guns once again had the best constructed and the largest bunker in the compound. Even though we had barracks, it was at our main bunker at the front gate where we spent the greater part of our day. Mamasan often came up to the front gate, selling candles, radios, watches, cigarettes and Cokes.

We designed the bunker to be an effective fighting position and a very comfortable place in which to spend our spare time. Every man in First Platoon, it seemed, came to help or otherwise contribute to its construction in some manner or another. They often would have to man the position during day gate-watch duty or wait there to catch a ride out to battalion or regiment.

While all Marines had their assigned working parties and work details, it wasn't uncommon for Jones, when he had work to do around the bunker, to bring out the music box; soon, Marines who had finished their work details came around. Somehow, Jones always seemed to sucker them into helping him do his work as well. They all knew what he was doing, but just the same, they kept adding to the bunker's construction.

The Seabees may have been great in general construction, but they were lousy at building fighting positions. When we were done, the perimeter looked nothing like the fighting positions they had built. We also set up fighting positions within the perimeter just in case we got overrun. With increased enemy activity in the area, we began having three-man watch positions. Two men would be stationed on top of the bunkers. One would stand watch while the other slept close by. The third man often slept inside the bunker.

Attack on Hill 25
Nong Lam (2), Hill 25 AT 839568
November 2, 1967, 0200 hours

Early on the morning of November 2, Aggie and I were standing watch at our front gate position at Liberty Bridge. A few miles away just the other side of the Song Thu Bon River where it becomes the Song Vu GiaRiver, on the barren little hill I first took notice of when I arrived on Hill 65. Mike Company's Second Platoon was being hit by a large enemy force.

From our position, we could see numerous illumination rounds lighting the night sky northwest of us. It was too far for us to hear any report, but the high burning flares revealed Marines there were engaged in a serious firefight.

While over a hundred hard core NVA soldiers from the Second Company, R-20 Battalion penetrated Hill 25's perimeter wire, the Marines on the hill were being pounded with mortars, recoilless rifle, grenades and automatic rifle fire.

Within minutes Marines inside the compound were engaged in a fierce fire fight as well as individual hand to hand battles with a well-disciplined enemy force. The enemy, were all wearing black shorts and red bandanas.

Outnumbered four to one, the twenty-eight Marines in Second Platoon, Mike Company on Hill 25, were fighting a fierce battle for the right to live.

Corporal Jim Meaney, a Marine that had been in First Platoon, India Company, and a survivor of the Gates of Hell, had been transferred to Mike Company just a few weeks before. He was leading an ambush squad near Hill 52 when that hill was also hit.

Caught in out in the open rice paddy fields, Meaney while leading his squad back to Hill 52 discovered a large enemy force set in ambush at the footbridge near Hill 52's southern entrance.

The enemy force numbering over a hundred was waiting for Marines from that hill to respond to Hill 25 Marine needs.[145]

As the large enemy force, began to destroy bunkers on Hill 25 by throwing satchel charges at the Marines in them, and targeting the bunkers with recoilless rifle fire, the platoon's sergeant, S.Sgt. Gilbert Bolton, gave the prearranged signal of two green star clusters fired into the air. It was the signal for the Marines on the Hill to seek cover while he called in artillery on top of the hill and on his own men.

The fire for effect airburst shells rained down hard on the enemy forces, outside the bunkers, and they broke contact. As they carried off many of their dead and wounded, the surviving Marines emerged from their bunkers and drove the remaining enemy soldiers off the hill. Puff showed up shortly after that to finish the job.

The following morning, there remained numerous dead NVA bodies scattered all over the hill, and the surrounding rice paddies. Of the eighteen Marines that survived that brutal encounter, half of them had been wounded.[146]

Ten Marines were killed that night on Hill 25.

KIA Marines; Amedola, Willet Rankin; Bates, Glen Douglas; Dearborn, Patrick John; Edinger, James Gard; Fiducioso, Stephano James; David Howard; Jones, Davis Allen; Kropidlowski, Gerald; Moore, Robert Everett; Pitts, Dana Allen; Shoemaker.[147]

CAC 2-2-1 Attacked
Liberty Bridge, South Vietnam
November 8, 1967, 0100-1500 hours

Early on the morning of November 8, Robert Tully, a Second Platoon Staff Sergeant set out with a squad of fourteen Marines to set up a night ambush, near the Song Thu Bon River. They had barely set in when they heard explosive fire to the north of their position. Over the radio he heard that CAC 2-2-1 was getting hit by an estimated fifty enemy soldiers.

A minute later the radio cracked with an announcement that the Army compound near the Dai Loc District Headquarters was also getting hit. In the distance he could see a huey gunship attacking the enemy and Tully began to move his men in the direction of the CAC unit.

Aggie was standing watch, and I was sleeping next to him at the front bunker position, the one nearest Liberty Road that led toward Battalion Headquarters, when the firing started. He woke me to say CAC 2-2-1 was getting hit.[148]

I got up and looked over the top of the bunker. It was one in the morning, and I ached from sleeping on top of the rock-hard sandbags. The blankets we slept on to cushion the hard sandbags did not make sleeping on them any softer.

Off in the distance, I could see that the village of Dai Loc was also getting hit as was the Army advisory compound near there.[149]

Explosions seemed to be occurring along the village's edge near Route 4.[150] Several illumination flares could be seen floating high over the old Dai Loc Bridge, as well as the CAC unit to the east of Hill 65.

Hill 65, with its battery of seven 105mm howitzers, could be heard unloading a barrage of outgoing artillery shells. Most recently, three new 155mm howitzers had been added to the arsenal of weapons there, and I wondered if they were now, being fired.

I missed Hill 65; to me, it was home. There was something rustic and wholesome that made it a pleasant place to be. The hill, without the military tents and bunkers, was just a barren, treeless mound of red dirt. During the monsoon season, the hill remained muddy, slippery, and wet for days, and it wasn't as pleasant then, but our old bunker that had been my first home in Vietnam was still there, and it held nostalgic memories of my first days in Vietnam.

Bright red and green tracers and white star clusters were lighting up the sky near Dai Loc, and Phu Loc (2). Hill 37 seemed to also be taking some mortar and rocket fire. I could hear the sound of numerous explosions going off in the far distance and a Huey gunship was busy crisscrossing the sky, between CAC 2-21, and Dai Loc firing off their machine gun and rockets.

Sgt. Tully meanwhile was maneuvering his squad to confront the enemy force attacking the CAC unit when all of a sudden his squad was taken under intense enemy fire. When he realized it was a very large force they had encountered, he quickly formed his squad into a defensive position, and hoped they would be able to hold on, until reinforcements arrived.

I felt a sense of helplessness, knowing Marines were getting hit while we were close by yet unable to help by returning fire. A reactionary force would soon be sent, I knew and I wondered if we would be going. The attacking enemy would know that a reactionary unit would be sent to the CAC unit, and they would be waiting for those Marines and probably had set up an ambush for them somewhere along the way. I was thinking. More than likely, the ambush would be set up on either side of Liberty Road if we responded that way.

Normally, a squad of Marines and a handful of PF's manned the CAC units in our area. The CAC unit being hit was located near the southeast corner of Liberty Road and Route 4. It was the CAC unit we had manned for a few days after Bro was killed. Most of the area in front of us was now ablaze with illumination, and numerous explosions were going off all along Route 4.

Rice paddy fields lined the right side of Liberty Road from our position all the way to the CAC unit. The closest tree line on the east side of the road was about 100 meters away. On our left side (the west side of the road) was a large cluster of trees near Hoa Tay where our old position used to be. If we responded alongside the road, the enemy could ambush us from that tree line. After that tree line, there was a small clearing, the thick jungle, and scattered small villages and homes that lined the roadway all the way to Dai Loc. More than likely, that would be the spot the enemy would choose to ambush a reactionary unit from if we sent one out from Liberty Bridge and used Liberty Road.

"I'll get Jones in case we start getting incoming," I said to Aguilar, as I rolled off the bunker's top and put on my Marine Corps cap, out of habit more than anything.

Most of us didn't wear a cap unless the sun got hot or we were told to wear them. One thing about being in a combat zone with an understanding platoon commander was the lack of concern for uniform appearances. Then again, we hadn't been resupplied as we should have been. Perry and Marty still hadn't received replacements for the trousers they tore during Operation Knox.

I crouched down low and ran toward the hard back barracks where Jones was sleeping.

As I crawled out, I could see a slow-moving plane circling over the CAC unit. The plane dropped a slow-burning flare that floated lazily downward. The flare bathed the entire area around the CAC unit in bright light. A cluster of small white parachutes held the flare high in the air. The flares being dropped burned for about three minutes as they drifted slowly downward and soon disappeared below the tree line. As the flare died off, the intensity of the exploding ordnance increased considerably.

When I got to the barracks, Jones and Dumont were fast asleep. I hadn't realized until then that the four-hundred-foot distance from our gun's position to the barracks was so far.

The other gun team, made up of Duran, Keeton, and Martinez, were at their bunker manning the other gun position near the river's edge. Like always, Jones had returned to sleep on his cot in the barrack after first watch. Sometimes, we took turns doing this as sleeping on the cot after standing first watch and not having to worry about watch for the rest of the night was like not having stood watch at all.

"Jones, Dumont," I yelled out as soon as I went through the door, careful not to startle them too quickly. Jones always slept with his M-16 nearby and Dumont with his .45 pistol under his pillow.

"The CAC unit is getting hit badly!" I shouted. "Mortars, rockets, and lots of incoming."

By the time I started back out the door, Jones had grabbed his shirt, a bandolier of ammo,[151] and with his M-16 in hand, was running alongside me back toward the bunker. Dumont fell in close behind, but then he turned and ran toward the CP.

By now, other Marines were running around the compound, putting on their helmets and flak jackets. Others who had returned to sleep in the barracks were picking up extra bandoliers of ammo, grenades, and flares and were running toward their assigned bunkers.

"A company runner came by as soon as you left," Aggie said when Jones and I arrived. "First Platoon is staying behind manning the perimeter with two-man positions for the rest of the night. Second and Third Platoons are going out as a reactionary force to the CAC unit."

An artillery round exploded in the tree line in front and to the left of us, then another and hundreds of red and white sparklers shot up like a giant white dandelion. A cluster of burning destruction was peppering the tree line on the left side of Liberty Road. It looked like the Fourth of July, except the fireworks were on the ground and destructive. Seconds after impact, a cluster of explosive rounds shot into the air. The string of glowing white sparklers showered down like hundreds of miniature rounds that seemed to explode on contact.

The miniature exploding balls reminded me of the new baseball-shaped grenades I had seen but had not yet been issued. Once you pulled the pin and threw the grenade, it exploded on contact. I wished we had some at our bunker's position. Hill 65 was dropping volleys of artillery rounds up and down the west side of the road where a likely ambush by the enemy might be set up against our reactionary force.

Within thirty minutes from the time Aggie had awakened me, the last men in Second Platoon left the perimeter wire. They were assigned to move out toward the left of Liberty Road, traveling north alongside the river's bank.

Sgt. Everett James Wilcox a Third Platoon squad leader was assigned the mission of reinforcing the CAC unit Marines. Wilcox had been with the company since mid-July. A tall, medium built Marine, with long arms, thick eyebrows, sidewall hair-cut and a sense of mission about him. He had already gathered a reinforced squad of Third Platoon Marines and they were loaded on board two amtracks that were already standing idle at the perimeter's wire.

The amtracks moved out traveling east toward a far tree line, then north along the tree line, rushing toward the CAC unit. They would come up behind the enemy forces and sweep through to the CAC unit.

The rest of Third Platoon, meanwhile, was double-timing toward the CAC unit along the edge of Liberty road.

As the last fire-team from Third Platoon left the perimeter wire, Jones and Aggie pulled close the thirteen-foot wooden-frame fence that was interlaced with concertina wire. The gate closed tight, sealing the perimeter securely. Aggie with his long arms reached up and hooked a simple piece of looped wire over the top of the connecting poles.

A simple piece of wire held the two gateposts together. They reminded me of how my grandfather used to hook the top of the chicken coop door in his backyard in Las Cruces, New Mexico, together and shut the chickens in for the night. My grandpa did that every evening before retiring. They lived on Mulberry Avenue near Solano Drive, and every evening, all the chickens came into the chicken coop on their own and he would be there to lock the gate that kept them safe from coyotes and other wild critters that hunted in the darkness.

I had fond and mixed memories of my youth when my grandparents lived there. I recalled when my grandmother died on my eleventh birthday, and a few days after the funeral, my grandfather had me sit next to him on a horse-drawn wagon, as we went into town for supplies. Like my father, he was tall and light skinned, had dark, long curly hair. Other than a thick grayish moustache, my grandfather was clean-shaven; the corner of his moustache was always stained brown from tobacco juice. That day, as we turned down Tornillo Street, he spat tobacco juice out and part of it struck the horse's rump and dripped off the wagon's dash rail. He handed me the leather reins and I smiled at him, feeling proud and privileged, to be driving the wagon into town.

On our way back we stopped at the corner family-run store and he reached into his overall's pocket and took out a nickel. He gave it to me and I went into that store and bought a handful of four-for-a-penny candy.

For the first time on Liberty Bridge, I realized the gooks didn't have to blow a hole in the front gate to attack us. All they had to do was, unhook the wire and swing the gate wide open. No wonder I couldn't sleep at ease during those nights out in the bunker.

Hill 65 fired off another series of artillery rounds, and I realized that's what I had missed about the hill: the sounds of artillery and large explosive rounds on their way out. It was the secure feeling of outgoing artillery; the sounds of war that kept the gooks far away, the coyotes from the chicken coop that made sleeping on Hill 65 so comfortable. On Hill 65, we were on the offensive; but on Liberty

Bridge, we were waiting for the enemy to strike. I sat down next to the machine-gun, prepared to fire.

Chasing Charlie
Liberty Bridge, South Vietnam
November 8, 1967, 0100-1500 hours

The two miles between the CAC unit and our position was thick with trees and deep undergrowth on the left side of the road. Only a small clearing separated our old position and the tree line that connected the clusters of trees that led to Dai Loc and the CAC unit farther up the road.

In the sky over the CAC unit, a Huey gunship was busy strafing the area around the CAC unit with heavy machine-gun fire.

"That's an Army searchlight firefly," Jones said. They keep a gunship there at their Dai Loc compound," he added.

I felt relieved at not having to go out with the other two platoons, but felt guilty at the same time that we weren't out there, while Marines were fighting for their lives.

Bro had gone out in my place, and he had been killed. I realized that it could have just as easily been First and Second Platoons or First and Third Platoons. Perhaps it was because we were more familiar with perimeter security around Liberty Bridge and had built up much of the bunkers that the captain felt we could do a better job of defending the bridge if we needed to.

Perhaps that's why he decided to keep First Platoon back. That thought eased my conscience, but only for a few seconds.

Third Platoon for some reason seemed to be the captain's favorite as their platoon commander often volunteered them for extra patrol or assignments, yet for some reason, they did not engage or made contact with the enemy any more than the other platoons.

Why hadn't Battalion HQ sent out a reactionary force? Lima Company was on Hill 65, and part of Kilo Company was sitting at battalion! Either way, I knew the gooks would have set up an ambush for any responding unit. They would be expecting someone from 3/7 to respond. It was the military base closest to the CAC unit.

I wished we had a radio to find out what was going on. Second and Third Platoons could easily end up caught in an NVA/VC ambush. Guns were usually the first ones to respond when the call for "guns up!" went out, but often we were the last to find out what was going on. Perhaps it was Captain Baggette who had volunteered the company, and now both Second, and Third Platoons were gone and First Platoon was left behind manning their bunker positions.

Dumont had gone to the CP to find out what he could about what was going on. *An hour had passed and not a word,* I was thinking when the short Frenchman came running toward our bunker.

Dumont, jumped on top of the bunker, and sat down;

"The lieutenant said not to open up unless we're getting overrun," Dumont said as he climbed on top of the bunker.

"What's going on," Jones asked him.

"The CAC unit was hit hard, and NVAs were over-running them when Third Platoon got there. The gooks also hit the surrounding villages and a reinforced company of them, wearing only black shorts and black headbands, attacked the security detail from Lima Company at Dai Loc Bridge. A platoon of Marines from H&S Company responded to assist Marines there. They've taken several KIA's."

"Are, we going to go," Jones asked.

"No, I don't think so," Dumont answered.

"They hit Battalion with mortars and recoilless rifle fire. It seems like they hit a lot of places at the same time. Battalion figured they might have set up an ambush for anyone coming down from Hill 37, but it seems Third Platoon caught them by surprise when they came from here.

I don't think they knew that we had all three platoons at Liberty Bridge, and we may now have them in a cross fire."

Gooks might have also set up at our old position so we might get some incoming.

"When Third Platoon arrived they shot and killed eight to ten VCs on the berm near the CAC unit."

"Where's Second Platoon," Aggie asked.

"The captain received a report from Third Platoon that gooks were running west across Liberty Road. And as they ran heading for the river, Second Platoon opened fire on them."

The whole place was now filled with burning flares high in the sky, smoke and air activity as two Puff planes flying overhead were working out with their mini-guns.[152]

"What about Lima Company? They were on Hill 65, what happened to them?" I asked.

Dumont took off his glasses, placed them on his lap, leaned back, and placed his hand over his mouth, his index finger pointing out.

"I think, I overheard the lieutenant say, that a platoon reactionary force came off the hill on two tanks, and they met a company-sized enemy force that was withdrawing from the old Dai Loc bridge going toward the CAC unit. They hit the enemy force from behind, firing several canister rounds at them. Some of them ran toward Route 4 where they ran into other Marine units—now a whole bunch of them are pinned down along both sides of that road. They are caught between our platoons."

Dumont dropped to lie on his side on top of the bunker.

"Man, I'm glad, I'm not out there," Aggie said, as he sat down next to Dumont, his long legs sticking out over the bunkers edge."

I moved to the edge of the bunker and joined Jones looking out. I could see Puff was working out, near Dai Loc along the river.

Dumont, looking toward where I was looking, went on to say;

"The NVA were set up on the east side of Liberty Road, to hit our reactionary unit, if we went out that way from here, but when Third Platoon used the amtracks and the tree line, to get to the CAC unit, the gooks left their ambush site, where they had been dug in. But as they withdrew toward the river, they ran into Second Platoon so, then they were forced to run toward Dai Loc and now Puff is working them over."

I was wondering how, Second and Third Platoons were doing;

How many casualties had we taken? How many will not be returning to Liberty Bridge. I could see the enemy was taking a beating, and they were fighting back. Would we be hit next? Were they planning to assault us next, since only one platoon was left to guard the bridge?

I was glad the enemies' ambush had been foiled; their tactics had failed when they tried the same thing on Hill 52, when they were set in to ambush Marines responding to the attack on Hill 25. We were very lucky, or someone was taking care of us. I checked the gun, it was loaded with a two hundred round belt, Aggie had seen to that. The belt was fan-folded evenly. Three other ammo cans were stacked near by, as were six-seven grenades. Aggie had strapped his K-bar to his leg.

"Hey, Aggie, you expecting a war," I asked jokingly, pointing at his scabbard and the extra ammo.

"Well, you never know," he answered.

"I better go, check on the other gun-team," Dumont said.

"Gooks might now be located at our old position so we might get some incoming," Dumont added, before he picked up his glasses and wiped them clean with the corner of his utility shirt.

The intensity of the firefight in the far distance had not let up; green as well as red tracers were bouncing and ricocheting and flying every which way high in the air so that we couldn't tell where the Marines were and where the enemy were.

Puff reappeared, spraying its destructive ray of bullets on Liberty Road and the area that used to be our old position. The plane moved back and forth flying on this side of the river and back across the river into the Arizona territory.

"It looks like the Charlie's stuck in the middle," Aggie said as he strained to look beyond our perimeter wire.

"Charlie got himself locked in between two companies of Marines with no way out," Dumont answered, thinking out loud. "Unless they try to overrun us or to swim across the river, they're dead meat. I bet that when Second and Third Platoon came around from the tree line, they probably cut off Charlie's escape route. Now I bet we got Charlie trapped on this side of the road. We got Charlie locked in," he said more forcefully as if to summarize in his head what he was realizing.

"The lieutenant says not to open up unless they try to assault us. We're spread pretty thin all around the perimeter," Dumont repeated himself. Then jumping off the top of the bunker, he said, "I'll be right back," and ran off, zigzagging his way back toward the CP, no doubt to share with the lieutenant what he believed might be happening to the enemy.

Reinforcements Arrive At the CAC Unit
Liberty Bridge, South Vietnam
November 8, 1967, 0100-1500 hours

When Wilcox's squad of Marines arrived at the CAC unit, it was being overrun by a large number of NVA soldier's dressed as Viet Cong. The enemy had secured the majority of the CAC unit's bunkers, and a large enemy force had breached the CAC unit's southeast corner, destroying a bunker there and heavily damaging the tower and the large bunker below the tower.

As they entered the compound, Third Platoon Marines were met by a barrage of incoming mortar, recoilless rifle and automatic rifle fire being directed at them and at the CAC unit Marines, but they had arrived just in time to reinforce the CAC unit Marines, and united they aggressively fended off the assaulting enemy force. In minutes Third Platoon had secured the center of the compound and the NVA began retreating.[153]

A half an hour later, Dumont returned with an infrared scope. He spoke as he searched out the tree line directly in front of us using the scope.

"The CAC unit wasn't overrun," he said.

"But a lot of the villages got burned by the VC and they killed a lot of civilians. Third Platoon is getting ready to hook up with the Lima Company Platoon that came off 3/7 on tanks. It seems like the gooks might be running our way." Dumont waited for a reply from us.

"We figured that," Aggie replied and reached out for the scope and Dumont handed it to him. Dumont looked at Aggie's response with a surprised look on his face.

"Well, where else would they be going," Aggie added, as if he wanted Dumont to note that he too had figured it out.

Aguilar's long, skinny fingers wrapped themselves around the scope's large plastic covering. He appeared funny, like goofy looking through the scope as if he was imitating an officer. Jones reached out and turned the infrared scope around for Aggie. Aggie grinned and Jones lay down, lit a cigarette, and offered me one.

I lit it off Jones' cigarette, cuffed it, and took in a long drag. Aggie asked for a smoke but lit it himself.

"It's bad luck to light three cigarettes from one match, huh?" he asked. Dumont turned to look at him, but did not answer. Aggie looked at us with a distant gaze; he was pondering saying something.

"What, Aggie, what are you thinking about?" I asked him.

"I don't want to be shot in the head," Aggie said, and we all turned to look at him.

"They say if you're shot in the head, you won't make it, so I don't want to be shot in the head."

"Well, then, where do you want to be shot?" Dumont asked.

"Well, nowhere," Aggie answered. "But if I get shot, I just don't want to be shot in the head."

"Well, we'll have to tell the gooks that, Aggie, if they are going to shoot at you, not to shoot you in the head. Would being shot in the foot be all right, then?" Dumont asked.

"No, I guess not," Aggie said. Aggie turned to look out across the dark field, this time looking through the infrared scope correctly.

I felt a slight sense of relief knowing we now had two different Marine companies involved in response to the CAC unit.

From the sounds of the battle off in the distant tree line, the firefight was subsiding a little. From our position, I could see where the majority of the fighting was going on. With the scope, we weren't able to see any movement out in front of us; but from that distance, I knew we wouldn't be able to tell if any figure appearing was friendly or foe.[154]

A short time later, a quarter moon emerged from behind us. It had been hidden for most of the night behind dark rain clouds. As its light lit our perimeter, I felt an eerie sense of danger.

Shadows were stretched out and the moon light covered the tree line in front of us with moving shapes and scattered patches of darkness warning us of hidden dangers. The light silhouetted Marines standing watch on top of the bunkers to the left of us, making them a clear target. When my watch was over, I slid down behind the safety of the sandbagged wall as Jones took watch. Dumont squatted down gook-style where Aggie and I were. He moved his hand around the outside edge of a sandbag.

"That platoon from 3/7 and the tanks are here," Dumont said, showing us by running his finger along an imaginary line on the edge of one of the sandbags. "They're moving toward the CAC unit to meet up with Third Platoon along Route 4," he said as he used the outward edge of the sandbag to indicate where Route 4 was. "Lieutenant Wilson said that at daybreak, a platoon from 3/7 with tanks, Second and Third Platoon would join up and make a wide sweep toward us." Dumont indicated on the sandbag where the tanks and our two platoons would stretch out along Route 4 and use Liberty Road as their left guide to sweep the enemy force toward us.

It was a large area, but the enemy would have few choices. If they tried to cross Liberty Road, Puff would slaughter them. If they tried to swim across the river, they would also get slaughtered by artillery or Puff; if they tried to overrun us they would have to cross the bridge and Echo Company 2/7 guarded on the other side of the bridge. Either way, what remained of the enemy force was now trapped, and they were going to be decimated.

Charlie Is Boxed In
Liberty Bridge, South Vietnam
November 8, 1967, 0100-1500 hours

"Captain Baggette is still leading this operation since it was our company that caused Charlie to be boxed in," Dumont continued. "It seems like we are going to push and squeeze the VC until we get him in a cross fire. We got Charlie this time, and he's not getting out. The lieutenant said that at daybreak, we might be going out along the north bank of the river to act as a blocking force, so start getting your gear ready. If we go, we'll do it at first light."

Our old position between us and the CAC unit must have been crawling with gooks by this time because Puff kept spraying that area relentlessly. For the next two hours, we stayed awake and watched him work out.

We were on 100 percent alert, and none of us would have been able to sleep even if we wanted to. Instead, we took turns peeking over the sandbags, watching, and waiting. We sat in silence, trying to distinguish the different sounds made by weapons being fired off in the distance.

We could tell when an AK-47 opened up, its kack-kock-kack, sound was loud and distinct compared to the quieter, duh-duh-dit of an M-16. At other times, it was just a smorgasbord of concentrated firepower.

I heard a series of engagements, silence, followed by another clash and then more silence. Off and on throughout the ordeal, I could hear sporadic small arms and automatic rifle fire and see green and red tracers being shot at Puff who, after a while, moved west of us and was working out along the banks of the Song Vu Gia River.

Just to keep us on alert, a few stray shots were now and then fired in our direction. So I knew some elements of the NVA/VC unit were now located in the cluster of trees in front of our gun position.

The NVA/VC was always well prepared for their missions. They practiced their assaults on our units over and over again before launching an attack. They had prepared for success but did not seem to have expected Third Platoon to come toward the CAC unit on amtracks from Liberty Road. Now, Second Platoon was knocking on their back door and they were boxed in.

The enemy force was divided and scattered all over the area, mostly concentrated on the west side of Liberty Road. They were surrounded by Marines to their north along Route 4. East of them was Liberty Road and open rice paddies. To the west was the Song Vu Gia River and to their south Liberty Bridge. They had no way out.

The NVA/VC soldiers caught running in the maze were being cut to pieces by artillery being fired from Hill 65 and when the barrage of artillery stopped, gunships appeared overhead. Little by little, information was filtering down to us on what was happening. Dumont filled us in as he ran back and forth between our position and the CP.

Ira Hullihen, First Squad, squad leader who had been listening to the firefight over the radio from the beginning, came by to get a firsthand look at the situation, and to check out what may be in front of our perimeter. He filled us in on what was going on in more detail. He told us that two local VC had been captured, and the Kit Carson Scouts had relayed over a separate frequency a lot of valuable information to everyone, about the enemy's strategy that night and their plans afterward.[155]

When the NVA/VC ambush platoon that had been set up on Liberty Road, realized Third Platoon had by-passed them by taking amtracks along the distant tree line, they abandoned the ambush site, just before the rest of Third Platoon used that way to get to the CAC unit.

They enemy force ran north toward Dai Loc, to tie up with their other forces and ran into the fleeing sappers and other NVA support units running from the CAC unit in their direction. The NVA were then seen running back and forth in between the villages.

A short time later a platoon from H&S 3/7 moved into position on the North side of Route 4 in support of the Dai Loc Bridge—and now the enemy was trapped in between Marine forces. Boxed in, the enemy turned direction, to run southwest toward the river.

When Sgt. Tully's squad of Marines found themselves confronting a large retreating enemy force, he quickly withdrew his men toward the river's banks and set up a defensive position, and the squad of Marines were assaulted with heavy machine-gun and grenade fire. Knowing his squad would not be able to withhold such a large enemy force, called upon the bird-dog pilot flying overhead for help.

"Basketball-814," an air-support flare ship, soon arrived on station and the bird-dog, dropped a smoke grenade to alert the flagship where the majority of the enemy force was concentrated. The ship lit up the area with flares and began to fire their mini-guns at the enemy.

In the heat of battle, the enemy, continued to run into each other. In desperation some tried to flee across open rice paddies, and from where we were, I could see Puff spraying the area with thousands of rounds. Most of the enemy survivors were now trapped in the trees in front of Liberty Bridge, and there, they continued to suffer heavy losses. When Puff broke contact, artillery from Hill 65 rained down again.

At 0345 hours, relieved and able to move his squad again, Sergeant Tully moved his squad into a blocking position as the rest of Second Platoon moved north toward his location. As the squad set in, his squad spotted three boats heading south from the north bank of the Song Thu Bon River. Each boat had two enemy soldiers desperately trying to row, across the river. The squad opened fire with machine-gun rounds and their M-16s, striking the lead boat. The second boat was also hit, but the third boat managed to make it to the other side of the river and its passengers escaped. Sergeant Tully had been with the company for only two months. A strong, short, husky Marine with a balding head, he had a fatherly disposition that quickly earned him the respect of the Marines in his platoon.[156]

As dawn arrived, the rest of Second Platoon moved out along the banks of the Gia River, and tied in with Sgt. Tully's squad. Stragglers from the VC/NVA battalion that had wiped out many villagers near Dai Loc were reported by a Bird Dog to be hiding in the tall grass near the river's banks, and Second Platoon moved out in that direction.

The bird-dog, meanwhile, called in the first of a series of fixed-wing bomb drops, and napalm was dropped where the largest concentration of the enemy was seen.

CHAPTER THIRTEEN

A Battalion Destroyed
Liberty Bridge, South Vietnam
November 8, 1967, 0100-1500 hours

At first light, Dumont came running out to our bunker. Around the perimeter, I could see the rest of the platoon saddling up.

"Saddle up, we're going," he said, as he jumped on top of the bunker. Both Jones and Aggie by then had strapped two hundred round belts across their chest, and with our flak jackets, and helmets on. We were ready.

Duran, Keeton and Marty came up. Duran was carrying the gun. First Squad who would be leading the platoon was already gathering at the gate.

"Keeton, you go with Cookie, and Aggie, with First Squad, I'll stick to Duran," Jones said.

"Why, you don't trust me," Duran shot back.

"You're carrying the gun," Jones answered, and they fell in behind the CP group.

We moved out the front gate, turned west, and traveled alongside the northern bank where the Song Thu Bon and the Song Vu Gia River merged. We set up as a blocking force a short distance from our compound along the river's edge.

A short time later, we moved out again and received some scattered incoming small arms fire, but we were told not to return fire because of friendlies in the area.

We set up near the riverbank waiting for Second and Third Platoon, as well as Kilo Company, to sweep the enemy toward our position.

A Lesson For the Corpsman
Liberty Bridge, South Vietnam
November 8, 1967, 0100-1500 hours

As Second Platoon moved out along the river's bank, an NVA soldier with his hands bound in a white rag emerged out of the tree line.

The soldier had his hands over his head as he started to run toward the point man. Sgt. Tully yelled out that the enemy soldier had a satchel charge and Lance Corporal William Thomas, dropped the soldier with ten rounds fired from his M-16.

Doc, Darrel J. Keller a twenty-two year old, U.S. Navy, Corpsman who had been with the company since early October, stood at awe in what he had just witnessed. In his mind, he couldn't believe what had been a living soul was so suddenly dead, just a clump of flesh, with thick bright red blood flowing into the dirt.

The Corpsman mesmerized by what he had just seen, just stood still. "Come on, doc," said, a Marine, walking by and shook the Corpsman's arm to rouse him out of his state of shock.

As the Corpsman hurried to catch up with his lieutenant, a skinny young VC with severe napalm burns on his face and body was sitting on the edge of a rice paddy dike. The VC soldier clad in only burned and tattered black shorts was crying out in agony, as the acid sizzled and burned through his body.

"Shoot him, doc," Lieutenant Faithful told the Corpsman, and Keller quickly drew his .45 pistol and took aim, the VC in great pain was nervously rambling on and Keller just couldn't pull the trigger.

"Shoot him," the lieutenant ordered the Corpsman to open fire, but Keller just shook, unable to pull the trigger. Faithful then walked up to the enemy soldier and pumped two rounds from his pistol into the young enemy soldier. The soldier fell forward, squirming and shaking on the ground.

All of a sudden the cracking sound of Ak47's filled the air and Second Platoon came under heavy and intense automatic rifle fire from across the river.

Terry Dixon out in the open was shot in the leg, and he went down. Bullets were striking all around him, and it was evident; the enemy was trying to finish him off.

Almost immediately, Doc Keller was out running toward Dixon. Marines provided covering fire for him, and he half-carried Dixon back while bullets were striking the sand, and grassy mounts all around them.

Medevac
Liberty Bridge, South Vietnam AT 909555
November 8, 1967, 0100-1500 hours

The medevac chopper landed out in the open field, and Doc Keller stepped out to help Dixon who was able to walk to board the aircraft. As they both got to the chopper's door, the enemy opened fire on them.

Bullets struck the helicopters side and the door gunner returned fire.[157] As soon as the chopper lifted off, great fear fell on Keller as he ran for cover. Bullets were impacting the ground all around him, and he began to realize the enemy was trying to kill him.

A moment later he found himself on the ground shaking uncontrollably from great fear and trauma. He could not hold back his bladder and as he peed in his pants, the Corpsman brought his hands up to his head and wept.[158]

Quick Draw VanCleef
Liberty Bridge, South Vietnam
November 8, 1967, 0100-1500 hours

The word was passed for Second Platoon to move out and short five-foot-three-inches tall L/Cpl. Darrel VanCleef, was walking point.

The patrol neared the river's edge and VanCleef spotted an area along the bank of the river where the elephant grass had been pressed down. VanCleef was new to the company with only six days in country, but he was a seasoned Marine who had taught guerrilla warfare stateside. He moved cautiously out to the edge. When he looked down, he saw footprints in the mud below.

VanCleef slipped over the edge and could see a small cave a short distance away. He raised his M-14 and silently moved toward the cave's opening, having to wade into the water waist deep. At the cave's entrance, he saw an NVA soldier standing in the water holding a Russian-made machine-gun.

VanCleef opened fire, striking the enemy soldier before the soldier could fire back. The Marine dragged the dead enemy's body out of the cave along with the machine-gun he had captured, and Sergeant Joel Williamson reached down to pull both the gun and soldier's body onto the bank. About the same time, VanCleef looked over to his right, and hidden in the tall grass was another enemy soldier with his weapon pointed at VanCleef, Captain Baggette and "Doc" Keller.

VanCleef dropped just as the enemy opened fire and the Marine emptied the rest of his magazine across the enemy's chest; the enemy's bullet struck the Marine's helmet, traveled down through his right ear and alongside the inside of his neck, and exited the left side of his neck. The wound was more of a flesh wound, but as Doc Keller dressed VanCleef's wound, the Corpsman noticed how his hands were trembling, and he wondered how he would survive another eleven months of duty, with the Marines.

A Battalion In Disarray
Liberty Bridge, South Vietnam
November 8, 1967, 0100-1500 hours

Over the radio we learned a reinforced NVA/VC battalion had struck several targets in the area. They had burned a number of villages and killed hundreds of civilians. They would have overrun the CAC unit had it not been for the quick response of Second and Third Platoons. During the firefight, Second Platoon captured the NVA battalion commander and from him, we heard over the net that the commander was in tears; he kept repeating the same words over and over again that his battalion had been wiped out. He blamed himself for the annihilation of his men.

Most of the villagers hid or fled their homes during the NVA attack emerged when they saw Marines and informed Second Platoon's lieutenant where the enemy was located, and this allowed for Second and Third Platoon to circle around, blocking the NVA/VCs escape route. The NVA units were then totally trapped.

We learned that while some civilians in some of the villages had been killed, most of them had escaped to a safe area. Instead of surrendering, however the NVA soldiers decided to kill as many civilians in the villages that they found. Old men, women, and children were shot and killed indiscriminately. Families who did not have hidden bunkers where the enemy could hide were massacred. Whole families were burned alive as they were corralled into their homes and their huts set on fire.

When Marine units cornered the enemy, the NVA and VC used civilians as human shields, forcing them to run alongside of them as they tried to escape. Puff was relentlessly firing upon all of them. From where we were, we could see green tracers being fired at Puff; so, we knew heavy enemy resistance remained.

In the shadows of the darkened jungle, it wasn't possible to see who carried weapons and who were civilians compelled to run alongside the fleeing enemy. Puff was firing into the thick tree line with its twin mini-guns. It fired endless bursts of machine-gun fire, and the screams of the injured and dying could be heard above the roar of the dragon's bullets being sprayed into the area. Friend or foe, the flying monster's bullets couldn't tell the difference. The screaming and the dying were all the same.

As Marines moved in, tightening the circle around the enemy, Puff broke contact. We were, by then, too close for him to provide any further firepower without the risk of hitting friendly forces. The rest of the enemy force would be left for us to seek out and destroy.

Shots rang out again in our direction and once again, we were told to check our fire. We were not to fire unless we saw the enemy coming in our direction.

By midmorning, we moved west then north, along the riverbank and set in out in the open with the river to our backs. By then the villages and populated areas had been cleared and Marines units were sweeping toward us. The enemy was completely encircled and those that continued to fight had no chance for survival, unless they surrendered.

We heard reports over the radio from Marine units involved in the sweeps that enemy soldiers were making their way toward the road or running toward the river and our location. I knew it would only be a matter of time before we would be engaged in an all-out firefight, maybe even hand-to-hand combat. The largest remaining pocket of enemy resistance seemed to be located in front of us. At least a hundred or more NVA soldiers were reported boxed in near the village of Hoa Tay.[159]

The only covering we had was weeds and foot-high bushes, barely enough for us to hide behind while lying flat. If the enemy ran toward us, we would be able to pick them off as they crossed an open field toward us, but they would have the advantage of numbers.

The gun was ready, and Aggie had attached an additional 100-round belt to the 100-round belt already in the gun. He checked them to make sure there were no long or short rounds and that all were seated flush in the belt. Aggie was in the A-gunner's position to the left of the gun. Keeton to my right was lying prone with another two hundred rounds ready if they were needed.

Over the radio, I could hear that Second and Third Platoons were capturing many prisoners. While I wanted to be able to cut down the enemy should they advance toward us, I was not looking forward to it.

Another radio spot report announced NVA/VC soldiers were dropping their weapons and walking out to meet Marines with their hands over their heads. Other radio reports were that the enemy was fighting hard and killing civilians.

We waited in the open fields while the three captains and Battalion HQ considered what to do. It would be a long, slow and heavy firefight if we decided to go into the thick forested area in search of them.

The amount of incoming bullets being fired at us was steadily increasing. Carbine, AK-47 and grenades from grenade launchers were being fired in our direction. The enemy knew where we were so we hugged the ground and waited as bullets flew overhead. Whatever decision the brass was going to make, they had better do it soon. We were not in a good defensive position, and if the enemy assaulted en masse, there weren't enough of us to repel them effectively.

We were out in the open, with not even a rice paddy dike to hide behind. I could tell that a large enemy force was gathering in the dense jungle in front of us. We were in the way of their closest route of escape; if they made a run for it, they would have to cross about 100 yards and then it would be hand-to-hand combat.

We were a platoon of about forty-seven men: three Marine rifle squads, two gun teams, a rocket team, and the CP, consisting of five men, including the lieutenant. If the remaining two or 300 enemy soldiers assaulted, some could cross the river behind us and escape into the Arizona Territory.

Walking With the Enemy
Liberty Bridge, South Vietnam
November 8, 1967, 0100-1500 hours

In front of me, I could see enemy movement. Groups of people were moving from left to right. They were armed NVA soldiers, but sandwiched in between them were civilians—women and children whom the enemy was pushing, pulling, and forcing to run alongside of them. The lieutenant once again passed the word for us to check our fire because Second Platoon was somewhere nearby, sweeping toward the enemies' position along the Song Vu Gia River.

The enemy, I could see, was moving in the bushes some seven hundred yards away. I sighted in. I knew I could single shoot the gun one round at a time. I had single shot the gun before. We did it at Liberty Bridge, shooting the gun that way for fun and practice. I knew I could hit selected enemy soldiers. I brought the gun up tight against my cheek. One of the NVA soldiers used his weapon to butt strike an old woman, and other soldiers nearby pushed children to the ground that were not moving fast enough, stepping on them as they moved on.

I wanted to squeeze off a round. If I held the trigger down too long, three or four machine-gun bullets would fire and I might hit a civilian. But I was confident I could single shoot it. Snipe at the enemy with the M-60, one shot at a time. I had hit floating debris in Song Thu Bon River many times that way, and the NVA soldiers were much larger targets.

I took in a deep breath, held it, and sighted in on a lone target. The gun was tight up against me; I sensed her willingness and confidence and I held her closer. I could squeeze off a round, shoot one of the soldiers, but maybe they didn't know exactly where we were and the shot would give away our position. I pressed my index finger up against the trigger. The gun had no slack and just a hair width kept the gun checked.

The NVA soldier I was sighting on turned and shot a young child and an old woman that had fallen down. Before I could fire, he grabbed one of the other children and shoved him forward. Other old men and women ran past the soldier to catch up with the child and the enemy force became surrounded by civilians. An NVA soldier stopped moving and began yelling out orders. He became perfectly positioned in my gun's front sight; the round would tear through his chest, and I visualized the bullet striking him and him flying backward. All I had to do was squeeze the trigger and he'd be gone. I wanted to fire just that one round. The NVA turned, and a group of soldiers with civilians ran by, weaving in between the enemy soldiers, bushes, and small trees. The enemy began to run again using civilians and shrubbery for cover and concealment. If we assaulted the tree line and the village, the enemy would use the civilians as shields and a lot of innocent people would get killed.

Keeton was lying on his back smoking a Kool cigarette. He motioned for us to look up. Two camouflaged phantom jets appeared out of a clear dark blue sky. They circled around and dropped straight down toward the tree line in front of us. The jets pulled out only a few hundred feet above ground level. The thundering roar of their exhaust shook the ground and left the trees vibrating.

A display of power like that must have had a demoralizing and fearful effect on the enemy, *but why didn't they drop anything?* I was thinking.

Keeton, as if in answer to my thoughts, said, "They were only marking their target. That was their dry run, now they'll come in for the kill."

No sooner had he spoken than we caught the sun's reflection off the shiny gray and green colored aircraft as they turned slowly, almost lazily, in the air and then dropped once again. They were two specks of silver bullets against a dark blue backdrop. The planes dropped effortlessly, coming in silent and swift. A few hundred feet off the ground, each plane dropped two long olive-drab barrel-shaped canisters. As the canisters floated slowly toward the earth, the planes pulled up smoothly. The noise of their exhaust engines was silenced by the explosive roar of the four powerful and violent explosions that followed in their path.

In front of us, the sky was ripped apart, the elements melting before our eyes and the tree line was swallowed by a fierce explosive ball of fire. A bright cloud of yellow and red flaming liquid exploded, spewing death and destruction over the entire area. It was as if a miniature atomic bomb had been dropped in front of us. The earth below us shook, bounced us off the ground as whining, sizzling, burning shrapnel flew through the air past us. A large chunk of metal embedded itself deep into the ground just a few feet from where we were.

"Goddamn 'em, don't they know we're here?" Perry cried out from behind the gun team. The planes had dropped four canisters of napalm.[160] When the napalm bombs exploded, an indiscriminating wave of flames engulfed both the enemy soldiers and civilians alike. A huge fiery ball rose high into the air, and the intense heat wave enveloped us, sucking the air out of the area. We were about a football field's length away from where the bombs had exploded; yet we could feel the heat and devastation the fiery inferno produced.

The phantom jets circled again and again until they had dropped the five or six loads they each had. The tree line was burning like the fires of hell, the flames lapping everything in its path, leaping and exploding blistering heat high into the air. The crackling fire muffled minute secondary explosions as it consumed and melted together trees, hooches, weapons, flesh and bones.

After they dropped their last load, the planes circled overhead once more, coming in slow, and then they turned high in the sky in a long, wide curve. The planes arched their wings until both were flying side by side in a clockwise direction. At about eleven o'clock, they flipped their wings, turning their bellies toward us, and the sun's reflective glow caught their silvery bottom. They dropped their right wings, and together waved good-bye to us twice as they accelerated and disappeared into the dark smoke-filled sky.

We got up and started a sweep straight across the tall elephant grass, not knowing what we would find. At the same time, Second Platoon began their sweep toward us from our left flank. We stopped at the tree line, and a platoon of tanks moved through the area in front of us. Their tracks churned the charred remains of what had once been a beautiful forest.

Chunks of shrapnel had ripped apart rocks and plants. Burned trees, gray-colored plants, branches and foliage littered the area. A powdery grayish white residue lingered smoking on the ground. All around us were scattered embryonic-looking clumps of flesh: charred bodies of a dozen or more enemy soldiers. There were dozens of small clumps of black and gray matter huddled together; the smell of burned flesh and bones rose above the smell of napalm, and we all knew what the clumps were. They no longer looked human, and it was hard to imagine that just moments before they had been living human beings.

No one said a word.

When Second Platoon Marines moved through in front of us, we fell in behind and together we swept through the area. The enemy's fighting power and their will to resist was snuffed out by the explosive air power unleashed. There was no more incoming or firing anywhere; we found only smoking remains, burned body parts, and dark blood-soaked weapons.

Sweeping Through A Charred Landscape
Liberty Bridge, South Vietnam
November 8, 1967, 0100-1500 hours

As we moved out the radio was buzzing with numerous reports of NVA soldiers turning themselves in as prisoners of war. As the sweep progressed, we began to pick up weapons and military gear the enemy had thrown on the ground. We stopped and then swung left toward the remains of the villages that once surrounded Dai Loc. Then we moved northwest in a counterclockwise direction toward Route 4.

It was now just a mop-up operation. Soon, we ran out of the forested area and started out across open rice paddy fields, and I was glad to be out of the smothering forest. Out in the open in the middle of a field, we saw enemy bodies; some were still smoldering. They had crawled out of the jungle to finish melting in the rice paddy fields. Napalm, once it got on you, is burning acid; it burns the body and there is no stopping it. The body of a lone NVA soldier lay next to a rice paddy dike. A Marine from a squad in Second Platoon, walking by the charred mass, saw that the soldier was still breathing. He swung his M-16 off his shoulder and pumped three or four rounds into it. The smoldering body twisted and jumped as the bullets slammed into it. When I passed by, I saw the full effects of napalm. The soldier may have escaped death at the tree line, but the napalm that had splattered on him had melted his face away. He looked as if he has wearing a distorted rubber Halloween mask. The NVA soldier would have died a slow agonizing death, had not the Marine ended his life.

By late afternoon, our platoon alone had recovered sixty-seven enemy rifles and grenade launchers as well as a number of satchel charges. The unit involved in the attack, according to the information the Kit Carson Scouts had obtained from captured prisoners, was the First Battalion, First Regiment (aka Seventieth Battalion). The operation was battalion size. The enemy was supposed to overrun the CAC unit and then sweep southeast toward Xuyen Trong Village in Duy Xuyen District then toward Go Noi Island, which was the main headquarters for the R-

20 Battalion. One of the prisoners said the attack was carried out by the Second Company, R-20 Battalion, which was the unit that attacked both the Tam Hoa refugee camp (AT 868564) and the Mike Platoon 3/7 on Hill 25 (AT 839568) on the second of November.[161]

The enemy involved in that attack on the CAC compound alone numbered from 70 to 150 VC/NVA, all were dressed in black; and attacked using AK-47s, mortars, recoilless rifles, B-40 rockets, satchel charges, as well as Bangalore torpedoes and grenades.

More than six hundred homes had been burned to the ground by the NVA/VC. They had killed more than two hundred civilians, wounded another sixty, and a hundred or more were missing. India Company suffered four WIAs, none of them serious, and no KIAs. First Platoon had no casualties. In true Marine Corps tradition, the number of enemy killed was underplayed. India Company was credited with killing thirty-one enemy soldiers; another thirty were credited to artillery. Three Marines had been killed at the Dai Loc Bridge and an unknown number wounded.

By late afternoon, we reached Liberty Road and turned toward home. Off in the distance, I could see that Liberty Bridge was burning and figured our compound had been attacked while we were away. Dark black smoke was rising high into the air. It was a long road and a long walk home, and I wondered what condition we would find our barracks in.[162]

Once the company had returned to the bridge, Second Platoon had to go back out. First Lieutenant Steven Matulich had lost his code book, and the platoon went back out to search for it. While our enemy prisoners credited us with the annihilation of the Lap Duc NVA/VC Battalion of 200 to 300 men, I hadn't fired a round.[163]

A Celebration
Liberty Bridge, South Vietnam
November 8, 1967, 1800 hours

That evening, for a job well done, Battalion HQ sent us two small trailers pulled by jeeps that were filled to the top with ice-covered beer. There were more cases of beer stacked inside the jeeps. We were to celebrate our victory and told not to worry about standing watch that night. The tank platoon that had accompanied us on the sweep would be manning our perimeter for the night.

We spent that afternoon celebrating, drinking beer, and eating barbequed steaks; and while the company commander and our lieutenant may have thought we were celebrating because of our victory, we were more elated to have been given the rest of the day off. We would not have to stand watch at night. That was a reward we appreciated. Late into the night, the sounds of the Beatles and the Rolling Stones played in the background while we all sat around enjoying cold beer.

The more we drank the braver and more foolish we became. We started sharing war stories, and soon we were all shit-faced, falling-down drunk. We drank and cursed. We slurred our words, and we talked about Swabbies, the dumb Seabee who burned the bridge while we chased after gooks; we spoke of stupid lieutenants and captains who were more interested in medals than in the safety of their men. By nightfall, the talk turned to cowards in the Corps and to Lieutenant Gen. Chesty Puller, the Marine Corps's most decorated hero, who once said, "You ain't a Marine until you've done time in the brig."

We talked about being busted and who had been busted the most as well as who had done the most time in the brig. Of Marines who had the most time in grade, Dumont won that distinction, and we cheered and slapped him on the back and drank to the French Canadian Marine who didn't mind being called Frenchy. We drank to little Sergeant Isaacs, called him a skinny four-eyed Jew. We drank to his bar mitzvah and to the wife he didn't have. We talked about love and war. We talked about girlfriends and wives who were unfaithful, women who never loved us back. We compared gooks we had killed with the ones that got away. We traded back and forth the enemy weapons we had captured; knives, helmets, pistols, carbines, and brand-new AK-47s were traded for permission to write a Marine's sister or for the latest *Playboy* centerfold. Later, Jones and Keeton got into a fight over the music box, and Marty cried over having shot holes in Jones' 45 rpm records and kept telling Jones how sorry he was for having done that.

At midnight, I asked Jones why we weren't standing watch. "I don't know, and I don't care," he answered and everybody laughed and Keeton hugged Jones.

"Hey, somebody ought to be out there," I said, and nobody answered. "Hey, this is serious," I insisted, but no one was listening. "Somebody ought to be on guard duty."

"The tanks are out there," Dumont answered.

"I didn't see any tanks," said Aguilar. "I just took a leak and there ain't any tanks out there; it's darker than hell, and there ain't any tanks,"

"Aggie, get the ammo. I'll get the gun," I said and I picked up the M-60 and headed for our gun's bunker position. We got to where we believed the perimeter wire should have been or at least where our gun's bunker should have been, but we were so drunk that we couldn't find the bunker. We decided to set up right where we were even though we couldn't see four feet in front of us.

Aggie took first watch, and I could hardly stay awake. When he lit his cigarette, I just sat there, too tired and drunk to tell him that he ought to cup his hands over a cigarette when he lit it. *But that's okay*, I thought. *If the gooks shoot at us, Aggie will kill them*, I reasoned as I passed out.

The following morning, the tanks' engines woke us. The sun was high in the sky, and it was almost ten in the morning. We had set up directly behind a tank, almost underneath it.

When I looked up, Aggie was shaking his head trying to wake up. We started to laugh at our bravery and stupidity, but we stopped immediately. Our heads hurt too much to laugh. We rolled out from behind the tank, grateful that they hadn't started up or backed up during the night. I picked up the gun, and he picked up the ammo. It hurt to bend over.

"Hey, Aggie," I said.

"Yeah," he responded.

"Now I know why it was so dark last night," I told him. We chuckled, shook our heads, and headed for the piss tubes. The raunchy, acid smell around the tubes was turning our stomach, so we held our breath while we pissed.

A Day in the Sun
Liberty Bridge, South Vietnam
November 9, 1967, 1300 hours

In the afternoon, we were called to formation and given small sundry packages that had come from a group of Good Samaritans in Fort Lauderdale, Florida. Among the items in my package were cookies, gum, magazines, toiletries, toothbrushes, and a small portable radio with batteries. The toothbrushes would be used for gun cleaning. Some of us that did not have them were finally issued the new lightweight utilities, including camouflaged shorts and new lightweight canvas-type boots. Even Doc Mac got new boots. They were a size 9 and he wore a size 11, so he carried them around all day before he was able to trade up with a Marine for a size 10. Keeton and Jones turned in their frayed and torn boots for new ones, but as soon as the supply sergeant left, they retrieved their old boots for trading purposes. An old pair of boots that had humped the jungles was a highly prized commodity to pogues in the rear. Some Marines wrapped them up and sent them home as souvenirs.

Aggie's Gunner's Test
Liberty Bridge,
November 9, 1967, 1800 hours

For the next four days, we were to run regular patrols and night ambushes or worked on reinforcing our bunkers. On the ninth of November, Aggie asked if he could take the machine-gunner's test because he wanted his MOS to be changed to that of a machine-gunner. Word had spread that we would soon be going on an operation into the Arizona Territory, and Aggie wanted to be a designated gunner. We had been kidding Aggie all along that if he could fieldstrip and put together the machine-gun while blindfolded, he would become a gunner and his MOS could be changed.

Rahm, Boyd, Pridemore, Boone, Perry, Keeton, Jones, Dumont, Duran, Marty, and myself gathered around the hooch and, with a bottle of hard whiskey, Cokes, and ice we had bought from Mamasan, sat around listening to the juice box, preparing for Aggie's gunner's test. Dumont went over the rules with him: he was to take the machine-gun apart, we would blindfold him, and he was to put it back together while blindfolded. He had to be able to name the part as he put the gun together. There would be no time limit, but it was desirable for him to do it within two minutes to qualify him for an MOS change.

Aggie disassembled the gun into its eight major groups without difficulty. Then we had him disassemble the barrel group as well. Aggie had torn apart, cleaned the gun, and had placed it all together numerous times before; but he had never been allowed to be the gunman out on patrol, something he often wanted to do. Both Marty and Aggie were good A-gunners; both took good care of the guns and the ammo, making sure the links and the ammo were clean. For Marty, it was almost an obsession. He would take hours to clean the gun and ammo. Marty had carried the gun out on patrol, but not Aggie; we still would not let him do so because we told him that he had to first pass the field gunner's test, which we had never required of Marty. But Aggie didn't know that, and there was really no gunner's test. Aggie, in the beginning, had not been as thorough in cleaning the gun, but after his encounter with the kids in Dai Loc, he had begun to take extra care of the gun, giving it as detailed of a cleaning as Marty.

The gun was disassembled and laid out in front of Aggie. Dumont blindfolded Aggie, and we all toasted him. Dumont said "go," and clicked the stopwatch. Aggie reached out with his long, skinny arms and first put together the barrel group. When he flipped it upside down, we could hear the piston move easily down the gas cylinder. From there on, he was on a roll. In less than two minutes, he had completely assembled the gun and removed his blindfold. Aggie surprised all of us, and we toasted to him and slapped him on the back. He asked Dumont if he would be able to carry the gun on the operation and Dumont answered, "Yes, if we need you, you'll get to carry the gun."

Boom Box Bombers
Liberty Bridge,
November 10, 1967, 0600 hours

The following morning, the small pocket radios filled the early morning air with a loud cry of "Goooooooooooood Moooooooooooorning, Vietnam! This is Armed Forces Radio, live from Saigon. For you, Marines, suffering from constipation . . ." That evening, we listened to Hanoi Hanna broadcasting from Hanoi, telling us how people back home were protesting against the war and supported the people's revolution in Vietnam. Before noon, a small plane dropped leaflets in the area between Liberty Bridge and An Hoa where Operation Arizona had taken place. Loudspeakers mounted on the low-flying aircraft broadcast announcements in Vietnamese for all civilians to evacuate the area. The leaflet bombers flew low over villages and hamlets, dropping leaflets and telling the VC and NVA to surrender under the Chieu Hoi program.[164]

The loudspeakers warned the enemy not to shoot at them because they would be *dich ban ruoc* (killed by the ghost ship); Puff was flying high overhead. If the plane with the loudspeakers received any incoming, Puff swooped down and opened up with devastating mini-gun fire. The enemy soldiers, like most Vietnamese were very superstitious so for the most part, they left the loud, squawking bird alone, fearing that to fire on them would anger the sky monster that had a loud roar and a deadly red sting.

The pamphlets announced that the Arizona area must be evacuated immediately. The area was considered to be completely under NVA/VC Communist control, and anyone deciding to stay would be considered a North Vietnamese sympathizer and treated as an enemy of the South Vietnamese government. The bird-dog announced the same message in Vietnamese over their loudspeakers. The pamphlets were also an announcement to the NVA and VC that we were coming and were prepared to fight them in their own backyard.

It was bold for us to announce that we were coming, but the leaflets also gave instructions on how a North Vietnamese soldier could surrender at any of the surrounding military bases. The bases meanwhile had received instructions on how they should take in and treat prisoners who surrendered under the Chieu Hoi program.

During the next couple of days, we were told to be prepared for an operation into the Arizona Territory. We were going to go there on a search and destroy mission in response to the death and destruction the NVA/VC had caused in Dai Loc on the eighth.

We were told not to expect much contact during the upcoming operation as more than likely, the enemy would leave the area. But when we went out on night ambushes near the river's edge, enemy forces contacted us from across the river, using loudspeakers to warn us to stay on our side of the river.

On the night of November 12, we picked up a broadcast by Hanoi Hanna. In her broadcast, she warned us to stay out of the Arizona Territory and she named our company by name: "Suicide India Company, Mahreene, if you come into Arizona Territory, it will be your suicide. We will be waiting for you. You will die in the rice paddies and a new GI that stayed home will marry your girlfriend. It will be suicide for you if you cross the river. We will be waiting for you in Arizona Territory."

That night, before putting out the candle lights, Lieutenant Larry Wilson, First Platoon's commanding officer, having returned from a divisional briefing at headquarters, taped Frag-Order 31-67, to the bottom of a chair in his bunker.

The Execution command outlined the order of battle to commence at 0900 hours on November 13, 1967.

Chapter Fourteen

Operation Foster
Liberty Bridge,
November 13, 1967, D-Day, 0600 hours

When we awoke on the morning of November 13, a thick blanket of fog covered most of the An Hoa basin. A few minutes later, scattered dark gray clouds dropped long, cold drops of rain on us. We were saddled up for the operation, but sat waiting. There were forty-seven Marines in First Platoon going in on the first wave of helicopters. Next to us were the Marines in 60's Mortars; Larry Pancake, George Buethe, Steve Puder, Patrick Gallagher, Sam Edge, Al Homan, and Sam Muszel.

We all just sat and waited, got wet, then got dried in the sun. Not much information was ever passed down to guns, so we just sat and waited.

I stuffed Marty's letters and pictures into my seabag along with most of the personal gear we always left behind during operations. Everything we didn't need was left behind.

"Marty, are you gonna keep fooling' around like this? What'll happen if I don't make it back? Who's gonna send the letters back to your folks?" I had asked him.

"Cook-San, you'll make it back," Marty answered as he stuffed his camera into his knapsack, pulling the straps tight. "You got something going. You'll make it. Besides, my girlfriend and I just split up, so I don't have anyone, but you do. You got that girl, Jerry's sister, that's been writing to you. You ought to think about her and get rid of your old lady. She ain't faithful, and she'll only drag you down. It isn't worth it. The pain isn't worth it. You'll make it back. You'll see,"

Marty picked up a 100-round belt of M-60 ammo. He used a toothbrush to clean out a bit of crust off one of the double links and then used a clean towel to wipe the rounds clean. He made sure that the rounds were seated properly in the links, and there were no long or short rounds. The first gun team would be Jones, Marty, and me. The second gun team would be made up of Duran who would be carrying the other gun. Aggie would be his A-gunner, with Keeton, his ammo bearer. Both gun teams had our asbestos bags packed full of gun-cleaning gear, gloves, and tools, and each bag held an extra gun barrel.

Marty had recently returned from R&R. He had planned on taking his leave in country at Cam Ranh Bay but changed his mind. The saying was, at that time, that if you couldn't go Stateside, Cam Ranh Bay was the very next best thing.[165] Marty instead, when he received the Dear John letter from his fiancée, decided to go home to Sacramento, California. He chose to take his R&R in Hawaii and paid for his own round-trip airfare to the States. He had never mentioned his fiancée before, and we were surprised to find out he had a girl back home. When he came back from the States, he told us that everything had changed back home.

"Everything is psychedelic," he said. "Girls are wearing miniskirts, and the college kids are protesting against the war, but Americans are holding counter-demonstrations in support of us."

Marty had brought back a stack of 45 rpm records to give to Jones to make up for the ones he had put a .45 slug through, and he bought himself a two-by-four-inch miniature chrome-plated 35mm Minolta camera. The camera looked like a little spy camera, the type James Bond would carry, and it took excellent 35mm color pictures.

As we waited, I wished I were as confident as Marty that I would make it back stateside. By now, it was hard to picture a different life, a different world outside of rice paddies and C-rations. Vietnam had become my way of life.

"Back in the world," we often said when referring to life stateside. But now, this was our "real" world. Our life here in Vietnam was temporary, but there were times the world outside Vietnam no longer existed. I had been here so long that this world of guns and ammo, night ambushes, patrols and filling sandbags was the real life that mattered. Sweating and humping around rice paddies, seeking an elusive enemy that chose when and where to fight, was what was now real. The "real" world in the United States was the world that was fading in my mind; it no longer seemed real.

Operation Foster
Liberty Bridge,
November 13, 1967, D-Day, 1300 hours

At 1100 hours, just about the time we were beginning to seriously think the operation might be cancelled, a strong wind blew over the mountains, dispelling the clouds overhead and filling the valley with moist, hot air. Moments later, the area was cleared of clouds and gloom. At 1200 hours, the hot Vietnamese sun was beating down on us. We moved out of the perimeter toward the dirt road to the west side of the bridge, and by the time we got there, we had dried up from the rain only to become drenched and soaking wet from perspiration. Across the river, jets were peppering Football Island, dropping high explosives on LZ (landing zone) Sparrow (AT 893521), the LZ where we would be landing. Marty took his familiar pose, and Doc Marren took his picture, then all of us gathered and posed for more pictures.

Captain Baggette informed Lieutenant Wilson the CH-46s had been grounded so we would be going in on 34s (UH-34Ds, capable of carrying only six Marines each), The Red Lions, with HMM-363, operating out of Da Nang, would be doing the helolift.

First Platoon would be the lead platoon, going in. That meant the first load of Marines would be on the ground alone for a time until the 34s returned to Liberty Bridge, loaded another bunch of Marines on board, and returned. It was going to take them a while to get us all into the operation area.

Moments later, six small grasshopper-shaped choppers appeared on the horizon. They circled overhead and landed on the dirt road a short distance away. No sooner had the first chopper touched down on the roadway than we were boarding the small grasshopper-shaped helicopters.

Operation Foster commenced. The search and destroy operation involved, India and Lima Company 3/7 and Foxtrot 2/7 OpCon (Operational Control) to 3/7. To the north of us, Operation Badger-Hunt also began with SLF 2/3 participating.

Only half of First Platoon was able to get on board the first few choppers, and at 1300 hours we lifted off the ground. The insides of the chopper rattled and shook a lot more than the large Chinooks we had used during Operation Knox. Within minutes, we were circling over a large village in the middle of Football Island.

Along the southern edge of the village was the Song Thu Bon River. The north side had a 200-foot wide, dry sandbar, which formed a natural border isolating the island from the rest of the area. North of the village were rich rice paddy fields, dry riverbeds, and densely populated small villages. Scattered clumps of tropical trees, tall clusters of elephant grass, and brushwood reached all along the southern edge of the Song Vu Gia River to where the river drew near Route 4.

Northwest of us, large bamboo patches and a thick-forested area clustered around a long, skinny, finger-shaped lake in the middle of a six-mile stretch of land that was sandwiched between the two rivers. This was the area known as the Arizona Territory where the Second NVA Division and the 620th Battalion operated. The enemy's division was supposedly composed of two NVA regiments, one VC regiment, plus the VC Sapper 402nd Battalion. Their combined strength was approximately nine thousand men scattered throughout Quan Nam Province.

As we began our descent, off in the distance we could see smoke and patches of small burning fires from the airdrops earlier in the day. The Arizona area was primarily flat with scattered small hills and laced with open rice paddies, small villages and clusters of dense thick jungle areas. To the west were mountains covered with heavy vegetation and a series of steep foothills.

Our gun team and a couple of First Squad Marines were going to be in the first chopper to land. Lieutenant Wilson and the CP group were directly behind us. Just as the chopper was landing, we took incoming rounds. A couple of rounds struck the undercarriage and one round struck the door just above the chopper's gunner position. Chips of metal fragments sprayed out from the bullet's impact and the gunner opened fire, spraying the area, as we touched down.

We landed on the east side of Giang Hoa (Football Island) and jumped out. Jones ran toward a small rice paddy dike while we took cover near a tree line close to a large village. To our right, a well-traveled trail led into the village. Immediately, our chopper lifted off. Duran's gun team exited the last chopper and set up on the other side of the trail on our right side; they also were facing the village.

As the sound of the choppers' rotating blades faded in the distance, we heard shots once again being fired at them. Soon they were far away and a deep sense of danger, of fear, and a desolate feeling of being forsaken crept over us. I sensed a gray cloud of doom over-shadowing us.

We stayed still while visually checking out the village before us. There was silence all around us, there were no birds in the sky, and even the wind seemed to be standing still. Second Squad, led by Corporal Stanley, moved in, his fire-teams leapfrogging their way in, moving closer to the village alongside a thin tree line on our right side. Duran's gun team was sandwiched in between the last two fire-teams as they skirted alongside the tree line; Duran was looking for an advantageous position where he could set up his gun. Once in place, we stayed where we were to wait for the rest of the company to join us.

An eerie unsettled silence descended around us. Sitting there waiting, we strained to hear any noise, wondered where the enemy was. Jones got up and had me move the gun into a more advantageous position. We were now facing the village with the river to our backs. The gun's barrel pointed down the wide trail leading from the river's edge toward the center of the village. I wondered how long it would take for the choppers to return. Only about twenty-four of us had been dropped off, half the platoon. We had our backs toward the river, and to our right, I could see scattered bamboo shoots and clusters of thick vegetation that covered a large swampy area leading to the sandbar I had seen from the air just before we landed.

On the other side of the sandbar, a number of rice paddy fields abutted a large brush covered village. I sensed it was from there our chopper had been shot at and from there the shots were fired when the choppers left.

Other than those few shots, we had landed without any enemy resistance on Football Island, in the Arizona Territory. We were in enemy territory—with only a squad of Marines, two gun teams, and the CP group.

About forty minutes later, the choppers returned. As they began to land, Lieutenant Wilson had us move forward and through the deserted small village. On the ground, scattered about, were pieces of clothing and miscellaneous personal items. The village had only recently been vacated. We didn't know if it had been occupied by civilians who saw us coming and went into the jungle ahead of us to hide or if the NVA/VC had been living in the village. Vietnamese rice farmers were politically minded; they would house, support, and give information to both sides in order to survive.

One of the goals of Operation Foster would be to relocate any remaining villagers out of the area. The South Vietnamese government had erected several refugee settlements where the people could find safety and be cared for and fed. In the back of my mind, I thought of how we, along with the South Vietnamese government, had not been able to save the hundred or more civilians that had been killed in the settlements at Dai Loc. Had the survivors of that day returned to this side of the river? And would we now be sending them back? The NVA/VCs raid through Dai Loc had left, over six hundred families homeless. It was all a vicious circle, and the cause was Communist aggression, plain and simple.

Over the years without mercy, the villagers had been killed, raped, their children taken away and their villages plundered on both sides of the river by the enemy. Either way, it was just another small conflict in the overall battle for Communist domination, and we were there to do what we could and it didn't seem like much. If the citizens had fled the area as the leaflets had instructed them to do, the NVA would not have them to use as shields. I would be able to fire without hesitation. Perhaps this time, I would shoot at the enemy for the Vietnamese people.

By mid-afternoon, the full company had been airlifted and dropped off at our location. Shortly after that, we moved out, sweeping west by northwest toward the lowlands. Along the way, we saw hooches that were completely covered over with bamboo and hidden among tall trees. They had been constructed so that they were invisible from the air. There was evidence that the hooches had been used recently, and many had tunnels or "spider holes dug in and around the dwellings"[166].

We tore down what covering we could, and engineers attached to the company blew them up as well as the tunnel enclaves we found. The primary purpose of the operation was a search and destroy mission. We were to seek out the enemy and destroy them. But I couldn't imagine they would have stuck around, especially not after they had been given prior notice by the flying loudmouth planes that notified them we were coming and had warned them so clearly that we were on our way into their area.[167]

The purpose of the announcement was to get the civilians out of the area so that we could operate in a free-fire zone, meaning that we would be free to fire upon anything that moved without fear of hitting innocent civilians. In a free-fire zone, we would be able to call in artillery or jet-air strikes to destroy an area being used by the enemy without hitting innocent civilians.

That evening, we settled in an old French village; it was from there we would be operating for the next few days. First Platoon and 60 mortars were assigned to guard the northwest side of the perimeter; Second Platoon, the south; and Third Platoon, the east side. The company's 81-mortars platoon had the northeast corner covered. The wide sandbar gave them a clear field of fire, and visibility was good. In front of us was thick jungle and heavy bushes with grass three to six feet tall in some places. If the enemy approached the village from where we were, they would be on us before we would see them.[168]

Search and Destroy
Operation Foster, Arizona Territory
November 14, 1967, D+1, 0700 hours

The following morning, we set off, and it wasn't long before we found civilians that had remained in the area. The CH-46 choppers that had been grounded were flying again and were being brought in to evacuate the remaining civilians by air and by amtracks out of the area. In one of the better-constructed cement buildings, we found writings and hand-drawn pictures painted on the walls of AK-47s firing at helicopters. The room appeared to have been used as a training classroom for soldiers. Elsewhere we found Communist printed anti-U.S. government propaganda leaflets thrown throughout the area. We found wooden AK-47 rifle replicas used to train enemy soldiers. The area we were in, it seemed, had been used as an enemy training camp.

We came across an old man lying on a bamboo stretcher inside a hooch where his family had abandoned him. Marines picked him up to place him on a chopper and his family protested—leave him behind, he is old, they said.

Lieutenant Wilson argued with his family members, and they finally gave in when they were told by a Kit Carson Scout that they wouldn't have to feed and care for him because the South Vietnamese government would assume that responsibility. It was then that they agreed for him to be evacuated with them.

Once the last of the civilians we could find were cleared from the area, we moved on and began to aggressively destroy villages where we found evidence of the enemy's presence. When we found weapons or punji stakes in a hut or village, they were burned.[169]

Brown Husked Rice For Dinner
Operation Foster, Arizona Territory
November 15, 1967, D+2, 0900 hours

The following day, we searched out more villages and traveled through numerous open rice paddy fields and followed jungle trails connecting hamlets and tree lines. For two days, the choppers were continuously evacuating Vietnamese civilians out of the area. Many civilians who said they were not supporters of the NVA did not want to leave their homes because of their religious beliefs. We had to reassure them that we were not going to burn their homes but they needed to be out of the area. They knew the NVA would not show any mercy to civilians that chose to stay behind, so while some hid, the great majority of the villagers were more than willing to leave.

"Ancestral worship was the reason many of the villagers did not want to leave their homes," a Korean Marine attached to our company explained to our lieutenant. Koreans had fought Communist aggression in South Korea for decades so they understood better than we did what the villagers and local officials had to endure from the Communist-trained soldiers that were invading their land. They understood the customs and traditions of the villagers and the position the populace were in. They also had ways of extracting information from them that helped identify Vietcong supporters as well as NVA Communist soldiers living among them. Many South Vietnamese families had sons or daughters serving in either the North or South Vietnamese armies or in both. Many of their youth, especially in the Arizona Territory, had been abducted by the NVA and forced into combat duty or hard labor. For some villagers, their loyalty to either side was as divided as their families.

We found an old woman and a young girl with a child in one small village. They were the only survivors of what had been an NVA purging through the area where the enemy had killed and raped innocent civilians in the village. When the South Korean officer started to question the young girl, it was evident to him that something suspicious was going on. Even though we did not understand the high-pitched, whining Vietnamese language being spoken by the Korean and the young woman, I could tell the grandmother and the young girl had been spared for some reason and the Korean Marine was determined to find out why. The woman revealed nothing and continued to say they had no information of value to us. The short, round-eyed Korean Marine officer who was questioning the girl was kind to her for a time, but once they gave him contradictory information, he snatched the child away and gave him to Sergeant Phu, the head Kit Carson Scout attached to our company.

Sergeant Phu, a round face short Vietnamese Kit Carson Scout took the child away against the young mother's outcry and screams. The Korean Marine then shouted orders to Phu in Korean but made sure that there were enough Vietnamese words interwoven with his messages so that the young mother understood that Sergeant Phu was being asked to prove his loyalty to the South Vietnamese government by shooting the child. The girl started to scream hysterically as Phu took the child out of the women's sight around to the other side of the house. The Korean officer then questioned the girl about her inconsistent answers. When he did not obtain a satisfactory reply, he shouted orders for Sergeant Phu to shoot the baby. A shot rang out; and the baby, who had been crying throughout the ordeal, immediately stopped crying. The girl screamed and fell on her knees crying when she saw Sergeant Phu emerge, carrying the soft bundle at his side like a bundle of tattered rags. The officer then ordered the old woman to be brought forward. He was about to repeat the process by having the young girl shot when the old woman started to talk. She told him which direction the NVA had fled, how many there were and where they might be spending the night. The baby had not been harmed, only silenced by a hand placed over its mouth and carried away. The plot was; however, an effective way of obtaining valuable information. A short time later, the mother, child, and grandmother were taken to an awaiting helicopter and flown out to the refugee camp. The girl and her child would never be able to return to the village of their ancestors. They had betrayed the NVA, and they would also not be easily accepted in the refugee camp since they had collaborated with the enemy.

The South Korean officer explained that the Vietcong in the area were not local men as had been the case years before. Most were from other villages; others were individuals that had left South Vietnam during the ten-thousand-day period when everyone was allowed to travel and settle in the North or in the South in whatever country they chose. Most of the VC operating in the Arizona area had been trained by Hanoi and were merely puppets of the North Vietnamese Communist government. The same thing had occurred in his country, he said. It had taken years to purge their land of Communist infiltrators.

The Vietcong would often deceive the local villagers into believing that they were the liberators and promised them land and peace once the war was over if they supported the cause. But just as often, they turned against them and used the villagers to help meet their supply needs. At other times, they would rape the women and massacre anyone they chose. Sometimes totally destroying a village they despised because they had no local connections to them and considered the people weak and useless. Once the enemy learned that they wouldn't be able to extract food or provisions from a village, or wouldn't be able to win it over to their cause, they simply eliminated the villagers so that they wouldn't be able to give information to the South Vietnamese government.

As we moved closer to the An Hoa mountain range, every hamlet or adjoining home had connecting tunnels that tied in with other huts. We found tunnels under small bridges or under large clay pot containers in the courtyards of many homes. Other tunnels connected hooches to jungle trails or branched off in any number of different directions. We found underground bunkers with large quantities of American medical or food supplies stashed away. These supplies were often easily accessible from a number of connecting tunnels throughout the villages.

By the third day of the operation, we were out of food and weren't being resupplied. While we were operating in the east side of the Arizona Territory near the Song Thu Bon and Song Vu Gia Rivers, BLT (Battalion Landing Team) 2/3 Marines were operating west of us near the An Hoa mountains, sweeping toward us. Other than Marines being wounded by booby traps, none of the units involved in the operation had so far encountered notable enemy activity.

The An Hoa basin was known in I Corps as the booby trap capital of South Vietnam. Sapper units who were experts in setting up the deadliest, most destructive antipersonnel mines found in Vietnam operated in and around an area known as the Triangle located between Da Nang, Hoi An, and An Hoa. Bouncing Bettys, punji stakes, trip wires connected to grenades, claymore mines, or even 250-pound bombs hanging from trees were not uncommon in the Triangle. When the point man found a trip wire, we waited while engineers moved forward to destroy it, and they usually found other explosive devices nearby also rigged to go off.

We settled in the late afternoon in an abandoned village. In one of the huts, we found bags of husked brown rice and a medium-sized pot that had been recently used for cooking. The cooked rice in the bottom of the pan couldn't have been more than a couple of days old. Before this operation began, the burned, caked rice at the bottom of the pan would have brought a disgusting frown from any of us. But we hadn't been resupplied for two days and we were hungry, so we searched the village for anything edible. We scraped out what rice we could from the bottom of the pan then boiled some water and cooked some of the husked brown rice in the pan. If the gooks ate the stuff, we figured we could also. For flavor, we threw in some salt tablets and a can of pork rings someone had. We ate only a little off the top because it smelled terrible and looked even worse. We wondered how the Vietnamese survived on eating this stuff and fish heads since that was what we mostly saw them eat. Dumont came by and, seeing what we had done, said we couldn't eat the stuff because the rice was still in the husk; it hadn't been separated from its shell.[170]

Invite A Pig To Dinner
Operation Foster, Arizona Territory
November 16, 1967, D+3, 0900 hours

By the sixteenth, we were beginning to find more and more evidence of NVA-controlled villages. AK-47 ammo and shells for NVA weapons were found hidden inside bamboo poles or buried in the tunnels that ran underneath homes and throughout the villages. Many hamlets had a number of trenches dug all around them so that civilians could run to them during air strikes, but the tunnels and bunkers we were discovering were being used to store military supplies and were constructed to serve a dual purpose. They served as elevated fighting positions for NVA units as well as hiding places during aerial bombardment. Recon inserts were also reporting a number of enemy sightings near the An Hoa foothills.

The sixteenth was pretty much spent in searching out and destroying a number of fortified hamlets where we found evidence of NVA support. We left intact some of the villages where no such evidence existed.

The South Korean Marine did not like leaving those villages untouched, and he argued that the NVA would come to the village and kill any civilians they found because if we didn't destroy the village, it was proof to them that the village was friendly toward the South Vietnamese government.

Later that day, we stopped near a series of hooches in a small village. Not having been resupplied, we once again started to look for food in the villages. There were little white chickens here and there, but they were hard to catch. Finally, a Marine from Second Platoon started chasing a small piglet and others joined in.

Stan Villarreal, a Marine from Second Platoon, threw a K-bar at the running pig. The knife struck the pig from behind, going in through the eye and coming out of its mouth. The piglet dropped, buried its head in the ground, and spun around in circles until George Martinez—a short, stocky Marine from Guam who spoke in broken English—grabbed the squealing pig and gutted it.

We started to roast it out in an open campfire started with cardboard, dry bamboo sticks, and C-4 as fuel. The hot fire burned part of the pig but it was cooking.

Doc Keller came by and told us not to eat the pig as we would get sick. Prescott, having cooked pigs before, told us that we weren't doing it right, but we paid him no mind. We hadn't showered or shaved in over four days, our utilities were soiled and torn, our boots had mud caked on them, and we hadn't even had a chance to change our socks so we really didn't care much about our health at that point. We were out of C-rats and were now drawing our water out of the village wells; we were hungry, and we were going to eat the pig. By the time the pig was beginning to turn a nice golden brown, the word was passed for us to move out. Some of us in First and Second Platoon took out our K-bars and cut chunks of meat off the pig that looked cooked to eat as we moved out.[171]

The Old French Fort
Operation Foster, Arizona Territory
November 17, 1967, D+4, 0900 hours

On the seventeenth of November, we went back to the old French fort. We laid our gear down on a cement slab, inside a large torn building. The area was littered with trash.

I sat down, lit a cigarette and as the smoke cleared I was looking at the village with a new sense of wonder.

The village had concrete-constructed stores that had been ripped apart by explosions and were war-torn and bullet-scarred. But, beyond the destruction, one could easily imagine the beauty the village once displayed.

White cement homes closely built together lined both sides of what must have been the main street of the village. Sharp pointed tile rooftops, and small brick footpaths, garden and grassy areas with benches to sit and rest, were still discernible among the ruins. It must have been a quaint little French village such as one might find outside Paris, I was thinking. Trees and shrubs had been purposely planted around and throughout the village instead of just having grown wild with a village developing around them, as was the case in many other Vietnam villages. We were told to dig in as we were going to spend the night there.

Corporal Perkins, Second Squad leader, found a hidden tunnel and Lucero volunteered to check it out. Meanwhile, a Marine everyone called 'Gimpy,' from Second Platoon, was looking for a place to dig a hole to relieve himself and began to dig in on the other side of the perimeter near a trail leading into the village. When his entrenching tool struck a burlap sack, he discovered a number of fifty-pound bags of polished rice as well as a large quantity of American medical supplies in a tunnel.

No one knew how Robert Wilson IV, a medium-built Marine with short, curly blond hair got his nickname Gimpy; it seemed, he brought it with him when he joined the Corps. He often played the guitar on Hill 65, and Marines from around the hill would, at times, come around to hear him play.

When Lucero emerged from the tunnel Perkins had found, Lucero said there were dozens of large bags of American rice stored in a large tunnel complex. The word was then spread for us to search the area to see if we could find similar tunnels or rice buried in the area.

By late that evening, we had unearthed seventy-five tons of polished rice. Some were in large 100-pound bags and stamped that they had been provided by the U.S. government. The bags were wrapped in burlap sacks and covered by black plastic to keep the moisture out.

Rice Pudding for Dinner
Operation Foster, Arizona Territory
November 17, 1967, D+4, 1300 hours

Since we had gone now for two full days without a complete meal, we were hungry and trying to figure out a way we could cook some of the rice. We didn't know if the shortage of C-rat supplies was due to our CO not ordering adequate supplies or the Corps' famous method of operation. We knew that the Corps was expanding operations into several areas of Vietnam, and we figured that was one of the reasons we had exhausted most of our available supplies. We not only had a shortage of food, but ammo and other critically needed supplies were also in poor supply. Many of us had been in country for months and had not received a full set of the lightweight jungle utilities that many other units had been wearing for some time. Army, Navy, and rear-area personnel had been wearing them for months before the grunts out in the field received a complete set. Some items we knew were available, but often the distribution process was flawed. The Corps was short of needed personnel as well as supplies—supplies that were of vital importance like weapons, food and ammo.

Some Marines had learned that maintenance parts to some of our equipment sat in crates in Da Nang or on ships offshore, and after a while, some of those supplies ended up on the black market and were traded for or bought outright by government officials linked to the enemy forces.

We were tired and hungry. Sweat, dirt, and grime stuck to our torn trousers and bodies. The monsoon rains made the operation cold, wet, and wretched. During the day, it was hot and humid. In the evening, heavy rain fell and the cold wind made us miserable.

Finding the whole-grain, 100-percent-pure American rice did give me an idea. My mother used to cook rice cereal for us when I was a kid. She would fill a pot with rice and water and bring the rice to a boil and then she would add sugar, milk, and cinnamon and serve it to us warm. I remembered how those bowls of hot rice cereal used to warm our bellies before we left for school during the cold winter months and how full we remained afterward.

Everyone in guns branched out in search of milk and sugar. A short time later, Jones and Aggie found a case full of Borden's Eagle brand sweetened condensed milk and some cinnamon sticks. They had also found magazines, cigarettes, and some lousy-tasting chewing gum. We found a large cooking pot. It was dirty and none of us wanted to cook the rice in it, but Keeton cleaned it out pretty well.

"Why don't we cook it in our steel pots?" Marty suggested.

"Have you ever cooked anything in those pots?" Jones asked.

"Marines have been doing it for a long time. It'll work," Marty said.

"Only in the movies," Dumont said. "It'll make you sick."

"Heck, if we get sick, we'll get out of the field," Marty added. Once the old pot was cleaned, Jones drew water from the village well and Dumont broke off a chunk of C-4 to burn; and before long, the water was boiling. I added the rice, covered it, and once it was boiling again, stirred, and moved it a little ways away from the heat. Once the water had boiled away, I added the canned milk and cinnamon sticks. We found dishes or empty C-rat cans to serve ourselves. Soon, we had eaten and were full and Marty was the only one who got sick; he puked his guts out and had the runs all night long. Despite Marty's theory, he wasn't taken out of the field.

As we settled in, reports were being received by intelligence from recon inserts that numerous enemy forces, battalion size or better, were being swept west toward our location by BLT 2/3 F and G companies. Hotel Company was then helilifted into the area, causing the large enemy force to move toward our location.[172]

Write You Last Letter Home
Operation Foster, Arizona Territory
November 18, 1967, D+5, 1600 hours

On the eighteenth, as we were loading the rice we found onto a Mike boat, old men, women, and young children were appearing out of the surrounding hills, jungles, and villages requesting to be taken out of the area. Some were loaded on the Mike boat and others on choppers that were called in to take them to the Dai Loc refugee camp. The civilians were telling us that the NVA were purging the area by slaughtering all civilians that they came in contact with. Other Marine units in the area were also beginning to encounter increased enemy activity, and the civilians wanted to be out of the area. Marine reconnaissance scouts had been reporting that a high number of NVA had been seen moving into the area we were in, and low-level intelligence reports indicated that contact was eminent.

Doc Keller from Second Platoon took it upon himself to get the Marines in his platoon to write letters home just in case something happened. Because we would probably make contact with the enemy the following day, Doc found some large crayons and distributed them to the men in Second Platoon, telling them to write home. It might be their last letter home, he told them. Some did this using the cardboard from the C-rat boxes to write on and then simply wrote "free" on the top right side of the cardboard box. Doc Keller picked up these letters and he sent the whole lot out on the helicopters that were evacuating the civilians.

It rained late in the afternoon, but as evening approached, the rain stopped and soon we saw Puff working out about a mile southwest of us. We had set in to spend another night in the old French village. Our gun team hadn't dug a fighting position as our field of fire was down a trail, and we had a cement wall for cover behind us. At night, those of us not on watch slept behind the lone-standing concrete wall no more than three feet behind the gun's position; it was a safe position to be in if we received any incoming fire.

The sound of Puff's presence working out nearby grew louder and closer, and after a while, we all went outside the building to look as Puff saturated an area with thousands of bullets. Then the plane suddenly turned, appearing directly overhead and shining its bright light on us. It was a mistake on our part to have stepped out into the open, and we scrambled for safety. Seconds later, thousands of rounds were being shot toward us. Puff was strafing the area with thousands of machine-gun bullets that were striking the ground and making its way toward our buildings and us.

Lieutenant Boyd Faithful, Second Platoon commander, scrambled to find the plane's radio frequency and seconds later was screaming into the PRC-25 radio, telling the Puff plane to break contact, to break contact as we were a friendly force.

"Cease firing, cease firing, break contact!" he screamed into the mike, his voice loud and determined. The plane slowly circled around for another pass, and we scrambled to find better cover. We were sure this time we were going to be taking some casualties.

I looked at Puff and was trying to determine the pattern of the bullets fired. If Puff opened fire again, I would be able to hide by pressing myself up against a standing wall until he passed overhead and then move to the other side. That was really the only cover guns had.

Puff got closer, and we dreaded to hear the sick, mourning sound I had heard months before followed by the red ray of light, but the plane flew silently overhead without unloading another blast. When we examined the destruction he had made, we found that some of the bullets had penetrated the building's walls and roof. The inside of the building was in shambles, and the wall and the partial roof were peppered with hundreds of holes. Had we stayed inside the building, we would have been hit.[173]

The Squawking Blackbird
Operation Foster, Arizona Territory
November 19, 1967, D+6, 0700-2030 hours

First Platoon saddled up early the next morning. The rest of the company was staying behind at the old French fort. The smell of wet soil clung to the air around us. As we moved out a thick fog covered most of the village and only the top of a cluster of trees a short distance away was visible; the trees' dark green colors hidden by the thickness of the troubling cloud surrounding us.

As we moved out, a lone blackbird, the only visible creature in the area, squawked loudly as it flew past us. It scurried from treetop to treetop, squawking in rage at having to move along ahead of us as we approached. Then the bird perched itself on the top branch of a tall wide-leafed palm tree. As we drew near, the bird looked down at us, looked behind his back, and hesitated at moving away once more. Then it squawked loudly at something behind it and quickly flew off over our heads, and I wondered if it was an omen of what the day would bring.

We traveled in a northwest direction, bypassing several small villages as we circled to come back to where we started. The area we were moving through contained thick hedgerows, heavy clinging vines, and clusters of tall trees that concealed many small trails, tunnels, hooches, and small villages. The platoon stopped, and we set up a blocking force at the northwest corner of Phu Long (1).

Phu, Vietnamese for rich and Long was the name local peasant farmers had given the village, one of two so named villages in the area. All the villages in the area were considered rich by the villagers. The villages enjoyed two large rivers close by, rolling hills, thick vegetation, tall trees, and rich farm land suitable for rice growing, and friendly hamlets. Close by a number of foot paths, cart trails and hooches were well kept and used.

We set in where a cart trail and two footpaths (trail) came together, and First Squad moved out, to envelope around in a wide clockwise direction to flush out any enemy and drive them toward us.

By noon, the squad had returned; Izzie and Chief reported having seen movement in the area, but they couldn't get close enough to substantiate if it was enemy activity or civilians that might still be hiding.

By 1500 hours, we returned to the village, and a squad from Second Platoon with a machine-gun team was going out. They were to patrol along the east side of Phu Long (1), circle around counterclockwise and return to our company's camp before nightfall.

Lieutenant Faithful, Second Platoon's commander, had begun the operation with the most undermanned platoon in the company.

He walked up to Corporal Neufeld and asked him how many men he had in his squad; five answered Richard Neufeld, a short-timer whom everyone called "Duke." With less than a month to go, Operation Foster would be his last operation.

Lieutenant Faithful then asked Corporal Sanders and Robert Sanders answered six as he was counting himself, and his squad was picked to go.

Sgt. Robert Tully would lead the squad and the new Corpsman HM3 Charles Robertson, who had been in county only two weeks, was chosen to go with them. Doc Keller asked the lieutenant if he could take Robertson's place, but Faithful said, no. With the men selected, the squad moved out.

You Are Invited To Dinner
Operation Foster, Arizona Territory
November 19, 1967, D+6, 0700-2030 hours

Shortly after the squad moved out, Captain Baggette summoned his platoon commanders for a ceremonial dinner meeting at his command post located inside a brick building at the French Ville.

From what his CP personnel had been able to gather from the rubble and from the spoils of war, an arrangement had been made to have a nice dinner. A table had been set, complete with lighted candles, dinner plates, eating utensils and other items company grunts had gathered from the vacated buildings in the old French village. Dinner was set for 1600 hours.

As Lieutenant Wilson, First Platoon, Lieutenant Faithful, Second Platoon, and Lieutenant Mullens, Third Platoon, made their way toward the CO's command position, the point man in Second Platoon's squad on patrol was nearing the tree line at the end of a long dike.

The cart trail located at the northeast corner of Phu Long (1) was used by locals as a trail to travel on between villages.

All of a sudden, the tree line in front of the point man erupted with automatic and machine-gun fire.

Second Platoon's Squad Is Pinned Down
Operation Foster, Arizona Territory Grid 872522
November 19, 1967, D+6, 0700-2030 hours

We gathered to listen to the radio to hear what was happening.

"We've been hit, we're pinned down, we need help and an immediate medevac," the squad's radioman was screaming into the net.

The squad was taking heavy incoming machine-gun fire near the northeast corner of Phu Long (1). They were on a large dike and had sustained casualties.

"Two men are shot badly!" he screamed into the mike, calling for a priority medevac. The sound of gun fire and small explosions could be heard over the open mike.

"Come, get us out of here!" cried out the radioman calling for an immediate medevac. Then, the radio went silent.

Within minutes, of the radio message Second Platoon Marines were gearing up, grabbing their weapons to get out to their men.

Captain Baggette asked his radioman, to ascertain the exact position where the squad was and told Faithful, he was sending out Third Platoon to the rescue. Ron Patrick, a Second Platoon Marine already saddled up, was listening to the radio, when he overhead the captain's order and pleaded with him to allow Second Platoon to go, instead.

"They're our men and we need to go," he argued almost to the point of insubordination, in front of his own commander.

Baggette remained determined to send out Third Platoon, when Ralph Keenan another Second Platoon Marine also interviewed. He also pleaded for the captain to let Second Platoon Marines go instead.

"How can we face those guys, if someone else goes out, instead of their own platoon," he said.

By then Second Platoon Marines were saddled up and ignoring the Captain they were lining up and were ready to move out.

Lieutenant Faithful looked at Baggette, waiting for an answer. The Captain stood with his hands on his hips, relented and gave him the go ahead.

Tall and lanky Sgt. Joel Williamson from East Meadow, NY, took point. Williamson was often called, "Ball" by members of his platoon, because he seemed to be always bouncing around the compound, helping out, fixing things and doing odd jobs for others.

Responding to the pinned down Marines, behind Ball, was 18-year old, Robert Bruce Wilson IV a short blonde haired Marine from Winston-Salem, NC. Everyone called him, 'Gimpy.' A very religious Marine, Gimpy loved playing the guitar and was naïve of many things in life, including sex, which was the main topic he was often kidded about.

As the unit moved out, Doc Keller fell in behind "Fat Pete," Mark C. Petersen, from Pierson, Iowa. Petersen was tall and a bit heavy, that wanted to play professional football. He was an intelligent Marine who was always full of laughter and humor, Petersen had dark brown curly hair, straight teeth, and wore thick eye-glasses. A battle-savvy Marine, he was on his last month out in the field, and Operation Foster was to be his last time out in the field

As the platoon moved out, Doc Keller in one of those moments in life when scattered thoughts cross your mind was stepping out behind him and recalled how

Petersen had once told him that for awhile he lived over a post office in a small town and had gotten the clap from a school teacher living there.

First Platoon didn't wait for the word to be passed down: we saddled up and were ready to move out in trace of Second Platoon. Our First Squad was being led by a new squad leader, Sgt. Evaristo Morales, a dark skinned Hispanic that had been with the company for some time, but was new to our platoon. Duran's gun team fell in right behind Morales followed by Lieutenant Wilson's CP group.

Jones sandwiched my gun team just in front of Third Squad's last fire-team. We were returning to the same area where we had been earlier that day. It was the place where Izzie and Chief had said they had seen possible enemy movement.

Get Off The Trail
Operation Foster, Arizona Territory Grid 872522
November 19, 1967, D+6, 0700-2030 hours

At the southern edge of Phu Long (1), Faithful's platoon turned right to travel around the southeast corner of the village counter-clockwise to come up behind their pinned down squad. Moments before Lieutenant Faithful's platoon reached their men, the enemy broke contact.

When Faithful arrived at the edge of the village, he could see some of his men spread out along the cart trail that ran north on the east side of the northeast corner of Phu Long (1). The wide dike, used as a cart path ended a hundred yards away where it entered a thick cluster of tall trees and heavy vegetation.

A couple of Marines who had been walking flank to the left of the dike were laying prone out in the open rice paddy field. Some were wounded, others had their backs up against the dike, and some were wedged solid up against another dike hugging its berm for what protection it could provide.

From where they were, it was hard for Faithful to tell exactly where all the men were and who was wounded or killed and who wasn't.

"Get off the trail, get off the trail," a wounded Marine cried out to the lieutenant and his CP group.

Immediately the machine-gunner behind Faithful peeled off to go left and set up along the edge of tree line while his ammo carriers quickly jumped to the right side of the trail.

Lieutenant Faithful stepped off the trail and stood surveying the area. Then he saw an enemy soldier get up from the base of the tree line northwest of him and take off running west to the left of where Faithful stood. Before he could say anything, Marines were already taking aim. Just then, another enemy soldier also took off running, in the same direction.

The Marines opened fire and saw the last of the enemy soldiers go down, at the edge of the tree line. There was no return fire.

Faithful knew that if he were to get his wounded men out and a medevac in, he needed to secure the far tree line where the enemy soldiers had disappeared into.

Corporal Charles Saunders' Squad Moves Out
Operation Foster, Arizona Territory Grid 872522
November 19, 1967, D+6, 0700-2030 hours

The job of securing the tree line was given to First Squad being led by Corporal Charles Saunders. The squad reinforced with other volunteers moved out to cut across on the left side and secure the base of the tree line where they had seen the enemy soldier fall.

Saunders moved out using a shallow ditch at the base of the wide berm (cart trail) that ran along the edge of the tree line. By then, Faithful had moved back up, and was standing at the end of the village where the dike began; open rice paddy fields were to his right, thick tropical jungle and Phu Long (1) to his left rear.

As the squad moved out, Saunders had his squad drop off their belts of machine-gun ammo at Cpl. Ralph Keenan, Pvt. John Webster and L/Cpl. Peter Lehr's machine-gun position. Webster had set up his gun to cover for them at the outer edge of the shallow ditch at the base of a wide berm in front of the tree line. He was to the west of Faithful's position and midway between the two dikes.

Saunders made his way west until he reached a wide dike fifty yards away. He gave the signal to the rest of his squad, and they all stood up to move north across the two parallel dikes. A fire-team stood up to walk midway across the open rice paddy field, in assault position.

At that time, there was no doubt in Saunders and Faithful's minds the enemy had opened fire and had now fled the area.

As the squad made their way across the open field between Phu Long (1) and Phu Phong (4), Faithful walked toward Sergeant Tully, who had been wounded in the hand and was still lying prone alongside the eastside dike (cart trail). Other Marines followed their lieutenant walking out on top of the dike. The dike ran straight north from the northeast corner of Phu Long (1) to another tree line about 80 meters away. Tully was about twenty meters out.

As the Marines moved out an enemy sniper placed Lieutenant Faithful in the center of his scope, took in a deep breath, held it, and squeezed the trigger.

Find Cover As Best You Can
Operation Foster, Arizona Territory AT 867519
November 19, 1967, D+6, 0700-2030 hours

Immediately the tree line in front of the Marines exploded with intense incoming automatic rifle fire.

Marines on the west dike jumped to the right side of the trail. Others hit the ground out in the open rice paddy field. The only cover available to Saunders was a distance away. He ran northeast across the rice paddy toward the nearest rice paddy dike, as bullets kicked up dirt following him.

Gerald Vealey walking right flank to Saunders' right front, dived for cover as the first volley of bullets flew by. He struck the muddy ground hard but recovered quickly.

As Saunders ran forward, Gimpy, Saunders radioman got up from where he had hit the ground and ran toward where his squad leader was running.

Vealey having found cover behind a rice paddy dike lifted his weapon to open fire and cover for them. When he pulled the trigger, his rifle exploded in his hand.

He lay there dazed for a second, but unhurt. He looked at his mud-stuffed busted barrel. His M-16 was now useless. Bullets flew by as he crawled in closer to the dike. Without a weapon, there was nothing he could do.

The enemy was shooting at ground level, and as Saunders ran a round struck him in his foot and he went down. While bullets struck the open ground all around him, Gimpy kept running until he found cover behind the dike Saunders had been running toward.

Sgt. Joel Williamson at the tree line dropped down to one knee at the onset of the attack and boldly returned automatic rifle fire at the entrenched enemy forces. He knew he was in an exposed position as bullets were being shot at him but there was no time to first seek cover. Instead he returned fire desperately trying to cover for his men. As he fired and re-loaded as fast as he could, two rounds entered his mid-section and he dropped to both knees.

Williamson, though seriously wounded, raised his weapon once more to fire off a few more shots when a sniper's bullet to his head brought him down.

Saunders could feel the pain from where he had been shot in the foot. He got up and tried to make his way to where his radioman, 'Gimpy,' Robert Bruce Wilson, had found cover but the distance was too great. He could hear his radioman yelling on the net, calling for help. As bullets struck the ground around him, Saunders began to crawl toward his radioman.

When the initial barrage of incoming fire was released, Sergeant Tully without hesitation quickly got up, reached out and grabbed his lieutenant, and brought him down to the ground.

Lieutenant Faithful, with Gary Reed, his radioman at his side, having been identified as an officer by an enemy sniper, took two of the initial fired bullets in his gut.

Tully returned fire while placing his body in such a position that he was also protecting his commander from any further impact. Tully the closest to the lieutenant held his M-16 close and tight trying to make himself as small a target as possible as he returned fire. By then the NVA sniper had zeroed in on Tully's head and pulled the trigger.

Other Marines got a hold of their lieutenant and pulled him further out of harms way. As they did, they could see where the bullets had sliced through their commanders' mid-section, and knew their lieutenant was seriously wounded.

The sniper's bullet slid straight across the open field in a southeast direction and struck Tully's M-16, ricocheted off and with a bouncing glance struck Tully in the chest giving him a flesh wound. Tully continued to fire, until his M-16 jammed.

Tully then turned to help other Marines move his wounded platoon commander farther out of harm's way, as he did a bullet sliced through Tully's buttocks.

George Matinez, the Pacific Islander from Guam, was standing behind Faithful's radioman, when the shooting started; he helped drag Faithful away from the rice paddie dike and into a more secure spot near a large grave mount.

By then, most of the squad committed to cross over the open field were pinned down out in the open and were receiving a concentrated volume of heavy machine-gun and automatic rifle fire. Martinez, trying to cover for them, to give them a chance to get out of their pinned down position, took careful aim and opened fire on the enemy position with his M-79. He and others by his side returning fire were soon also receiving an intense amount of incoming fire.

Corporal Ron Patrick in charge of guns had set up the second machine-gun, at the intersection where the cart trail that ran along the tree line turned north at the northeast corner of Phu Long (1). From there the gun team he felt would be able to fire across to the far left tree line and to right of the trail near where the enemy originally ambushed the squad.

He got behind the gun and barely opened fire when a bullet struck the machine-gun and it stopped firing.

As Saunders was slowly crawling on his belly toward Bruce Wilson, his radioman, Wilson was on the radio frantically calling for help, calling for a medevac, telling whoever would listen that he had been shot, and other Marines lay wounded or killed, he was desperately crying out for a priority one emergency medevac, and he wanted them there, now.

"We're-pinned down, and can't return fire, and we're taking heavy casualties," he cried out over the net as he pleaded for help to come quickly.

Ironically Gimpy had been scheduled to go on R&R but his orders had been cancelled an hour before the operation and now, seriously wounded he was calling out for help, describing what was happening, over the net over and over again.

Don't Move, Doc. Robertson
Operation Foster, Arizona Territory AT 872522
November 19, 1967, D+6, 0700-2030 hours

The enemy's main firepower was well directed; they continued to fire at the pinned down Marines keeping them trapped, while still maintaining much of their firing directed at Lieutenant Faithful and his men. The platoon commander's radio antennas made the CP group an attractive target for the enemy.

Doc Robertson, lying at the edge of a narrow dike had already been shot and each time he moved a sniper shot at him again, and again. When Tully saw that, he grabbed hold of Lieutenant Faithful's M-16 and opened fire drawing attention away from the wounded Corpsman, but then Faithful's M-16 also jammed and as Tully went down to clear it, the enemy opened fire with .50 caliber and recoilless-rifle fire at Tully's position. The explosive ordinance blew away the edge of the dike where he had been only seconds before.

Because of the fierce incoming fire Marines were also pinned down inside the shallow ditch that ran in front of the tree line. Some were wounded and unable to return fire, others were calling out to Robertson, the wounded Corpsman, trying to tell him to stay still, crying out to him to stop moving, but the bullets kept coming and as the Corpsman moved, more bullets would strike him.

Marines knowing the Corpsman was being used as bait by the sniper couldn't do anything but sit-and-watch as the Corpsman moved and the sniper's bullets would strike him again and again until he stopped moving.

Ron Patrick's Rocket Team
Operation Foster, Arizona Territory AT 872522
November 19, 1967, D+6, 0700-2030 hours

As they continued to take incoming fire, Ron Patrick, and his A-gunner took their rocket launcher as forward as they could and found a small bomb crater they crawled into. They loaded the launcher and he fired off a couple of rounds from the bazooka rocket launcher, before the other two rocket rounds they had wouldn't fire. With the rocket launcher now useless, and the enemy targeting their location, the rocket team crawled as low as possible back to the tree line.

With Faithful seriously wounded and Sergeant Tully already shot twice. Sgt. Douglas Isleb, "Sergeant Gus," as he was called by his men, assumed command of Second Platoon.

The thin faced, small frame giant of a man held his men's respect from the first day he joined the company in early July. An easy going, tough Marine that was very cautious of where he was and what his troops were engaged in.

The burden of assuming command of Second Platoon in the middle of a fire fight while they were taking casualties weighed heavily upon his shoulders, and he wondered what was best for his troops.

Marines were being hit left and right by sizzling shrapnel from exploding rocket fire, grenades as well as from bullets being unleashed by a well-trained and disciplined enemy force. Some Marines lying out in the open had already received multiple hits. There was no doubt by now that the enemy force they had encountered was bigger than platoon size.

No sooner had Ron Patrick and Thomas Cole slipped into a safe spot, Sgt. Gus called them over and asked them to move up as far forward as possible, and if they had a chance to try to get wounded Marines out of the kill zones they were in. They both looked at each other. They had just come from there.

As the two moved out, the enemy spotted their movement and both became pinned down by intense incoming fire.

Some Marines that were unable to return fire, without fear of being hit, so they were laying their M-16s flat on top of the dikes and returning fire. They didn't dare look where they were firing for fear of being hit. They just opened up with the M-16 laid out over the rice paddy dike and fired away.

With the enemy's concentrated fire being aimed at anyone who moved or responded to the incoming fire, Gus realized he had limited fire power, and ordered Keenan, Webster and Lehr's machine-gun team to cease firing. They were drawing too much incoming fire, he told them. Gus also told the other members of Second Platoon to cease firing unless they saw the enemy, and had a clear target or they were directly fired upon. He wanted them to conserve their ammo and wait until the rest of the company caught up.

First Platoon's Response
Operation Foster, Arizona Territory
November 19, 1967, D+6, 0700-2030 hours

No sooner had we saddled up, and moved out in trace of Second Platoon, Lieutenant Wilson called for us to double-time out to their location.

We were running on the same trail that we had traveled often over the past few days in our patrols throughout the area. The trail ran across rice paddy fields leading to Phu Long (1). As we ran across I couldn't help but to think it was a perfect place for the enemy to ambush us, as both sides of the trail offered no cover.

The wide berm was large enough for a water buffalo to walk on but not a cart. From the French fort the trail shot out in a northwest direction then inclined slightly northeast through the village and the tropical jungle surrounding it. At the end of the trail, a wider berm used as a cart trail ran east and west, in front of a tree line at the northern edge of the village. Often in the past when we arrived at that berm, we turned left toward Phu An (1) then followed the trail north again between a large rice paddy field toward Phu Binh (3) where the trail once again ran east and west along the tree line the enemy now had Second Platoon pinned down from. Behind the tree line was a thick forested area that extended all the way to the base of Finger Lake.

As we moved along I felt the enemy could be anywhere along the trail.[174] The rice paddy to the right of the trail was flooded; another field further up mud filled. The rice paddies to the left of the trail were dry. A series of scattered grave mounds could be seen to the left of the trail where it ended at the southern edge of the village of Phu Long (1). There was a gradual rise in elevation from where the long dike began to where it ended near the grave mounts. To the right were open fields and further northeast of us was a larger graveyard. Just a short distance away from there, Second Platoon was engaged in a fierce firefight with the enemy.

As we entered the thick vegetation and village area of Phu Long (1) we could hear gunfire and we quickened our speed to get there.

The End of the Trail at the Edge of the Tree Line
Operation Foster, Arizona Territory
November 19, 1967, D+6, 0700-2030 hours

Before our platoon arrived at the contact area, the shooting stopped. L/Cpl. Lee McCullough, Second Squad's point man was leading the platoon, and he stopped at the tree line where the trail ended.

Out in the rice paddy field, he could see other Second Platoon Marines lying out in the open or pressed up against rice paddy dikes, others were lying in the wide agricultural ditch to the right of the trail.

When he stopped, the rest of the platoon stopped behind him, and immediately Second Squad peeled off going to the left of the trail and began to set in at the northern edge of the tree line behind a wide berm. They set in facing the open field and the tree line on the other side, of two large rice paddies.

McCullough was a big Marine that liked walking point for his squad. He and other Marines now stood out in the open along the cart trail running east and west on the other side of the tree line.

Our platoon had reached the tip of the trail by going through Phu Long (1). To the left was the dike in the middle of the rice paddy fields we had often used; the trail led north to the far tree line to Phu Binh (3) and its thick forested area. To the right and east of the trail were Second Platoon Marines. Some were in the shallow ditch at the base of the trail that ran in front of the wide berm used as a cart trail that ran along the edge of the tree line. Other Second Platoon Marines were set in behind the tree line.

Just passed them was the beginning of the trail the original squad was on when they were ambushed.

Duran's gun team, with Aggie as his A-gunner, followed Second Squad as they peeled off, going to the left

Duran began looking for an advantageous position from where to cover for the Marines from Second Platoon he could see lying out in the open. He chose to set up the gun on the berm near the end of the west trail. A fire-team set up to his left, on the other side of the trail.

Keeton, carrying two hundred extra rounds of gun ammo, had fallen back and was standing to the left near the edge of the trail behind Chief and Izzie. To

Keeton's right, the platoon's CP group including Sgt. Isaacs was stopped on the trail.

Keeton felt something wasn't right, so he quickly got down on one knee, eyeing an old bomb crater to the left of the trail as an advantageous place to jump into if they got hit. The rest of First Platoon, having stopped, behind the CP group also got down to the left of the trail we had followed out. We waited to see where we would be deployed.

As we sat down to catch our breath at the tail end of the platoon, Jones began to check out the area.

Clusters of thick bushes and tall tropical trees filled the area on both sides of the trail with small patches of clearing here and there on both sides of the trail.

We were in the midst of a tropical jungle with no buildings or dwellings nearby, and no place for us to find cover if we were hit from any direction. Jones was looking around to see where I could set up the gun, in case we got hit.

A Premonition—Of What Was About To Happen
Operation Foster, Arizona Territory AT 872522
November 19, 1967, D+6, 0700-2030 hours

Lieutenant Wilson stepped off the trail and joined other Marines who were standing behind the tree line using it for cover. He was looking at a map of the area.

Wilson had, had a premonition about the area ever since we first started running patrols in the area and had instructed our squads not to cross the open fields using the east trail where the Second Platoon's squad now lay pinned down. That reservation had now come true and as he took notice of that forewarning he wondered what to do.

If Second Platoon had been hit twice, Wilson wanted to make sure we weren't caught in the same situation. No telling where the enemy was or if they were still in the area. Most of the time, the enemy would hit and run, but it seemed this time they had stuck around long enough to hit Second Platoon twice. That meant they might have a large enough force that was willing to take on a platoon or a company of Marines. When we arrived, the shooting stopped, which might indicate the enemy had decided to leave.

Wilson, like Lieutenant Faithful, realized we needed to get across by way of the left (west) side to cover for our men and to get them out of the kill zones. To use the east trail the Marines were originally on was not an option as that was where the majority of the enemy's concentrated fire power seemed to have come from.

If the enemy were still there, we were going to have to secure the area by enveloping around to the left side to come up behind the tree line where the enemy was.

Earlier that day, First Squad had come back on that berm after circling around to our left. Wilson eyed the options he had. To the left of that trail, thick tall bamboo and four foot height elephant grass covered the area. To go around meant First Platoon would have to go pass that trail the long way around and would have to cut across a wide open field on the other side of a cluster of the tall grass and bamboo patches.

Meanwhile, if the enemy was still there, First Platoon would have to engage the them from the tree line for a long period of time, and he wanted to get to the wounded Marines and get them medevaced as soon as possible.

A direct assault would be costly, Wilson knew, and as he pondered all this in his mind, wounded Marines lay out in the open some thirty to one eighty meters away. It was hard for him to tell where all of Lieutenant Faithful's men were.

As I sat waiting for the word to move up, Captain Baggette and his CP group ran past us.

Wilson by then had already deployed the remaining Marines from his CP group and Second Squad to his left along the well-beaten berm that ran parallel to the tree line. A fire-team from first squad including Chief and Izzie had also positioned themselves in that area. The rest of first squad was deployed to the right of the trail and reinforced Second Platoon's men.

They Are Going Into Spider Holes
Operation Foster, Arizona Territory AT872522
November 19, 1967, D+6, 0700-2030 hours

Lieutenant Wilson knew a priority medevac chopper was needed for Lieutenant Faithful, and other seriously wounded Marines. To do that, the area needed to be secured; he decided it would be advantageous to send out two squads at the same time.

Sergeant Isaacs would take a fire-team of Marines and go out along the right (east) dike and Third Squad would go out along the west trail while the rest of First Platoon would provide cover.

Sgt. Lawrence Isaacs was technically smart. He once said he wanted to go to Israel and fight for them during their Six-Day-War. Small and skinny, he had big ears, was thin faced, and wide eyed. He told his squad, he was a country boy from Tennessee or Kentucky, no one really knew, as he mentioned several other states at different times. When he arrived at Liberty Bridge, he was assigned squad leader to Second Squad and quickly got them busy in cleaning out their barrack and the surrounding area. No sooner had they done that, the typhoon hit, washing out the sand bags they had laid out to reinforce their bunkers. All their work wasted.

He moved out with one of his fire-teams, going east on top of the cart trail that ran east and west in front of the tree line. He wanted to get as close to the Marines that were out in the open as quickly as possible. If the enemy opened fire again, he had instructed the Marines with him, to try and get Lieutenant Faithful and the other wounded Marines out of the kill zones.

The wide shallow ditch was to their left. Keene was walking point, Walsh walking behind him and they could see Marines laid out prone at the bottom of the ditch. Some seemed to be wounded; others were using the ditch for cover.

When they arrived at the tip of the cart trail that ran north from the tree line, they could see where Lieutenant Faithful was.

I sat and waited. We were spread out along the trail and still a good distance from where everyone else was at the front where the trail ended at the tree line.

There was an eerie silence present in the area as a reinforced Third Squad fireteam moved out along the wide berm on the west side. To their right McCullough, Lucero and another Marine stepped off to get across assault style.

Marines from Second Platoon and their Corpsmen in the shallow ditch began to crawl out to get wounded Marines out of harm's way. The majority of Sergeant Tully's squad still remained out in the open along with Lieutenant Faithful.

Corporal Boyd had assembled his rocket launcher and was moving up to the tree line on the left side of the trail when he saw movement across the paddies along the far tree line.

Boyd set down the rocket launcher and ran back to tell Lieutenant Wilson what he had seen. As he was making his way back, he caught a glimpse of a quick, jerky movement near some bushes close to the right side of the trail the area was behind where everyone else was located. He took out, his .45 pistol and walked over where he had seen movement. He found a hidden tunnel and at its entrance a shirt the type NVA soldiers wore, he called out to Dumont.

When Captain Baggette arrived at front of the trail, Wilson turned to consult with him.

Doc Gibbs, Captain Baggette's CP group Corpsman, immediately sensed that something was wrong, something was very wrong, and something was about to happen, and it was going to happen very quickly. The Corpsman decided to promptly move to the right to get off the trail.

"Dumont, there's someone moving in that far tree line across the ways," Boyd told Dumont as he walked up to the CP. "And I saw some movement behind us, by a tunnel over there,"

"Show me," Dumont said, and in French he called out to the Kit Carson Scout assigned to our company to follow him and Boyd.

The Kit Carson Scout examined the torn shirt and disregarded it as unimportant, the scout did not examine the tunnel any further, and they all returned to where Lieutenant Wilson was.

Boyd once again looked across the open rice paddy field to where he had seen movement before and again spotted movement.

"Lieutenant, look over there," Boyd said to Wilson.

"They're going into spider holes." Across the rice paddy field, NVA soldiers were moving forward into concealed positions. Lieutenant Wilson strained to look where Boyd was pointing, but there wasn't any further movement.

That Sense of Danger—That Is In the Air
Operation Foster, Arizona Territory AT 872522
November 19, 1967, D+6, 0700-2030 hours

As Doc Gibbs placed the stock of the M-16 he was carrying on the ground and knelt on one knee, he was struggling with the foreboding sense of a very present danger. Unable to ignore, the escalating sense of a serious threat nearby, he looked across the open rice paddy fields to the far tree line, where the sensation of evil was coming from.

The tree line across the open rice paddy fields suddenly exploded with intense small arms and automatic rifle fire.

Gibbs jumped with the sound and destructive force that was unleashed. His body struck the dry grass hard and he slid sideways as bullets whizzed pass his ears.

Bullets were being fired toward where the majority of First Platoon Marines were and others were being walked up the trail toward where Lieutenant Wilson, Captain Baggette, and their CP groups were gathered.

Instantly, Marines were hit along the tree line, on the berm, in the open field, and on both trails.

Boyd and Rahm simultaneously jumped into the same bomb crater, Keeton had eyed earlier.

Ward Keeton, with his back to the open field had just stood up, and was facing Lieutenant Wilson, when the sounds of gunfire erupted.

He began to twist and duck to dive for the crater when he was hit by an enemy round.

The bullet struck his right shoulder, tore through the base of his neck and lodged in his spine. The impact of the bullet spun him around and he fell headfirst into the crater.

Wilson, standing in the middle of the trail, turned to his left to dive for cover and was hit by a bullet that struck his flak jacket and glanced off striking his chest.

The impact of the bullet on the flak jacket was enough to knock the lieutenant to the ground.

Before the artillery Forward Observer carrying a TAC radio could hit the ground, he also was hit.

Anthony Vigil the Marine sniper who had been with us on Operation Knox was standing out in the open next to Rahm when the shooting started; he also jumped into the crater, almost landing on top of Rahm and Boyd.

Vigil recovered quickly, got up on one knee and began to sight in on the enemy across the field. When his scope found a suitable target, he held his breath and squeezed the trigger.

Rahm and Boyd scrambled at the bottom of the large crater to prepare the rocket tube for action. The crater was old, and large, probably from a B52 strike, months ago.

Several Marines were already in there, when Wilson crawled off the trail and slipped into the same crater. Feeling pain from the bullet's impact, he touched his chest with his hand, fearing what he might find.

When he withdrew his hand he saw blood at the base of his palm. He tore open his shirt, fearing to look at or touch the wound.

Keeton while struggling at the bottom of the crater managed to right himself and sought a comfortable position to sit up. The pain in his shoulder was intense and nauseating.

Everyone around him looked out of focus, as if they were in a fog. As his head began to clear, he could hear an echoing sound as Wilson was asking him a question.

"How bad am I shot, how bad am I shot?" Lieutenant Wilson asked Keeton.

Keeton steadied himself, tilted his head back and saw his helmet lying next to him at the bottom of the crater. He could hear Marines at the lip of the crater, and elsewhere returning fire, and he thought of getting it, but the pain returned. He shifted his weight to sit upright and focused on Wilson, half kneeling next to him.

He leaned over to look at the lieutenant's wound.

The bullet that struck Wilson's flak jacket had glanced off his chest, leaving behind only a flesh wound. With an encouraging word, Keeton said, "It's just a pimple of a hit, Lieutenant."

Keeton then leaned back to take off his own flak jacket and utility shirt to have a look at his own wound.

On the dike/trail to the west of First Platoon, enemy firepower was peppering both sides of the dike. The rounds were steadily making their way toward Marines lying prone on top of the dike.

Other bullets were striking the area where McCullough, Lucero and another Marine were laid out in the open rice paddy field. All three had been hit.

Behind them the top of the berm in front of the tree line was being struck with relentless explosive incoming gunfire.

Cpl. Robert Howard from First Platoon had just crawled out and gotten hold of a wounded Marine who had been hit in the initial firefight. Sergeant Gus had set up two Marines to provide cover for him in case he was fired upon; As Howard was bend over to pick up the wounded Marine, the enemy opened fire.

Instead of providing cover, the Marines that were suppose to provide cover, jumped out of the safety of the swallow ditch and ran out under intense enemy incoming fire to help Howard carry the wounded Marine back to safety.

Out in the open, one of the Marines knelt on one knee near the fallen Marine and returned fire. Behind them, Sgt. Gus also exposed himself to enemy fire and provided cover as they all ran back.

Howard and the other Marine carried the wounded Marine out of harm's way and into the safety of the wide agricultural ditch.

They made it back, without getting hit, and as Howard and Sgt. Gus helped get the wounded Marine into the secured tree line behind the wide berm, other Marines were returning fire.

Other Marines, both from Second and First Platoon, were now being hit by enemy fire and were calling out for help or calling for the Corpsman.

Lucero, out in the middle of the rice paddy, was curled up with his head, arms and whole body drawn in tight. He was screaming hysterically, calling and crying out for help as bullets struck the ground all around him.

"Get us out of here! Get us out of here! We're all going to die! We're all going to die!" he kept crying out.

The platoon could hear his screams above the uproar.

Sgt. Isaacs moved his fire-team back to rejoin First Platoon where the enemy was concentrating their fire power.

As they were crawling their way back, Keene dropped off where Lieutenant Faithful was. He told Walsh, to go on he was going to stay there next to Faithful and did so.

Duran's Response
Operation Foster, Arizona Territory AT 872522
November 19, 1967, D+6, 0700-2030 hours

Duran, with Aggie as his A-gunner, was sighting in to cover for the Marines moving out when the shooting started. He immediately stiffened his hold on the gun pulling it in close while tightening his grip on the gun's trigger mechanism. He sighted in and opened fire toward where the majority of the incoming fire was coming from.

Aggie quickly took up the A-gunner's position and immediately they began to take heavy incoming fire.

To keep his head down and with fear his head might get hit, Aggie lay down on his back to be as low to the ground as possible. While lying on his back, to the left of Duran, he was making sure the rounds were not touching the ground and were being fed evenly into the gun's feed tray.

Duran was shooting over the heads of Marines that were lying out in the open rice paddy fields in front of him.

The enemy's firing began to get closer to his gun and he could tell a number of enemy soldiers were targeting him. Bullets began whizzing by only inches away.

Duran zeroed in on those firing at him until he silenced them or they stopped shooting. He had control of his gun and was steadily sweeping the area with intense machine-gun fire, spraying the far tree line from left to right, raking the enemy line of fire with a steady flow of fiery red tracers. He held the trigger down and bullets rapidly exited the gun's barrel.

The enemy; however, seemed to have responded to his firing with the same amount of relentless firepower; and for a few seconds, blue, green, and white machine-gun tracers crossed the same rice paddy dike as Duran's red fiery tracers. Duran's response was accurate and some of the incoming fire subsided, but only for a few seconds before a number of other high-powered enemy weapons turned their attention and fired toward Duran's M-60 machine-gun position. AK-47's and automatic weapons opened fire in his direction, including 30mm caliber machine-gun fire.

Duran responded without reservation, firing at the enemy with pinpoint accuracy; then from his left side, from the grassy area to the left of the western dike, the enemy opened up, shooting at Duran and other Marines from that side.

Duran, seeing where the new incoming fire was coming from, turned to his left to engage them; but in order to effectively return fire in that direction, he had to rise up, lifting the gun's barrel to do so, and as he did, he exposed himself from the waist up.

As his finger squeezed the trigger, incoming bullets began to tear up the top edge of the dike he had been laying behind. The bullets were crisscrossing and striking the dirt in front of his machine-gun position and began to climb inching their way closer toward him.

Aggie was preparing to link another 100-round belt to the gun when he felt dirt and debris falling on him. The incoming bullets were repeatedly striking the same area in front of their position; he looked at Duran and saw, how much Duran was exposed to the incoming bullets.

"Get down, get down!" he screamed at him, but no sooner were the words out of his mouth, a snipers single bullet tore through Duran's right side and exited his front and Duran went down.

Boyd and Rahm, with the 3.5 rocket launcher ready to fire, rolled out of the crater and moved out to the edge of the berm near where the trail ended. Boyd rose to one knee to fire the rocket. Rahm moved out from behind him to avoid the backblast the rocket was sure to create, and he patted Boyd on the helmet, clearing him to fire.

Boyd pulled the trigger and nothing happened. By then, the enemies' bullets were moving toward them. Bullets began to strike the edge of the berm, and both Boyd and Rahm dropped down for safety as bullets struck where they had been, showering them with debris.

They crawled back to the crater and checked the trigger and wiring and then rolled back out to try and shoot the rocket again.

As Boyd rose to fire, he aimed for the center of where the intense firing was coming from. It was the same location he had seen the gooks disappear into earlier.

He pulled the trigger, and the rocket's round once again failed to ignite. As the incoming rounds all around them increased in intensity, they both dropped back down and waited for the onslaught to die down.

Larry, What Do We Do Now? What Do We Do Now?
Operation Foster, Arizona Territory AT 872522
November 19, 1967, D+6, 0700-2030 hours

Captain Baggette and the Marines from his CP group had also jumped into the crater and were hugging the ground for safety. Others were set up along the tree line and against fierce incoming fire were returning fire when they could.

Captain Baggette moved over to where Lieutenant Wilson was and cried out excitedly, "Larry, Larry, what do we do now? What do we do now?"

Lieutenant Wilson, buttoning his shirt, answered with what he had been pondering in his mind.

When the enemy opened fire from their entrenched position, firing toward where Faithful and his Marines were, Wilson had seen where the enemy bullets were striking, and got a better view and understanding where most of Boyd Faithful's forward men were located. Some of the Marines in Second Platoon on our far right were pinned down some as close as eighty feet from the front of the tree line where the enemy was entrenched and firing at us from.

He could see that where they were, they were too close to the enemy and if they moved, they would surely be killed. It would also be hard to bring in air support, but something had to be done. He could see that Marines from his platoon's First Squad and what remained of Second Platoon were spread out across the open rice paddies in front of us. He counted six Marines still out in the open and others pinned down on the trails. From where he was, he couldn't tell who was dead and who was wounded.

"We need to drop artillery on the left side of the tree line of where the enemy is firing from. It seems as if from there, they are also supporting the enemy force firing at Second Platoon to our right. We need some air cover but right now, we have Marines too close to the tree line for that. Maybe we can envelop around to the enemy's left side. Where's Third Platoon?" Wilson asked and Baggette got on the radio.

Boyd rose again for the third time to fire his rocket; they had checked the rocket's wires and trigger and were sure it would fire this time.

He shifted his weight and got on his knees to fire. As he did, a sniper high in a tree across the field was waiting. He set his scope's crosshairs dead center on Boyd's head, and squeezed the trigger.

Boyd turned his head, to sight in with the bazooka when the bullet penetrated his helmet. The bullet's impact twisted Boyd around lifting the giant Marine clockwise, as the bullet glanced off his forehead.

Stunned, he dropped the rocket launcher as another bullet struck him in his right shoulder.

The second round hurled him backward. The impact of both bullets left Boyd dazed and bleeding spread out on the ground. Rahm quickly dragged him from where they were back to the safety of the crater.

Some Marines from First Platoon along the tree line had moved up behind the wide berm to their left and were providing good response fire, but their M-16's response to the enemy's incoming rounds was weak compared to the loud and powerful sound and impact the AK-47s were making. The enemy was unleashing a wall of lead, and the company was taking casualties. The enemy soldiers were firing mortars, RPG rockets, .30 and .50 caliber and automatic weapons at us, and our weapon's return fire, paled in comparison.

Wilson realized we had met a new and very aggressive enemy force. The enemy had chosen to stay and fight. They were well disciplined, effective, and the area was ablaze with bullets and exploding grenades as well as incoming mortars that were beginning to explode in the rice paddies in front of us, and most of our response was with little Mattie Mattel's.

Out in the open fields, Marines lay prone hugging the ground, trying to get behind any cover they could find. For the most part, they tried not to move, not to draw attention to themselves. The enemy had planned their ambush well. It was a classic L-shaped ambush that had been successfully deployed.

The enemy's main force was entrenched at the tree line directly in front of our company with only their heads rising up long enough to fire then ducking back into their spider holes or trenches while others would rise from their tunnels and from where they were hidden in the hedgerow to fire at us. The smaller leg of their L-shaped ambush force was set up to our left, and from there, they were engaging Marines from behind tall elephant grass. They were hard to detect until they fired their weapons. They had already shot Duran when he fired in support of the wounded Marines, and any Marine rising to return fire became their target or the target of a very successful sniper or snipers.

The Sniper's War
Operation Foster, Arizona Territory AT 872522
November 19, 1967, D+6, 0700-2030 hours

By the time the second bullet was shot at Boyd by the enemy sniper, Vigil our Marine sniper was looking for the well hidden enemy sniper.

Concealed snipers had been hitting the company with extreme accuracy. One of them was expertly selecting his shots, and Vigil was looking for him. Already two of our radios, a machine-gun, an officer, a Forward Air Observer, two sergeants, Duran, our machine-gunner, and Boyd, our rocketman, and perhaps others as well, had been shot by him or other snipers. Vigil had already successfully taken out two enemy snipers, who were selecting their targets to shoot at from well concealed positions.

"Both head shots," Vigil had told Ralph Keenan, the Marine nearest him after he had taken out the two snipers. Vigil set up next to a tree near Keenan's machine-gun position. If the enemy targeted them, he wanted to be able to take out the sniper.

Bullets, grenades, and RPG rockets continued to hit all along the tree line and berm where Captain Baggette and most of India Company's command group, as well as First Platoon, were located.

Baggette meanwhile was busy directing our 81mm mortar fire on the enemy's position.

By now the crater was full of Marines, mostly Baggette's CP group. Wilson, Doc Mac, and the other Marines decided to get out of the crater and run for the safety of the tree line. Doc Gibbs, seeing Wilson's radioman antenna poking high into the air, warned Wilson of the sniper firing at selected targets.

Wilson decided to go for it; they all were going to make a fast dash, but as soon as they got up, new intense incoming fire caused them to exit the bomb crater low crawling while scrambling for cover. Had they stood up when they ran out of the crater, the enemy would have had a good shot at all of them. They found themselves in a small garden with a wired fence that halted them from advancing. As the lieutenant looked up from his prone position, wondering what to do, he saw Izzie and Chief looking toward him unsure what the lieutenant was doing. Both Izzie and Chief had good cover and were responding effectively to the incoming fire when they could. Ira Rahm, who had joined the lieutenant and was now lying prone next to him, spun around and with the heel of his boots kicked the garden fence down and all of them moved up.

As the fence came down, Wilson, Rahm, and other Marines crawled out to the edge of the cart path where they could get a better look at the battlefield.

Two Corpsman, Snipers—Who Should Go?
Operation Foster, Arizona Territory AT 872522
November 19, 1967, D+6, 0700-2030 hours

Doc Gibbs and Doc Marren lying prone inside the crater decided where each of them would go to tend to wounded Marines calling out to them. Marines were calling for the Corpsman from both sides of the trail.

To their left, Duran had been hit and they had heard Aggie cry out for a Corpsman. As the Corpsmen sought out the best way to get to where Aggie was. Aggie saw that they were getting ready to risk their lives to get to Duran so he yelled back at them, "No, don't come, you'll get hit. Don't come."

Gibbs could tell from the urgency in Aggie's voice that there was a need for a Corpsman. Aggie wanted them to be there to tend to Duran's wound but was concerned for their safety as well. As Gibbs got ready to go, a new barrage of intense incoming bullets forced both Corpsmen back into the crater.

The Explosive Sounds Of War
Operation Foster, Arizona Territory AT 872522
November 19, 1967, D+6, 0700-2030 hours

While my gun team as well as the rest of Third Squad had not yet joined in the firefight, we could hear the explosive sounds from the weapons being discharged and the bullets as they sliced through the air overhead. The word by now had been passed down to us that First Platoon Marines were also pinned down and were out in the open rice paddy fields. I knew it would only be a matter of time before we would be called up to the front, and the look on Jones, it seemed, was that he was anxious to enter the battle, to be up front to do something, instead of just sitting and waiting.

As we waited, Third Platoon relieved of security for battalion back at Football Island showed up. They fell in behind the last fire-team to the right of where I was sitting.

Lieutenant Wilson, meanwhile, had called and deployed the first fire-team from Third Squad to the right of the trail. He figured that if they could provide cover, he would be able to lead Marines around to the left and recover our Marines that remained pinned down. Once the fire-team from Third Squad had crawled into an advantageous position, they unleashed a fierce volley of firepower toward the enemy, but it wasn't enough. As each Marine opened up, the enemy matched the increased firepower with their own concentrated fire. AK-47 bullets roared across the rice paddy fields from the entrenched enemy force, striking the berm and dirt where the fire-team was, causing them to seek cover. For Marines to shoot back at the enemy from the top of the wide berm was difficult because of the openness of the dike and because of the fierce incoming rounds striking the top of the cart trail. Who-ever was in charge of the enemy force had well prepared for this battle, as much of our response fire was quickly matched.

The tut-tut-tut sound of an enemy's M-50 machine-gun could also be heard above the uproar. The sickening sound the large bullets made as they split the air overhead or struck small trees and split them in two had a fearful effect on all of us.

Large branches were splintered into pieces and flew off every which way. The enemy's other machine-guns—both .30 caliber and Russian-made 7.62 machine-guns—could be heard as well, and green or white tracers flew overhead and embedded themselves in the jungle's thick foliage. The enemy bullets were striking canteens, flak jackets, helmets, knapsacks, radios, rifles, and officers and enlisted men alike.

Flatten Yourself, Hope and Pray
Operation Foster, Arizona Territory AT 872522
November 19, 1967, D+6, 0700-2030 hours

Marines out in the open flattened themselves as much as possible and hoped and prayed the cover they had was adequate to keep them safe. Those who could, found cover, rolled or embedded themselves farther into the sides of the rice paddy dikes. The rest, out in the open, lay motionless, hoping not to draw enemy fire; we didn't know if they were dead or alive.

The NVA remained heavily entrenched in the narrow trench lines on the other side of the rice paddy fields, they were in command of the battlefield. They had successfully pinned down Marines from Second and First Platoon and were targeting Marines who tried to go out and drag our wounded back to safety. The enemy before us was well disciplined, and they were utilizing their cover to their best advantage. Once in a while, they would fire an occasional round of bullets near a fallen Marine to agitate them or entice us, to try and rescue them, while concentrating on keeping the rest of the company engaged in battle.

Sgt. Gus had seen through all that, and had instructed his Marines to stop firing unless they had a clear target. "Let artillery and air wingers do their job, but if you can try to get our men out of harms way," he told them.

Cpl. Charles Saunders, First Squad leader from Second Platoon was one of the Marines still laid out in the open. His squad remained pinned down about sixty feet in front of a large bomb crater far out in front of the tree line.

He was too far out to be able to crawl back to safety. Members of his squad also remained pinned down near him. Saunders was in his twelfth month in Vietnam, and he wondered if he was going to get out alive. He had seen this scene repeated over and over again during his tour of duty.

To his right was Gerald Vealey. Vealey was another veteran, an old-timer in his eleventh month in country. Not since the Gates of Hell on January 30, 1967, had Vealey encountered as fierce a firefight as he now found himself in. Both he and Saunders were there during those days of intense fire fights during Operation DeSoto. It was ironic that during that operation they had ended up with their rifles covered with mud and malfunctioning as well. History was repeating itself.

A Radioman's Last Transmission
Operation Foster, Arizona Territory AT 872522
November 19, 1967, D+6, 0700-2030 hours

Lieutenant Wilson called Dumont over to where he was, near the tree line.

"I need a gun team out there," he told Dumont and pointed to the edge of the ditch just to the right of where the trail ended. The site was an open area from where a gun team would be able to effectively return fire. The area was slightly exposed, but a gun team at that location could give the company a chance to put out the firepower it desperately needed.

Wilson could see that there were a couple of Marines laid out in the open in front of that position, and he needed to get word to those Marines to let them know what was going to happen. He could see that they had a radio with them. It was Corporal Saunders and his radioman.

As Dumont ran back to where we were, Wilson got on Second Platoon's radio frequency.

Saunders's radioman called out to him that our lieutenant wanted to speak with him over the net, the sniper across the field saw Saunders move and shot at the Marine who had his back up against a dike. Saunders's response was to reach out, grab his M-16, and laying it over the dike popped off a few rounds at the enemy to show them he was still there; and as he did, the sniper shot the M-16 out of Saunders's hand.

Gimpy, his radioman, rushed over to where his squad leader was and Saunders rogered our lieutenant's transmission.

Wilson told Corporal Saunders to keep his squad's heads down as a machine-gunner would soon be firing over their heads. The gunner would be laying down suppressive fire to give others time to get those we could out of where they lay wounded.

It was not what Saunders, already being fired at from the front, wanted to hear. Now a Marine machine-gunner would be firing over his head from behind him.

Vigil, seeing the radioman's antenna moving above the rice paddy dike, knew the radioman would soon be the next target of the enemy sniper. Using his scope he began to look for the sniper that had been targeting certain Marines. The sniper had been very selective, firing only when he had to, choosing his targets well and keeping his position hidden as much as possible.

Saunders yelled out orders to his men to get farther down into the dirt and hand signaled for other Marines who could see him to do the same. The enemy sniper zeroed in and shot at Saunders while he was still speaking on the radio. The bullet shot off Saunders left index finger.

"A machine-gunner is going to be shooting over our heads, so keep your heads down," Saunders, while in great pain still yelled out orders to his men. Gimpy picked up the handset to roger another transmission but decided to answer the message himself instead of handing the handset to his wounded squad leader.

The sniper then shot at Gimpy as the radioman was finishing rogering the transmission.

The bullet struck the radio's handset and the side of Gimpy's head. As Bruce Wilson slumped gasping for breath from that bullet's impact to his head, another round struck the young Marine and he slowly slipped into the rice paddy's muddy bottom.

Guns UP!
Operation Foster, Arizona Territory AT 872522
November 19, 1967, D+6, 0700-2030 hours

"Guns up! Guns up! Gun team up!" Dumont's call was relayed back to where we were. Before Dumont reached us, Jones said, "Let's go," and he picked up his M-16. Dumont seeing Jones was already getting up, stopped, "Come on," he said, as he quickly turned around and started running back toward the front.

Jones was right behind him; I followed and Marty fell in behind. As we ran forward, I could see in between the trees and heavy underbrush up ahead that Marines were pinned down out in the open. Bullets were kicking up dust in the rice paddy fields in front and to the side of them. As each round struck the dirt, Marines tried to bury themselves deeper into the ground or to move in closer to the rice paddy dikes for cover. Some Marines were not moving at all.

As we ran forward, I saw Marines prone alongside of the trail that led to the tree line at the end of the trail. We ran past Marines in a hunched position as fast as we could while incoming rounds cracked overhead. The Marines along the trail looked at us as if we were crazy.

With bullets whizzing by, we were running toward the direction from which the rounds were coming. I knew I would soon be engaging the enemy with the M-60 in a firefight, and the gun was willing.

The gun thrown over my shoulder was crying out to be heard, and she knew I was carrying her into battle. Firing with the trigger held back, I knew I could put out a wall of burning hot lead, and we were determined to do just that. We would get Marines out of harm's way by shooting at the enemy, and that was what we trained for.

Sometimes the safest place in a firefight was behind the M-60 machine-gun; sometimes, it was the most dangerous.

By this time, I could disassemble and reassemble the gun in a matter of seconds. Both Marty, Aguilar, and I had drilled and drilled on taking the gun apart and had timed each other to see who could do it faster or shoot the gun more accurately. A twenty-round burst was the Marine Corps preferred mode of response firing in combat. There was, however, a burst of fire with which I had gotten comfortable with; but I never tried to count the rounds. I just fired, and I could sense when I had fired an effective burst and would then let up.

The fact that a machine-gunner's life expectancy was only a couple of seconds once the first round was fired in combat did not trouble me. I had practiced flipping the gun with its bipods folded down off my shoulder and hitting the ground, ready to fire, so fast that I figured if the first round didn't get me, I knew the second round would not find me in that same position. If the enemy's bullet didn't get me with the first few rounds, by the time I hit the ground, I knew I'd be firing a burst of automatic machine-gun fire directly at them. From then on, I would not give them a chance to fire back. Whoever put out the most rounds was the person in charge of the firefight, and the one who would most likely determine who would live and who would die.

As we ran past the Marines laid out along the trail, I saw a glance of admiration in some of their faces. In others, I saw sympathy. We were either being looked upon as saviors and heroes or as fools rushing headlong to our death. It all depended on who was looking and how long they had been in country.

"Guns up" meant the machine-gun was needed. The platoon was pinned down, and we had to put out some heavy firepower against the enemy. We needed to gain fire superiority. I knew I had trained well, and I was ready. This was what the gun was designed for—to give a Marine rifle squad the advantage of superior firepower over the enemies' determination to have that edge.

As we raced forward, I was calling back to memory what I needed to do, what I had been taught. This was where I was supposed to put into practice what the Marine Corps had taught me at machine-gun school. It was what I had been trained for. It's weird what thoughts flash through your mind. I guess the Corps didn't know search-and-traverse response fire was useless in the jungles of Vietnam because it was difficult to deploy a tripod-mounted gun in an ever-changing battle zone where the enemy laid low and sometimes in layers and constantly shifted positions. Even using the gun's bipod legs, a machine-gunner would have to shift his body as often as his gun's position.

The way we had been trained to fire the machine-gun was only vaguely comparable to the reality of firing the gun in battle. I had learned to effectively fire the gun on my own, I learned how to handle it, and Bro's gun responded to my touch, and its accuracy was outstanding. It was functioning as it should, and I had confidence in myself and in the gun and I was determined to do what was required, using what I had learned. I needed to get Charlie's head down, so we could gain fire advantage over our enemy. That would let us get our wounded out of harm's way.

With half of Second squad pinned down and out in the open, Sergeant Isaacs had tried to direct his men to open fire from where they were. he opened up with his M-16 to provide covering fire for them, but because of the intense incoming firepower the enemy was unleashing it wasn't enough to provide the cover needed for him to run out and rescue Marines.

In front of where he was, just a short distance away Isaacs could see Big McCullough, lying out in the open field, and his heart ached for his friend. When he first got to our Platoon, Little Isaacs, and Big McCullough had hit it off, and each, the little and the big had promised each other to do anything they could to help each other out if they got into a tight situation.

A Sniper's Battle
Operation Foster, Arizona Territory AT 872522
November 19, 1967, D+6, 0700-2030 hours

In the crater the Corpsman could hear Aggie calling out again to their far left for a Corpsman. As Doc Marren and Doc Gibbs were deciding which one of them would go Doc Gibbs saw our Marine sniper L/Cpl. Anthony Vigil, step up behind the berm, get on one knee, and aim his rifle at the enemy sniper he had finally located. The Marine was a short-ten-feet away, from Gibbs.

As Vigil took careful aim, the sniper's face exploded as a round hit him dead center at the bridge of the nose and Gibbs saw the Marine fly backward as the bullet, blood, and brain matter exited the back of Virgil's head.

Lance Corporal Darrel VanCleef, who everyone called goat or lucky after he had been shot on November eighth, saw the Marine fall backward, and rushed over to Virgil's side. He grabbed him, and started to drag him toward Ralph Keenan's machine-gun position. Keenan jumped up, and ran to help VanCleef and then both of them dragged the Marine toward Doc Gibbs who by then was rushing toward them.

When the Corpsman reached the Marine, he saw a small hole where the sniper had gotten hit in the front of the face. As he turned him around, he saw there was hardly anything left of the back of his head.

Gibbs then asked VanCleef and Keenan to lift Vigil and take him back and they placed him up against a small tree, a short distance away.

The Crater at the Edge of the World
Operation Foster, Arizona Territory AT 872522
November 19, 1967, D+6, 0700-2030 hours

The edge of the tree line came up quickly, too quickly. As we ran forward and incoming rounds whizzed past us, I could hear trees cracking on both sides of the trail as bullets embedded themselves deep inside the soft tissue of the palm and banana trees.

Some trees were being split and torn apart by the .50 caliber bullets striking them; other smaller caliber rounds were whizzing past us.

It's funny what you see, what your mind takes in, when the adrenaline flows and opens our minds. Everything slows down, and you catch a panoramic view of what is happening all around you. You can see, hear, and smell things like never before.

Large banana leaves were being split apart by bullets. Others were being ripped from the trees by the bullets' impact. On my right, I could see a cluster of small trees filled with short, stubby, round bananas. *Round bananas? Nothing is normal in Vietnam,* I was thinking as we broke out into the open field.

Bullets were striking the ground to my far left near fallen Marines. Other bullets were hitting out in the rice paddies filled with water.

The incoming bullets were kicking up thin geysers of water high into the air. As we ran forward, I noticed that the enemy's fire began to change direction. The bullets were shifting, moving slowly toward the direction we were running.

I hadn't been told where we were going; I was only following Jones and Jones was following Dumont, and Dumont did not stop where the lieutenant had indicated he wanted the gun placed. Instead, he ran past Baggette's crater and the tree line, ran past where Wilson was and the big berm and the wide shallow agricultural ditch and ran out into the open field.

We cleared the tree line, and I couldn't stop my feet from running. Out in the open, they ran faster, trying to catch up with Jones. Jones was trying to catch up with Dumont, and Dumont was running as fast as he could toward a large bomb crater that was at least 300-feet beyond the tree line.

Bullets were whizzing by; others were kicking up dust in front of us as we ran toward where the bullets were coming from. Then the enemy's firing crossed over from the left to my right side. They missed Jones and Dumont as both of them dived into the large bomb crater at the edge of the world.

As the enemy's bullets began to change direction again from right to left, I saw Marines from our platoon, where they were pinned down and I realized we had just passed the safety of the tree line where the rest of the company was located.

As the front of the crater came into view, I could see Marines lying prone in front of the crater. One Marine was looking my way; others weren't moving. They were pinned down and not moving. Another Marine from Second Platoon was farther out to my right.

Somehow before reaching the crater, perhaps while I was still in the air and jumping forward, the machine-gun was flipped off my shoulder and it was firing, responding to the intensity of my mind's determination to put out lead.

The gun, seemingly with a mind of its own, was spewing out its first burst of bullets while I was still in the air diving toward the crater's forward edge.

The enemy's bullets were not selective about who or what they struck. Pieces of shrapnel were flying every which way and as I hit the ground the sounds I had been hearing all of a sudden increased in tempo into a roar that filled the air all around me with terror and fear.

It was the noise of death and destruction, the sound of a sick symphony, a musical composition hidden and secretly playing selected tunes of suffering and pain behind jungle foliage. The music played in the hearts and minds of Marines who had no choice but to listen to the songs of agony being played out for them as they hugged the earth. Most accepted their pain and their lot in life as they spilled their blood on the hard Vietnamese soil.

Some turned their thoughts to home and the words of a friend, a schoolteacher, an employer, and the memories of Mom and Dad, brothers and sisters, wives, daughters and sons and home came to their hearts and minds. Those comforting thoughts, however, could not stop their pain or their blood from slowly flowing from the tablets of life to where they met death, and thoughts of tomorrow and yesterday faded as did their lives. HM3 Corpsmen Charles Edward Robertson, Lance Corporal Robert Bruce Wilson, Corporal Mark Carson Petersen—all from Second Platoon—took in their last breath and died.

Battlefield Engagement
Operation Foster, Arizona Territory AT 872522
November 19, 1967, D+6, 0700-2030 hours

Seconds before I struck the ground, my first burst of rounds had gone wild, spraying the air at treetop level.

The gun was laid flat on top of the crater's edge, the bipods legs hanging over the edge, not touching the ground. The newly created bomb crater was huge, dirt on top and on the sides was still loose.

I brought my gun in closer, tightened my grip and squeezed down on the trigger. The first burst of controlled fire swept across the wide tree line where the enemy was entrenched.

Sixty feet away, Corporal Saunders was lying and as the bullets flew by him, he hugged the ground and inched in closer to the dike. I held the gun in tighter, firing only inches above the rice paddy dike and prayed Saunders and his men didn't move.

The sound of Bro's gun reverberated loud and clear. Sizzling red-hot tracers shot straight out of the gun's barrel at four, three, two feet off the ground; bullets were striking tree branches slightly above the enemy's head just as Bro had taught me. Then as I started to sweep the machine-gun's bullet across the battlefield, they were barely clearing the top of the dike where Marines were laid out prone hugging the dirt.

The sound of the enemy's AK-47s had dominated the battle scene. Our M-16's returning fire had paled in comparison, so the initial burst of fire from my machine-gun being fired at them from out in the open seemed to have startled the NVA. An immediate pause followed my initial burst of fire as the enemy ducked to avoid the deadly onslaught of incoming machine-gun bullets being fired at them, just inches above their heads. It was only a couple of seconds of silence, an instant state of confusion as thoughts were gathered in the enemy's mind, but it was all that was needed.

In those seconds of hesitation, I gained the time we needed. I fired the gun with a controlled burst of machine-gun fire and all the months of Marine Corps training and fam firing on Hill 65 and at Liberty Bridge kicked in. I swept the area using what I had learned on my own and what the Marine Corps had taught me. Searching and transversing machine-gun firepower swept across the open fields without the use of a tripod or the gun's bipod legs. The gun was swinging free, flat on the crater's edge. It was firing as if on its own, as if it was in control, and it was singing a new song the enemy didn't like or understood.

I brought the gun in closer and tighter up against my cheek the way I liked her and draped my left hand over the cover assembly to hold her firmly in place. It was what I had found gave me the best control over the gun, and she was spitting bullets out her mouth, with every fifth round a red-hot burning tracer full of anger and screaming death. She filled the battlefield with chaotic devastation, with revenge that rose from her heart as a self appointed judge waging war and dispensing justice without reservation against the forces of depraved soldiers who without mercy massacred innocent lives. She had the power to demolish their strongholds and to avenge Marines stuck in filth and caught in the mud and blood filled crevices of the earth. This was her time, her moment what she desired.

Jones linked another 100 rounds to the belt rapidly moving through the gun's feed tray.

We belonged together the gun and I, as she spit out sizzling-hot lead. Was she in control or was I—it was hard to tell; she had a mind of her own and together we were singing a death song, steadily and evenly as bullets sailed across the open rice paddy fields, destined to find a target, to inflict injury, to silence the enemy, to save Marines. Each bullet had its own tune to hum; each tracer unleashed its own fine, thin, fiery-red beam of agony, misery, and pain. They sliced and tore apart bushes and small shrubs at the base of the tree line, occasionally the enemies' head, eyes, ears, and nose; wherever they arose to fire upon us, wherever the enemy's gunfire came from, there our bullets found them. They flew across the battlefield just inches above the dikes Marines had huddled up against for protection, and sought out slanted eyes poking out of spider holes.

To my left and below me in the crater, I could sense Jones' presence as he scrambled to hold up the tail end of the belt of ammo rapidly moving through the gun. In those first few seconds, I had expended over 300 rounds. Jones kept feeding her and I kept firing. The enemy tried to return fire, but as they did, I opened up and effectively silenced the area from where their bullets came from.

Suddenly, the incoming came at us from our left and right side at the same time and then more fiercely from the center of the tree line where the majority of the enemy was located; and the gun met each challenge without hesitation, silencing each encounter, and the Marines caught in the middle prayed once more as bullets flew by them from friend to foe. The bullets didn't care who was in between, so Marines pressed their bodies closer to the earth and held their breath and didn't dare to move or they would die.

Get Me Out Of Here
Operation Foster, Arizona Territory AT 872522
November 19, 1967, D+6, 0700-2030 hours

"To your right, to your right!" cried Doc Gibbs from behind me, and I moved the gun's muzzle to the right, firing almost at ground level in order to keep the enemy from firing back. I swept the gun's fire from left to right then right to left, sweeping the area with bullets that were ripping through the tree line looking for a target. I sensed that the intensity of the incoming rounds had lessened although it remained fierce.

Isaacs had been anxiously waiting at the edge of the swallow ditch. Big McCulloug was the closest Marine to the tree line but had been hit four or five times, in the chest, back and legs, moving little, McCullough was crying out in pain.

Isaacs got up and ran to where McCullough lay, sliding in headfirst as bullets followed him. He crawled over to his friend's side. When he got to the Marine, McCullough, looked up at Isaac and with sad, and painful look in his eyes, pleadfully said;

"Get me out of here, Sarge, Get, me out of here."

A short distance away, lying out in the open, Isaacs could see Lucero with blood oozing out of one of his ears. It looked like his ear had been shot off. Lucero kept crying out, for someone to get them all out of there.

The rounds being fired at us began to increase again as the enemy recovered from the surprise of an M-60 opening up at them from out in the open from an area where they did not expect someone to open fire at them from.

The gun firing to the right was what the Marines behind me were waiting for so they could run out to get our dead and wounded out of the open rice paddy fields.

It was also the cover Ron Patrick's rocket team needed, and both he and Cole rushed forward, low crawling as fast as they could toward Faithful's position.

As they ran out the enemy was prepared, they had waited and were seeking revenge against the rocket team. They had seen where Ron had fired their rocket at them from and they had their orders, to sit there and wait, that was their assigned duty, to sit and wait and now, as Ron and Cole got up to run, they took careful aim and fired an RPG rocket round at them.

You quickly learn in war to distinguish the sounds different weapons make. You could hear the difference between the M-16, the M-60, and the enemy's carbines, AK-47s, and their powerful 7.62 machine-guns. Recognizing the difference can save your life.

As they heard the welcome sounds of the M-60 responding to the enemy's fire, Marines recovered from their pinned-down positions and were once again returning fire from out in the open rice paddies and from the tree line or shallow ditch. Some that had been in the kill zone and pinned down had managed to crawl back into the safety of the ditch or the tree line, and they too were now firing back at the enemy.

The RPG rocket exploded next to Faithful's CP crew just as the two Marines arrived there, and both Marines were blown off in opposite directions.

Cole felt like he had been hit in the back by a powerful blow from a thick two-by-four as he flew through the air. Ron struck the ground hard. Lying on his side, he lifted his head and his helmet fell off; his face was covered with blood.

Isaacs hearing the machine-gun opening up and the sound of the huge rocket explosion on the opposite side of the field causing the needed distraction in the battlefield quickly picked up Big Mac and started to run back to the tree line with him over his shoulders.

As he did, he felt a drag on his leg. Lucero had grabbed hold of him and was holding on.

"Get me out, get me out," Lucero, cried out.

As Isaacs pushed on, rounds were kicking up dirt and dust all around them. The distance was only about forty yards and Lucero tried to hold on, but finally lost his grip. Even with the adrenaline rush, Isaacs continued to run but a short distance from the wide ditch his legs gave out because of the Marine's heavy weight.

Isaacs went down on his knees and then tried to drag the big Marine the last ten yards.

"You don't drag a Marine, Izzie was thinking, and he and Chief were about to run out to help, when Sgt. Stanford and another Marine ran out, to help Isaacs.

Chief, knelt behind a tree near the wide berm, and provided covering fire with his M-14.

The Marines while under intense incoming fire, managed to get McCullough and the exhausted Sgt. Isaacs out of the kill zone and into the safety of the wide and swallow agricultural ditch

Behind Chief standing behind the cover of another tree, Izzie was popping off round after round of M-79 grenades across the rice paddy field. The launched grenades were exploding on line where the intense fire being directed at Isaacs and the others was coming from. No sooner had one grenade left the tube than Izzie was loading another one, and he kept looking for an advantageous target, all the while moving swiftly in and out of cover to avoid long exposure to the incoming bullets. He kept repeating the process, loading and firing, loading and firing.

Isaacs helped Doc Gibbs patch up McCullough's wounds and when he was assured the Marine would be taken care of, he looked over to where Lucero was.

The small Marine was curled up tight in the fetal position his hands tightly wrapped over his head with his legs raised up against his body. He was now more fully exposed, out in the open and enemy bullets were striking the ground all around him using him as bait. Lucero wasn't moving

Jon Q. Nelson, an old-timer with the platoon, got up from the agricultural ditch to seek better cover behind the tree line, where Keenan's gun team was located. As he turned to jump into the small crater the gun team had moved their gun into, a bullet struck him and Isaacs saw him spin around like a top from the bullet's impact and fall forward into the center of the crater. Isaacs rushed over to help.

When he got to him, he saw that the Marine, had been shot behind his right ear. When he turned him over he saw that the bullet had exited through his right eye.

"What's you name," Isaacs, asked him

"Nelson," the Marine responded and Isaacs called for the Corpman.

Over to his right Isaac could see two Marines of their back, lying next to an M-60. A disassembled 3.5 rocket launcher was lying next to them. The Marines weren't moving and he didn't know if they were also wounded or dead.

The incoming fire continued to increase striking along the edge of the wide agricultural ditch. Isaacs could see other Marines farther out, taking heavy incoming fire. He figured with the right direction they might be able to provide out-going fire.

He picked-up the M-60 and 300 rounds and ran toward where Marines were located over on the far right side. He was going back, to where he had been before, but now had an M-60.

More Ammo, Please
Operation Foster, Arizona Territory AT 872522
November 19, 1967, D+6, 0700-2030 hours

Jones cried out for more gun ammo from inside the crater, and Marines low crawled as close as they could to us then risked their lives to throw machine-gun ammo into the crater. A Second Platoon Corpsman and others behind me continued to cry out to me to shoot to my right so that I could keep the enemy's head down while they ran out to get wounded Marines out of harm's way.

I increased my firing to the right, and immediately felt the enemy's bullets being fired at us from my left grow with renewed intensity.

Bullets were coming fast and fierce from our right as well, I needed to shoot in two different directions at the same time. I shot at those that shot at me and returned their fire and prayed that they learned their lesson and stopped firing back.

At times it seemed they hesitated, only to be replaced by another NVA team who took up the slack and opened fire at the gun from a new spot. They were new; this was their introduction to war and their commanders were encouraging them, urging them, to fight, directing their fire, taking casualties, and telling them to be brave and if they had to, to die. They had come from the north, a three months journey for this very hour for this purpose, and this was their destiny and what they had been trained for. Now was their moment for honor, a time to fulfill their own dreams of glory.

Isaacs had moved Second Platoon's gun into the center of where the fierce incoming fire was striking. He found an advantageous position on the side of a dike that went across the open fields. Some of the men from Second Platoon were laid prone just to the right of his position. It was the same location Ron Patrick's machine-gun had fired from, earlier.

In front of Isaacs, bullets continued to strike near where Doc Robertson lay and the sergeant wondered if he was still alive. He could swear he saw the Corpsman move, but also wondered if it was just a muscle spasm causing the dead body to twitch.

If he could fire enough rounds to get the enemy's fire to subside, on his side then perhaps maybe Marines pinned down might be able to crawl back to the ditch and the tree line, he was thinking.

Isaacs opened fire with the M-60 across the field to the far right almost in line with the trail that led into the center of the enemy's position that had initiated the original ambush. This caught the enemy by surprise, but they immediately returned fire in his direction.

When, I heard the sound of an M-60 firing behind me, I breathed a sigh of release, another gun was opening up, and I wondered who it was.

My machine-gun's barrel was glowing red hot and smoking; dust was being kicked up in front of it. I had never seen those results coming from the gun's flash suppressor before, but then I was firing near the bomb crater's edge and because the crater was deep and too steep for me to be able to get down flat, I was firing back from a half-crouch position. The bottom of the gun's forearm assembly was lying flat on top of the crater's edge and the gun's flash suppressor was close to the ground so with each round it spit out, dust was kicked up, clouding the area.

It must be the loose dirt in front of the gun's barrel, I was thinking. The dirt and dust billowing around the front of the gun at times made it hard to see where I was firing. I responded to the increased incoming fire with as many rounds as I could, holding the trigger back harder for the gun to spit out more bullets, and she did so willingly.

Jones kept hooking up belts of ammo to the gun and I kept firing them as fast as he snapped them together.

We kept this up as dirt and debris flew every which way in front of the gun. I fired at the enemy's muzzle flashes when they fired at us and they were silenced for awhile, then it was someone else's turn to die and as they opened fire the gun met their bullets sometimes half way across the rice paddy fields and the gun's bullets caught enemy soldiers sometimes in-between breaths and life was taken in seconds and if their number didn't come up to die that day, their bodies were riddled and torn, and ripped open by the explosive force of the 7.62 caliber round that entered soft flesh and tore limbs, and body organs to sheds and when that happened there was silence but only for a short time, as others were moved forward to take their comrades place to live or die, what ever their lot in life was. It all depended if they fired their weapons and the gun found their muzzle flashes.

They say that you never hear the bullet that strikes you, the sound it makes comes after the round has penetrated your flesh and pain conceals the sound from you. Suddenly, a series of M-79 grenades exploded near our gun and Jones had to let go of the belts he had been linking together and slid down and huddled into a little ball at the bottom of the crater. Behind us, I could hear Marines opening fire spraying the area to my left with hundreds of rounds.

Isaacs had only shot a burst of about forty rounds from the machine-gun when a sniper's bullet from behind struck the gun's butt stock.

The bullet bounced up and entered Isaacs's left shoulder.

The bullet came from a sniper hidden somewhere to his right, from the same place a sniper had earlier shot and hit Ron Patrick's M-60.

As Isaacs lay back, collecting his thoughts he could hear mortars being dropped, and could see they were being walked along the ditch line. Marines who had found refuge there were now jumping up and running for cover behind the safety on the other side of the wide trail and the tree line. For the wounded Marines still out in the open, hope for an immediate rescue faded.

An RPG round exploded to our left side near the crater's edge. Dust, dirt, shrapnel and debris filled the air.

"I can't see where to fire," I yelled down to Jones.

"Just fire low," he yelled back at me as he tightened his arms over his helmeted head and hugged the crater's bottom. From the exploding ordinance all around us a pile of dirt and hot showering shrapnel fell all over us. Dumont was also huddled up but compressed into a smaller ball. Farther into the crater's bottom, Marty was curled up tight. A cloud of dust at the bottom hid most of him from view.

No sooner had Keenan, VanCleef and Doc Gibbs's set Vigil's dead body down near a small tree behind from where most of the company was located when shots rang out.

The first bullet struck Vigil in the head near where the other round had entered earlier. Two more were fired into his chest. The bullets had come from behind our lines.

All three got down seeking cover and since they didn't have their weapons with them, they lay motionless and waited. It was hard to see where the bullets had come from. Probably a spider hole, they reasoned. No other incoming rounds were fired. There was no doubt in Keenan's mind, that the Marine sniper had been especially targeted for assassination. A vague message that could not be lost to either side, that there is a price to pay by those assigned to shed blood in secret.

When they got back near where everyone else was, Gibbs asked for a poncho to cover Vigil and VanCleef called out to see if anyone nearby had a poncho.

The wounded FO in the crater said he had a poncho they could use. Keenan went over to retrieve the poncho and the first of a series of air strikes dropped high ordnance on the enemy position across the field. As the plane lifted up, green tracers could be seen being fired at the plane.

As Keenan waited at the creator's edge to get the poncho from the FO, he caught a sniper's round in the thigh and went down. Shaken, Keenan found himself laying on top of the trail exposed to enemy fire that was being walked in his direction.

Instinct, told him to protect his left side and he grabbed his M-16 and pulled the weapon close to his side as a series of bullets struck the M-16 smashing the rifle into pieces.

Keenan began to slowly drag himself toward the muddy agricultural ditch, to find cover. Doc Gibbs seeing Keenan hit rushed over, grabbed the Marine and rolled with him into the shallow ditch, getting him out of the enemy's line of fire.

When they hit bottom an enemy mortar round struck the center of the ditch only a few feet away from them. The round embedded itself deep into the soft mud and didn't explode.

Isaacs, saw where the jet's bombs had landed and as he and other Marines around him continued to get a heavy volume of incoming fire, he felt the fixed-wing aircraft had missed the mark by a good 200 meters. He called out from the hole he had found cover in for someone to get him a radio.

A few minutes later, Sgt. Isaacs, while lying on his side with his shoulder wounded could be heard screaming into a radio's mike, trying desperately to get the jets coming in to drop a load of ordinance, further to the right of where they had dropped their first load.

A birddog overhead tried to calm the grunt sergeant, so that he could relay the message to the F-8 pilot.

"Okay, Serge, you need to calm down. I can not hear you, if you scream into the mike. You need you to talk to me calmly, like we're sitting down drinking coffee."

Isaacs took in a deep breath and calmed down but he was still wound up, and the bird-dog pilot could tell, so he came back on the air.

"Serge, the F-8 will be coming in for a dry run, almost tree top level, and from there you will be able to tell me for him to come left or right and where you want him to drop, the napalm. Think of the plane as a clock, with the nose of the plane being twelve o'clock."

The Phantom jet came in slow and smooth, flying west along the tree line. When he was over the targeted area, the gooks opened fire up with automatic rifle fire, shooting at the plane.

Once he cleared the area, Isaacs, had calmed down enough and was talking to the bird-dog pilot.

"About 200 yards to the left, at nine o'clock not even half way across, from where he dropped his first load, is where we are getting most of the incoming fire from," Isaacs said, over the radio very calmly.

The F-8 pilot came back around and when he was about a quarter of the way to where Isaacs had said, he dropped two napalm canisters and as he hit his afterburners, shooting straight up, green tracers were fired at him. Seconds of silence followed, and then the tree line exploded into in a bright white devastating inferno of white flame. The pilot had dropped them right on target.[175]

Aggie, had managed to drag Duran over to where Doc Marren was. Marren and Aggie used the path Rahm had cleared near the small garden to drag Duran away from the tree line and the line of fire. There was another smaller bomb crater hole behind most of the Marines but farther away and Doc Marren laid Duran up against a tree next to that crater. As the Corpsman began to examine Duran's wound, Aggie crawled back to his gun's position. Marren did what he could to dress Duran's wound and told him to stay where he was until he was medevaced. Doc Marren then left the Marine there and returned to the front. Duran, dazed, could see no one else around him. No other Marines were close by, so he took out his .45, cocked it, and waited alone.

The Realization of Vulnerability
Operation Foster, Arizona Territory AT 872522
November 19, 1967, D+6, 0700-2030 hours

Black smoke filled the air in front of the crater we were in, and I heard the roar of the jet as it accelerated away from us. That sound was followed by a huge explosion.

No sooner did the smoke clear the enemy began to fire once more in our direction. The incoming rounds were concentrated and focused, as if the enemy before us had specific targets and each team was assigned to cover certain area and it seemed that more then one team was assigned to silence my gun.

I could see that some of the men from Second Platoon and from our squad in First Platoon had been able to move back and were now out of harm's way,

I held down the trigger once more responding more forcefully to the increase in incoming fire. Soon, the gun's barrel was glowing hot, so I eased up a bit adjusting my firing selectively to a twenty, thirty, forty round burst. It was controlled firepower, and the gun was singing the tune I was playing. At times, the volume went up to meet the enemy's response; and increased in tempo according to the pitch the enemy's bullets were rendering.

I could sense the platoon behind was also putting out a steady response to the enemy's incoming fire and I knew we had gained fire superiority. The enemy was no longer in control of the battle scene.

At times, the gun seemed to be firing of its own free will. It was responding in kind to each burst of incoming fire according to the intensity of the rounds being fired at us. It was an intense battle between weapons of war, between machine-guns, automatic weapons, and a defiant foe determined to win that day. Whoever was their commander, or company leader it was evident he had a well-trained and disciplined force.

I cursed the dirt flowing up in front of my gun, as the intensity of incoming enemy fire began to increase again. A powerful new force was being unleashed and I returned fire holding down the trigger until the gun's barrel was glowing white. This time, I was determined not to let them gain the title to the battle, and we fired away once more, at each other, neither one letting up.

The battle continued and hot lead flowed both ways with an intense determination on both sides to win and I wasn't going to let up so I held the trigger down and the gun released a powerful destructive force that was seeking death and destruction with vengeance.

In the midst of the battle, I suddenly realized that the bomb crater's edge had eroded away from the impact of incoming rounds. It was then I saw the rounds from my machine-gun were dropping only seventy to eighty feet away. They no longer had the power to go on. I had melted the gun barrel.

I had been firing from a kneeling position at the crater's edge and was now exposed from my chest up.

Most of the covering, I had earlier had been ripped away from the crater's edge. More dirt was now being kicked up in front of me, and the small pieces of rocks and sharp splinters were flying every which way as the NVA soldiers concentrated renewed firepower on my gun. The bullets and shrapnel were crisscrossing and ricocheting at the crater's edge, kicking up dust and dirt in my face.

"*Dang,*" I said, to myself, the word barely out of my mouth, when I more fully realized the danger I was in.

I grabbed the gun and slid straight down into the crater as the crater's edge burst into a bright white fiery ball.

An incoming RPG rocket exploded where my gun had been only seconds before, the force shoved my body down hard into the center of the crater.

The explosion at the crater's rim, demolished the front section of the bomb crater and rained dirt, dust, and pieces of rocks and shrapnel on Jones, Dumont, Marty, and me.

As the smoke and dust cleared away, I spit out dirt and little pieces of rocks and brushed off the dirt and mud particles from my mouth and eyes. My ears were ringing, I felt dazed, I could taste the sulfur and black powder from the explosion in my mouth, and everything was out of focus.

Over to our left side near the tree line, I could faintly hear an M-60 open up. *It must be the other gun,* I thought. I couldn't remember hearing it before. *They must have been pinned down,* I thought, and I closed my eyes to relax, feeling guilty I wasn't firing; but at the same time, I was in no hurry to get out of the crater to fire again.

Aggie had seen the explosion where my gun had been; angrily, he reloaded the M-60 and was now firing away at an angle across the open rice paddy field where he saw the RPG round fired from. His firing must have surprised the enemy because as soon as he opened up, all the NVA firing ceased and a long silence followed. I feared the enemy was now moving to our left to engage Aggie's gun.

Air Strike With A Vengeance
Operation Foster, Arizona Territory AT 872522
November 19, 1967, D+6, 0700-2030 hours

We sat there in silence at the bottom of the crater covered with dirt and residue. Jones sat up and shook his head; pieces of dirt and dust flew off. Only the place where he covered his eyes with his arms was still black; the rest of him like everyone else was covered in fine tan-colored soil. Dumont sat up, he started to stand up but decided instead to squat and sit next to Marty who still had his butt up in the air; he hadn't moved, and we couldn't tell if he was praying or cussing. All of us were covered in filth. If it wasn't for their bodily form, all three would have blended in with the crater's wall. No one was willing to stand up and look out over the crater's rim. The thud of an M-79 being fired could be heard followed by the sound of the round exploding at the enemy's tree line, and more silence followed.

Moments later, close air support reappeared and a series of jets dropped thousands of pounds of bombs along the tree line and in the jungle from where we were getting hit. The exploding ordinance shook the ground below us.

Seconds later, a thundering roar split the air above us. We looked up and saw the jet planes' exhaust darken the clean blue sky above. A large explosion shook the ground and Marty hugged the ground anew, Dumont buried his head in his chest, and Jones covered his ears; I sat there still dazed.

The Marine phantom jets coming in from the east peeled off to the right going north as the heat wave from the fiery ball flowed over the top of the crater. The jets turned back for another pass then returned and dropped more high explosive ordinance, and then they returned and strafed the tree line with canon fire. As the jets continued to come in, from the bottom of the crater, we could hear the report of the enemy AK-47s shooting at them and I could see green tracers going up following after the planes' trails. We lay there in the bottom of the crater as plane after plane dropped their load on the enemy's position. Then other jets came in and dropped two to three loads of napalm on the entrenched enemy forces. Before long, the tree line where the enemy was located was engulfed in flames.

After the bombing ceased, there was silence, Jones and Dumont stood up. The layers of dirt rolled off them in waves of fine dust. Marty stirred, and as he stood up, a shovelful of dirt fell off of him and billowed up before settling back down.

With the realization that a great majority of the final incoming rounds being shot at us had been shot at me, I hesitated to stand up. For the first time in combat, I was beginning to fear; I felt an alarm clicking in the back of my mind, as if the enemy's bullets could be waiting if I stood up or looked out. I was too scared to move. I wanted to just move away from the gun and at the same time, I wanted to embrace it, to kiss it for what it had done.

Maybe Jones, Dumont, or Marty would look out over the top. I knew I wasn't going to move, so I sat there and waited. I didn't want the gun; it had been a target.

The enemy had shot at it with bullets that had crisscrossed in front of me and fired rockets at it that had torn apart the lip of the crater where I had been only seconds before. We were down six to seven feet below the surface, and I had no desire to get out of that hole. Others can carry on the fight, I was thinking.

Jones held the gun while Marty changed the melted gun barrel and inserted a new one; Dumont examined the one I'd used. He flipped the barrel upside down. The piston wasn't moving. The barrel was worthless.

"Barela, they're going to make you pay for the barrel you melted," he said, and Jones chuckled. Jones unfolded the new gun barrel's bipod and put the gun back down at the bottom of the crater next to me. Marty, sitting up, took the gun, opened the gun cover, and inserted a 100-round belt of ammo, checking the rounds to make sure there were no long or short rounds.

Priority Medevac
Operation Foster, Arizona Territory AT 872522
November 19, 1967, D+6, 0700-2030 hours

Behind us, Doc Gibbs was working to keep Lieutenant Faithful alive. Jackie Williams and James Keene had helped pull Lieutenant Faithful and other wounded Marines back to the safety of a secured area.

"Do you have water in your canteens," the Corpsman asked Williams and Keene, without waiting for them to answer, Gibbs told Williams to pour water over Lieutenant Faithful's guts that were exposed and hanging out.

"Is it safe to pour water on them," Keene asked. "Yes, the water is clean, you need to keep his intestines wet, can you guys keep doing that, Gibbs asked.

Both nodded in agreement, and the Corpsman went off to treat other wounded Marines.

"Move out," the command from Captain Baggette came, and I could hear Marines moving all around us. I looked up as I sat at the bottom of the crater; and James Keenan, from Second Squad, came up to the edge and hesitantly looked down. He ignored the others until he saw me stirring at the bottom of the crater, looking up staring at him; he shook his head at me in disbelief and then moved on.

Lieutenant Wilson stepped up to the right edge of the crater and also looked down at us. He seemed glad to see we were still moving. He looked to his right. "Third Squad," he called out, "move out." And Third Squad Marines began to move across the rice paddy field on-line on our right side. Jones was the first to climb out of the crater; Marty and Dumont followed. I picked up the gun and handed it to Jones, hoping he would carry it for the rest of the day. He placed it down near the crater's edge and reached back to help me out.

When I got out, I saw Marines from Third Squad running zigzag patterns across open rice paddy fields until they reached the right side of the tree line and secured it. Marines from Sergeant Isaacs's squad were also getting up and moving on along the east dike. There was no more incoming.

Jones turned and walked off toward the tree line behind us; and I picked up the gun, folded down its bipod legs, adjusted the sling, and held it next to my hip, barrel pointed down. Perhaps the enemy, if they were still present, would not see the gun for what it was if I carried it pointed down.

We stopped at the edge of the tree line, and as we picked up more ammo, Marines were helping wounded Marines get back to the tree line. Others, despite their own wounds, were also helping.

Saunders was limping on his own back toward where the rest of the company was; he was walking behind two Marines who were carrying Corporal Wilson's limp body toward the shallow ditch. Corporal Boyd and Ward Keeton, wrapped in white bandages, were being moved toward the medevac area where the wounded and the dead were being collected.

Jones walked past the shallow ditch then turned right, going west walking parallel to the tree line along the topside of the wide berm. In front of the berm, in the ditch where Marines had laid wounded, torn Marine Corps clothing littered the ground where the Corpsman cut and tore apart military uniforms to work on the wounded. Clearly visible were large dark spots where their blood had soaked into the earth.

We walked past where Aggie was. Rahm had joined him; the gun was set up near the edge of the tree line. Aggie was lighting up a smoke.

"Hey, Marty, what happened to you?" Aggie asked, grinning. Marty gave back a smirk and walked over to where Aggie was seated and dusted himself off. Loose dirt and grime fell from his clothing over Aggie and Rahm. Jones turned right, falling in behind James Keenan's fire-team.

We started across, walking on the west dike toward the tree line where the majority of the enemy soldiers had been firing at us from. We were moving north on top of the west dike in the same direction Saunders's squad had earlier traveled to get around to the left flank of the enemy's force.

Far over on our right side, part of Second Platoon Marines had reached the tip of the far tree line. Second Platoon then began to move along a small trail in front of that tree line, moving counter-clock-wise toward us.

Behind us, the rest of the company was saddling up and getting ready to move across in our tracks.

On the far side of the battlefield, the distinct sound of a UH-34 chopper could be heard. The sound was coming from our far right side, east of us and I knew it was a medevac chopper coming in to take out our wounded, and that was a comforting thought.

The only secured area for them to land was fifty meters away from the northeast corner of the village.

Sgt. Stamford popped a green smoke grenade, for the choppers from HMM-364 and HMM-362 to land, and that also was a signal for Keene, Williams and two other Marines, to carry Faithful, and Ward Keeton out to the first chopper. Another chopper was coming in right behind to pick up others.

To my right front, I could see Marines from Second Platoon moving along the edge of the tree line, where I had fired the majority of my machine-gun's bullets at targets there. Marines had not yet gotten to the center of where the entrenched enemy had shot their most concentrated fire at us from. I popped open the gun's bipod legs and shifted the gun onto my shoulder.

Immediately I remembered just before the rocket explosion, I had seen the enemy moving to the left, which would mean they would have been moving toward the center of the dike we were now walking on.

A Visit and A Dance With the Angel Of Death
Operation Foster, Arizona Territory AT 872522
November 19, 1967, D+6, 0700-2030 hours

A harsh hot and painful east wind swept across the field toward me, making the hairs on my arms and neck stand on end. It was a bitter wind that turned my blood cold and filled my mind with the dreadful spirits and voices of lost souls. Sin, sickness, hatred, terror dreams and the promise of sleepless nights, all rushed to my side. It was as if the demons of war had poured on me the knowledge of the existence of evil since the beginning of time. It was the fearful presence of thick darkness among the company of immoral anguish and the foul smell of the angel of death arrived to walk by my side.

Next to the radioman, and officers, the machine-gunner is among the most attractive target. The man carrying the gun a worthwhile prize to take out in battle, and if the machine-gun's machine-gunner has just rained hellfire and brimstone upon you or shot up some of your comrades, payback is warranted. The NVA always sought revenge.

Immediately, I flipped the machine-gun off my shoulder and lunged forward as the sniper's bullet with its beelike sound whizzed by where my head had been a microsecond before.

A dozen more bullets followed me half way to the ground. I struck the top of the hard pressed dike hard, hitting my head on the gun's frame. The gun bounced out of my hands as a second volley of concentrated enemy bullets struck the ground near me kicking up dirt and debris. Another barrage of AK-47 automatic and machine-gun fire zeroed in closer, striking the top of the rice paddy dike near my helmeted head. From where I was lying, I could see Marines from Second Platoon, also taken by surprise were scrambling and diving for cover along the tree line to our far right side.

The bullets were quickly getting closer to where I was, and I realized I was still on top of the dike.

As the incoming bullets zeroed in, I grabbed the gun and threw myself off to the right side of the dike. Bullets struck the top of the dike and ricocheted sideways and skyward. Most of the bullets were striking the ground where I had been split seconds before. Small slivers of splintered shrapnel, and shattered pieces of small rocks struck my helmet, neck and arms. Bullets flew by, inches away and buried themselves into the soft rice paddy field at my side.

On my back, I pressed myself up against the hard wall of the rice paddy dike, squeezing myself against it for life. More automatic and small arms rifle fire peppered the other side and the top of the dike where I was. I pulled the gun in, and held her close, as I crawled on my back moving away from the impact zone.

As the first medevac chopper took off, I felt a sense of relief until I saw it start to fly overhead. Half way across it immediately turned to their right to avoid being shot at from the tree line from where we were now receiving fire. As I breathed a sigh of release, that they were safe, the enemy shot at them.

As the pilot in the first chopper circled around, gaining altitude he broadcasted to the Huey gunships escorting, where he was getting fire from and a Huey gunship swooped in from behind him and opened fire with his machine-guns on the enemy force shooting at the chopper. In defiance, enemy soldiers fired at the gunship as well.

The Huey gunship being piloted by Maj. David L. Ross with Lieutenant Col. Marsh Fulton as his copilot, quickly circled around, then came back and released several rockets into the enemy's position.

Ward Keeton, looking out of the circling medevac chopper above them and seeing the battlefield as Marines exchanged gunfire below, wondered in his heart what was to become of the Marines he was leaving behind.

So many bullets were being fired at us I dared not try to turn around to get on my belly and crawl. Instead I kicked with my feet and together with Jones, we edged our way toward where I had seen two rice paddy dikes intersect twenty meters away. Bullets were coming from our left front, near the grassy area the enemy had shot and wounded Duran from. The enemy was now located farther north and slightly to the west of their original position.

Jones was lying on his belly pushing himself forward; only his feet moved, the rest of him was hard pressed up close to the dike's wall. He inched himself closer and closer to where the two dikes connected to seek better cover as bullets whizzed overhead. Marty, behind me, wasn't moving; his head was buried in the dirt as bullets ripped apart the top of the dike near him.

The enemy was about sixty yards in front of us and was effectively shooting at both platoons of Marines and those they had caught out in the open. This time, there was no squad of Marines out on our left flank or in front of us. We were the left flank and we were up front. This time, we were the bait.

Then the enemy for some reason stopped firing toward Second Platoon and Second Platoon, I noticed, wasn't returning fire. Some of the Marines were laid out in the open in the rice paddy fields to my right, but they also didn't seem to be getting any serious incoming rounds. It seemed as if the enemy was firing just enough bullets at them to keep them pinned down, and to keep the rest of Second Platoon from advancing.

Whereever I was; however, it seemed a concentrated volley of bullets was striking the dirt dike directly over my head, and the enemy incoming fire was clearly aimed at where I was with my gun. The rice paddy dike I was lying behind was less than a foot high. Just a little way up at the intersection of the dikes, the height was about two feet. I knew that if I wanted to survive, I needed to crawl closer to where the two dikes intersected. It was there Jones was slowly crawling toward. It was a safer spot, so I kicked out with my feet to move closer to the security of the intersection of the two dikes. As I scooted along on my back, to my left I could see the form of a fallen Marine. He wasn't moving, and I strained to recognize him. It was Lucero.

Terror In the Presence Of War
Operation Foster, Arizona Territory AT 872522
November 19, 1967, D+6, 0700-2030 hours

When the others had been picked up and moved out of the killing zone, Lucero and another Marine were the last that remained to be picked up, and as Marines were about to get to him the shooting started all over again and now Jerry was left once again out in the open and bullets were striking the ground very close to where he was. Above the sounds of the bullets striking the dike near my head, I could hear Lucero crying. He was sobbing with deep moaning sounds like a man that had been seriously hurt, physically and emotionally wounded as well. Lucero was sobbing with sounds coming from deep inside; and it was a desperate hopeless wailing sound full of pain coming from him as if someone near him, someone in his immediate family, a deeply loved one had died.

"Are you all right?" I called out to him, but there was no answer. I turned on my belly and began to crawl out to him and as soon as I did, a new volley of incoming rounds kicked up dirt and small pieces of rocks and dirt clogs in front of me. Lucero remained pinned down out in the open field and bullets were striking the ground all around him. The enemy was using him as bait. I looked at Lucero and saw he was visibly shaking. He was more exposed to the incoming fire than I was; yet I knew that if I tried to get out to him, the two of us would make a bigger target. So I stayed back at the safety of the dike.

Men from our platoon who were able to return fire at the enemy were doing so, and they exchanged bullets, grenades, and automatic rifle fire for a while. As I turned to get on my back again, making me a smaller target in that position, another barrage of automatic rifle fire peppered the other side of the dike near where I was. I moved in closer to the dike, embedding myself into the side of the rice paddy dike until I couldn't move any closer.

I held the gun in close to my chest, keeping it out of the dirt. The gun's barrel smelled like solvent and fresh oil. It was clean and dry; and I sensed that the gun wanted to return fire, wanted to join in the battle, desired to be part of the firefight and unite with other Marines who were returning fire and were fighting back for the dead and for the wounded that we had suffered. I noticed that I had unconsciously folded down the gun's bipod legs.

There was no doubt in my mind that my gun was one of the enemy's primary targets. Whoever was shooting at us was shooting low. He knew he had Jones and me pinned down and was making sure that if either of us moved, we were going to get hit. The enemy was determined to take out the gun to keep it from responding and to kill the Marine behind it that had caused them so much pain. Payback was on their minds.

Lucero remained out in the open, exposed to the enemy's bullets that were kicking up dirt and little geysers of water when they struck sitting rice paddy water near him. I looked at him and realized that he was in a far better position than I to open fire.

If he would only start firing, then it would give me the advantage I needed to open up. That's all I needed, just a minor distraction nearby; if Jerry would turn and shoot at them, they would not be expecting it, not from out in the open. All I needed was a little bit of time and cover so I could turn around and open fire, and then he would be able to get out of the kill zone.

Aggie's gun was behind us on lower ground so I knew he couldn't open up and help from where he was or engage the enemy effectively from where they were. We were also in his line of fire. If anyone near me would start firing at the enemy just long enough to get the gook's head down for a second, that's all the cover I would need to flip the gun over and open fire.

I crawled toward Jones, hoping not to draw fire, exhausted from pushing with only my legs I lay there on my back and brought the gun in closer. The gun's bipods were still down, so I knew I would be able to lay the gun down flat on the dike the same way the gun had laid on top of the crater's lip. I knew right there and then that I was going to open up, and those first few seconds were going to be intense. I might get hit, but there was no doubt in my mind that I was going to open up. Jones, seeing what I was about to do, brought up his M-16; and I knew that he was going to cover for me to give me the advantage I needed and he would be risking himself at the same time.

Before today, I had never fired the gun without it resting on its bipod. I hadn't practiced shooting the gun that way. But I also knew that I needed to stay as low to the ground as possible. It had worked before, it would work again; all I had to do, as I had before, was to hold the gun in tight with my hand holding its frame down hard on the top of the dike. It would work again; the bomb crater had taught me that. I just had to make sure the gun's flash suppressor cleared the edge of the dike, if not there was going to be a lot of dust and debris around me, and I wouldn't be able to see my targets.

Mud Marines and Little Green Tracers
Operation Foster, Arizona Territory AT 872522
November 19, 1967, D+6, 0700-2030 hours

Jones flipped his M-16 over the dike and opened fire toward where the concentration of fire was coming from. It was all I needed. As the enemy returned fire in his direction, I flipped the gun over, laid it flat on top of the dike, and opened fire. I was shooting toward my left from where most of the automatic rifle fire was coming, fire that was being directed at Jones' position. Forty, fifty, sixty rounds, I shot off in seconds. I slid the gun to my right and engaged the enemy who were firing at Jones from that position. Then I fired at the enemy soldiers who had Lucero pinned down as I opened fire on that enemy force, I caught a glance of Jerry still out in the open field.

"Come on," I yelled out to him, "Jerry, get out of there!" I turned the gun back and fired again at the enemy to my left once more. As I fired away, I sensed that Jerry wasn't moving, so I concentrated on the enemy firing at us.

I had seen blood oozing from his left ear and wondered how bad he was wounded. Either Jerry had been seriously hurt or he was stuck in the world of fear and pain. Perhaps it was better for him to stay in that self-made protective environment, where he had closed-out the real abnormal world we were living in.

The enemy increased their firepower, and I began to receive concentrated incoming fire in front of us as well as from our left side. I flattened myself as much as possible and brought the gun in closer. Held her tight and kept firing, her bullets sailed steadily across the open fields, slicing through the air, a red fiery beam of death and destruction. I could see enemy soldiers using grave mounts for cover, and I targeted them.

I shot at one target and then another, searching and traversing my firepower the way the Corps had taught me to respond in a firefight. I was putting out as much firepower as I could, and it was all coming together. Marine Corps training, my own survival skills and instincts, and a willingness to do what was right, it was all working together: I was firing low, and the red tracers were striking at ground level right where Charlie's head would be.

I was no longer interested in just keeping Charlie's head down: I wanted to stop him from firing and the only way to do that was to kill him, and the gun was determined to do just that. Jones crawled back toward me and handed me his 200-round belts. I had already fired most of the two hundred rounds I had been carrying. I didn't remember connecting them or perhaps Marty had, as he was now connecting the other belts of ammo Jones had handed us.

Flashes of green and white sizzling tracers shot past me, and I turned to fire in the direction of the enemy's machine-gun position. I fired with a new determination to knock out their machine-gun position. The rounds were flying past me toward where Lucero was; and for a split second, I feared my firing was placing Lucero in grave danger. Diana's picture flashed in my mind and I thought of how her brother's death, if he were killed, would affect her, and perhaps it would have been my fault.

My trigger finger pulled back harder and the barrel spat out more bullets. Hot and angry, bullets were being fired without reservation and without mercy. I didn't know if Lucero was seriously hurt or just too scared to move, but I knew he needed to get out of that area and the sooner the better. I fired a concentrated burst of fire at the enemy's gun position and kept firing until the machine-gun's bullets were exhausted.

I quickly reached out, flipped the cover open, pulled back on the cocking lever handle and Marty slapped in another 100-round belt. I closed the cover and knew, at any moment, the enemy's bullets would be ripping across the terrain to my gun's position; but nothing happened. I looked over the dike, aiming the gun's barrel at the base of the far tree line, searched the grave mounts, nothing.

I waited for the puff of smoke, for the sound of the enemy's incoming rounds to shoot past me; I waited while seeking a target, but there was none. I kept the gun moving slowly back and forth, moving it left and right without firing. Those moments of silence were disturbing. Then the tree line exploded in front of us.

The captain had called in artillery fire from Hill 65, and 105 rounds were exploding all along the far tree line where the enemy had been firing at us from. After the last barrage of artillery rounds exploded, three, four, five minutes of silence followed before the lieutenant called out for us to once again move out.

From my right, Marines emerged out of the dirt and mud, out of the clay where they had sought refuge. I hadn't seen them there before, but now they rose like little statues being formed by an invisible hand into Mud Marines; they came out of the dirt and muddy rice paddy fields in which they had buried themselves. Jones got up, and so did I. Once again, we started across.

Shoot At Them For A While
Operation Foster, Arizona Territory AT 872522
November 19, 1967, D+6, 0700-2030 hours

Lucero still wasn't moving. I felt like going over to him to where he was. As I got closer, I could see him trembling, in quick short shaky movements. I didn't know if it was from the physical wounds he had suffered or from what he had experienced. I could hear him sobbing within from the terror and the torment he had endured for so long and wondered if perhaps he would be caught in the shadows of fear, death, and the terrors of war forever. But he was alive.

I moved on, leaving him to the loneliness of lost innocence that surrounded him. I didn't understand it, but I knew he needed time without anyone being next to him. He hadn't moved, he hadn't disassociated himself from the danger that had engulfed him and that madness still held his soul in the shadows between life and death, between fear and sanity. He had touched the untamed demons of hell and they still held him in their grip. I feared having to face my own demons of hell. It was the first time I had seen the terror of fear grab someone like that, and it was real. I wondered what I would have done had I been shot at as he had, had I been the one fully exposed and tested or used as bait; my life and last breath dependenting upon the mercy of the enemy's next bullet.

This time, as we moved out, I kept the gun at my side pointed down, allowing it to swing freely from the sling draped over my shoulder. It wasn't the normal way gunners carried their guns, but this way, it looked less like an M-60. I knew I had been a target, and I didn't want to be one again. I didn't want to give the enemy the advantage or an opportunity to spot it.

Up ahead, James Keenan's fire-team had made it across to the tree line in front of the dike. The Marines turned right to hook up with Second Platoon. As we moved out, I suddenly felt another sense of great fear and once again, I began to drop to the ground before the first rounds of the enemy's bullets flew by.

Jones dodged the bullets as well, as he fell backward, and rolled off the dike.

The incoming firepower was once again heavily directed at our machine-gun team; their bullets aimed at my gun. I had only taken a few steps when the enemy opened up again. They had been waiting.

"Damn them! Damn them," I said as I slid into the side of the nearest dike. The rounds shot in my direction were intense but this time I had a little better cover, but I still dared not move again and flattened myself as much as possible.

Let 'em think they got me, let 'em think they got me, I thought as green and white tracers struck the top of the dike I was hiding behind and they kicked up dust, dirt, and chips of rocks off its surface. Grenades exploded with a violent force directly in front and on our side of the dike, pelting the area with little pieces of sharp metal. I pulled the gun in closer. The barrel was still warm, the smell of gunpowder still present, and I embraced and held her close as bullets struck inches from me on three sides of where I was. The majority of the incoming rounds were clearly being fired at the gun and me.

For the first time in war, fear started to grab hold of me, fear like I had never experienced; but I wouldn't let it enter my mind.

I took in a deep breath and let it out slowly, but I feared to take another deep breath worried that the movement would expose me to more incoming rounds, so I buried myself deeper into the dike and waited.

This time, I decided to lie still. This time, I wanted someone else to do the fighting. This time, I couldn't move and I wasn't going to; I didn't want to. This time, I knew I was not going to fire back.

Let the gooks shoot at the other Marines for a while, I said to myself. *Damn them! We're not even halfway across. So this is what Lucero was feeling, what it meant to be totally helpless and unable to move.*

I began to think that the enemy might have a personal vendetta against me or they were determined to take out the gun because of the death and destruction she might have caused. The intensity of their concentrated firepower at my position was evident. It was revenge, on their part, plain and simple. They wanted to kill me, to destroy the gun I was carrying, and I wasn't about to move; I wasn't about to give them that chance and satisfaction. I cradled the gun in my arms and held her close as I hugged the earth for safety.

Bro had said if this happened, and if I wasn't able to move, to just stay still. Others would respond. I hoped they would; I wasn't going to move. This time, others would have to fight to keep me alive.

Why can't they shoot at some of the other Marines for a while? I thought as I buried myself deeper into the ground and inched my way farther into the soft side of the rice paddy dike. I was able to crawl into an area where I felt the incoming rounds couldn't get me. The dike's height was higher there and Jones was lying nearby, on his back only a few feet ahead of me.

I turned on my back and pushed myself up next to him. While bullets continued to impact the area around us as Jones, while lying on his back, lit a cigarette and handed it to me. Unable to move, we just laid there smoking his cigarette as bullets kicked up dust just inches above our heads. Neither of us moved or said a word; we just smoked Jones' cigarette, knowing neither of us this time was going to return fire, not this time.

A short time later, we realized from the shifting of the incoming fire and the impact of where the rounds were hitting that the enemy had moved back toward the front end of the dike. That meant they had pushed Keenan's fire-team back as well as the remnants of Second Platoon.

They're trying to get over to our right from where they would be able to get a clear shot at all of us on the right side of the dike, I thought as bullets started to strike the top of the dike closer to where we were and now, more dirt and dust was falling on us. A few more inches closer and I knew both Jones and I were going to get hit.

As the bullets got closer, I knew there was nothing we could do.

Izzie, lying on his back in front of Jones turned on his belly and fired his last shot from his M-79, right where the enemy was starting to shoot at us from.

Once more I could tell, we were the target and it was only a matter of time, as the bullets came closer and with Jones and Izzie in the way, I wouldn't be able to shoot back. To move out in the field would make me a clear target.

Then someone behind us, opened fire with an M-60, firing the machine-gun's bullets directly over our heads. The gunner was shooting a beam of well controlled red tracers in a direct and smooth sweeping path right over the top of the dike inches from where we were.

Other Marines took up the battle and opened fire from our right where they had been pinned down. The M-60 once again had made a difference, and both platoons began to return fire.

I wondered where Third Platoon had been all this time. Were they still at the tree line with Baggette?

The firefight continued with a heavy exchange of firepower for the next ten to twenty minutes, and I could hear Chief's M-14 popping off selected rounds at the enemy, but I didn't know where he was.

Whoever was on the gun, behind us, was good. He kept an effective fire going and was keeping the enemy away from us. Twenty minutes is an awfully long time to lie still, to keep from moving. I stopped thinking about the danger and began to regret not firing back. I thought to myself, what if I got hit and this time I hadn't fired back?

Green and white tracers from the enemy's weapons crossed path with the red tracers responding to their firing. Both sides were shooting only a foot or two above our heads, and at times they were only inches away.

Since the time Second Platoon was first hit, we had now been engaged in the firefight for close to three hours. It would soon be dark, and I wondered how we were going to get out of where we were. Soon all the firing had stopped, both incoming fire and from the machine gun team that had been firing over our heads A helicopter gunship appeared overhead, and they sprayed the tree line where the enemy had been firing at us from, and I breathed a sigh of relief. Another medevac must be taking place, I was thinking, and was thankful for the escorting gunships. But, as they flew overhead, we could see green tracers being shot at them.

The Huey returned with another gunship at his side and they both came in low making several passes. They opened up with machine-gun fire and dropped rockets on the enemy positions and then there was silence again.

We stayed where we were; Jones, Marty, and I remained buried in the dirt. No one had gotten up; no one wanted to. A half an hour passed, and I heard voices in front of us. There were American voices where the NVA had once been.

Tree Line Secured
Operation Foster, Arizona Territory AT 872522
November 19, 1967, D+6, 0700-2030 hours

Third Platoon under the command of Lieutenant James R. Mullens had managed to help secure the rest of Second Platoon Marines from where they had been pinned down and had maneuvered all the way around the left flank and was now moving in the tree line in front of us where the enemy had once been. Mullens was the tallest platoon commander in the company. Tall, muscular, with a rugged look, short curly hair with large hands he seemed to always be in command mode. He stood at the tree line with his radioman at his side, his utility jacket sleeves rolled up above his elbows. He lit a cigarette taking in a long puff. The rest of the company was now getting up, and everyone was moving across the open paddy fields in a long scrimmage line. India Company was assaulting the tree line; there was no more incoming.[176]

Izzie got up and swung his empty M-79 over his shoulder. To my right, I could see part of Second Platoon, being led by Sergeant Gus, walking toward us along the trail in front of the tree line, where the enemy had been. Other Marines were sweeping on line across the open rice paddies, toward where Mullen's Third Platoon was. Soon both platoons were joined in front of us. The enemy was gone.

I still didn't want to move. Both Jones and I peeked over the dike at the same time. Marines were standing at the end of the dike thirty yards away near the tree line where the enemy had been firing at us from. Other Marines were standing only a few feet from us; they were out in the open rice paddy fields. They were casually walking around, standing, smoking cigarettes.

I felt embarrassed to still be lying there in a prone position, my back up against the dike. I looked back to the tree line to the ditch at the end of the dike where the company had sought cover from the enemy and where the enemy had relentlessly sprayed us with their bullets and saw that our platoon's CP group and the company's CP group were standing nonchalantly in front of the tree line, on the wide berm. It seemed like just seconds ago we were in the thick of hell's fire, and now Marines were walking around the area as if nothing had happened; we were company-size again. I was feeling bad that I had been pinned down this time, and I had not returned fire.

At the tree line, in front of us, Al Homan and Sam Muszel from 60 mortars were walking to our left past the front of the dike. They must have reinforced Second Platoon and came around with them.

Homan looked my way, recognized me, smiled, and waved. His broad grin reminded me of the experience we had shared at mine and demolition school after graduation. I still owed him a couple of bucks from that night. His mortar team was bringing up the rear of Second Platoon. Marines from our platoon were busy checking out the area in front of us from where we had been hit. They were looking for weapons and dead enemy soldiers.

The rest of First Platoon by now had gotten up and had moved up to the tree line in front of us and were standing idle, waiting for our lieutenant to join them. Other Marines were moving back and forth across the open rice paddy fields checking on fallen Marines and picking up discarded weapons left behind by our dead and wounded. It was starting to get dark, and I knew we wouldn't be able to check out the area fully in front of us until the following morning.

Jones and I got up to join our company; first Jones, then I hesitantly followed. When I stood up, I noticed a Marine had been standing next to me for awhile. I didn't recognize him at first.

"Good thing, you didn't move," Borgman said, as I recognized, then realized it was him, who had shot the M-60 over our heads. I wanted to hug him.

"Hey, you shot better, then I did, in machine-gun school, so, I knew I would be alright," we chuckled and he half smiled and stepped off, to join his platoon. I never got a chance to thank him, or to ask him, where Dustin was.

As it was starting to get dark, our trip across the field was not completed because Lieutenant Wilson called the platoon back to the tree line we had left earlier. As we made our way back, Marines from First Platoon helped the Corpsmen pick up wounded Marines. Other Marines from the company followed us back across. Since we hadn't checked out the area, it had been decided to set back in the area we were familiar with where we had been pinned down for so long. We would be spending the night there.

We were supposed to be fighting VC, insurgents, and Communist revolutionaries trying to overthrow the government of South Vietnam. There was no doubt in my mind that the enemy soldiers we had faced were hard-core NVA Communist soldiers.

As we made our way back, Marines from Second and Third Squad from First Platoon, who had quickly checked out the immediate area where the enemy had fired at us from, said they were unable to find any dead enemy bodies. They found only a few bullet casings. Thirty Spider holes and they had seen splatters of blood, as well as thick globs of blood drippings from large plants and the ground along the tree line was washed in blood, but no dead enemy soldiers. The area also did not seem to have been disturbed by a large enemy force.

The NVA soldiers were worthy opponents. We had engaged at least a company-size or a reinforced company-size enemy force, and to prove their discipline, all of their dead and wounded had been carried away and the area policed of almost all their brass and evidence of their presence before they moved out.

This had been a hard battle, and I knew we had wreaked havoc upon them, but where was the proof? Where were the bodies of the enemies dead?

Psychologically, their cleanup of the battle site was disturbing to us because we had so little evidence of the damage we might have inflicted upon them.

We started moving back, and I went over to where Lucero was. He was still lying out in the open in a scrunched-up fetal position.

Sergeant Stamford was talking to him and had called for the Corpsman. Lucero was still sobbing in long, deep, mournful sighs. His mouth was quivering, and a dull glaze covered his wide-opened eyes. Lucero was combat scared: he wasn't speaking or moving. He was just laying there mourning. I wanted to reach out to him, to say something and encourage him, but I didn't know what to say. Doc Gibbs and Sergeant Stamford got him up and moved him back toward our side of the tree line.

Dumont spoke to some of our wounded before they were medevaced. Boyd had been shot twice—a clean shoulder wound and on the left side of his head. The bullet that struck his head went through his helmet and ricocheted off his skull.

They medevaced him with the others, but he'd probably be back after a while. Duran had taken a round to his side, but his flak jacket had stopped most of the impact; he might be back. Keeton had a serious shoulder wound and Dumont didn't think Keeton would be back.[177]

As evening fell, a night medevac was still needed, and Sgt. Stamford flagged in the choppers using strobe lights and they medevaced out the last of our dead and wounded. They were our evidence of the enemy presence and of their destructive force.

India Company had sustained five KIAs including L/Cpl. Anthony Vigil, and fourteen wounded. Second Platoon had the four KIAs: L/Cpl. Robert B. Wilson, Sgt. Joel S. Williamson, Cpl. Mark C. Petersen, and Corpsman HC3 Charles Edward Robertson. There were six WIAs: Second Lieutenant Boyd L. Faithful Jr., S.Sgt. Robert E. Tully, Cpl. Ronald Patrick, Cpl. Charles R. Saunders Jr., Cpl. Robert White Jr., and Cpl. Ralph P. Keenan. Others were wounded, but their wounds were not serious enough for them to be medevaced.[178]

Among First Platoon's eight wounded were L/Cpl. Ward S. Keeton, Pfc. Felix L. Duran, Cpl. Jonathan H. Boyd, L/Cpl. Lionel "Jerry" Lucero, Sgt. Lawrence M. Isaacs, L/Cpl. Jon Q. Nelson, L/Cpl. Thomas J. Cole, and L/Cpl. Lee H. McCullough. Third Platoon suffered no casualties.

George Of the Jungle
Operation Foster, Arizona Territory AT 872522
November 19, 1967, D+6, 0700-2030 hours

Back at the old French Fort only a handful of Marines had been left behind. Most were mortars Marines. Just before nightfall one of the Marines there was bitten by a snake, and the Marines send George Buethe to contact the company, to have them call in a medevac. When George didn't return, the remaining Marines figured out on their own, how to call in a medevac.

The Marine was evacuated without a problem. Buethe, meanwhile had gotten lost, and instead of wondering out in the area in the dark, he found himself a place to hide and stayed there all night. When daylight came, Muszel saw him coming up the trail, toward the CP. He didn't bother to ask him where he had been, he just said, "Well, if it ain't George of the Jungle."[179]

A Night Full Of Fearful Recollections
Operation Foster, Arizona Territory AT 872522
November 19, 1967, D+6, 0700-2030 hours

Dumont, Jones, Marty, and I set up the gun exactly where it had been earlier in the day, out in the open at the lip of the bomb crater. We were again out in front of everyone else. Aggie and Rahm were on the other gun behind us in the tree line where they had been most of the day.

There was a profound disturbance present when we set in for the night. The full moon overhead, added to the gloom and loneliness we all felt. Second Platoon had suffered the most, in the battle. Some of those men had experienced hopelessness, felt helpless, and suffered the depressing consequences of war.

We stood watch while others slept then slept while others stood watch, but it was an uneasy sleep. Some slept for only minutes while others didn't sleep at all. The memories of the day of our dead and wounded, was still very real, in our hearts and mind.

The loss we had suffered were the most casualties our company had suffered in a single operation since Operation DeSoto.[180]

We had all experienced and witnessed war at its front door. We had felt distress at seeing Marines killed or wounded. It was baptism by fire for many of us. We were no longer young and inexperienced men, but Marines who had been scared, experienced deep fear, faced death and had fought back.

We had done what men have done since the beginning of time: we had met the enemy on the battlefield of life and death and had survived. Our doubts about war and manhood, fear and courage, had been met in the fields of fire and we had performed as was expected of us. The proud and the brave were among us, so were the fearful and humbled; we were one and the same. We were men of war and many of us had also conquered the fear of uncertainty. It was the sorrow, fear, and the pain of war that made us a united military fighting unit that day. While we didn't look forward to what tomorrow would bring, we no longer feared that we might not respond to the battle cry.

CHAPTER FIFTEEN

Chicken-Dancing in the Old French Fort
Operation Foster near Giang Hoa (2) (870520)
By the Song Thu Bon River
November 20, 1967, D+7, 0800 hours

The following morning, it was raining, and we moved out on a platoon-size hour long patrol. We patrolled in the same area where the firefight had occurred and found no bodies, just discarded blood-soaked NVA uniforms, some casings from AK-47s, and a .30 caliber machine-gun.

We hadn't been resupplied with food and were wet, tired, and hungry. We had been out for a week, and we smelled like it. When we returned to the French fort the sky above cleared. It wasn't long, before we were told news reporters were coming in from Da Nang to cover the found-rice story, and we would also be getting new reinforcements. While we waited, Lima Company 3/7 landed not far from where we were. Lima Company was to set up near by, reinforce our positions and take on a more active part in the operation, during much of the operation the company had been designated as a reactionary unit. With us having made contact they were now deployed.

Fresh Marines, I was thinking as the reinforcements landed. How many were veterans? How many were new men? How many would freeze up in a firefight? The helicopters lifted their tails and as quickly as they had landed, they were gone and the new Marines began to make their way toward us.

Lucero had fought until he was wounded and then fear had taken over. I now understood the fear of being pinned down and being unable to move. When he was medevaced, Lucero had that far-off look in his eyes that many called the thousand-yard stare that usually comes upon veterans of many firefights. Before he was medevaced, Lucero had sat alone not talking, not moving, and I didn't know what I could have said to him. I regretted not having told his sister Diana that we were going out on an operation. Perhaps Lucero would be sent home. She would be glad that her brother made it home. I also knew I would stop writing to her. We sat around the village hungry and tired, waiting for the news reporters to show up.

Then a skinny, slow-moving chicken made the mistake of walking in front of us. Two more similar size but skinnier chickens were walking right behind her; they were walking in a column. The first one seemed a bit larger than the others in comparison. Jones, Rahm, Aggie, and I looked at each other and then back at the chicken that was walking point. The chickens stopped to peck away at small grains of seeds or whatever it is that chickens' peck at on the ground, and the idea struck all of us at about the same time.

They were huddled together, as most chickens do when they feed, and were ignoring our presence. No longer moving, the chickens made an inviting target. I moved toward the one that had been walking point. She was the biggest of the three, while Dumont moved in behind her and Jones and Rahm circled around. I moved in closer with my eye on the largest of the birds, but the chickens quickly got wise to our intentions; they must have had a chicken sense of danger when a threat to their existence draws near, and all of them went on full alert. They stopped pecking and looked up at us; and as we sprung our ambush, all three squealed hysterically, flapped their wings, and flew right past us. We spun around and gave chase. Chief and Izzie, who had seen our failed ambush attempt, sat laughing at the fiasco that was unfolding before their eyes.

"You're not going to catch them," Chief cried out, chuckling as we ran past him.

"Go, chicken, go!" Izzie yelled out at the skinny little chickens, encouraging them to run faster.

Then other Marines joined in taunting us, crying out, "Go, chicken, go! Run, chicken, run!" and the fluffy white chickens twisted and turned every which way to get away from the fierce squad of Marines from weapons but we did not let up, and continued to chase them throughout the village. We were not about to let a fire-team of enemy chickens which had infiltrated our lines escape.

Not having made any progress in capturing even the smallest of the lot, Dumont called us together to formulate a plan. Jones and Rahm would sweep around and flush them toward Aggie and me. Dumont would hide behind a bamboo fence near a small building and catch any that ran that way. We waited quietly near the building's wall while Jones and Rahm walked toward the chickens, forcing them to move in our direction. When they were close and we were about to spring our ambush, Lima Company Marines came walking through the middle of our ambush site.

We broke ranks and gave chase to catch the chickens again. The fresh, full-bellied, clean-shaven, green-booted Marines walking by shook their heads at First Platoon Marines from India Company as we ran around the village chasing chubby, potbellied, full-feathered, overweight mouth-watering white chickens. Then Marty and Perry joined in the chase.

ARVNs who were with us on the operation had gotten hold of some long poles and were also seen chasing chickens, but we weren't about to do that, it wasn't fair to the chickens.

We would catch our chicken American style and so when Marty was able to corral the nice, fat big one, Aggie, Rahm, Jones, and I surrounded it.

We formed a small semicircle and moved toward the squeaking, panic-crazed, double-chinned chicken.

We knew we had finally cornered it and could already taste it in our mouths. No way was it going to escape.

Then the bird did what chickens are not supposed to do: she flapped her wings, rose up into the air like a helicopter lifting off, and flew up over our heads.

Aggie cried out, "It's a gook chicken!" And with that declaration of war, we took out the M-16s and as Rahm and I set up a scrimmage line Marty and Jones encircled the chickens once more.

We moved out on line, all seven of us, and finally had the biggest, fattest one cornered; and without hesitation, while it was in the center of the circle, we opened fire on it with our M-16s.

We shot off about twenty rounds of M-16 bullets at the squealing, super size, high-flying, and fast-moving chicken; but once again, the chicken flapped her chicken wings and soared through the air across our perimeter, then zigzagged while dodging our bullets.

The rounds struck the hard ground and bounced off the cemented walls of nearby buildings, while the mammoth-size chicken zipped back and forth on the ground. Half scared out of its wits and exhausted, the chicken stopped and looked at us.

She remained motionless, eyeing us to see what we would do next. For now, she remained unharmed and alive.

Jones took aim and opened fire, but the chicken keeping an eye on his trigger finger, waited until he started to squeeze the trigger and she jumped straight up, flapped her wings hysterically, as the bullets sailed pass her and she would have gotten away had that dumb chicken not decided to fly out of the kill zone by way of flying low and over the shortest Marine on line.

Dumont, clobbered it with a large wooden board.

The hen dropped flat at his feet. The chicken's head a mangled mess while the body flipped and flopped and danced around in circles on the ground until it stopped moving.

Within the half hour, we had plucked, cut up, and boiled the chicken. Meanwhile, Perry and Marty had cooked a pot full of white rice; someone threw in some salt tablets into the chicken soup, and we sat around and ate our well-deserved meal. A short time later, it started to rain again and so we sat there by the building with full bellies, keeping watch down the trail for the enemy while the rain came down.

Aggie's Revenge
The Old French Fort by Giang Hoa (2), Football Island
Operation Foster
November 20, 1967, D+7, 1500 hours

Shortly after noon, the rain stopped; we were told we would be on standby while Lima Company saddled up and went out on patrol. With time on our hands we decided to go out and explore the French village. Aggie stayed behind standing watch with the gun and equipment at the edge of the village. With Lima Company Marines gone, India Company CP waiting for the newspaper reporters to arrive and report on the rice we had found, it was going to be an easy day for us. The lieutenant and his CP group were set up at the center of the old French village, and Wilson was about to get some quiet well-deserved sleep.

It was a quiet afternoon. Aggie had just finished cleaning and reloading his M-16. He had laid out his poncho and was arranging his gear to lie down next to the gun. Pridemore was catching a nap, next to him, almost at his feet. Everything was prepared so that Aggie could also catch a quick nap when we returned. He got up and went over to get his canteen when he heard Vietnamese voices coming toward him.

It was laughter coming toward him from outside our perimeter. Knowing ARVNs were in the area and had been seen chasing chickens, he was about to dismiss them; but the voices were coming from the old trail, a trail we hadn't been using but where we had set up the gun to cover just in case.

Dumont, sitting close by, also heard the voices; both of them looked over the four-foot tall elephant grass to get a better view. The voices grew louder with the laughter increasing. As the talking soldiers came into view, Aggie was about to call out to them and challenge them but was not sure who they were, so just in case, he ran over picked up the M-60, and kicked Pridemore awake as he did so.

Dumont saw the first of the soldiers come into view. It was a uniformed female NVA soldier. She was wearing the traditional NVA tan uniform, carrying an AK-47 and walking point.

The rest of the NVA soldiers walking behind her were also dressed in their NVA uniforms and wearing hard cardboard sun helmets with the exception of the third man in line who was shirtless with a red bandana wrapped on his head. He was wearing green trousers.

The female soldier saw Dumont, and as she contemplated what was going on, Dumont said, "It's a broad."

"La Dai!" Dumont called out to them, and as soon as the female NVA soldier realized Dumont was a U.S. Marine, she turned and ran but not before Aggie opened up with a forty round burst of machine gun fire.

Dumont quickly grabbed his M-16 while Aggie swept the area with the M-60 mowing down the grass in front of him and fearing others might have been walking their flank, swung the gun and opened fire from left to right, letting loose with another thirty to forty rounds. He was firing from a kneeling position toward where he had seen the enemy and where he believed there might be others.

On the other side of the village, Jones had just found a case of French-brand cigarettes in a building that at one time must have served as a drugstore when we heard the outburst of gun fire. Jones, Marty, and I ran toward Aggie where the M-60 was firing.

"Outgoing, Outgoing!" cried out O'Neil from First Squad. O'Neil had been sitting nearby and saw Aggie raise the M-60 and open fire. Dumont also opened fire then ran to find and notify the lieutenant.

By the time we got to Aggie, the firing had stopped. He was kneeling on one knee; the gun was smoking from the hundred rounds that had just been fired.

"Gooks," he said, pointing down the trail when we got to him.

"Lots of t-t-them, I shot t-t-three of them," he said, stuttering as he spoke.

At first, with his hard breathing and stuttered speech, we didn't understand what he had said.

"NVA," he said. "A whole bunch of NVA, they were walking down the trail, coming this way, and I shot three of them." We looked down the trail but saw no one. No movement or sound was coming from where Aggie said the enemy soldiers had been, and no incoming fire.

"They were all walking in formation," he said, opening his eyes wide to show us he wasn't lying. "I hit three of them, probably killed three or four of them," he said.

"Sure, Aggie," Jones said, and we dismissed it as Aggie's revenge against us for having left him on duty guarding the gun. Pridemore was standing next to Aggie, with his M-16 in his hand but he hadn't seen anyone. None of us believed him.

Lieutenant Wilson, who had just lain down and was falling fast asleep when the gunfire erupted, came running over. With him was Arthur Toy, his radioman. When he got to where we were, he saw Jones talking to Aggie about what had happened.

The lieutenant, realizing that it was Aggie who had opened up, began to shake his head back and forth and said, "This had better be good, Aguilar. This had better be good. I better see some bodies, Aguilar."

Aggie did everything he could to convince Lieutenant Wilson that he had indeed opened fire on a column of NVA soldiers.

The lieutenant, recalling how often Aggie had in the past exaggerated incidents or embellished issues, remained hesitant to believe him. Still, there was something about the urgency in Aggie's voice that said there might be something to what he was saying. Either way, the incident would have to be checked out as Captain Baggette had already radio Wilson to look into what was going on.

The captain wasn't too pleased with First Platoon, not since the dog in the wire incident and after he heard of us shooting at chickens earlier in the day. Wilson knew he would have to give Baggette some account about the latest First Platoon shooting. Just then, Dumont showed up and verified what Aggie had been saying.

"Okay," the lieutenant said. "Get a squad together with men from all three squads and take a gun team with you and check out the area."

"But don't go too far before reporting in," he told Dumont.

Wilson did not like having to send a squad out alone after what had happened to Second Platoon the day before, but with a gun team and the squad going only a short distance, he would have something to report to the captain even if it was just to say that no VC bodies were found. "Make sure you check in with me right away if you find anything," Wilson added.

"Yes, sir," Dumont responded, and we saddled up.

Stimulus Equals Response
Operation Foster AT 875516
November 20, 1967, D+7, 1500-1900 hours

A short time later, we moved out. Dumont was leading the Squad, and Keene was walking point followed by Welsh and Parisi.

Edward J. Welsh from New York, of medium built, had straight hair, and a large oval-shaped face. A very likeable Marine who had been with the platoon since early September, he reminded me of Audie Murphy. He stepped off, with a spring in his gait, falling in right after Keene.

William L. Parisi had been in country since early April, I didn't know him. He fell in next, followed by Dumont, Pridemore and the radioman.

I picked up the gun, and Aggie picked up two hundred rounds of machine-gun ammo, strapped them across his chest, and stepped into formation in front of me, walking behind Pridemore and the radioman. Marty fell in behind me in front of James Keenan's fire-team, which was bringing up the rear.

About thirty yards away, we found blood splashed all over the area.

Globs of thick blood were still flowing down the center veins of a plant that had broad leaves. The blood was slowly dripping falling on the trail's surface. We could see where the thick elephant grass had also been hard-pressed against the ground by a fallen human form. The dark green leaves clearly revealed where a pool of blood was smeared when they dragged the body away.

Keene, walking point, stopped, looked at the blood, and silently moved on. Dumont reported back to the lieutenant that we had found blood and were following the blood trail left by a bleeding enemy soldier. Wilson radioed back for the squad to follow, but not too far, and he passed the word for the rest of the platoon to saddle up.

Keene hunched low and moved more cautiously along the trail.

We followed the blood trail until we found it split into two different directions. Most of the pools of blood led in a northwest direction on top of the wide trail on the berm that crossed open rice paddies leading to Phu Long (1). It was the same long, wide berm that we had crossed to get to the thick jungle and Second Platoon the day before.

Smaller pools of blood led west along a thick tree line that ran parallel to the Song Thu Bon River. At the beginning of the trail leading across the open field, Dumont picked up a bloody bandage.

Part of a skull and brain matter fell out. Aggie had indeed hit someone, and more than likely, that person was now dead. Aggie turned around to look at me, and I nodded my head without speaking, saying, "I know, I know" to Aggie.

We decided to follow the largest concentration of blood droppings on the dike that ran across the open rice paddy fields toward Phu Long (1). Drops of blood as well as drag marks where the enemy was helping one of their own along the way were clearly visible on the top of the trail and along its side.

On the right side of the berm, the rice paddy fields were filled with small weeds, water, and mud.

A small agricultural water ditch ran alongside the left side of the berm. The trail to Phu Long was well beaten from frequent use; we had used it many times over the past few days. The fields on the left side were dry, except for where the rain had fallen earlier; most of it seemed to have been collected in the small agricultural ditch.

The trail/berm we were on led through the village past the thick tropical jungle we had ran through the day before. A cluster of tall trees, scattered huts and a small clearing could be seen to the left of the trail. To the right the tropical jungle was thick, full of vegetation, palm and banana trees.

When we neared the second of three wide rice paddy fields, Keene walking point, stopped. Parisi and Welsh moved up to join him, and they all stooped down.

We all stopped out in the open on top of the berm, and I got down on one knee, placing the gun down on top of the dike. I did not like stopping, certainly not out in the open.

Keene was about three-fourths of the way across the rice paddy fields when he noticed the blood trail suddenly stopped.

I started to look ahead, where the gooks might have gone. Thoughts cross my mind.

We are out in the open. There is quite a distance, we still need to go. We are too much out in the open.

A deep sense of danger seemed to be moving toward where I was kneeling, like a wave moving across the field. The rest of the squad is to my right rear, so that was covered. I began to look behind me, toward my left rear.

I could see Keene walking back and forth on top of the trail, checking the edge of the berm.

Keene found where the blood trail left the berm, where it cut across the small agricultural ditch to our left and pass a dozen or so grave mounds. As Keene was trying to see exactly where the blood trails led, Dumont filled in the lieutenant over the radio.

"Why is he stopped on the trail?" Wilson asked over the net. Dumont then asked Keene why he was stopped.

"Gooners," answered Keene.

"Gooners?" Dumont asked.

"Yes," Keene replied. "Gooners—I can smell them."

"He smells gooks," Dumont reported into the mike.

"Well, tell him to get off his ass and out of there," Wilson said over the net, fearing we were too much out in the open.

Keene could see that the blood trail led west toward the southwestern edge of Phu Long (1). The enemies whom Aggie had shot up had cut across the last rice paddy field, dragging their dead and wounded into the village. As Keene stood up to move out in response to Wilson's order, so did the rest of the squad.

I stood up, and threw the M-60 over my right shoulder. As soon as we all stepped forward, the enemy opened fire.

Keene, Corporal Howard, Dumont, and Rahm as well as most of Third Squad quickly jumped to the right side of the trail as bullets struck the ground directly in front of where they had been.

Parisi had the experience of having been out on a number of patrols, and like others with time in country, he had been shot at often. As the first rounds shot past him, he saw bullets strike the top right side of the berm he was on; the bullets striking near him had come from his right, so he jumped to the left of the trail that had the small agricultural ditch running parallel to it.

Ira Hullihen, the tallest Marine in the squad, was walking behind the radioman and was struck by the initial volley of bullets. The bullets spun Hullihen around and around, and with each impact; he was twisted counterclockwise like a rotating top.

When he stopped spinning, Hullihen fell facedown on top of the dike. Charles Miner Taylor III, a new man in the platoon, stood motionless, mesmerized by the way Hullihen was being twisted and turned as the bullets struck him; Taylor was still standing upright on top of the dike, exposed to incoming fire when both Howard and Dumont grabbed Taylor by his ankles and pulled him down just as a new burst of automatic gunfire flew past him and others struck the dirt where he had been standing seconds before.

As the men in the squad sought refuge on the right side of the dike, Hullihen, knocked down by the impact of the bullets, listlessly rolled off the berm like a smooth slithering snake as an RPG rocket exploded in the dry rice paddy fields to the left of him. The explosion shot out shrapnel, dirt and debris up and over the berm and on the Marines in front of us. Most of the shrapnel landed in the flooded rice paddy field to our far right.

When the shooting started, I saw Parisi jump to the dry left side of the trail as bullets kicked up dust to his right.

The enemy was firing at us from both sides of the trail that led from Phu Long (2) into Phu Long (1), and bullets were striking in front of Aggie and I, tearing up the hard-pressed ground. The bullets were being fired at us from our right and were making their way toward us. I followed Parisi's movement, and so, did Aggie in front of me, and both of us jumped to the left side of the dike and quickly sought cover in the middle of the small agricultural ditch that ran parallel to the trail. It was the only covering available.

Stimulus equals response, I was thinking as my body struck the mud at the bottom of the small ditch. The thought was a flashback to a high school teacher's lesson on Newton's theory of relativity: *objects in motion tend to stay in motion until acted upon by another force.*

Sergeant Nelson had expounded upon that theory during our training at MCRD: "If you analyze the area where you are and look for both an advantageous position for cover and where to return fire from, just in case you get hit and if you have already searched for spots that might present a danger, when the shit hits the fan, you will be prepared to respond and will have already found cover. If you wait until the first round is fired to look for protection, it will be too late."

Mentally and subconsciously, I must have been searching, thinking, and cautiously preparing myself for the scene that was now unfolding. I had been preparing for contact while we were still out in the open, on top of the berm. Every object in a state of uniform motion tends to remain in that state of motion unless an external force is applied to it.

Stimulus equals response. As we move forward, the enemy opens fire, and we hit the ground. I'd done this before.

When, I dove for cover I saw, Prescott and other Marines to his right lying out in the open on the wet side of the berm near where the rocket had exploded.

They must have been walking our right flank, I was thinking. My mind had created a quick panoramic view of the whole scene, as it all happened. It was as if everything was happening in slow motion, but in split seconds.

Bullets were striking the ground near Marines up front. The rocket exploded, shrapnel and clods of dirt shot out, struck the flooded rice paddy fields, and their impact shot geysers of water high into the air. Marines lying out in the open area had only the cover of little green-colored rice plants and the soft mud below them for shelter.

As I buried my head in the ditch, I could hear the dull thud of bullets striking the water on the other side of the dike and bullets burying themselves deep into the mud near fallen Marines.

Caught in the Enemy's Cross Fire
Operation Foster AT 875516
November 20, 1967, D+7, 1500-1900 hours

I heard an M-14 open up, fully automatic; the sound was followed by the sound of M-16s as other Marines opened fire as well. No sooner had Aggie and I hit the ground we were showered with automatic fire from both sides of the trail, where the path entered the tree line at Phu Long (1). The enemy had definitely seen the gun. It was an M-60 that had opened fire on them and which had caused them the loss of one or more of the comrades. I crawled deeper into the small agricultural trench as bullets struck the side and lip of the wide berm above us. Other bullets were striking the hard dry dirt wall only inches away from my head.

With Marines out in the open rice paddy, I knew I needed to open up so that they could get out of harm's way. I prepared myself to open fire to the right toward the tree line at Phu Long (1). The majority of the incoming seemed to be coming from that spot where the bloody body had been dragged into, and most of the incoming was targeting our guns' position, from that location. I quickly brought the gun up and opened fire in that direction and then the incoming shifted a bit to the left. The majority of the incoming fire was coming at us from the left near the grave mounds near the tree line. I shifted my fire in that direction.

Seconds later, another barrage of incoming rounds exploded near us; they were AK-47 bullets being fired at us from our left rear behind us, not from in front of us or from the Phu Long (2) side of the clearing.

The new incoming fire was coming from the direction of the blood trail we had chosen not to follow behind us, southwest of us, from the tree line near the Song Thu Bon River. The AK-47 fire was striking the berm just to the left of my head. As the bullets struck the edge of the agricultural ditch, puffs of dry dust and pieces of chipped rocks and small particles of dirt shot off into the air. The NVA had us in a cross fire. Marines were pinned down on the right side of the dike and were taking incoming fire from their right front and from their left. We that had jumped to the left of the dike were taking incoming from our left front and now also from our left rear. We had jumped on the wrong side of the dike.

We were on the same side of the dike where the majority of the NVA were, and the only cover we had was the small water channel we were in. The tributary was somewhat dry, but parts of it had fresh mud from the morning rain as well as hard-pressed mud I could feel below me. The ditch was two feet wide and about a foot deep. The rice paddies on our side of the berm were dry, and I wondered if that was the reason I had chosen to jump on this side of the trail. The berm we jumped off of was at least four feet higher than the small ditch we were in. The height might as well have been six feet; it was too high for us to try and jump back over from a laid-out position. We would have to get up onto the berm, run across its width, and get down on the other side without getting hit. Aggie, lying prone a few feet in front of me, was busy trying to un-jam his M-16. Bullets were kicking up dirt and mud between us, and we were also being showered with dust and small pieces of rocks and debris as bullets struck the dike's wall above us.

Bullets continued to come at us at an increasing pace from our side of the dike and I could hear Marines at the same time beginning to engage the enemy with increasing return firepower.

I turned my body and fired a twenty-round burst at the enemy's position that were firing at us from our rear, and more green tracers from their machine-gun was their response. The rounds came in a steady flow, striking a foot or two in front of my gun. I squeezed the trigger again, held the gun in tighter, and held the trigger down, zeroing in for a tighter pattern shooting at the source of the enemy's tracers.

I could see my red tracers moving in closer and tighter toward where the enemy's green tracers were coming from until my bullets met the spot from where they were originating.

Then the enemy's green tracers shot off high into the air away from us, spiraling upward in a spastic pattern, then struck the ground way out in the middle of the rice paddy field to our far right, and I knew I had hit their gun.

As I was firing away at the enemy behind us, the intensity of the incoming rounds coming at us from across the flooded rice paddy near Phu Long increased. I could sense that someone else behind the berm had also opened up and was responding to their incoming from our right rear from near the French fort. Someone from behind us was shooting over the heads of the Marines on the other side of the berm. I could also tell that enemies' bullets were now being directed at him as well.

Aggie unjammed his weapon and opened fired toward our right front at the enemy entrenched along the Phu Long tree line. I switched the gun around to engage the incoming fire the enemy was shooting targeting him with. As I turned, new incoming gunfire, .30 caliber fire, and RPG rounds were added to the AK-47 gunfire already being fired at us.

The rounds were exploding near Aggie and I, but Aggie kept firing until his M-16 jammed again.

Behind us, the volume of bullets being fired at us once again began to increase. I couldn't shoot the gun in both directions at the same time so I fired back at what seemed to be the heaviest concentration of incoming firepower where the majority of the bullets were coming from. Aggie crawled backward to where I was, unhooked his two 100-round belts, lay on his back, and hooked the links together to make a 200-round belt for the gun, and handed them to me.

Our response gunfire on the right side of the berm was intense as Keene and the other Marines on the right side of the trail returned fire as the enemy's firing increased. They were on higher ground then us so they could provide better coverage for us. Then, I realized that the enemy was firing at us almost in line with the ditch, but just a bit to the left of where I had seen Parisi jump into the ditch.

On the other wet side of the dike in front of us, I could hear a Marine fire off an M-79 round. It was a smoke grenade, and exploded near the enemy's Phu Long firing position on our side of the dike. A short time later, I heard a series of small thuds and heard our mortar rounds flying overhead racing toward the enemies' position. The mortars were coming from the French village where our mortar squads were located.

I hoped the mortars would cause the enemy to flee, but as the mortars ceased, they unleashed yet another round of intensified firepower at us. All kinds of dirt, dust, and mud as well as ricocheting bullets were now being sprayed all over us.

By now, I knew the routine: I had to stop firing and hug the ground. And I did.

As I got down and backed off from where I had been shooting, a fresh volley of incoming rounds claimed the embankment from where I had been. I turned on my back to keep the gun clean and out of the mud and felt the warmth of the gun on my chest.

"Aggie, Aggie," I called out to him.

"Yeah," he answered.

"Aggie, we jumped on the wrong side of the dike."

"I know, I know," he answered. "How did we do that?" he asked, unbelieving and almost comical in the way he posed the question. I didn't know if he was trying to be funny or if he really didn't realize the world of hurt we were in.

"Is anyone still out in the open?" I asked.

"Yeah," Aggie answered, as he adjusted himself to get deeper into the center of the little ditch we were in. "I saw Jackie Williams and another Marine who were walking on our right flank hit the dirt; they were out in the open. Parisi jumped on our side of the dike," he added.

"I know," I answered. Parisi was shorter than Aggie or me and a bit chunkier. I wondered how he could be squeezing himself into the same skinny little ditch we were in.

"We can't stay here," I cried out to Aggie.

"Yeah, I know," he answered softly, his voice fading as he realized what I was saying. Just then, another group of bullets struck the wall of the berm just above our heads, and we hunched our heads farther down. Aggie would have to move fast when I opened up again, and he knew it. He yelled out to Parisi to tell him that I was going to open up so he would be able to jump over to the other side of the berm as well, but there was no answer. Aggie called Parisi's name again and cried out loud that the gun was going to open fire and for him to jump over to the right side of the berm. Still there was no answer.

"I only have about fifty rounds left," I said to Aggie, and I could see the worried look on his face. Fifty rounds would be fired off before he would be able to get completely across the wide berm.

Pridemore, who had been bringing up the rear, had jumped to the right of the dike; and like other Marines who found themselves stuck deep in knee-high mud, all they could do for a while was bend over at the waist as bullets flew overhead until they were able to break free and pull themselves out of the muddy trap and find cover at the edge of the berm.

I called out to see where Marty was; he had been right behind us when the shooting started. He would have two hundred rounds with him. Marty answered from our side of the trail. Shit, I said to myself. I didn't know he was on this side, yet I had felt a Marine's presence behind me. Both he and Keenan had also jumped on the wrong side. But, Keenan had jumped over to the other side when I first opened fire, Marty said.

Now I knew who it was that had been shooting over our heads at the enemy to our right front.

"Marty, can you throw me your gun ammo?" I asked and as Marty scooted up, bullets peppered the area between us. Unable to get in any closer, he tossed me first a 100-round belt then another.

"Hey, Keenan," I called out. "Keenan," can you cover our rear when I open up?" I yelled out. I waited there was no answer.

"Yeah," I can do that, he answered. But I realized that to do so, he would be exposing himself to the firing coming from our front near Phu Long (1).

"Just give me a minute," he said. "I can get a better shot if I move back. I'll have to shoot over Marty's head," Keenan said. "Marty, don't move until I open up so you'll know where I'm at."

"Hey, Cookie," Marty called out urgently. "My rifle's jammed."

"Can you jump over?" I asked.

"Don't know," he answered.

I linked up the first hundred rounds Marty had given me to the gun, and waited for Keenan to set up. Then for some reason, there was a pause in the shooting and Marty leaped over the embankment and slid across the top of the wide berm.

"God *damn* it!" I could hear Keenan yelling at him. "I almost shot you, damn you, Marty, you scared the shit out of me!"

Marty, without answering, leaned his back against the dike and began to tear apart his M-16 to unjam it.

"Okay," Keenan yelled out, and we both opened fire so that Aggie could jump over.

This time, I held the trigger hard, pressed against the trigger guard, and a steady stream of red burning tracers slid evenly across the rice paddy fields. The bullets sailed straight across with a deadly slicing ray of stinging pain. The rounds I was putting out were traveling about a foot off the ground and impacting almost at ground level along our right front where the path to Phu Long disappeared into the tree line. Bushes and tall clumps of elephant grass near the tree line were being mowed down as if an invisible reaper's sickle was swiftly moving across the wide terrain. While I concentrated on shooting to the right, I could hear Keenan's bullets being fired toward the enemies' position to our rear.

New incoming bullets were beginning to kick up dust all around the gun with renewed intensity. I was being hit by chips of ricocheting bits of bullets and small pieces of rocks and loose dirt clods from the incoming bullets' impacts near me. They stung my face and bounced off my helmet as I fired away. I yelled at Aggie to go.

Aggie got up quickly and jumped up to try and get over the berm. He had underestimated the height of the berm, his right leg never made it to the top, and he fell back into the ditch.

Marty opened up, shooting along with Keenan at the enemy behind us. Then Keenan's M-16 jammed. Aggie, who had unjammed his weapon, got back up, and opened fire toward the NVA on our right side; but the enemies' incoming rounds were hitting all around us with such ferocity that all Aggie could do was to open fire without daring to look where he was firing. He just slung his M-16 over the top of the ditch, pointed it in the general direction from which the bullets were coming from, and opened fire.

Aggie's firing was answered with renewed automatic gunfire. The small dirt embankment both of us had been able to hide behind was being slowly eroded by the intensity of incoming bullets. I scooted back, moving away from Aggie to find better cover. As I did, the embankment I moved away from was being peppered with direct enemy fire, and I wondered why I hadn't been hit.

As I moved back, I could see a fist-sized dirt clod sitting at the edge of the ditch. It was the best covering for my helmeted head that I had found since the firing begun. It was only about four or five inches in diameter, but to me, that dirt clod looked like a large boulder. It was something I could hide behind. The dirt clod was large enough to cover the left side of my head, so I backed up to get behind it and opened fire with a steady burst toward the tree line on our right side. I fired away until my bullets were spent, then loaded the last hundred rounds of ammo, closed the cover, and opened fire again. All of a sudden the dirt clod shattered.

A high-caliber bullet had struck it. The bullet had come from our right front. It was a single shot, and no others followed.

"Sniper!" Aggie cried out, and I got down farther but kept firing to my right toward where the round had come from.

All of a sudden, I could sense I should be shooting more to the left as that was where the bullet had come from. As I started to move to shoot in that direction, the machine-gun in my hand shook violently.

The bullet's impact caused the gun to quiver in my hands, sending a throbbing electrical sting up my forearm and down my back, and the gun jammed.

A Sniper's Prize Realized
Operation Foster AT 875516
November 20, 1967, D+7, 1500-1900 hours

"Damn it!" I said and rolled over on my back, pulling the gun to my chest. The sniper's bullet had struck the gun dead center on its right side and had split the locking pin in two. Only half of the thin metal locking plate remained attached. It slid off into my hand, and the gun's trigger housing group fell out. Without the locking pin to hold the trigger housing group in place, I could no longer fire the gun.

I lay there holding the gun on my chest as bullets continued to whiz by all around us. The majority of the rounds continued to come from our right front on the Phu Long side where the majority of the enemy was located. There was silence on my left side or at least not as many bullets were being fired in our direction from our left rear, as well.

Perhaps Marty and Keenan's return fire had done the job. With the gun silenced, the enemy may have counted me as dead. Behind me, I could hear voices followed by sporadic gunfire; the noise was coming from the French village from where the rest of the platoon was. A moment later, a machine-gun opened fire and from the distance, lying on my back, I couldn't tell where it was or where it was firing, but I recognized the sound as outgoing fire. It has to be Jones, I was thinking or hoping. He must have been firing at the enemy's position by the river to our left rear.

Aggie called out to me, "I think the platoon's coming."

"Where are they?"

"I don't know," he answered.

"Aggie, the gun's jammed," I said, and there was silence from him.

"There are still gooks in front of us." I knew that Aggie was probably lying on his back as I was.

"Yeah, I know. They're NVA, a whole lot of them," he said.

"Hey, Aggie," I called out.

"Yeah," he answered.

"I think you pissed them off."

"Yeah, I know," Aggie answered. "'I'm out of ammo," he added.

It was not what I wanted to hear. "Shit!" I said. "I was hoping you'd be able to kill all the gooks if they assaulted our position." I heard Aggie chuckle.

Then he said seriously, "Do you think I could?" And I chuckled too, afraid the enemy might see us moving.

"I have to go pee," Aggie said, and I laughed to myself.

"They're not going to stop shooting at us so you can go pee," I said. "Go in your pants."

"I guess I could," he answered as new incoming rounds struck nearby. The enemy must have seen us move. On our backs amidst all the gunfire, it was hard to tell where the bullets were coming from. Then all of a sudden, the sky above us rattled and vibrated as a set of fixed-wing aircraft pulled out. I could see bullets following after them. The enemy was shooting at the jets even as their destructive load began to explode. Then the ground shook, and a huge explosion filled the sky with the flash of a fiery ball.[181] Somewhere, a Bird Dog overhead had called in an air strike for us.

The jets came in again for another pass, and this time, the enemy did not open fire on them. I heard movement behind us, and I wondered where the enemy was or where the rest of the company was. I unsnapped my holster, took out my .45 caliber pistol, and laid the machine-gun down next to me. The gun's barrel was still smoking.

I always kept a round in the chamber of the pistol so that in an emergency, all I had to do was cock the hammer back and pull the trigger without having to pull the slide backwards to chamber a round.

I didn't like the noise the sliding motion made at night, and this way, the pistol was ready to fire when we were out on night ambushes. I turned my body slightly so that I could look toward our rear.

I couldn't see anything except the wide side of the berm and the sky above.

Over my head, I could see black smoke billowing upward from where Napalm had been dropped. The smoke was expanding, and I hoped the enemy was gone. I laid the pistol on my chest, holding it tight. All I could do was lay there and wait.

I was getting used to being out in the open behind rice paddy dikes while being shot at. I couldn't understand how we were going to win this war if we couldn't see them in the tree lines when we shot at them and if we were able to stay out of their bullets' paths by hiding behind rice paddy dikes. In Vietnam, there were plenty of tree lines and there were plenty of rice paddy dikes.

I wasn't very good with the .45. I had shot only marksman with it. The Corps called that medal award "the toilet-seat award." The Distinguished Expert Medal was the preferred medal for machine-gunners to earn. I had shot sharpshooters once, but the corporal at Edison range at Camp Pendleton hadn't recorded it. I hadn't qualified with as high a score after that. Now I was wishing that I had shot better, medal or no medal. Shooting at the enemy now would depend on how close they got. Marksmanship qualified you with the pistol in the Corps, but that's not what mattered now. I wished I had practiced as much with the .45 as I had with the machine-gun. The .45 pistol is not very good at long-distance shooting unless you've mastered its recoil. At twenty yards or closer, I felt confident I could hit the enemy at that distance. The pistol's 100 percent stopping power at that close range would do the rest. I was prepared to shoot the first person that appeared on the berm in my direct line of fire. I knew if there were more gooks after that first shot, I would be killed, and I felt helpless.

I was expecting the enemy to run up from behind us from where they had been on our left side. They would run by shooting at us. I wondered how many Marines from the squad had been wounded, how many had been killed. The majority of the enemy might still be across the wet rice paddy field where the sniper had been. Aggie was a short distance away, but he was out of ammo. *At least I have my .45 pistol,* I thought, and I felt better. I didn't know where our platoon was, but I hoped they would come up the trail that we had followed and find us.

I wondered if they were going around trying to get behind the enemy force that had fired at us from our rear. If so, the enemy might be flushed out and have run toward where we were. They might make a mad rush for it and use the wide trail to get quickly across. If they did, it would be the last thing I would see—a gook on the trail. I would fire a few rounds at them and then it would be over. I had seven rounds in the pistol; maybe I'd get lucky and hit at least two of them.

I wished I knew what was going on, where the platoon was, but I didn't dare move to try and look out. The last barrages of intense incoming rounds had come from both sides of the berm. I didn't know what to expect. *What damage did the jets do?* I wondered. The arrival of the jets had at least showed me that someone knew where we were. I lay there silent, waiting.

Then I heard footsteps on the hard surface of the berm.

The sound was coming closer. At least, they weren't running across.

I took the pistol off my chest and pulled back the hammer, extending my arm as I pointed the .45 pistol in the direction from which the sound was coming.

I took up the slack on the trigger, and my hand pressed down on the gun's grip safety. The weapon was ready to fire; all I had to see was the target.

I was ready to drop the hammer, when the camouflaged helmet and dirty face of Keenan appeared as he stepped up into the berm. He stepped up in front of the Marine whose steps I had heard moving in our direction. Keenan came over to where I was, looked down at me, saw my gun in pieces, and my .45 pistol extended. He saw that I was also caked in mud but alive. He shook his head. "Unbelievable," he said and moved on.

I drew a deep sigh of relief, brought the pistol back across my chest, and held on to the hammer as I released the trigger, dropping the hammer down slowly so that the gun wouldn't go off. I heaved a long sigh and silently thanked God.

Another Dance For The Bandaged Gun
Operation Foster AT 875516
November 20, 1967, D+7, 1500-1900 hours

Other Marines materialized walking on top of the dike. They were First Platoon Marines. I got up, and on the other side of the trail, I saw that Second Platoon Marines were walking across in a small scrimmage line. Farther east, the rest of India Company was moving in a column along the top of a dike toward the southeast corner of Phu Long (1). It was Third Platoon and a platoon from

Lima Company. To their left, a squad of Marines was sweeping across on line, protecting their left flank.

I holstered my .45, picked up my machine-gun, and Aggie got up. He fell in line in front of me. Marty came up behind us, and we moved along with Second Squad on top of the berm toward the tree line where the trail ended.

We walked past Hullihen who was having his wounds looked at by Doc Marren. Hullihen was sitting upright on the right side of the berm; bullets from a carbine had struck his flak jacket in several places. Despite the violent force that had spun him about, he only had some dark bruises on his chest and a slight flesh wound on one of his arms: he was all right. He looked up as we drew near, and I could see a slight smirk at the corner of his mouth.

"Lucky," I said, only moving my mouth not saying the word while shaking my head in disbelief. He grinned wider and nodded in agreement.

When First Platoon's Second Squad got across, they peeled off to the right of the dike. Jones, First Squad, and the lieutenant as well as his CP still hadn't started across from the other side. Perhaps the lieutenant was being cautious and did not want a lot of Marines out in the open walking together on the dike.

We passed Parisi who was still lying in the ditch near where our point man, Keene, had originally stopped before the enemy opened fire. Welsh was lying next to him, both were on their backs smoking cigarettes. Only then did I realize that Welsh also had jumped on the wrong side.

"Hey, Parisi," I asked, "how'd you get so dirty?"

Parisi didn't answer. As he exhaled the cigarette smoke, he released a long sigh and grinned. He was glad to be alive. He and Welsh were so close to where the enemy had been that I realized why he hadn't answered before during the firefight. His silence had been caused by the fear of giving away his position.

"Hey, Welsh, what are you doing on that side of the dike? The gooks are on that side," Aggie said to him.

"Yeah, I know," Welsh answered in his New York accent. Welsh and Parisi got up, and I could tell that both were still visibly shaken. Welsh's M-16 rifle was in pieces and full of mud. It had jammed up, and unable to move, he hadn't been able to dislodge the round that was still stuck in his M-16's chamber.

That's probably what saved his life, I thought.

Welsh would have kept on shooting despite the intensity of the incoming rounds and the closeness of the enemy to his position. I reached down to help Welsh up out of the ditch, and Keene got up onto the berm from the right side where he had ended up.

As Williams and the other Marines that had been pinned down to the right side of the dike reached where we were, Welsh reached down to grab his gear. All of a sudden there was an explosion at the end of the trail. Parisi jumped up, and we all jumped to the right side of the trail as enemy bullets whizzed by. Some Marines I could see were out in the open field. They ran toward the berm or toward the nearest dike as bullets kicked up small water geysers high into the air near them. The incoming was not intense.

This time, Aggie and I had better cover. We propped ourselves with our backs up against the berm and sat up knowing the thick wall would protect us; we felt safe.

Someone near where the explosion had occurred called for a Corpsman. The M-60 was in pieces, and Aggie was still out of ammo. Welsh crawled over to where we were and propped himself up next to us. His broken and mud-soaked M-16 was useless. All three of us were among the closest to the enemy and, except for my .45 pistol none of us had a weapon capable of firing back at them.

If I could find a way to hold the locking mechanism in place, maybe a piece of wire or a string, I would be able to fire the gun. I held the gun's trigger guard in place and pulled back the cocking handle. It worked. Aggie raised the cover and dropped in the 100-round belt of ammo that Welsh had been carrying. Aggie closed the cover, and the gun was ready for firing. I laid the gun over the dike while holding the gun's trigger housing group up tight against the gun. I pulled the gun in tight and pressed down on the gun as I opened fire. The gun fired off four quick rounds before kicking the firing mechanism out of my hands and jamming. By this time, the rest of Second Platoon who had been out in the open had managed to move up to the berm's edge, and those that were able to were returning fire.

All Aggie, Welsh, and I could now do was to sit there with our backs up against the berm and wait. We each lit up a cigarette and just sat silently smoking while bullets sped through the air overhead and other Marines fired back. There was nothing else we could do.

In the rice paddy fields, Marines were getting up and running for cover, zigzagging across the fields as enemy bullets kicked up dirt or little spurts of water into the air where they struck the surface. Some Marines ran straight for the safety of the berm where we were, and when they got close, they dove for cover as bullets continued to zip by. Others ran right by us or stopped, dropped, then got up and ran again toward the front of the trail.

Mud Marines and A Photo Shoot
Operation Foster AT 875516
November 20, 1967, D+7, 1500-1900 hours

"Corpsman!" somebody yelled again from near our end of the berm, and Doc Marren began to make his way in our direction. He was with our CP group at the end of the trail. He stopped and dropped a couple of times before he got close to where we were. He dropped again when incoming rounds struck the top of the berm. No doubt the enemy was zeroing in on him because his head kept bobbing up and down along the dike; no one else was moving, and he was the only visible target for them as he made his way forward.

The Corpsman was breathing hard when he stopped at our position. Beads of perspiration were flowing freely on his forehead and there was a deep fear in his eyes. It was too risky for him to move on as bullets struck the top of the berm above us, so he just lay there not moving.

"Hey, Doc, you got to run fast or stay down or they're gonna get you," I said, and his eyes grew wider. It was not what he wanted to hear, reminding him of his mission.

"You got any tape?" I asked. "I need tape to hold my gun together." And I showed him the pieces. Doc Marren rolled on his back, reached into his Corpsman's bag, and gave me a roll of white tape. He seemed relieved to be able to provide some service and not be running forward.

Aggie held the gun out of the mud while I pulled the cocking handle back, and he dropped the ammo belt into the feed tray. I closed the cover, and we taped it together as best as we could. It looked like a wounded Marine.

While I was wrapping tape around the gun to hold it together, I sensed someone out in the open field to my right. It was a news reporter and his assistant. They had been running along with the Corpsman, and the Marine photographer or news reporter was kneeling out in the open field a few feet away focusing his movie camera on what Aggie and I were doing. A few more rounds zinged by and we ducked while they kept shooting their film.

By then, Third Platoon, with the Lima Company Platoon, had crossed over and reached the southeast corner of Phu Long (1) while the squad of Marines that had still been sweeping across on their left flank scrambled for cover. Some made it across; others were still out in the open fields.

Marines that had reached the tree line were now sweeping west along the tree line from the southern edge of the village, toward us.

When the explosion occurred, some Marines had found cover near some fallen trees and others along the side of the tree line. They were about forty yards from us and were starting to move cautiously toward the tree line, while waiting for Third Platoon to come along their side before moving on.

The area once again exploded with incoming RPG and mortar rounds as well as .30 caliber bullets and AK-47 gunfire. Before the enemy fire increased, Marines that had been sweeping across had found better cover. The enemy was now fighting back, and they were advancing, pushing toward us. As both units moved forward toward each other, the firefight was growing in intensity near us. First Platoon Marines who had reached the edge of the trail were firing back, so there was a three way fire exchange.

I crawled on my belly up onto the edge of the wide berm then moved forward just enough to get a clear field of fire and opened fire with a forty-round burst and then let up, I was glad the gun was firing again. Aggie crawled up next to me and linked another belt to the gun. I raised my left arm to hold the ammo belt up, and he draped the rounds over it and moved away from me.

There was room for him where I was, but he would be exposed and since I could, with my arm extended, act as my own A-gunner, there was no use in both of us getting hit. Meanwhile, Doc Marren had made his way over to where the call for the Corpsman had come from.

Squatting next to Aggie, the cameraman continued to roll his film. We were mud Marines doing what we had been trained to do with whatever resources we had, and it was all being filmed. The enemy's incoming bullets struck the top of the berm in front of us and smoke rose from the barrel of the bandaged machine-gun, but I kept firing and the combat news photographer kept filming.

Recon By Fire
Operation Foster AT 875516
November 20, 1967, D+7, 1500-1900 hours

From the other end of the trail, Jones' gun opened fire, and his tracers shot across the rice paddy fields at a right angle toward where I was firing. Jones was zeroing in and shooting toward where he could see my red tracers were going. My gun was shooting at an angle, striking the edge of the tree line across the graveyard from where the enemy was firing at us from. This time it was Charlie, not us, in the cross fire.

Third Platoon meanwhile was moving forward along the tree line. Marines spread out to our right were steadily moving forward, shooting on line and advancing toward the enemy's positions. When they aligned with our position, my gun fired an additional twenty more rounds then the trigger mechanism became loose and the gun stopped firing.

As I checked it and decided to back myself off the berm, the gun's cocking handle cracked and vibrated as the gun was ripped once more from my hands.

The gun had taken another direct hit from a sniper who had fired on us from our far right side, from a tree near the huts in the village. Third Platoon Marines the closest to the snipers fire. They sighted in on the sniper in the tree and opened fire in his direction. Enemy resistance continued, but soon Marines had secured the area and were deployed along the trail as it entered the jungle area.

Meanwhile, the rest of Lima Company that had gone out on a long patrol, earlier were moving south toward us along the trail, we had been on the day before. As they drew near, the enemy broke contact.

After the arrival of Lima Company, all of India's First Platoon were gathered at the end of the trail and Lieutenant Wilson; from there, along with Lima Company Marines on our right, had us get on line and move out on line.

Those of us with defective or broken weapons took the weapons from our CP group and got on line to advance forward. "Recon by fire" is what the lieutenant called it as we moved through the area firing our weapons as we went. While we only found pools of blood in as many places, we did find three dead NVA bodies. Welsh and Williams recovered their weapons.[182]

Lima Company, on line with us to our right, swept in the area from where we had received the majority of incoming fire and also found only blood trails, discarded NVA clothing, and backpacks.

First Platoon suffered three WIAs: Cpl. Gerard Dumont, Cpl. Ira H. Hullihen, and Cpl. Robert W. Howard. None had wounds serious enough to warrant a medevac. Hullihen, with just a flesh shrapnel wound and bruises, remained. Dumont and Howard were wounded in the explosion at the end of the trail. A Marine had tripped a booby-trapped grenade the enemy had left behind. After others that had also been wounded that day were medevaced, the company moved back to the old French village for the night.

That evening, we were resupplied with rations, and a late incoming chopper brought in three new men and another machine-gun for First Platoon.

The new men we received were to replace the eight that had been wounded and evacuated from First Platoon over the past two days of fighting. That brought our platoon strength to forty-two men including the CP group.

An Extreme Makeover For An Old Friend
Operation Foster AT 875516
November 20, 1967, D+7, 1500-1900 hours

Aggie and I sat up in the same location back at the village from where he had opened up on the gooks. Dumont spent the night with us rather than with the CP while Jones and Marty joined First Squad on the other side of the village.

In the battles we had fought over the past two days, the NVA had paid a great price. We may not have found bodies as evidence of our effectiveness, but I knew they had paid a great price in the battles they had fought against us. The war, I realized, was going to go on long after I was gone; other Marines would come and fight, some would die. Some might even step on the brass I left behind, but for now, it was important to me to fight to keep as many Marines alive as long as possible.

The Vietnam War was a war of attrition, Dumont had once told us. Body counts were important, but not to the enemy. Their dead, lost in battle meant nothing to their government. Their government did not value life as we did. We may not have seen the bodies of the dead enemy soldiers whom we had killed in our two days of battles, but I knew they had lost a lot of men. Aggie alone, had done them great harm. The NVA had far too many soldiers they considered expendable and whom they were willing to sacrifice in the theatres of war.[183]

That night, as we settled in, I felt that the enemy would remain in the area. They weren't going away.

They would seek revenge, they always did, and tomorrow was as good a day as any. We didn't know where the wounded enemy soldiers had gone, who had been firing the AK-47s at us from our rear. Nor had we pursued them or searched the area where that other blood trail had led.

The special enemy work detail that had wondered into Aggie's gun no doubt had been sent there to gather supplies, probably the rice we had found, they then were to regroup with the unit we had now divided.

We hadn't pursued the large enemy force that had engaged us for most of the afternoon. The battle we had waged today, I felt, was not finished.

We were supposed to turn in Bro's gun as replacement for the new one issued. Instead, we stripped down the new gun, took what parts we could scavenge from it, including the cocking handle and locking pin, and Dumont turned in only the new gun's stripped-down frame and butt stock. Aggie and I tore apart Bro's gun, cleaned it, and did an extreme makeover on it. The gun was reconstructed with new parts, and we kept other parts as extras just in case. Bro's gun was ready for another day.[184]

Movement At Night
Finger Lake AT 867523
November 21, 1967, D+8, 0200 hours

In the early morning hours of the twenty-first of November, at approximately 0200 hours, the remnants of Second Platoon—twenty-six men including the CP group being led by Sgt. "Gus" Douglas Isleb—saddled up and got ready to move out.

As the platoon was ready to leave, Sgt. Gus asked Captain Baggette about meals, since they would be set in, hidden for most of the day and wouldn't be getting re-supplied. Baggette told them to grab a few cases of C-rats, they could figure out individual distribution once they set in, he wanted them out and set in long before daylight. The platoon grabbed the cases of food and moved out.

First Squad, with the gun team made up of Jones and Marty saddled up and went with them. When Second Platoon turned left at the entrance to Phu Long (1), where we had engaged the enemy the day before, First Squad was dropped off.

Second Platoon, meanwhile, was to circle in a clockwise direction following an old northbound cart trail for easy traveling and set up as a blocking force on the west side of Finger Lake near where the narrow finger-shaped lake bent to the left, about two klicks northwest of our location.

With enemy presence still expected to be in the area, First Squad with the gun team was set in to cover for the company when we would later cross over the long dike.

A couple of hours after Second Platoon moved out, India Company, reinforced with a Lima's platoon saddled up and we moved out.

First Platoon took point, and Lima's Platoon was bringing up the rear. We moved out along the same wide berm we had fought on the day before, while First Squad already set in across covered for us.

At the end of the trail where it met the tree line, First Platoon peeled off going left where we met up with our First Squad Marines. When Third Platoon in our trace reached where we turned, they turned right. Captain Baggette and his command group followed them as did the platoon from Lima Company that was now sandwiched in between him and our platoon. We were to set in for awhile and at daybreak when the company moved out, we were to bring up the rear.

The company at first light, with First Platoon bringing up the rear, was to move out and sweep north along the eastern edge of Finger Lake, circle around its tip and then head south toward Second Platoon which would be set up as a blocking force on the west side of the lake. The main enemy force, according to intelligence reports, was supposed to be located on the right side near the top of the lake. The company size movement sweeping north would force the enemy around the lake and into Second Platoon's blocking position.

We set up out in the open about ten yards from the tree line, using the grave mounts and the drop in elevation for cover. A small trail ran east and west along the edge of the tree line at the end of the wide berm. We settled down and in the process, lost contact with the Lima's platoon. They were supposed to set up to the right of the trail and stay in contact with us on the west side of the trail, but they had moved out too far to the right and now there was a wide gap between First Platoon and the rest of the company.

Lieutenant Wilson inquired over the radio about the gap that existed between our platoon and Lima's platoon, and the captain informed him to stay to the left of the berm. He was not going to move back to hook up with us. We were to stay where we were until daybreak. Then we would all move out.

We set in and went on 50 percent alert. Aggie and I were on the far left side at the western edge of our platoon's formation. Jones and Marty remained where they had set up earlier that night; they were to the east of us at the edge of the berm near where the enemy's blood trails had cut across the grave mounds the day before.

Come, Join My Parade
Finger Lake AT 867523
November 21, 1967, D+8, 0500 hours

When the darkest hour before daylight arrived, before it began to give way to the first rays of gray twilight, Lieutenant Wilson realized we were too far out in the open. We needed to move up and find cover in the tree line. Wilson stirred to pass the word for us to move forward when he saw movement to our right rear. Marty saw it at about the same time and jarred Jones awake and told him he had just seen a bush on top of the berm run past us.

Aggie, on watch to my left, had also seen the movement and he jarred me awake. I couldn't see anything and disbelieved him at first. Then a large bush ran hurriedly down the berm and turned right along the edge of the tree line. Shortly afterward, another smaller bush followed then another. I was trying to figure out what we were seeing. Then four, five, now six uniformed little soldiers very quietly moved rapidly along the top of the dike and this time, they turned to the left. They were now only about twenty feet in front of us.

The enemy soldiers had moved across the wide trail in a crouched position. They were silent and swift. As I tried to figure out if they were our people, ARVNs or what, Aggie whispered, "They're all the same size."

I pulled the gun in tight; the majority of them were gathered right in front of my gun's position.

With the platoon on line, we had them, and they wouldn't escape. Jackie Williams and Pridemore had seen them as well and were ready to open up. All we had to do was squeeze the trigger.

Wilson, was cautious, not fully knowing what we had, he radioed Baggette to reassure himself.

"One Actual to Six Actual, do you have people moving?" Wilson asked.

"That's a negative," Baggette replied. "No one from our units is moving."

Another squad of six to eight semi-camouflaged enemy soldiers ran across the dike and also turned left; they stopped along the tree line just a few feet in front of us. By now, we had counted over twenty-seven of them. They were gathered only ten to fifteen feet in front of us. If I opened up, it would be a major slaughter.

Convinced of what we had, Wilson radioed Baggette, again.

"We got enemy movement right in front of us." Wilson was ready to engage the enemy, but hesitated because he didn't know the enemy's strength or how many others were still behind us. Our platoon might be sandwiched in between a large enemy force. We were too much out in the open with very little cover. After the initial engagement, we could become trapped, with an enemy force, in front of us, to our right and behind us as well. Wilson asked Baggette what he wanted to do.

"Let them go," the captain said.

"We don't want to give away our positions and we'll get them later. We'll push them ahead of us into Second Platoon."

When what seemed like the last of the NVA soldiers had crossed over and with dawn fast approaching, Wilson passed the word for us to quickly move forward into the tree line. We were about to do that when a couple of NVA soldiers returned. The returning enemy soldiers were camouflaged as bushes.

They called out to the first group of soldiers that had turned and set in to our right, to cover for their comrades while their unit came across.

Then another small group of NVA soldiers crossed over from behind us and then two more small groups followed. The last two soldiers turned to the right at the end of the trail and a squad member from the group in the tree line called out to them and they turned back and joined him.

The other NVA soldiers that had turned right then got up and joined them. The group was now standing between one of our fire-teams to my right and my gun.

The last soldier had seen Jones lying on the ground next to Marty.

He called out to the other NVA soldiers and they stood fast in front of us, waiting for the group of Marines they mistook as their own soldiers to get up and join them.

In Vietnamese, he called out to Jones: "*Anh lai ây cüng! Anh lai ây cüng!*" (You come too! You come too!) He then motioned for Jones to join him. Then another NVA soldier from his left called out in Vietnamese and the last enemy soldier turned quickly rejoined the group, and they moved on.

We now had about forty to fifty NVA soldiers between us and Second Platoon.

Move Out Toward Finger Lake
Finger Lake AT 867523
November 21, 1967, D+8, 0640 hours

At first light, Captain Baggette passed the word for us to move toward Finger Lake. We were to move forward and then join him at the tip of the lake and together we would move out along the eastern side and in a long stretched out column, flushing enemy soldiers northward and then around the tip of the lake, toward Second Platoon.

We moved out, but soon got bogged down in heavy underbrush. We were supposed to be moving abreast of the company on their left side moving north together, flushing out the enemy toward the top. However, we were stuck in an area covered with thick jungle growth that required for us to move in a column. We had a fire-team walking our left flank, and it was hard to keep visual sight of them at the same time.

Once the company arrived at the tip of the lake, the Lima Company platoon swept through the company to take lead.

Before the rest of the company could move out and follow and before we could move to the right to catch up with them, the Lima Company Platoon surprised a team of NVA soldiers set in near a small shack. They killed three of the four VC, and captured a K-44 rifle.

Because of the thick vegetation we had to move left and ended up circling around the small tip at the bottom of Finger Lake. When we moved back in to try and connect with the rest of the company we found ourselves on the left side of the lake.

Lieutenant Wilson, informed Baggette that the lake was now to our right and if the Captain wanted us to come back around.

Baggette's group meanwhile began to take long distance sniper fire from huts near the village of Phu Binh (1). He was convinced now more then ever the majority of the enemy force was before them. He told Wilson to continue sweeping north on the west side of the lake and reinforce Second Platoon while he, Third Platoon, and the Lima Platoon would continue to move north on the east side of the lake.

The company traveling on the east side of the lake, had easy going and were moving north at a more rapid pace through open areas. There were scattered huts and clusters of trees, before them, but they had no thick jungle to have to contend with. Captain Baggette, reinforced with the Lima Company Platoon, were moving freely alongside the east side of the lake area where it was mostly open terrain, the company continued to take sniper fire and the sniper kept moving northeast, drawing India Company away from the lake.

At times, we had to move away from the lake because of the thick growth at the lakes edge or wait for our left flank fire-team to catch up, as they were encountering thicker barriers. During those times, it was unknown what was in front, behind, to the left, or to the right of us.

On our side, because of the thick, heavy jungle vines there were very few paths to follow. As we moved through the foliage, Wilson saw Private First Class Taylor moving slowly across a small clearing. Wilson, concerned of the whereabouts of the enemy we had seen earlier, said to him, "Taylor, you're going to have to move faster than that out here!"

"Yes, sir!" Taylor replied as the tall Marine picked up his pace and caught up with his squad.

Charles Taylor from Little Rock, Arkansas, was a healthy-looking Marine with long arms and a quiet disposition. His father, we had been told, was a lieutenant colonel in the air force and had given his son a chrome-plated .45 pistol to carry. Taylor like most others in the squads was carrying two bandoleers of M-16 magazines, three grenades, a hundred rounds of machine-gun ammo, his M-16, gas mask, two canteens of water, and his cartridge belt holding what-ever-else he could strap on it.[185]

His backpack was mostly empty of meals, except for perhaps a can of a meal he might have saved, we were suppose to be re-supplied before noon somewhere along our sweep, but now we were separated from the rest of the company. After two hours of struggling through the thick jungle, we made radio contact with Second Platoon and advised them we were close by.

Where's Charlie?
Operation Foster, Finger Lake AT 867522
November 21, 1967, D+8, 1000 hours

By late morning, we neared Second Platoon's location, on our side of the lake. They had walked most of the night carrying several cases of C-rats with them. The C-rats was enough food to last the platoon the whole day, as they would not be re-supplied and would be laying in wait for us to sweep the enemy toward them.

As they sat and waited, they were tired and hungry, but Sergeant Gus, realizing we were making our way toward them without meals would not allow his platoon to break open the cases of C-rats, until we joined them.

We made contact with Second Platoon and as is customary in military operations, the sweeping platoon moves through the blocking force, but before moving through, we picked up our meals and took the lead, arriving at the edge of a thick tree line.

Wilson, asked Sgt. Gus if they had seen or heard anything, no, nothing Gus answered. Then Wilson told him about the enemy force we had seen earlier and now we all wondered what had become of them.

What had happened to the large enemy force we had seen and was supposed to be in between us. Where had they disappeared to? I now wished more then ever, I had opened fire on them, but then again, they were well organized, silent and well disciplined. They had sent over a team to cover for them, until the majority of the unit crossed over, and staggering everyone, as they crossed. Still I could have shot 10-15 of them, right there and then, they were so close.

A few feet past the tree line was a thick strand of a camouflage barbed wire fence. The fence ran the length of the tree line from the edge of the lake where the fence was buried in the water running westward for about 300 meters. On the other side of the fence barrier were a number of well-beaten paths lining the borders of a series of rice paddy fields. A large hooch that was more of a house than a thatch-roofed hut stood isolated at the apex where the lake bent northwest. Between the fence and the house on the lake's west bank was a wide sandy beach. The beach area ended where the barbed-wire fence disappeared into the lake.

Keene, walking point, checked the wired fence; he was looking for a gate and possible booby traps. The fence seemed to have been originally built to keep water buffaloes from wandering off into the jungle; but the fence was overgrown with thick vegetation that was now holding back the jungle from the cleared rice patty fields on the other side. A bulging hedgerow, a variety of crawling vines and thick bushes covered the fence, and in its center were strands of concertina and rolled barbed wire.

There was no village nearby, so it was unusual to find such a large house sitting all by itself. For safety and security reasons, most peasants clustered together. The owner of this large house more than likely conducted most of his business by boat, probably by floating his trade down the lake toward the Song Thu Bon River as no roads ran near his home. Well-maintained rice paddy fields to the south side of the house ran west for about a mile until they connected to a distant network of tree lines that had scattered clearings in between. To the northwest of the hooch were a number of grave mounts followed by a thick jungle area that ran north along the west side of the lake all along its edge to its tip a good distance away.

About sixty feet from the edge of the lake, Keene found a small opening in the fence that was barely large enough for one man to pass through. The Vietnamese were small people, and the small path through the barbed wire ran in a zigzag pattern, first northeast and then in a northwest direction.

First Squad made their way through the fence one man at a time, and quickly set up on the other side to provide cover for the rest of us. Another squad followed.

Once on the other side, Second Squad turned right toward the lake and set up at the nearest dike to use it to cover while the rest the platoon followed.

As I went through the gate, that uneasy feeling of danger returned. I sensed that the enemy was watching us and that something was going to happen. The fence barrier was about ten feet wide. Once on the other side, I noticed, the fence had recently been reinforced with new strands of concertina wire. Things just didn't seem right; it was that human instinct or insight alarm within us—distinctively the human sense that we rarely pay attention to or understand—but I knew something was going to happen and it was going to happen soon. The dread of defenselessness drew to my side as I exited the fence and entered into another world.

The opening emptied into the middle of a rice paddy field. A wide dirt embankment large enough for a water buffalo to walk on ran along the length of the fence line. When you emerged, the only covering available was a rice paddy dike; the nearest one some twenty feet away. Another dike north of the opening was sixty feet away. Anyone running for cover once they came through the fence opening would be an open target for the enemy if they were in the tree line located northwest of the opening.

We arrived at the hooch without incident. Once all of First Platoon had passed through the fenced gate and entered the courtyard in the front of the house without incident, I felt relieved. Third Squad checked out and cleared the house before moving on and setting up along the tree line behind the house. First and Second Squad with the platoons' CP and our two gun teams stopped in front of the house in the open courtyard; it seemed to be the most secured spot.

The house appeared to be well kept but abandoned. Not a soul in sight. The ground surrounding the house was hard-pressed dirt, concrete solid, from having been walked on often. The hard ground had been swept clean and it curved around the house in a horseshoe pattern.

The front entrance to the house faced the lake with a large cleared courtyard that reached all the way to the edge of the lake. To the left of the house, as you faced the front, was a small garden enclosed by a Two inch thick bamboo fence The fence and garden separated the house from the rice paddy fields and the sandy beach, the fence placed there no doubt to keep the water buffaloes and small pigs away from the hooch and out of the garden.

Several five-by-ten-foot-wide round woven bamboo threshing-winnowing disks were leaning against a larger bamboo fence at the rear of the house. The backyard of the house was only about ten feet wide with the rear bamboo fence separating the house from two water-filled rice paddy fields behind that ended at the tree line and the thick jungle beyond. Scattered grave mounds dotted the landscape near the hut, others were further away near the tree line, some at the edge of a large rice paddy.

A tiny trench line ran all along the rear of the house, but the channel wasn't deep; it seemed to have been constructed more for rain runoff and to divert rice paddy water around the house than for protective cover. Most hooches throughout the area we had noticed were well fortified and honeycombed with dug out trenches or spider holes near by, but not this hooch. Still, I eyed the small channel as a good defensive fighting position if I needed it; after all, it was a bit deeper than the agricultural ditch I had buried myself in the day before.

The village huts further in the jungle area were widely scattered among tall skinny palm trees, heavy leaf laden trees with vines and tropical vegetation at ground level. The jungle ran along the edge of the lake for as far as one could see.

The tree line that abutted the rice paddy fields behind the house was about 300-feet wide. There was considerable heavy tropical foliage past the tree line. Wide leaf elephant plants and other thick and colorful plants surrounded other huts a short distance away that were located beyond the tree line deep in the jungle.

From the southwest corner the tree line ran west and began to widen until it was at least a quarter of a mile wide about a mile northwest of the house near where the lake turned once more north. A gradual rise in the terrain from there continued for about 500 meters to the northern tip of Finger Lake.

The area was beautiful and secluded, the home a simple wonderful place to live. We had entered into a peaceful environment that was very inviting, a haven of rest that seemed far away from the terrors of war.

Break For Lunch
Operation Foster, Finger Lake AT 867533
November 21, 1967, D+8, 1030 hours

We received word to break down for chow. I placed my gun down to the side of the front of the courtyard, near the edge of the fence close to the lake and dropped my flak jackets and gear there. Jones, Aggie and Marty did the same. A short time later, the Lima Company Platoon showed up across the lake from us. They set up at the north end of Phu Binh (1) with their backs to the lake as ours were. In this way, with the lake between us, we could defend each other's backs. Just northwest of Lima Company, the tropical forest ended abruptly. Beyond was a series of open rice paddies that stretched out for about 300 meters followed by the village of Quang Hue.

Northeast across the lake, the open fields were scattered with a number of small villages and open rice paddy fields until they reached the Song Vu Gia River two klicks away. The view from the front of the house was beautiful in any direction you looked.

The exterior walls of the hooch were stucco, partly built of cement, unlike the hooches in the surrounding villages which were made mostly out of wood straw and bamboo.

Jones, Aggie and I entered the house to examine it from the inside. The house was constructed of solid mortar, cement, dirt and straw. The interior walls were plastered with a smooth cement finish, and the dwelling was clean inside and out. When you entered the front door, there was a large living area with a family ancestral altar in the center of the room. A skinny bamboo bed, barely a foot off the ground was set alongside the back wall. Aggie laid down on it. The bed ended where his knees began.

"Man, that's not very comfortable to sleep in," he said. "Don't they put anything soft on the bamboo to sleep on," he asked, not really looking for an answer, as he bend over to look over the candles and incense sticks at the family altar. He picked up a clay jar, and Jones, told him, "You better put it back in just the same spot, facing the same way, because it represents the spirit of the dead, that are hungry." Aggie hurriedly put it back.

"There goes your beans and franks," Dumont added, as he walked through the door. "You'll never enjoy them the same from now on, some angry hungry ghost will lick each bean as soon as you open the can." Aggie, looked at Dumont, "Naw," he said, half believing him.

A separate cooking place was located in an adjacent smaller room to the left of the entrance. An open window in that room faced south toward the fence where Second Platoon was located. A doorway in that room opened to the rear of the house; from there, you could see the rice paddies, the graveyard, and tree line behind the hooch.

We went back through the living room, and to the right of the front entrance was a door that led to a small bedroom. The house was built at an angle set according to the bend in the lake. The bedroom's open window had a good-sized view of the bend in the lake, and if you looked out the window, you could see the corner of the tree line behind the house. From there we could see, Prescott, Pridemore, Welsh and a Marine from Third Squad standing, sitting, or walking in the area, near the tree line.

The lieutenant had placed a listening post a short ways into the jungle along our right flank next to the lake. Both positions were visible from inside the hooch's bedroom window. The platoon was spread out all over the area. Around the house, inside and out, at the banks of the lake, and out to the left along some grave mounds near a large flooded, reed-filled rice paddy field.

From the bedroom window, you could also look across the lake with a view of the deep-forested area where the platoon from Lima Company was located. A small trench line ran alongside the inside wall of the bedroom with what looked like a drainage hole on the north end.

Standing there, one could stand upright and look out the window at what would be the normal height of a Vietnamese man. I had to duck down to look out the window but not Jones. Because of his height, he was able to look out at a perfect level.

Whoever the owner was, it was evident he was one of the wealthier landowners in the area. From such people, the NVA extracted heavy taxes or they considered such landowners to be supportive of the South Vietnamese government and eliminated them. Where the owner of the house was, we didn't know; perhaps he had been evacuated like so many of the other homeowners in the Arizona Territory. Since the beginning of the operation, by now over seven thousand Vietnamese had been evacuated from the area; many others had come to us asking to be taken out of the area for fear of being killed by the NVA.

We hadn't bothered to set up the machine-guns at the tree line as we normally would have. For some reason, I really didn't want to be near the tree line. There was something there that troubled me and perhaps Jones as well as neither he nor Dumont pressed for the gun to be set up at the tree line, and that was unusual.

While I sensed some guilt for not setting up the gun as additional security, as if I was shunning my duty, I welcomed the break. We were, after all, going to move out right after chow. We had Second Platoon on our left (south) side and Lima northeast of us across the lake.

We sat down to eat under a small porch in the front of the house, thankful for the peaceful moment, why not take a full break.

It soon became one of those rare moments in life, a time for the building of friendships and for laughter, of sharing home life, dreams, and experiences. We sat and warmed up our meals, Aggie, Jones, Marty, Dumont, Rahm, Perry, Pridemore, Whiteside and myself. We were, just a group of Marines, whose friendship was forged by our time in life, by the clouds above, by the wind and our lives across the sea.

We spoke and listened to each other, shared thoughts about loved ones, places we've lived, cars and guitars, and of the good times we had shared together as a unit. We talked about how, in the past two days, we had lost eight good men and had gained three new ones, Marines whose names we still didn't know.

Sgt. C. J. Whiteside broke out his pipe and was jiving, joking, laughing.

We sat quietly eating our C-rats, enjoying the peace that surrounded us. Marty broke out the camera and took a picture of the hooch, the tropical jungle, and the lake. I was thinking to myself what a beautiful visual representation of the moment to capture on film. Marty sensed the same beauty as he turned toward us, and with a wide grin on his face, he raised his arms like a musical conductor. "Ain't this great? You can almost hear the symphony playing in the background," he said.

"I went to a symphony once," Aggie said, and we all turned to him in disbelief.

"Come on, Aggie," said Dumont. "You went to a concert, to hear a symphony?"

Yeah," Aggie answered with a hurt look on his face because we didn't believe him. "I went with my girlfriend and her mother in Los Angeles, but we left early," he added.

By now, we were all listening intensely; we knew that what was coming was going to be good.

"There was nothing but old people there," Aggie said. "And I told my girlfriend what the old people were doing, and she said they were old and couldn't help themselves so I went outside. Then we left." Aggie was holding our attention, and he thought we knew what he was talking about. In disbelief, he exclaimed, "They were all farting! How can you listen to music when old people sitting in front of you are farting? Seriously, come on!" By then, we were rolling on the ground with laughter.

During this time, members from Third Squad were going back and forth between the house and the tree line, relieving the men in the tree line stationed at the listening outposts so that they could take a break and eat. We ate, rested, and shared some quiet time together and some of us caught a moment's rest. Sergeant Stanford went and sat on the ground with his back up against the house, he took out a Stars and Stripes, newspaper to read.[186]

Saddle Up
Operation Foster; the Battle at Finger Lake AT 867533
November 21, 1967, D+8, 1130-1940 hours

The word was passed for us to saddle up. It was time to move out. Wilson received word from Captain Baggette that he wanted us to come around to their side of the lake and they would stand still and be our blocking force, so Lieutenant Wilson radioed Sergeant Gus, Second Platoon's leader, and suggested that First Platoon lead off and Gus's platoon bring up the rear. Gus agreed.

The air was humid, so I took off my utility jacket, wrapped it up and placed it inside my backpack, put on my flak jacket, with the knapsack and cartridge belt attached, threw on the extra belt of ammo across my chest, and waited to fall in line.

The plan was for us to travel north along the west side of the lake to the top where it ended then turn south getting on line and sweep toward Lima's Platoon and our company on the other side. Jones and Marty were to fall in at the tail end of First Squad, which would be leading the platoon, followed by the CP group. Aggie and I were going to fall in between Second and Third Squad.

By now, most of the platoon had saddled up and we were ready to move out when Chief found a toy rifle made out of wood inside the hooch by the bedroom. As the lieutenant examined it, Jones and Marty decided to search around in the kitchen area to see if they could find other items of interest when Marty felt something under his feet.

He removed a large double-sided mat and discovered a tunnel under it. Prescott who was a tunnel rat volunteered to go in. He preferred a K-bar in his hand instead of a 45, and quickly disappeared into the hole to check it out; when he called back to Marines inside the hooch, his voice response could be heard coming from the hole near the inside bedroom wall, where the vent was. It was a breathing hole. Wilson then called for us to stand down while the tunnel was checked further and cleared.

With the delayed wait, Jones was beginning to feel uneasy and said we needed to set up the gun near the tree line. Since I was carrying the gun that would be bringing up the rear, Marty, feeling a bit proud for having discovered the tunnel, volunteered to go and check out the area to see where he could set up Jones' gun.

Meanwhile, Jones set down his gun near the front of the hooch and Marty set down his M-16 next to it; he dropped his gear, flipped out his soft cover and walked satisfyingly down the dirt trail on the right side of the hooch, talking to Marines along the way that were saddled up and waiting to move out.

Aggie, assigned to be my A-gunner, turned to me and said, "I have to go." I looked at him, wondering where it was he had to go, when he added, "You know, to relieve myself."

"Thanks, Aggie, I needed to know that," I answered.

"Well, each time I eat C-rat frank and beans, they do that to me. Do you get that?" he asked. I didn't feel like standing all saddled up talking to Aggie about bowel movements.

"Just go, Aggie," I said to him, and he laid down his weapon and gear and walked off, rubbing his stomach and looking around for a place to go, finally deciding to go behind one of the small grave mounds between the rear of the house and the tree line.

Prescott came out a few minutes later and reported the tunnel was clear, small, but well constructed. The tunnel ran toward the lake where there was an opening into the water's edge. In between and near the corner of the house, the tunnel turned north toward the tree line and another link in the tunnel seemed to swing around the front of the house along the edge of the lake toward the fence where Second Platoon was located. Prescott didn't follow the tunnel that far, but he believed that there might be other entrances and a different network of tunnels somewhere along the edge of the lake.

Lieutenant Wilson decided to have the tunnel blown up and asked the engineer attached to us to blow it up once Second Platoon passed by and we have all cleared the area. Others headquarters support Marines with the CP group and the engineer dropped their gear and sat-down, on the small trail next to the hooch.

CHAPTER SIXTEEN

A Household Full Of Chaos
Operation Foster; the Battle at Finger Lake AT 867533
November 21, 1967, D+8, 1130-1940 hours

Most of the platoon had remained saddled up when Lieutenant Wilson called out to us to move out again. Aggie, having relieved himself was pulling up his trousers just as Marty was turning to make his way back from the tree line.

Prescott had just stepped down the embankment, when the word was passed for the platoon to move out. Prescott turned back around to get back up unto the trail to move out, when Pfc O'Neil stepped out in front of him.

O'Neil, in First Squad, started to move out on the trail leading toward the tree line and into the jungle. Prescott fell in behind him. Chief became irritated that O'Neil was at point leading the platoon.

"Hey, is Stringbeans, going to walk point?" he asked Izzie.

Izzie moved up to ask O'Neil what was going on, and O'Neil answered that Morales was now his squad leader and he was told to walk point. O'Neil turned and moved out.

As Marty stepped away from the tree line, he caught a glimpse of uniformed enemy soldiers as they stood up.

The NVA soldiers opened fire as they rushed forward assaulting toward the edge of the tree line, where Marines were standing.

Two of the bullets from the initial blast of the enemies' machine-gun tore into O'Neil's chest, and he went flying backwards.

Prescott only a foot or two away from him fell back as more bullets ripped through the air, and a team of NVA soldiers rushed past him.

Chief, who was stuffing the toy wooden rifle inside his shirt, dropped it, knelt on one knee, and opened fire with his M-14 at the rushing enemy.

As he got down, Izzie, standing behind him, fired off a round from his M-79 grenade launcher, into the group.

He immediately chambered another to fire as the grenade exploded behind the advancing enemy soldiers that were rushing toward them from the tree line.

The explosions caused the NVA soldiers to pause as grenade fragments struck them from behind, the explosion sending them flying to the ground.

As Chief fired the last of the twenty-round burst of fire from his M-14 at the advancing enemy, another blast of concentrated enemy bullets flew past him and Izzie.

An AK-47 bullet struck his left arm and he went down. Jackie Williams and Morales to their right had struck the ground and both were returning fire.

Izzie, already on the ground on one knee as the bullets flew by, was chambering yet another round into his grenade launcher.

He rapidly fired off five more rounds and raised his arm to fire another grenade further into the tree line when his arm got caught in a low-hanging branch.

He jerked to free it and as he did out of the corner of his eye he saw a skinny NVA sniper in a tree to his left about twenty yards away. The sniper with his eyes opened-wide was lining up his scope, sighting in on Izzie.

Izzie turned to move away, as the sniper fired off his first round.

The bullet tore off the branch that had caught Izzies arm. The second bullet tore through Izzie's body striking him at waist level going in one side and out the other. He immediately felt the pain.

Keene, having heard the word to move out, had just gotten up. Both he and Welsh had been sitting at the listening post near the lake.

Welsh had just slipped on his flak jacket and were reaching for his weapon when shots rang out from the enemies' automatic rifle fire.

Both Welsh and Keene, turning to see where the gunfire had come from, saw a team of enemy soldiers rushing toward the tree line, to their left.

As bullets flew by them, Keene flipped his M-14 off his shoulder, brought the weapon up, and took careful aim at the rushing attackers. Welsh by then had turned his M-16 switch to full automatic, and both Marines unleashed their first full magazines of automatic rifle fire at the assaulting NVA soldiers.

The bullets they fired tore through the jungle foliage, striking the lead group of soldiers rushing forward, about the same time Izzie's grenade exploded behind them.

As soon as both Marines emptied their weapons they changed magazines. A barrage of enemy incoming bullets struck the area all around them and both hit the deck at the same time. Having reloaded before they hit the ground, they shot back then sought better cover as they saw another wave of NVA soldiers rushing toward the Marine's positions located at the tree line.

Marty, weaponless was running full speed toward the safety of the hooch. Pridemore, who had been standing out in the open was also running full speed a few steps ahead of him, toward the hooch.

Marines at the tree line dropped to one knee and returned fire, striking several enemy soldiers as they tried to run through their positions.

Other Marines standing in the column that had been saddled up and were ready to move out hit the ground where they were and returned fire or scrambled for cover.

Jones, who had been standing in front of the hooch when the shooting started, picked up his gun and ran toward the entrance of the cemented house.

The peaceful scene where we had enjoyed our lunch was now covered with clamor and war, blood, death, and destruction; and the platoon was desperately fighting to stay alive.

Pridemore was heading to the side of the hooch, when he saw Marines scrambling away from there. He saw that the rear door was closer, and he rushed through right in front of Aggie that was running toward the hooch while trying to hold up his trousers.

Aggie arrived at the hooch's rear doorway at the same time Doc Marren did. Marty, who was also running for the same doorway at the same time, struck them both at the door's small entrance, and all three of them went through the doorway striking the floor inside the hooch as a barrage of bullets struck the sides and top of the doorway only inches above all of them.

Doc Marren and Marty crawled into the inner safety of the hooch as bullets coming through the doorway struck the wall inside the kitchen.

Aggie, knocked down found that he was laying on the ground at the doorway, he could see both Marty and Doc Marren crunched in a ball in the middle of the kitchen while bullets ripped through the air and struck the hooch's walls outside and inside the hooch. He decided that instead of joining them in the kitchen of the hooch, he would crawl along the outside wall along the small ditch to get to the front where our gun and his weapon were located.

A Devastating Blow to First Platoon
Operation Foster; the Battle at Finger Lake AT 867533
November 21, 1967, D+8, 1130-1940 hours

I had just shouldered the gun and was waiting for Aggie to return when the enemy opened fire.

In front of me were Toy (the platoon's radioman), Lieutenant Wilson, and Doc Mac. The Corpsman and other Marines were standing out in the open courtyard pulling on their packs and adjusting their straps when the initial burst of gunfire tore though the air.

Within seconds, the roar of fierce and destructive incoming bullets was tearing through the air. Concentrated mortars, RPG rocket rounds, grenades, small arms and automatic rifle fire were all being unleashed at us all at once.

Bullets, mortars and exploding grenades were all delivering a very devastating blow to First Platoon Marines.

Caught out in the open, Marines were being struck with small arms, shrapnel, and machine-gun fire. Everything was perfectly timed. Bullets tore through the loose straw at the top of the house and struck the walls and roof as well as along the bamboo fence in back of the hooch where Marines were standing.

Out in the open fields, bullets were being walked systematically toward Marines running for cover. You could see the bullets striking the ground behind Marines as they ran seeking protective cover.

Everything was happening at a very rapid pace, yet to me, it seemed as if I was seeing everything in slow motion. The sounds followed long after the action had occurred.

To the south of the hooch, toward the barbed wire fence, bullets were striking the ground where Marines were laid out in the open rice paddy fields.

To my right on the north side of the hooch just past the bend in the lake, a fierce barrage of bullets were ripping apart the foliage and the dense cluster of shrubs that ran along the trail near the water's edge. Marines were scrambling to find cover and concealment wherever they could. Some had made it to the safety of the front of the hooch. Two sides of the hooch, were receiving severe incoming gunfire.

The bullets were striking small trees and bamboo poles as well as the hard, dry ground and garden plants. Splintered pieces of the roof, plaster, and shrapnel were flying off over our heads as mortars struck the hooch and the ground all around us.

I saw a Marine from one of the supporting units struck by a bullet in the leg, and by the time his body hit the ground, it seemed as if two or three other rounds had torn into his side and back. He lay there twisting, torn, and bleeding on top of the rice paddy dike. Another Marine who had already found cover behind a dike reached out and exposed his upper torso to the onslaught of bullets tearing up the dirt mount directly in front of him. He recoiled from dust and dirt being kicked in his face, and leaping forward while under intense enemy fire, he pulled the wounded Marine out of harm's way. The wounded Marine's head, arms, and legs were limp and lifeless as he was dragged out of the kill zone.

A Marine in Second Squad, about twelve feet in front of me on the south side of the hut, was struck in the shoulder and he went down.

Toy, was standing in front and to the left of me. He had just put on his backpack and was adjusting his radio pack when the enemy opened fire.

He turned and ran as fast as his little legs could carry him toward the safety of the hooch's front wall. I swear his feet were kicking up dust as the bullets were ripping the ground where he had been standing only seconds before.

I struck the ground so hard it knocked the air out of my lungs, and I gasped for air while crawling to get away from the area being impacted by the enemy's bullets.

A couple of Marines in the front of the hooch were looking up, trying to see if the dry bamboo stalks that covered the house's roof were strong enough to support them. They wanted to climb up on the roof where they would be able to shoot down at the enemy from that advantageous position.

Those who had made it to the inside of the house were already appreciating the strength of the hooch's plastered walls. While bullets rained all around, the foot-thick walls were taking the full impact of automatic and machine-gun fire being fired at us.

On the other side of the lake, I could hear Marines from Lima Company crying out, "I'm hit, I'm hit!" and others were calling for their Corpsman.

Lima Marines were yelling out to other Marines who were trying to figure out what was going on, that it's India Company across the lake that was taking fire. However, they were also impacted by the bullets that bypassed us. It wasn't long before they too were targeted with RPG and mortar rounds as well as automatic rifle fire coming from their northwest.

RPG and mortars were exploding at the water's edge as well as landing in the center of the Marines from Lima and their platoon's CP. They scrambled, looking for cover and an advantageous position so that they could return fire. A seasoned Marine ran south then north along the edge of the lake trying to figure out a way he could return fire without hitting us. With our platoon in front of their line of fire, Lima Company Marines weren't able to open fire upon the enemy from where they were.

Several First Platoon Marines had been instantly hit in the initial barrage. Three of them were not seriously wounded and were lying with their backs up against rice paddy dikes, bleeding, while other Marines were trying to bandage their wounds. Others were laying facedown out in the open. Some weren't moving.

O'Neal, Izzie, Parisi, Ezell, Howard, and Sergeant Whiteside had all been hit in the initial outburst of incoming rounds. Incredibly, we could hear the cries for the Corpsman from wounded Marines above the turmoil of the battle.

The roof of the porch attached to the front of the hooch was being ripped apart as 81-mortar rounds began to strike it. The dry splintered bamboo sticks were being ripped apart from the crossbars and became sharp flying needle shaped pieces of wood that sailed through the air and embedded themselves into the hard-pressed ground.

The incoming fire grew in intensity as did the number of mortars and M-79 grenades striking the area all around us.

On my belly, I tried to appraise the whole situation before me, to try to determine where I could best set up the gun and return fire.

The only safe area to return fire that I knew of was from inside the house from the window in the bedroom.

Marines that had found cover at the northern edge of the hooch weren't able to open up because other Marines were still out by the tree line or were lying out in the open rice paddy field or by the grave mounts along their line of fire.

Some Marines out in the open were pinned down and unable to move or return fire. Those at the base of the tree line had no choice, but to stay there and they were fighting for their lives at almost point-blank distance against a large force of NVA soldiers that kept getting up trying to assault their positions.

Unable to return fire, Marines that had secured cover turned to try to move the wounded to cover as well. Some Marines in the open could have easily left their position and made a run for the safety of the hooch, but wounded Marines would have been left behind. Instead, they moved over to be closer to where the wounded Marines were and without exposing themselves to direct enemy gunfire, tried to provide cover for them. Staying close by the wounded Marines and returning fire as best as they could.

This was notable all around our perimeter: Marines covering for Marines, staying by the wounded and assuring the wounded Marines to hang on, telling them that they were not going to leave their sides.

The Battle For Survival
Operation Foster; the Battle at Finger Lake AT 867533
November 21, 1967, D+8, 1130-1940 hours

The continued intensity of the incoming rounds striking all around us was overwhelming. The NVA were trained to ambush a squad-size patrol by using a platoon-size ambush or higher. For a platoon, they used a company-size ambush and for a company, they would use a reinforced battalion. Since they had attacked two Marine platoons, the size of the enemy would be at least company size, or reinforced company size. When they attacked, especially at night, they came in waves. When they struck at daylight, the practice was to get in as close as possible to the Marines to prevent us from raining in mortar, heavy artillery, or calling in jet strikes on them.

Unknown to us grunts, intelligence before the operation had estimated eight hundred to one thousand NVAs in the area, not counting a newly arrived battalion size force and local VC.[187]

Within minutes of the initial burst, a third of First Platoon had been shot and wounded. Marines were bleeding, limping, and seeking medical attention; the wounded Marines unable to return fire were being assembled in the courtyard in front of the hooch. Others were returning fire while desperately trying to get help from other Marines to get the wounded near them to safety. Some wounded Marines were disregarding their own wounds and were assisting others or they kept firing, ignoring their own medical needs. Every Marine was trying to survive, and we were fighting for our lives and for the lives of those around us.

Second Platoon's Response
Operation Foster; the Battle at Finger Lake AT 867533
November 21, 1967, D+8, 1130-1940 hours

As First Platoon fought off the NVA assaults, Second Platoon was scrambling for cover on the other side of the barbed wire fence.

Dennis Imperial, Second Squad's point man in Second Platoon, had just stepped out of the zigzagged wired gate to follow in trace of First Platoon as we moved out, when all hell broke loose. A mortar round exploded close by and shrapnel struck him in the head, knocking him down.

Marines never leave their wounded behind. We knew this, and the NVA knew this. As Marines from Second Platoon tried to reach him, they came under intense automatic rifle fire, from the tree line, across the open rice paddy fields. While First Platoon Marines responded, it was not enough fire-power to keep the enemy's fire suppressed. Two Marines from Second Platoon disregarded the danger and rushed through the gate and took up defensive firing positions out in the open on top of the broad dike. When they opened fire, bullets fired at them, tore the area up all around them, but they kept firing.

As they returned fire, two other Marines along with Doc Keller rushed out of the gate, grabbed Imperial, and pulled him back through. Bullets zipped overhead and ripped through the overhanging vines as they dragged him back into the safety of the tree line behind the barbed wire fence. The two other Marines broke contact and slipped back through the wire as well, as M-79 grenades and automatic rifle fire followed them into the fence line.

From the other side of the barbed wire fence, Marines from Second Platoon were desperately trying to return fire across the open rice paddy fields. They were shooting in a northwest direction toward the tree line where the NVA were shooting at them from, not knowing our Marines were at that same tree line firing back at the enemy, and Second Platoon bullets were coming dangerously close to where First Platoon's Third Squad was fighting off the NVA assaults near the southwest tip of the tree line.

To the south of where I was, on the left side of the house near a small grave mound, a Marine fire-team was bunched up trying to put out what firepower they could. One Marine was visibly shaking as he was frantically trying to repair his jammed M-16.

The Marines had already moved back from where they were originally when we got hit but now had limited use of the corner of the grave mound; they were returning fire as best they could while still staying under what protective cover they could. Because of the limited avenue of space from where they could return fire, they were taking turns returning fire one man at a time. One Marine would shoot from the corner and empty his M-16 then another would take up his place and the process would be repeated. Each time they did this, the Marine returning fire was taking great risk as the enemy kept zeroing in on their position.

The Battle Scene From the Ground
Operation Foster; the Battle at Finger Lake AT 867533
November 21, 1967, D+8, 1130-1940 hours

To my right, on the north side of the hooch, Marines were firing as carefully as possible over the heads of Marines who were lying on the ground near the small trail that ran alongside the north side of the hooch. As they returned fire, they exposed themselves to enemy fire.

Ezell, already wounded, stood on one knee to provide cover for Chief who was dragging Izzie to the safety of the corner of the hooch.

Once Chief got Izzie to the front of the hooch where Doc Mac was caring for other wounded Marines, he returned to help other Marines get out of their kill zones and then returned and picked up Izzie's M-79 launcher, where Izzie had dropped it. Chief took the weapon's safety off and fired the grenade still inside the launcher into the tree line where the concentrated enemy fire was coming from. The round flew by only a few feet above where Marines were laid out prone while they were returning fire at entrenched NVA soldiers that had moved into spider holes. From there the enemy soldiers were now taking turns popping up and shooting at Marines.

The lieutenant and his radioman were huddled up against the front of the house near the door. Wilson was on the radio trying desperately to convince Captain Baggette that we had made contact with a superior enemy force and we needed help.

"We're under heavy enemy attack, we are taking casualties, and we need assistance!" he screamed into the mike, trying to raise his voice above the sounds of the battle zone. He told Baggette that because of our location, we could put out very little gunfire and Second Platoon was in no position to come to our rescue. We needed the help of the rest of the company and we needed it right away.

Wilson had already heard Second Platoon had taken casualties and were calling for a medevac on the other side of the barbed wire fence. If Second Platoon tried to make it through the zigzagging gate, they would suffer heavy casualties.

If they took the long way around along the fence line, they would have to travel straight north along the edge of the tree line for about 300 meters and then they would be exposed to the same hostile firepower we were receiving if they tried to cross over open terrain across three long rice paddy fields.

But, if they decided to do that, then our south side would be unprotected, and we still didn't know where the group of NVA soldiers we had seen earlier had gone or if the enemy we were engaged with was that same group.

Had the enemy planned to get both First and Second Platoon in the kill zone we were now in?

Sergeant Gus, on the other side of the fence, was directing his platoon to withhold their firepower from where they were on the other side of the fence as it was ineffective. Meanwhile some of his men were sent out to search for a better position from where they could provide better cover for us, while at the same time, he set up others to protect their backs.

Shortly after we recovered from the first volley of fire, both Jones and I headed toward the front door of the house at the same time. We both were headed for the side bedroom window that had an advantageous firing position.

From there, we felt we could return fire with the machine-gun. Jones was a step ahead of me, and reached the front door first. Once inside the hooch, I saw Doc Marren and Marty on the floor to our left in the kitchen.

Marty was rolled up in a ball near the hooch's south wall as bullets entering through the open rear door struck the side of the wall nearby. Other Marines were moving through the hooch, seeking areas from where they could return fire. The open doorway was an easy target and the enemy bullets were flying into the hooch through it. The bullets were striking the wall inside the hooch and raining dust and debris off the plaster onto Marty and the Corpsman that was hunched over on the floor next to him.

Other Marines were crawling on the ground coming in from the back of the hooch moving through the open kitchen doorway toward the front yard.

Jones and I turned right toward the side bedroom window. When we got there, Jones placed his back up against the wall near the window and took a quick peek out.

The open window on the north of the bedroom offered an excellent and advantageous firing position for the gun. He popped his gun with a 200-round belt already linked together on the window's edge.

The window and the gun's firing position were perfect for his height, and he was well protected there. The window was a practical place to put the gun and fire back at the enemy, but it was not large enough for both guns to fire back.

Jones pulled the trigger, shot off about a twenty-round burst, and immediately had a misfire. His gun jammed, and as he pulled the gun back to un-jam it, a grenade exploded on the outside of the hooch directly below the window; the explosion did not faze Jones who quickly got his gun back up, sighted in, and opened fire again. The initial burst of machine-gun fire was enough for the NVA that were advancing to withdraw.

As soon as Jones opened fire again, he was met with intense incoming gunfire, and the window's ledge was peppered with the enemy's automatic and machine-gun fire. The crisscrossing bullets were beginning to ricochet inside the house as well. Evidently, the NVA knew that position well and had set up a machine-gun to open fire on that window if we used it. They had clearly prepared for us to return fire from there as evidenced by the intensity of their firepower. I realized that the window location and the open door in the back of the house were not safe positions to return fire from. Still, Jones held back the trigger and unloaded a wall of lead at the enemy's positions.

I needed to put out some firepower of my own, and it needed to be done right away. I ran back outside and moved toward the lake. Perhaps from there, I might be able to return fire.

Here, Listen To This!
Operation Foster; the Battle at Finger Lake AT 867533
November 21, 1967, D+8, 1130-1940 hours

As I went out the door, I could hear Lieutenant Wilson, with alarm in his voice, shouting into the handset, calling for the company commander to come to our assistance. It appeared that he was not getting the response he wanted and was raising his voice as he screamed into the mike. Finally, he keyed the PRC-25 handset and cried out, "Here, listen to this!"

Explosions and ricocheting bullets and the clamor of war was growing in intensity all around us. Marines could be heard crying out for the Corpsmen as bullets flying every which way could be heard cracking the air overhead and impacting their hot lead into the hooch's plaster-covered walls. The sound of the NVAs incoming firepower was loud and destructive. Whoever was on the other end of the radio the lieutenant was talking to could certainly hear the sounds and the chaos of war as well as the fighting going on all around us. They could hear the incoming as well as the Marine counter-engagement we were involved in.

Wilson brought the handset back to his mouth, shouting, "Now, do you believe me?" Frustration overshadowed his face as well as disbelief as he received a response he didn't want to hear: "Calm down, Larry, calm down, we're getting some incoming too!"

To the left (west) of us, the dense foliage and thick vines interwoven throughout the heavy strands of the barbed wire fence kept Second Platoon on the other side of the fence. They continued to have a difficult time trying to find a clear spot to return fire while keeping out of harm's way. They soon realized they could not return fire through the wired fence as the raised berm on our side was higher, and this prevented them from firing in the prone position from the tree line behind the fence. The only other option they had was to go ahead and follow the tree line out to where it ended then sweep out across and assault the tree line, but such an assault would be costly to a platoon already heavily undermanned. The area between them and where the tree line ended could possibly also be heavily booby-trapped, and it remained unknown how many of the enemy may be in that jungle area and may have set up to ambush them if they tried that.

The NVA knew that Marines were trained to attack rather than take a defensive fighting position. Marines were an offensive fighting force, and the NVA always set up several other defensive positions if we attacked their primary positions. The second entrenched position was usually a more heavily defended position, and it was always within close proximity of the first. They did not like giving up ground; if we attacked, the first line of defense may get up and retreat, but we would soon find ourselves encountering another more heavily defensive enemy position, sometimes only a few feet away and in well-hidden positions.

The enemy that had attacked us had moved into their first well-fortified positions, and they were deeply entrenched. They were prepared to engage us at the tree line or if we assaulted their positions from a secondary position. The NVA/VC always planned, planned, and planned. They practiced their assaults and being assaulted by Marines. They tried to figure out how we would fight and how we would engage them in battle. They had a well laid-out plan, and we had fallen into it.

Our only hope now was to push them back so that we would be able to call in artillery or air support. This was why they had moved in to be as close as possible to us. They had already scored a major victory. Marine bodies were laid out in the open, not moving. They had pulled off a very successful ambush. Often the enemy would hit us and then retreat. This time, it looked like they were staying. They had a platoon of Marines in their hands, and they were not about to let us go. I wanted to do something, to respond, to hurt them for the pain they had caused, for O'Neil, for Chief, for others I had seen bleeding with deep and fearful pain in their eyes.

With the increased contact we were encountering, from his operation headquarters, Colonel Barnard decided to commit Lima Company to swing around the lake and come to our rescue.[188] However, Lima Company, was finding it difficult in maneuvering to try and get over to help us. They had hoped to swing around the top of the lake and then south to our location. However, when some of their Marines reached the edge of the tree line on the other side of the lake, open rice paddy fields and heavy incoming fire from across the open paddies with little covering kept them from advancing. They were also receiving incoming fire from the northwest corner of the tree line across the lake near where Keene's and Welsh's listening post had been.

We would not be receiving help anytime soon from Lima or the rest of our company. The enemy had chosen their ambush site well.

CHAPTER SEVENTEEN

NVA Enemy Soldiers Running Among Us
Operation Foster; the Battle at Finger Lake AT 867533
November 21, 1967, D+8, 1130-0940 hours

On the other side of the barbed wired fence, Sgt. Gus had requested a medevac for his wounded men. It seemed that area was some what secure enough to bring in a chopper.

No sooner had the medevac chopper appeared overhead it began to take on incoming fire, from our side, from the enemy force we were engaged with.

An escorting armed UH-1E helicopter, under the command of Captain John Nelson Shinnick, could see where the incoming fire was coming from, but was unable to make contact with Lieutenant Wilson. None the less Shinnick and his crew took the enemy under fire with a series of rocket and strafing runs. While the medevac extraction was successful, the aircraft had sustained battle damage and Shinnick escorted the battle damaged medevac chopper to An Hoa.[189]

A bird-dog plane flying overhead and Second Platoon Marines on the other side of the fence were seeing NVA soldiers running among us in between Marines that were lying out in the open and those hidden behind clusters of weeds and the grave mounds. Other enemy soldiers were gathering at the tree line, getting ready to assault. I could see some of them moving in, slipping into the hidden trenches at the base of the tree line.

A group of Marines were bunched up at the southwest corner of the house. They had their weapons at chest level. They were standing upright, as the enemies bullets struck the house wall on the other side of them. I could tell they were waiting for an opportunity to return fire, but the incoming fire had grown so fierce they couldn't even sneak a look around the corner without getting hit. Meanwhile, the running enemy soldiers were moving in to their left to outflank them, to get them in a crossfire.

There's a Place in the Sun!
Operation Foster; the Battle at Finger Lake AT 867533
November 21, 1967, D+8, 1130-1940 hours

I moved toward the lakeside of the house, looking for an advantageous position to open up, but there was no room. Marines who had very little cover occupied the narrow passage and small trail from that side of the house that led north to the tree line. Some were desperately trying to return fire over the heads of other Marines that lay prone out in front of them.

Cpl. Evaristo Morales, First Squad's leader, was standing with his back up against the corner of the house. He stole a quick glance from the corner, saw where the enemy's incoming fire was coming from, popped his head back around the corner of the hooch and opened fire at that target.

He quickly moved back as a barrage of bullets struck the side of the wall from where he had fire from.

He shouted orders for one of his men, laid out along the trail to get down.

I came up to him and asked if he knew where I could put the gun. He looked scared, looked over the area and shook his head no.

There was no advantageous position from there where I could open fire. I went back to the lieutenant who was still busy on the radio.

"Where do you want the gun?" I asked him, not bothering to say "sir." This was the first time I had ever spolen to the lieutenant. The first time I had asked an officer for directions.

He was too busy talking over the radio net to answer me.

I went over to the left side of the house where I had seen huddled Marines taking turns returning fire at the enemy from that corner of the house.

The only good position I could see from where I would be able to return effective machine-gun fire seemed to be out in an exposed position in the open about eighty feet to the left of the house.

The position would be in the center of the kill zone between the fire-team that was out in the open behind a small embankment and the bunchedup Marines huddled at the corner of the house. It would be an excellent, but a very dangerous, position for the gun.

What I needed to do was to put out a lot of lead, and that location would give me the opportunity to do so.

Aggie by now was at my side; he had been there all along as I ran back and forth seeking a place from which to fire the gun. I had only sensed his presence before, but now I acknowledged him. He gave me that "you're not really going to go out there, are you" look.

When the fire-team that was out in the open behind the dirt embankment looked my way, I held the gun up high for them to see it over the bamboo fence and pointed to indicate that we were going to move the gun to their right front.

They nodded acknowledgment. There was a slight rise on the ground where I wanted to set up the gun. A lone Marine rifleman lay out in the prone position there, his head buried in the ground as bullets struck the ground nearby. I could see that the rise in the ground there was providing him some protection.

Perkins's fire-team, were the bunched-up Marines at the corner of the house, and it was his man that was lying out where I wanted to place the gun.

When that lone Marine looked up, Perkins motioned for him to come in. Perkins opened fire, covering for him. The Marine rolled to his right, unleashed a burst of automatic rifle fire, and ran for cover joining his squad behind the hooch.

As he ran, two men from the fire-team that were out behind the small dirt embankment also opened fire. Another Marine behind them got up on one knee, lifted his M-79's barrel and fired a grenade over their heads at enemy soldiers who had advanced forward and were moving out of the northwest corner of the tree line using some of the grave mounds for cover. It looked like the enemy was positioning themselves to assault our positions. They were setting up to outflank the Marines firing at them from the tree line.

When Perkins's men opened up, it was my chance to go. I grabbed the machine-gun by its carrying handle and ran forward in a hunched-down position. I was hoping the enemy wouldn't be able to see that it was a machine-gun I was carrying. The covering fire for us was very effective.

As Aggie and I ran out into the open, we were shot at. Seconds later, the incoming fire grew fierce, and we both dropped and hugged the ground.

Aggie, running behind me, ended up on my right side. It was the wrong side for an A-gunner to be on. The incoming rounds were intense, steady, and well concentrated, making it impossible for him to move from where he was without getting hit.

He crawled in closer and in the midst of bullets striking the ground all around us, managed to hook up a 200-round belt of ammo to the belt already hanging from the gun. I hadn't realized until then that another Marine was lying prone just a few feet to my left. He was laid up against a small broken down bamboo fence. He wasn't firing, he wasn't moving. He was lying on his left side, wide-eyed and breathing hard.

Wilson Takes Forward Command
Operation Foster; the Battle at Finger Lake AT 867533
November 21, 1967, D+8, 1130-1940 hours

With the enemy running among our fighting positions, Wilson was more deeply troubled about what was happening to his platoon. As his men fought back, fighting to stay alive, he knew he had to do something.

Recognizing that there would be no immediate assistance coming from our company commander, Wilson decided the best help he was going to get was going to come from his own ability to control the battle scene; he needed to get an overall view of the battle zone. With his radioman Toy at his side, Wilson ran from the safety of the hooch southeast toward a large grave mound out in the open; as he ran across the open field, bullets followed him and his radioman. Exposed to enemy fire when they hit the ground, Wilson got up again and ran toward the safety of an open crater and a more secured spot. They were now in between the hooch on his right and the fence barrier on his left where Second Platoon was.

It was a small crater, barely large enough for him and his radioman, but it offered good cover and it was a great spot from where he could observe where the majority of the enemy's firepower was coming from. No sooner had they relaxed to catch their breath, the enemy identified his new leadership position by Toy's radio backpack.

Unlike other platoon leaders, Wilson carried an M-16 in addition to his .45 pistol to make himself look more like a trooper than an officer. Art Toy his radioman had often disguised his radio when out on patrol by bending the radio's antenna down, but now the antenna was up to be able to broadcast and receive distant communications and the lieutenant was busy using the radio trying to contact Second Platoon.

As the enemy continued to zero in on their position, it allowed Wilson to better pinpoint some of the enemies' positions. As Wilson looked over the battle scene a bullet struck the dirt embankment in between him and Toy. Both looked at each other laughed and got down.

I hadn't noticed until then, but there were other Marines to my right laid out in the prone position sandwiched in between the rear of the house and another small bamboo fence. Chief, with a white bandage on his arm, and another Marine were prone out on the ground. The only cover they had was the slightly elevated threshing floor in the backyard of the hooch and a small lattice bamboo fence that was being peppered with bullets. Chief and the Marine next to him opened fire at the advancing enemy soldiers that were trying to break through by way of circling around the grave mounds.

I crawled up to be on line with that bamboo fence so that I could get a clearer field of fire and so that Chief was to my right and not ahead of me. I was looking for other Marines to make sure they were not going to be in my line of fire.

The dirt was soft there, too soft, so I backed off a little and lost what little cover I would have had from a grave mound on my right; but my new position gave me a wider field of fire.

To my right side toward the lake, I could see Marines in the open field with their heads down as green tracers flew wildly over their heads. A Marine had his back hard pressed against a rice paddy dike; he was alive but barely moving. Marines a little to my left in front of the gun were looking in my direction, and they realized I was about to open fire over their heads, at the grave mounts to their left. I could see they were scared, but I could tell that they wanted me to open up so that they would be able to crawl out of the kill zone they were in. Jerry Souble and Ira Hullihen were among those Marines.

To my immediate right, a dozen or so circular bamboo disks of various sizes used to sift rice were lying on the ground. Some of them had already been torn apart by the exploding mortars, bullets, and grenades. A smaller disk that had been hanging on the lattice bamboo fence was jerked out of its position when an enemy's bullet struck it.

Just before the round disk struck the ground, another bullet's impact sent it violently spinning clockwise toward the house. The disk bounced off the solid wall at the rear of the house, sailing silently out into the flooded rice paddy. The incoming bullets were coming from an enemy's machine-gun's position, to my left.

Prescott who had been laying out along the trail next to the house had made his way back to where Morales was. He could see the fierce incoming fire striking the window where Jones was firing from. All of a sudden an RPG Rocket struck just below the window and the explosion rained shrapnel all over the trail he had been on.

He jumped across the trail and ran into the hooch. Jones was sitting on floor dazed but ok. He was grinning.

"You OK?" Prescott asked. "Yeah!" Jones answered, clearing his head. Prescott had earlier tried to get Jones to open fire over their heads, while he and James Keenan were laid out in the open, it was from where the RPG rocket had come from, but Jones wouldn't, fearing they were too close, and he might hit them.

He told Jones there was an advantageous firing position for him and the gun if Jones would follow him through the tunnel. Jones did, and emerging at an opening at the corner of the hooch. It was a perfect place for the gun. He could fire low, and he had plenty of cover

Across the field, the enemy, shooting in a southeast direction, was able to keep Second Platoon from coming to our rescue. Green tracers were being fired at them from farther up the tree line, far to my left. It seemed like the enemy was entrenched in an inverted L shape with the long stem of the L along the tree line in front of us where Marines had been before the firefight started.

From my location, I could see where the enemy was and from where they were firing. I could also see them moving back and forth five to ten feet behind the tree line.

Keene and Welsh had moved up on the right side of the house near the trail, and I could see them firing at the enemy at an angle. Keene looked my way and realized that I was getting ready to open up; he reached up and snapped off the twenty-round magazine he carried upside down on his helmet. The heavy-duty inch-wide rubber band that held it tight against his helmet snapped back in place. Keene fired off a few more rounds, emptying his magazine, then quickly released, and changed the magazine in his M-14.

I pulled the gun in tight and took off its safety. The gun's bipods were buried in the soft dirt at just the right height. I could see new enemy movement in the tree line. The enemy was moving in closer, shifting positions, getting ready to assault.

Vengeance is Mine, Saith the Gun
Operation Foster; the Battle at Finger Lake AT 867533
November 21, 1967, D+8, 1130-1940 hours

I raised my left elbow so that the belt of machine-gun ammo would slide easily over my raised upper arm, then pulled the gun in tight up against my cheek, I held down the gun's frame with my left hand, and pulled the trigger.

The first rounds sailed straight and struck just above the base of the tree line—leaves, branches, and splinters from thick trees being struck by my bullets flew every which way, and I held her tighter and pulled back harder on the trigger, sweeping the length of the tree line where the enemy was entrenched. Left to right, then right to left.

My machine-gun's explosive entrance into the campaign roared across the landscape and added a thundering sound to the chaos of war.

The sound vibrated across open rice paddy fields and the new song she was singing before her audience sent waves of fear and guilt across the land all the way to the foothills of the An Hoa mountain range and across the river to base of Charlie Ridge. Its echoing sound bounced back loud, announcing boldly to the enemy the gun had entered the battlefield.

I held the trigger down, spraying the area with a steady flow of controlled automatic machine-gun fire at ground level where the main enemy force remained entrenched, where their heads were.

It was what the gun wanted, what we had been longing for—to unleash its blazing firepower so we could mingle new blood from the enemy with other lost souls who were foolhardily rushing to knock at hell's back door.

I was angry, determined, and spiteful. The gun had recovered from her wounds from the sniper's bullet the day before and now the sword was drawn and she sought vengeance.

It all felt so natural, so right, as if God was walking in our midst as if He was the one holding my hand while a steady flow of bullets shot out and called out for the death angel to follow them across contested terrain.

The machine-gun was doing what she did best. I held her pressed hard against my cheek, and I had full control of her vindictive firepower.

Red-hot tracers were being spat out her mouth with an intense hatred that only those who have fought in war seeking retribution can understand. I wanted, needed, desired to wreak havoc and destruction upon the enemy.

To kill and take men's last breaths and if possible, to strike at the same wound twice and to steal from the enemies' minds those last thoughts of life, of friends, families, and foes.

I wanted to rip apart all those memories of life from their minds and to seal them in pain so they would wish, they had never been born, had never seen this day, and to brand their hearts with the scars of terror, fear and the horrors of war forevermore.

Over to my left, a Marine firing from behind an embankment cried out, "Yeahhh!" and others took up the battle cry and unleashed their own fiery and violent discharge of pent-up frustration and explosive anger that had been silent while they had laid pinned down by the enemy's bullets.

It was the wrong time for the NVA to begin their assault. They had just gotten up, to attack when the gun opened up.

The enemy soldiers to our left, who had advanced to the grave mounts were the first to feel the sting. As they got up, they were slaughtered by Marine responsive fire power. Those that could, ran back to the safety of the tree line. Others trying to help a wounded comrade were met with a blast of M-16 bullets and they went down. Marines summoned to battle clicked on to full automatic, and in the next few moments of life, we unloaded a destructive force of firepower that wreaked revenge and punishment upon the enemy for the pain they had inflicted upon us.

Marines stood up and threw grenades, at the advancing enemy. M-79 grenade launchers were fired in rapid succession dropping several rounds where the enemy stood.

Marines with true grit, courage and determination to cease the enemy's bloody thirst for victory, took on the offensive, declared their will to engage, to demolish and destroy and the world around us trembled.

These were consecrated warriors. Men of war, Marines, who had experienced, the terror, horror and devastation encountered in the battlefield. They were Marine warriors, hand chosen for this battle, for this time, and today we would not be defeated, we wanted to taste their blood and count their dead.

Keene got up on one knee having inserted the magazine he had carried with him for over three months. He opened fire full automatic from his M-14, and unleashed the magazine's twenty red tracers at the base of the tree line where a group of NVA had just stood up for the assault.

Less then a minute later, another cluster of red tracers was fired from my left side and I thought that it was a machine-gun from Second Platoon opening up in the rice paddy field, but it was Perry.

He had followed Keene's lead and had also switched magazines, and unloaded his magazine full of red tracers at the enemies' position.

The ricocheting red-hot bullets mixed in with every fifth red tracer round I was firing, combined first with Keene's then with Perry's red tracers had filled the air with a wicked display of fiery menace.

The enemy, not understanding what they had just been hit with, got up; and I saw a number of them running to the right, shifting positions, retreating into the thick jungle, moving further back.

Marines emerged from the dirt and mud and arose firing, running to find more secured positions from which to return fire. I hadn't seen the fire-team to my left until they opened fire. They had been assigned to walk our left flank when we were moving out and had been lying out in the open rice paddy to my left, unable to move, but now they took advantage of the gun's firepower and began to respond. Some got on their knees and opened up while the others began to leapfrog their way back toward the hooch, providing cover for each other until all of them had reached the safety of a large dirt mound near where the lieutenant was.

To my right, the same thing was happening. I saw a wounded Marine limping back while others helped carry another wounded Marine out of danger. Sometimes, it's not just the firepower that makes the difference in gaining fire superiority in a fierce firefight, its guts, and sheer determination. It is Marines willing to take chances over overwhelming odds. Sometimes, it is pure anger and hatred fueling a deep determination to set things right that compels individuals to do what must be done. They pin medals on individuals like that and call them heroes. They are decorated with honors and glory, but all too often, they were like we were: scared and fighting or engaging the enemy simply because we had no other choice. When it came right down to it that day, it was them or us, and most of us were determined to make sure it was not going to be us.

The real heroes of war were the wounded and those killed fighting for a just cause, individuals that paid the ultimate price by the shedding of their blood. This is what I was seeing, what was happening in front and all around us. Marines were covering for each other, exposing themselves to harm's way, and placing their lives in danger for the life of others. They were helping one another and returning fire against a well-concealed foe and exposing themselves to fire while doing so. They were Marines doing what Marines do best: fighting and killing the enemy that dared to engage us in battle.

With the enemy's lapse of fire power, we had gained fire superiority, and it felt great, but the victory was short-lived.

Moments later, NVA reinforcements were rushed to the front and they released their own dreadful surge of firepower to meet the new challenge with their own AK47 bullets, Russian made machine-guns, grenades and communist supplied B-40 rockets.

The battle rage increased but the sound of Bro's gun continued to roar above the enemies' clamor, while the cry of the wounded on both sides filled the air with pain, death and shattered dreams. U.S. Marines and well-trained Red Communist Soldiers were locked in the heat of battle, and no one was giving ground.

NVA in the Tunnels and Lake
Operation Foster; the Battle at Finger Lake AT 867533
November 21, 1967, D+8, 1130-1940 hours

Shortly after the first rounds were fired, Second Platoon's commander, Sergeant Gus had assigned one of his fire-team leaders, Richard L. "Duke" Neufeld, to set up his fire-team near where the barbed wire fence disappeared into the water. Gus also asked Duke to see if there was another way to get over to where we were besides the zigzagging gateway. After having determined there was no other way to get through the fence to us other than the gate, the team set up near the water's edge and it wasn't long afterward that they spotted six NVA soldiers, as they emerged soaking wet, from a tunnel on our side of the barbed wire fence near the water's edge. The NVA soldiers had hugged the water's edge and had made their way through the tunnel complex, coming out behind First Platoon's position.

Duke signaled to his men to pull back and wait until the last men in the NVA squad began to move toward First Platoon along the sandy shore on our side of the barbed wire fence. The enemy soldiers would be emerging behind Lieutenant Wilson's command location where he had his back toward the lake.

Sergeant Gus, at about that same time, had just ordered his men to grab a bite to eat as it was unknown when they would get a chance to eat again.

On his makeshift stove was his favorite B-2 unit meal, spaghetti and meatballs; he had used two heat tabs to warm it nice and hot, the way he liked it. He opened the accessory pack and found the four-smoke pack of Chesterfield cigarettes; it couldn't get any better. He grinned to himself as he grabbed hold of the warm can by the bent metal lid he had left attached. He stuck his spoon into the spicy red spaghetti sauce, whirled the spoon around, and spooned out a mouthful of spaghetti; he blew on the food-filled spoon to cool it off. Just as the smell reached his nose and the spoon was about to touch his mouth, Duke's fire-team opened fire, striking the enemy soldiers from behind.

Gus dropped to the ground and the full can of food fell on his poncho liner and the wet earth. Noticing there was no incoming, he cried out, "Who's firing, Who's firing?" And someone answered, "It's Duke, down by the lake."

Gus grabbed his M-16 and, with his radioman at his heel, raced down a small trail toward the spot he had assigned the fire-team to keep secure. Near the edge of the lake, he saw Marines from his platoon shooting at two NVA soldiers as they dove into the water. On the beach, a short distance away, he saw four dead NVA soldiers lying at the edge of the sandy beach.

As Sergeant Gus stepped off the trail to cut across an open field to get to his men, he slipped and fell on his behind then rolled down a small embankment. He got up and looked back where he had stepped off the trail and noticed that he had slipped on human waste that somebody had failed to cover up.

"*God* damn, you people!" he cried out. Duke, thinking his platoon commander was yelling at him for the shooting, cried out, "But, Gus, they're gooks, gooks that were sneaking up on First Platoon!"

"Not that," Gus replied. "This shit. Who the hell didn't cover up their shit?" Gus's trousers and utility shirt were soiled not only from the mud and rain but now from where Gus's body had slid on top of the human waste. For the next few seconds, the fire-team didn't know whether to keep looking for the NVA soldiers to surface or feel sorry for their soiled platoon commander. No one in Duke's fire-team fessed up to having relieved themselves.

"Damn, damn, damn," Gus said as he looked toward the lake. The drop at the edge of the lake on his side was too steep for him to jump in to get clean, and they didn't have a rope to get him back out if he jumped in to wash himself off.

"Shit," he said as he turned to get back toward his CP; there was no telling when he would be able to get washed up and get his clothes clean. As they walked back, Gus removed his shirt and held it at arm's length; while his radioman stayed a good distance behind and could only chuckle to himself.[190]

Duke's fire-team had killed four of the enemy soldiers, but two had managed to dive back into the water and escaped. Due to the barbed wire barrier, Duke and his team were unable to pursue them.

Doc Mac Needs Your Help
Operation Foster; the Battle at Finger Lake AT 867533
November 21, 1967, D+8, 1130-1940 hours

With the unleashed firepower we had released, Marines were able to move forward, using the grave mounts for cover and taking advantage of the slopping terrain, when they could. The majority of the enemy were soon forced to move back and settled into secondary entrenched positions ten meters from the front of the tree line.

However, NVA soldiers could still be seen moving into some areas near the front of the tree line. They were moving in snipers and sappers with satchel charges.

Cpl. Morales, having deployed his men as best he could, turned his attention to helping deploy other Marines into positions where they might be more effective. He went over to where Doc Mac was working on O'Neil.

"Need any help, Doc?" Morales asked.

"Find Doc Marren, I need his help, and tell the lieutenant that I have two priority medevacs and one routine that need to be taken out now." Izzie, lying nearby, grabbed hold of the Corpsman and said, "How many priorities?"

"Two," Doc said.

"Three," Izzie said.

"Make that three," Mac said, and Morales turned to find the lieutenant and the other Corpsman.

Morales ran out to where the lieutenant was and notified him of Doc's urgent request then turned to find the other Corpsman.

He entered the hooch and found Marines huddled at the rear door, taking turns returning fire at the enemy. Doc Marren and Marty were still huddled in fear in one corner of the kitchen. He shook Marren and the Corpsman looked up. He was scared, a vacant look in his eyes, disconnected from what was happening. He was trembling and perspiring profoundly.

"Doc, Doc," Morales said as he shook him again. "Doc Mac needs your help, just right outside the hooch. He's just right out the hooch." Morales nudged the Corpsman to move. Marren, though scared and in a daze, made his way out of the hooch and over to where Doc Mac was busy trying to keep O'Neil alive.

"Marty," Morales called out and Martinez looked at him, "here, take this." And Morales handed Marty his M-16 rifle. Marty looked at it, brought his trembling left hand to his mouth and his right up to his chest and then moved both to his mouth, cupping both of them there. He was scared, petrified, and unresponsive.

"Here, take this," Morales said again, a little more forcefully; and Marty's eyes looked down and then away, a faraway look shadowing his mind.

"Take it," Morales said loudly, and Marty took the weapon.

"I want you to go out to the left of the hooch and cover the area by the edge of the lake, Calderon is there," Morales said to Marty.

Marty took the weapon and ran to the front door then toward the lake, down the small path past Marines in the prone position who were busy returning fire, and past Leonard Calderon, Calderon had been in country now for eleven months and this he figured would be his last operation. He was sitting near the banks of the lake alone guarding that side of the lake wondering if he soon would be the only Marine left standing. He was feeling very much alone and was there just in case the enemy tried to swim along the lake's edge and up the beaten path that led to our right flank.

Marty stopped right in front of Calderon, took the weapon off safety, and fired a twenty-round burst at the tree line then turned around and ran back to the hooch. He was out of ammo.

Wilson heard what Morales had said, but also knew there was nothing he could do to get a chopper to land in a hot LZ. Wilson's priority was first to gain control of the battlefield or no one was going to get out alive.

"See if you can get a medevac chopper in," Wilson said to Art, his radioman, and called Sgt. Stanford over.

The tall Sgt., came running over and slid as much of his body that he could into the small crater Wilson was in, "find a spot for a medevac," he told Stanford and Toy got on the radio.

As incoming fire continued to increase and our casualties were mounting, Wilson feared a medevac on this side of the wired fence may not be possible. Perhaps if Second Platoon could get through the fence and reinforce us, the medevac might be possible. He contacted Actual Two, Sergeant Gus, Second Platoon's leader, and quickly relayed to him the situation we were in and suggested that Second Platoon mount up and join us.

Sergeant Gus was concerned, but disheartened. His platoon was in no condition to offer much help. They also had taken casualties.

Gus responded by saying that he would join us if Wilson really needed them. But with the few remaining men he had in Second Platoon and casualties that hadn't been medevac he felt it would be better for him to stay where he was where his platoon would protect our rear and left flank. As it was, Gus told him, his men were stretched pretty thin in doing just that. Returning fire when they could, they had already engaged a number of enemy soldiers who had tried to come around and behind our position. If Second Platoon tried to get to us by way of the zigzag gate, the platoon would pay a heavy price in casualties.

Artillery by the Handful
Operation Foster; the Battle at Finger Lake AT 867533
November 21, 1967, D+8, 1130-1940 hours

Wilson, troubled about not being able to get the help our platoon needed, nonetheless agreed with Gus about leaving Second Platoon where they were.

At least our rear and left flank were protected by Lima Company across the lake and our left side by Second Platoon, Wilson thought.

With Second Platoon unable to come to our assistance, Lieutenant Wilson still had to do something. The Forward Air Controller (FAC), Artillery Forward Observer (FO), and Aerial Observer (AO) Teams were all with the Company Command Group across the lake.

Without an FO, Wilson would have to call Hill 65 for an artillery missions himself. He knew he would not be able to call in the rounds too close to where the NVA were entrenched because that was near where his men were. A long or short round could be disastrous.

By the time he asked for the mike, Toy anticipating the Lieutenant's request was already switching to a long range antenna.

The PRC-25 radio signal with its small metal tape measure looking antenna was usually good for only three miles or about five klicks. With the longer extended antenna the range was good for 12-18 miles, depending on ones elevation.

Normally, it was Battery India, Third Battalion Eleventh Marines located on Hill 65 who provided artillery support for the Seventh Marines. With 2/3 also involved in Operation Badger Hunt/Foster, north of us, the artillery-fire mission fell on Battery B, First Battalion Twelfth Marines. They were the unit assigned to provide artillery support for us during Operation Foster but, just as often, artillery was provided by the Eleventh Marines who were more familiar with the area and they fired their 105 Howitzers with pinpoint accuracy, and it was them, India Battery that responded.

As the artillery high explosive rounds began to land behind the enemy's entrenched positions, the ground below us trembled and shook. The beehive rounds were right on target.[191] The artillery rounds tore up the deep undergrowth and mowed down small trees in the dense jungle just behind the enemy. Some of the fired artillery rounds had a delay fuse inserted so that the round would first strike the ground, embed itself deep before exploding and releasing hundreds of secondary explosive charges into the air. They would then explode seconds later upon impact.

The artillery rounds turned the jungle floor into a burst of deadly, shattering pieces of explosive fiery hell. The enemy, however, remained close to us and the barrage of artillery only temporarily caused them to cease firing as they sought cover from the exploding rounds. The only thing we could hope for was that the artillery barrage would keep enemy reinforcement away from the battlefield.

Seconds after the last barrage of artillery fell behind enemy lines and while smoke from their impact was still on the ground, the NVA opened fire again.

Lost Bait
Operation Foster; the Battle at Finger Lake AT 867533
November 21, 1967, D+8, 1130-1940 hours

With artillery impacting the forested area behind the tree line, a group of Marines to my right got up out of the kill zone and ran for the safety of the corner of the house, the enemy opened fire in their direction. The enemy had lost the Marines they were using as bait and decided to take them out instead, but they were too late. All of a sudden, automatic rifle fire coming from other Marines nearby was enough covering to get our Marines out of harm's way. As the enemy shot at the fleeing Marines, their rounds were also met by the clamor of Jones' machine-gun opening fire.

I opened fire at the origin of the enemy's green tracers, and now both M-60 machine-guns were firing together. For a time, Jones' red tracers swept across from my right toward my center field of fire, crisscrossed with my line of fire, and the red fiery tracers kissed in the middle of the rice paddy fields as they tore apart the edge of the tree line and wreaked havoc upon the enemy.

We fired, and fought our war, and we did just as we had been trained to do in machine-gun school. It was controlled interlocking machine-gun fields of fire; it was powerful and very effective. We continued to fire for a time until the enemy stopped firing, and then we stopped. We had finally gained the fire superiority we needed.

Chief, Howard and Welsh had set up two strong defensive positions near the left side of the hooch, from where they had a clear view of the battle scene before them. Prescott moved up and joined them. Prescott moved up next to Newman.

"Hey, Cuch," Prescott said, "yeah," Chief answered.

"I was scared." Cuch looked over at the Marine. "I was scared, so I hid right after Stringbeans was hit. I fell backwards when he was hit, and when the gooks ran right by me, I hid in the bushes."

"At least, you're alive," Chief said, and with that, Prescott took in a long sigh, and returned his thoughts to the battle before them.

Lieutenant Wilson called in another barrage of artillery fire. The sounds of artillery exploding behind the enemy's line caused them to seek better cover, and for a while, the enemy ceased firing altogether. The lieutenant adjusted the rounds, bringing them in closer and closer to where we were. It was the only way we were going to be able to overcome the large enemy force that had hit us and who remained close by. As Wilson walked the rounds in closer, some were beginning to have an effect upon the enemy elements that were entrenched close to the tree line.

We could hear them calling out to each other and I saw some getting up and moving out. The sound the rounds were making as they exploded in the thick foliage sounded as if a giant fire-breathing dragon was slowly stomping toward us in the jungle.

With each succeeding step, the dragon's fire exploded from its mouth, destroying those before it while its steps shook the earth.

The earth shook under me as I lay hard pressed against the ground. The destructive power the artillery rounds were causing was devastating. But the rounds could only be called to a certain distance and the enemy knew this, and that was the reason they had gotten up close to us. Even as the fiery dragon walked in their midst and released a thundering roar while breathing out smoke, death and destruction, the well-disciplined enemy soldiers moved back in and when possible closer to us and continued to open fire in our direction to keep us from assaulting their positions.

One thing for sure, the NVA military unit we had engaged was not going to leave. They were courageous and brave soldiers. They were determined to stay and fight and inflict as much damage as possible on a Marine platoon they had cornered, and they remained determined to destroy us.

An Unrelenting Battle
Operation Foster; the Battle at Finger Lake AT 867533
November 21, 1967, D+8, 1130-1940 hours

The battle continued; we shot at them, and they shot at us. We ducked their bullets, and they avoided ours. We went back and forth like this, and we danced with each other and were forced to listen to the music each of us played. Sometimes, I opened up fully automatic and the sound carried with it a wall of lead and sang loud with a powerful voice, and the enemy's music would fade. Then as they responded to the song my M-60 was playing, they would sing a new song with a new tempo and a new sound of determination and firepower. The enemy fought back fiercely, and we tried to kill each other. At times, it seemed like it was our own little war: some moments I felt as if I was the only one firing and sometimes I was. We lost time and space, memories and fear. The rain came and went, but the sun never shined with its full strength; it was determined long ago that this day was to remain a gloomy day for all.

When I stopped, the bullets would come and then the grenades would come then others would join in the game and fire upon the enemy because it was now their time to sing and to dance with the song of death, or to sing a different song and to feel the pains of war. And so we fought our war, and Marines were shot and wounded while the NVA rapidly carried away their dead and wounded and just as quickly, they buried them in quickly dug, shallow graves, sometime some were buried while their last breath was still in their lungs. Other soldiers were then quickly moved in to take over the same forward fighting positions their dead once occupied at the base of the tree line or in spider holes, filled with blood.[192]

For hours, we danced and sang our songs together although neither of us liked the music being played or the offensive odor of gunpowder that mingled with the smell of fear, blood, guts, death, pain, burning plants, grass and flesh, we kept firing at each other. I hated most of all the sizzling green tracers that blazed a trail other bullets followed. It was a show, a theater, a deadly musical game we were playing and the music played different tones; each time a round was fired, all was not understood, listened to, or embraced.

The enemy was now concentrating a greater part of their firepower solely on my machine-gun or on Jones' machine-gun position depending on which gun was silent and which was shooting. When Jones opened up, I stopped and the NVA gunners would then open up on his gun position and I, in turn, would open up at the enemies' firing position and Jones would stop fighting. Then the enemy would start concentrating on my gun's position, and Jones would open up on that shooting target. While I had a clearer and wider field of fire and could cover all of the tree line the enemy was firing at us from, Jones' gun could only cover a third of the tree line to the right of my center field of fire.

Soon the enemy realized this, and they moved their firing position to the left and unleashed a new wave of firepower aimed only at my gun's position. For a time, Aggie and I stopped firing and we hugged the ground and waited when the incoming got too fierce and each time we did that it seemed the enemy opened up with new machine-gun positions and then there was silence and it seemed they were once again gearing up for another assault.

A Bird In the Sky
Operation Foster; the Battle at Finger Lake AT 867533
November 21, 1967, D+8, 1130-1940 hours

Lieutenant Wilson knew we needed to get choppers in to medevac our dead and wounded, but the area remained to hot for them to be able to come in.

We continued to take incoming, from a couple of machine-gun positions. To get a medevac chopper in, those gun positions would have to be eliminated. Wilson called for the rocket team.

A Bird Dog pilot listening in on the medevac channel, heard Wilson checking on the possibility of getting in a medevac. The pilot came on line via that frequency and asked if he could help.

Wilson advised him of our situation, and the location of our enemy. The Bird Dog pilot flying overhead was an Army First Lieutenant by the name of Ray Caryle, a savvy veteran with many flight experiences. The Marine Captain observer at his side was Rob Whitlow, both were on their second run of the day, flying in an Army O-1G bird-dog aircraft.[193]

Whitlow responded that the enemy was too close for regular bombs. He could get napalm in, but Marines may get hit. Wilson told him that we were in fear of being overrun and we needed air support; if we didn't get help soon, we wouldn't have a chance.[194]

"I have a flight of Air Force Phantoms coming down from the north after aborting a bombing run, and they are carrying bombs and napalm," he told Wilson.

"They will not drop the bombs but will give you the napalm if you'll take responsibility for the results." Wilson agreed, and through the Bird Dog pilot, he began to vector the Phantoms in.

The rocket team of Perry and Rahm got to the lieutenant's position, and Wilson pointed out a small hut a good distance away along a narrow stripe of hedgerows. As he was pointing it out, the machine-gun opened fire in their direction, and they got down to avoid getting hit.

Looking at Perry, the lieutenant asked him; "Can you put a rocket, at that machine-gun position."

"Sure, can do, lieutenant," Perry said, and both he and Rahm moved out to find an advantageous position to do so.

From a small crater a short distance to the left of the lieutenant's position, Perry and Rahm, quickly assembled the rocket launcher. Perry rose with the rocket on his shoulder and took careful aim at the target. When he had it in his sights, he pressed down on the trigger. The rocket didn't fire. The enemy, however, having seen him, with the rocket launcher on his shoulder zeroed in on him and he went down just as the bullets struck the edge of the crater, they were in.

He and Rahm checked the rocket's cable, contractor latch assembly, firing mechanism and electrical circuit, everything seemed ok.

Perry got back up, took careful aim, and pulled the trigger.

Once again, the rocket misfired, and his position was again peppered with enemy machine-gun fire. It was the last rocket the gun team had, so both he and Rahm worked on cleaning the rocket's trigger mechanism. Then Perry got up again and took careful aim.

At about this time, the first of the Phantom jets dropped down for their first bombing run. The enemy took cover, and with no incoming fire, Perry stood firm and took careful aim. He fired, and as the rocket took off, the Phantom jet's first canister of napalm was dropped. Both impacted the enemy's machine-gun position at the same time.

When the rocket was fired, a thick cloud of dust from the rocket's back blast covered the crater Rahm and Perry were in.

As the cloud dispersed, Perry was lying at the bottom of the crater. His head was spinning, a glazed look on his face, blood was oozing from his ears.

As Rahm dragged the half dazed Marine toward the Corpsman, he stopped to catch his breath at Wilson's crater.

"What happened to him?" Wilson asked, as Rahm, was attending to Perry's wounds. Toy, broke open a First Aid bandage and gave it to Rahm. Rahm, answered; "Back blast. He was too close to the back of the crater when he fired the rocket."

The second jet came in just behind the first, and he dropped napalm as well. A fiery yellow and white burst of burning, blistering death enveloped the enemy's entrenched positions. The drops were dangerously close to the Marines closest to the tree line, and Wilson feared that they might have gotten hit as well.

Keene and Welsh, the two Marines closest to the tree line, felt the heat of the napalm as it sucked the air out of the area. For the first time since the battle began, the enemy's guns were silenced. It was a good thing because Welsh was out of ammo.

It wasn't long before the enemy incoming fire began to increase again, and the bird-dog pilot who remained overhead called in an artillery mission where he could see the enemy fire coming from.

Having stuck around, the Bird Dog pilot got back on the radio and advised Wilson that he had another flight of aircraft that had made themselves available. They were Marine A-4 Skyhawks carrying napalm and snake-eyes.[195]

As the AO overhead briefed the A-4 flight leader, Wilson was marking our positions with a yellow colored smoke grenade. Caryle then dived on the target and fired off one of their wing-mounted rockets, to mark the enemy's position with a white phosphorous rocket. It hit twenty or so meters from the enemy position.

The lead A-4 thundered in from the northwest on about a 150 degree heading and passed only a few hundred meters in front of our positions. Their bomb run took them roughly parallel to the outline of Finger Lake, so that the bomber would not pass over our positions.

After their last load was dropped Wilson asked if the jets had cannons, and the Bird Dog pilot told him that twenty-millimeter cannons were available on them. Wilson asked for a run of this, and both aircraft came in blasting away at the tree line one after the other. Wilson realized this now gave us the best opportunity to assault the enemy's position.

Wilson asked for more, but the Bird Dog pilot advised him that the fixed-wing aircraft were out. Our lieutenant then asked for the jets to make a dry run. He figured that when the jets would come in, the enemy would have their heads down, and it would be a perfect time for us to assault. The word was passed for us to prepare to assault the enemy.

Doc Mac wanting to make sure the lieutenant was aware of how desperately we needed a medevac had crawled over to where the lieutenant was. To be heard above the roar of the battle, as we began our assault, the red-faced Corpsman screamed at the lieutenant,

"O'Neil has to be evacuated; his lungs are falling out of his back. I've wrapped tape around his upper torso, but I don't know how long I can keep him alive."

Wilson looked helplessly at the brawny Corpsman.

"Lieutenant, you've got to get him out of here. He's not going to make it," Doc Mac cried out louder, hoping that with an urgent request, the lieutenant would be sure to get in a medevac chopper in somehow. Wilson had never seen the always-calm giant of a Corpsman so upset. He understood what Mac was saying, "Doc, I'll get a medevac area set up, as soon as I can" he told the worried Corpsman, and with that assurance, the Corpsman crawled his way back toward the hooch.

"Bang, Bang, Bang, Bang"
Operation Foster; the Battle at Finger Lake AT 867533
November 21, 1967, D+8, 1130-1940 hours

We were Marines, and this is what we were trained to do: assault the enemy in their entrenched positions and secure the area.

We were to assault while the jets were flying in. He believed that the enemy would have their heads down to protect themselves against the cannon bursts while we charged at them. As the jets were bearing down, the lieutenant called for us to assault. Some Marines were hesitant to do this at first, not knowing that the jets wouldn't be firing, but they obeyed our lieutenant's command and got up from out in the open from behind rice paddy dikes. From behind the house and behind grave mounds, Marines rose to assault. I opened fire from my forward position, covering our assault from the left side.

Welsh, without bullets in his weapon, tried to get the lieutenant's attention to tell him that he was out of ammo. But as the other Marines arose to assault, he also got in line with the other Marines and assaulted as well. As the jets hit their afterburners to pull up, First Platoon Marines were on line and assaulting the tree line.

When we went through ITR training at Camp Pendleton, we practiced assaulting enemy positions. When we ran out of the blank ammo we used in training, the instructor ordered us to keep assaulting and to call out, "Bang, bang, bang, bang," in support of other Marines assaulting.

Calderon, on line with the assaulting Marines, dropped on one knee and shot an enemy soldier fleeing the scene; other Marines were opening fire on enemy targets as they got up to leave their entrenched positions.

Over to his left, Calderon saw that the Marine closest to him was assaulting but wasn't firing. It was Welsh, and he was crying out, "Bang, bang, bang, bang," as they moved forward.

The enemy had gotten up and, seeing the advancing Marines, had withdrawn from their secondary positions. But the battle was not over.

The NVA quickly regrouped next to the banks of Finger Lake, and they moved other enemy soldiers to hide in the number of hooches to our left near the open rice paddies to cover for them as they withdrew.

As the platoon entered the right side of the tree line, they could see uniformed NVA soldiers running away. Then all of a sudden others appeared: a full line of enemy soldiers had gotten up from another trench line further back and were counter-assaulting the Marines. I had crawled up closer and had set up the machine-gun on a large grave mound and saw the enemy as they moved toward the Marines. There were about a dozen of them running, shouting, and shooting toward the attacking Marines.

Marines stopped, got on their knees, and continued to shoot while others fell flat on the ground to fire from the prone position. As the enemy advanced, others arose to reinforce their comrades.

Marines in the prone position then provided cover for Marines as they fell back. Some Marines turned and fired back, giving Marines who had fallen time to get up and join them; Keenan and Prescott had advanced the farthest and were both on the ground and out of ammo as the second wave of advancing enemy soldiers stood up and assaulted, the enemy soldiers ran past them.

Keenan, realizing they were now behind enemy lines and in the midst of the assaulting enemy, quickly turned to Prescott and told him to play dead. Prescott, seeing that the enemy was close by, closed his eyes. His thoughts went back to what he had done earlier, and feared this time he would be killed, probably by the same enemy soldiers that had ran past him the last time.

"Open your eyes and stick out your tongue," Keenan said to him, as three of the NVA soldiers came rushing back to where they had seen both Marines lying on the ground.

As I saw the assaulting Marines withdrawing from the tree line as bullets were flying past them, Aggie and I quickly moved the gun forward, placing it on top of a grave mound near the tree line, and opened fire across the tree line at an angle to cover for them. The enemy stopped their assault before reaching the tree line and turned to get away from the gun's fire.

As the enemy retreated, they stopped by the two Marines, dropped to their knees, and opened fire at us while kneeling next to Keenan and Prescott. They then grabbed the two Marines by their flak jacket and dragged them into the dense jungle.

Once they had the two Marines behind their lines an NVA soldier, talking to the others, reached down and grabbed Keenan's rifle; Keenan's hands tightened.

Let go, he told himself, and his hand snapped back as the enemy took the weapon.

Oh no, he said to himself, *he saw me move.* The enemy soldier took out his knife and carved a large *X* in the middle of Keenan's forehead. He did the same to Prescott, carving the *X* dead center on his forehead. Keenan imagined the next sound he would hear would be that of a bullet entering his head. He waited for the bullet to explode in his head.

Click, he heard the NVA soldier's hammer strike an empty chamber. They, too, were out of ammo. The NVA soldiers grabbed the weapons of the Marines pretending to be dead and began to strip them both of their clothes as well.

As the enemy turned Prescott's body around to take off his shirt, NVA soldiers started to run past them. Rahm, Pridemore, and Keene, knowing Marines had been left behind, had turned back and counter-advanced, causing the NVA soldiers kneeling over the two Marines to retreat. As Keene kept firing at the fleeing enemy, Rahm reached down, grabbed hold of Keenan, shook him, and called out his name. He was alive. Prescott, lying next to him, got up from pretending he was dead, and all five ran back as other Marines came on line to cover for them.

Doc Marren, saw the fear of death and the ashen color on both Marines, those were wounds he was not prepared to care for. As the Marines huddled near the back of the hooch, the Corpsman went off and sat by himself in a small bomb crater, His arms over his knees, he sat alone a distant look on his face.

The bird-dog pilot flying overhead contacted Wilson over the medevac radio and told him that he counted over eighty dead enemy soldiers near the tree line, nearly double the size of all of First Platoon, earlier that day.

A short time later, the Bird Dog pilot with the call sign of Benchmark 11 came back on line and reported seeing over 125 enemy soldiers advancing toward our positions. He told Wilson to have our troops move as far away as they could from the tree line as he had another flight of jets coming in. As the jets turned over the horizon to come in, the enemy opened fire at us from all along the tree line. It was perfect timing for us; as their volley of bullets left their weapons, the jets came in and dropped their load of bombs near the enemy's position.

Try Another Medevac
Operation Foster; the Battle at Finger Lake AT 867533
November 21, 1967, D+8, 1130-1940 hours

The lieutenant regrouped the platoon near the hooch and set up a defensive line to protect the medevac area. He called in again for the evacuation of our wounded, including Private First Class O'Neil who was the most critically wounded

Marine and was close to dying. By now, we had been involved in the firefight for close to three hours. The enemy's fire had died down, and the word was passed to stand by to provide cover for the choppers. We didn't know how many of the enemy remained close by as we took defensive positions from where we were.

It wasn't long before we heard the drone of the Korean War-vintage CH-34 helicopter coming in for the first pickup. Sergeant Zaryl Stanford popped a red smoke grenade near the edge of the lake by the sandy shore, and we saw the first of the medevac choppers approach the designated landing spot. The chopper came in along the open rice paddy fields, circling in from the north, and I felt uneasy about him coming in that way. The enemy, if they remained in the area, would be just to his left as he approached.

As Sergeant Stanford was waving the chopper in and as it got within a few feet of touching down, we could only hear the roar of the helicopter's engine laboring to settle into the landing zone.

This was going to be the first medical evacuation since we had gotten hit. Many of the wounded needed to be evacuated. It seemed like eternity, yet at the same time as if it all had started only a few moments before. Normally, it doesn't take long to medevac a wounded Marine, but because of the intensity of our engagement, no one had been able to come in and remove our wounded from the battle scene. While the rest of Second Platoon remained behind the fence, they had managed to bring out their most serious wounded out to the landing strip as well.

Many Marine helicopter crews would go in any time, any place; others were overly cautious and very hesitant to come close to a hot LZ. It was all up to the pilot.

During Operation Knox, just a couple of sniper rounds had caused the re-supply choppers to pull out. This time we had some seriously wounded Marines that needed to be medevaced. Critically wounded Marines who required urgent care were always medevaced first. Those who had sustained wounds that were life threatening, like a sucking chest wound, or those who might lose an arm or leg were why a priority system had been set up for air evacuation needs. But to land in a hot LZ where the enemy was still present was an option left entirely up to the medevac pilot. A hot LZ was usually marked with a red smoke grenade while a safe landing zone was marked with a yellow marker. Doc Mac had pled with the lieutenant that if O'Neil wasn't medevaced, he would die. The chopper, as it was about to land, would be O'Neil's only hope.

Each Marine had been trained to do whatever he could in providing first aid to "stop the bleeding and keep 'em breathing." Doc Mac evidently had done whatever he could.

The chopper's approach for evacuation was along the corridor between the house and the fence.

Chief and Souble, along with Doc Mac, had moved the seriously wounded Marines to the LZ, O'Neal was first, then Izzie which they carried out to the LZ in a poncho. Others were serious but not serious enough to be listed as a priority call; they would have to wait for the next chopper.

Sergeant Stanford was standing upright directly in front of the landing chopper using hand signals to help the pilot land on the sandy beach. The area had a large enough slope that offered some cover.

The chopper landed on the south side of the house and just north of the barbed wire fence line where Second Platoon remained on the other side.

The "wop-wop-wop" sound of the chopper's blades dissipated in preparation for full landing. When the chopper's tail was settling, both Aggie and I were looking at the chopper and heard behind us the distinct sound of incoming rounds.

The NVA had opened up with heavy automatic rifle fire, directed at the chopper and we turned to engage the enemy.

The chopper's crew chief was standing on the doorway, waiting to help lift our wounded on board. When the bullets struck the chopper, bits and pieces of shrapnel flew off; and a sniper shot the crew chief.

As Stanford was peppered with flying pieces of metal fragments from where the bullets were striking the chopper, it roared back to life and lifted off.

An RPG rocket round directed at the chopper struck the ground in-between Izzie and Chief, but it didn't go off, the impact of the rocket round struck the toy rifle Chief had dropped and it flew off, spinning counter-clockwise and struck Izzie in the forehead.

Lieutenant Wilson, a distance away couldn't hear the incoming fire the chopper was receiving because of the chopper's noise. Not realizing the chopper was taking incoming fire, the lieutenant yelled at the pilot over the radio handset demanding an explanation.

The pilot yelled back that his crew chief had been shot in the head. He was leaving for An Hoa and would not return until we could assure him that the LZ was clear.

As soon as the first rounds were fired, both Aggie and I opened fire at the source of incoming fire.

I fired at the NVAs machine-gun position with a burst of forty to sixty rounds of machine-gun fire. By the time that burst of fire had been expended, the medevac chopper was gone.

"Damn them," I said, realizing no one had been medevaced, and held down the trigger, spraying the whole area, left to right, then back again. I was angry and wanted to get the enemy that had shot at the chopper.

The second chopper close at hand decided not to come in and so our wounded were taken back to the edge of the house as was O'Neil.

After I opened fire, I noticed the enemy was not returning fire. For some reason, the enemy didn't open up with the intensity of fire I felt they were capable of delivering. They were still there, I could hear them talking, whistling and saw some of them moving through the deep underbrush behind the thick tree line.

I took careful aim at a target in the tree line, and was about to pull the trigger, when all of a sudden behind us the same Huey gunship that had escorted the first medevac reappeared.

The gunship crew had refueled, rearmed and were back, coming in low wreaking the ground and the enemy in front of us with machinegun and rocket fire. The gunship made pass after pass.

The Huey gunship remained unable to make contact with us, but still remained over head returning to An Hoa, refueling, rearming and coming back several times.[196]

"Sure would like to have been on that medevac chopper and out of here," Aggie said, verbalizing what I had been thinking.

"Yeah, except I wouldn't want to be wounded," I answered.

Aguilar got behind the gun while I crawled back toward the hooch to find more ammo. Where was the enemy coming from? By now, it was late in the day, and darkness was not far away. We had been fighting for over five hours and while we now had some control of the tree line, the enemy was still close by; I could sense it, and I could hear them.

One thing I was learning about our enemy. They almost always returned to the same spot, almost always traveled the same route, always seemed to set up their ambushes in the same places, and above all else they always sought revenge for the casualties they took.

Most NVA/VC squad leaders wore a leather thong with a hook around their wrists, which was used to drag their dead and wounded from the battle zones. The NVA squad leader would throw out the line to hook any part of their comrade's clothing, body, ankles, hands, neck, anywhere they could hook the metal piece into the body or clothing in order to retrieve their fallen comrades. Often they took great chances, even at the risk of death, to take dead bodies out of the battlefield. This was done more to deprive U.S. soldiers of an actual body count than to provide their comrades a proper burial. They looked upon the death of their comrades as martyrs having died for the cause and revered them as heroes for having done so.

Second Platoon Machine-Gun's Response
Operation Foster; the Battle at Finger Lake AT 867533
November 21, 1967, D+8, 1130-1940 hours

On my way to the hooch, I saw Doc Mac working on wounded Marines under the small porch beside the house. Blood had soaked the hard-pressed dirt where about a dozen wounded Marines had been gathered.

I found Jones on the side of the house; he was in an excellent defensive position and had plenty of ammo left. I picked up two hundred rounds of machine-gun

ammo from inside the hooch where Marines had placed them for us and went
back to join Aggie.

As soon as I went out the front door, I heard Aggie open up with about a forty-
round burst. I crawled out to find him shaking. Rounds were kicking up dust close
by, so he had moved the gun back about ten feet. This posed a problem because I
could no longer fire at a ninety-degree angle but was limited to a forty-five-degree
fire zone to our direct front. It was also not a safe spot for us to be in, and the
ground we were lying on was hard-pressed compared to where the gun had been
before. We would be too exposed to fire from that position.

Aggie told me that he could see enemy movement all along the tree line, and
some were moving toward the grave mounts again. We moved the gun forward by
crawling closer to the fence where I had been before. I wanted to go back out to
the open space from where I had originally opened fire from, but incoming rounds
prevented us from moving any farther out to where the gun had been earlier.

We moved out as far to a forward position as we could, and then I slid my body
into the soft ground. It felt good to be back behind the gun, and I felt refreshed.

Just that little time away from the gun had relaxed me. Unfortunately, it had
also opened my eyes to the misery of war, particularly to the pain and sorrow that
fellow Marines were enduring while they waited to be medevaced.

I began to believe the possibility existed that I might get hit, killed, or wounded.
I didn't like that feeling and tried to shake it off. But at the same time, seeing our
wounded renewed my determination to wreak havoc and hell upon the enemy. I
became more determined to keep firing no matter what. Once I touched the gun,
it became a part of me again. Touching the hard piece of metal gave me great
comfort and reassurance as well as a secure feeling as if my destiny was somehow
related to how I handled that gun and it knew how to respond in my hands.
While many feared being behind or near the gun under fire, I felt at ease and a
part of the destructive force it was capable of releasing. It was as if the gun was
an extension of my arm, of my life, and I knew we belonged together. Together,
we could put out that wall of lead, and I knew I had done that. Today, Charlie
wasn't going to win.

By moving away from the tree line, we had gained the artillery and air support
advantage. Sometimes there would be a pause in the firefight, but as soon as there
was any movement on our side, or we saw movement in the thick bushes, someone
would open fire. The firefight would then go on for a while and then die down. This
was repeated again and again sometimes only because neither of us could stand
the silence and we feared the unknown, so we opened fire. We had gained some
ground in our assault, and air drops but it remained unknown where the enemy
had moved to, what their strength was, or how far away they were from us.

My immediate right flank remained blind. The small bamboo fence was obscuring
my view; I could no longer see the edge of the tree line to my right. I only hoped
that Jones or other Marines would be able to cover that area. I hated to depend on

others, but I had no choice. I didn't want anyone to take any chances to protect my right front and that was why I was so glad when the Marines had gotten out of there. They had been too exposed lying down in the back part of the house.

The Marines that had been covering that area were able to get out when I first opened fire. It was a dangerous spot to be in, but also a great spot from which to return fire. Now no one was there to cover my right side, the gun was exposed should the enemy choose to come at us from that direction.

Once again, like in the bomb crater incident, our gun was in the most forward position of the rest of the men in our platoon. I continued to open fire without hesitancy when ever I saw the enemy moving in the tree line. Wherever and whenever the enemy opened up, that spot became my primary target, and I fired effectively and with extreme prejudice until the movement ceased or the incoming from that direction stopped. Then the enemy returned a heavy volume of automatic rifle fire at me and when it became too intense I would stop firing and wait and see what their plan was. At times, they fired and I did not return fire.

A short time afterward, a gun team from Second Platoon opened fire across from the open rice paddy fields to our left. The gun team was behind the barbed wire fence, and they weren't visible. They were shooting to our right front at enemy soldiers they saw moving along a second tree line to the south side of the dense jungle. From where they were they could see the enemy moving forward. That tree line facing south ran west toward Phu Phong (2). There was a wide gap between the fenced wire and that tree line. Evidently, Second Platoon had penetrated a part of the wired fence and had cleared an area so that they could respond to some of the incoming rounds that we were receiving. It was a comfort to know that another machine-gun team was firing and covering a section of the tree line hidden from us.

I opened up toward where they were firing to get the enemy in a cross fire, but we were immediately met by intense incoming automatic rifle and machine-gun fire from my right side. The fire was so fierce that it was evident that the enemy had been reinforced and was back for more.

A streak of glowing, burning white light shot across the rice paddy field from the middle of the south tree line that ran west. It was an RPG round that had been fired toward Second Platoon's gun team position. I turned my gun to fire at the origin of the rocket round, but it was too late. The machine-gun team in Second Platoon received almost a direct hit from the Soviet RPG-2 antitank rocket, and they went silent.

"Did the enemy have some type of overall plan?" I wondered. I had hoped that they would have left by now. Forty meters to my direct front, the back blast from the RPG was noticeably visible. It was near the front of the tree line near a hooch, and the smoke marked a spot upon which I could concentrate my machine-gun fire. I opened fire in that general direction and a barrage of fierce incoming rounds met me immediately.

The incoming fire was intense and fierce and came at me from two areas. With only about fifty rounds left, instead of continuing to draw fire, I just stopped firing and laid low as bullets whizzed by at a steady flow, some only inches away, their sibilant sound ringing in my ears long after the bullet had gone by. I realized that Jones' gun had been silent for a long while and wondered if they were conserving ammo or if Jones and Marty had been hit.

Aggie, who had crawled out to get more ammo, returned with 300 rounds gathered from Marines around the perimeter. He also had bad news. The reinforcements we were hoping for weren't coming, at all he said.

Some of Lima Company Marines had made it across the lake but ended up with Second Platoon; the rest of the company wasn't coming around the lake because the enemy was set in across the open fields and if they tried to swim across, snipers would shoot them in the water or if they set in along the edge of the lake. Then Aggie added, "The lieutenant believes the gooks may try to overrun us."

"Are Jones and Marty okay?" I asked.

"Yeah, but a lot of guys are wounded, almost everyone," Aggie said with a look of fear that we may be next in his eyes.

I added a 200-round belt to the gun, Aggie had put together. There were now over 250 rounds hooked up to the gun. It would be foolish for the NVA to try and overrun us; the gun would wreak devastation upon the enemy if they tried to assault our positions. They would pay a price. But I was worried about my blind right side; I only hoped Jones would be able to cover some of that area.

Charlie's Assault
Operation Foster; the Battle at Finger Lake AT 867533
November 21, 1967, D+8, 1130-1940 hours

All of a sudden, the enemy opened up with renewed intensity. Green tracers were kicking up dust all around us while grenades were exploding directly in front of the gun's position and among the grave mounds. The enemy was yelling, screaming, and a group of NVA soldiers were getting up from the trench line in front of the tree's edge.

Second Platoon Marines had a clear view of the enemy and the battlefield as they saw the enemy get up and began their assault. NVA soldiers could be seen running in front and to the west side of our defensive positions. Marines from Second Platoon opened fire on the advancing enemy soldiers.

Blurs of stirring movements shuffling back and forth in the dense jungle in front of us could be seen on my right. Other movement in the area wasn't as clear.

They might have believed that they had silenced my gun and were now brazen in their assault as they moved forward. Some enemy soldiers were crawling, others half hunched over moving in closer toward the edge of the tree line; other enemy soldiers were using the grave mounds and dikes on my left side for cover. I saw two, three, four of them; they seemed taller and healthier than the local Vietnamese people. I pulled the gun's butt stock back and held it tight up against my right shoulder, but I knew I had to wait so I didn't open fire—I wanted more targets.

More of them in blatant view began to stand upright in front of the tree line, and they started to move across the open rice paddies toward us. Behind and between them, the tree line opened fire on us with renewed fury. A great number of the rounds were also being fired at Second Platoon, which were located to our left along that tree line and behind the thick fence line. The enemy was now running toward us along the rice paddy dikes while their comrades shot at us from the tree line.

Charlie's In Our Midst
Operation Foster; the Battle at Finger Lake AT 867533
November 21, 1967, D+8, 1130-1940 hours

To my right I could see Williams and Morales firing at the enemy soldiers. They were unleashing their own response. I took in a deep sigh, exhaled; with so many targets now in view, pulled the gun in tight, I sighted in, concentrated on three enemy soldiers grouped together and pulled the trigger.

The gun shook and spewed out a stream of bullets that flew out whistling the names of the soldiers they would strike and take the lives of. Aggie also opened up with his M-16 on a group of NVA soldiers that had moved to his right front and into the gun's blind spot. The NVA were assaulting our positions in scattered waves.

Jones' gun began spitting out burning hot lead like I had never heard it fire before. I was wondering if the enemy was trying to move toward him along the edge of the lake just as a steady stream of red tracers slid evenly across the open field from Jones' gun position toward the assaulting enemy force. His line of fire was steady and purposeful. He had several targets in mind, I was thinking. As the enemy advanced, they began to pay a heavy price. I don't believe they expected both guns to open up as ferociously as we were doing. With every fifth round being a tracer round, the stream of bullets cutting across the terrain seemed like a steady beam of light crisscrossing and cutting down the advancing enemy force. The lead we were putting out was unparalleled, severe, and effective and the forward enemy movement stopped suddenly. By then, however, some enemy soldiers had reached the area midway between the tree line and the hooch.

To my right was Aggie and to his right Ira Rahm; both were returning fire as well and selecting targets closest to them. Since the beginning of the battle, Ira had been all over the battlefield, mostly getting ammo from other Marines for the gun or directing fire at enemy positions. As the enemy withdrew, Ira told Aggie to cover for him as he was going to go get us more ammo, and Aggie opened up as Rahm ran for cover.

Clear Fields of Fire
Operation Foster; the Battle at Finger Lake AT 867533
November 21, 1967, D+8, 1130-1940 hours

There are times when life-threatening danger is so near the mind records minute details with unique clarity. It's as if you have acquired a new sense of perception: smells, visions, time, space and hearing—all your senses become unified in such a way that everything is crystal clear. It seems that everything is occurring in slow motion. Your physical reactions are functioning at rapid speed and your mind is unveiling and recording unfolding events in slow motion and in precise details. The physical body is reacting and adjusting rapidly, but not fast enough so that it appears the action you are responding to is slow compared to the action being recorded by the mind.

I heard a pop to my right from my blind side and I turned to see what it was; in slow motion, it seemed, I saw an NVA soldier raise to his feet from my right side; he was looking my way and was throwing a brown cylinder-shaped canister over the small bamboo fence.

Aggie, who was the closest to the enemy soldier, was busy looking down, changing the magazine in his M-16 so I leaned on my left side to turn and shoot the NVA soldier that had thrown the smoking canister. He was on the other side of the bamboo fence only fifty feet away; by then he was on his knees staring at me, and I could see his eyes grow large as the gun's bullets tore through the bamboo poles and embedded lead and bamboo splinters into his upper torso, ripping his chest open. The bullets' impact shoved him backward, his body twisted around, and I noticed that he was unarmed and felt bad that I had shot an unarmed soldier. But why had he thrown what he did? It didn't look like a grenade, just a can of dirt.

"Where was his weapon?" The canister he had thrown struck me in the chest when I had rolled onto my left side to fire at him, then the canister slowly rolled down the slight incline and stopped rolling under my right thigh while I fired at the soldier.

I came back down flat on top of it and caught a glance of an advancing human form running toward us from our left side. I turned that way.

The canister felt uncomfortable lying under my thigh, and I was wondering why the enemy soldier had thrown the skinny tan-colored canister. It looked like the can was odd-shaped and full of dirt as dust was bellowing out when he threw it.

Over on my left side, the lone uniformed NVA soldier that was rapidly running toward our gun position came into focus. At first, I thought it was a Marine. *What is he doing out in the open rice paddy?* I was thinking. Then I realized that he was a green uniformed NVA soldier rushing toward us. Somehow, he had crawled alongside of the rice paddy dike and was now in an all-out assault, firing his AK-47 in full automatic at our gun's position. A large tan-colored smoking satchel charge was strapped to his right shoulder.

The bullets he was firing were going over our heads, way over our heads, and I realized he was running scared toward us and nervously shooting his weapon in our direction. I leaned heavily on my right side while turning to fire at the rapidly advancing enemy soldier. My right index finger was hard pressed against the gun's trigger guard. As bullets were being discharged, I swept the gun's fire toward my left side to shoot at him.

I had to lean completely on my right shoulder in order to get the gun's barrel pointed toward the assaulting enemy soldier. The gun's left-side bipod's leg came off the ground, and the gun skipped and bounced off the ground as the bullets exited the barrel. When he was about sixty feet away, four machine-gun bullets struck him at almost the same time. The first two impacts were at chest level, and he started to fly backward as two more 7.62 rounds slammed into his midsection. Blood and guts spilled out of his mouth and the right side of his head where one of the rounds exited. I could see pieces of flesh, blood, and clothing being ripped from his body. The fifth round to hit him was a red tracer; it bounced off his chin and cart wheeled away. Then he exploded as another round hit the satchel charge he was carrying. Under me, the canister-shaped grenade the enemy had thrown exploded.

The explosion lifted me up and threw me backward about fifteen to twenty feet in the air. As I was flying backward, dust and dirt and shrapnel showered Aggie, and he twitched with pain from the impact of the small slivers of dirt and sharp steel as they entered his body.

Rahm, running to get the ammo, was shoved to the ground by the grenade's explosive force. He felt small pieces of shrapnel enter his legs, but figuring the grenade had landed between him and Aggie and no real damage was done, he got up and continued on his mission.

Nothing Is As It Seems To Be
Operation Foster; the Battle at Finger Lake AT 867533
November 21, 1967, D+8, 1130-1940 hours

When the dust cleared, I felt okay and tried to get up, but I couldn't move. My legs were numb, I couldn't move them. I turned over on my stomach to get back on the gun and saw Aggie crawling toward the hooch. I couldn't feel my legs so I was crawling using only my arms; as I tried to scoot forward, I suddenly felt nauseated, my stomach was turning, great drops of perspiration were dropping from my forehead and neck. I felt weak so I turned on my back for relief from the pain then blacked out.

Someone shook me, and I felt drowsy and weak as if I had just awakened from a deep sleep. I felt as if I was floating, coming through some clouds from a dream world and to a reality of suffering and pain. While I lay there on my back, the ground was spinning and my head was trying to get a clear understanding of what was going on.

Sounds and visions, time and perceptiveness were slowly becoming synchronized again. Doc Mac's voice and form was slowly coming into focus.

The enemy had taken great pains to silence the gun by launching a combined frontal attack on the platoon and a grenade and satchel assault on the gun. Two NVA soldiers had crawled out separately. One along the outer edge of the rice paddy dikes, and the other out, sneaking around from the grave mounts. When in place and the signal to start the frontal assault was sounded, they did what they had been sent to do.

The enemy soldier I had shot to my right had thrown a ChiCom grenade. The ChiCom (Chinese Communist) grenade was of the old potato-masher type. When I turned to shoot at the running NVA coming at me from my left side, my right thigh had pressed down hard on the canister, shoving it into the soft ground. When the grenade exploded, the concussion threw me backward; and as I flew backward, the released shrapnel showered Aggie with dirt, dust, and small pieces of sharp metal.

I tried to get up in order to get back to the gun, but my legs wouldn't move. I looked down at them; both were still there, but I didn't have any control over them and I couldn't feel them. They were completely numb, I couldn't feel or sense that my toes were moving but I was not worried, just numb; I was trying to figure out what to do next.

The Corpsman had found me, or someone had dragged me over to him; I didn't recall hearing someone call for him. He checked me over with a worried look on his face and then tagged me by pinning a yellow casualty evacuation card on my flak jacket on the tag he had written my name, taken from my dog tags as well as the date/time and cause of injury. Grenade explosion, fragmentation and shrapnel, both legs.

When he moved on to another wounded Marine, I crawled toward the front of the house and propped myself up against the wall. I didn't want to be with the dead and wounded. I sat there looking out toward the lake. Behind me, the firefight was still going on. Wounded Marines were laid out all over the place. Some were in shock. Others had a faraway look in their eyes, and you knew that although the person was there, his mind was a world far away. It seemed to me that about six of the Marines had serious wounds. They were laid out in the open courtyard behind the hooch; all were awaiting evacuation.

Then I heard Doc Mac say to Rahm, "Cookie got hit, he's paralyzed, and he can't move his legs. Go get his gun!" And I didn't like the words Doc had used.

In a daze, I saw Rahm crawl out, out into the open field and while under fire, he returned with the gun in pieces, cradling it in his arms. As he drew near, I dozed off.

A New Life For An Old Friend
Operation Foster; the Battle at Finger Lake AT 867533
November 21, 1967, D+8, 1130-1940 hours

Aggie had managed to put the gun back together and Pridemore had joined him near the grave mounts not far from the hooch. It was further away from where I had gotten hit, but it gave Aggie better cover. A few minutes later mortars began to fall near them and they had to move the gun. A short time afterward mortars were falling near them again, they seem to be following the gun and fearing that the mortars were being dropped in preparation for a ground assault, Aggie moved the gun once more away from the grave mounts to behind the hooch.

No sooner had they gotten behind the hooch, the enemy opened up again, with rocket, mortars and automatic rifle fire.

Seeking a better location for the gun, Pridemore moved to the edge of the hooch, where Morales had been standing earlier. As he looked around the corner a sniper's bullet struck his helmet and glanced off his head. He went limp, and fell to the ground, his head covered in blood.

Thinking he was dead, Aggie and Rahm, were dragging him back when Keith awoke for a minute shook his head, said to Rahm; "What are you doing," Rahm dropped him, saying, "Hey we thought you were dead," hearing that Pridemore fell into unconsciousness again.

Bodies Floating In the Water, Or Was It A Dream?
Operation Foster; the Battle at Finger Lake AT 867533
November 21, 1967, D+8, 1130-1940 hours

I awoke to see bodies floating in the lake; they looked like dead Marines, or were they NVA soldiers in green uniform? I could see other bodies lying on the far bank; some were lying face down on both sides of the shoreline. Lima Company must have tried to cross the river and had been cut down or the enemy may have assaulted Lima's position and it was enemy soldiers in the water, I was thinking. It was all blurry and hard to distinguish what was what, what was true, real, or was I just imagining it all?[197]

L/Cpl. Vaughn T. O'Neil
Operation Foster; the Battle at Finger Lake AT 867533
November 21, 1967, D+8, 1130-1940 hours

My head wasn't clear, so I crawled back toward where Doc Mac was. When I got near him, I could see that he was working frantically on a wounded Marine, trying to keep him alive. I wondered if I could help.

The Marine he was working on had an open chest wound, and blood was gushing out. Doc's hands were full of blood, and another Marine to his left was assisting him. Doc Mac looked scared; he had run out of battle dressings and bandages. He looked around and asked if we had any pieces of gum. Izzie, in pain, was lying nearby but he began to search through his pockets, searching for sticks of gum.

"I need the foil," Mac cried out.

I reached into my flak jacket's pocket and held out four sticks of gum. He took one, tore off the wrapper, discarded the gum; much of the thin white paper peeled right off the foil and what remained of it was stuck to the stick of gum. Doc Mac stuck the aluminum foil into the Marine's sucking chest wound. I began to peel the others as he tried to plug up the gaping holes with four pieces of gum foil.

The next thing to being dead out in the field is a sucking chest wound. I knew the Marine wasn't going to make it unless he was medevaced right away. His face was already turning an ashen color from the loss of blood. It was O'Neil, and he was dying while Doc Mac was anxiously doing everything he could to keep him alive.

In desperation, Doc Mac lifted O'Neil's head and began mouth-to-mouth, attempting to breathe life into O'Neil's lungs. With each breath, O' Neil's chest wheezed, followed by a sucking, bubbling sound as blood and air mixed inside his body. Then the bandages slowly slid off O'Neil's body. The Marine was no longer breathing. The Corpsman with tears streaming down his cheeks grabbed hold of the dying Marine and just held him in his arms as O'Neil's limp body surrendered his spirit to another world. Izzie closed his eyes and cried.

Private First Class Taylor
Operation Foster; the Battle at Finger Lake AT 867533
November 21, 1967, D+8, 1130-1940 hours

The platoon began to receive new incoming machine-gun fire and mortar fire. It seemed as if the enemy kept reappearing from out of nowhere. This time, it was from a small hooch bordered by a cluster of trees sixty yards away. The hooch was located just a bit from the southwest corner of the tree line near where they had shot the RPG rocket at Second Platoon earlier.

A United States Army Huey gunship by the call sign of Alley Cat-6, the same unit that had been there on the eighth of November when the CAC unit had been overrun, had heard our plea for assistance over the medevac radio and came on line offering his help.

The lieutenant attempted to tell him several times where the hooch was from where we were receiving incoming fire from, but he just couldn't see the hooch from the air. The pilot fired smoke into the area, trying to determine by its position the hut's location. But the hut wasn't visible from above as thick foliage covered most of it, and he was unable to pinpoint the target.

Wilson called Corporal Dumont and told him to take some men and get close enough to the hooch to mark it with a yellow smoke grenade. Dumont selected his men from the few that remained unwounded.

Among them were Howard, Taylor, Welsh, Ezell, Rahm, and Keene. The lieutenant called Private First Class Taylor over; remembering how Taylor had been slow in moving earlier that day, so he personally cautioned the new Marine to follow every order given by Corporal Dumont.

"Taylor, if you are told to move, don't hesitate but go immediately," Lieutenant Wilson said to him.

Taylor responded with a "yes, sir, I'll do that," and the team of six Marines moved out.

Soon, the Huey pilot saw the plume of yellow smoke rising from the area to the right of the hooch. He came back around and fired a rocket to verify the location. After the lieutenant gave him the affirmative, the pilot then unloaded several rockets on the structure, destroying it and the machine-gun that had been firing at us from there.

The enemy firing ceased and Corporal Dumont and his men returned. When they arrived, Wilson saw that Pfc. Jerry Ezell was carrying a Marine over his shoulder. When they got to where the lieutenant was, Ezell laid the Marine down and the Marine's helmet fell off. A bullet hole was clearly visible on the top of the Marine's head. It was Private First Class Taylor.

As the team rushed through a small opening, a sniper was shooting at them; Dumont reported to the lieutenant.

When it came time for Taylor to run across, a sniper got him. When Taylor was hit, he looked up, and Welsh and the others told him to stay where he was, that they would get to him. Taylor then just laid down. When they got to him they knew he never had a chance, he had received a fatal head wound. They had accomplished their mission but at a great price.

Doc Mac rushed over to Taylor, tilted his head back, and saw the gaping hole. In disbelief, with sobs and an outcry, Mac was about to give Taylor mouth to mouth but Ezell held him back; Taylor's head wound showed there could be no life left in the Marine's body.

"No No, No! Not again, Please, Not again," cried the giant Corpsman as he bent his head, broke down, and wept.

Who is Red Dancer?
Operation Foster; the Battle at Finger Lake AT 867533
November 21, 1967, D+8, 1130-1940 hours

With the report that our platoon received another casualty, our battalion commander, Lieutenant Colonel Roger H. Barnard assumed control of the activities occurring in our battle. First Platoon, India Company, had been engaged for most of the day in a fierce five-hour battle with a large enemy force.

The rest of the company on the other side of the lake was being delayed in getting to us. Second Platoon was unable to get to us without exposing themselves to heavy enemy fire, and according to the bird-dog pilots in the air, enemy forces were still close at hand.

The R-20 Battalion and Q-14 Company were known to be operating in the Arizona area, and low-level intelligence reports before the operation had indicated a newly reinforced NVA battalion-size unit had recently moved into the area where we were.[198] From earlier reports, Barnard knew the enemy had prepared several sites in the area from where they would try to engage Marine units. If they destroyed a whole platoon of Marines, it would be a great victory to them, and that was what Charlie wanted to do, and Colonel Barnard was not about to let it happen.

It was evident that we had encountered a superior enemy force. A number of artillery strikes, three air strikes, one by Air Force Phantoms, and two others using Marine A-4 Skyhawks and a U.S. Army Huey gunship had responded to our call for assistance as well as the call from the Bird Dog pilots.

For close to 5 hours, medevac helicopters had tried to land to get our wounded out; two different H-34s had gotten shot up trying to come in. One Bird Dog pilot alone had expended thousands of machine-gun rounds and forty-eight rockets in that same tree line because of the large enemy presence they saw there. Colonel Barnard had heard all this over the radio as well as how two separate Bird Dog pilots had described the battle scene. One counted at least eighty dead enemy soldiers at the battlefield and another over 125 uniformed NVA soldiers moving toward our position.

"The only thing that Wilson hasn't used is naval gunfire," Barnard said to First Lieutenant Charles Chritton (Red Dancer) the acting Commanding Officer for Foxtrot 2/3, that day.[199]

"Can you get your men in there before nightfall?" Barnard asked him.

"Prep up that zone with air strikes, artillery, Huey gunships and get those choppers in here to pick up my men, and we'll be at your platoon's front door by 1700 hours," was Red Dancer's reply. It was then 1620 hours.[200] BLT 2/3 (Second Battalion Third Marines) had Echo, Foxtrot, Golf, and Hotel companies and their supporting elements assigned to Operation Badger Hunt/Foster from the beginning; the Marine companies had been reassigned to An Hoa and from there had been hopping on helicopters from one hot spot to another during the operation.

Now, Foxtrot 2/3 was being Sparrow hawked in to help us out.

"Cam-Kook, Cam-Kook, Mahreene, Tonight You Die!"
Operation Foster; the Battle at Finger Lake AT 867533
November 21, 1967, D+8, 1130-1940 hours

Just before 1700 hours, NVA soldiers moved in as close as they could to the tree line and began yelling out to us, "Cam-kook, cam-kook, Mahreene, tonight you die!" Then the enemy opened fire on us with just a few rounds of harassing fire. A couple of Marines responded with a few rounds to let them know we were still there.

The words *cam-kook* was words we often used to ask the Vietnamese for their ID. The words meant "show me your government-issued identification card."

The enemy was telling us that at one time, Marines had stopped them and asked them to show their South Vietnam identification cards. By using the words *cam-kook*, they were mocking us, telling us that they had fooled us when we had asked for their ID cards and we had let them go. Such boldness could only come from seasoned soldiers, individuals who could keep their wits in the midst of battle, and that battle was not over.

Break Out the Gas Masks and Wait For the Enemy's Assault
Operation Foster; the Battle at Finger Lake AT 867533
November 21, 1967, D+8, 1130-1940 hours

We were by now about an hour from darkness and had suffered severe casualties. Lieutenant Wilson had us pull in our perimeter into a tight area. There weren't many Marines, that weren't wounded. Some were seriously wounded others had wounds that did not require for them to be medevacked.

We broke open our gas masks and tear gas canisters. The gas was normally used for tunnel searches and clearing. Marines that had them checked their gas masks to see if they worked. Those that didn't work were replaced by finding some that did among the dead, or among the gear of the wounded, that were not going to be able to defend themselves.

Other weapons and gear were stockpiled in preparation for the heavy enemy assault that was building up at the tree line. As the gooks continued to cry out to us, Jackie Williams took out his K-bar and attached it to his rifle, a dreadful look revealed the fear going through his mind. Other Marines followed. The wounded that could fight were given weapons to protect themselves.

I no longer had my .45 pistol on me to protect myself. I had given it away earlier to someone who needed a weapon with ammo. We all knew it was only a matter of time before the enemy would try to overrun us; and the platoon, now down to about eighteen fighting men, would use the tear gas to protect and help us all survive the assault. It would be hand-to-hand fighting, and I couldn't stand up. I could only crawl by using my hands and arms, so we lay there waiting—we were all prepared to fight to the end, but I didn't have a weapon, and many of us that did have a weapon, were low on ammo.

A short time later, Captain Baggette advised Wilson that he was unable to get to us because of enemy forces between his position and ours, and they continued to receive incoming fire.[201] He did advise Wilson that reinforcements could be flown in to assist if Wilson felt he needed them.

Wilson advised him that our situation was not good for making it through the night without assistance as the enemy remained in the area and their size remained unknown, and may have increased.

No sooner, had Wilson mentioned this over the radio, Lima Company on the other side of the lake was desperately trying to get to us.

Marines were out in the open rice paddy fields, firing from behind rice paddy dikes, others were assaulting across the field to a far tree line. Others were lying out in the open not moving at all. *Lima Company is suffering heavy casualties trying to get across or around the lake to help us,* I was thinking.

Sergeant Gus, meanwhile, asked Wilson what he wanted his platoon to do. Wilson told him to stay put; once it got dark enough for them to come safely through the fence, we would unite and set in for the night reinforced. No sooner had Wilson said those words than the enemy soldiers once again called out, "Mahreene, Mahreene, tonight you die, Mahreene, Mahreene, tonight you die."

It was starting to get toward the evening, and it didn't seem as if we were going to be able to get out before nightfall. "Cam-kook, cam-kook, Marine, tonight you die!" could be heard again and again, and I wished that I was behind the gun.

Rahm and Keene meanwhile had moved up near the tree line to see if they could get a shot at the NVA soldier calling out, and when he cried out again, "Mahreene, Mahreene, tonight you die!" Rahm, who was the closest to the gook, yelled back, "You booku, dinky dou, you dinky dou!" and popped off a couple of slugs at the NVA soldier with his .45 pistol.

The soldier hiding behind a grave mound scrambled back into the jungle as Keene fired off a few rounds at the running soldier from his M-14. A large enemy force returned fire, and both Rahm and Keene ran back to our location.

Those of us that had not been medevaced were dragged back out of the LZ and taken toward the safety of the front of the house. We were all laid out, at the southeast corner of the hooch. It was the most secure area, protected form enemy fire by the hooch's location. It was now about 1650 hours, and it would soon be dark.

Giant Green Grasshoppers
Operation Foster; the Battle at Finger Lake AT 867533
November 21, 1967, D+8, 1130-1940 hours

A lot had happened in the hour since I was wounded. As I lay on the ground with other wounded Marines, all of a sudden the tree line was rocked by a barrage after barrage of intensive artillery fire coming from the artillery batteries on Hill 65. For fifteen minutes round after round was dropped in the area, and I wondered how anyone could survive a bombardment like that. Yet, I wondered if it was enough to keep the enemy away.

When the artillery stopped, several UH-34s and four CH-46 helicopters appeared overhead and began to circle above.

We're all going to be helilifted out, I was thinking, as the choppers began their descent. I knew that if they landed, we were going to have to make a run for it. At the same time, I wished that I was behind the gun to provide cover for the choppers as they came in. The LZ remained hot, I knew that.

While I wanted to be medevaced out, I also feared that the choppers were going to be shot at and wanted to wave them away from the danger I knew was still present. They didn't know the strength of the enemy force in the tree line; they wouldn't be able to land and take us all out without getting hit hard, and I feared what was about to happen as soon as they started to land.

It will be a slaughter if they try to land where the medevac choppers had tried to land. The greatest danger for a landing chopper was at those last few seconds just before touching down while it was hovering just a few feet off the ground. The enemy knew this, and we knew it. I wanted to get back to my gun, but I didn't know where it was or what condition it was in. I had last seen Rahm carrying it in pieces into the house where Jones and Marty were. The grenade's concussion had caused my legs to become paralyzed. They were cold and numb; I couldn't feel them at all. They wouldn't respond when I tried to move them. I wondered if the gun was repairable. It had been hit three times already on this operation.

As the helicopters circled overhead, the enemy increased the barrage of automatic rifle fire being fired at us. Green tracers were once again being shot at us, at a steady flow and someone from Lima Company opened up in response. They were firing red tracers across the lake toward the enemy from the east side of the lake near where the tree line ended and the open rice paddies began. They were firing to our right where we had sensed the enemy buildup was occurring near the edge of the tree line and the lake.

It must be a sixty; it sounds like one of ours, I thought. I felt useless seeing the exchange of bullets and not being able to shoot back. If the supporting Hueys needed a smoke grenade to mark where the gooks were, the green tracers they were firing at us gave the enemies' position away.

Two Huey gunships came in low over the lake at treetop level. They appeared directly behind Lima Company and began strafing the tree line directly behind the house on our side of the lake. The choppers were flying barely above the top of the hooch when they fired their rockets into the thick underbrush. As the rockets exploded, and the choppers pulled off, a barrage of green tracers were shot at them in return. [202]

At the same time a group of NVA soldiers opened up at us from our left side from along the tree line that ran south away from us toward Phu Phong (2). This time, Second Platoon responded with machine-gun fire from across the open rice paddy fields and the enemy intensified their firepower directing their fire power toward them with renewed determination, at the same time they were firing at Lima Company, and us.

I started to think that when the Hueys come back to strafe the area, the helicopters would be landing near the embankment to the left of the hooch as it remained the most secure location possible for an evacuation of all of us. I didn't know how I would get to the choppers, but somehow I knew we all would make it.

The Hueys came in again and again, flying in low and slow, strafing the tree line in front of us and the south tree line that ran toward Phu Phong (2). The Hueys then fired rockets into a tree line about five hundred yards away from our position.

They must be seeing other enemy movement, I was thinking. The enemy in the tree line in front of us and along the southern tree line near us must have felt secure enough to believe the Hueys would not open up on them because they were so close to us, but the helicopter gunships opened fire on them from the side and in response, the enemy opened up on us with increased viciousness. The NVA appeared to have received new reinforcements, and they were not leaving; they were sticking around to finish off the platoon they had cornered.

The helicopters all of a sudden descended rapidly. Like giant green grasshoppers, they dropped right into the middle of the open rice paddy fields a klick southwest of us.

The first chopper landed with its tail end facing toward the south edge tree line. It was about 300 yards away from us and had landed about eighty yards from the tree line.

They're going to get hit bad, I was thinking. *They're landing right smack in front of where the majority of the NVA are.*

At the same time, I was thinking that they had landed too far away for any of us to be able to be run out to the choppers to be evacuated.

Marine Masters Of the Trade
Operation Foster; the Battle at Finger Lake AT 867533
November 21, 1967, D+8, 1130-1940 hours

As soon as the first chopper touched ground, screaming, yelling, shouting Marines came flying out. It was only then I realized that the choppers were not intended to get us out but to bring Marines in.

Foxtrot 2/3 under the command of First Lieutenant Charles Paul Chritton, had landed. Immediately their First Platoon under the command of Lieutenant Charles Woodard, took heavy incoming fire, they engaged the enemy and moved in quickly to envelope around, cut-off any enemy that might try to escape north and moved in to sweep from along the river's banks. The other two platoons, Second Platoon, Lieutenant Brian Schmalz, and Third Platoon under the command of Roger Gunning, were sweeping in toward the tree line.

The Marine assault by helicopter must have taken the NVA by surprise as well because there was a pause in the outgoing gunfire being shot in our direction and in the direction of Second Platoon. It was not what they were expecting, and the NVA now switched their fire to engage the landing Marines, but it was too late, by then, the first squad of Marines having landed out in flooded rice paddy fields, had already cleared the open area in front of them and were by then about fifty yards to their right front. Some had secured cover behind rice paddy dikes, and all were engaging the enemy with heavy automatic fire power. Their concentrated fire was directed at the edge of the tree line where the enemy laid entrenched.

A machine-gun team was right behind the first squad of Marines that landed, and as the machine-gunner with the gun in his hands jumped out of the chopper, he landed with both feet planted firmly on the ground before he started running with the machine-gun at his hip.

A veteran, I thought as I saw him and his A-gunner run from the chopper. They crossed thirty yards of open terrain in seconds. Bullets kicked up small geysers of water and mud in front of the gun team as they ran for cover. When they got near a dike large enough to provide them protection, they dove forward, and immediately—almost before the gunner had fully hit the ground—the gunner had opened up with a forty-round burst of machine-gun fire. His A-gunner at his side had already unstrapped the 100-round belt from his chest to link to the ammo being expended through the gun. To their right, their ammo humper was already firing away at the enemies' position with his M-16, covering for the gun team as they finished setting up and unleashed their first barrage of concentrated machine-gun fire.

The sound of the gun echoed loud and clear. The rapid hail of machine-gun bullets pierced through the valley with a song of revenge and power, smoke, heat, fear, and pain. The song of death and destruction, vengeance, freedom, and life was being sung by another machine-gun in the same basin, in the same theater we had sung our song just hours before. I treasured the sound. The gun's bullets were slicing through heavy undergrowth where the enemy was hiding and doing what it was meant to do.

The United States Marine Corps trains men to be masters of their trade, and now The Marines red fiery tracers sliding evenly across the rice paddy fields toward the enemies' entrenched position was evidence they were masters of the trade. The red-tracers crossed fields with the green tracers being shot in their direction. The enemy's tracers were sporadic, uneven, and wild. The Marine's fire was direct and constant. There was no jerky movement, no wild shooting—just even, destructive, pinpointed, and effective firepower being directed at the enemy at ground level right where they were hiding. Any enemy looking up from their trench lines and spider holes was going to get wasted.

Other choppers were landing, and Marines were disembarking and assaulting on line toward the tree line. The Marines were disciplined, coordinated, and professional unlike any movie could portray.

Crazy Marines, I was thinking. *Crazy, crazy Marines.* And I wished I was out among them, assaulting instead of being where I was lying on the ground, helpless and paralyzed. But I was only paralyzed in my legs; I could fire the gun, and I realized I understood what Sergeant Nelson had told us, "You don't die until you kill the bastard that killed you." I had shot and killed the enemy that had thrown the grenade at us as well as the other enemy soldier carrying the satchel charge. I'd seen the bullets tear through both of them, but I wanted to do more, I wanted to finish the job.

Squads of Marines all on line were advancing, firing their weapons from the hip in semi—and fully automatic rifle fire. M-79 men were lobbing grenades into the tree line in front of them. Farther up, a machine-gunner was firing his M-60 from the hip as he advanced John Wayne style just like in the war movies, yet here it was, all so very real. The bullets were real, and the enemy was real.

About 300 yards farther west of where the first wave of Marines had landed, I could see other helicopters landing and more Marines unloading and moving toward the tree line that was farther away from us and from where the first platoon of Marines had landed.[203]

Marine Revenge
Operation Foster; the Battle at Finger Lake AT 867533
November 21, 1967, D+8, 1130-1940 hours

The enemy was boxed in with their backs to the lake. As soon as the choppers cleared the area, Hill 65 began to drop artillery rounds across the lake. Recon inserts were calling in the artillery barrage, adjusting the rounds for the cannon cockers on Hill 65 as enemy soldiers were attempting to escape by swimming across the western tip of Finger Lake.

Huey gunships soon were strafing the tree line, closer to us, ahead of the advancing Marines. Farther out, you could still see green tracers being fired at the Marines and the gunships and I realized we had truly engaged a professionally disciplined and worthy opponent.

The Huey gunships then turned around and strafed the area east toward the advancing Marines, catching the enemy from behind. Another Huey gunship shot off rockets into the dense jungle area. It seemed as if when one gunship lifted up, another ship took his place. Two, three, four gunships; it seemed were all in a row working together on this side of the lake, moving in a northeast direction while unleashing their destructive and ferocious firepower into the central part of the thick tropical forest.

Smoke rose up from where the rockets exploded and I was glad the battle with the exploding rockets, grenades, and automatic fire was occurring far from us. It was heartening that others were now fighting the enemy force that had earlier engaged us in battle.

Were there that many enemy soldiers? I wondered as 100 yards west of us, Marines were beginning to enter the tree line. That distance and firefights going on indicated a larger force than I had thought had been present. Were the enemy spread out that far? After the Marines entered the tree line, much of the incoming fire being shot at us stopped. The first squad of Marines I had seen land closest to us still remained out in the open rice paddy field, providing cover as other Marines west of them moved into the tree line to sweep east toward our position.

A yellow smoke grenade was popped, an indication they had taken casualties, and soon a medevac chopper landed out in the open field and a wounded Marine or two were loaded on board.

Squads of Marines remained out in the open and continued to provide cover, waiting for the sweeping Marines to come abreast of them. Their landing and initial firepower had caused the enemy to run northwest into the heart of the tropical jungle, but there, the NVA ran first into the gunships. Some tried to swim across the lake, others ran into the main Marine assault force that had landed farther west of us and were now moving southeast toward our location. The enemy was now scattered throughout the dense jungle, and they were being systematically destroyed.

We could hear hundreds of rounds being fired in the deep and dense jungle about two hundred meters in front of us. Grenades were exploding in the deep underbrush, and their muffled sounds were followed by automatic rifle fire. The enemy may not have expected this type of heliborne air assault and now they were caught in a trap. When all seemed lost, Marines had gotten Sparrow hawked in to rescue us, and they were now wreaking revenge; I wondered who they were.

Medevac Our Wounded
Operation Foster; the Battle at Finger Lake AT 867533
November 21, 1967, D+8, 1130-1940 hours

With so many ground troops in the area, Wilson called for a medical evacuation, and the word was passed to get ready for those who could to provide cover for them. While the area was not totally secured, Wilson wanted to get out our priority one wounded Marines out.

Doc Mac had those wounded taken out to the medevac area according to the seriousness of their wounds. Jackie Williams and Morales carried me and Pridemore over to the side of the embankment near the sandy shoreline. Pridemore had been out cold for the longest time, but now he seemed alert. Both of us were laid out among the last of the wounded from our platoon that were to be medevaced.

I heard Doc Mac tell the Marine assigned to get us both on board that I was to be loaded on a chopper and not left behind. There was fear that the enemy might try and assault us one last time, if they were cornered, and he wanted to make sure both of us were evaluated.

Marty a short distance from Doc Marren near the hooch had been guarding and responding to incoming fire from that area when he heard a gunshot go off, and a short time later saw the Corpsman come out limping out of the small crater he had been in for awhile.

A Huey gunship escorted the first chopper that came in, and as they circled overhead the chopper landed and wounded Marines were loaded on board by priority according to their wounds. The first medevac went off without a hitch. The wounded were loaded on board and a second chopper came in, and they too came in and were gone without a problem.

With the medevac of Marines, the choppers also dropped off food and ammo for the platoon and medical supplies for the Corpsman.

As I waited, I still couldn't move my legs, but I could still fire the gun and wanted to, still things were not clear, as if I was seeing things and hearing things through thick fog.

The last chopper for the night came in and dropped off supplies, and both Perry and Pridemore were loaded on board. There was room for one more the door-gunner said as they were the last chopper for the night.

Jackie Williams and Morales picked me up, and while I was being carried over Doc Marren came limping up from a bullet wound to his calf. He said that he needed to be medevac instead of me. The Marine door gunner on the chopper protested that I had already been tagged, but the Corpsman insisted he needed medical help while all I had was a concussion from a grenade that wasn't serious. Doc Marren insisted I could be evacuated early the next morning.

As they were arguing the chopper began to take incoming fire, and with much hesitation, the pilot said, he was lifting off, no sooner were the words out of his mouth an incoming M-79 grenade exploded near the chopper door and the door gunner, took some shrapnel, with that the Corpsman jumped on board and the chopper lifted off and I was left behind.[204]

Morales and Williams brought me back to the corner of the house. Doc Mac was furious, and he questioned how Doc Marren could have gotten hit and had received a small bullet wound in the calf when throughout most of the battle he had never left the safety of a small hole in front of the hooch.

The Marines of Foxtrot 2/3
Operation Foster; the Battle at Finger Lake AT 867533
November 21, 1967, D+8, 1130-1940 hours

An hour later, all incoming fire had ceased. Aggie had been reassigned by Sgt. Whiteside to guard our right flank near the small trail on the right side of the hooch that led into the tree line. Somehow, Aggie hadn't gotten the word that Marines were moving toward us. He had just inserted a new twenty-round clip of ammo into his M-16 when he heard and saw movement in front of him.

Aggie rose to confront whomever it was that was coming toward him from the tree line. As he did, his M-16 got tangled in a low-hanging branch. When he pulled it free, he pressed down on the trigger. His rounds struck the dike's dirt embankment just as a Foxtrot Marine emerged out of the tree line.

"Don't shoot, Don't shoot, it's us! We're friendlies" cried out the Foxtrot Marine as he emerged out of the tree line.

"Man, I could have shot you," Aggie argued in an angry tone to conceal what had happened.

"Man, you almost did," replied the Marine.

The rescuing Marines emerged victorious. They had wreaked havoc and destruction upon the NVA soldiers that had ambushed us and had chosen to stay till the end. No prisoners or wounded enemy soldiers were taken; all the NVA they had encountered had been wasted. Not one surrendered or was given that opportunity; the sweep had been swift, powerful, and deadly. No time to stop and ask questions, just time to take names and do the job they had been trained to do. Death is the nature of war and today it was vengeance unleashed by the wrathful hand of Marine warriors, Marines who had tasted the pains of war and had hungered to pay back what was due.

The Marines of Foxtrot Company 2/3 were Sparrow hawked in to kill the enemy. That's what a Marine is trained to do, that's what a Marine grunt does best. A Marine kills the enemy; it's all part of the training coupled with pain and sorrow. It is part of the victory and part of the Marine Corps's pride to do our share, our duty for our country, and more if we get the chance when we are released to fulfill our own individual dreams of glory. It's what warriors have done in war, what the Marine Corps has done since its birth. It was moments like this when Marines are allowed to take the initiative to attack and be victorious that wins wars and makes the Marine Corps proud. War is cruel, filled with wrath and fierce anger, that's what won America's freedom and gained her glory. Compromise and holding back, has only added misery, fear, and more death. Failure to fight her wars with the goal of completely destroying the enemy into total submission only brings her shame and displays of weakness.

Today, Marines had done what Marines do best: they had been victorious and they had killed those who would have destroyed us without mercy and they had made us proud.

As the first Marines walked by, I wanted to run up and kiss those dirty, skuzzy, smelly Marines. I wanted to thank them, hug them; but you don't do that in war—you don't do that to a Marine. They were dirty, they were filthy, and they were well-seasoned Marines that had saved our lives. They were angry, and they had unloaded their fury upon the enemy.

The Marines of BLT, Foxtrot 2/3 had been told that we had suffered heavy losses that the NVA were crying out to us that they were going to finish us off that night. They knew that we were destined to die unless they came in and helped us out, and they had determined that this time, the enemy wasn't going to get away.[205]

The Marines of Foxtrot 2/3 landed with vengeance in their hearts and a thirst for blood. They were going to strike a heavy blow against the enemy, nothing was going to stand in their way, and they did just that. Many of them were veterans of many battles in Vietnam; some may have been there during Operation DeSoto, at the Gates of Hell, and in many other battles where they never saw the enemy, never saw the fruit of their labors, never saw a wounded or dead enemy soldier because they were quickly carried away from the battle scene.

But now, I could see that they were proud to have been allowed and finally been given the liberty and the opportunity to fight back against an enemy that didn't get away. They finally were able to see the enemy and were given that rare opportunity not often available in Vietnam to effectively deal Charlie a fatal blow and to see the evidence of the battle, the bodies of dead enemy soldiers, were there for them to see. It was an opportunity many Vietnam veterans longed for. Victory without seeing the evidence of your labors is not as sweet and strangely unsatisfying, especially when you have taken casualties.

Once you lose a friend in battle; once you see a Marine, a fellow American that has been fighting for freedom, die next to you—or you see him lying wounded at your side, righteous indignation arises within and the hunger for blood becomes part of your soul. The frustration of months of pain and the sorrows of war has a way of blinding your vision and sense of reason, but it's also that lack of concern for personal safety that dictates victory.

At the dawn of victory, there is no time to stop and reevaluate, to question what is right or wrong. There's a time for war and a time to kill, a time to eliminate your enemy, and to make sure he's dead. In the heat of battle, it's amazing what destructive power a lone Marine rifleman or a machine-gunner can wield. None of the NVA soldiers that chose to remain and fight survived the slaughter the Marines let loose that day.

Some NVA/VC troops took extra pains to police all their casings so that only the smell of their presence remained after a firefight and very little else. Not this time, while they remained Marines on the offensive shot at and killed a visible, viable, and tangible enemy. This time, we knew where the enemy was, and they weren't about to let any of them escape. And they didn't.

They Should Have Gotten Medals
Operation Foster; the Battle at Finger Lake AT 867533
November 21, 1967, D+8, 1130-1940 hours

When the Marines of Foxtrot 2/3 walked by us, they were grinning from ear to ear. They walked by me and the other wounded Marines and gave us the thumbs-up sign and the nod of comradeship. They had seen the dead enemy soldiers we had killed, not a small number by their estimation. The enemy force that they had encountered and killed, they said, was also worthy of confrontation; they were proud of us and only wished they had been with us during our firefight. They felt proud of themselves that they had been chosen to rescue other Marines, and they had done so and we were very proud of them. I would have gladly pinned a medal on each one of the men of Foxtrot Company, Second Battalion Third Marines.

If it hadn't been for them, we would have been killed that night. First Platoon, India Company would have ceased to exist. That evening, the enemy had the manpower, the opportunity, and desire to do just that. It would have been us at the end of the badgers' fierce and merciless hand; we had seen what they had done to innocent civilians, their overwhelming numbers would have ended a Marine platoon's existence and we would have gone down in history as one of the Corps' worst losses in Vietnam.

But today, the battle belonged to us, today was our day of victory, our day of glory and rejoicing, and Foxtrot had annihilated the enemy who in the end had misjudged and stayed too long to fight a platoon of Marines. They had not figured how a Marine platoon would respond when cornered. They had played a loser's hand while holding on to a full deck of cards, and they waited too long to lay their cards down. Perhaps they just didn't know our full strength or that only a few of us remained to fight or they misjudged our own determination to live because we held them back time and time again and had prevailed.

The enemy had planned and waited; that is what the NVA did best. They had patience and determination, but they got greedy today and wanted their fish heads with their rice and a side dish of spicy sauce. Because of this greed to kill off an entire platoon of Marines, they paid a heavy price. They had planned and waited, and the taste of the initial victory lingered in their mouths too long. They stayed to savor the victory in full. They waited a bit too long and while they danced with us, they were caught by surprise with the Marine's new tactical air assault operation.

It was the new Marine Corps way of doing things. It was what Vietnam had taught us. You dropped in on your enemy from the air by way of helicopters and right into the lion's den; you walked right through their front door through their living room and right into their family's altar. This was now twice that we had, through the results of our platoon's actions or inactions, eliminated a large NVA military unit. The hunters had become the hunted. This was war, what war was all about. This was how you kill or are killed in war. Today, it was their turn to die and they died.

The Brave and the Proud Among the Shadows of Fear and the Presence of Death
Operation Foster; the Battle at Finger Lake AT 867533
November 21, 1967, D+8, 1130-1940 hours

When Foxtrot Company came through the tree line, they joined up with the fire-team of Marines nearest the tree line who had rescued Keenan and Prescott. When they joined us, I could see the terror still present in the eyes of the rescued Marines. Their clothing had been torn; I could see how the enemy had torn off and taken some of their clothing and web gear. Prescott only had his trousers on. Dry blood covered Keenan's left shoulder where he had been shot.

Both of their faces were ashen in color as if all the blood had been drained from them. Keenan's eyes were fixed, his mind someplace else. His voice was muttering something, and his body was shaking. He had been dragged away from us by the enemy and had played dead to live. They both had been stripped of their weapons and most of their clothes. They had played possum in the midst of a fierce firefight between Marines and hard-core NVA soldiers and lived.

The NVA thought both Marines were dead; we thought they were dead. They could hear and smell the enemy bending over them, kneeling close by as they shot at us. They never moved while the enemy fired at us and while we fired back. Their faces now revealed the shadows of fear and the presence of death. Both Marines had an X carved into their foreheads, where the enemy had planned to put a bullet through their heads. But now they were alive but would forever have the presence of the death angel at their side.[206]

Red Dancer Does Not Travel At Night
Operation Foster; the Battle at Finger Lake AT 867533
November 21, 1967, D+8, 1130-1940 hours

As Foxtrot emerged out of the tree line, Second Platoon Marines made their way through the small opening in the gate with their wounded and joined us on our side of the wired fence.

As darkness began to fall, Captain Baggette got on line with Foxtrot's radioman. Foxtrot's CO was standing near where the wounded Marines were lying on the ground. A humble and cautious man, who chose his words well, he was talking to the wounded encouraging them. His company had taken, four casualties, since they landed. Two were high priority medevac and two routine medevacs. His radioman relayed the message from Captain Baggette, that India Six Actual wanted Foxtrot Six Actual to come around the lake with First and Second Platoons and meet up with him.

"Tell India Six that Red Dancer does not travel at night," replied First Lieutenant Chritton and once that message was relayed, the radio went silent.

Foxtrot 2/3 Company's CO then told our lieutenant to have our guys stand down; his men would stand perimeter watch and watch over us for the night.

Across the lake, Lima Company, with the help of artillery and fixed-wing air strikes, had finally driven the enemy from the far tree line at the outskirts of Quang Hue. The enemy had stayed and fought and had prevented Lima from coming around to help us, and the enemy had paid a heavy price. Late that evening, we could see the helicopters' blinking lights as two medevac choppers landed on the other side of the lake and picked up two of Lima's emergency wounded.

A short time later Captain Baggette called for a priority medevac. Cpl. Leroy Chambers and L/Cpl. Herbert E. Whitaker, from Third Platoon, were among those wounded that day and medevaced out.

Recap Of the Day's Events
Operation Foster; the Battle at Finger Lake AT 867533
November 21, 1967, D+8, 1130-1940 hours

When the realization began to set in for those of us that had survived the battle, we began to take count and inventory of our wounds and took into account of who had survived, and how many of us had been wounded. Of the thirty-five Marines in First Platoon, that had entered the battle area that day, only twelve remained that had not been seriously wounded. When the engineer assigned to our platoon, took off his web gear, he became aware of a bullet hole that went through his blasting cap's pouch. When he opened the blasting cap tin, he noticed the bullet had gone through the only spot a blasting cap was missing. Had the bullet struck any of the other caps in his pouch they would have exploded and he would have been a dead man. [207]

Of Coco For Aggie, And A welcomed Rain For Sgt. Gus
Operation Foster; the Battle at Finger Lake AT 867533
November 21, 1967, D+8, 1130-1940 hours

As Marines began to gather around, Aggie walked into the hooch, picked up the bamboo bed and placed it in the corner of the kitchen. He then placed a straw mat he had found down on top of it and his flak jacket and gear. Soon the hooch and area all around it was packed with Marines settling in for the night. With a fresh supply of meals and ammo, Aggie, using a small chunk of C-4, fixed himself a hot cup of cocoa from a C-rat pack. He poured the instant powdered cream that came in the small accessory packet into the canned tin cup, and stirred it. He had found himself a warm and secure spot inside the hooch in a corner of the kitchen area to sleep for the night and he sat down there to enjoy his cocoa.

It will be a nice place to sleep," he said to himself when he sat down on the bed and drank his cocoa. As he sat enjoying the quite evening, he looked up and there just a few feet away, was the rear door of the hooch, where what seems days ago, he had rushed through as bullets impacted the area all around him. He sat back against the wall, took in a deep sigh, and sipped his cocoa.

After we ate, Jones, grabbed two of the large six-foot round bamboo disks the Vietnamese used for threshing rice from where they had been in the rear of the hooch and rolled them out into the center of the courtyard in front of the hooch, where the dirt was hard packed. He laid one down then laid out our flak jackets on top and any extra utility shirts we had. Next, he laid our ponchos on top of the other disk. He and Marty then carried me over and laid me down in the middle of the disk. He took out my utility shirt from my backpack, and laid it over me, as well as his poncho liner, then he got in on one side and Marty on the other. Then they pulled the second disk with the plastic poncho coverings over us. Moments later it started to rain. With the realization that Marines were on watch, we fell into a deep sleep.

Once Second Platoon had settled in, Sergeant Gus came out from under the tree covering where the remnant of his platoon were gathered near a corner of the hooch and he stood out in the rain until he was soaking wet.

Our KIAs, O'Neil, Vaugle T., Taylor, Charles N. III.

Our Platoon's WIA's; Aguilar, Steven., Barela, Refujio., Cuch, Newman.,Jones, Michael., Sgt. Stamford, Zaryl, Sgt. Whiteside, Calvin, LaJeunesse, Herman, Keenan, James., Perry, James, Pridemore, Keith, Ezell, Jerry D E,

Purple Hearts For the Wounded
Operation Foster
November 22, 1967, D+9, 0800 hours

The following morning, although my legs remained partially numb and painful, circulation had returned and I was able to stand up and a short time later was able to walk around. The word was soon passed for those wounded and not tagged for evacuation to come up to the CP for evaluation. Colonel Barnard was coming out to our positions; we were told that he wanted to congratulate us personally and wanted to ceremoniously acknowledge those wounded with the award of the Purple Heart Medal.

Aggie went to Lieutenant Wilson and showed him the gash he had received on his leg when the grenade exploded and wounded both of us. Surprisingly, Aggie had no other visible wounds; after the Corpsman examined the cut and removed some of the shrapnel still embedded in Aggie's leg; the lieutenant approved his Purple Heart. Aggie was officially labeled WIANE (wounded in action not evacuated). I still had the large cardboard yellow medevac tag attached to my flak jacket, and was waiting to be medevac. We were instructed to get on line and await the colonel's arrival.

We stood waiting along the narrow trail near the lake's bank between the tree line and the back of the house where third Squad had been pinned down for most of the battle the day before.

Aggie and I were the farthest away in formation, and with my legs still weak from the explosion, I sat down on the dike to wait for the military brass to arrive. Other than a few cuts and bruises, my legs looked okay. I felt okay except for the throbbing pain down my legs and now and then a quick sharp needlelike pain that would shoot up and down my legs and spine.

Captain Baggette and the rest of the company by then had made their way around the lake and had joined us.

The first chopper landed and the colonel got off and walked toward the hooch on top of the rice paddy dikes where we had fought our fierce battle the day before. Others accompanying him stepped off into the muddy rice paddy fields, and they walked on line toward the hooch, something they wouldn't have been able to do twenty-four hours before.

A large Chinook helicopter landed out in an open rice paddy field, and out poured a number of individuals from the press and other high military brass and Vietnamese government officials. As they made their way around to the other side of the hooch, I felt they were desecrating sacred ground by walking so nonchalantly where we had fought our fierce battle the day before.

Captain Baggette greeted the visitors, and Colonel Barnard asked the captain about our battle the day before. Baggette began to tell him of the sniper that had him pinned down for a while on the other side of the lake, but the colonel interrupted him and asked about the battle on this side of the lake.

"Oh, you mean Larry's little thing," Baggette responded, and the veins on our lieutenant's neck stood out as he held back a verbal response to Baggette's snide remark.

Lieutenant Wilson gave the colonel a brief rundown of the battle and the enemy's determined will to stay and fight while emphasizing what his men had endured during the day and his gratefulness for sending out a Sparrowhawk unit to assist us.[208] The colonel listened and then moved on to ceremonially acknowledge those that were wounded and not evacuated.

As we waited, I sat there on the dike behind the hooch and watched the muddy rice paddy water bump up against the dike's wall. The blood shed by

Marines the day before was still flowing leisurely on the water's surface. News reporters had cut across the flooded rice paddy field on the other side, and their steps had stirred a wave that slowly nudged small bits of caked blood over the trampled-down rice plants and pressed it into the crevices of the dike's slippery wall.

Only a few feet from where I sat, Pfc. Vaughn T. O'Neil had been ripped open by machine-gun fire. Not far from where I sat, Charles N. Taylor III's body had been laid down after being shot in the head by an enemy sniper. Izzie and other Marines had been seriously wounded at the tree line and behind rice paddy dikes and grave mounds nearby, and their blood had been spilled on this battlefield of honor.

Many Marines from First Platoon were wounded and two killed the day before. They were the real heroes of yesterday's battle, those that died in war and who fought for life. They deserved the Purple Heart. I didn't feel I deserved it. I felt unworthy to receive the award among such Marine warriors.

Without looking around, I reached up with my left hand grabbed hold of the medevac tag Doc Mac had attached to my flak jacket, gave it a quick jerk, and it came off in my hand just as the colonel came around the corner of the hooch making his way toward where the wounded stood.

I crumpled the tag in my hand and quietly reached behind me, burying it on the other side of the dike in the bloodied rice paddy field. I buried the tag deep in the mud of yesterday's battle and sealed it in the back of my mind as a closed chapter in the battle of Finger Lake. When I withdrew my hand, it was full of mud and stained with the blood of fallen Marines. I quickly dried it on the green towel I wore around my neck and then dropped the soiled towel in the field behind us. Aggie, looking at what I had done, asked, "What are you doing?" I was embarrassed that he had seen what I had done.

"I'm not going to take it," I answered.

"What? You were wounded," Aggie said, "in battle!"

I shook my head no.

"You deserve it," he said, encouraging me to take it as the colonel's presence drew near. Aggie looked me in the eyes and shook his head, saying, "Man, you're brave!"

We stood up and turned to face the colonel and came to attention as he drew near. The colonel made his way down the line of Marines, congratulating and shaking the hands of the seven of us that remained in First Platoon that were wounded and not medevaced. As he made his way down, I was looking at those that remained of the original platoon. Counting the CP group, only twelve of us remained. He congratulated Aggie and came up to me as I was still standing in line, in formation. He asked if I was wounded, and I shook my head and said, "No, sir." He looked puzzled, but turned and made his way back. A short time later, we moved out.

Move Out and Count the Bodies
Operation Foster
November 22, 1967, D+9, 1100 hours

"Fire in the hole!" a Marine engineer shouted, and we covered our ears as the engineers blew the tunnel Marty had found inside the house. The tunnel had an outlet into the lake; One of the engineer's attached to the company had stripped down to his trousers, jumped into the lake, and explored its entrance. Then the engineers had him place a charge of C-4 at its mouth, and they blew it.

Late that morning, we swept in a southwest direction toward BLT Echo Company 2/3's position. Echo had been helilifted to establish a blocking position two klicks southwest of us (AT 840519). As we prepared to move out, the helicopter pilots that had dropped off Echo Company reported that a large enemy force was seen fleeing northwest from the top of the lake from the southern tree line where we had engaged the enemy the day before, and plans were changed to try and engage them.

India and Lima Company 3/7, reinforced with BLT Foxtrot 2/3 Marines, now swept on line through the area the enemy had moved their troops through the day before to attack us at the bend of Finger Lake. As we moved through the area, we began to get sniper fire, which was the usual ploy the enemy used to stall any advance on their positions. This often gave them the time they needed to withdraw from the area. To counter this, Hotel Company 2/3 was helilifted at 1435 hours and dropped off a couple of klicks north of us (AT823538), where they set up a blocking force as we swept toward them.

Meanwhile, Third Platoon, India Company, was given the task to sweep south along the south bank of Finger Lake and they found fifteen fully clothed dead enemy soldiers. Some were partly buried. The dead enemy soldiers were found at the corner of the lake and tree line where they had first launched their attack upon us and later mounted several assaults from that location. Third Platoon also recovered their weapons and other equipment.

The company then swept back to that location, then north again until we came into a clear area, and I knew that we would pay a heavy price if we swept out across the open rice paddy field without knowing where the enemy actually was.

The battalion commander, who was getting situation reports from recon inserts, was informed that indeed there was a high concentration of enemy soldiers in the tree line in front of us.

While we waited, the recon team called in artillery and then a bird-dog called in air strikes into the dense forested area. Echo and Golf companies then swept around the tip of the lake and then in a southeast direction, counterclockwise toward us. After the air strikes, Hotel 2/3 swept toward us through the strike area as did Echo and Golf companies. There was no enemy contact.[209]

That evening, India, Lima, and Hotel set in together for the night. We set in the same area near the hooch where we had engaged the enemy the day before. We were west about a quarter mile west of where the hooch was, that was blown near where Taylor had gotten killed. We sat in for the night in the thick jungle.

As I set up the gun, I was looking south through the leaves, bushes, over-hanging vines and tall palm trees and caught a glitter of sparkling lights coming from the blinking helicopters tail lights landing out in the rice paddy fields. Soon a number of Marines came running out and the CP set in at the tree line directed them toward First or Second Platoon positions. Thirteen new men reported in, to our platoon.

Back to the Old French Fort
Operation Foster
November 23, 1967, D+10, 0700 hours

Early the next morning, we started sweeping on the west side of the lake back toward the house by the bend in the river where we had been ambushed on the twenty-first. As we traveled through the heavy tropical jungle that abutted the lake, I could smell the enemies' presence. The smell of *nuoc nam* sauce remained in the air.

Fear was also in attendance, it hung suspended in the air, and I didn't know if it was the enemy's fear or mine. The area brought back memories and fears I had not acknowledged the day of the battle, it was fear our new replacements hadn't experienced. The new men as they walked ahead of me smelled like Dial soap, and their brand-new utilities, were making too much noise. I feared enemy soldiers were hearing and smelling their freshness in the bush.

Over half the platoon hadn't been under fire, and I was wondering how they would react. One thing about combat was that you never know how you're going to react until the bullets begin to fly. I feared for the new Marines and what they might soon experience; once we were hit, with something other than sniper fire. We swept through the area without incident.

When we arrived at the hooch, we stood by as First Reconnaissance Battalion divers made a detailed search for underwater caves at the west banks of Finger Lake near the hooch, but no significant findings were uncovered.[210]

As we made our way back to the old French fort position, it seemed to me that it was all of a sudden surprisingly quiet. This was a different type of cautious concern, as if the oceans waves were withdrawing from the seashore, as if someone was holding back the winds from the four corners of the world.

Recon inserts had also reported a decrease in enemy sightings as well as enemy activity, and that was disturbing.

Our platoon's strength now stood at twenty-seven men, including the new men and the CP group. We were once again low on supplies and hadn't eaten all day. When we arrived at the French fort, it started to rain, it rained all night.

A Heat Tab Lesson For the New Kid
Operation Foster
November 24, 1967, D+11, 0700 hours

The next morning, it was still raining, mostly a light drizzle. Dumont had secured C-rats for us, and one of the new kids sat down next to us and broke open his box of C-rats. He made himself a heating stove from the small can that held the crackers like he had seen us do. Then he went and got his poncho and heat tab. We all knew what was going to happen next, and everyone started to gather around him.

Being proud of his new stove, he looked at us assemble around looking at him, while the drizzling rain came down.

He smiled, and then did what new guys often do. He lit the heat tab, placed his can of C-rats on the stove to heat, and to keep the rain out, he pulled his poncho over his head and over the stove to keep the rain out.

In less than a minute, the smokeless chemical tablet had released its obnoxious sulfuric acidy smell and his poncho came flying off.

He stood up, his mouth opened wide, gasping for air. His eyes were watering, and his nose had turned a bright red. He looked at us as we sat nearby and all in unison were shaking our heads in disbelief at him.

As he looked on, we lit small round chunks of C-4 to heat up our meals. The C-4 burned hot, clean and fast. In less than a minute, our meals were ready to eat.

When it started to clear, we moved out. Company-size, soaking wet and muddy, we swept in a counterclockwise direction along the north bank of the Song Thu Bon River, crossing numerous rice paddies and open fields.

A Bird Dog pilot circling overhead, dropped down low and tossed out his window a small package into the middle of the rice paddy, near us.

A Marine ran out and secured the package, and brought it back to the CO. The package was, a Leatherneck Magazine wrapped around a can of Budweiser.

We turned to move out toward the area where we had made contact with the enemy on the nineteenth.

A short time later, Second Platoon, walking point, made contact with a small enemy force. First Platoon was right behind them and we deployed to envelop around, but the enemy quickly broke contact and disappeared. We stayed deployed in the flank position as a medevac was called. Two Marines were wounded from Second Platoon: Cpl. William C. Burdge and Sgt. Frank Joslin. Both had been in Second Platoon for some time.

After the choppers lifted off, Second Platoon moved out, and we continued our sweep. As we headed back, we were bringing up the rear.

For some reason, I felt the enemy had panicked and had opened up before Second Platoon had fully walked into their ambush. Perhaps they also had gotten in new men, and the inexperienced soldiers had opened up prematurely. First

Platoon took no casualties and only received a few sniper rounds that were shot in our direction.

By midafternoon, we moved toward the southeast side of Phu Long (1) and a number of choppers began to land out in the open fields. They had brought out hot chow for us. It was turkey, mashed potatoes, gravy, and biscuits in hot portable mini-tubs. It was Thanksgiving Day, and we didn't know it.

By the time First Platoon's turn came up to enter the chow line, only biscuits and gravy remained, but we were glad to get that. The last men in the line were Dumont and Lieutenant Wilson.[211]

Search and Destroy
Operation Foster
November 25, 1967, D+12, 0700 hours

The following morning, we moved out company-size, searching for the NVA. By the end of the day we had little contact. However, recon inserts high in the mountains overlooking the area continued to report enemy soldiers moving away from our units, as we swept through an area.

Our mission for the operation was to capture and destroy enemy forces within the operations area, to destroy their supplies and facilities. We had destroyed much of their fortified facilities, many of the hamlets had been honeycombed with tunnels and fighting positions. We had captured a quantity of their food supplies, over 84 tons of processed rice, ready for consumption and by removing much of the population from the area we had deprived the enemy of the labor force they often forced into service to meet some of their military needs. Other than our platoon's contact with a large enemy force, for three consecutive days, the operation had not had much success in capturing or destroying the enemy.

CHAPTER EIGHTEEN

The Battle Plans Are Drawn
Operation Foster AT 873517
November 26, 1967, D+13, 1120-2350 hours

At 0800 hours, we moved out early to be a blocking force for two platoons of Marines from Lima and Foxtrot Company that were sweeping from Phu Long (2) toward Hill 11 located northeast of us. India Company was to sweep along the river, then north toward Hill 11 and depending on who flushed out the enemy, the others were to then set in as a blocking force or sweep along to force the enemy toward who ever had the advantage. The rest of Foxtrot or Lima Company would join in later if they were needed.

Shortly before noon, a platoon of Foxtrot Marines, from 2/7 (Second Battalion Seventh Marines), were sweeping south toward a small hill and made contact with a small number of enemy soldiers. The point of contact was located on the west side of the hill half a klick from where we had gotten hit out in the open rice paddies on the nineteenth and the twentieth. The enemy however, quickly broke contact and the lead Foxtrot platoon aggressively went in pursuit of the unit as well as the enemy snipers they had spotted near the top of the small hill.

Ten minutes later, the Lima Company platoon from 3/7 sweeping west approaching the same hill also made contact with an entrenched squad-size enemy force. The Lima Company platoon counted twelve entrenched enemy soldiers, on the east side of the small hill, and this time the enemy wasn't moving. They were less than a klick (nine hundred meters) away from the Foxtrot Platoon that had made contact on the north side of the same hill. The hill had an elevation of only 10 feet above the rice paddy fields that surrounded it, but it was heavily forested with several levels of grades, and cut out that made it difficult to judge the full height of the hill.

The Foxtrot Platoon in pursuit on the west side of the hill was being led by Lieutenant Krebs, a pug nose, medium built Marine, that commanded his troops by the book. They had estimated the enemy sniping at them to be a squad-size group of enemy soldiers that didn't seem to be heavily armed as they had only been fired on them with carbine and small arms rifle fire. As the platoon made its way through thick brush, all of a sudden, a couple of enemy soldiers ran in front of the platoon, into a thick jungle area.

An aerial observer (AO), R. Lararmy, Benchmark 15 was on station at the onset of both firefights. From above he observed fifteen to twenty-five well-equipped NVA soldiers wearing green uniforms and foliage as camouflage, laying in wait for the Marines, further up the hill. The pilot, John S. Longo, fired off four 2.75 WP rockets on the enemy force, and the AO immediately called in and directed air strikes on the entrenched enemy positions. With the hill surrounded by rice paddies, Longo noted that this time, the enemy "shouldn't get away."

The Foxtrot platoon commander at about this time ordered his platoon to assault up the hill, after the fleeing two enemy soldiers they had seen running away from them.

As soon as the platoon hit the tree line, they began to get heavier rifle fire, but the platoon commander kept pressing on. Once they were a good distance into enemy territory they came under heavy enemy fire.

When our captain heard that both platoon's from Lima 3/7 and the Foxtrot 2/7 had made contact, he hurried us to set up our blocking force position on Hill 11. The hill was located about a klick away from Hill 10, where the other Marines had made contact. They were supposed to be sweeping toward us, and we were supposed to be set in on Hill 11, waiting for them, but things change quickly in war, and so we quickly swept through the long tree line along the sandbar that ran on the north side of Football Island and hurried to get to our blocking position.

Captain Baggette believed all along the NVA main force was located on the east side of Finger Lake. Hill 10 he figured may very well be the place where the major company-size battle of Operation Foster was going to be fought; it might be there where the elusive enemy force our recon inserts had been spotting and we had been searching for might make a stand and engage us in a company-size firefight. Intelligence reports had indicated all along that the enemy had been setting up battalion-size ambush sites, hoping to engage a large Marine unit in battle. On Hill 10, they seemed to have set their boundaries, bunkered down, and got their wish.

Battle Plans Executed
Operation Foster AT 873517
November 26, 1967, D+13, 1120-2350 hours

We moved out, quickly sweeping east then stopped before crossing over a large open series of rice paddy fields between the sandbar and Hill 11; we would have to secure that hill to set up our blocking force on the other side.[212]

We moved out in three columns across the open fields and easily reached Hill 11 without incident. We swept over the hill, and once on the other side, we could see smoke still rising from where the gunships rockets and the artillery he had called in had taken place. On two sides of that hill enemy forces had engaged two platoons of Marines.

Before us were a number of rice paddy fields and several graveyards with a series of various-sized grave monuments. As usual, the graves were grouped around the corners of the rice paddies with several grave mounds at each location. Another series of grave mounds ran alongside the base of Hill 10. [213]

The Lima Platoon managed to secure the tree line on the east side of Hill 10, but kept getting hit by sporadic gunfire that kept them from advancing forward.

The landscape surrounding the small hill was covered with a series of rising tiers of elevations each forty to fifty yards in width. In-between and on each tier were grave sites, large bushes and dirt cut-outs, from erosions and some were man made. The landscape would present a problem as well as advantageous covering sites if we made it to that point.

Meanwhile the Foxtrot Platoon was now pinned down and was coming under heavy sniper fire as well as a heavy volume of automatic weapons and small arms fire. A short time later, the enemy began to drop 60mm mortar rounds on them.

With the Foxtrot Platoon pinned down under heavy machine-gun fire, the Foxtrot Company commander deployed his two other platoons around the hill to envelope around counterclockwise in an attempt to outflank the enemy soldiers.

As we sat and waited, as to what we were going to do, I recalled having seen the Foxtrot2/7 Platoon commander whose unit was now pinned down back at Liberty Bridge, before the operation. At that time, he was having his platoon fall in and out as well as having them march in formation. He had them, practicing assaults with fixed bayonets and doing flanking movements the type that would never be effective in the jungle terrains of Vietnam. He seemed gung ho and inexperienced and I wondered how his troops were doing.

In Vietnam, there really weren't any organized battles where we knew for certain where the enemy was dug in and waiting for us to attack. Firefights often began by chance meetings, but just as often, it was the enemy who picked the time and place. But once the firefight got going, things never worked out the way anyone might have planned. I had learned that after the first round was fired, anything goes; prior decisions made by company commanders, lieutenants, or squad leaders could have great as well as devastating consequences especially if they tried to follow through on their plans when the enemy hadn't read the same script and wasn't responding as predicted or as may have been planned. One minor change of plans and a unit could end up being the hunter or the hunted; it all depended on a minor decision by a Marine, a squad leader or platoon commander and that could result in fatal consequences or great victories on either side.

Semper Fidelis
Operation Foster AT 873517
November 26, 1967, D+13, 1120-2350 hours

Shortly after noon, a priority emergency medevac was called for a wounded Lima Marine. As the HMM-363 chopper prepared to land, they took heavy gunfire and were unable to medevac the wounded Marine. A Huey gunship flying escort also took fire. They responded by unloading over four thousand rounds of machine-gun fire into the entrenched enemies' position. A landing strip for the emergency medevac would have to be secured before another attempt was made.

At 1300 hours, another gunship appeared over the entrenched enemy's position being piloted by a Marine named Lyons and an AO by the name of Wanner. They called in three air strikes, marking the spots where they had seen enemy activity with four WP rockets.[214] The called in air strikes destroyed six structures and five meters of a trench line.

The NVA knew the Marines' personal code of conduct "Never leave a wounded Marine in the battlefield and never surrender," and they always planned to use this knowledge to their advantage. The NVA would often open up on a patrol and then wait for reinforcements to come to the rescue and then ambush the saviors. In this manner, the NVA had learned to use wounded Marines as bait and lured others into a predetermined kill zone. Another tactic that seemed to be working well for them was to use runners to bait a unit to go in pursuit of them. They had done this on the nineteenth, twentieth, and twenty-first; and now they were using the platoon from Foxtrot as bait. Meanwhile, it seemed as if they were a large enough unit to keep the Lima Platoon bogged down on the east side of the hill as well. They would have also known by now, we were a short distance away but would have to cross open rice paddy fields to get to the south side of the small hill.

On the other side of the hill, Foxtrot's two platoons had started their offensive movement to get around to assist their pinned-down platoon. They did not receive any resistance until they were a good distance away from the base of the hill. Once they had advanced well into the bushy and tiered northwest section of the hill, the disciplined and well-equipped entrenched enemy soldiers opened fire on them, hitting them from the top of the hill and from their right side with grenades and heavy automatic rifle fire.

It was a classic L-shaped ambush, and Foxtrot's two platoons were now caught smack in the middle of it.

Marines are trained to "fight until we kill our enemy or until he kills us." Even then, according to Sergeant Nelson at MCRD, we weren't allowed to die until we killed the bastard who had killed us.

Semper fidelis, Latin for "always faithful," the Marine Corps's motto, was adopted in 1868. It was a constant resolution of ours. It was part of our training, part of our life, an anchor in a sea of turmoil. You might fear death, but you did not leave Marines in the hands of our enemy. You did not run or hide. You killed or were killed; there was no retreat, and you never surrender your weapon. James Keenan, who had been medevaced to the rear after the Finger Lake battle, was rescued by Rahm and Keene because of Marine faithfulness. They knew where he and Prescott were and ran back into the enemy's den to get them out. Yet Keenan had to give a written account of why he had allowed the enemy to take his weapon and clothes. He had to itemize all the equipment the enemy had taken from him. He had let go of his weapon, something you are trained from boot camp never to do; but sometimes, circumstances are beyond mottos, beyond tradition, comprehension, bravery and honor. It is then, that wisdom plays an important part in a Marine's life, and because of that, Keenan had survived because of his presence of mind in the midst of battle and in the process he had also saved Prescott's life.

Semper fidelis to grunts, besides meaning "always faithful," also meant corporate pride, mutual dependence, and brotherhood. Keenan had exemplified this. There is a sense that you belong to one another, and you know you can depend on your fellow Marine and that he can depend on you. This belief is what is also meant by the Marine Esprit De Corps, a common spirit and bond of camaraderie, enthusiasm, and allegiance. It is often mingled with pride, unity, blood, and guts. That was what, to the Marine Corps grunt, made victory at war possible against overwhelming odds. It was all part of the dreams of glory in fields of fire. It was honor and despair, joy and shame—it was all the same part of the common bond Marines share in war.

Marines are trained both to follow orders and to be independent warriors. In the Marine Corps, there was no absence of leadership. We were trained to take the war to our enemies' front door, if necessary, to achieve our objectives or to rescue the life of a fallen Marine against the odds. It was this type of action in the heat of battle that made Marines unique men of war. Trained to go on the offensive, Marines attack when ambushed—they don't dig into defensive positions, but attack. We follow orders, and today, First Platoon, India Company was ordered by our commanding officer to stand up and assault across open fields of fire to the base of a small hill where the enemy was waiting and entrenched in fortified bunkers. The enemy had successfully pinned down more than a company of Marines, so, we knew they were well armed and disciplined and they were waiting for us; and we got up and made ready to get on line. This time, there would be no cover for me or the gun, this time I knew I would be carrying the gun at the hip, and we would be assaulting while firing and the enemy would be firing back at us.

Assault Across A Graveyard
Operation Foster AT 873517-873522
November 26, 1967, D+13, 1120-2350 hours

The enemy had the two platoons from Foxtrot 2/7 in a killing zone while the other platoon remained pinned down under heavy enemy fire 300 meters away. At the same time, on the east side of the hill, they were unleashing a barrage of fire on the Lima Company platoon that was trying to move up Hill 10.

At 1300 hours, India Company was committed to join the battlefield. We were no longer a blocking or a sweeping force but an assault force, and we prepared to move out.

The NVA had attacked defenseless civilian villages. The civilians meant nothing to them, but they attacked and killed them in our TAOR;[215] and we came out to find them, to search them out, and to destroy them. They knew it, and they remained and were prepared to engage Marines in battle. This was the day of battle, they had chosen, and we were Marines and committed to do battle. Back at headquarters, Colonel Barnard, wondered about our units, how well we were trained, how we would do.[216]

Chance encounters with the enemy like the one we had experienced at the old French fort on the twentieth had a way of escalating into full-blown battles. Mistakes made on either side can be costly. The NVA were entrenched on a small hill. They knew Marines were on the north side of the hill, where some of their elements had a platoon of Marines pinned down, they were also keeping the Lima platoon Marines from advancing on them from the east side of their hill.

Now, as they looked across open rice paddy fields, they could see a company of Marines getting ready to cross over to engage them. They had laid out their battle plans; it was their battle game that was going to be played out. The pawns on both sides with their specialties and fire-power were being moved into position. The officers, the squad and team leaders, the grenade launchers, the automatic rifleman, the sniper's and machine-gunner's, were being placed at certain spots and as we all wondered what the enemies tactic were and I knew it was their chessboard we were playing on.

The hill we were to take was an island surrounded by rice paddy fields on three sides. The terrain leading to the small hill had a gentle rise to it, but at times there were layers of dirt cut out between the two hills.

A network of tree lines and deep tropical jungle area covered the hill's west side. From there, the tree line connected to the dense forested area at the base of Finger Lake. If we approached the hill by moving clockwise around that tree line, the enemy could pin us down for hours as they had Second Platoon on the nineteenth, and that route would take too long. Securing the base of the hill for medevac extractions was a priority. Already two medevac choppers had been shot up, trying to come in to extract Foxtrots wounded.[217] Surely they would not expect an assault across open rice paddy fields. If they had, it would be a mistake, it seemed to me, to entrench themselves on the small hill without a way out. Mistakes like that made in combat cannot be recalled once the battle begins.

As we prepared to move out, Lyons and his AO, still flying overhead, spotted seven to ten NVA in full uniform, with packs and rifles, moving into trench positions, across the field from where we were. They informed Beechnut 6, our company commander, they had air support available for us; but our captain chose instead to call in an artillery strike, and once the artillery rounds began to land, the ground FO adjusted the rounds until they were impacting the area where the enemy soldiers had been spotted.

At 1300 hours, as most of the smoke cleared away, we were ordered to assault. We got on line and moved out.

While we had not received any incoming, there was uneasiness present as we started across on line in assault positions. The journey across was not going to be easy. Some of us could use the dikes, others would have to cross over flooded rice paddy fields, still others would have to maneuver around large bush clusters, as well as scattered grave mounds. As we stepped out, I knew it was going to be a long day.

Behind us, some of the ARVNs became uneasy at the silence and began to fire M-79 rounds over our heads and into the base of the hill and the tree line in front of us. A fired M-79 round fell short and dropped at the feet of a Marine walking on a dike. It exploded and threw him back a few feet. He called for the Corpsman as did others around him. Shaken and dazed when Doc Mac got to him, neither the Doc nor the Marine could find any wound.

"Check again," he cried out to Doc. "Check again!" But still, not a wound was found. The Marine got up and rejoined the assault.

As we got closer, we began to get scattered carbine fire. When we were fifty yards from the hill, the enemy opened up with automatic and machine-gun fire.

Third Squad advancing online to our left, instead of getting down and seeking cover, returned fire as they ran forward across the rice paddy fields. The rest of the platoon did likewise, advancing as we fired at the enemies' entrenched positions. It may not have been what the enemy had planned.

Their initial fire had been fierce, but then it quickly stopped. The enemy may have been taken by surprise at what we were doing. They may have planned for us to get down while out in the open and from there return fire. Most military units would have done that. Then they would have plenty of time to keep us pinned down for a while as they fired upon us; but now the platoon was rapidly advancing on line firing at them, and they stopped firing and adjusted their positions.

A couple of NVA soldiers on both sides of the tree line kept firing at us as we advanced toward the base of the hill. Our M-79 men on both sides of the platoon targeted those positions and they soon went silent.

We continued to advance as new incoming fire peppered the rice paddy field in front of us. Lieutenant Wilson, with his radioman at his side, was a prime target and a sniper's round struck the lieutenant's left foot. He felt the pain as other incoming rounds kicked up dust and dirt all around us. At the time, he was hit, the lieutenant was talking on the radio to Third Squad, which was advancing ahead of the rest of the platoon on our far left side. Wilson was worried the squad was getting too far ahead of everyone else and wanted to keep his platoon on line during the assault when the bullet knocked him down.

Art Toy, his radioman, a step ahead of the lieutenant kept moving until the cord on the handset jerked him back. As Toy fell backward, he thought he had been hit. When I saw both of them fall, on my left side, I thought both had been hit.

While it was not a good position for the gun, I dropped to one knee and opened fire at the enemy; others to my right also stopped and began to do the same.

Third Squad was now ahead of all of us and they just kept moving toward the hill. I shot my machine-gun rounds in front of them to provide cover, and together we sprayed the area, while I swept machine-gun fire to their right, sweeping the base of the hill left to right, right to left. A hundred rounds left the gun quickly, and Marty scrambled to load another belt as the gun's bullets flew through the gun and ripped the air across the rice paddy fields.

Jones with Aggie carrying the other gun were advancing to the left of us; they were sandwiched in between First and Third Squad on Wilson's left side.

Aggie, hearing my gun open up, stopped on a grave mound and opened fire, John Wayne style, from the hip. He had already attached a 200-round belt, and he just kept the trigger pulled back, firing at the base of the hill in front of Third Squad. His red tracers were bouncing off the top of rice paddy dikes ahead of the Marines assaulting the hill.

After he had expended most of his bullets, he saw the gun's barrel smoking and feared he may be burning up the barrel. But he didn't want to stop firing. He hurried to get on line with the Marines advancing on the hill, expended the last of his rounds, and then sought cover by a small tree.

Jones, thinking Aggie had stopped to reload the gun or because he had a misfire, dropped on his knees and provided cover for him.

Aggie fearing he might melt the gun barrel decided to get on his knees and change the barrel. He unhooked the locking latch and grabbed the barrel with his bare hand. Suddenly feeling a burning pain, he remembered he was supposed to use the asbestos glove to change the barrel. With a badly burned hand, he still managed to change the barrel, reloaded the gun, and ran to get on line with the Marines that had by then reached the base of the hill.

As soon as Third Squad reached the tree line, the NVA soldiers seemed to have re-grouped and they unleashed another volley of incoming rounds from the west side of the hill.

The enemy must have reached their secondary fighting position, I was thinking, and were now firing at us from that location.

While we were still out in the open field, Third Squad continued to press forward, and one of their fire-teams was rapidly moving up a crest of the small hill.

Rahm, at the center of Third Squad's advance, had almost reached the second layer of raised ground from the base of the hill when he found himself all alone and ahead of everyone else. He looked back and saw that some of Third Squad members had stopped at the base of the hill and others were waiting for the rest of the platoon and the platoon commander to catch up with the squad. Ira decided he better get back and join them, and as he quickly made his way back, bullets started striking in trace of his footsteps flying over his head just past the first layer of raised ground. He stumbled and fell headfirst into the first trench the enemy had abandoned.

Abe Metzler and Dumont noticed the increasing volley of bullets being fired in their direction as they advanced so they dove for cover into the hedge grove at the base of the hill.

"Help, help, heeelp!" they heard someone cry out in front of them as a mortar striking nearby, exploded shaking the whole area around them. Dumont was hit with shrapnel in his legs, and when both he and Metzler looked up, they saw a pair of booted legs sticking out of a hole. "Help, help," they heard the outcry, again.

Abram Metzler was a short, chubby Marine with a round face and big round eyes and a cautious spirit about him that made him valuable to the platoon. Abe looked over at Dumont and they both chuckled.

Rahm, carrying two hundred rounds of machine-gun ammo, six grenades, his flak jacket, two bandoliers of M-16 ammo, his helmet, three canteens of water, and a number of other items attached to his cartridge belt, was stuck upside down in the trench line. The trench dug for small Vietnamese men was too small to give him any wiggling room, and he couldn't move. "Help, help, get me out of here," Abe heard Rahm cry out; and while bullets struck the ground all around them and grenades exploded nearby, Metzler and Dumont struggled to get Ira Bruce Rahm, also known as Timber Wolf, alias Combat, and now Rabbit, out of the hole he had fallen into.

Souble to their left had also advanced past the first layer of ground beyond the base of the hill when a round struck his flak jacket, knocking him down. The bullet didn't penetrate his flak jacket, but he felt a burning pain near his chest. He opened his shirt and the bullet that had struck him fell into his hand. He thought it amusing and placed the bullet in his shirt pocket and, as he did he looked to his right and about two hundred feet away saw the enemy sniper taking aim at him.

The bullet tore through his leg, and the sniper zeroed in once more. There was no covering available for Souble to hide behind, so he took his M-14 rifle and placed it out in front of his head, extending his arms as far as he could to have the rifle shield him from the sniper's bullet he knew was coming.

The bullet struck the rifle's recoil pad, shattering the stock and trigger firing mechanism before embedding itself into Souble's hand.

The bullet that had struck Wilson had only grazed his boot, and while thankful he wasn't hurt, he realized that now some of his men were laid out in the open field with him while Third Squad had reached the base of the hill and some were still advancing up the hill. Wilson got up quickly and told us all to get up and assault and we did.

A Place For the Gun
Operation Foster AT 873522
November 26, 1967, D+13, 1120-2350 hours

We reached the base of the small hill while it was still smoldering from the artillery bombardment, by now most of the incoming fire had stopped.

Once our platoon settled in at the base of the hill, Lieutenant Wilson sent my gun over to protect our right side. Second Platoon filed off, setting themselves to Wilson's left as did Third Platoon. Baggette's CP, however, remained set up on Hill 11 from where he could have a wider view of the battle scene.

Marines now encircled the hill on three sides, and it seemed that much of the battle continued over on the other side of the hill, where Foxtrot remained engaged in a fierce firefight. While we weren't receiving fire, we could hear the report of extensive gunfire occurring on the other side of the hill.

The L-shaped ambush site the enemy had set up for the initial Foxtrot Platoon had a network of tunnels connected to a secondary set of tunnels farther up the hill. Once the Foxtrot Platoon was committed and had passed the first trench line, they were met by a fierce onslaught of incoming firepower from the top of the hill and also from a thick knoll on their southeast side where the enemy soldiers were well hidden in dense forested terrain. The NVA soldiers were now pouring out automatic and machine-gun fire on them. The platoon from Foxtrot Company could do nothing but stand still and when they could return fire while fighting for their lives.

I set the gun up where the lieutenant said I should set it up, but it didn't seem right. To our right was a fire-team, and they had connected with the Lima Platoon we could see to our far right front just a little ways up the hill.

After we set in, another attempt was going to be made to get out some of Lima's wounded, they had brought around. To our left, about 100 yards away, someone popped a yellow smoke grenade, and the sound of the medevac chopper was soon heard coming in from the west side. As the chopper prepared to land, the enemy as was expected opened fire with automatic weapon's fire. A Huey gunship escorting the chopper returned fire, and as the medevac chopper pulled away, abandoning their mission, I could see green tracers from an enemy's machine-gun being fired at both choppers.

At the base of the hill where I was, the gun wouldn't be able to provide much cover or be able to engage the enemy where they were set in higher up the hill. I thought of staying where the lieutenant had placed us. But the gun was useless there, so I moved out and away from the base of the hill and the small bend there that had provided good cover for the gun. Out in the open rice paddy field I found cover behind a three-by-six-feet oval-shaped grave mound. The grave mound was a perfect spot for the gun; except for some trees that were partly in the way, at the base of the hill, the location provided an excellent overall view of the hill as well as giving me an opportunity to cover for the platoon to my far left. It was a very advantageous firing position.

Medevac the Wounded While You Bleed
Operation Foster AT 873522
November 26, 1967, D+13, 1120-2350 hours

We had taken some causalities and this time when the medevac chopper landed, there was no in-coming, and India Company's priority wounded were loaded on board. As Rahm helped Doc Mac prepare Souble for the next medevac chopper, the Corpsman noticed Rahm was bleeding from his legs. Rahm, up until that time, hadn't noticed the wounds he had received when the grenade exploded while his legs were up in the air. It wasn't the first time during the operation that Rahm had been wounded with only slight shrapnel wounds. From mortars on the twenty-first as well as from the grenade explosion that threw him forward when I had been hit; Rahm never bothered to have his wounds cared for. He had simply dismissed them before, but this time, his trousers were soiled with fresh blood. Before the Corpsman could look at Ira's wounds, the second chopper coming in to land was met with heavy enemy machine-gun fire.

The enemy's gun was dead center and up the hill about eighty yards from our platoon. The chopper was getting hit bad and had to abort the mission, and as they pulled away, green tracers followed after them. The escorting Huey opened fire on the enemy's position with their machine-guns as did our platoon below.

Marty had crawled up next to me, his wide-eyed look revealing the fear he had about us being out in such an open position. As First Platoon Marines opened fire on the enemy shooting at the chopper, the hidden enemy force responded by unleashing a heavy barrage of automatic weapons fire down on the platoon all along the base of the hill. The enemy, entrenched and well concealed in their fighting positions was unloading a heavy load of lead, grenades, and mortars on the platoon.

I was surprised this time by the full realization of the raw strength and firepower the enemy revealed. Had they not exposed their firepower, we would have been slaughtered had we tried again to assault them even at company strength. This was going to be a heavy battle, and I brought the gun in tight and prepared to select my targets.

It's Time To Dance
Operation Foster AT 873522
November 26, 1967, D+13, 1120-2350 hours

As the enemy at the top of the hill was shooting straight down, First Platoon at the bottom was shooting straight up, and we were at a disadvantage. The enemy had not only the advantage they were in control of the battlefield. Not only on our side of the hill, but also with the Lima and Foxtrot platoons.

With my cheek up against her stock, I cradled the gun, bringing her in close, draping my left hand over her cover, and I could almost feel her throbbing spirit, waiting to be released. She was ready for full engagement so I tightened my hold on her, and at the peak of her excitement, zeroed in on my target and pulled the trigger. She released her desires with intense pleasure. Her screaming bullets came flying out. Marty, checking the links, released them as soon as I opened fire, so that they could sail smoothly into her feed tray. The bullets being spit out went straight and true, seeking the enemies' hidden positions. The rounds struck the entrenched enemy at an angle; and as their machine-gun turned their fire in my direction, I had already concentrate my fire power on them and holding the trigger back; I send a solid stream of red tracers straight into their fixed position, and their gun went silent. Others that returned fire were also met with the sting of the gun's anger.

The machine-gun's fire from out in the open, from behind a grave mound in the rice paddy below, came at the enemy once again as a surprise; for a few seconds, they stopped firing.

Above us, the Huey gunship escorting the medevac chopper followed my red tracers and opened fire with his guns and then marked the entrenched enemy's position with a fired WP rocket. As the smoke rose into the air, Skyhawk jets came in fast and swift, blowing a good part of the enemy's long trench line into shreds.

The line of flames from the explosions ran the full length of the trench line, wiping out a whole line of NVA soldiers that had been shooting straight down on us.

We didn't know the full strength of the enemy we had encountered. From the visual Bird Dog and recon reports, our commanders would know them to be well-equipped hard-core NVA soldiers. At present, we as grunts only knew they were a large enough force that they were able to control four separate combat zones, two different skirmishes with Foxtrot, one with Lima, and one with us.

They were engaged in firefights with Marines on three sides of the hill, and both Lima 3/7 and the Foxtrot 2/7 platoons were receiving not only small arms fire but also full automatic rifle fire as well as .30 caliber machine-gun fire and .82mm mortars were being dropped on them.

By now, the enemy had survived a number of WP and HE rockets fired at them by our Huey gunships, thousands of .30 caliber machine-gun rounds from those same choppers, over six air strikes, and four or five artillery bombardments. Over fifty yards of their trenches had been destroyed in the process, yet their strength remained unrelenting.

The enemy's rain of bullets upon our platoon was frightening; as the planes came in for the air strikes, we could see tracers going out to meet them. With the volume of power displayed by the enemy, First Platoon Marines realized how vulnerable we were at the bottom of the hill so many of the platoon quickly shifted locations, moving to find better firing or protective positions; even with air cover above dropping in high-explosive bombs, the enemy still kept us scrambling for cover and continued to prevent us from returning effective fire.

I adjusted my firing, selecting the target that was unleashing the most fire on the platoon, holding down the trigger, letting the enemy know that if they fired they would be responded to. Marines along the base of the hill returned fire as well. To my right, a lone soldier fired in my direction, his bullets striking near the gun's barrel. I turned to respond with a twenty-round burst but as I did the Marines to my right, fired on him as well and his firing stopped. What little incoming from then on I was receiving I was able to respond to immediately and most of that incoming ceased coming my way.

It wasn't so for the troops below; the enemy was well entrenched, and their targets below were choice targets to them. The enemy moved as far as they could away from my firing position and adjusted their firing positions opening fire once again on the platoon below them with massive automatic weapons fire.

I kept firing, and soon, Aggie on the left side of the platoon began firing his machine-gun toward where he saw my red tracers traveling. Soon our tracers began to cut across the battlefield, traversing the trench line from where the enemy was firing at us from, and once again there was a pause in the incoming fire we were receiving, but such relief lasted only for a short time as it was soon renewed with a shift in their positions and more firing.

The guns now however had most of the enemies firing positions in a cross fire and we had a slight advantage if we could keep the bullets flying as I noticed the enemy wasn't returning fire with the strength they once revealed they were capable of delivering.

I feared that soon they would move around to our right and try and knock out my gun from that area, but Lima Company was supposed to be there; I hoped they were. For now, I was able to return fire on the enemy's positions and the bullets were ripping their defensive entrenched position to shreds, forcing them to keep their heads down, and you could tell they weren't able to return fire as they had been doing before, because they had, had to move. But if Aggie or I let up, the incoming fire would increase.

First Platoon was shooting up from the base of the hill, and my gun was shooting across the enemies trenches at an angle from their right. I had been shooting steadily for some time and it had provided our troops the time they needed to find better cover and locate positions from where they could engage or return the enemies' fire.

The NVA in their trenches and fighting positions were limited to shooting straight down. They were not prepared nor had they set up their fighting positions to shoot across to their left. Their east flank was also busy with trying to keep the Lima Company platoon from advancing up that side.

The knoll at the bottom of the hill offering me some cover disappeared about sixty feet up so that it was not possible for me to shoot at the enemy if they moved down; it provided me with some cover, but if they arose to shoot back in my direction from above, from where the majority of them were, they would have to expose themselves to the platoon's fire from below and would also become exposed to Aggie's machine-gun fire, which was set up to fire at them from their left. The little bend at the base of the hill made all the difference for me, and Aggie's gun was covering the crevice in the hill behind the little knoll. Both guns were in perfect firing positions from where we were. If the enemy moved down to shoot at my position, they would have a clear shot at me, but other Marines guarded that approach as did Aggie's gun. Marty and I had a great firing position, and once again, the enemy did not consider what a machine-gun located out in the open could do.

The enemy chose, for the most part, to ignore shooting at my gun and concentrated on keeping the platoon pinned down at the bottom of the hill; they were determined to keep the platoon from advancing toward them as the platoon's advancement presented the most danger and at the same time their best target.

From the sound of firing going on the other sides of the hill, the enemy continued to be engaged in a heavy firefight with both the Foxtrot and Lima Company platoons. If our platoon was able to advance up the hill, we would split up their forces.

Once More With Bravo
Operation Foster AT 873522
November 26, 1967, D+13, 1120-2350 hours

A Huey gunship suddenly appeared overhead and to my left, I could see another medevac chopper approaching. All of a sudden, a barrage of extensive firepower was unleashed upon the platoon and at the choppers. The platoon responded, and I held down the trigger as bullets flew out of the gun's barrel with a fierce determination to put an end to the enemy's incoming fire. But the enemies' firepower continued, and in response, I held the trigger down and sprayed the area left and right, expending hundreds of rounds. I had learned quite well that we must gain fire superiority to avoid casualties and I was determined to do that. As the enemy increased their fire, I was able to pinpoint their location and responded at that target without prejudice; Aggie was matching my determination, and together we kept up our firing until most of the incoming stopped.

The medevac was again unsuccessful but the enemy finally ceased firing for a while and I knew we had gained the advantage. I fired a couple of more rounds at a new target I saw move and noticed my rounds fell short of the target. Other Marines then responded to the target I tried to fire at. I brought the gun down and noticed the gun's barrel glowing white-hot; it was warped. I had melted my second barrel.

Another Attempt To Assault
Operation Foster AT 873522
November 26, 1967, D+13, 1120-2350 hours

An hour later, several medevac choppers were able to come in and evacuate some of our wounded; they landed at the base of the graveyard just to my left in an area that was free of incoming fire. The choppers dropped off emergency supplies and new men while the firefight continued with both sides exchanging fire superiority back and forth for the next two hours.

From my position, I could hear medevac choppers constantly come in and lift off. We continued fighting in this manner for the next couple of hours until shortly after 1700 hours when we were told we were going to attempt another assault.

At 1715 hours, Captain Baggette called for Second and Third Platoon to assault up the hill while First Platoon was to remain at the bottom and provide cover. With Third Platoon to our far left (west) and Second Platoon in the middle, India Company Marines got on line to assault up along the west side of the hill.

As soon as they started moving, the enemy unleashed a heavy barrage of machine-gun and automatic rifle fire on them as well as mortars.

Third Platoon Marines who had secured themselves among the graveyard at the base of the hill were receiving most of the mortar fire that was being dropped on the company. Cpl. Gary Brown, an old-timer with less than a couple of months to go, got up to assault, and a mortar round struck a cement grave mound near him. The granite monument absorbed much of the impact, but it was still powerful enough to whirl Brown through the air.

Brown, who everyone in Third Platoon called Chief because of his Indian heritage, shook his head and the dirt and dust fell off him. He sat up. His ears were ringing, and his knee was bleeding. Others around him were scrambling to find cover from the barrage of incoming mortars. The enemy was shooting down at Third Platoon Marines from farther up the hill, it was not from the location the enemy had been engaging them before. They seemed to have moved to yet another higher fighting position.

I adjusted my firing to shoot higher to strike the enemy force where fire was coming from. Meanwhile, half way up the hill they had left behind a number of NVA snipers to harass India Company with sniper fire to delay any advance up the hill.

A Corpsman found Brown and the Marine had him quickly brush off the granite and metal fragments and just bandaged him up so he could rejoin his platoon which was once again maneuvering to resume the assault.

The platoon, once on line, moved out. To Brown's right was L/Cpl. Gerald Anthony DeMunda. Both Brown and DeMunda had a machine-gunner's 0331 MOS. DeMunda from Niagara Falls, New York, had only been with India Company for a couple of months but already was well liked. He had earned the nickname of Curly because of his bald head.

As Third Platoon advanced up the hill, making their way through thick underbrush and along crevices at the base of the hill that were filled with water, Brown was firing his gun from the hip. DeMunda, standing next to him, to get a better shot at the entrenched NVA soldiers' positions, raised his gun to fire from the shoulder; with both M-60's blazing away, the platoon advanced. They hadn't gotten but a few feet before a sniper's bullet struck DeMunda and he went down.

By the time Brown got to him, DeMunda shot through the heart was dead. There was a contented smile on his face as if he was sleeping. "At least his war is over," thought Brown as he turned to once again engage the enemy.

DeMunda's A-gunner—a tall, heavy set, black Marine whom they called Chubby, stood silent, nearby, he was scared frozen as bullets struck the ground all around them. Corporal Brown had to shake him and to get him to pick up the gun to get out of the kill zone.

Prescott was the last Marine in First Platoon at the end of the line. He saw Second and Third Platoons get up to advance; and minutes later, the wounded from both platoons were being brought back down to the CP as was DeMunda's body. With the fierce incoming fire striking the area all around him, Prescott had had enough, he bent over and began to weep.

The intensity of the incoming increased with grenades exploding in front of second and third platoons as they moved up the hill at a slow pace in the dense foliage. The platoons tried to find as much cover as possible while still advancing, being cautious of booby traps the enemy might have left behind. The best cover they were able to find came by way of scattered bomb craters and grave mounds that offered some protection from the rain of enemy bullets. A fire-team would deploy into the scattered shelters and from there, provide cover for the others as they moved up. In this way, the platoon was slowly leapfrogging advancing up the hill.

In some areas, the NVA soldiers were unable to see the advancing Marines because of the jungle terrain below them so they began to blindly lob a barrage of grenades at them. The majority of the grenades, however, were falling short; they were either duds or exploded in the thick bushes eighty to 100 feet in front of the platoons. When the grenade assault ceased, the captain called for First Platoon to join in the assault by bringing up the company's right flank.

Dumont came over and said for me to keep my gun in place at the bottom of the hill because the gun remained in an advantageous position to cover the company's advance and would keep our right side secured. I told Dumont we had melted one barrel and the other barrel wasn't working right, we would need a barrel replacement soon.

As First Platoon began to assault, the enemy, which was concealed in trenches on the far right side of the hill, unleashed yet another onslaught of automatic rifle fire that blanketed the ground in front of First Platoon. Bushes and thick grass shoots were being ripped out of the jungle's floor, from their roots. Exploding mortars were causing soft-tissue trees to be split apart. Thick banana trees were being torn in half; their heavy branches laden with unripe fruit were ripped apart by grenades, mortars, and bullets.

We returned fire, and I kept opening up with machine-gun fire focusing on what I saw as the main source of the incoming fire. While my firing was constant and heavy, it was not as effective as I would have liked for it to be. I couldn't tell what real effect my firing was having upon the enemy because they weren't firing at me, and I had to wait to see from where they opened fire before I could respond.

Soon I was firing only a few feet over the heads of Marines that were crawling up the hill while scattered enemy snipers were trying to pick them off one at a time. The small knoll in front of me now prevented me from seeing where the Marines from Second and Third Platoons were.

Then the enemy unleashed another barrage of automatic rifle fire at First Platoon as the platoon tried to advance up the hill toward their entrenched positions. I opened up with as much firepower as I could unleash to cover our side of the hill, holding down the trigger, allowing the gun to fire off as many rounds as she could. I knew the bullets were causing the enemy to keep their heads down because it was then that their main volume of fire being shot at us decreased only to increase elsewhere.

When You Meet Your Limit
Operation Foster AT 873522
November 26, 1967, D+13, 1120-2350 hours

As the platoon advanced, a recently arrived Marine who had been moving up behind the point man in Second Squad stopped, turned around, and ran back down the hill. He dropped his rifle and was screaming hysterically, running past other Marines. He was darting from one place to another crying. He stumbled and fell, got up, and kept running down the hill as if the demons of hell were whispering in his ear that his time had come. He ran toward the LZ where the helicopters had been, but they were long gone. He turned back toward the base of the hill where the platoon's CP was located and fell on his knees sobbing. A drizzling rain began to fall, adding sorrow to the sight.

Marines walking by the CP stopped, looked at him, and then among the explosions and fierce firing still going on, they turned to join in the assaulting Marines. Before long, the intensity of the incoming fire was so fierce it prevented the company from moving forward and Marines just found cover where they were, stopped and waited.

From my distant position, I had seen Porter scampering around carrying supplies from the LZ toward the CP. In one of his trips, he stopped by the kneeling crying Marine, and even from that distance I could see Porter's eyes opened wide and he looked scared but he didn't say a word to the young Marine. He merely moved on. Lieutenant Wilson and the other men assigned to the platoons' CP left the kneeling Marine alone to battle his own war as they concentrated on the battle before them.

Welcome to Nam, I was thinking. While I felt sorry for him, I couldn't help but think how others had frozen the first time in battle or when they found themselves pinned down had peed in their pants. I remembered what had happened to Lucero when he froze and also remembered that Lucero was the Marine who had had the dirty trick played on him at Liberty Bridge with the dead gook they had hoisted up from where he had been floating in the river. That incident alone could have easily messed up anyone's mind. Still, I didn't want that new Marine next to me. *Take him out of here,* I was thinking.

Stop the War, I'll Be Back
Operation Foster AT 873522
November 26, 1967, D+13, 1120-2350 hours

With Foxtrot and Lima Company still under fire, one more attempt at an assault was planned. New men were coming in, and it was hoped that with the reinforcement, we might be able to take the hill.

At 1830 hours, emergency medevac choppers began to come in; they came in, dropped off new men, and took with them our wounded. As the choppers landed, Marines fell on line and we began to assault once more.

One of the last choppers that landed stood idle, waiting for Marines up the hill that were carrying down on a stretcher a seriously wounded Marine to be loaded on board. Meanwhile, a new Marine that had landed with the first chopper had ran to join a fire-team from Third Squad that was advancing up the hill. As the squad slowed down to move around a small bomb crater, he caught up to them. He grinned as he fell in, about that same time, he got hit with an incoming round that struck his flak jacket. The round spun him around, and he fell flat on his face. He got up; as bullets kicked up dust all around him, he looked at his torn flak jacket, laughed, and ran quickly around the crater to once again catch up with the squad. No sooner did he reach the fire-team than he was hit in his right foot.

He went down again, looked at his foot, no blood was visible; only his boot was torn at the heel, so he got up again and ran toward the Marines who were now standing still looking at him. When he reached them, they turned to advance once more up the hill; and when they had advanced only a short distance, he was hit a third time.

This time, the round caught his flak jacket hard enough to throw him backward for a few feet. He sat up; blood was slowly coloring his shirt a darker shade of green. He tried to get up but couldn't, so he just sat back down, a disappointed look on his face. The advancing squad of Marines had stopped for him, and now two of the squad's team members picked him up and carried him back down the hill. When they got him to its base, he let go of them and limped by himself over to the last chopper that had just loaded the seriously wounded Marine on board, and the chopper lifted off.

For some reason, I knew that Marine would be back. A Marine that gung ho, that didn't get a chance to fire his weapon, would be back, I knew. If for nothing else, just to pop off a few caps in this war.

As our company assaulted the hill, we were taking heavy casualties. Above us the choppers seemed to be stacked in line, one on top of the other, circling overhead like hungry vultures waiting for the prey to drop so that they could swoop in and claim their victim. They looked like little tadpoles swimming overhead in circular formations. The landing zone was constantly busy now as choppers came in without hesitation or worry of taking incoming fire. They easily picked up the wounded; dropped off reinforcements, food, water, and emergency supplies; and were gone in minutes. The dead were pulled to the left of our position; they would be medevaced later.

Then the enemy unleashed another volley of fierce firepower so heavy they seemed to have been reinforced with other more experienced enemy soldiers; our platoon once again became pinned down under heavy well directed enemy fire and could no longer advance. Like Lima Company on the east side of the hill, we were being prevented by the fierceness of the enemy's incoming firepower from pressing forward. The same held true for Second and Third Platoon.

As Marines stopped where they were or moved back down to find protection or fighting positions, two Marines came down the hill near us.

They were assisting a third Marine who was wounded. He was a new man who had been with us for only two days and had been advancing with the platoon up the hill with First Squad when he was hit by shrapnel in the head, the worst place to get hit in combat; but like Boyd, who had been hit in the head on the nineteenth and lived, the Marine was also lucky. The helmet had taken much of the initial impact from the shrapnel.

The Corpsman had wrapped his head in clean white battle dressing, covering his eyes and leaving only a small opening near his nose and mouth. The crisp whiteness of the bandage contrasted sharply with the dark green jungle background and gloomy gray battleground he emerged from.

Other choppers were landing on the other side of the hill southeast of Foxtrot 2/7's location. While Lima and the Foxtrot Platoon continued to receive mortars as well as automatic and machine-gun fire by now both platoon were finally able to medevac out their wounded.

Like Ducks In A Shooting Gallery
Operation Foster AT 873522
November 26, 1967, D+13, 1120-2350 hours

By now, we were almost out of ammo for the gun and the gun was beginning to misfire; it needed a good cleaning, but I didn't have the equipment to do it right. Marty volunteered to clean it as best as he could, so while he stayed with the gun, I ran along a small path that ran along the base of the hill looking for more ammo. As I ran, bullets struck the ground following me. The faster I ran, the more the incoming rounds seemed to grow in intensity.

As I ran, I eyed a small bomb crater ahead and jumped into it. Only when I landed did I realize the crater was full of Marines.

It was Welsh; he now had a squad assigned to him, and one of his fire-teams was huddled together as bullets whizzed overhead.

The platoon remained pinned down and immobilized. A couple of his Marines inside the crater had broken down their M-16s and were trying to un-jam them.

"What are you doing," Welsh asked. Getting ammo for the gun, I answered, and we both got down further to avoid getting hit by incoming rounds. He told his fire-team leader to remain where they were and to keep their heads down, "I'm going with you," he said, and we took off.

We dashed from one Marine position to another, and before long, we realized we were the only ones moving and, of course, Charlie's bullets were following us from one place to another. As we ran, the incoming grew in intensity, and we dropped often and as quickly as possible. We stopped near a tree that was quickly splintered by the concentration of the enemy's incoming rounds, so we took off again.

As soon as we took off, the bullets were at our heels, so we both hit the ground. I hit so hard I turned on my side and spit out pieces of grass and dirt. It was too close, so we both decided to just lie there in the bushes with the wet earth underneath us and wait as bullets whizzed by.

As we waited, a light rain began to fall then it turned to a steady flow. A beautifully fine feathered gray, tan, and black-striped duck landed at the edge of the rice paddy a short distance away. The duck stuck his head into the edge of the dike and pulled out a large wiggling bug, dropped a large white load of waste, looked up at us, and as he jerked his head back to take notice of us lying there in the grass and mud, a stray enemy's bullet struck the mud and splashed rainwater up less than an inch away from him. He squawked, flapped his wings, and flew off. The enemy sniper had shot at him, and I realized where we were lying made me feel like the duck; we were sitting there like ducks in a shooting gallery.

Every year, the Ringling Bros. and the Barnum and Bailey Traveling Circus would come to Casa Grande, Arizona, and set up their large tents on Trekell Road. For a nickel, you could shoot BBs at cutouts of metal ducks that moved back and forth in the shooting gallery. I remembered how some ducks in the middle of the field hardly had any white paint left on them. The constant barrage of pellets had chipped away most of their paint. Those ducks were more exposed than the other ducks farther back. The ones in front moved slower, and you got very little points for hitting them. The ducks farther back moved faster and were partly hidden behind cutup pieces of scenery. They were the prize ducks to hit, but they also moved and dropped faster. If you took the time to take aim at them when they appeared or all of a sudden popped up, by the time you pulled the trigger, they disappeared just as fast as they appeared and the chances were slimmer of hitting them and winning the bigger prize. The white paint on those ducks looked almost new in comparison to the ducks out front.

As with the unpitted ducks, to move fast and drop often was the answer to avoiding a gunshot wound. We were trained to do that, and by the time the enemy shot where Welsh and I were, we were no longer there. By the time they saw where we were and shot at us, we were gone and had hit the ground or were running again.

It is funny how so many things can cross your mind in times of danger. Your mind wanders for split seconds that seem like hours, and it travels back and forth between thoughts of the real world back home and this world so dissimilar to the world we grew up in. All this thinking occurs in the midst of battle in images and quick memories of home, and you take in a deep sigh and that glimpse of safety and loved ones gives you hope and a will to fight and survive.

Weeks before, I had sent away for our weekly hometown newspaper and had received a few issues, then they stopped coming. Pat Frye, a high school classmate working for the *Casa Grande Dispatch* newspaper had inserted a note in the first newspaper I received. She said she remembered who I was and wished me well.

I remembered her. She had short jet-black hair and an oval-shaped face with a wide smile and full lips. She had always been friendly in high school as had most of the female classmates I could remember.

Debbie Echeverria came to mind. I knew her brother, and I often wondered if she was friendly toward me because of that or if she was flirting. Her friend, short little Donna Johnson, was a fireball and always smiling, and I liked her. There was a whole group of them that hung around together: Pat Frye, Debbie Echeverria,

Sharman Ethington, Vicki Early, Natalie Gifford, and Veronica Alvarez who reminded me of Annette Funicello in the Walt Disney's *Mickey Mouse Club.*

Then there was Sandy Erdmann—man, did I ever have a crush on that girl! I could sit and stare at her for hours. And just as often, she seemed to stare back during much of the classes we had together in high school. She was someone I would love to have been writing to. Then there was Cathy Majors. Cathy in grade school taught me that girls were different.

We were both in sixth grade and used to poke and make fun of each other while attending Saint Anthony's Catholic School. One day as she was sitting in front of me, she leaned back and gave me the cap of a Bic ink pen. I was puzzled, and she turned to me and whispered, "Smell it." I was too naïve to understand, so I pulled her hair, and she stabbed my knee with her pencil. It wasn't until my wedding night that the recollection of that smell came back to mind. The pencil lead was still embedded on my right knee.

Eddie Ornelas, Michael Andrade, Martin Rodriguez, Gil Palacio, Timothy Acuff, Robert Antone, Mike Kakar, Pixler, Polsun, Jim Prettyman, Steve Nava—I wonder what happened to them? Had they joined the service? Would they soon be in Vietnam? Had they graduated? We were all friends living a life of freedom and safety in our little corner of that world.

What a difference a few months had made. I had dropped out of school a year and a half before, had gotten married, and now I was fighting a war that many of us in high school never knew existed. I remembered when I received the first newspaper from home.

Pat Frye, and most of the other girls whom I remembered, lived in the rich part of town, the area we called Evergreen. That was where the upper class of people lived; most of them would be going off to college. I used to wash windows, do yard work, and mow lawns in that part of town for spending money.

I had sent off a few dollars to receive copies of my hometown newspaper, and reading the *Casa Grande Dispatch* newspaper helped fill a need and longing for home. Even Prettyman's Supermarket advertisements with the logo of the little man with a large pencil behind his ear made me feel at home. Mom used to shop there every first of the month when we received the welfare check from the government. She would collect the S&H green trading stamps at the checkout counter, and we would lick and paste them in a book she traded for gifts at the Sperry and Hutchinson corner store on Fourth Street. She once got me a white cowboy hat with those stamps, and I was the only kid in the neighborhood that had a white cowboy hat.

It is amazing how much simple things like Prettyman's or Basha's Market advertising can mean when serving in the military far away from home. The Paramount movie house where Gil had worked and where I had helped him run the movie projector was advertising the latest movie. After working there, whenever I've been in a movie theater, I have been able to tell when the movie projectionist was about to change reels because of the discolored burn marks that appeared on the upper right-hand corner of the screen. That was the signal for the projectionist to start the next reel. When we didn't do it on time, the screen would go blank.

I was wondering what Martin and Gil were doing. Both were friends who graduated from high school a year before I was supposed to. If they had joined the service, they too would now be here in Vietnam. Every day after school, we all used to hang out at the A&W Root Beer stand on Florence Boulevard.

When my sister Connie was dying of leukemia, I dropped out of high school and went to live with her in Sanger, California, to help her. It was there I met Dorothy, my wife, but it was her sister Cecilia I had been infatuated with. So many different paths my life could have taken.

One thing happens, and it affects many other people's lives. I joined the Marine Corps in San Jose, California, so more than likely, my hometown newspaper never announced that I had been accepted into the Marine Corps or that I graduated from boot camp and was sent to Vietnam. What a different world Casa Grande was.

Debbie Echeverria's father had owned a large ranch there. What would have happened if I had asked Debbie or Sandy Erdmann out? If only I had gathered up the nerve to ask Sandy to go out and if we had gotten together, I probably never would have left Casa Grande. What a different life I would have lived!

A grenade's explosion rocked the earth close to where Welsh and I where, and we hugged the earth in the mud and rain.

I checked the area where we were to run to, and we took off as another explosion occurred nearby and sniper bullets followed us. We dropped just as another grenade exploded where we had been only seconds before. The enemy was lobbing grenades and sniping at us as we ran along the base of the hill.

Grenades exploding in the underbrush sounded much like the dud smoke airburst of the yearly Fourth of July fireworks show. I leaned back against a thick tree trunk, bracing myself steadfast against its secured position as I took in a deep breath to catch up with my heavy breathing. I ignored the battle going on all around us to allow my mind once again to race to thoughts of the comforts of home.

The picnics and barbeque festivities at the city park in Casa Grande were community events where the whole town came out to celebrate Independence Day. A twenty-foot heavily greased aluminum pole was always erected in the middle of the park and a crisp brand-new $20 bill placed at the very top. Dozens of kids would try to climb up the pole to get the prize. It wasn't long before we became as slick and slippery as the pole. Everyone stayed at the park awaiting nightfall to watch the fireworks exploding overhead. That's why I was here in Vietnam: my country had called, I had answered, and now I was fighting against Communism in Southeast Asia. It was to preserve that type of freedom we enjoyed back home, but now, grenades and incoming mortars were exploding all around us and sending sparkling red-hot shrapnel into the air.

We waited in the wet soil and damp leaves, protected by a small sliver of a cutout on the side of the hill that protected us from the enemies' bullets. By then my trousers were covered with greasy reddish yellow Vietnamese mud. Over the past few months, the sun, sweat, and countless hours of humping across rice paddy fields, dikes, and endless tree lines have made my utilities, once they got wet, as slick as my trousers had looked after trying to climb the greasy pole back home.

Back in the States, it had been Martin, Gil, and I that hung around and played together as friends, cruising in a tan-colored '52 Chevy down Florence Boulevard and then Main Street checking out the girls. Here in Nam, it was Marty, Jones, Aggie, and I patrolling rice paddy fields and checking the ground for booby traps, trip wires, and smelling the air for gooks. There, life had a different meaning: it was carefree and fun. Here, the game we were playing was called life and death. Back home, it was a pencil lead stuck in my knee; here, it was the burning hot lead from bullets I was trying to avoid.

No Covering Fire For the Medevac
Operation Foster AT 873522
November 26, 1967, D+13, 1120-2350 hours

Welsh, lying on the ground next to me, was adventurous enough to cause the enemy great pain but cautious enough to warrant respect from other Marines. When another grenade exploded nearby, he crawled in closer under better covering where I was. Welsh had great respect for the M-60 machine-gun. He had seen what it could do in battle. When I fired out across the open rice paddy the time I had jumped on the wrong side of the dike a few days earlier, he had been one of the Marines that had also jumped on the wrong side of the dike, and the M-60 had covered for him when the enemy had drawn very near to where he was. It was the gun's firepower that kept the enemy away. He had also seen the gun's response at the battle of Finger Lake. He was appointed a squad leader after that day and now made sure each member of his squad carried two hundred rounds of machine-gun ammo; that ammo had long been fired, and now we were out searching for more from among the other Marines in the company.

We found Aggie, and he had 300 rounds of ammo left. We took a 100-round belt and with another belt we had found made our way back to the gun.

As a new series of medevac choppers began to approach to land closer to the base of the hill, we started to get incoming fire from a couple of snipers, and Lieutenant Wilson called for us to provide cover for the priority evacuation.

Marty had cleared and cleaned the gun, but as soon as I test fired it, it was still misfiring; the dirty ammo didn't help. I could only shoot a few bullets at a time before the gun would jam. We waited a few minutes then took the barrel off and unjammed the bullet, hoping we didn't have a "cook-off."[218]

As the choppers began to land, a sniper opened fire on them and the lieutenant called for us to lay down suppressive firepower in that direction so the chopper would be able to land safely.

I opened fire and the gun jammed again. I could no longer put out the firepower we needed. To our left, the platoon opened fire, but then, most of the M-16s began jamming. The M-16 rifles had been giving us trouble before, but now, they were really jamming up with the rain and mud. Expended rounds became stuck in the chamber and soon only one or more M-16s were firing at a constant rate, and most of those belonged to the new men. Besides them, only Keene, who still carried the M-14, was still firing.

I unjammed the gun, reloaded, and opened fire. The machine-gun responded, but only for a few short bursts before it stopped firing. The choppers came in, and the platoon was barely able to keep the sniper's head down during the critical part of the evacuation. As they took off, the sniper opened fire again.

On the right side, the east side of the hill, other choppers were landing. It was the rest of Lima Company being dropped in to assist their platoon.

Catch A Falling Sniper
Operation Foster AT 873522
November 26, 1967, D+13, 1120-2350 hours

Welsh came by with another hundred rounds of ammo for the gun. I told him the gun was no longer working. The gas cylinder wasn't operating right. Welsh laid down his M-16 it was covered in filth and mud, he looked at me, and said, "I know where the sniper is. Do you want to go get him? I have my M-16, but it keeps jamming," he said.

"I have my .45," I said, and with that, we both took off while Marty remained with the gun and once again tore it apart to clean it.

Welsh and I went over toward the left of the hill, then up a short bend and again made our way up by using the tall grass and shrubs, to move toward where he had seen the sniper. We finally came up close to where the sniper was. We could see him: he had camouflaged himself with foliage and was protected by large tree branches. When the sniper opened fire again, Welsh shot off four rounds at him before his M-16 jammed. I popped off five rounds with the .45 but didn't hit anything. The sniper was well protected from us by the thick tree he was hiding behind. If we tried to go around, other enemy soldiers would have us in their sights.

"We can get him with grenades," Welsh said, and as I reloaded, he took off down the hill and came back a short time later with five grenades. By then, I had moved up closer to the tree the sniper was in. I still hadn't seen him clearly, but I could hear him moving in the tree about eighty feet away from us. Welsh pulled the pin on the first grenade and threw it. The spoon flew off, and the grenade exploded at the base of the tree. I stood by with the .45 in hand to shoot the sniper if he moved into view, but nothing happened. I gave my pistol to Welsh and threw the next one; it struck the tree, bounced off, and never exploded. It was a dud grenade. Welsh then pitched another one, and right after its explosion, the sniper opened up in our direction from behind the tree. The bullets struck the tree we were hiding behind.

To get him, we would have to pull the pin and then time the throw of the grenade so that it would explode at just the right height and distance. With only two grenades left, we decided to throw them together. Perhaps they would explode in close enough proximity to the sniper with an explosion large enough to knock him out of the tree. We pulled the pin and held the grenades close.

"At the count of three," Welsh said. The spoons flew off in different directions as we released the handles, and the fuse ignited. The metallic sound of the spoons flying off alerted the sniper to where we were. He opened fire on us, a steady steam of bullets flying out of his AK-47, as the seconds on the grenades ticked off, and we stepped out from behind the large banana tree and threw them. As the grenades traveled through the air, we hit the ground. A series of bullets struck the tree where we were at knee level.

The explosions were loud, but not loud enough to cover the loud cry of pain as the sniper fell from his tree. At the same time, another sniper farther up the hill opened fire on us. He was far up and to our left in the area covered with deep jungle. As we crawled back down the hill, I realized that was the first time I had heard the deep cry of pain coming from an enemy soldier. I didn't recall ever hearing Marines that I had seen get hit cry out in such pain. I never saw the enemy soldier, just heard the cry of pain we had inflicted on him and the sound his body made when it struck the ground. As we made our way down to the bottom of the hill, Marty opened up on the second sniper; I could see the machine-gun's tracers working their way across open space and then striking the tree where the sniper was. The bullets made their way up, then there was an explosion, and the sniper's torn body flew out of the tree.

I left Welsh with his squad and made my way back to our gun's position at the base of the hill. I passed two rows of dead Marines that were laid out in a large bomb crater near the center of the graveyard.[219] Doc Gibbs and Doc Mac were attending to the wounded that were clustered near the company's CP about fifty yards from my gun's position. Just before nightfall, Marty was walking around trying to find a cigarette, and Doc Gibbs went over to a dead Marines body, and took a blood soaked pack of cigarettes from the Marines flak jacket pocket. He opened the pack and with blood soaked hands gave Marty a cigarette and took one for himself. They both sat down at the edge of the tree line quietly smoking a cigarette as a light rain began to fall.

Friendly Fire At the End Of the Day
Operation Foster AT 873522
November 26, 1967, D+13, 1120-2350 hours

Late evening and choppers landed on the east side of the hill and the word was passed that the rest of Lima Company had landed to join their stranded platoon on the east side of the hill.

We could hear that on the other side of two small knolls at the very top of the hill a fierce battle was being fought. The battle continued for about ten minutes then silence.

A few minutes later, the northwest and southeast sections of the hill became heavily engaged in fierce firefights. The entrenched enemy was being very effective in keeping both Lima and Foxtrot platoons pinned down, but soon Lima Company began to advance along a fingerlike slope of the hill between our gun's position and Foxtrot's location. Once they got near the top, they became engaged in heavy fighting with NVA soldiers.

While Lima Company had visual contact with us, they couldn't raise the Foxtrot platoon on their radio frequency, which were supposed to be at the base of the hill on their right flank, more or less in the same position we were but on the opposite side of the hill. Unknown to Lima Company, the Foxtrot 2/7 Platoon had managed to get out of their pinned-down position and had moved back down the hill, traveling clockwise and were now near the thick tree line close to the top of the right side of the hill. The objective Lima Company had been given was to assault from the east, westbound, and take the top of the hill; and before nightfall, they were determined to do that.

As Lima Company advanced, the enemy stopped firing at us. At the very top of the hill, we could see the enemy getting up, popping out of their spider holes in the ground, and moving out in clusters of twos and threes running southwest to our left toward the heavy tree line on the other side of the hill; they were going toward the side of the hill where our Second and Third Platoons were located. Had the Foxtrot Platoon remained where they had been most of the day, with Lima Company advancing, we would have had the enemy boxed in. With Foxtrot out of the way, the enemy found a way out.

Just before nightfall a fierce firefight erupted at the top right side of the hill, and about a hundred or so bullets snapped sharply over our heads. We hit the ground but did not return fire. With Lima Company moving up the hill and without knowing where they were, we held our fire. The firefight at the top of the hill continued for about ten to fifteen minutes and then silence followed.

On the other side of the hill, three BLT 2/3 companies were being dropped off to assist us. If the large enemy force was still present in the morning, they would be slaughtered.

Just before dusk, as the day's troubles and events began to return for reflection in the mind, Marty and I were sitting out alone, still out in the open, when Marty asked if we should move the gun back to the base of the hill and join up with the fire-team that had been protecting our right side. We didn't know what the company was going to do, so we moved the gun in. Once we arrived at the base of the hill and set in, someone cried out from the tree line in front of us: "Don't shoot, don't shoot! We're coming down."

It was the point man from Lima Company 3/7. The rest of Lima Company came down that side of the hill, filing past us in solemn silence. A Marine walking by was visibly upset, fuming mad. Something was wrong as none of the Lima Company Marines had said a word, as they filed past us.

"What happened?" I asked.

"We got in a firefight with Foxtrot Company at the top of the hill," one of the Marines answered.

The enemy had opened up on both Lima and the Foxtrot Platoon and then pulled out, allowing the two Marine companies to advance on each other. Because Lima Company was operating on a different radio frequency than Foxtrot, they never knew who they had engaged until they heard Foxtrot Marines calling out for a Corpsman.

As the rest of the company walked by, I wondered about Foxtrot's platoon commander; they had suffered a devastating blow, taking a number of KIAs and WIAs. Gone were yesterday's hopes of honor and fame for their platoon commander; any dreams of victory or visions of honor were stolen by the shadows left in place by the pains of today's battles and defeat. A miscalculation, misjudgment of the enemy's strength, determination, and quickly made plans had been costly. We were fighting a very shrewd enemy, and the price we had paid in today's battle was very high.

As the retreating enemy force tried to make their way west, they came across Third Platoon, which had managed to secure most of that side of the hill, and a fierce firefight ensued with them and Second Platoon who moved up to engage the fleeing enemy soldiers. Then just before nightfall all the firing stopped.

Choppers were landing on the other side of the hill southeast of Foxtrot 2/7's location. By 1830 hours it seemed both Foxtrot and Lima Platoon's were finally able to medevac their wounded.

Shortly after dark Lieutenant Wilson appeared to our left, popped off a canister of yellow smoke, the smoke barely visible in the evening light. A short time later, our wounded were medevaced out and two CH-46 Sea Knight helicopters landed with an emergency supply of ammo, water, and C-rats. In the darkness of the night, while their strobe lights were flashing, eighteen dead Marines were loaded on board. As the choppers lifted off, their throbbing taillights mocked the life that disappeared into the darkness of that night.

Counting the Dead Among the Alive
Operation Foster AT 873522
November 26, 1967, D+13, 1120-2350 hours

When full darkness fell, we settled in for the night. Lima Company hooked up with us, and the Foxtrot Platoon joined the rest of their company, which had relocated to the northwest side of the hill.

Dumont came over with a new gun bag and gun barrel. Marty was right behind him, carrying ammo and a case of C-rats. Dumont told us to dig in; we were staying put for the night. Aggie and Jones joined us and we decided to keep the gun teams together for the night. I broke down the gun and began cleaning it.

Dumont's left arm was bandaged from shrapnel. "India Company lost two machine-gunners, both of them were in Third Platoon," Dumont said. "The gunner was killed while his A-gunner, a guy by the name of Dustin, was wounded.

Prescott, Morales, and Souble from First Platoon were also wounded and medevaced." Some of the other men who were wounded and medevac Dumont didn't know. They were new to our platoon. Our platoon was down once again to only eighteen men, he said. This included six new men and the CP group. Wounded this day from India Company were fifteen Marines and one KIA. Rahm and Dumont, both WIA from mortar shrapnel, were not evacuated. Dumont, noticing the big bandage on Aggie's left hand, asked, "What happened to you?"

Aggie responded, "The barrel was melting when I was assaulting, so I had to change it real quick. It's a really bad burn. You know, I kept firing even though I was hurt. Do you think I should get a medal for that?" Dumont just shook his head and walked away.

I did not feel comfortable being so close to the tree line, so I moved the gun back to the grave mound where we had spent most of the day. In guns, we never carried the all-purpose entrenching tool, so we borrowed one from a man in Lima Company who had set up to our right. We dug into the side of the oval-shaped grave mound that had served us well during the day as an effective fighting position. As we dug in, bones of whoever was buried there became exposed.

Dumont came back around, he was taking count of the enemy dead to call in a spot report to battalion. I told him of the two snipers we had killed, and he wrote the number down.

Aggie asked Dumont if the company was going to count the body in the grave as an NVA killed in today's battle.

"Why not?" he answered.

"If it's a gook's body and he's dead, we might as well get credit for the kill." We'll count him as a VC and not an NVA, he said. The bones of the body that was buried were long dry, but they were counted that night among the enemy we had killed.

We sat up late, not really talking, mostly just wondering, unable to stop secret thoughts from running through our minds.

Individually, we recalled the events of the day in the silence of our minds, in aching fearful hearts; we breathed deep sighs and prayed for our dead. We moved with slow acknowledgment of our own survival, coupled with the knowledge of tomorrow's sorrows when loved ones across the sea would be notified that their Marine wasn't coming home. Here, his friends and those that fought at his side were lost in time once shared as the darkness of the night arrived at our doorstep. We lost friends, and the darkness of the night added to the isolation we all felt.

Aggie didn't want to spend the night anywhere near the grave mound with the exposed body in the grave, so he moved higher up near the base of the hill and chose to sleep out in the open rice paddy instead.

"It's the living you have to worry about," I said. "The dead can't hurt you."

We had encountered a well-equipped, well-trained enemy force. The top of the hill remained unsecured, and in the morning, I knew we would take the hill.

Enemy losses for the day remained unknown; we had eighteen Marines that had been killed and sixty-six wounded.

Just before midnight, we stopped fighting for the night; up until that time, we had continued to receive sporadic fire. No one called a cease-fire or called for a truce; no understanding existed between us to leave each other alone for the night—we just stopped firing at each other. We stopped returning fire, and they stopped firing at us. Maybe both sides were too exhausted to keep going, and I wondered who won.

Who won the battle? All firefights in Nam were inconclusive. Most of the battles I had been involved in we had prevailed, but what did it all mean when we rarely saw the spoils of war? Body counts brought little consolation. There were numerous tunnels that interlocked all over the battlefields. Some went down deep into long passages with many chambers. The NVA used them for many reasons; tonight I hoped the enemy had used them to move away from the battlefield. Twenty-seven Marines had been killed and over a hundred wounded since Operation Foster/ Badger Hunt began. India Company alone had suffered much of the wounded during the operation. None had suffered more then First and Second Platoons.

Foxtrot's KIAs were the following: Donald Albert Basalla, Hank John Conrad De Hommel, Michael Daniel Deeson, Danny Lee Frye, Manuel Hernandez, William Henry Prothero, Lonnie Lee Silver. Lima Company's KIA, Wesley David Day.[220]

Sweeping Through Yesterday's Battle Scenes
Operation Foster AT 873522
November 27, 1967, D+14, 0655-1500 hours

Early morning at 0655 hours, I woke up before dawn as Lima Company already saddled up was making their way through our positions. Marines with full gear, fresh ammo, clean weapons, were moving out, ready for a new day of engagement.

We hadn't gotten the word what we would do or how we were going to do it. I only knew that the little knoll of a hill less than ten feet in height had been the site of much pain and suffering yesterday; with the new day, I wondered what was in store.

Before dawn, I moved the gun back to the base of the hill. Aggie was sitting up drinking hot cocoa from his canteen cup. He had cut a small hole on the side of the pound cake canister, dropped a few drops of water into it, and was now warming the can slowly with a heat tablet. Peaches and pound cakes that came in our C-rat packages, though not together in the same packaged meal, was always our favorite; warming the pound cake made it soft, moist, and a special pleasure because you had the time to warm it so you knew you had the time to enjoy it.

"Do you like Chesterfields?" Aggie asked me, throwing me the small four-cigarette package that came with our meals.

"Sure," I said and opened the small package and lit a cigarette.

"I thought you smoked," I asked Aggie. "I do," he answered, "but that's that new filtered Chesterfield cigarettes, and you can read what it says on the pack."

For months we had been eating old left over Korean vintage C-rats, the new C-rats we had been receiving lately were different, packed with different varieties of meals, accessory packets and they tasted better.

"Caution: Cigarette Smoking May be Hazardous to Your Health," I read to Aggie what was imprinted on the package of cigarettes.

"There you see it's hazardous to your health. None of the other packages say that."

"Aggie, they all say that now. You're getting shot at every day, and you're worried about your health from smoking a cigarette?" I laughed. Aggie looked up at me, "Oh, yeah," he said.

I lay back where I was sitting, to enjoy the early morning smoke. Above us, a cloudy gray sky added a sense of gloom to the day before us.

As the last man in Lima Company passed our gun's position, the word was passed for us to saddle up.

Aggie took his last bite of the pound cake and washed it down with his cocoa then poured water into his canteen cup and drank it, washing the last traces of the chocolate out. One of the new men in the platoon came by carrying the red mailbag, policing up our trash, to be buried. We had left the grave mound open, not bothering to cover up the exposed body we had unearthed the night before. I felt like going back and covering it up, but with daylight, I would be exposing myself out in the open field.

Lima Company had moved out to envelop around the east side of the hill, traveling in a counterclockwise direction toward the same area they had occupied the day before. I put on my backpack, draped a new 100-round of ammo across my chest, and picked up Bro's gun. The smell of Hoppes cleaning solvent mixed with the all-purpose military gun oil I had bathed her with the night before gave me a strong sense of confidence in the gun. She felt strong, smelled clean; the new barrel had never been fired, but I had taken it apart and cleaned it. The piston now flowed smooth, evenly and tight; she would do well in a firefight and I knew she was ready.

We had now been out in the field for two weeks; we hadn't showered or shaved and looked and smelled like it.

As Lima Company moved into position a good 400 meters from us, they were fired upon. Almost simultaneously, on the other side of the hill northwest of us, Foxtrot 2/7 was also hit with small arms fire and they began to receive a number of 60mm mortar rounds.

We had already started to move out when we heard the new sounds of battle going on in the distance; the noise filtered through the thick jungle foliage between us, and our gait quickened. We were moving west to circle clockwise around the hill and hook up with Foxtrot 2/7. Then we were to sweep up and over the hill, two companies together, to where Lima had set up as our blocking force.

The enemy once again had revealed their determined presence. A few stray rounds were fired on us from the very top of the hill, but today we were not going to play their game. This time we were not going to fight them on their terms; we ignored the snipers' rounds and kept moving. While both Lima and Foxtrot companies entertained them, we wrapped around to move in to assault their entrenched positions.

I noticed that this time the battle was being fought by the enemy from a distance. They were mostly firing M-79 grenades and dropping 60mm mortars on both companies and using small arms fire. Noticeable was the missing presence of the many AK-47s and machine-gun fire we had heard the day before. I knew then that the majority of the enemy had fled and only about thirty to forty had remained or been left behind as sacrificial lambs and they would be killed; they knew it and were willing to die, and we were on our way to make their dreams came true.

This time, no air strikes or artillery fire was called in. Instead, India Company began a cautious advance north, slowly sweeping toward Foxtrot 2/7's position. Third Platoon was leading, followed by Second Platoon, and First Platoon was bringing up the rear. Soon we would all be on line, sweeping together to overtake the enemy.

Within the hour, we had aggressively moved toward our objective and had taken three casualties. This slowed our platoon's advance until the priority wounded were medevaced and then we continued on.

At 1040 hours, we linked up with the rest of our company as well as with Foxtrot 2/7 then together we swept toward Lima Company's position.

Just before noon, we started to encounter some heavy resistance near the top of the hill and Lima Company started to take some casualties as some enemy soldiers fleeing our location were trying to get through their lines.[221]

By noon, BLT Battalion 2/3 ordered a heliborne assault of three Marine companies in support of the engagement we were encountering. All three companies—Golf, Hotel, and Foxtrot 2/3—landed by helicopters southeast of us between Hill 10 and Hill 11, and began sweeping toward our positions. As they advanced they discovered well-fortified enemy defensive bunkers some with four-foot-thick earth coverings at the base of Hill 10. The tunnels were found at the base of the hill where we had spent the night. Some of the bunkers and honeycomb tunnels discovered went under the graveyard and some ran along the small trail at the base of the hill. They were all destroyed by BLT's demolition Marines.[222]

By 1330 hours, we had secured the hilltop and were beginning to make our way toward Lima Company; by then we were receiving only sporadic gunfire and most of that was not directed at us. Once we reached the top, all the incoming had stopped. As we went through the battle area of the day before, we found seventy-nine dead enemy bodies including their weapons and packs and two Russian-made machine-guns. All of the dead soldiers were hard-core NVA soldiers. All wore the distinguished NVA military uniform, green in color, Russian-made web cartridge belts, cardboard beige helmets, boots; not one of them was dressed in VC black. The dead soldiers had clean uniforms on, they were all clean-shaven, and seemed to be dressed more for a parade than for battle. The fact that they had left so many of their dead behind made me realize we had encountered and fought against a very large enemy force the day before. It would remain unknown how many of the enemy had been wounded or killed, how many of their dead had been dragged away and buried; both Foxtrot 2/7 and Lima Company Marines, as well as our own, had fought under extreme incoming firepower and in terrain that favored the enemy.

Lima Company was credited with much of the body count for the day, but they had also lost the most: four men KIA and five priority WIAs. Foxtrot 2/7 had two KIAs and nineteen WIAs.[223]

Get Off the Hill and Continue the Operation
Operation Foster AT 873522
November 27, 1967, D+14, 0655-1500 hours

India Company swept through Lima Company's line then turned left going northwest, to sweep north along the eastern edge of Finger Lake. First Platoon was bringing up the rear then, Lima Company was to follow in trace.

Three-hundred yards away, a helicopter was coming in to land when he began to take some incoming fire from an enemy force near the tree line that ran along the east side of Finger Lake.

An escorting gunship flying ahead of the chopper quickly turned, banked left, circled around, and opened fire on the tree line. At the same time, I could hear Lima Company sweeping southwest of us, get hit. A heavy volume of gunfire was being exchanged. We had just swept east of that area, and now the enemy had attacked Lima Company, behind us. It seemed as if the whole area was infested with enemy soldiers.

About half a klick away, a bird-dog flying overhead fired off a couple of WP rockets toward the lake's edge; and a short time later, a jet appeared overhead, swooped down, and dropped a load of napalm at the tree line to the north of the WP smoke. Once the smoke cleared we continued on, sweeping through the village of Phu Bihn (1).

Sniping With the M-60
Operation Foster AT 873522
November 27, 1967, D+14, 0655-1500 hours

By mid-afternoon, the three BLT 2/3 companies turned to sweep away from us, going southwest, toward the Song Thu Bon River. Meanwhile, we reached the outer edge of a large hamlet we had traveled through near the bend in the lake; this time, we were on the east side along with the rest of the company.

As we emerged at the edge of the tree line between two thick tree lines some six hundred yards away, someone pointed out a squad of NVA soldiers running away from us. They were too far away to shoot at accurately with the M-16's. We were told to just keep moving as they were running away from a sweep another Marine company was conducting toward yet another Marine blocking force east of us, which they would run into. The gooks out in the open were too choice a target.

I raised the gun to my right shoulder, held her firm, sighted in, and squeezed off a single shot. It struck just behind and short of the running gooks. The nine soldiers quickened their pace, and I sighted in through the gun's sight again. When I had the second to the last one in line aligned in my sights, I held the gun in tight and held her firm, her hard body feeling solid, rigid, itching determined to strike a target. I pulled the trigger, and the bullet flowed through the bore smoothly.

The second to the last soldier went down, and the last men behind him quickly hit the deck. Two others ran back, picked the downed man up, and all three dragged the limp body into the dense tree line where the other NVA soldiers had disappeared into.

The M-60 was not made to be single shot nor was it designed to be used like a sniper's rifle, but there are a lot of things we did with the M-60 machine-gun in Vietnam that the gun was not designed to be used for. The moving NVA targets had been too inviting, and I couldn't see just letting them go; we had done that before and suffered greatly for it.

The bird-dog, flying recon overhead, eyed the struggling enemy soldiers out in the open; as they desperately tried to escape by entering a tree line, he fired off a WP rocket into the same spot. Seconds later, one of our FO's took over calling in an artillery mission. The first rounds were on target, he adjusted the impact site, and called for a fire-for-effect and the whole area exploded under the barrage of artillery fire.

We had now been out in the bush for two solid weeks, seeking the enemy, humping from one village to another, crossing numerous rice paddy fields, small hills, and thick jungle terrain. We had swept through the area in the morning, afternoon, and evening. In the sun, at night, in the rain, and in the mud. Before the operation, it had never occurred to me that the enemy would stick around to engage us in a firefight. We were Americans, from the world's wealthiest nation, and we were supposed to have overwhelming military firepower at our disposal. We had naval and fixed winged-aircraft firepower as well as mortar and heavy artillery. What chances would an enemy infantry unit have against such odds? We had dropped thousands of leaflets into the area announcing our intentions. Surely the enemy would have left the area. I hadn't seen a single VC. All the individuals that we had come across, seen, engaged in firefights or found dead, had been dressed in dark green or dark tan NVA uniforms. Not one VC in black pajamas was among them.

NVAs were hard-core fighters many of whom had been in the bush for a while. The enemy force we had encountered were highly skilled and determined. They were well-trained enemy soldiers and were much better equipped to fight against us than the local VC. Whoever their commanding officer was, he was a worthy opponent and had run the battlefield with great expertise, conducting warfare against us expertly, and deploying his men with noble skills. The NVA planned their battles well, and we had seen how well in the past few days of fighting.

The NVA soldiers that walked into Aggie's line of fire back at the old French village were moving down the trail in formation. Somehow, they hadn't gotten the word that we were in that area. But then again, we also hadn't been told that an NVA division was operating in the area we were patrolling in. The NVA it seemed just happened to be one step ahead of us in many ways. I wondered where the majority of them were now located, where had the majority of them disappeared into.

Later that day, we went to cross an open field of rice paddies and advanced to the top of yet another small hill near Quang Hue (Hill 12).[224] There were a series of tree lines and scattered bushes and beyond the hill, another series of rice paddy fields. We were to take the hill and set in. The enemy, we were told, might be entrenched in a far tree line on the other side of the hill. First Platoon was assigned to advance on line while the rest of the company would cover for us.

I feared that if we got pinned down, we could be pinned down for hours. Yet, the platoon got on line and we began our assault and once committed, the enemy opened fire.

The platoon as before instead of seeking cover, rushed toward the enemy positions.

I ran with the gun toward a near tree line to our right and found some cover behind an embankment there and covered for the platoon as the rest of them caught up with us. As we took cover we kept getting sporadic incoming fire until the rest of the company moved forward then all the incoming fire stopped. A short time later a medevac priority mission was called in, so I knew we had taken casualties.

We stayed in the tree line while the choppers came in and took out the wounded. On the choppers were new supplies and some of the men returning to the platoon who had been wounded earlier at the beginning of the operation or had returned to the company from other assignments. Among them was Corporal Boone who had recovered from an injury he had received just before the operation began.[225]

The company moved out along the tree line then turned north along another tree line, First Platoon was walking point. A small well-beaten path ran beside the tree line, and while we were on that path, we were once again hit with heavy incoming fire. The platoon was stretched out along a thick tree line. The rest of the company remained around a turn in the trail a good distance away, and were already maneuvering counter-clockwise to outflank the enemy.

As we lay on the ground, just inside the tree line waiting for the rest of the company to be deployed air strikes were called in and as they began their first run, Boone came walking behind me. Scattered bullets were still being shot at us here and there, but Boone was walking around as if nothing was going on. I was lying on my back waiting for the sniper taking potshots at us to stop firing when Boone stopped, and stood directly over me.

"What's going on?" he said.

"Get away from here, Boone," I said to him. "You'll draw fire." He knew I was serious and wasn't taking his gallantry as valid behavior but pure foolishness on his part. There were times like that that Boone really irritated me. For some time now, he no longer seemed to care if he lived or died and he now was carrying an antagonistic attitude as if he was privileged or should be afforded some special courtesy because he was black, or because he had time in grade. But with that mind-set, he might get others killed.

I knew Boone had wanted to be promoted to sergeant and had asked Lieutenant Wilson if he could take over First Squad, but when Wilson refused, Boone attributed that to mean no because of his skin color. Walking around as he was, showed me he was not qualified to lead, and now I further questioned his leadership abilities.

We waited while another Marine company was called in, and they swept in from our far right side coming in abreast of our company as they made their way around. Once the two companies united the incoming fire ceased. The platoon meanwhile had taken three WIAs, but only one was medevaced.[226]

Jungle Rot
Operation Foster
November 28, 1967, D+15, 0800 hours

On the morning of the twenty-eighth, we received reinforcements and with the new men, swept north toward the Song Vu Gia River. We had started Operation Foster with forty-seven men in First Platoon and three times now, had been reinforced with new men. Twice, we had gone down to less than twelve men in the platoon. With the new replacements, we were now up to thirty-two; twenty of them were new replacements. Some came and were gone during the operation, and I never saw their faces. I never knew they had been assigned to our company or platoon. They were Marines and they did their duty, were wounded, and had been medevaced. Operation Foster was a search and destroy mission, and while firefights had for the past few days become a daily occurrence, there was no getting used to war. Each firefight was different; every battle was experienced differently by each of us. Marines that came and went in such a short a time would remember this war so differently.

When we arrived near the river, we stopped to rest and Doc Mac came around checking our feet for "jungle rot." If you don't change your socks often—a luxury you don't get in the bush—chances are good that your feet will turn a greenish blue color.

"Jungle rot will eat a grunt's foot right out," Marty had once said. When, I took off my boots my feet were swollen, waterlogged, and had turned a greenish purplish color. Welsh, Marty, Keene, Rahm, and a new man by the name of Mark Saylor, as well as another Marine from Second Platoon, were tagged, to be medevaced out of the field. Saylor was tagged to be medevac because of a wound he had received from shrapnel during the graveyard assault.

As we waited to board the choppers, two NVA prisoners were also loaded on board. Both were blindfolded and had their hands tied behind their backs. An ARVN was with us as well as a Korean military officer and an ROK Marine who was in charge of the prisoners. The Korean officer moved both prisoners toward the chopper's open door while yelling at them in Vietnamese.[227]

Just before we landed, the chopper made a wide turn and stood still hovering in the air. The Korean Marine that had been interrogating the prisoners asked one of them a few questions. The prisoner refused to answer. The ROK Marine then shoved him out of the door of the chopper while it was about 100 feet or more off the ground. He screamed as he fell onto the helipad below. Before we landed, we hovered twenty feet above ground and the other blind folded prisoner was blabbing away, answering the Korean ROK Marine's questions.

We landed on the helipad at 3/7 and were met by a full bird colonel, news reporters, and other officials. The welcoming committee were greeted and saluted by an officer who had also been on board the chopper.

We got off, walked around the group and were more intent on making our way to the chow hall then going to the Battalion Aid Station, but one of the medical doctors there wanted to see us first. He examined our feet and separated a few of us from the rest.

CHAPTER NINETEEN

First Medical Hospital
Da Nang, South Vietnam
November 28, 1967, 1300 hours

At 1300 hours, a couple of other Marines and I were loaded on board medevac choppers and landed at Da Nang's first medical hospital. The other Marines left behind at 3/7 were to be sent out the following day by six-by trucks. Seven of us landed at the hospital the night of the twenty-eighth and most of us were infected with a serious case of jungle rot. Some there at that hospital ward were Third Marine Division Marines who, like myself, had been out in the field for long periods without having taken off our boots much less changed our socks. I hadn't realized how bad my feet were until the nurse examined my feet.

That evening, those of us in the same hospital section gathered around and began to compare the color of our feet and the various stages of infections we had. Soon, we were comparing other diseases encountered in country: malaria, leprosy, and all kinds of social diseases. We compared the marks left behind by cuts and bruises, infected eyes, insect bites, and the color of the pus we had seen as well as the size and colors of snakes and animal bites Marines had received. We spoke of the weird, multicolored, and noisy birds and animals we had seen.

We spoke about the disease caused by leeches when they were plucked off and left their heads embedded under our skin. We spoke of the largest rats we had killed and how many roosters, chickens, dogs, and rock monkeys we had shot. We spoke of the number of rounds it took to bring a large-size water buffalo down. We went from there to the types of food we had eaten, which included large insects, wild boars, snakes, dogs, rats, monkeys, water buffaloes, pigs, chickens, ducks, fish, and husked (brown) rice. We shared stories about what we had encountered in the bush: gorillas, monkeys, elephants, wild boars, and tigers. Some Marines spoke about the war and the dead Chinese and Russian advisors whom they had killed, gooks we had seen or killed, and the many colorful clothes and different uniforms the enemy wore. The enemy we had engaged in battle came in all sizes and shapes: there were tall ones, skinny ones, fat ones, stinky ones, and clean-cut, well-dressed enemy soldiers. We spoke of the black-teethed women that followed their men into battle and who often died alongside their men.

While we sat around talking, a Third Marine Division Marine got up and walked into the adjoining room looking for the head to relieve himself. He had been in Vietnam for over eight months, and most of that time, it had been in some remote outpost on the fringes of civilization. A couple of minutes after he had left the group, we heard a loud scream echo down the hospital's hallway.

We rushed over to see what was going on, and on the way there, we heard the Marine scream again. It was a loud cry full of anguish. As we went through a set of double doors, we found the Marine sitting on the floor next to a commode.

We stood there, silent, looking at him; then he pulled down the toilet's handle, and the water flushed, and he screamed again, "*aaaahhhh!*"

It had been so long since he had seen a toilet that pushing the commode's flush handle gave him great pleasure. His screams weren't from pain, but from shock and pleasure. It was civilization; it represented home, and it was as American as ice cream and apple pie. It gave all of us a sense of the real world, life, and American living.

It's funny how such simple things like a toilet can be taken for granted and how we don't realize what comfort we have back in the real world until we have to do without. It had been five months since I had last seen a toilet, and I could easily associate with the joy the Marine was feeling and the high he was getting just sitting there on the floor flushing the toilet. He must have flushed it ten to twenty times before he was satisfied that it was real and it wasn't going away. We then took turns flushing the toilet.

Flushing that toilet was more therapeutic than a whole week of psychological counseling. We stood in line to flush that toilet and saw it as a rite of passage. It was the introduction of association that we needed to turn our minds back toward the real world. The words John Niederinghaus had once shared with me came back once more to remembrance: "For those who have fought for it, life has a flavor the protected will never know."

A new, young medical doctor making his evening rounds came by to see what was going on. He walked away shaking his head and muttering to himself, "Crazy grunts, crazy Marines."

That night was the first night out of the bush for many of us in many, many months. For the most part, most of us had come from recent combat operations or firefights, and as we gathered around that night to watch television programs broadcast by the Armed Forces Network, the program everyone wanted to see on television was the then-popular weekly TV series *Combat*. We sat there and watched the program, and it didn't bother us; it was so far removed from the real world of war we had experienced.

It was comforting to have spent the first night out of the bush at first med in Da Nang with many of the war wounded. Many were hurting in more ways that can be imagined as not all were suffering the physical pains of war but of those invisible wounds found deep within the soul.

I slept in a real bed with a real mattress with a clean white sheet on it, but when the lights went out, I couldn't sleep. It was too quiet. I tossed and turned, unable to sleep until about eleven that night. Off in the far distance, I heard the distinct sound of artillery fire going off. On some faraway hill, somebody was firing off artillery rounds, and I silently fell fast asleep to the sounds of war.

Slimy Yellow-Colored Feet
Da Nang Hospital
November 29, 1967, 0800 hours

The morning of the twenty-ninth was spent with doctors examining us and with nurses dressing our feet. One Marine's feet had been so caked with grime and filth that the doctors used surgical scissors and tweezers to pry off his socks while wearing a face mask because of the smell. That Marine was in the bed next to mine. Both of his feet were tightly wrapped in puffy white bandages that had been soaked in oily yellow ointment. He was told that he would undergo prolonged and extensive immersion foot treatment and would be sent out to another medical facility for further treatment. While my feet were likewise soaked, they didn't seem as damaged as his. That evening, while some Marines were sent back to their companies, those of us requiring further medical treatment were staying and were allowed to go see a USO show.

First Army Hospital
Chu Lai
November 30, 1967, 1300 hours

The next day, twelve of us, the ones with the worst cases of immersion foot, were loaded on board a C-130 cargo plane and transported to the First Army Hospital at Chu Lai for long-term treatment. Among those from first platoon were Welsh, Keene, and myself.

The hospital was made up of long wooden billets, some attached to each other, others were located just a short distance away, so for some treatment you had to go out one barrack then turn around and go into another for different treatments.

On the morning of December 2, I was able to take a steamy, hot shower—the first hot shower since I arrived in Vietnam. The medical personnel at the army hospital treated us well. Some had became fascinated by the color my feet had turned, and they took numerous Polaroid color photos to show and tell what the results of humping rice paddy fields without taking time to rest or to air out your feet or change socks would do. The doctor in charge told me that I was going to spend at least a week there, and he and the nurses cleaned and dressed my feet and cleaned out what pieces of shrapnel they found in our bodies. They wrapped our feet in puffy white bandages that had been soaked in a smelly, oily yellow ointment. The doctor in charge of my care seemed to like me, and when I told him that I had a friend stationed in Chu Lai assigned to MAG 13, the doctor said he would try and contact him for me.

On the third, Ted Asher, the Marine airman friend of mine, came to the hospital to visit. That afternoon, I was allowed to visit his barracks and couldn't believe the type of life air wingers lived. They had spacious air-conditioned barracks with four-inch thick mattresses. Some of them wore new camouflaged utilities or camouflaged shorts.

That evening, as I waited for Ted to come over to take me and the other Marines to the MAG 13 club, Welsh and Keene decided to go over to the club by themselves. When we arrived at the club, Keene and Welsh were sitting outside and told us that grunts were not allowed in the club unless a Marine airman escorted them. When Ted tried to get us all in acting as our escort, he was told that he was allowed to escort only one Marine grunt into the club and he quickly contacted a friend of his, by the name of Dallas and grabbed hold of a passing air Marine and all three of us were escorted in.

It wasn't long before pilots there found out we were grunts. As we spoke and shared with Ted and his friends what we had experienced during Operation Foster, pilots and crew chief members along with others in the Air Wing gathered closer and listened. Then one of the pilots grabbed a chair, joined our table, and ordered drinks for all of us.

After a while, a pilot said how envious he was of us to be able to meet the enemy on our level eye to eye. In the sky, he said, they weren't given that opportunity to use his flying skills against the enemy as he had been taught and wanted to engage the enemy in a firefight.

We, in turn, toasted them and honored them for supporting us, for being there when we needed air strikes and when our wounded needed to be medevaced, and we acknowledged how they often took great chances to help get us out and how they often took hits on their planes and helicopters while giving us that close ground support we needed and appreciated.

Keene told the pilots, "I sure would like to meet the pilot that helped us out on the nineteenth of November." Keene told them how we had been pinned down by a very effective sniper located in a treetop that we couldn't see.

The jets came in low, real low; while the pilot was talking with one of our sergeants on the ground, that pilot on the net then brought in his plane almost at treetop level. He made one pass, and then on the second pass, he hit his afterburners near where the sergeant told him the sniper was and the plane shot straight up in the middle of the tree line from the spot where we were getting sniped.

"Damn if we didn't see the whole treetop light up and the sniper was thrown out of the tree as the jet's afterburners tossed him out. It was the most awesome thing that I've seen," Keene told them.

We drank some more and shared more stories with the Marine airmen who kept buying us drinks, and soon, other Marine grunts that had been evacuated with us and transferred to Chu Lai showed up and this time they were allowed into the club without an escort.

After a while, the air crew members left and one of the grunts told us how he had tried to get a pair of camouflaged shorts from the supply sergeant at the army base but had been denied because he wasn't assigned to the MAG 13 (Marine Aircraft Group) unit. On our way back to our barracks, as we passed the supply shack, it was decided to use the opportunity given us and so we helped ourselves to as many camouflaged shorts and utilities as we could carry. Our mistake was that some Marines returned to the club to celebrate their good fortune, with the borrowed clothes stuffed in their shirts and trousers, and there they continued to drink and celebrate.[228]

Hidden To Stay
Army Hospital
December 4, 1967, 0900 hours

The following morning, the base commanding officer, upon hearing that someone had broken into the supply shack, ordered our barracks searched. Before the searchers arrived, the medical doctor in charge of my case had me pack up my gear, and he transferred me to another barrack. When I returned later that afternoon, everyone was gone. All the Marines that had participated in the break-in had been sent back to their units. I alone remained. Keene and Welsh, while sent back, had managed to hide some of their tropical utilities and took them back to our unit.

My doctor decided to keep me there as my feet were too raw, and he and the others treating me at the hospital remained fascinated by the color and condition of my feet. The next couple of days I spent with Ted and Dallas. The area there was serene and peaceful. If it wasn't for the background noise caused by the constant planes landing and leaving the air station, it seemed impossible that just a few miles away, a war was going on. The beach, for as far as we could see, was deserted. A U.S. naval ship was anchored about four miles offshore.

On December 10, the doctor discharged me and that night, Ted took me over to the officer's club once more. While we were there, some of the pilots gathered around me and treated me like a celebrity. I was a grunt; it was my red tracers that helped them pinpoint where the enemy was so that they wouldn't open up accidentally on our own men. I never realized how much pilots feared dropping a load of ordnances on *friendlies*. They were fascinated by the accounts of the battles I shared with them.

While they saw the action from above, fighting the ground battle to them was a thrill they hadn't experienced. As much as they loved flying, to be able to exchange rounds with the enemy blow for blow was something many of them desired. I noticed that most of the pilots carried .38 caliber pistols with them and asked Ted about them. I shared with him the incident with the .45 in the rice paddy, and he asked me to stay another night. I missed my flight out that day and stayed as Ted had suggested. That night, we went back to the officer's club, and the air Marines that frequented the club presented me with a .38 pistol and a shoulder holster as a gift.

On the twelfth, I caught a C-130 flight into Da Nang and arrived too late to be picked up by the battalion runner. On the thirteenth, I returned to Battalion HQ, but I had to wait until the fourteenth to get out to where First Platoon was. Marines there told me that India Company was split and Third Platoon was now at Seabee Bridge while First and Second Platoon were on Hill 65, temporarily manning Lima Company's lines as they were at battalion preparing to go out into the northern section of the Arizona area on Operation Citrus.

Return To Hill 65
Hill 65, AT 878577
December 14, 1967, 1200 hours

I rode out on the mail truck to Hill 65, and the area seemed different. The villages had lost their beauty, the simple life of the villager I once saw was now marred in the shadow of gloom that hung unspoken over the whole area.

The first person I saw when I got off the six-by on Hill 65 was Sergeant Dumont. "Glad to have you back," he said as we shook hands.

"We're back to Hill 65?" I asked.

"Only for about another week, we're on loan to 2/7. Lima and Kilo Company are at Battalion getting ready to go on Operation Citrus in the old Foster area. India Company is scattered all over, First Platoon does most of the road sweeps in the morning on Route 4, Liberty Road and sometimes, up Highway 5 (Convoy Road). Lieutenant Wilson is gone to battalion, and he'll be going on R&R soon, so we don't expect him to return to the platoon. We're waiting to get a new lieutenant. We got in a bunch of new guys, so most of the platoon is new. I'm the new platoon sergeant. Jones is on R&R, so I guess you're the new squad leader for guns, for now."

Lieutenant Wilson had been an outstanding officer.[229] Together, we had gotten into several tight situations. He cared about the safety of his men while he did the job assigned to him and expected us to do our job as Marines. He didn't take unnecessary chances with his Marines. With a high score when he graduated from

OCS, he could have chosen any field for duty, but he chose to lead combat Marines in battle. He had once sat with us in guns' hooch at Liberty Bridge and just sat around with us talking. I had heard him say at that time that once his enlistment was over, he planned to join the FBI; he's halfway there, I was thinking.

"Some of the wounded from Foster have returned, but we're still short of men," Dumont went on to say as he turned to walk with me down the hill toward guns' hooch.

"The company doesn't keep men in the CAC unit in the village anymore. They have been renamed CAP units and have their own headquarters and run their own security details. First and Second Platoons are on the hill, and Third Platoon is assigned to provide security for the Seabee Bridge at Battalion. As soon as we get some new men, we may go back to Liberty Bridge. The squads have, at the most, eight men in them so fire-teams are small, three or four men each. Sometimes only eight men go out instead of the twelve that used to go out on a squad-size patrol. Guns has two new guys, Eddie Williams on loan from patrol and Herman James. James has a 0331 MOS."

I was glad to hear that. At least one of them would have been trained on how to break down and fire the gun. Both Eddie Williams and another Marine by the name of Raul Serrato had joined First Platoon in December just before we left Liberty Bridge. We called Serrato "Chino" because of his round nose and almost slanted eyes that made him look Asian. Serrato had been raised in East Los Angeles and grew up on Brooklyn Boulevard, but even the gang fights in the barrios hadn't prepared a street-smart Marine like him for war. The fear in his eyes revealed how young and innocent he was.

"How did the operation end?" I asked Dumont as we made our way toward the mess tent and the trail that would lead toward guns' hooch.

"After you left, we stayed out for another two days," Dumont replied. "We lost a couple more men."

I slowed my pace and turned my head to hear the bad news. Who had been killed ran through my mind. I stopped. Dumont stopped and said, "Only wounded," he said. "I don't even know who they were. Twenty-one men were killed and 137 wounded during Foster. They gave us credit for killing 125 of the enemy, but that was for the whole operation. Who knows how many of them First Platoon actually killed?"

In the back of my mind, I figured that if there had been 125 actual bodies counted, that meant at least twice or three times that many had been killed, so at least another hundred or two of the enemy would have been wounded. I knew we probably killed at least that many at the graveyard battle. It didn't seem like they counted those we killed on the nineteenth through the twenty-first. I knew that we caused them great pain in those days of battle. I wondered how many, I had actually killed, wounded? Even the two that I knew were torn apart by my machine-gun remained unconfirmed kills because their bodies were recovered by the enemy. Unless the body was there in the morning and we stepped over it, no one counted it as a confirmed killed.

"With you back, only twelve of the original First Platoon remains. I had to pack and ship off the gear of all the Marines in our platoon that were wounded or killed and weren't returning. Right now, there's you and Aguilar and the two new men in guns. You also have Porter and Rahm assigned to guns."

"Porter?" I questioned.

"We don't have a rocket team anymore," Dumont said. "It's been dissolved. Everyone now carries the new LAWs (light antitank weapon rocket). We only have one gun team, but with you back, we'll have two gun teams. Porter and Rahm may be reassigned elsewhere, but for now they're in guns. But I don't know what the new looey will do."

"Congratulations," I said, pointing to his new sergeant stripes.

"Thanks," he answered.

Porter had always been jittery since he'd been in country. He protested every assignment and was always scared stiff whenever we went out on patrol. But still, once on patrol he was alert and ready for battle, so I knew I could count on him when it counted. We stopped near the trail leading down toward guns' bunker. Eddie Williams was coming down from the chow hall, and we slowed down our gait to meet him where the trail led down to guns' bunker. He had a small body, a short black Marine with straight, thick, greasy hair combed straight back. He walked past us without acknowledging our presence. William's air of arrogance and haughty disposition was clearly evident in his demeanor as he walked by.

"Somebody's going to knock the shit out of that kid," I said to Dumont before I turned and walked down to the hooch alone.

Life In Guns Would Never Be The same
Hill 65
December 14, 1967, 1300 hours

Williams had walked into the hooch before me and turned on the juice box that Jones had left behind. The music was loud. I walked in behind him and turned it off. He arose in protest, was about to say something but held back as his anger quickly turned to caution, his round eyes betraying his fear of the unknown, and he decided to sit back down. I picked up my mail and walked back outside. I figured when he saw Dumont and me together he knew who I was. I walked out and saw that Williams had taken over "Bro's" old cot in the corner.

I removed his blanket and gear, turned the cot upside down, shook out all the dirt and caked mud out of its bottom, then propped myself down on it to read my mail. Life in guns wasn't going to be the same.

There were four letters from my wife and a couple from Diana. I read Diana's letter first. The letters from my wife I was not looking forward to reading. While she shared with me stories about my son, there really wasn't much more in them that I looked forward to reading. After I had finished reading all my letters, I toyed with the idea of having Williams carry the gun. There's nothing like hell's fire to straighten out a Marine's priorities. But I realized that if shit hits the fan, he might freeze and would be useless in a firefight. *Perhaps I'll have him hump it then take over if we get hit,* I thought. Williams acted like an old salt, but the fear I had seen in his eyes had betrayed his inexperience as well as the fear of the unknown. I wondered if he was a draftee. I hated draftees, especially ones who came with attitudes.

When I joined the Marine Corps, it was just coming under pressure to take in draftees. While some Marines had joined the corps in fear of being drafted by other military services, the pride of the Corps was that they volunteered and were accepted into the Marine Corps family; they deliberately made a choice to serve in combat as a Marine because that's what Marines do, but a draftee was just picked out of line and sent to the Corps.

Private Johnny T. Reysack was a draftee that had been rushed through the recruitment process by a recruiting sergeant from Iowa. Reysack did not truly know his left foot from his right foot when he first arrived in boot camp, and when you explained it to him, he forgot a minute or so later, it seemed, mostly because of the pressure and the way he was treated as a draftee by the drill instructors in Boot Camp. The drill instructors often told him that he would never be a Marine.

Reysack often showed up in formation with boots on the wrong feet or unlaced; his trousers were baggy, wrinkled, and his cap two sizes too large. The drill instructors never bothered to get him the proper size of clothing. "Why bother as he will never be a Marine" seemed to be their reasoning.

One day, during a quiet Sunday afternoon time for the platoon, drill instructor Sergeant Nelson, who had seen my artistic abilities, had me draw the outline of a naked woman on his pillowcase. I drew it for him using a felt-tip black marking pen. When I finished the drawing, I presented the pillowcase to the drill instructor and Private Reysack was there, having been assigned house mouse duties to clean the drill instructor's Quonset hut for the day. Nelson showed Reysack the picture I had drawn on the pillowcase and asked him if he liked it. Reysack grinned, and as soon as he did, Nelson told him that it was a dirty picture. Then he bellowed, "Marines don't look at dirty pictures, Private Reysack! Do you like looking at dirty pictures, Private Reysack?"

Private Reysack looked away like a shamed puppy instead of looking down as most would do. Nelson then opened his wall locker revealing a large naked picture of a *Playboy* model. It was Miss July 1966. "Private Reysack," he said, "is that a good picture or a dirty picture?" Reysack's eyes opened wide, and he displayed a broad grin, nodding his head yes. At that time, I wondered if Private Reysack was smarter than the drill instructor believed. "Reysack!" Sergeant Nelson yelled. "That's a nasty picture! Marines aren't supposed to look at dirty pictures, are they, Private Reysack?"

"No, sir," Reysack answered loudly, snapping to attention, taking special efforts to look down at his hands and place his arms at his sides as he was supposed to. He made sure his thumb was at his trousers' seam before he looked up again. His shirtsleeves were rolled up because the sleeves' arms were too long for his short arms.

"Then close that locker, Reysack," Nelson ordered. Reysack quickly reached up and closed Sergeant Nelson's wall locker's door. "You were looking at that dirty picture, weren't you, Reysack?" Nelson asked. "You're never going to be a Marine, Private Reysack, if you keep looking at dirty pictures." Poor Reysack didn't know how to answer. Nelson then picked up his pillowcase with the drawing of the naked woman I had drawn on it. "Do you like my pillowcase, Private Reysack?" he asked again.

This time, Reysack shook his head no.

"You don't like my pillowcase, Reysack?" Nelson barked out. "There's nothing wrong with my pillowcase, Reysack! It's a beautiful picture. Reysack, you have a dirty mind, Reysack. You're not going to become a Marine if you have a dirty mind. You have to be clean, clean in body and clean in mind. You shower, don't you, Reysack? The Marine Corps only wants clean Marines in its service. If you go to Vietnam, Private Reysack, are you going to be thinking of dirty pictures? If you're thinking of dirty pictures when you should be shooting gooks, you're going to get Marines killed in Vietnam, Private Reysack. You don't want to be responsible for getting Marines killed in war, do you, Reysack?"

Reysack shook his head no. Tears were beginning to form at the corner of his eyes, but he held them back.

"You better give up trying to be a Marine in the Marine Corps, Reysack!" Nelson commanded. "You have a dirty mind, and Uncle Sam doesn't want Marines with dirty minds fighting and killing gooks. The enemy deserves to die with honor and dignity. But if you're thinking of dirty pictures when you kill the enemy, that's not right. Would you like to get killed by a gook that is thinking of naked women when he shoots you? Get out of my office, Reysack. Go take a shower, Private Reysack, clean out your mind, Reysack!"

With that, Reysack ran crying out of the drill instructor's Quonset hut and headed for the shower. I often wondered whatever became of Private Reysack, and prayed he wasn't send to Vietnam.

Aggie's Gun Team
Hill 65
December 14, 1967, 1600 hours

Aggie, returning from a patrol, came walking up the path with James, the new guy. James was carrying the gun, and Porter was behind him carrying two hundred rounds of ammo. Aggie and Porter never liked each other, so I was tempted to put Williams and Porter together but that would be a disaster and dangerous to the squad they would be out with. We had already lost one gun to the gooks, and I didn't want to be responsible for losing another.

Shortly after "Bro" was killed, his family wrote to the company requesting that someone write to them. I wanted to write, but how could I tell his family that I was alive because their son was dead, because he volunteered in my place? The NVA had taken that gun, but there was nothing he could have done about that. A squad should have been sent out instead of a four-man fire-team. But we didn't know that an NVA regiment had been operating in the area. That they had lobbed over fifty Soviet-made 122mm rockets at the Da Nang airbase just days before. We didn't know then what we were up against.

"Here comes Combat," Aggie said, as Ira Rahm[230] came walking down the hill. Rahm certainly looked like a walking "combat Marine" because of all the stuff he was carrying.

Later that afternoon, we all sat around and talked about Operation Foster and what had happened to the platoon since then. James sat around and listened. Williams had left and was visiting a friend on the other side of the perimeter. When he was about to leave, Williams went over and moved his gear that I had removed off of Bro's bunk and placed them inside the hooch. He came out a few moments later and said that he was going to visit a friend of his in First Squad. While it was not a request, it was the beginning of acknowledging the rank structure, and he had to give an account to me as my position as guns' new squad leader. I nodded yes and he left. I still hadn't spoken to him, but he clearly understood who was in charge.

As Rahm, Aggie, and I talked, Porter contributed little to the conversation concerning the firefights in which the platoon had been involved. Rahm, Aggie, and I knew that when Boyd was medevaced, Porter became attached to the CP. Dumont had then made him the platoon's runner so he hadn't been as involved in some of the more serious firefighting as that the rest of us had experienced. He may have been as scared as I remembered but he was there and did his part.

Rahm ran down for me who was left from the original platoon before we went on Operation Foster.

"Only a few are left from the original platoon," he said. "In First Squad, only Abe Metzler. In Second Squad, Chief, Chino. Perkins is now with the CP. Lucero never came back. Welsh is still here. He's Second Squad's squad leader. Boone is the squad leader in Third Squad, only Cobb remains of that original squad, I forget who else is left. Bruce Alan Cobb was from Bradford, Pa, a short Marine, with stocky arms, round face, and a quite disposition, and I remembered him.

In guns, it's me, you, Aggie, Porter, and the two new guys, Williams and James—oh yeah! Marty went back to Third Squad. Pridemore is also back.

"After you were medevaced," he continued, "we had companies of Marines all over the place and only ran into light ground fire, but it was more harassment than anything else. Nothing like what we saw, but this time we called in a lot of artillery and air cover.

I think the NVA took off back up the mountains after the graveyard battle. We found out we had some Marine scouts working in the mountains who had spotted whole columns of NVA moving down out of the mountains into the Arizona area days before Operation Foster was launched, but no one passed down the word to us. They were looking for a fight and knew we were coming into the area; they had it well planned. A couple of days after we pulled out, B-52s dropped hundreds of bombs in the mountains, where their base camps were located. It was a real arc-light show."

Night Ambush At Mamasan's
Hill 65
December 15, 1967, 1800 hours

On the morning of the fifteenth, Aggie and I were standing watch at the front gate of Hill 65 when two incoming .57 recoilless rifle rounds hit the hill. One of the large high-explosive rounds missed the guard shack by only a couple of feet and struck a dirt embankment behind us.

Dumont came by late that afternoon and said a gun team was needed to go out with First Squad on a night ambush. Almost immediately, an argument ensued between James and Williams as to who was going and whose turn it was to carry the gun. I listened for a while as James pointed out that he had carried the gun out the past two times. It didn't seem like James was scared to carry the gun, but that Williams and Porter needed to carry it also. Since the Marine who carried the gun becomes a favorite target for the enemy, I understood his concern. Aggie seemed glad that I was there, so he didn't have to intervene. I could tell he had gone through this before. He also knew I would not send him out with the gun.

I liked James. He, like Porter and Williams, was a black Marine, but he had a common sense attitude unlike the other two. I could see that James might have been shafted by Williams before and wasn't going to be taken advantage of again. James was a Marine anxious to do a good job, but somehow, he had gotten sucked into the bickering that had developed in guns while I was gone. He would make a good gunner if I could help keep him alive. Williams and Porter were men assigned to my gun squad not because they wanted to be here but because we needed bodies. I knew I would treat them equally while expecting them to display the same type of professional service required of a Marine in combat. Williams looked scared at the prospect of carrying the gun out on a night ambush, and I understood that. I was determined not to let petty squabbling interfere with guns' integrity. Our lives and the lives of the platoon depended upon it.

"Aggie," I said, "you take charge of the watch tonight. It'll be you, Williams, and Porter standing watch. I'm taking the gun out with James and Rahm. James will be my A-gunner." I could tell that Porter and Williams were pleased with the arrangements, but I wasn't too sure about James. He seemed to welcome the opportunity to go out with me and to know that he wouldn't be carrying the gun, which released some of the tension he had been under. I nodded to James and half smiled; he welcomed it.

The eight-man rifle squad and my three-man gun team left the perimeter wire just before sunset. The gooks would be keeping their eyes out to see where we would go. Ira Hullihen, First Squad's leader, was a veteran and had less than two weeks to go before he would be going home. He had been promoted to corporal and should have been in the rear awaiting a flight date. Most Marines were pulled to the rear when they had less than a month to go, but Ira wasn't.

After Foster, because of the heroic deeds Wilson had shared with Baggette about what our men had done at the battle of Finger Lake, Captain Baggette had told Wilson that Wilson had a choice to make. He could award medals to a few Marines or promote almost everyone that was eligible for promotion in the platoon. Wilson chose to have his men get promotions to higher ranks and most did.

As we moved out, Hullihen's new radioman was calling in a radio check. The radioman was a short, red-haired, freckle-faced young Marine with barely ten months in the corps. His light-colored face shone brightly in comparison to the rest of the veterans who were sunbaked with a golden tan.

I decided that as soon as we got back, I was going to get to know the men in First Platoon as well as spend some time with Williams and James. I wasn't going to get close to them, but I was determined to get to know more than just their name, to find out at least a little bit about who they were and where they came from.

Sometimes, when a Marine is killed, the officers ask for someone to go into Da Nang and identify the body before it's shipped home. I would hate to be called to do that and have to say that I really couldn't tell if it was one of my men in guns.

Ira went out about half a klick and then it started to rain. We walked by a village, and there was something eerie about the weather and the village that we were passing through—something didn't seem right. Marines were visibly silhouetted against the dark jungle background with rain pouring down on us, and we could clearly see into the kerosene-lit village huts where the Vietnamese were gathered eating their evening meal.

Often, we had passed through similar villages in similar times and the families were always talkative inside their homes. There was a sense of family unity and sharing that gave you a feeling that the family was at peace and they were simply eating their evening meal together. But tonight, their silence betrayed their fear and knowledge that something was amiss. Ira also had an uneasy feeling about the area and tonight's patrol. It may have been because he was a short-timer or maybe it was that sixth sense of danger you learn to pay attention to, so he stopped and called his two team leaders together and they talked for a while.

A moment later, he turned his squad around and we zigzagged back in a circular pattern. As a result of this, we weren't far from the hill. After two hours, we had only gone about a klick from the perimeter wire.

We were supposed to be on a night ambush three klicks away by then, but we set in temporarily alongside a tree line while it rained. From there, we could easily see all around us so we sat and waited. At 1930 hours, we heard distant firing and we moved again.[231] You always set in an initial place for a night ambush and then wait until it gets dark and move again. The reason for this is that if Charlie was tracking you and he had made plans to attack your ambush, then he would spring it but there would be no one there. You set up and then move out to a better ambush site that you had pre-selected earlier.

This time, Ira had us set up in Mamasan's hooch, which was the home closest to a break in the perimeter's wire and just down the village on the north side of the hill.

I had greater respect for Ira that night. Squad leaders, especially squad leaders with time in the Nam, would know if the gooks were close by; their desire to keep their men safe was more important than to foolishly walk into an ambush site because some pogue officer sitting in the rear decided that this was what our route should be and plotted it on a map over a piece of land that they had never walked over and weren't familiar with.

It's hard to smell the presence of gooks when you're sitting in the comfort of a bunker miles away. Ira could have easily followed the mapped-out route that had been given to him; it was a preferred route of travel and easy traveling, but it also was very predictable. It would have been easy for the gooks to figure out our route of travel and return.

The captain or whoever had assigned us the patrol route had included plenty of checkpoints along the way. It gave us little leeway for deviation from the path we were assigned to follow. By the time the platoon or company would have reacted to a squad in trouble three klicks away and in the rain, the unit could have been annihilated. By ditching the patrol and neglecting to go out according to the assigned route, Ira was taking a chance on being court-martialed. At the same time, Ira was teaching new Marines that certain orders could be disobeyed because a Marine's life was more important than a few missed checkpoints. A lot depended upon the individual Marine and his squad.

To some, shortening the patrol because of possible danger only further raised their fears of war, especially if they were untested. But to Ira, their lives were more important at this moment and he was determined to keep them alive.

Trusting your instincts in Nam was the way of survival and victory. I'm sure he secretly hoped that they would not turn out to be afraid to face the enemy in a battle because of his diversion from the original plan. He knew what he was doing, but it's hard to instill the experience he had upon others. Sometime soon, they would be called upon to fight, and at that time, it was hoped that they would react as Marines and not as fearful kids who were afraid because their squad leader had not taken them where he believed the enemy might be or because his instincts told him differently than a few notes written on a piece of paper by someone that was not out in the rain or in the field with Charlie.

All these things, I knew, weighed heavy upon Ira although he never said it. Tonight, his squad was safe; tonight they would live and tomorrow they'd fill sandbags, but they would be alive.

Sometimes it was just common sense. At other times, you just had that sixth sense of danger and Ira, Rahm, and I seem to have, perhaps others did as well, or perhaps it was just fear.

We didn't discuss it; we just supported his decision, but I am sure if either Rahm or myself had said something, Ira still would have continued on to the ambush site.

We spent the night in Mamasan's hooch calling in our regular hourly checkpoints while we were no farther than fifty feet from the perimeter's wire. Second Platoon, whose responsibility it was to cover the side of the hill, knew that we were just below them in Mamasan's hooch. Perkins, was assigned that night to the CP's radio watch, he had received the code from Ira that designated where we were and had passed the word down to Second Platoon.

In Vietnam, you survived by Marine training, instincts, and mutual support from others that had experienced similar troubles and found solutions that might be contrary to military standards, but they worked and kept Marines alive.

Hill 55
Seventh Marine Regiment, Bridge Security
December 16, 1967, 1300 hours

First Platoon rode out to regiment HQ, Hill 55, on the sixteenth of December and relieved Third Platoon while they went out as a blocking force to look for the enemy that had shot at them the night before. We stood watch on Golden Gate Bridge that connected the route that ran from regiment to Route 4. We were also serving as a reserved reactionary force for a company patrolling in Dodge City.

I didn't particularly like bridge watch at regiment. The bridge had big floodlights that remained on all night. It was supposed to illuminate an enemy that might try to swim up the river to blow the bridge away, but what concerned me were the distinct silhouettes that the lights created of Marines walking up and down the bridge. A good sniper could easily wreak havoc.

At 2145 hours that night, Rahm spotted an NVA soldier kneeling on the road between the bridge and Hill 55. We figured he was planting a mine in the roadway, and James got on the gun and opened fire with about a thirty-round burst at the enemy soldier. The enemy fled, and we didn't know if James had hit him.

Early the following morning, while Williams was supposed to be on watch, I found him sound asleep at his post. I took my magazine out of my .45, removed the chambered round, and dropped the pistol's hammer right next to William's ear—*Click*. He awoke startled, his eyes focused on the barrel of the .45 pointed in between his eyes. I inserted the magazine, pulled the pistol's slide back, and chambered a round. His eyes grew bigger, and for a second, I thought of firing a round next to his head. Instead, I slipped the pistol back into my holster and never said a word to him and walked away.

Hill 55 And Our New Lieutenant
Dodge City Patrol
December 17, 1967, 0850 hours

The following morning, as Third Platoon moved out to provide security for the road sweep, we told them about the gook we had seen on the road the night before and about two hundred feet from where Ira had spotted the enemy soldier, the road-sweeping detail stopped and, using a mine detector, found a twenty-five-pound box-type mine, which they destroyed in place.

Later during the day, our new lieutenant joined the platoon, a small-framed but stocky Marine with a shaky voice. The first time we locked eyes, he looked nervously away. I knew I had changed, things were different, and rank no longer meant respect in a combat zone; the new lieutenant would have to earn it. I had a funny feeling that things weren't going to be good for the platoon.

That afternoon, we were Sparrow hawked into Dodge City to assist Kilo Company. They had encountered a large enemy force and were in need of a unit to set up as a blocking force while they swept toward us. I hated to be out in the bush with a new looey who hadn't been tested. The lieutenant hadn't bothered to introduce himself to the platoon. He assumed command and had yet to address his troops. Fortunately, we came back that same night without having made enemy contact.

Liberty Road Explosion
Liberty Road Sweep Explosion
December 18, 1967, 1010 hours

On the morning of the eighteenth, Marines in third Squad, Third Platoon had just gotten in from a night long patrol. Two of them Paul Yurgen and Frank Prasifka, needed to go into Regiment. Yurgen hadn't been paid for over four months, and Prasifka had a bad toothache, and needed to see the dentist.

Tired from their patrol, they laid down, and asked to be awakened when the mine sweeping detail showed up, so that they could catch a ride into regiment.

That morning H&S 3/1 was providing security for the Seventh Engineers who were sweeping Liberty Road near Hoa Dong (AT 922551).

When the mine clearing team completed the road sweep, half of the team quickly jumped on board the tank to return to battalion. Prasifka and Yurgen were awakened just as the tank turned around, in front of the gate. They grabbed their gear and ran for the gate, yelling for the tank to stop.

Too late, by the time they arrived at the gate the tank was already moving down the road and was a good distance away, both Marines, yelled and cussed at the tank crew for turning around so fast, they hadn't been able to get on board.

As they turned to walk away they heard a loud explosion. The tank had run over an eighty-pound mine.

Two Marines were instantly killed and five others seriously wounded.[232] Two medevacs were called. The first chopper evacuated four of the wounded while the second took one of the WIAs and the two KIAs.

The explosion left behind a ten-foot-wide-by-five-foot-deep hole in the roadway. A Marine from Second Platoon had earlier tried to hitch a ride on the tanks but had been unable to. He stood by the gate grateful that he also had missed that ride.

Squad-Size Patrol
Liberty Road
December 20, 1967, 1415 hours

On the twentieth of December, we were out on a day patrol with Second Squad when we got sniped at. The carbine was too far away for it to do any damage, and I realized that it was more harassment fire than anything of serious concern. It was probably a local VC test firing his weapon in our direction. The VC would often be seen working in the rice paddy fields as we went by, then a short time later, they would reach into the muddy waters of the rice paddy and take out their weapons that had been sealed and buried in a watertight canister. They would then pop off some caps at us then hide their weapon once again in the same or another secondary location. As we neared the CAC bridge, I felt that the rounds flying overhead were of so low a velocity that even if they hit us they wouldn't do any real harm. Perhaps I was just feeling invulnerable or no longer cared.

The following day, we went out on an early road sweep with the battalion's engineers as they cleared the roadway between Liberty Bridge and An Hoa.

We found a 100-pound bomb in the middle of the road that had been set up as a booby trap for heavy vehicles. Four feet away, we found another bomb, but this one was command detonated and designed to be triggered by the enemy when the engineers or others gathered around the dead and wounded from the first bomb. Fortunately, the enemy was not around to set it off. As the engineers prepared to blow both bombs in place, we moved off the road and across an open rice paddy about one—hundred yards away.

We sat and waited at the base of a thin tree line, waiting for the engineers to complete their mission. Behind us were open fields and scattered huts. I could imagine how Charlie might often come to the tree line we were in and watch the daily sweeping detail or they would snipe at us from here then disappear into the thicker grove of trees, then slip into the small villages farther out.

Thirty minutes later, we heard the engineers cry out, "Fire in the hole," and seconds later, both bombs exploded. A large cloud billowed upward, and shrapnel flew every which way. A second later, a buzzing, hissing sound was coming toward us and its sound was increasing in velocity. I sensed I needed to move my left leg, and a split second later, a large chunk of smoking, burning metal five inches by seven inches struck and embedded itself deep into the dirt embankment where my leg had been. If I hadn't moved my leg, the flying burning piece of metal would have all but severed my leg.

An Honest Conversation With Boone
Liberty Road
December 21, 1967, 1300 hours

Every third day, one of the squads was out on patrol. With increased enemy activity in the area, platoon commanders were being given greater flexibility as to where and how long their squad patrols would be. They were given a general area and objective, and it was up to the platoon leader to choose the route. Since there were only two gun teams that meant every other day one gun team went out. Every day that a squad went out, they received sniper fire. Charlie wasn't particular about whether it was First, Second, or Third Squad they were shooting at. Thus, every other day, someone in the gun team was being sniped at. I knew it was only a matter of time before a squad would be hit or a sniper would hit a gunner. That evening, when Boone showed up at gun's hooch, I decided to share with him what had been bothering me.

"You know, Boone, your squad's gonna get hit," I said to him. Boone had been taking too many chances with his squad and I wanted him to know how I felt. I poured a shot of Colt 45 whiskey over iced Coke and offered it to him. He refused as he sat back to listen to what I had to say. James had purchased the whiskey when Dumont had sent him out on a supply run into Da Nang. James was fitting perfectly into guns. He was alert, perceptive, and cautious. These were qualities desired in a Marine assigned combat duties, especially one assigned to guns, and what was as important, he and Aguilar got along great. But I could see he was at times subjected to Boone's negative influence. Porter had been reassigned to the CP where they used his strength and abilities to help out with CP duties and for carrying supplies. Porter welcomed his new assignment as he now wasn't going out on patrol with the rest of the squad.

"It's easy for the gooks to study the squads that go out every day and figure out that every third day a particular squad goes out," I said to Boone.

"Take a look at your squad, a gook can easily figure out that you're the squad leader because you make sure that the radioman sticks to you like glue. The gooks can see that you're in charge because you're always giving commands all around you. He can also tell that you're more careless in taking chances than the other squads, and he knows that the squad led by the black Marine is more predictable.[233] He goes out longer and deeper into their territory than the other squads. More than likely, they will try to knock you out on your return trip. Your weak point is that if you go out long, you have to come back long. You always make your return trips on a run because you're always in a hurry to get back. The gooks would be wise to hit you on your way back."

Boone sat back and listened, and I couldn't tell if he was feeling angry, defensive, insulted, or was really interested in what I was saying. Either way, he knew I was going to tell him what I felt.

"Both Ira's and Welsh's squad would be hit on the way out because the men are inexperienced and they can tell," I pointed out to Boone.

"Those squads stick closer to base, so they might not be as attractive a target for the gooks, but it's also easy to tell that the majority of the squads are made up of new men. Your men are also new, but you've taken the time to train them, and the difference is noticeable. They go out, don't talk and keep their interval. I can tell the difference when I go out with your squad than when I go out with the other squads. If a squad gets hit, it will probably be a squad that is out by themselves," I said.

"The gooks will hit your squad just as you're turning back, and if they knock you out with the round fired at you and your radioman, then your squad is going to be in a world of hurt because you don't trust anyone else to be in charge. Even your radioman doesn't say anything or call in checkpoints on the radio because you're always taking command. Your squad's trained to survive but only on your commands. If you're gone, you've trained them only to follow your orders."

Boone realized that what I had shared with him was true and just said, "You're right, I have to watch out for the guys." What was also disturbing me and was stuck in the back of my mind was that there was something bothering Boone that was affecting how he ran his squad. He seemed to be taking the dangerous routes and more chances for some reason. I knew that something was worrying him, but he wouldn't let on as to what it was and I didn't know how to approach that subject. Sometimes, a guy would act like Boone was acting when he got a Dear John letter or bad news from home. When the rest of the platoon was promoted, Boone wasn't; he remained a corporal in charge of Third Squad and supposedly a squad leader was supposed to be a sergeant.

Boone had changed; he had separated himself from the rest of the platoon, seeking to hang out and urge "the brothers" to stick together. "Bro" had taken on a new meaning; it now meant being black, a soul brother, and the lingo was changing, jiving, and chuckling, mixed with a militant spirit that made you want to stay away. It was not good, and it was beginning to divide the platoon. Segregation was setting roots, but it was Boone and some of the blacks who seemed unfriendly, who had separated themselves from the rest of the platoon. I had first seen it in Eddie Williams when he arrived, and there was a bit of it in Porter but only when he was with the "bros." Up until that time, we used words like *black*, *negro*, or *colored* interchangeably to describe a black Marine with no negative feelings attached to the words. We were Marines first and foremost, and that was what was important. It wasn't just in blacks; some Latinos now wanted to be classified as Chicanos, whatever that meant. In war, there was no space or time for such foolishness.

I knew Boone felt he had been overlooked because of his color and indicated that belief often among other blacks in the platoon. Before Foster, that type of belief wasn't present.

"Look," I said, "I'm concerned because one of my gun teams has to go out every other day, so they are more apt to become involved in an ambush than others in the platoon because we're out in the bush more often than the rest of you guys in the platoon." I realized then that I was arguing what Bro had argued with Lieutenant Cortaze months ago, and perhaps I needed to point this out also to the new lieutenant.

We sat around, and Boone drank with us and relaxed; later that night, Boone let it slip that his folks were talking about a divorce and he wanted to go home on R&R as soon as possible. However, he had already used his R&R in Bangkok. Boone said that if he re-upped for another six months in the field, he could get a leave now and then another one in March when he was supposed to rotate back and he would be promoted to sergeant. He also mentioned that maybe that was the only way for him to get promoted because the corps was prejudiced to blacks.

"I don't think so," I said to him. "Look at Whiteside and half the other sergeants in the company, they're black. It's you that needs to change, Boone, you blame everyone for your troubles. Unless you change, you'll always blame it on someone discriminating against you because of your color. If someone has a problem with your race, you go around them. It's their problem. It's the same thing with Mexicans. Some blame the corps for them not being promoted. Lucero used to say the same thing, but it was all in his head. Unless you personally change, those problems of the past will always be there present with you in whatever you do. The corps doesn't hold you back; you'll get promoted if you deserve it in spite of your color. But if you mess up or can't hack it, others will get it."

Boone had injured himself a day before Operation Foster and hadn't gone with us on that operation until the last two days before the operation ended. But its things like that that will hold a guy back from promotion. While I couldn't see sticking around in Vietnam if I didn't have to, I could understand Boone's desire to get home right away. But it would cost him another year in country; that was a high price to pay. I figured it was going around it the wrong way.

On the twenty-second, everything was normal as usual. We were out on a routine patrol, and while crossing an open rice paddy not far from Liberty Bridge, we got sniped at again. Sometimes we would go after the sniper; this time, we didn't bother going out to look for him nor did we bother to call in a spot report. At night, we ran ambushes and during the day our daily patrols. But Charlie continued to be evasive to our limited patrol activities, but we knew it would only be a matter of time before we would engage them in a firefight.

Vietnamese In The Wire
Hill 65
December 23, 1967, 1300 hours

We were now standing watch on a regular basis at night at our guns' position on Hill 65. Much had changed since I was last here. The friendly village below didn't look as friendly anymore. When we passed by the villagers during our patrols, they were distant, evasive, where as before they seemed friendlier. The area, however, still looked as beautiful as ever and I enjoyed what quiet time I could find sitting out on the front porch of our old bunker on top of the hill. We normally didn't stand watch during the day at our bunkers; there was always too much activity going on around the hill, so anyone coming up to the perimeter's wire would be noticed as the villagers always stayed away from the base of the hill and our perimeter's wire. The afternoon of the twenty-third, while I was sitting on my cot overlooking the village below the hill, I noticed a Vietnamese man walking near the perimeter wire. He appeared to be probing along the wire looking for weak spots. I noticed that he would stop, look around, and then move on. We usually didn't see Vietnamese get that close to the wire, so I grabbed an M-16 and got a hold of a Marine from artillery and both of us went down to the wire; but we couldn't find him. Then we saw where he had ducked into a small crevice and was slowly crawling along the wire. We went down to where he was; when he looked up, I was standing over him with the M-16 pointed at his head. The old Vietnamese quickly got up and began to bow and bow, trying to convince us that he was old, confused, and just lost.

He had no ID on him, and we found a hand-drawn small map of our perimeter in one of his pockets. The map pinpointed by measurement our artillery and machine-gun positions. We brought him to the CP and a chopper picked him up and took him to Battalion HQ for interrogation. A Marine in one of the squads had said that he saw the Vietnamese man earlier in the day near the wire and thought of shooting a round over his head, but by the time he had gotten his weapon, the man had disappeared.

Return To Liberty Bridge
Liberty Bridge
December 24, 1967, 1300 hours

Following the early morning road sweep, we returned to Hill 65, gathered up our gear, and First Platoon was returned to Liberty Bridge.

A Christmas truce had been called, which meant a general stand-down: we would not be taking any offensive action against the enemy unless they fired upon us. It was not known if Charlie would comply with the truce. In the history of Vietnam's struggle for independence, the North Vietnamese government had broken every truce and agreement they had made with the South Vietnamese government so none of us expected a true truce. We would comply; the U.S. government always lived up to those agreements. As Marines, we just saw those special days as a welcome rest. It meant we only had a 50 percent chance of getting killed or wounded during this time as we would not be initiating any operations, patrols, or action. The enemy almost always used the occasion to take some type of offensive operation, to move supplies and weapons out in the open before our eyes, knowing we would not fire on them. We almost expected them to come out of the tree line to the banks of the Song Thu Bon River and dance for us as they knew we would not fire.

Late that afternoon, two large handmade Christmas wreaths came floating down the river. Second Platoon Marines fished them out cautiously as they might be booby-trapped. But they weren't. They were a present to us from Charlie. The wreaths were made from local foliage, decorated for Christmas with colorful streamers, ribbons, and held together by large bamboo poles. One had a large handwritten Christmas banner attached to it. A handwritten Christmas card was attached with North Vietnamese symbols and a Christmas greeting:

Christmas Greetings;

The National Liberation Force offers Holiday greetings, for Marines of India Company we offer, this bounty for Marines of India Company.

> *For officers of Marines*
> *Lieutenant and higher 30,000 piastres*
> *Sergeants 20,000 piastres*
> *Corporal and lance Corporal 50,000 piastres*
> *Marine grunts 200 piastres . . .*
> *DEUT1—DOS*

A list followed with some Marines from First and Second Platoons listed by name and rank. The list also contained the names of other Marines whom over the past few months had been assigned to provide security at Liberty Bridge. It also included some of the names of Marines who had been either killed or wounded during Operation Foster and were no longer with us.

The list of names we figured must have been obtained from the Vietnamese women that came weekly to pick up and deliver our laundry at Liberty Bridge. The clothing was washed and laundered in Da Nang.

Some of the Marines were angry not because their names were known by the enemy or because their names were listed but because the Vietcong were offering such a low amount of money as bounty for them to be killed. Two hundred piastres were less than two dollars. Quite possibly that was the reaction the VC had hoped for. In their insulting offer, they may have wanted the Marines to feel insignificant and resent the distinction they made of importance between us and our officers.

Christmas Eve had deposited a festive spirit on us. Without having to go out on patrol, we had a chance to sit and joke around and relax and just spend some time with each other. There was no beer or hard liquor around, only the friendship we had established with each other; and as the evening hours arrived, we welcomed the silence that followed. We could have been on any base in the world.

Marty had received a small artificial Christmas tree from home, and we set it on a small table in the front end of the barrack. Three large foot-long red-colored candles, fifty-cent-piece size in diameter, burned in the background. The glow cast the tree's life-size shadow against the barrack's canvas.

Two boot bands held together a C-rat box where I had stuffed two new M-16 magazines for Ira and Marty. Next to it, Aggie had torn out some advertising pages from *Playboy* and had wrapped a can of gun oil and a brand-new cleaning rod for the M-60. Supplies he had managed to borrow from battalion supply when the sergeant in charge wasn't looking. Aggie's gift was a bath-size towel bought from Mamasan and stuffed into an empty green ammo can. Perhaps now he would stop borrowing ours. Before retiring, while Aggie was pouring foot powder on his feet, he took some of it and sprinkled it on the Christmas tree. For a while, we sat in silence staring at the tree then Rahm blew out the candles and said, "And a Merry Christmas to all and to all a good night."

CHAPTER TWENTY

Christmas Night In The Boonies
Return to Football Island
December 25, 1967, 1800 hours

Christmas Day and both Paul Yurgen and Frank Prasifka, Third Platoon Marines were on watch on the tower at Liberty Bridge and reported seeing a lot of enemy activity along the banks of the Song Thu Bon River. There were some NVA and VC soldiers boldly carrying their weapons, some getting on boats and traveling along the river resupplying their reserves. Because of the Christmas truce, we couldn't fire on them.

It seemed strange that we would pause in this war when the North Vietnamese soldier wasn't supposed to be here in the first place.

In the battlefield of Finger Lake, I knew there had been a pause in the enemy's fighting because they needed to pick up their dead and wounded. While that was never confirmed, it was one of those rare moments in time, those unspoken-about moments in war when firing stopped. I recalled how at that time, for some reason, I had seen the enemy moving in between the tree line and while they had a clear shot at me and I had a clear shot at them, we didn't shoot at each other. I saw them bending over and moving away only to resume their fighting a short time later. How I understood or they understood it to be a time or a pause in the battle to get out our dead and wounded, I don't know. But when they got out their dead and wounded, fighting resumed. Perhaps that was another reason that I had opened up so fiercely at them when the chopper came to medevac our wounded because they didn't honor our warriors as we had theirs. Now, it just didn't seem right. We stopped firing at the enemy during the Christmas truce but knew they would violate it at will.

At 1800 hours on Christmas Day, the truce ended and the company, already saddled up, got on Mike boats and moved across the Song Thu Bon River in a search and destroy operation.[234] The boat beached itself on the south side of Football Island next to two small boats. We were back in Arizona Territory, not too far from LZ Sparrow where we first landed at the beginning of Operation Foster.

490

As the boat was dropping its ramp, one of the navy gunners opened up with the .50 caliber and another of his mates fired the .30 caliber at an abandoned village. Waiting inside the track for the boat's ramp to fully deploy seemed like it was taking forever; when the ramp finally opened fully, we moved out, entering the nearest tree line, and encountered no resistance.

The company deployed, searching for the enemy that had been spotted earlier, carrying weapons and supplies, but found no one. As we headed back to the beach to be picked up by amtracks, a third platoon squad of Marines found two tons of polished rice hidden in tall grass, along with some cooking utensils and other NVA gear. The rice was camouflaged with green plastic and weeds. Since it was already late, that squad and First Platoon stayed behind while Second Platoon and the rest of third platoon went back to Liberty Bridge. It was believed that the enemy force, would believe that all of us had left, so we stood still and waited for nightfall. At first light the amtracks would return and we would load the rice on board, and go back to the bridge.

It's Christmas Past
"Chieu Hoi" (I Surrender)
December 26, 1967, 0100 hours

Shortly after midnight, a Marine in Third Platoon heard an NVA soldier call out, "Chieu Hoi, Chieu Hoi" and Dumont called back to him in French. A minute later, the soldier emerged out of the darkness of the night and surrendered. He was wearing brown khakis, had no ID card, and was carrying no weapon. He was about thirty years of age and scared. He didn't seem like the other NVA soldiers we had killed in war; his facial feathers were narrower. He was taller than the round-faced, short NVA soldiers we had seen. No sooner had he crossed over than we began to get our perimeter probed by enemy scouts. Then they began to taunt us as they had before by calling out loudly: "Hello, hello, Marine. Tonight you die, cam-kook, cam-kook."

I wondered if these were the same NVA soldiers that we had engaged at the firefight at the house at Finger Lake on November 21. If they were, we would soon be in for a fierce firefight. A few minutes later, the Marines in Third Platoon heard the sound of a boat as it crossed the river from Phu Nhuan (8) toward our position. As soon as the NVA soldiers got out of their boat, the squad of Marines opened fire. All three of the NVA soldiers were immediately hit and seriously wounded. The squad of Marines destroyed the boat and they held on to the prisoners. Drag marks could be seen at the location and it seemed another boat had been just behind the first boat and they had escaped in the darkness. Sgt. Wilcox the next morning said that one of the prisoners was a VC officer and all night long he had sat out by the river moaning with pain and due to his head wound but had died before he could be evacuated at first light.

The Lieutenant's Assault
Arizona Territory
December 26, 1967, 0600 hours

At 0600 hours, we began to search the area near the ambush site and found fifteen tons of rice as well as other NVA gear.[235] As Second Platoon loaded the rice and gear found onto the Mike boat that had returned to pick us up, First Platoon was assigned to search the surrounding area.

At 0830 hours, we found an NVA cartridge belt, two NVA canteens with covers, six ponchos, assorted waterproof gear, and a pack containing three medical kits.

By now, the lieutenant seemed to be getting uneasy; we certainly were deep in the enemy's storage bin and things didn't seem right. I felt the enemy's eyes on us and perhaps only our size prevented them from engaging us right there and then in battle.

A few seconds later, a sniper opened fire on the Mike boat and we all hit the deck.

The new lieutenant ordered an assault on the tree line across an open and wide rice paddy field from where we had received the sniper fire from. He stood up to lead the charge.

Without waiting for all of us to get in line, he took off across the paddy with his radiomen at his side. Nobody else moved.

The enemy sniper shifted his fire from the Mike boat toward the clear target moving out in the open. The lieutenant, realizing he was alone and out in the open, hit the deck just as bullets came flying at him. No one had moved out with the lieutenant, and now he had to crawl back as we provided cover.

When the lieutenant had ordered the assault, the enemy had been engaged in shooting primarily at the Mike boat. He might have figured the enemy force were probably just a couple of local villagers and nothing more. But without an idea of the enemy's strength and no one assigned to provide cover for us and no reserved unit in case we got pinned down during the assault, no one else had moved out. The fierce return of fire shot at him when he moved out on his own, revealed a far larger force was waiting behind the thick tree line, he had ordered us to assault.

The lieutenant now ordered us to move toward the Mike boat as quickly as possible. As we moved out, a Marine fell in a hole and more rice was discovered. We dragged the rice out into the open, but the lieutenant by now was visibly shaking and told us to leave it and just head for the Mike boat.

"What about the rice?" Dumont asked.

"Just leave it," he answered. When Third Squad walked by the rice, Boone opened the bags with his K-Bar and quickly spread out the rice and then threw grenades into the pile. After they exploded, he buried smoke grenades deep in the remaining piles of rice and pulled the pin. The lieutenant was walking in front of me, and I could tell that he was irritated; he had a lot to learn from veteran Marines, and one of those lessons was that we certainly weren't about to die foolishly in an assault across an open rice paddy from where we were getting incoming fire. The tree line hadn't been peppered with artillery or an air strike. No Huey gunships or Bird Dogs were in the air to possibly help determine the enemy's strength, and we were not about to leave food for the enemy.

As we got on the Mike boats, we were beginning to take more incoming fire from yet another enemy position. Had we assaulted, we would have been caught in a crossfire.

As the Mike boat moved out along the river, the lieutenant didn't bother to call in artillery on the enemy's position and the platoon's radioman, having already learned not to make suggestions that might make the lieutenant look inexperienced regarding such simple a situation, just remained silent.

When we neared Liberty Bridge, it was a welcome sight. Seeing the bridge and our defensive positions from the middle of the river, I could see some vulnerable spots that Charlie could find advantageous for probing or gaining easy access into our compound. Actually, the whole perimeter looked defenseless, and I realized how easy it would be for Charlie to attack us from this side. I looked over at the lieutenant to see if he was taking note of the view our location presented us with, but he was busy writing notes into the personal journal he carried.

Conflicts With The New Lieutenant Increase
Liberty Road
December 27, 1967, 1415 hours

For the next couple of days, we were assigned to build up our defense positions at Liberty Bridge. Something was coming down, but we weren't being told much. There was deep tension in the air. Dumont had fallen out of favor with the lieutenant when he had argued to leave Perkins behind before our last operation because Perkins was due any day to rotate Stateside, but the lieutenant had argued that he needed Perkins out in the field because he felt Perkins knew the area. He wouldn't listen to Dumont or other veterans in the platoon, so most of the squad leaders avoided him. In return, we received very little information about what was going on, where we were going, when we went out, or any of the other information we used to receive about possible action before we went out. I believed the lieutenant was scared; he feared something, and it wasn't only the enemy. Some of us believed he feared his own lack of confidence, which was a weakness that caused the men to mistrust his judgment.

Lieutenant Wilson used to keep his squad leaders informed and abreast as much as possible of what was going on, and he let his squad leaders make suggestions. The new lieutenant wasn't giving out much information either way. Dumont was all but ignored by the lieutenant, so he asked for R&R and the lieutenant granted him his request. Marines who had been in Perkins's squad were especially angry with the lieutenant because he had kept Perkins out in the field until the very last day before his tour was up.

Lieutenant Nowicki from the onset wasn't well liked. He slobbered and slurred when he drank and he drank a lot, but when he did, he stayed away from us. We likewise avoided him as much as possible. He had a distance about him that showed a lack of leadership.

Saddle Up
Liberty Bridge
December 29, 1967, 0600 hours

On the morning of the twenty-ninth, the platoon was ordered to saddle up; we were only told that we would be going out on a two-day platoon-size operation for which the lieutenant had volunteered us. Other than that, we were told we should prepare accordingly. Whatever that meant to the lieutenant, no one knew. No one dared ask the lieutenant any questions. We just took what we normally would have taken for a two-day operation. Usually we were given some guidelines. Should we take gas masks? Will we be resupplied with water and food? Did we need entrenching tools? No frag order had been received, so we knew it wasn't a major operation.

I had been in country now for more than six months, and I was beginning to feel the weight that comes from being in country for so long. The new lieutenant's arrival didn't help matters. What was it that Bro had said? "Be careful when you get in a new looey, especially when they try to do things by the books. It doesn't work in Nam. The looeys who try to run things like they learned in officer's school by the books will get Marines killed. They're ninety-day wonders."

Our new lieutenant was a mustang, a lieutenant that had come up the ranks, so one would figure he was in tune with the grunt's way of life; but it didn't seem that way. Already we had heard that he had ambitions of one day becoming a general. Not on the backs of dead Marines, I was thinking.

I was beginning not to care anymore in one way or another as live or die it all seemed the same to me. The real world was a distant and a faraway world that no longer seemed to exist. This world—the world of gooks, grenades, mortars; artillery, firefights, snipers, sappers, the smell of gunpowder, and the ashen color of death—had become my real world. It was in this world that I needed to belong to and live in to survive. I had come of age, I had changed, I knew; but I still needed to take that step between the real world I lived in and the dreams of tomorrow. Live or die that world or this, at this point it no longer mattered.

We patrolled and passed through villages and open rice paddy fields at a fast pace. Then we slowed down for a while but soon picked up the pace again as if we were in a hurry to get somewhere—but nobody knew where or what we were to do once we got there.

We traveled east along the north shore of the Song Thu Bon River past Giao Thuy (1) and Giao Thuy (2), following a well-worn trail around a small hill. The lieutenant seemed to like following trails.

With the river on one side and the hill on the other, we were smack in the middle of a perfect ambush site, but the enemy didn't spring one.

I reasoned they were in the area without reinforcements close by. We passed by Phu Tay (1) and Phu Tay (2) and then stopped on the outskirts of Phu Tay (3).

I wondered if the lieutenant would have us cross the vast sandbar where there would be no cover.

I thought the lieutenant might be lost. Then I saw the FO, a Marine by the name of Rick Oglesby, assigned to our platoon for the two-day operation, approached him and showed him where we were on the map.

The FOs were usually on Hill 37 assigned to a group called The TAC Party or Tactical Air Command Party. The FO team's presence with our platoon gave our lieutenant the capability to engage the enemy with jets and helicopter strikes until help arrived.

Just the fact that an FO team was there with us indicated that battalion felt something big was out there and that there was a good chance we might engage them in a fierce firefight. It was a tactic of our military commanders seemed to use. Send out a small unit into places where we might engage a large enemy force and then a larger reactionary unit already on stand-by would respond. This is why we believed the FO was with us.

We broke for lunch out in the middle of nowhere, and then moved out again, following the wide trail past Tuy La (1) where the huts were all deserted and the rice paddies overgrown with weeds. We hadn't seen one soul all day long. Charlie may have wondered why we were in such a hurry to get to wherever we were going. We passed on the other side of Giao Thuy (2), and we stopped to spend the night between two Buddhist shrines that belonged to the idol worshippers of Giao Thuy (3).

Move Out
Liberty Bridge
December 30, 1967, 0600 hours

Early the next morning, we swept north toward the CAP unit (Tiger no.1) then east into an area we rarely ventured into. The area looked risky and something was not right, but the lieutenant kept pressing on. He still had not been under fire, so he seemed to be looking for one. In the direction we were going, I knew it would only be a matter of time before we made contact. The FO's presence with us was unusual but necessary if we got into a firefight. Perhaps Baggette wanted to get Nowicki under fire so that he could prove himself, and having an FO with us was one way of securing the platoon under a new commander. Or perhaps we were just bait. We were in Charlie's country, at his back door, and we were looking into his bedroom windows. At any time, I expected him to walk into the room.

The trail we were following ran alongside a thick tree line that abutted a long skinny lake on our south side. We were traveling east; to our left (north) were several scattered hooches and the village of Loc Thuong. Thick elephant grass four to eight feet high covered much of the area. Scrub brush with a little rise in the ground and little hills as well as bigger dirt mounds separated some of the jungle area. North of where we were traveling, though, the land lay flat with a rise in the ground here and there that gave the area character. Yet this place was not pretty like the rest of Vietnam: it was as if this part of the country had been abandoned and neglected. The dry scattered interlaced rice paddy fields lay in waste; they hadn't been worked in years.

In the midafternoon, the point man found a ChiCom grenade lying on the trail we were following (At 935555). When the grenade was destroyed, the explosion vibrated across the flatland. If the enemy didn't know we were there, they did now.

Perhaps the lieutenant wanted to prove himself under a combat situation to his men. But he was going about it all the wrong way, and instead of obtaining our loyalty, he was already receiving our discontent. By now we had ventured out into NVA territory where I knew we shouldn't be unless we were company size. If we got into a firefight out here, a responding unit would have to be Sparrow hawked in.

We set in for the night and Ira Hullihen, First Squad's leader, came by to tell us not to dig in for the night. Battalion had just informed us over the net not to dig foxholes as there was a report of a large enemy force in the area and we needed to be as quiet as possible. Tomorrow would be Ira's last day in the bush before he would be going to the rear as his ticket home was already punched and waiting for him at battalion. We were all glad for him, and as the lieutenant had said, this was only a two-day operation and tomorrow we would be heading in. We all looked forward to that.

For the first time, I wished it was one of those nights I hated where the moon's glow would assign sinister shadows to the plants, trees, and dark vegetation all around us. October through late February were wet months in our area, and for the past month, we had been receiving scattered rain during the late afternoon and early evening hours. We settled in and the night became pitch-black. The dark clouds above hung like the dark demons of the night that nobody sees but I sensed their presence.

There were no stars visible above, no lights on the ground or in the sky above, and no one lit a smoke while on watch—no one said a word. We were on 100 percent alert because we knew the enemy was near. At 0300 hours, battalion gave us a wake-up call as they dropped in H&I rounds near our position. No one had bothered to tell us that they were going to do that. A recon unit had reported a large enemy force was seen moving rapidly toward our position and artillery was dropped on their location.

Lost In Circles Around Giao An
Liberty Bridge
December 31, 1967, 0600 hours

There are sounds and smells made in a jungle environment that although dangerous are welcomed as they reveal natural animal activity instead of enemy activity. Vietnam had its own sounds and smells, and the silence that came with the sunrise every morning was unique and welcomed. Vietnam is a beautiful country especially at that time of the day when everything is clean, crisp, innocent, and quiet. The land begs to be recognized and admired for its beauty, and this morning we all awoke with a sense of achievement for just having survived another night in the jungle and we were now ready to get back to Liberty Bridge.

We settled up early and moved out alongside of an extremely dense series of tree lines. Then the trail turned and brought us back toward where we had started, and we wondered if the lieutenant knew where he was going. We continued and soon we were following a small trail that turned going east and we passed the village of Thuong Phuoc and a little hill near Tuy La (1) hamlet. It was pretty much the same area we had entered two days before.[236]

By midmorning, we were coming around the hook at the end of the lake and swinging around the northeastern tip of a small hill when the point man saw a young male talking to a Vietnamese teenage girl. The girl, was wearing a blue top and black pants. Close to her, stood an older woman of about thirty-five and a younger girl of about nine wearing a sweater. The male was about twenty to twenty-five years old and dressed in black pj's; he also had on a helmet, a bandolier of ammo, and was carrying a carbine. He looked up as the patrol approached, and immediately the point man ordered them to halt. All four took off running northwest toward the small hill. We searched the area and found the two women and the girl but not the young man. The girls all had similar ID cards that were unlike those that were issued by Dai Loc officials.

As soon as we resumed our patrol, we spotted a young man of about sixteen years of age pretending to work the rice paddy field with a hoe. He was wearing green camouflaged utilities, and we detained him as well. With the prisoners in tow, we continued our patrol. They would all be turned over to the Battalion S-2 for questioning once we got back to Liberty Bridge.

A Loss That Could Never Be Replaced
Liberty Bridge
December 31, 1967, 1130 hours

We continued our patrol going east along the well-worn trail. On our right side was a small hill and to our left were open rice paddies and a tree line a short distance away. A number of small mounds scattered throughout the area hid numerous blind spots, hamlets, small hooches, and trails. It was one of those days where things were not lining up right.

The platoon was walking in a staggered column. There were so many new men in the platoon, and they were making an extraordinary amount of noise. Although the lieutenant did not seem concerned about the noise, the squad leaders were. Since we were on the move in a hurry to get to wherever we were going, no one said anything.

We passed a series of rice paddies on our left, and soon we were forced to walk in a long column alongside the base of a small hill that was quite steep on the right side with a bend at its center. James, carrying the other M-60, was in front of the lieutenant followed by the CP group, and Aggie and I fell in behind them. The FAO, a Marine by the name of Rick Oglesby, had been assigned to the platoon for this mission and was walking in front of my gun team. It was unusual to have an FAO with a platoon; usually they accompanied a company-size movement.

Up ahead of the platoon, two Vietnamese males came around another bend in the hill. There was a good interval in between them and both were wearing black pj's and carrying AK-47s. The point man dropped to his knees and opened fire; bullets ripped through the body of the first Vietnamese and he went down as the other took off running. Other Marines opened fire and a series of shots struck the second soldier, knocking him over an embankment.

By the time we got to the first soldier, he was dead; in his possession was a pack full of laundry and miscellaneous military papers. The point man held up the brand-new AK-47 as his war trophy.

The lieutenant dispatched part of Ira's squad to go after the other soldier we had seen shot and had fallen over the embankment. As the lieutenant called in the spot report and examined the papers found on the dead soldier, Ira Hullihen and Jerry Ezell moved out. I approached the lieutenant and asked if I should cover for them and he said no, for me to stay where I was, and to set up the gun facing southeast away from the location. Chief also ran up to the lieutenant and asked to go along with Ira and Ezell and the lieutenant also told him no.

"The other guy was shot at least twice," Ira had told Ezell as they made plans on how to approach the area where the enemy had gone down. This was also going to possibly be Ira's last chance to take home a war trophy, and he wanted the AK-47 he saw the enemy was carrying so he was anxious to move out.

Abe Metzler, it was decided, would go around clockwise to the left while Rahm would go to the right side of the site counterclockwise and both would cover for them. Abe had been with the platoon since Foster and was now a fire-team leader in Ira's first squad. He wouldn't ask anyone in his fire-team to do what he himself wouldn't do. Both he and Rahm moved out quickly to get into a position where they could look down into the gully the enemy soldier had slipped into.

Ira and Ezell moved up before Metzler and Rahm had gotten into position, and as both Ira and Ezell looked down into the embankment where they had seen the enemy fall, a burst of automatic AK-47 fire tore through both Marines. The first round struck Ezell in the forehead, exiting through the tip of his helmet, and he went flying backward. The next round also struck Hullihen in the head, killing him instantly.

Both Metzler and Rahm rushed over to where the enemy soldier was lying, and as Metzler shot the enemy soldier twice with his M-16, Rahm emptied all the rounds in his .45 pistol into the quivering soldier's body.

As the radioman called in the casualty report to battalion headquarters, on the other side Lieutenant Wilson, who had become 3/7's S-3 officer, was listening to the spot report coming in concerning his former platoon. The phonetic spelling of Ezell's first and last name came over the net as a WIA. India-Romeo-Alpha (Ira) came next over the radio, and Lieutenant Wilson knew there were only two Marines in the platoon with that first name. One of them, Ira Rahm, had just come back from R&R where they had spent time together; the other was his former squad leader. The platoon's radioman continued on to finish phonetically spelling out the name of the Marine that had been killed: "Hotel-Uniform—" and Lieutenant Wilson's heart sank; he walked outside the bunker to be alone.

As Ezell was helped to get on board the evacuating chopper, four Marines slowly lifted Hullihen's dead body and also placed him on board. As the chopper lifted off, Metzler turned his face away so no one would notice the tears in his eyes. The new lieutenant looked at him and said, "Why are you crying? It's his fault he got killed."

It was New Year's Eve, and we headed in.

CHAPTER TWENTY ONE

R&R In Hawaii
Liberty Bridge
January 1, 1968, 1300 hours

New Year's Day and Marines in First Platoon were walking around the compound in sober silence. The death of Hullihen lay heavy on our hearts, especially since he had only one day to go before he was scheduled to be sent to the rear and home.

It was uncommon for us to talk about the firefights we had participated in or to talk about those lost in battle, wounded, or killed. We did not speak about the emotions and personal feelings we felt, and if someone leaned toward recognizing that hurt, we embraced that protective shield of disassociation and blocked the sorrows of war that made our hearts ache and eyes water. At times like this, silence was our chief comforter.

Silence always followed those emotional moments where dreams were shattered, and the facts of life and death didn't correspond with the feelings embedded deep within our hearts and minds, of life and love and liberty; the release of deep sighs were the only signs of hidden thoughts and buried sentiments.

No one ever spoke about the number of kills they had made, the enemy soldiers encountered in battle, and no one claimed glory for having done some heroic deed while engaging the enemy in fierce firefights. Other branches of the U.S. military service pinned medals or ribbons on a serviceman for actions that were normally required for us to do as Marines. We didn't seek medals or awards; we just fought to protect each other, to engage the enemy, and to win.

Since I was scheduled to go on R&R on the seventh of January, I needed to go into Da Nang to make a MARS phone call home to make the final arrangements to meet Dorothy in Hawaii. Before I left, Lieutenant Nowicki called for me to come up to the CP and asked if while I was there I would identify Ira's body at the morgue. He could have ordered me to do it, but instead he asked. Perhaps he had seen how upset I was, how upset we all were at the death of a Marine we respected, a Marine the lieutenant didn't know. Already I had a dislike for him, and perhaps it was beginning to show, causing him to ask rather than order or direct me to do it. Perhaps it was the look in my eyes of disdain. The next few months with the lieutenant in charge of our platoon was not going to be pleasant, this I knew.

The ride into battalion arrived too late to allow me to catch the mail run into Da Nang, and that evening, Corporal Boone showed up at battalion and said the lieutenant had sent him to find me to say that he would identify Ira's body as he had some personal supplies Boone was also picking up for the lieutenant. Boone then added that he was now First Squad's squad leader. I was glad about not having to go to the morgue to identify Ira's body and glad Boone volunteered to do that, but wondered how it was that Boone had been picked to replace Ira.

Battalion Mortared
Hill 3/7
January 2, 1968, 0200 hours

Early morning, on the second of January, battalion was hit with fifteen mortar rounds that struck the compound near the heliport, the communications bunker, and the motor pool. I didn't like being in the rear and felt unprotected; it was safer out in the field.

The MARS station was well staffed and in no time they had me connected with my wife in Sanger, California. While it was 1300 hours in Da Nang, the afternoon of the second of January, back home it was 10:00 p.m., New Year's Day.

Dorothy did not want to bring my son with her when she came to Hawaii to meet me on R&R. I wanted to see him, hold him, and see what it felt like to be a father. Against my wishes she had named him after me, perhaps because of the urging of her mother; just in case something happened to me, he would have my name. I was named after my mother's brother and wondered how he felt about his name. At least she had also given him the name Troy; I had wanted Paul, but without me being there, she made the decision herself.

After a while, she agreed to bring him and said she would go ahead and make the arrangement to be in Hawaii when I arrived. While military servicemen were allowed to take their R&R in Hawaii, they were not allowed to go to the continental United States, so spouses had to meet their mates in Hawaii. Counting the seconds of delayed silence on the handset that followed after we said "over" to let the person on the other end know we had finished speaking, our phone conversation was over in less than three minutes. In that time, we had said all that needed to be said as there was no exchange of sentimental love talk, the normal conversation that would reveal the presence of a healthy love relationship in a marriage. We just talked about the arrangements that needed to be made.

I wondered what the American ham radio operators stateside thought of our conversation compared to others they had heard when they made similar connections for them.

Afterward, I headed for the naval compound on the other side of the airstrip to do some trading. I had brought with me some of the NVA uniforms and equipment the gun team and others had captured during Foster to trade with pogues in the rear.

A large Chinese Communist-made knife I had taken from a dead enemy's body I knew would bring a good prize from those in the rear that collected captured weapons. I traded the other goods I had with me without any problem: the NVA knife ended in the hands of an air force chef for four cases of beer, four cases of soda, four bottles of Colt 45 whiskey, a pair of sunglasses, and a Green Beret cap, which he had gotten from trading with someone else. The air force chief was pleased to have the knife in his possession and couldn't thank me enough. I wondered what war stories the rear pogues would tell about how it was that they came into possession of the enemy's equipment. It was too late to catch a ride back to battalion so I stayed overnight at transit.

Da Nang Rocketed
Da Nang Transit Facilities
January 3, 1968, 0300 hours

At 0338 hours, the Da Nang airfield was impacted with twenty-two 122mm rockets. The rockets had come from south of the air base from our TAOR, launched like before from near where Bro had been killed on July 19, 1967, that date would forever be embedded inside those secret chambers of my mind. God had to be a warrior. He must have a special place for warriors like Bro, who die, so others may live.

I arrived at battalion early morning of the third and traded a bottle of whiskey with a mechanical mule driver for a special run to Liberty Bridge; another Marine jumped on board to ride shotgun for the mule driver. Since November 8, when we devastated the NVA battalion in that area, there had been more incidents of sniping along Liberty Road.

That night at 2315 hours, Liberty Bridge was hit with heavy automatic weapons fire and twelve rounds of mortar fire from an estimated twenty NVA/VC. For three days now, wherever I was, the place was being hit with mortar or rocket fire.

Early the following morning, Lieutenant Nowicki sent word for me to come see him and told me to go into battalion. He wanted to make sure I would be there on time to catch my plane out. My flight out of Da Nang wasn't until the seventh so I welcomed the break and caught the first mule run into battalion where I turned in my weapon and waited for the clerk to complete the necessary paperwork for my five days of R&R.

That night, battalion once again got hit with incoming mortar and rocket fire. I didn't know which was safer, Liberty Bridge, battalion, or Da Nang.[237] I decided it would be safer for me to wait at the transit facilities in Da Nang, so I caught the first run into Da Nang the morning of the fifth.

Da Nang Air Base
Da Nang, RSVN
January 5, 1968, 1300 hours

I spent the fifth and the night of the sixth in Da Nang waiting at transit for a plane ticket. With Da Nang getting rocketed often, the sergeant in charge said he could get me out the night of the sixth, but the plane was destined for Okinawa where I would have to change planes but wouldn't get to Hawaii until late the following day. If I wanted to wait, he guaranteed me a ride on the seventh straight into Honolulu. I chose to wait and that evening went to the Seabees' watering hole for a beer. It felt good to take a real shower and to get cleaned up. A Marine coming back from Hawaii, where he had spent the days with his wife, mentioned that he wasn't able to buy liquor as neither he nor his wife were of age. Here we were fighting for our country but couldn't purchase an alcoholic beverage in the state of Hawaii. At least my wife was old enough. She would be able to buy hard liquor while we were there.

R&R In Hawaii
Honolulu, Hawaii
January 7, 1968, 1500 hours

On the afternoon of the seventh, I boarded the flight and arrived fifteen hours later in Honolulu, Hawaii. Because we had crossed over the International Date Line, it was late in the morning of the seventh, the same day I had left Vietnam.[238]

We disembarked and grabbed our bags. The wooden building was painted white. Hawaiians were walking around in colorful printed shirts and muumuus. Signs on the wall at the airport gave military personnel directions to the staging area where we were to meet our spouses.

I followed the signs, wondering what my son would look like. He would now be four months old, and I still hadn't seen a picture of him. The signs led us into an open area outside the airport. As we exited the doors, it looked like we were in an outside parking structure. Dorothy was standing to my left; she had no makeup on, was wearing a purple pantsuit, and her long uncombed hair was merely pulled back and held in place with large bobby pins. In her arms was a chubby bald-headed baby boy.

The baby had on a white shirt and fluffy brown-colored corduroy pants. His chubby cheeks, big round eyes, and small nose accentuated his bald head.

Where's his hair? I was thinking and felt a bit of a negative response toward my son because he was bald. I quickly reached out and took him from Dorothy's arms to avoid any rejection in my mind. As I held him in my arms, he didn't cry; he just moved his head back to get a look at the stranger holding him. He had a sad expression on his face. He didn't know who I was and I didn't know who he really was, but he was my boy and I held him out at arm's length to see what he looked like. I wanted to hear him and see what he was like.

"That's your son Troy," Dorothy said as I examined him and then turned to look at her. "You wanted me to bring him," she said, raising her voice in an argumentative tone. But then she paused, looked at me, raised her eyebrows, and squeezed her lips tight. "So here he is."

"Where's his hair?" I asked.

"Babies don't have hair," Dorothy answered scornfully as she took Troy from my arms, shaking her head slightly.

"We got here yesterday," she said with a disgusted tone in her voice.

"I forgot about the date difference," I said.

"Troy got sick on the airplane and wouldn't drink from his bottle. One of the Hawaiian ladies that help servicemen helped me. They contacted the Marine Corps, and the colonel from the base sent his jeep to take us to the dispensary where they gave Troy some medicine."

"Where did you stay?" I asked.

"The Marine Corps placed us in a shelter overnight. They said you would be coming in early this morning, and we've been waiting here all day." She paused and spent a moment in thought before she continued. "After the first two planeloads of Marines came in and you weren't on them, I was ready to go home. If you weren't on this plane, we were going to go back today." I listened, but I wasn't really hearing what she was saying. She seemed disturbed to be there with me, but my thoughts were on where we would be staying.

"They gave us a list of places we can rent for a week," she said and handed me a piece of paper with a list of local housing units made available to Vietnam servicemen on a short-term rental agreement. We called a couple of places on the list before we found one that was available. They asked if we had any children with us, and I mentioned we had one. The very helpful manager said that there was a stroller and a crib in the apartment and it was within walking distance of the beach.

We rented the small apartment for the week. It was a single-room dwelling with a bathroom and a shower. The bedroom, living room, and kitchen were all in one room, much like a hotel room but supplied with a small apartment-size four-burner stove, a small refrigerator, and a table. After we settled in, Dorothy fed Troy and said she had something important she wanted to tell me.

"Okay," I said and waited.

As she thought over what she was going to say, Troy spit up, and she rushed off to grab a hand towel. I took the towel from her and wiped his mouth and chin then started to dab him with the towel back and forth, and he smiled, a dimple appearing on his cheek. As I continued to play with him, he cracked up laughing. He had a big smile and a new gleam in his eyes and laughed out loud. I grabbed him and rolled with him on the bed, and he giggled and laughed loudly. We played like that as I held his arms up then crossed them in front of him, moving them back and forth, and he laughed and seemed happy and content. Dorothy went into the kitchen and prepared another bottle for him. I held him in my arms and fed him until he seemed to be closing his eyes, so I laid him down. Dorothy placed a small towel under his bottle to support it while he lay on his side drinking from it.

"We're going to need some milk for Troy's bottle," she said.

"I saw a store at the corner of the block; do you want me to get you anything else?"

"No," she answered.

"I was hoping we could go together, so I could get some beer," I said. With a look of disbelief, she shook her head and dismissed what I had said.

I walked down the streets and both sides of the road were filled with medium-sized well-placed trees and clean sidewalks. There was both a sweet-and-sour smell in the air. It was the damp smell of the ocean and a cool breeze brushing up against the many colorful flowers in the area. I felt good, full of strength and accomplishment walking free without a weapon down a street that looked much like many neighborhood streets in America. The street signs had Hawaiian names on them, but this was America. There were cars parked on the streets, and the homes were made of cement and some of wood with front porches and wooden doors. Some homes had large plate glass windows with pulled-back curtains on each side, and the people on the street were Americans. An old man was walking his dog and stopped while the dog sniffed around some bushes, lifted his leg, and peed only to move along only a few steps, stop, and once again repeat the process. A lady with a headband, sweats, and tennis shoes was walking briskly down the street; she smiled as she walked by.

The small store had limited items in it; it was a small deli with liquor bottles behind the cashier. Wine bottles were up front in wooden bins, and a good-sized cold-beer-and-beverage display cooler was located in the back. A large two-tiered refrigerated produce-and-vegetable display case lined one side of the wall. I took two apples and an orange, four twelve-ounce-sized cans of Coke, a half gallon glass bottle of milk, and a coconut-covered jelly roll cake to the cashier. The cashier bagged the groceries into a paper bag and thanked me. A cold, swift breeze chilled the air as I walked back toward the apartment. When I got back, Dorothy had changed into a long faded loose-hanging flannel nightgown.

There was ice in the freezer, and I filled a long glass with it, pulled the pop-top off the can of Coke; it hissed and the soda fizzled and bubbled as I poured it slowly over the ice.

Dorothy handed me a paper shopping bag from Sears; in it were two shirts and two pairs of pants, a package of white T-shirts and jockey briefs. I hadn't worn briefs in years; I hadn't worn underwear in months. I took a shower, put on a clean white T-shirt and the briefs, and got under the covers. We hadn't really talked much, and Dorothy now started to talk about her folks and her work while I played with Troy. Finally his eyes started to get tired, and he started to cry.

"He's hungry and needs to be changed," she said. She spoke to him as she changed him, putting a small nightshirt on him. She had already prepared his bottle and held him close while he drank it. When he finished, she turned him over and burped him, and he soon fell asleep. She laid him down in the crib, turned off the light, and crawled into bed next to me.

In the dark, I could smell the baby's spit-up on her neck and realized she hadn't bothered to shower. I touched her, and she said she was really tired with the time change and with Troy getting sick.

I woke up early the next morning and realized I had slept through the whole night. I took a long hot shower, shaved, and put on the new clothes and my military shoes. Troy woke up, and I changed his paper diaper, glad it was only wet with urine. I then warmed up his bottle as I had seen Dorothy do, bent the nipple to squirt a dab of milk on my wrist. The milk was warm, not hot, and I held him until he finished drinking it. I placed him on his stomach, and he burped on his own and laughed. As we lay on the carpeted floor and played around, I could tell he was a bright kid; he held on to my fingers and hands, tried to crawl, and seemed like he really enjoyed the attention he was getting from me.

When Dorothy woke up, she rushed into the bathroom and stayed there until she had showered and gotten cleaned up. She came out wearing the same flannel gown she had worn the night before.

"Are you hungry?" I asked.

"A little," she answered.

"There's a café close to that store around the corner if you want to go there for breakfast," I said.

"Okay," she answered as she took the same pantsuit she was wearing the day before into the bathroom to change; she came out without bothering to put on any makeup.

The café had round booths, and small metal push-button jukeboxes were sitting on the Formica-covered tabletops. We sat down, and the waitress brought over a high chair for Troy. I looked at the music titles: "They Call Me Mellow Yellow," "Mountain of Love," "Mr. Sandman," "Sign of the Times" by Petula Clark. I flipped the charts—"Another Saturday Night," "As Tears Go By," "Baby I Need

Your Lovin',," "California Girls." I inserted a quarter and pushed two buttons to hear "California Dreamin'" by the Mamas and the Papas.

After breakfast, we walked around, went to a nearby park, and then window-shopped at a nearby mall. I asked a stranger to take our picture and he did. We spent the afternoon at the beach, and once again Dorothy mentioned that she had something she wanted to tell me but never said what it was.

Our time together was not like I had hoped it would be; we rarely kissed and never spent intimate time together. She avoided that, and I wondered if that's the way it was supposed to be after such a long time apart. I really had not missed sex, the physical release, that is; with more important issues to deal with in a combat zone, survival dictates one's mind to be focused elsewhere. What I craved for, however, was intimate time. To be touched, loved, cared for, to feel secure of love where I could rid my mind of where I've been, what I've seen, done, and for a time, forget that other world I now lived in.

Dorothy never asked about what was going on in Vietnam, where I was, who my friends were, what I had experienced. If she had asked, I probably would have told her I had been wounded and in the hospital but she didn't ask, and I didn't tell her. I just left it in the back of my mind and decided to enjoy the time away from working parties, sleepless nights, guard duty, patrols, and war. That night, I played with Troy until he got tired and fell asleep and then I watched TV. When it came the time to go to bed, Dorothy went into the bathroom and showered but didn't come out until I had fallen asleep.

R&R
Honolulu, Hawaii
January 9, 1968, 0900 hours

We rented, a beige colored Dodge Dart to tour the island, and our first day was spent mostly in and around the downtown area. We picked up some groceries and relaxed at a nearby park and ate sandwiches that Dorothy had put together from our purchases.

The following day we spent most of the time at Sea Life Park, a Marine life attraction where dolphins jumped high into the air, penguins performed, and a young Hawaiian girl in a small canoe with her dog treated us to supernatural tales of ancient gods who saved Hawaii from one disaster after another. She told the story of the warrior King Kamehameha that won battles and unified the Hawaiian Island. His goal was to maintain peace and the traditional values of his ancestors. What battles he must have fought went through my mind, how many had he killed in war, how many had I. His war was over, he had won, conquered his enemies; mine were still alive and waiting for my return.

We learned from the stories the Hawaiian maiden shared about friendships forged between animals and the people of the island. I enjoyed meeting the people of Hawaii with their colorful clothing, wide smiles, and straight teeth. Women in short grass skirts stopped and said what a handsome boy we had and what a beautiful family we were.

In the evening, Polynesian drums sounded a call to relax and enjoy life; beautiful women danced and sang under a clear sky full of stars. Food was served with patience, more stories were told, and songs shared; for a time, I got lost in the magical paradise of Hawaii and relaxed as I held my son tightly.

On the eleventh, I wanted to explore more of the island, and we went sightseeing in a southeast direction away from the city along a beautiful highway filled with wide-open spaces. A lush green-forested area was on one side. Purple and pink-colored orchids; yellow, white, and orange soft-tip tulips; dark red and bright yellow flowers bordered by rich dark green foliage as well as red and bright lime-colored plants lined both sides of the highway. Hawaii was an island paradise, and I was enjoying its rich beauty.

I turned off the road to get away from the traffic and enjoy the solitude of the countryside, so we drove along a deserted small road. We traveled with no particular place to go and found some large estate homes nestled up against small hidden valleys. I slowed down and rolled down the car's window to enjoy the quietness of the area, the fresh smell of the surrounding farmlands, and to feel the cool ocean breeze as it flowed through the car's open window when all of a sudden, shots rang out.

I hit the brakes, slammed the car into park, and looked for my weapon as more shots were fired. I quickly opened the door, got out, and was reaching into the back of the car for Troy when I looked up at Dorothy who was sitting on the front passenger seat and wondering what was happening. She looked at me quizzically, bewildered by our sudden stop and my actions.

I stood back then leaned with my back against the car's door, tilted my head back, closed my eyes, and wondered if what I had heard I had imagined it in my mind. Then off in the distance, I could hear the rifle-range instructor giving direction to the next batch of shooters. Seconds later, they fired their volley of bullets in the outdoor rifle range we had stumbled across. Dorothy by now had gotten out of the car and was walking around. She looked at me strangely, puzzled by my odd behavior. I took in a deep breath, looked at her, and said, "Its okay."

We drove back to the apartment in silence. I never said a word of why I had acted the way I did, and Dorothy never asked.

The following day, we returned the rental. That evening, Dorothy said she needed to tell me something and I waited, but she hesitated and never said anything. By now, I had figured she had been with her old boyfriend again or someone else and I really didn't want to hear what she had to say, not now, not when I was preparing my mind and getting ready to going back to Vietnam. We hadn't been intimate at all and she had shown no desire to be so. She was here only because I wanted to see Troy, and for the past few days, he had been my world; for that I was grateful.

Before she left that afternoon, she said what had been bothering her was that she and her sister Cece had been shopping and they had been arrested for shoplifting. The charges had been dropped, but she just didn't know how to tell me as she didn't want to disappoint me. I knew that was not what she had held back; it was not the real reason why we hadn't been intimate nor why there was no sensual or sexual desire or interest in being together that way. She hadn't bothered to try to make the Hawaii trip a romantic one, even in pretence—but then again perhaps that was better for me. As she boarded her plane, I turned, picked up my duffel bag, and headed toward my plane. I couldn't wait to get back to war.

Back To Vietnam, Back To War
The Island of Guam
January 14-15, 1968, 1300 hours

The plane stopped in Guam, and I called Dorothy. She sounded happy and glad to be home. I landed in Da Nang late on the fifteenth, and on the sixteenth, there was no mail truck. On the seventeenth, I was finally able to catch a ride on a six-by ammo-truck run to 3/7 headquarters. At battalion, I learned India Company had been reassigned to the industrial complex at An Hoa. I wouldn't be able to catch a chopper ride to the new company area until the following day. I went to supply to draw a weapon, but the supply sergeant wasn't around. The corporal in charge said I would get a weapon issued to me at An Hoa, and while I didn't like being at battalion without a weapon, I knew I would have my hands on one soon enough.

Rejoin The Company
An Hoa AT 874473
January 18, 1968, 0800 hours

On the morning of the eighteenth, as I made my way through the mess hall line at battalion, a familiar voice cried out, "Cookie!"

Marty, wearing a large tapered white apron came running around from behind the counter and gave me a hug. I shook my head at Marty who was grinning from ear to ear.

"What are you doing here?" I asked.

"Malaria," Marty answered. "I got sick at An Hoa, and they didn't know what it was. I kept shaking all the time and they put me in the hospital there for about a week. Finally a doctor said it was malaria, wrote me off, and I was sent here. I'm out of the bush! Doesn't that beat all? After all the stuff we went through, they sent me to the rear because of malaria."

"Who's in charge of guns?" I asked.

"Rahm," he answered, Dumont is the new platoon sergeant." I felt good that it was Rahm in charge of weapons.

As I sat with Marty, he brought me up to date as to what the company had been up to for the past two weeks. While we sat and talked during breakfast, the company supply sergeant came up to where we were. I recognized Sgt. Wilcox from being a squad leader for either Second or Third Platoon, before Foster. He had been there during Operation Noah's Ark.

"You're Barela?" he asked. I nodded yes.

"Come see me at battalion supply before you leave to join our company," he said and walked off. On my way to supply, I figured I was going to get the modified new M-16 with the chrome chamber and the new buffers everyone seemed to be wanting because they were experiencing less malfunctions with those modified weapons, but instead when I got there, Sgt. Wilcox wasn't around another supply sergeant said I would get my weapon at An Hoa and handed me an asbestos pouch filled with gear for the machine-gun. I didn't know the sergeant nor did I recognize him. I didn't understand why he was giving me the bag, but I was grateful and reckoned we needed the items in guns. As I stood by the helicopter pad waiting for my ride, I noticed the landing pad was bigger, wider.

A Marine I didn't recognize was also waiting to hitch a ride to India Company. "You going to An Hoa?" he asked. I nodded yes.

"A C-130 was hit yesterday as it tried to land there," he said.[239] I looked into the eyes of the young Marine. He turned, looked away, and decided not to say anything else in the face of my silent indifference.

I opened the asbestos pouch to check out what was inside. It contained a brand-new M-60 barrel, two new cleaning rods, wire brushes, and oil for the gun. A small sealed manila envelope was at the bottom. I opened it and out fell a brand-new locking pin all by itself. I smiled, looked at the young Marine, took in a deep breath, and placed the locking pin inside my shirt's pocket.

At 1100 hours, the chopper lifted off the helipad. In the distance north of Hill 52, artillery shells were peppering the base of Charlie Ridge. I wondered what Marine unit was stationed on Hill 65. To the southeast was Liberty Bridge, and as we circled around, I saw to the southwest of the chopper was the An Hoa mountains with their beautiful background and the home of many NVA units.

Along the south side of the Song Thu Bon River, three Huey gunships were strafing a thick tree line west of Football Island. One released a series of rockets into deep undergrowth in the heart of the Arizona territory. The new Marine's eyes were glued on the battle activity going on below us.

As we passed overhead, the smoke from the exploding ordnance rose past us to blend in with the gray clouds hanging over the basin.

That's what, was missing while I was on R&R, I was thinking—the noise, the clamor, the hype, fear, anger, and the uncertainty of life.

I was home.

As the chopper prepared to land in An Hoa, I could see that the airstrip had been damaged. The airfield, composed of steel matting, had huge sections curled up and blown apart. Marine and Seabee engineers were busy patching up the gaps, pulling off the damaged hard steel matting and replacing it with a new plank of matting much like putting together a large jigsaw puzzle.

First Platoon's assigned area was located on the north side of the compound. When I arrived, most of the men were at chow. The mess hall was a large barrack; there were very few Marine faces I recognized. There was that new guy by the name of Cobb that had joined us on Foster. Welsh, Keene, and Aggie were standing in front of the line getting served. I didn't recognize the others around them.

"Hey, man, you're back!" Aggie said as he looked up when I sat down to join them.

"This is a nice place," I said.

"Yeah, but we had to build new bunkers," Aggie said.

"It's not bad at all," Welsh added. "We have been able to find some pretty good stuff lying around to make ourselves some comfortable bunkers where we stand watch at night."

"I saw the new type of two-man positions for standing watch along the perimeter," I said. "Not much of a bunker, they look like large piss tubes." Everyone chuckled.

"Not the type we're used to," said Welsh.

"They're supposed to blend in so Charlie can't see them from the air. The main thing we're doing now is standing perimeter watch and going out as security for the road sweeps between here and Liberty Bridge and then back again. We have the north side of the camp and the ARVNs the South side, but we don't trust them so we have to watch our backs," Keene said.

Who's Lieutenant Dan Walker?
An Hoa AT 874473
January 18, 1968, 1300 hours

While we sat still talking Rahm showed up; "Hey buddy," he said, with a small grin at the corner of his mouth.

"Hey, Ira," I answered back.

"I heard, you were back, so I thought I'll come by and see how your R&R went," He asked.

"It was alright, but wife wouldn't buy any liquor in Hawaii, so, it all didn't go, the way I thought it would. Get this, while I was there, driving around, I ended up near a rifle range and hit the deck," I said and laughed.

"Check out, who I hung out with on R&R?"

Before I could answer, Ira said, "the Lieutenant. We ended up on R&R together and since, he didn't want me to call him sir, or Lieutenant Wilson, or Larry, in case it slipped out, when we got back. We were trying to think up of a name for him to use and since I had ordered a shot of Johnny Walker Red and he, Jack Daniel's we named him, Dan Walker, and that's what I called him." "Lieutenant Dan Walker," I said and we all laughed.

"Our new lieutenant is not well liked right now," Welsh added.

"When we first got here, the lieutenant didn't like seeing 'Elvis' (Alan K. Kates) with long hair, so he sent Boone into Da Nang to bring back scissors and an electric hair trimmer. He then had First Platoon line up and started to cut everyone's hair, giving them, sidewalls and leaving only a small patch of hair on the top of their head. Some guys made a complaint to the sergeant, and he notified someone at battalion and they called down and put a stop to it. The lieutenant said we were his platoon, and they told the lieutenant he didn't have a barber's MOS. By then the troops were pretty mad at him and he at them for going around him to battalion. Some Marines said they would shoot the lieutenant for humiliating them that way."

"He overheard me say that," Keene said. "And he told me that if that's the way I felt, I'd better watch my back as well."

"We lost two more men (WIA), new men," Aggie commented, and I didn't bother to ask him their names. It didn't make a difference: if I heard their names, I wouldn't recognize them nor remember ever meeting them. They had become only numbers in the war. But they were Marines, and that counted for something. I was just glad that I hadn't gotten to know them, but when the others said their names, I regretted that I couldn't recall what they looked like or if I had ever met them. Where's Jones, I asked Aggie. "On the day you left for R&R, he broke his wrist, and was sent to First med in Da Nang, he only has a month to go, so, I don't think, he's coming back."

As we made our way back, the guys filled me in about the An Hoa base. I was surprised to find out that among other things at An Hoa, there was a large medical facility on base. German nurses were walking around and going in and out of large barracks that had a small wall of sandbags near the entrances.

"Round eyes!" said Keene.

"But they are off limits," added Welsh.

"I don't care, I still talk to them," said Aggie. "I mean, it doesn't hurt anything, and who knows? What if you get killed today? At least you talked to a good-looking woman!" We all laughed quietly at Aggie's reasoning.

One young nurse stopped where Dumont was sitting on the ground near a tree next to a barrack and began to speak with him in French. We stopped there, and Dumont acknowledged my return.

"It's okay to talk to you, ain't it?" Aggie asked her, and she looked at him, puzzled.

"I mean, its better speaking to a woman that is not slant-eyed and who is also very beautiful," he added, and she laughed, continued to talk with us. After a few moments of her laughter, we forgot about the war as we stood listening to the talkative, laughing German nurse.

There was an orphanage on base, and a Catholic nun walked by us with a group of young boys and girls.

The Catholics were in Vietnam long before the French. They continued to run the orphanage in An Hoa, which they had done that for many years. I noticed among those in the ranks the small boy with the missing left ear that I had seen at the dump at battalion headquarters when I first arrived in Vietnam. He was still wearing the same old Mickey Mouse T-shirt except that it was no longer brown. It had been washed, and now, the Mickey Mouse logo was clearly visible against a faded yellow background. His hair was no longer matted and dirty; his face was washed and clean. The column stopped as the Catholic nun spoke to the German nurse, and the boy looked up at me inquisitively. Then a broad, toothless smile came across his face and his eyes widened when recognition came to his mind. I saw his hand rise slightly, and he waved at me. It really felt good to see him again, to know that he was still alive, and someone was taking care of him.

When we got back to guns' barrack, I found both M-60s were filthy. When I asked Aggie about it, he said that the platoon has been out so much that they hadn't had a chance to clean them. The guns could take a beating and they did in Vietnam, but they needed a thorough cleaning. I asked Aggie to join me as we walked over to the CP. There, I mentioned to Dumont that we needed to clean the guns thoroughly so that they would not be going out on patrol or ambushes that night. He told me to go ahead and that he would tell the lieutenant so that guns wouldn't be sent out.

Aggie and I obtained two five-gallon containers, one we filled with heavy oil and the other we filled with aviation fuel. I had Eddie Williams and James join us behind one of the barracks. Bro had shown me how to clean the gun by using aviation fuel; the stuff was potent. We stuck both guns in the aviation fuel and a few minutes later, when we pulled them out, almost all the rust, dirt, grime, and built-up carbon had dissolved. The biggest problem we would have once we scrubbed and cleaned them a few more times was to make sure we thoroughly oiled all of the guns' inner parts. A couple of hours later, we had the guns completely back together and they were ready for the toughest of inspections. I had told Williams and James to keep the guns saturated with oil overnight and then to wipe them down completely in the morning.

Since the lieutenant had been told that we would be busy cleaning the guns, we weren't counted in with the night's perimeter watch for that night so guns had the night off.

Concerns About The New Looey
An Hoa AT 874473
January 19, 1968, 1300 hours

The next day, we began to build up the bunkers and defensive positions as well as to dig trenches around the perimeter. The area had been spared pretty much from enemy assaults. An Hoa, it seemed, hadn't been a high-priority target for the enemy for some reason; but with the coming Tet celebration, chances of us getting hit had increased greatly, we were told.

Dumont had decided to set up the platoon's M-60s to cover the northwest section of the perimeter. A .50 caliber was set up to protect the northeast section where our perimeter bunkers hooked up with the ARVN's security section so that the .50 would cover that area as well as ours.

On the evening of the nineteenth shortly after 6:00 p.m., when curfew commenced, villagers were still out in the rice paddy fields. Curfew was well known to be at dusk, so I opened fire with a couple of rounds, including a tracer over the Farmer's heads. As I did, a Marine standing watch at the bunker nearby shouted out, "We don't do that here," but it was too late, evidently curfew had not been observed in the area.

That evening just before night fall, we heard a loud noise in the wire near the bunker to our left.

As a Marine, popped a flare overhead, Jackie Williams also assigned to that bunker could see a large form, near the wire.

He quickly dropped down on one knee and took aim with his M-79 where the sound had come from, and fired off a round.

As the flare exploded overhead, the M-79 round struck a large water buffalo that had ventured into the perimeters fence.

The following night, all the villagers had left the field and were herding their livestock out of the fields in front of our positions. They were all out of sight long before dusk.

For the next few days, First Platoon and tanks provided security for the minesweeping assignments between An Hoa and Liberty Bridge. Whether we would make it back to An Hoa in one day or stay overnight at Liberty Bridge depended on the time we left, mines detected, and when we completed our mission.[240] Second and Third Platoons during this time were assigned to run the majority of patrols and ambushes in our newly assigned TAOR. At least that was what was supposed to be happening, but not only were we assigned as security to the daily minesweeping convoys between An Hoa and Liberty Bridge, we were also running patrols and ambushes at night and standing perimeter watch during the day and at night.

The platoon was still undermanned so sharing the patrol responsibilities with second and third platoons made some difference. One comfort was that patrols were now platoon or two squad size, which meant the lieutenant, would go out with us. Ambush units, however, remained for the most part squad-size or smaller. A squad-size ambush was more mobile, quieter, and could easily hit a target and escape to a predestinated area or quickly assemble to get back to the perimeter. They also would have the combined firepower to hold off or attack a good-sized enemy force.

On the morning of the twenty-third of January, James and I went out with two squads assigned to the road sweep. We returned riding on tanks along with the engineers who had found only a couple of mines on the roadway. Before blowing up the mines they had found, the engineers showed James and I how the NVA/VC had taken to sawing apart dud artillery or mortar rounds and were using the inner explosive charge to make several smaller booby trap mines they then laid on the roadway between An Hoa, Liberty Bridge, or Battalion HQ. Many of the booby traps that the NVA/VC laid were duds, and the triggering mechanism was often faulty. Others were quite good and very well put together and those were the most dangerous type to clear, the engineers told us. Riding back, one couldn't help but wonder or hope that the engineers had found all the mines or that after we swept the roadway, the enemy hadn't planted new mines. But we returned to An Hoa without incident.

Late in the afternoon, I could see something was bothering Dumont. I didn't have to ask.

"You know, since the new lieutenants arrived, two men have been wounded needlessly while on separate patrols," he said.

"This lieutenant is trying to run the war according to what he had been taught in officer's candidate school and he doesn't listen to the squad leaders. It's his way, and there's no way around it no matter what, and the troops are blaming him for what has happened and fear he's going to get them killed. There has been some talk of fragging him," Dumont said, "and I'm worried that somebody might try to do it."

Dumont looked at me with his head cocked to one side, a serious look on his face, his round eyes getting bigger as he spoke. "There are other ways of obtaining the same results without having to resort to that," he said. Perhaps with Dumont telling me, he felt others would listen to me and not do it, or he just needed to share his thoughts with someone. I wasn't sure why he told me as he wasn't always that bold in expressing those type of concerns; except when it came to us, I knew he wasn't hesitant to speak up to the lieutenant when it came to weapons' needs. He always looked out for us.

"I know what happens if someone frags a lieutenant, that unit is singled out as a problem platoon even though it's the lieutenant's fault.

You're branded, and you'll get all the shit details from then on and for years to come, you'll carry that label. I've met some shitty lieutenants, but this guy is weird, he's a lifer, is seeking medals, wants to be promoted to captain and become a general, can you believe that! So, he'll take chances with his men and volunteer the platoon for anything. That's why we are getting so many details and he's putting the platoon in danger for no reason. I'm afraid pretty soon he'll piss off a Marine and something will happen," Dumont said.

"He seems to leave weapons alone," I answered, and Dumont contemplated what that meant and why.

Chapter Twenty Two

Lessons For The New Looey
Liberty Bridge
January 24, 1968, 2300 hours

On the night of the twenty-fourth, the platoon was assigned to stand security at Liberty Bridge while Hotel Company 2/7, op-con to 3/7, went out as a blocking force for Kilo 3/7. Lima Company 3/5 had taken over Kilo Company lines during this time. Kilo's primary assignment had been shifted to conducting saturation patrol in the area Ira had been killed in near Liberty Bridge as well as in the Dodge City area.

That night a little past midnight while we stood watch at Liberty Bridge, the lieutenant decided to check the Marines standing watch. The night was quiet and one could easily hear low whispers being uttered from bunkers nearby. Three days before, while at An Hoa, the lieutenant had split up Third Squad's three-man hole watch at each position so that only two men were on watch at each position. No one knew why he had done that when the other squads had three men to a hole, but then again we were spread thin and we figured that was the reason why.

Lieutenant Nowicki, however, had made sure Keene and Kates were among those holding two-man watch details. Some thought that it was possibly because he resented Keene's anger over the haircutting fiasco and the fact that Kates' Elvis-like long hair remained uncut.

Alan "Elvis" Kates was a tall, muscular, handsome Marine with large hands and a pointed nose. When he smiled, a dimple appeared only on his right cheek. He dressed his wavy hair in a pompadour Elvis Presley style. On the morning of the twenty-fourth, both he and Keene were dog-tired from having gone on the daily road sweep where an enemy force had opened fire on the road-sweeping detail and tanks accompanying the detail had responded; they had also been on a patrol and an ambush the night before. The men of First Platoon were taking a beating, and Third Squad Marines were standing two-man hole watch which made it difficult for them to stay awake.

Klick-Clack, Lock-n-Load
Liberty Bridge
January 25, 1968, 0100 hours

Shortly before 1:00 a.m., Kates woke up Keene early to ask him if he would stand watch for a while as he could no longer keep his eyes open and feared he might fall asleep on watch.

Each hole-watch position manned by First Platoon was not allowed to keep our weapons locked and loaded, including our machine-gun positions, by order of our lieutenant. Nowicki might have feared with a loaded weapon an angry Marine might make good on the threat of accidentally shooting the lieutenant. He of course told the platoon that it was a safety issue, and if we got hit, we would have enough time to load up and return fire. At night when you're standing watch, however, you would want a round in the chamber. If you hear anything, you don't want the noise of the round being chambered to give away your location or alert the enemy. You want to be able to react quickly and not have to wait until the enemy opens fire before responding, but the lieutenant didn't see things that way.

The lieutenant came by our guns' position with Corporal Boone at his side and was somewhat social. Guns had also been ordered not to keep a belt of ammo loaded in the gun while we were in our bunkers unless the lieutenant gave the word that we might be getting hit. Intelligence earlier in the month had indicated that there was a large enemy buildup occurring in the area and that we might get hit any day by an aggressive enemy force, still the lieutenant insisted that our weapons not be loaded.

While standing in our bunker, the lieutenant saw that the gun was fully loaded with a 200-round belt attached to it. He looked at the gun and then at me then back at the gun a couple of times, and I could tell he wanted to say something but for some reason he remained silent then quickly left.

Perhaps he will mention it to Dumont in the morning, I was thinking, but it wouldn't make any difference to me and I had hoped he had seen that determination in my eyes when he was in our bunker. Both he and Boone left to check the bunker to our left. It was the bunker manned by Keene and Kates from Third Squad.

When the lieutenant tried to sneak up on them, Keene heard him, and called out, "Who's there?"

"Lieutenant Nowicki," was the reply. k*lick-clack-ssshhh-klick-clack* could be heard coming from the bunker. It was the distinct sound of a rifle bolt chambering a round, and I knew Keene had locked and loaded the second he heard the lieutenant's voice.

"Corporal Boone is with him! Corporal Boone is with him," Boone cried out loudly.

Silence followed then the rifle's bullet was cleared and the magazine removed from the weapon. The lieutenant never bothered to go farther but turned and walked away, heading back to the CP at a fast pace.

"I guess he decided not to check any more positions," I said to James and Aguilar who laughed.

Eddie William's Day with Destiny
Liberty Bridge
January 28, 1968, 1600 hours

Increased enemy activity had made it necessary for at least two squads and a gun team to accompany the early morning road sweeps. Williams's gun team went out with the road sweep on the morning of the twenty-eighth; when they returned, Porter came running to our bunker and Williams came up behind him with a sober look on his pale face. He was visibly shaking, and he had a distant look in his eyes.

Porter spoke up, "We were on our way to An Hoa when Williams stepped on a twenty-pound mine lying on the right side of the road. Everyone heard the loud click the mine made when the primer struck the charge, but it didn't go off. Eddie froze and, man, he turned white right there and then when he saw it was a mine he had stepped on. I have never seen a black boy turn so white so fast in my life!" Porter laughed then went on. "When the engineers blew it up, the mine left a five-foot-wide hole where Eddie had been walking and, boy, did he start to shake after that! He was lucky he walked right off of it. If the firing mechanism hadn't been faulty, at least three of us would have been killed."

Porter went on to tell us that one of the tanks had then seen three NVAs wearing black uniforms carry weapons in a far tree line and opened fired with a 90mm round. When the round hit, there was a secondary explosion.[241]

On their way back, the tank Porter and Williams were riding on hit a forty-pound command-detonated mine.[242] The explosion blew the track clean off, knocking Eddie off the tank; four Marines were also reported wounded. Pridemore and another guy with tanks were medevaced. Roberto Perez and another Marine who were also wounded were not evacuated and we continued on with the disabled tank to An Hoa.

Perez had been in First Platoon since November, a replacement Marine during Foster, and I hadn't gotten to know him.

Williams looked pale; he was scared, and he knew he could have been killed. He was trembling as he sat down. I wondered to myself if his attitude would now change; perhaps now he wouldn't be as difficult a person to deal with. Sometimes that happened to a person. A near-death experience and they begin to appreciate life, their attitude changes, and they become more humble, less demanding, and more in tune with how their life and actions affect others.

The following day as the platoon cleared the road to An Hoa, the squad that had returned to An Hoa began a patrol toward us along the road; it wasn't long after they had left the perimeter wire when they were hit by sniper fire. The squad returned fire, and when things cleared, a Marine lying next to Perez noticed blood oozing from one of Perez's ears. Perez was returned to base, and the corpsman found that Perez had a busted eardrum. He and another Marine who had lost his hearing on the same tank the day before were kept at the first aid station that night and were to be medevaced to first med in Da Nang at first light.

As they slept at An Hoa, the base got mortared. Perez could barely hear the sound of the incoming mortars but felt the earth tremble below him, and when he went outside the barracks, he saw the flashes of the impact. He woke up the other sleeping Marine who couldn't hear a thing and Perez tried to explain to him what was happening. Finally understanding what Perez was telling him, the two deaf Marines couldn't decide what to do. Where could they go where sound wouldn't make a difference in determining how secure they were? After searching for a place to crawl into for safety, they found a secure place to sleep. It wasn't until daylight that they realized they had spent the night inside an ammo bunker. Perez was medevac, then given a chance to get medical attention in Japan but instead wanted to remain at battalion so he could return back to the platoon as soon as possible, he was never returned to the platoon.

Tet Offensive NVA/VC kill Village Civilians
An Hoa
January 30, 1968, 0945 hours

On the morning of the thirtieth of January 1968, the perimeter security at the northeast corner of the An Hoa complex began to receive heavy incoming fire. For the next half hour or so, the base came under heavy mortar, rocket, small arms, and automatic rifle fire. As the fighting increased, some ARVN units assigned to their section of the compound abandoned their positions and ran. Marines were soon engaged in fighting off NVA soldiers that had come through the ARVN's sector. From where we were, we could hear the exchange of gunfire going on, and it wasn't long before we started to get some incoming fire at our positions as well. Some of the incoming fire was coming from inside the compound. A short time later, we were getting heavy fire from outside the perimeter that was directed at our machine-gun positions and both M-60s returned fire.

The base tower was soon directing our eighties and sixties mortar sections on NVA soldiers they could see coming through the wire near where the ARVNs positions had been. A large enemy force could be seen waiting for the mortar fire to stop so that they could advance on the compound; before they were able to do so, a heavy barrage of artillery shells were dropped on their location.

The firefight continued sporadically until just before daybreak when civilians began to show up at our gates reporting that a large NVA/VC enemy force was sweeping through their village, firing at and killing civilians without hesitation or mercy, including children, women, and old men.

At daybreak, as soon as the word was passed for us to saddle up, we were ready to move out. As soon as we got the order, we moved out, passing first through the base area most heavily hit by the NVA. The tower had taken several hits from RPG rounds as had a number of choppers and at least two Bird Dog planes parked at the airstrip.

We made our way out the front gate, down the hill, and moved out northwest toward the village of Phu Da (2).

Civilians in the villages reported that an NVA/VC platoon had swept through the village located to the northeast of the An Hoa complex. The NVA/VC had sought out PFs, civil servants, their relatives, and any civilian of high profile to kill. In the villages, we found unarmed civilians that had been slaughtered, deliberately cut into pieces while still alive, and horribly killed; a young child with arms severed and a slash across his face we found barely breathing but alive. I don't believe he could see us because of the dried blood that covered his face. Other children had also been shot or stabbed to death. We loaded both the dead and wounded in the village onto six-by trucks and some were transported to the German hospital at An Hoa.

It was the eve of the Tet holiday, a truce that had been in place since 1800 hours on the twenty-eighth of January; and the holiday was supposed to bring happiness, hope, and peace to the Vietnamese people. Instead it had brought death and destruction.[243]

Throughout our area, the enemy had launched a series of well-coordinated attacks on almost every base in the TAOR. Hill 65, 52, 55, 37, 10, 41 as well as all the CAP units reported getting hit.

The worst incidence of casualties we suffered occurred that morning when a squad of Marines from Charley 1/7 went on a patrol just a couple of klicks from Hill 41. They were soon caught in an L-shaped ambush by a company-size enemy force. Twelve Marines were killed as were three navy corpsmen some of which had responded, along with a squad of Marines, to support the embattled Marines.[244]

Promotions For The Company
An Hoa
January 31, 1968, 1300 hours

The company was called into formation and while Lieutenant Nowicki was at Division attending leadership school, our old platoon commander Larry Wilson was present for his man's promotions and the issuance of awards mostly for the Foster battles. The awards were handed out by LtCol. Roger H. Barnard, Commanding

Officer, 3/7. Sgt. Victor R. Delarino and Cpl. Ronald S. Patrick each received the Bronze Star with Combat V for actions against the Viet Cong on a company sweep of October 12, 1967. Cpl Gary L. Reed and l/Cpl. Peter J. Lehr were awarded the Navy Commendation Medal with Combat Distinguishing device for actions of the same date. Fifteen India Company Marines were presented the Purple Heart Medal. Recipients of the medal were; Sgt. Richard L. Fludd, Sgt. Calvin Whiteside, Sgt. Zaryl F. Stamford, Cpl. Robert W. Howard, Cpl. Gary L. Reed, L/Cpl. Ira Rahm, L/Cpl. Peter J. Lehr, L/Cpl. Darrel W. Vancleef, L/Cpl. Steven P. Aguilar, Pfc. Jerome V. Souble, Pfc. Mark S. Saylor and PFC Richard E. Olson. Recipients of the Gold Star in lieu of the second Purple Heart were Sgt. Gerald N. Dumont, Cpl. Ronald S. Patrick, L/Cpl. Dennis G. Dustin and PFC. Jerry D. Ezell.

Platoon-Size Night Ambush
An Hoa
February 2, 1968, 2015 hours

For the next couple of days, we searched the area for the enemy, but they had fled. Recon units, however, continued to report large enemy sightings; and on the second of February, the platoon saddled up to go on a platoon-size night ambush near the An Hoa complex. It wasn't a good idea to be moving through any area at night, not platoon-size. I recalled what Red Dancer had said at the Finger Lake battle: "Red Dancer does not move at night."

The lieutenant hadn't passed the word if we were going after a sighted group of enemy soldiers or just looking for a chance encounter. [245] We figured it would be a fairly large-size engagement we were looking for if the platoon was being sent on an ambush at night. We had an FAO Marine with us, which meant if we made contact, he would be calling in artillery, naval, or an air strike on the enemy's location. A platoon-size movement at night was not advantageous in Vietnam unless the platoon was well disciplined and well trained to operate together. Recon units often traveled in a larger than squad-size formation, but they were well trained and prepared to carry out secret and silent operations in the dark. We had too many new Marines in the platoon that hadn't been trained to go out even as a small fire-team or silent killer teams at night. Many of the new men had not been involved in a firefight, and if we got ambushed, it would be chaos. None of the new squad leaders had passed the word down on what individual members of each squad should do if we got hit or how we were to perform together as a unit. As we moved out of the perimeter's wire, shortly before midnight, the noise the platoon was making added to that concern. I brought the gun down off my shoulder, adjusted the strap, and carried it at my side.

We moved out in a southeast direction toward Cap N-2 located half why between An Hoa and Liberty Bridge on An Hoa road. We stopped near a dry creek bed at the southern tip of a skinny lake. I figured we would stop and then move out again as we would normally do, just in case we were being followed. However, the word was passed to set in for the night. No outposts were sent out as an early warning safeguard. Instead we just set up on that spot (AT 888482). It was going to be a long night.

One of the first basic lessons a new Marine is taught when he is going to go on a patrol with grenades hanging on his belt or flak jacket is to crimp back the safety locking pin on the grenades he carries, much like a cotter pin is crimped back so that the grenade's pull ring can't be pulled out accidentally if it gets caught up on a tree branch or a low-hanging vine. I had seen grenades pop off a flak jacket or a cartridge belt when a Marine got tangled up with a tree branch or hanging tree vine. Fortunately the pin was always crimped back, and this held the grenade's handle in place.

Someone had forgotten to share this simple jungle safety tip with the new lieutenant and no sooner had we set in at our ambush location when he took off his flak jacket with his grenades still attached and the jacket got caught in a low-hanging vine. He yanked the jacket to disengage it, and one of his grenades fell out. A second later, the handle flew off and the striker struck the grenade's primer. The primer exploded, igniting the delay fuse; seconds later, we knew the grenade would explode.

Dumont saw what happened, yelled grenade, and threw the lieutenant's flak jacket over the grenade as everyone dove for cover. The grenade's explosion lit the dark night then another grenade also attached to the jacket exploded.

The dual explosions ripped the jacket into hundreds of slivers of thin fiberglass. The flak jacket was totally ripped apart, looking much like shredded paper. The hole left in the ground was deep and had cleared a pretty good-size patch of underbrush. Fortunately no one was hurt. Dumont, without reservation, started yelling at the lieutenant much like a father would a kid. He was reaming him up and down before he calmed down and in frustration walked away. That night, I saw a side of Dumont I had never seen before, and I realized then and there why he hadn't been promoted to his present rank before. With our night position now compromised with the explosions, we had no choice but to move out.

"Six Actual, this is One Actual," the lieutenant's shaken voice cracked over the radio's mike as he tried to speak as quietly as possible and we all laughed to ourselves at the foolishness of his action, trying to be quiet when the whole valley probably had heard the explosion and now knew where we were.

"Six Actual, this is One Actual."

"One Actual, go," the captain's radioman at An Hoa answered on the radio. The voice was loud and clear, and the lieutenant turned the radio's knob to tone down the volume.

"Six Actual, Six Actual, this is One Actual, be advised that we're coming in."

"Six Actual to One Actual, is there a problem?"

"Six Actual, affirmative will explain upon returning to base."

"Six Actual, roger, will alert the gate."

The point man led us back in record time, and I feared we might be ambushed along the way but we returned to base without incident.

Since it was late, everyone was dismissed for the night. While we welcomed the rest that we would get in not having to stand watch that night, talking about what had happened to the lieutenant kept us awake and laughing for a while. When some of the company's men that had been left behind to man the lines were told of the reason why we had come in early, they joined in with our laughter. As the story was retold over and over again, it kept getting funnier and funnier with each retelling. Pretty soon the whole company was in an uproar with tears of laughter streaming down our cheeks. The bennies to the lieutenant's blunder was that we would not have to stand watch that night. As we crawled into our racks, we all silently thanked the lieutenant for the needed rest, and Dumont, that little Canadian Frenchman, had grown in stature before all of us that night.

Chasing The NVA
An Hoa TAOR
February 3, 1968, 0500 hours

Early the morning of the third of February, as dawn broke over the An Hoa basin, Marine recon inserts reported seeing four to five hundred NVAs surrounding the ambush site where we had set into the night before (AT 887490-890486-888473); the recon unit called in 105mm and 155mm artillery rounds from Hill 65 on the enemies' positions with good coverage. Forty minutes later, enemy soldiers opened fire on CAP N-2 with AK-47 and K-44 bullets fired at the platoon-size combat base. An Arty Mission with Willy Peter 105mm artillery shells were then dropped on the enemy's position, and they broke contact.

During the night of the second and early morning of the third, NVA soldiers swept through the villages nearby where they burned numerous hooches. We saddled up early, platoon size, to sweep through the area. We entered villages where the NVA/VC had torched some homes after demanding food for Tet. They had killed innocent civilians and children, leaving their bodies where they fell. Some you could tell were shot in the back as they tried to flee. As we entered one village after another, the villagers told us where the enemy had gone and we kept chasing after them. For most of that morning and early afternoon, we pursued them but made no contact.

At 1400 hours, a detail from Second Platoon assigned road sweep near the intersection of the road south of Liberty Bridge and the road that ran east and west on the south side of the Song Thu Bon River observed three NVA soldiers carrying weapons, packs, and cartridge belts. They opened fire on them with a 3.5 rocket and small arms fire. As the platoon made their way back to An Hoa, a platoon of enemy soldiers, having followed them, opened up on them with automatic rifle fire. The incoming fire was coming from a tree line on the south side of the road. Second Platoon was pinned down for a while until an artillery mission was called in and 105mm rounds were heavily dropped on the enemy's position. Due to the lateness of the hour, the tree line was not checked for enemy bodies. When they made their way back, both our platoon and Second Platoon arrived in An Hoa at the same time.

That evening just before sundown, a Vietnamese male approached the An Hoa perimeter and reported the VC had planted two mines just outside our perimeter's fence. The following morning, a command-detonated satchel charge was found lying forty meters from our front gate's position. The charge had been triggered, but it had not exploded.

Enemy sightings in our TAOR area continued to increase as were the mining incidents and sporadic short firefights along the road. It appeared the enemy was avoiding full confrontation in the An Hoa basin, and battalion began to shift Marine positions around to better confront the enemy movements throughout our area. Mike Company was moved from Hill 52 to Hill 37 and was placed under operational control (OpCon) of the First Battalion Seventh Marines.

Metzler's Broken Black Heart Of Darkness
An Hoa
February 4, 1968, 1300 hours

We went out on the fourth of February on a platoon-size patrol near where the first village had been destroyed by the VC during Tet. Metzler was walking point for his fire-team. The village normally filled with activity was silent and deserted. A wide foot path near the village entrance was blocked by a wide broken bamboo gate lying on its side. Bushes of varied sizes and shapes lined the trail as Metzler walked around the obstruction to enter the village when the enemy set off a command-detonated claymore mine. The mine exploded, sending out seven hundred steel bearings in a sixty-degree angle for about fifty yards. The shrapnel tore pieces of flesh out of Metzler and the two Marines standing behind him; all three fell seriously wounded by the explosion.

Metzler had twice turned down promotions because he didn't want the responsibility of commanding a Marine rifle squad. He feared getting Marines hurt or killed by a foolish decision he might make as a squad leader more than he feared getting hurt or killed. As we awaited the medevac chopper, Metzler sat on the trail silently, somehow he felt responsible for the explosion and then he slowly began to cry and all the pent-up emotions of months of combat just came pouring out. His emotional outburst echoed through our souls as well and it deeply troubled us. The sentiments he was feeling and releasing was like our own pent-up emotional turmoil's of war, of worry and fear, of deep frustration, of not being able to find and destroy the enemy responsible for the death and destruction of innocent villagers, lost Marine lives, and wounded comrades. While we all knew Metzler was not responsible, we took in long, deep sighs and no one said a word to him or to each other as we sat and waited.

Twenty minutes later, three helicopters appeared on the horizon. As the flop-flop-flop sound of their rotating blades increased in volume, a sigh of relief was released from all of us. We knew Metzler would soon be medically treated for his wounds and silently wished his other wounds, those found deep inside, could be treated as well. How can those wounds ever be identified? What treatment is there for those who will forever have to deal with the evil guardian spirits of the sorrows of war? Who can touch that emotional state of the mind once it has been embedded with hatred, evil desires, anger, and lamentations for the poor and helpless souls lost in war and the conflicts of life? Who can venture into those secret chambers of the mind where fear, forgotten dreams, and lost souls dance with demons well into the night? Why wasn't a military medal, a broken black heart, or a seal of honor issued to those warriors that have smelled death on the other side of God? They were men of war, warriors who had held and slept with the angel of death in their arms. For such wounded souls, there is no peace, no honor, or cure.

Because of increased enemy activity in the area, two Huey gunship escorts appeared alongside the medevac choppers. The command-detonated explosion meant the enemy was in the area, and no sooner had the choppers lifted off the ground we began to get incoming sniper rounds from a heavy tree line to the north of the village. I pointed out to James where the rounds had come from, and he opened fire in that direction. The enemy responded by increasing their firepower; we returned fire and, for a while, our firefight continued. As we continued to exchange fire, the machine-guns' red tracers pinpointed the enemy's location and the gunships swooped down and sprayed the area and the tree line where the enemy was hiding with hundreds of machine-gun bullets, and then unloaded a series of rockets into the thick jungle. As dark gray smoke spiraled upward, the word was passed for us to move out. We didn't bother to go after the enemy we had just engaged in battle or to search for evidence of enemy bodies we might have killed; the lieutenant wanted to get out of there fast, and we did.

The Claymore Marines
An Hoa
February 5-8, 1968, 2350 hours

CAP N-3 near the Song Thu Bon River got hit with grenades, heavy automatic rifle fire, and 60mm mortar rounds. As the CAP unit returned fire with both .50 and .30 caliber bullets, Third Platoon was sent out as a reactionary unit, but the NVA cut off contact before they got there. Two Marines from the CAP unit were wounded, and a sweep through the area the following morning by Third Platoon found no evidence of the enemy having been there.

During the day February 7, we received two incoming RPG rocket rounds and some small arms fire at our security position at the An Hoa Air Base. Intelligence had informed the platoon that a squad of enemy soldiers, were to pass through an area near a village close by. Two First Platoon Marines volunteered to go on a two-man ambush killer team. They loaded fifteen claymore mines into two backpacks and set out early that evening. At midnight, the Marines set off all fifteen mines, devastating a reinforced NVA rifle squad, and ran back to the perimeter wire safe and sound.

At 1150 hours on February 8, we were sent out as a blocking force for three reinforced Army Ranger companies that were sweeping with tanks through the area. At 1255 hours, as the first elements of the sweeping force approached our location, a squad of enemy soldiers opened fire on us from the west side of the road near a tree line. The enemy fired two hundred rounds at us and we returned small arms fire, and fired several LAWs in their direction. As the firefight continued, the tanks got into position and opened fire on the enemy force with their .30 caliber weapons. As the Army ranger swept passed us, we moved in and searched the area and found only blood trails leading away from the tree line.

New Commanding Officer For India Company
An Hoa
February 10, 1968, 1300 hours

On the tenth, we received a new commanding officer for India Company, Captain Reeder, and he came around checking on his people. I knew that I was going to like him. He seemed down-to-earth, and we were told he had some combat experience. A tall, husky Marine with a round face, he wasn't afraid to be out in the field with his men. He seemed to favor First Platoon for some reason.

For the next twenty days, First Platoon and Second Platoon were reassigned to Liberty Bridge, as we built up our bunkers and fighting positions there and stood watch at night while Second Platoon was assigned to the road sweeps from Liberty Bridge and Third Platoon handled night ambushes and day patrols, at An Hoa.

Those days were relatively quiet for us. It was as if we were being held in reserve but weren't told why. In Vietnam, the infantrymen were rarely given any information about what was going on elsewhere in country or in the surrounding area. I never read a *Stars and Stripes* or a *Sea Tiger* newspaper. We received only bits and pieces of information from friends in other companies that we happened or chanced to meet during supply runs or operations. Like many things in life, scuttlebutt was always mingled with half-truths and rumors that rarely proved to be true. We knew something was up, and our lieutenant never told us anything other than order us to reinforce our bunkers, dig our trench lines, work on our fighting positions, and be ready to move out at a moment's notice. We wondered what was really going on.

On the night of the twenty-third, we received twenty incoming mortar rounds, and like with the previous barrages at the compound, no one was hurt. During those attacks, we locked and loaded and waited for an enemy assault that never came. We, however, had confidence in the defensive positions we had built. The wire out front would slow them down, and we would be able to withhold a large attack. After such mortar attacks, Captain J.R. Reeder a tall, fluffy cheeked, heavy set commanding officer that immediately won the respect of his men. He would often come around personally checking the lines after a mortar attack, to see if we were alright.

Reactionary Force
An Hoa AT 875475
March 1, 1968, 0900 hours

On the first day of March, we found ourselves back at Liberty Bridge. We were placed on reactionary standby; for the next three days following our road-sweep details, we practiced falling in and out of formation with full gear just in case we were needed to respond in a Sparrow hawk assault we were told.

At first, our gear was checked and serviceable items were checked; missing items, or items that needed servicing, we were told to go to the supply sergeant and get them replaced, but there were no replacements available, so we just did without. What was, checked every time were our Geneva Convention cards and our dog tags.

In our packs, we were supposed to have a protective gas mask, an E-tool, toilet articles, two bottles of salt tablets each as well as one bottle of iodine water purification tablets, three pairs of socks, and an extra pair of trousers. Of course, none of us had those items. Those of us that had gas masks knew they were old and would probably leak if we ever had to use them. No one bothered to check the gas mask pouches we carried. If they had, it would have been found out that we usually stored other items in the gas mask pouches. Aggie did have a full bottle of salt tablets and a bottle of halizone tablets, but when he opened up the small dark brown glass bottle to check and see how many water purification tablets were in it, one lone tablet fell out along with some powder residue.

We were each issued three C-rat meals that were to be kept in our backpacks and not eaten. What other items we were supposed to have we normally wore on patrol anyways: our flak jackets, two canteens of water, helmet, weapons, and ammo.

Evidently the lieutenant didn't like how long it took us to fall into formation, so he would at a moment's notice call for us to fall out with full gear and assemble in formation on Liberty Road. He did that several times before we figured out how to offset the overall time it would take for us to fall out. We just kept our backpacks filled with the three C-rat meals and all the other supplies needed hooked together. That way, when formation was called, we just slipped on our flak jackets. Everything was already attached, so all we had to do then is grab our weapons, helmet, and ammo and we were ready to roll. However, this meant we manned our bunker positions without our flak jackets, but the lieutenant didn't seem to notice. He was just pleased that once the word was passed for formation, we were able to fall out and were ready to move out at a moment's notice.

On the Morning of the Third, First Platoon saddled up and we escorted the mine sweeping detail to An Hoa and were told to stay there that night. Something was up, but no word was passed around as to what was going on.

Civilians Butchered By The NVA
An Hoa
March 4, 1968, 0145 hours

At 0120 hours, on the morning of the fourth, we once again got mortared. Over thirty 60mm and 82mm mortar rounds were dropped on the An Hoa compound. CAP N-3 and the Duc Duc district were also hit with a series of mortar rounds and small arms fire. At first light, we moved out to sweep through the village of Phu Da (3), which was also known as the Duc Duc Resettlement Village located just southwest of us. During the night, NVA enemy soldiers had swept through the village and killed every villager they could find. That morning, we counted over seventy civilians who had been killed and another eighty-eight seriously wounded. Most of them were medevaced for emergency medical treatment in Da Nang. Another sixty-five villagers were treated and released at the An Hoa hospital complex.[246]

As we swept through the village, we found groups of women, children, and old men huddled together in several sections of the village where they had been gathered and massacred. Others were slain in their huts. Naked old and young women were found lying dead out in the open, and it was evident the women had been raped then shot in the head. Some had their body parts carved with a knife, others had an *x* carved on their foreheads and bullet entrance wounds near the marks. The villagers' survivors told us the NVA had attacked their village in order to force the people across the river into the Arizona area to grow rice for them. They also said the NVA had come through the village looking to kill PFs.

On the fifth of March, Mike Company 3/7 came in to man the lines at Liberty Bridge and Third Platoon was sent to battalion headquarters while First and Second Platoons returned to An Hoa.

CHAPTER TWENTY THREE

Operation Rock
First Platoon, India Company
March 6, 1968, D-Day, 0915 hours

Early the morning of the sixth, at 0915 hours, fixed-wing aircraft were prepping LZ Robin across the river in Quam Nam Province in preparation for our landing. This was the operation First Platoon had been preparing for, but we hadn't been told about.[247]

At 0940 hours as the jets pulled off, 115 Marines from First and Second Platoon as well as India Company's CP command group were loaded on board Six Sea Knight choppers (CH-46); a short time later, we lifted off the tarmac at An Hoa.

At takeoff, one of the CH-46s developed mechanical difficulties and was detained at An Hoa, but the rest of us continued on with our mission. "Operation Rock," a battalion-size operation, had commenced and we were on our way back into the Arizona/Foster territory.

As the choppers circled to land, smoke was still rising from where the air strikes had prepped the area. As the choppers began their descent, I could see we would be landing at the northern tip of Finger Lake. It was less than a klick from where we had fought our battle of November 21. I was anticipating a battle, another fierce firefight or a series of them.

The chopper's ramp was already down and level by the time the chopper touched ground. At times a chopper crewmember would point out to us where we should proceed toward or where enemy firing was coming from. The chopper landed in a hot LZ and we were getting hit with fierce incoming automatic weapons fire. As Marines scrambled out, I looked at the crew chief, and he threw his hands up in the air because he didn't know where the firing was coming from or where we should go.

As we ran out the ramp, the distinct sounds of bullets fired from AK-47s and other high-velocity machine-gun bullets sizzled past us. Dirt, mud, and grass were being plucked off the weed-covered ground as we scrambled out of the chopper's rear door. In front of us were open rice paddy fields and a tree line was just a short distance away. We were out in the open with no cover from where we could return fire.

With the noise of the chopper's blades reverberating the air around us, as the chopper accelerated its engines to lift off, it was hard figuring out where the majority of the enemy's fire was coming from. Seconds later, I realized we were getting hit from two sides. Bullets were coming from our left where Second Platoon was advancing ahead of us and also from our front. The majority of First Platoon had landed on my right, and Marines were beginning to advance on line. We had landed in a hot LZ. I stepped forward with them, all of us firing as we moved forward. Off in the distance, I could see fixed-wing aircraft dropping a load of ordnance as a Bird Dog plane circled around. The jets were preparing another landing zone.[248]

To my right, James opened fire with his M-60 from the hip; the red tracers were slicing across the open field, heading straight for the edge of the tree line where we were receiving the majority of incoming fire from. As the platoon advanced, the enemy stopped firing. Minutes later, we had secured the tree line and surprisingly, no one in our platoon was wounded or had been killed during the assault under heavy enemy fire. The enemy opened fire; but were now gone. A short time later, recon inserts reported a twenty-man enemy force fleeing our location traveling toward the river.

Within the hour, the same choppers that had dropped us off dropped off Lima Company 3/7 in LZ Blue Jay, the area the jets were prepping earlier. They landed on the other side of where the enemy soldiers had fled toward; the enemy soldiers were now between Lima Company and us. Lima Company however landed without incident.

Hotel 2/7, Third Platoon, India Company, our 81mm platoon, and a platoon of PFs were then picked up from Hill 37 and all were dropped at our landing zone. By 1105 hours, everyone involved in the operation was on the ground in the Arizona/Foster area and Lima Company was already sweeping toward us.

A short time later as Lima Company stepped out of a tree line they were hit with friendly fire. Two Huey gunship rockets were fired on them, but they took no casualties. Meanwhile, Hotel 2/7 captured a badly wounded NVA soldier.

The soldier was carrying two ChiCom grenades, ten M-79 rounds, and a .45 caliber pistol with three magazines. The soldier was clean and smart looking, and battalion personnel had determined he was probably an NVA officer; but as they waited for the chopper to medevac him, he died of his wounds and was just left there.

We hooked up with Second Platoon, and set in as a blocking force for Lima Company, Second Platoon had not been as lucky as we had. They had suffered one KIA in the initial assault: a machine-gunner by the name of Francis Capezio. Capezio, a new man in second platoon had less then a month in county. An NVA sniper shot the Marine in front of Doc Keller, by the time the corpsman got to him, there was nothing he could do, to try and save his life.

At the base of a small hill as they swept toward us, Lima Company captured two NVA Soldiers[249] and also took their first casualty. A Marine was shot in the head and killed by an enemy sniper. By mid-afternoon, Lima Company had swept through our perimeter and we all set up for the night on the lower east side of Finger Lake.

Lima Company Gets Hit Bad
Operation Rock
March 6, 1968, D-Day, 1945-2310 hours

Our defensive positions were set near the bottom tip of Finger Lake. Aggie was with me and Eddie Williams was set in with James. They were on the other end of our platoon's perimeter. It was very near the same location we had spent Thanksgiving Day during Operation Foster and close to where we had fought our fierce two-day battle on the small hill where three companies of Marines had taken many casualties.

At 1945 hours, Lima Company's defensive position began to get incoming fire. They were set up to our left, and the volume of fire steadily increased. Soon they were taking heavy incoming enemy fire, including numerous 81mm mortar rounds and hundreds of small arms and automatic rifle fire.[250] As they returned fire, their response was met with a heavier barrage of intense incoming rounds. The incoming rounds were so intense and close we felt the enemy would soon be attempting to overrun their positions.

For the next four hours we sat still and listened as Lima continued to get hit and no one passed the word down for us to move out to reinforce their positions. The sound of the enemy's AK-47 bullets roared above the sound the M-16s made as Marines returned fire. It sounded like a lion's roar and a mouse's reply. I wanted to move my gun over and engage the enemy with its firepower, to do something, to respond in some way.

Grenades, rocket fire, and mortars were also being dropped at Lima Company's defensive positions, and we just sat silent. We were set up in a two company-size defensive position with India Company on the right bottom side of the circle from six to nine on the clock. Lima was set up to our left from six to three on the clock. It was to our left near the midsection of Lima's lines that was getting hit the hardest, somewhere between five and four on the clock.

Hotel Company was set up a klick away near the tip of Finger Lake and they, like us, were not receiving any incoming fire. We didn't know the size of the enemy force in the area or where the majority of their force was located so we sat and listened—there was nothing else we could do.

While Lima Marines held on, we waited and no word was passed for us to move in to reinforce their lines.

Whoever the enemy force engaging Lima Company was certainly larger then a platoon, judging by the fire power and quantity of firepower they were releasing.

The Q-14 Company, and the R-20, was known to be operating in the area; their company strength was seventy to one-hundred men each. We knew that at times the NVA/VC control center was located at O Gia village (AT 870550), just to the north of us and a little more than a klick away from where Hotel Company was located.

There was a possibility we had enemy force on three sides of us. The enemy was attacking Lima Company with 81mm mortars, 57mm recoilless rifles, M-79 automatic and machine-guns; it was evident they were determined to inflict heavy casualties on Lima Company Marines that night, but with Finger Lake behind us, they would be foolish to try to overrun them or us.

Clock-wise, my machine-gun team was located at about six-thirty. We could hear Lima Marines returning fire with a clear message to the enemy force before them that if they attacked, they would be paying a heavy price.

We sat, listened, prayed, and wondered how the Marines of Lima Company were holding out. Above us, a half-moon was giving off its light and I was wondering if the Marines being hit appreciated the light from above shining upon them or on the enemy. I hated nights like this where the slight glow of moonlight shines on small objects and bushes and they in turn hide the dark shadows resembling humans and shapes of helmets and cone hats. On nights like this, one has to rely upon one's sense of smell and hearing as well as seeing what can be seen. Tonight, the moon's light was giving illumination to the battle scene where Marines were being shot at not far from us. Perhaps soon it would be our turn. So we continued to sit and wait and listen to the sounds of war, pain, and sorrow going on just a short distance from us.

Artillery was being dropped heavily on the enemy's rear position, most of it ineffective as their main force was too close to Lima's lines. Still, as soon as the artillery let up, the firing resumed with more intensity. Finally at 2350 hours, there was silence. The battle had ended for the day.

Early the next morning, long before dawn, we heard then saw the emergency medevac choppers landing near Lima's position. Already on this first day of the operation, we had lost one man as had Lima Company; now, the choppers were landing to medevac another KIA and five more of their WIAs. As they medevaced their dead and wounded, we saddled up and the second day of the operation began.

Got Hit Again
Operation Rock
March 7, 1968, D+1, 0845 hours

During the night of the sixth and early morning hours of the seventh of March, recon insert "Chile Pepper," high on the ridge overlooking our area, called in extensive artillery barrages to the west of us. The recon team had observed a number of enemy forces moving throughout the area, heading west toward their mountain retreat. It was a large enough force that everyone seemed to have been called into the action as artillery, naval gunfire, and air strikes were dropped in on the enemy force as they moved through the area.

With first light, we moved out going north to continue in our search and destroy mission. As we entered an area filled with scattered bushes, small trees, and open space, a command-detonated mine was exploded by the enemy, wounding a navy corpsman assigned to Hotel 2/7 (AT 864541). We quickly set up a defensive position for the medevac, and as the wounded corpsman was being medevaced, we got hit.

Lima Company a short distance away (AT858542), got hit with heavy automatic rifle fire and took a direct hit from 81mm mortars rounds. They became pinned down out in the open field unable to move because of the intensity of the incoming enemy fire. Two Company B tanks swept around to support us in the battle, but they too were soon hit with enemy sniper and RPG fire (AT857545). They returned 90mm fire, and that helped Lima Company get out of the kill zone but not before Lima had suffered another KIA and ten WIA's.

The enemy all of a sudden was popping up from out of nowhere and everywhere at the same time. They were behind us, in front of us, and to our sides. We opened fire at sites where we could identify the enemy had fired on us from, but often they were just separate spider holes from where the enemy would pop up, open fire, and disappear. We began to discover a network of trenches that connected hamlets and tree lines together. Many of the trenches had heavy-duty covers over them that offered the enemy protection from artillery and air bombardment. The hamlets were heavily fortified and well designed to provide strong defensive fighting positions as well.

We moved out, taking sporadic fire here and there. A Marine rifle squad would investigate where the shooting came from and then eliminate the lone enemy soldier, sacrificed for the effect of delaying our movement or to confuse our mission. In each hamlet we passed through, we found bomb shelters built nearby. The shelters hadn't been there during Operation Foster but now the small hills around us were honeycombed with a tunnel complex that varied in size and length. One particular tunnel we found ran for three thousand meters under and alongside the same trail we had used often during Operation Foster. The tunnel ran from the bottom of Finger Lake, south toward Phu Long (1) with an opening where Boyd had seen the enemy soldier disappear before we got hit on November 19. That seemed like ages ago; so many firefights had been fought since then, so many Marines killed or wounded, and now we were here again at the very same spot we had been four months before. The tunnel complex ran past and under where Aggie and I had been pinned down and had taken fire from two sides; I recalled how Aggie wanted them to stop shooting so he could go pee and I chuckled as we stood by and tunnel rats continued to follow the tunnel as it turned southwest, running parallel to the Song Thu Bon River and ending at the base of a small hill near Tan Phuoc (3).[251]

As we crossed an opening along a tree line, James pointed out a group of NVA soldiers moving in a far tree line. Lima Company had just stepped out into the open field to cross that open area and so had most of our platoon, so I told James to open fire, on the enemy soldiers.

On and off enemy engagement continued and by noon we made it across but were sweaty, dirty, and thirsty. The water in our canteens was gone or hot, and the temperature over 110 degrees. Somewhere as we were spread out between villages, the crossing of the open rice paddy fields, and the battle, Eddie Williams had collapsed from heat exhaustion and along with the wounded from that morning's battle was medevaced. With Williams gone, I picked up the M-60; and it felt good to have my old friend at my side once again.

Flamethrower Shot
Operation Rock
March 7, 1968, D+1, 1300 hours

We swept through the area Lima Company had gotten hit from then swept through the area where the snipers had fired on the tanks. I was pleased to have tanks and amtracks all around us, but that didn't stop the enemy from popping out of spider holes and selectively firing on us. Like evil jack-in-the-box puppets, the enemy soldiers fired at us and then disappeared. It was hard to tell where the bullets were coming from with tanks around us or when you were fired at from the rear from an area we had just passed through, while there were still Marines behind and to our sides. Unless we saw them, it was hard to find their covered spider holes.

Sometimes only the rifle barrel poked out of the hole when the enemy opened fire. The company called for backpack flamethrowers to clear areas we believed the holes may be and the area was sprayed and set on fire. As we moved through an open area, one of the flamethrowers, a tall Marine, came up walking alongside of me. My gun team was sandwiched in between two fire-teams as we slowly moved through the area.

As we came across an open flat surface, there was a sense of danger in the air. I tightened the grip on my gun, ready to bring it up, and slowed my pace. The flamethrower, with the tanks on his back, stepped away from me then turned and looked at me with a puzzled look. He turned to walk away toward one of the tanks, and as he took a step, he was shot in the back. As he went down, I turned and opened fire at the enemy's spider hole. Marines on both sides of me also saw the gook and fired on him as he dropped into his hole. Rahm ran up to the spider hole, pulled the pin on a grenade, lifted the cover, and dropped it into the hole. The grenade exploded and forever sealed the dead gook in his self-made grave. We never bothered to lift the cover or look inside.

Early that afternoon, the tanks and the amtracks began to experience mechanical difficulties so First Platoon was held back to provide security for them while repairs were made. The rest of the company moved on with Lima and Hotel continuing the sweep through a hilly section of the valley.

Before setting in, we searched the area around us and found groups of dead civilians left out in open rice paddy fields. Others, including women and children, had been horribly butchered and some had been thrown into the local village wells by the NVA. Many of the dead civilians we found were riddled with AK-47 bullets. They had been executed, by the NVA.

At 1600 hours, the tanks and amtracks were pulled off the operation, and we provided security for them as they crossed the Song Vu Gia River and headed for Hill 37.

Water Buffalo Attack
Operation Rock
March 7, 1968, D+1, 1700 hours

We moved out to rejoin the rest of the battalion, and as we passed through a small village near Finger Lake, we stopped to take a break. Two Marines standing near a thick cluster of bushes were drinking from their canteens when all of a sudden, a heavy bush in front of them was split apart as a large water buffalo came charging at them out of the dense vegetation. They jumped back just in time as the beast shot past them. The old water buffalo turned back and put his head down, preparing to charge them again. The Marines leveled their M-16s on the beast but didn't open fire.

"Aggie, is this a free-fire zone?" I asked.

"Yeah! Anything moving is fair game," he answered.

"Aggie, is that water buffalo a VC water buffalo or is he a friendly?"

"If he's here and moving, he's VC," Aggie answered. "I think that water buffalo is VC. He just attacked those two Marines," Aggie added. By now, two other Marines were pointing their M-16s at the water buffalo, waiting for him to charge. I knew the M-16's bullets would not stop the monster that was breathing heavily, and tightening the muscles on his broad shoulders.

He charged at the two Marines, and they opened fire. Their bullets went deep into his huge body, but the beast just kept coming at them. They jumped out of the way and the beast quickly turned to charge at them again. Four Marines opened up with more rounds. But the animal, unimpeded, turned and charged again, and they barely moved out of the water buffalo's path as he tried to strike them. Then the mammoth creature stopped, standing still looking at all of us. He had at least ten to fifteen bullet holes in him and they hadn't budged him a bit. One of the Marines opened up with two more bullets. A veiled thud was heard as the bullets went deep into the hard water buffalo's skin. Rahm stepped up, and fired two .45 caliber rounds from his pistol into the beast; the bullets seemed to bounce off his head, as the buffalo didn't seem to be shaken by their impact. Doc Mac stepped up and fired two shotguns blast into the animal, still the damage the bullets were doing didn't seem to trouble the beast.

"Shoot him in the back! You have to break their spines to bring them down," Welsh said as three more bullets were fired at the water buffalo and the beast bent his two front legs a little. Three more rounds entered his neck and he sat down. I opened up with six rounds from the M-60 machine-gun, and you could hear the beast's back crack and he fell headfirst into the mud. He twisted and turned, tried to get up, and then lay down on his side. He tried to get up once more then turned to face us; the water buffalo bawled loudly then stopped moving. Chino in Second Squad was carrying the M-79, and he fired a grenade into the beast. It exploded, sending chunks of meat flying off in several directions. The huge creature's feet went straight up into the air; he kicked out and stopped moving. Another smaller water buffalo about forty yards away, hearing the grenade's explosion, bellowed and high-stepped away, disappearing into thick bamboo.

"Well, that VC got away," Aggie said, and we all laughed.

A short distance from us at 1735 hours, Hotel 2/7 was hit with heavy M-79 fire and took two WIAs. They opened fire on four enemy soldiers they saw running away, killing one of them. However, in the process, one of their own was wounded by M-79 friendly fire.

Not far from them, a short time later, while two of Lima Company's platoons were boarding choppers to be helilifted out of the field to the An Hoa complex got hit; as the last chopper lifted off, they were hit with heavy small arms fire and took yet another casualty.

As evening fell, we hurried to find and hook up with Hotel Company. We were a little more then a klick from where they had gotten hit, earlier that day.

We set up on top of a small knoll northeast My Binh near the tip of Finger Lake.

The small hills surrounding us were covered with knee-high broad-leaf plants, newly grown bamboo shoots, and small banana trees. Some of the sides of the hills had steep drop-off edges where the local farmer had managed over the years to cut into the side of the hill in order to extend his rice paddy fields, which allowed water to flow evenly to water his fields. Before full darkness fell, we hadn't had a chance to visually check out the area in front or near us nor did we know where Hotel Company's positions actually were. For the most part, the two companies were set up on the large round tip of a fairly barren hill with no one set in to the west of us. To our northeast, the PF platoon was located and they were linked to Hotel Company. Hotel and the rest of India Company had arrived on the hill in the late afternoon and had pretty well dug in for the night.

We hooked up with them from their last position, stretched out counterclockwise from their location, followed by the Lima Company platoon who covered the northwest side of the hill.

Night Ambush In The Arizona Territory
Operation Rock; AT 858548
March 7, 1968, D+1, 2100 hours

We had barely dropped our gear, when a squad with an M-60 gun team was needed to go out and set up a listening post/ambush site. The lieutenant chose Third Squad and Aggie and me as the gun team to go with them.

We hurried to move out before the first rays of the moonlight would expose our squad's silhouettes moving through the night. The night had a deep, uncertain darkness to it, so we quickly found what gear we needed to take with us and moved out.

We moved out into the open rice paddy fields following the faint outline of the Marine in front of us, walking as silent as we could. We were traveling west along a wide rice paddy dike toward a small hill's outline some 300 meters away. The top of the hill was barely visible in the distance, its skyline just a shade darker than the faint blue tint of its background. Shadows within shadows, outlines that faded and disappeared, and it was hard to tell what was what, where the skyline ended, and the ground began. All of it was sheltered in various shades of shadows. Soft grays merged into dark green blacks and darker tones of thicker black shades with no beginning and no end. Earlier, before darkness had fallen, before we reached the hill the company was on, I had seen a cluster of trees and clumps of tall elephant grass at the base of the hill we were now traveling toward. I had seen them as good places for the enemy to be set up in a great place for them to fire upon our hill, and from where to ambush a unit traveling toward that location as we were. We were like blind mice slowly moving into that area, silently hoping they weren't already there. With each step, we drew closer to the black shadows of war where the demons of conflict dwelled and where the horrors of hell waited, a void in space where displaced spirits were assigned to hide in their own shadow of darkness, evil spirits waiting to snatch the lives of those that walked by.

After a while, the point man felt a cluster of bushes at his feet, and he pulled off to his right along the base of the hill; the rest of the squad followed. There had been a slight elevation in our path as we drew near the hill, so it seemed we had now reached our destination and would soon be setting in for the night.

When our gun team and the tail end of the squad came to the turning point, at the base of the hill, a chill ran down my soul; as the word was passed for us to stop, move forward a few feet, and set in, I sensed the presence of evil, death, and fear.

It was too dark to see anything in front of us; the vegetation at our feet was spongy, and soft loose dirt was on the ground. The foliage in front of us consisted of hearty broad-leaf plants that made no noise when you moved them aside. We slid into the undergrowth and blended in with the shadows of the night. The still air in front of us seemed to indicate there was some sort of clearing or thick tall plants in front of me. Either way, we figured we would be able to hear anyone coming our way although we may not be able to see them until our eyes adjusted to the darkness; but once they did, and if we were alert and listening, we would be able to hear or smell them for sure.

With Aggie set in on my right and the squad's last fire-team set in to my left, we sat still and silent. Aggie and I had done this together so many times we seemed to breathe and listen as one. The absence of any sound in front of us worried me, and I knew Aggie was just as troubled. The darkness was unlike what we had experienced during Operation Knox. Here there was no breeze, no air was flowing through the bushes or through the thick vegetation at our feet, and no sounds were coming through the bushes that were supposed to be in front of us. It seemed as if we had reached the doorway that led to fear and uncertainty. It was a place where spiritual darkness could be felt. We remained silent and still, afraid to move, then both Aggie and I turned to face each other when we smelled the death angel's presence. We knew we had set in at the threshold where demons dwelled, at the pinnacle where barren dice were tossed across time and space, heaven and hell, life and death; and we waited to see where the dice would end, but we knew it would make no difference how they fell. This was war, and so we tightened our grips on the weapons at our side and that gave us the confidence we needed to sit in the dark in the shadow of death.

Soon the quarter moon would come out of the dark clouds above and we would be able to see more clearly and then know what lay in front of us, but for now we waited and listened and wondered about life and were thankful with each breath we took and wondered how many more breaths we would take before daybreak.

Close to midnight, we heard a noise; it sounded like someone was crawling toward our position. The night remained bathed in blackness, the moon hidden behind thick clouds, so we strained our eyes to see, our ears to listen.

Damn it, I was thinking. *We're going to touch before we can see each other.* I pushed the gun's barrel forward and held her close and remembered I had left my K-bar behind.

We could hear the enemy moving in front of us, and knew they were close, very close. No doubt they were aware where our companies had set up for the night, so they might be moving toward the base of the hill and toward us.

We lay silent, waiting, just silently breathing while listening. We could sense their presence; but they, like us, remained silent. Hours passed then Aggie tapped me on my shoulder, and I leaned my head toward him. In the darkness of the night with only a sliver of faded light shining through thick clouds from the half-moon above, I could see his finger tapping his nose. I took in a deep breath and caught a slight smell of something foul. It was the odor of the enemies' unwashed body, the stench of oil and sweat, mixed with the foul smell of garlic and dead fish. It was a live human body's stench and I favored the smell of death instead.

We listened with renewed alertness and could faintly hear Vietnamese voices. The sound was farther back than the presence of the enemy soldiers we knew were near us. Probably their squad or platoon leader giving out instructions, I was thinking. The enemy soldiers near us were probably a listening post, or their ambush party.

To my right, a Marine moved and we heard a whispered, "shhh," and wondered who said it. We then heard the enemy move, the sound of damp leaves being pushed aside followed by silence and heavy breathing, ours or theirs I couldn't tell, then the smell of passed gas, and one of the enemy soldiers shoved his comrade. There was a muffled Vietnamese chuckle then silence again.

By now, I knew they were right in front of us and they must have heard us move as well, but we still couldn't see each other or detect any real movement. They couldn't see where we were and we couldn't see them, yet we could hear each other move and the noise was close, very close. Then a stern voice in Vietnamese whispered a command and the enemy got up to move from their position. At the same time, a Marine to our right opened fire.

Open Fire
Operation Rock; AT 858548
March 8, 1968, D+2, 0100 hours

Dirt, dust, and pieces of rock and shrapnel were kicked back in the face of the Marine who opened fire. Someone next to him felt the debris and fearing it was incoming, also opened up. Welsh, who had prepared for an enemy assault, had already un-crimped two of his grenades. He pulled the pin from one and threw it, then another and threw that grenade as well. Both exploded in rapid succession behind the enemy's forward position, and the enemy opened fire into the darkness in response to the attackers they couldn't see.

Green tracers flew five to eight feet above our heads, and I wondered why they were firing at us so high off the ground and knew that at any moment bullets would be slicing through the bushes and plants toward us. Both Marines and the enemy threw more grenades. The enemy's grenades exploded far behind us. An enemy soldier cried out in pain, and another used a harsh word to silence him. Then his comrade yelled at us in the dark and sprayed the area with automatic weapons fire. The bullets flew by high over our heads.

Northeast of us, where, the friendlies were, someone opened fire in our direction and the enemy returned fire at them; soon, bullets were crossing overhead five to eight feet above us and I wondered if we were in a large bomb crater with the enemy above us. The enemy and the friendly forces behind us exchanged fire over our heads for a few more minutes then our forces behind us stopped firing. Someone must have reminded them we were out here in front of them.

Something was wrong, and I couldn't figure it out until Aggie opened up with his M-16 and his bullets immediately struck something right in front of us. The bullets buried themselves deep into something thick and solid and at the same time kicked back pieces of dirt and dust. He held back the trigger and kept firing, and the intensity of the debris coming back at us increased and I figured his bullets were striking a solid dirt wall.

We had set up directly in front of a dirt embankment at the base of the hill. Above us, and only a few feet away, the enemy had set in. We could have reached up and grabbed them, but we could not have shot at them from our position. Aggie took a grenade and threw it high over the embankment, and the explosion shot its blinding flash over our heads and I could then for that split second clearly see the embankment and Marines huddled below. Then the enemy stopped firing. They didn't know where we were, and in the distance behind them, we heard a loud whistle then some commands in Vietnamese followed by the rustling of bushes and the sound of the enemy as they fled through the thick jungle.

"Pull back, pull back," Welsh called out and we all retreated backward. I was waiting for the enemy to shoot at us, but they didn't. In the dark, we had set up directly in front of one of the embankments a farmer had cut into the side of the hill. Had the point man gone another five feet before he turned, he would have hit his nose on the dirt wall. The edge of the embankment was about six feet above us, and that was where the enemy soldiers had been and the reason why we could hear and smell them but couldn't see them. They were only a few feet above us, and they didn't know we were just a few feet below them. Had they known, they could have dropped grenades on us and we wouldn't have been able to do anything in return.

When we all were about a third of the way back toward our company's line, someone on the hill popped a white flare directly over us. We dove for cover and froze out in the open, hugging the side of the rice paddy dikes or burying ourselves out in the open rice paddy fields hoping the enemy wouldn't see us and open up on us from behind.

We were out in the open not daring to move. As the flare's light faded, several of us now became separated from the others in the darkness that followed; with our night vision gone, there was no telling where everyone was. As the last sparkles of the flare died out, a voice called out, "Over here." The sound came from our left. Aggie, who had buried himself on the other side of the dike I was on, looked up and I asked Aggie if he could see where the squad was.

"Yes, on our left," he said.

"Let's go." I jumped over the dike, and with Aggie leading the way, we quickly low crawled toward the squad. As soon as we seemed to be getting near the squad, someone popped another flare and I buried my head in the ground, hugging the side of a dike so I wouldn't be seen.

Once the flare had burned itself out and I was about to get up, I could see a bright streak of light flying high overhead. It was an illumination flare fired by artillery on Hill 65. The whole area was now bathed in bright light. I closed my eyes and buried my head in the dirt to retain my night vision. Before the flare died out, another followed it, then I heard a third flare being popped overhead. After the last flare had burned itself out, I opened my eyes and could no longer hear or see any Marines. I looked over the dike; there was no one there. Third Squad and Aggie had followed each other toward the hill. The flares had helped them find our friendly positions. There was no one around. I was alone.

I released a long sigh and began to crawl slowly toward what I hoped were our lines. I heard movement to my left and hoped it was other Marines. I listened but didn't dare to call out. Then there was silence, and I wondered if the movement I had heard was Aggie or if he had stayed with the squad and had moved on. I hoped he had.

The night remained in pitch blackness, the moon hidden behind dark rain clouds. I had closed my eyes during the time the flare burned overhead to protect as much of my night vision as possible, but with pitch darkness all around me, it really hadn't made much of a difference. I had crawled about twenty meters when I heard a loud swoosh and hit the dirt again. I knew it was another flare. A handheld pop-up flare that exploded overhead was about 150 yards to my left front.

Damn those new Marines! I was thinking. *They're making us a prime target for the enemy to shoot at us from behind.* I buried my face in the dirt again with the gun's barrel directly in front of me. The flare's light caused the gun's shadow to move across in front of me as the flare floated high overhead, slowly descending, which caused the shadow to cross over again and again. I hoped the sticklike stretched-out shadow wasn't noticeable as a weapon by the enemy behind me. As it died down, it was followed by another flare. Finally the second flare burned itself out and it became dark once more. I didn't have time to move before I heard another flare going up. *Damn those new men! Why do they keep popping off flares? It only makes it harder for us to move.* I decided to wait where I was then crawl slowly forward, pulling the gun in under me. At least now I had an idea where the companies were, and it seemed I was moving in the right direction.

I wondered if I would have to crawl the rest of the 150-200 meters to the hill. I didn't want to stand up or low crawl as that would make too much noise; I decided to continue to crawl as I had been and take my time doing so.

What a night it had been. We had to lie silent without moving for hours, hearing and smelling the enemy that were close enough for us to touch and smell, and now I had no idea where they were or where I was. I didn't know if any other Marines were still crawling forward or if they had all already made it back. I was just hoping I was crawling toward our own lines and not those of the enemy; in the dark it wasn't hard to get turned around.

I wondered what would happen if I was captured by the VC. I knew I would not play dead and would not be taken alive. I would be killed before I would let the enemy get a hold of the gun and wished I had an incendiary grenade with me. I had Bro's M-60 with me, and that was a comfort. We had fought many battles together and knew that together we would at least be able to hold off any attackers for a while, at least 200 rounds worth. I reasoned that I would be shot once, twice and maybe more before they would rush me and the gun; I imagined even if I was killed, the gun would keep firing.

I made up my mind to absorb the impact of those bullets and just keep firing. Which way was I crawling? I feared what I could not see or hear. I feared that the enemy had seen me crawling out in the open and had seen the gun I was carrying and were now crawling toward me, and I feared the struggle that would ensue if I got jumped from behind. Was anyone crawling up behind me?

I would stop often and listen and strain to see what was behind me and hope that in the process, I didn't get turned around. Was Charlie crawling up behind me? That question kept returning with each forward movement, and I wished I had my K-bar with me. I had my .45, and the snub-nosed .38 was holstered inside my flak jacket. At close range, I could use them. The .38 would be first because that would be easier to get out in a struggle and then the .45 would give me the time needed to flip the gun around and open fire; all those plans, ideas, thoughts were racing through my mind as I moved, listened, and slowly crawled forward.

The darkness was both my friend and foe. I hadn't heard any movement near me and felt that now I was truly alone. For once I looked up seeking help from above, hoping for the moon to release just a sliver of its light, but she remained hidden behind dark clouds; the night, while it didn't seem possible, got darker with a thickness I could feel.

I could no longer see, so I felt my way forward and hoped I was moving in the right direction. I had found out what it felt like to be on the receiving end of a popped-up flare. The flares light up the area in front of you, and you welcome the visibility it gives when you are the one that has popped the flare, sitting in a defensive position, looking out, searching for movement, and looking for any unfamiliar shape in the night. But when you are on the other end and you didn't want to be seen, the flares become a threat to life.

Finally after an hour and a half of slowly crawling through the open rice paddy fields inches at a time, I felt a slight rise in the ground level below me and knew I had arrived at the beginning of the base of the hill, but which hill?

I continued to crawl forward and slowly started to climb up the small hill, hoping that I had reached the correct hill and the correct side of that hill where Marines would be on watch, listening and waiting for all to be counted. I hoped that the Marines on watch were not trigger-happy that they had gotten the word and were waiting.

When I heard movement up ahead, I stopped and listened. I hesitated but finally called out, "India Company." There was no answer. I crawled forward a bit more and listened and heard some whispering noises coming from my right, just a short distance to the right of the hill. But something didn't seem right. I didn't feel right about going in that direction; certainly someone was over there, but who? I knew the majority of the company should be to my left. Still, I didn't know where I was.

I waited, listened, and was about to call out "India Company" again when I heard the distinct telegraphic-sounding voice of a Vietnamese. They were trying to whisper in the night, but the rapid argumentative tone in their voice hadn't changed. I hoped they hadn't heard me or what I had called out. They were probably either a listening post or a group moving in to attack our position. Where was I? I crawled backward, off the hill, and then moved toward the left where I believed the company was, hoping that in the process I hadn't somehow gotten turned around.

I crawled along the base of the hill, moving up a few feet at a time, probing, then down again, up again, then down again hoping to hear someone before they heard me, and opened fire. Then I heard voices; and I moved in that direction, waited, and listened. I then heard the distinctive soft, slow sound of American voices. They were just whispers in the night so I listened, crawled closer with the gun ready to open fire, and finally called out, "India Company."

I waited in silence, more whispers, then somebody answered, "Over here." The voice had come from my left, and I half crawled while hunched over quickly toward that direction then stopped and dropped. I wanted to make sure they were friendly forces. I called out again, "India Company," and they answered, "Lima Company."

I responded, "Semper Fi," the words just came flowing out and the Marine on duty crawled out of his foxhole, quickly sliding down the hill to where I was. I don't know who was happier to see each other.

The Marine was a corporal and a squad leader assigned to the platoon from Lima Company that was attached to our company. I was sure glad to see him. In the darkness, he asked if I was okay and asked my name.

"Barela," I answered, and he motioned for me to follow him but at the same time almost half carried me up the hill. As soon as we got to his foxhole position, he was on the radio reporting that the last unaccounted-for Marine had made it back, and our company's radioman rogered the transmission. The Marine said that everyone else had made it back hours before. It didn't seem like I had been gone that long. My last name had come over the net alphabetically, he said and since they were the last post out, they hoped that I would turn up there and hoped the enemy hadn't taken my M-60.

"There are some gooks about a hundred meters to your left," I said to him, "near the base of the hill." He looked concerned and wondered what I had experienced.

Then he got on the net, got cleared, and called an Arty Mission on the spot. The arty rounds were right on target right where I had heard the voices.

Following the artillery barrage, Lieutenant Nowicki was on the radio calling for me to come up the hill and report to the CP. But the corporal took the handset from his radioman and said, "That's a negative, there are enemy forces in the area," and added they would utilize my weapon at their location. The lieutenant rogered the response, and there was no further communication made.

The corporal, a medium-sized slightly heavy-built Marine, was wearing a soft cover and looked a little like Bro. Another Marine, thinner and an old-timer judging by his clothes, was on watch; he looked me over, and the pleasant look in his eye made me feel that he also was glad to see me. The corporal turned to me, touched my shoulder, and said, "You're not going anywhere, your lieutenant can wait. We got the watch tonight, you get some sleep." I was grateful to that Marine, acknowledged his generosity, and crawled into a small corner of their foxhole. The corporal sat down next to the other Marine and both sat up standing watch. I leaned back and, knowing Marines were on watch, fell into a deep sleep.

Lima Company Returns
Operation Rock
March 8, 1968, D+2, 0845 hours

On the morning of the eighth at 0845 hours, Lima Company was helilifted from the An Hoa air base to LZ Canary. They landed just behind and above Hill 38. From that LZ, they had a commanding view of the Arizona Territory below them. No sooner had they landed than their forward element spotted a large enemy force moving toward the foothills along the south bank of the Song Vu Gia River. An artillery mission was dropped on them, and they were scattered. Lima Company moved out to set up a blocking force while our reinforced company began a sweep west along the river's bank toward them. Hostage 40 (a Huey gunship), observing several groups of NVA soldiers running away from our location as we swept toward them, called in an artillery barrage from the Eleventh Marines Battery on Hill 65. That barrage was also right on target. We then were told to stop as yet a larger enemy force had been seen behind us. We reversed course and reached the hill we had just left where we had spent the night before when we were told to halt and wait for Hotel Company with the PF platoon to sweep past us and take the lead.

As their last men passed our gun's position, I sensed the presence of immediate danger. Seconds later, their point man was hit and Hotel Company became engaged in a fierce firefight. They were pinned down and taking heavy incoming fire from the location I had heard the enemy soldiers the night before on the right side of the hill (AT 859543). As we prepared to maneuver around clockwise to outflank the enemy's positions, the enemy unleashed heavy automatic weapon fire, M-79s and mortar fire on the stalled Marines. The firefight continued for about fifteen minutes then, all of a sudden, the enemy broke contact.

A short time later, Beechnut 4, a bird-dog, flying overhead spotted twenty-five NVA soldiers running west from AT 850549, the same spot where our squad had set up our ambush the night before where the embankment had been cut away. When a gunship was called in to engage the enemy, they were fired upon and an air strike was then called in.

As Hotel Company moved through the area where they had gotten hit, they captured five males and one female, all NVA/VC suspects. One of the captured suspects said over forty NVA soldiers had left the area at 0800 hours that morning. They were members of the Q-14 Company and had crossed the Song Vu Gia River at AT 830547 on the fifth and in the early morning hours of the sixth. The soldiers were from the Second Battalion, Third Regiment, Second NVA Division. They had now gone west into the mountains. They were the same enemy soldiers recon inserts had reported seeing traveling northwest wearing uniforms, packs, and helmets. Recon had reported groups of NVA soldiers numbering fifty to seventy-five strong moving in that area a day before the operation was launched. Another of the captured NVA soldiers said the incoming mortars we had been receiving for the past two days had come from soldiers assigned to the Q-14 Company which had been left behind to engage us with mortars and small arms fire.

Both civilians and captured enemy soldiers seemed very willing to speak about the enemy force activity in the area; however, civilians were hesitant to speak in a group or when the captured NVA soldiers were nearby, but individually they revealed what they knew. From them, we found out that Q-14 local force guerillas that lived in the area along with about two-thirds of the NVA soldiers from the Second NVA Division had left the area a day before the operation. The local villagers had also told us that the NVA had told them Marines were coming the following day and they were leaving but would return. The NVA were expecting for us to take the civilians out of the area as we had done during Operation Foster, and they had told the civilians that if they left the area, they would be found and killed as they were needed now to harvest the rice for them. So they were supposed to go into hiding when we came by; if they left, the PFs at the refugee camps would not protect them because they were NVA.

Many of the civilians we had extracted out of the area during Operation Foster had returned on their own to their homes because the South Vietnamese government had not provided for their needs at the refugee camps. What provisions they did receive they had had to pay for.

The rice crops in the area were ready to be harvested, so they had returned to take their chances with the NVA, but the NVA taxed them heavily on their rice production up to 80 percent of what they harvested. Still, they said it was better than staying at the refugee camps.

Search And Destroy Continues
Operation Rock
March 9, 1968, D+3, 0845 hours

The following morning before we moved out, the twenty-two-member PF platoon was no longer needed and they were detached from the operation. As we waited for them to be helilifted out, we figured someone had finally figured out they were the reason the enemy knew we were coming the day before the operation started.

We moved out heading toward the foothills, burning abandoned villages, and destroying tunnel complexes and bomb shelters the enemy was using. By evening, no one had made contact, and except for a few suspected NVA/VC stragglers we found here and there, no major engagement was made.

Move out and leapfrog
Operation Rock
March 10, 1968, D+4, 0700 hours

Early in the morning of the tenth of March, Hotel 2/7 was helilifted to the southern edge of the Song Thu Bon River and the village of Bac (1). There they detained Dang Thi Phat, a member of the Second Battalion Thirty-first Regiment Second NVA Division, and he said the division's morale was low due to the lack of food in the area and the heavy casualties they had suffered for the past few days. On several occasions, the captive said, he had carried rice from the area to the Huu Rien Mountains; while there he had seen many wounded NVA soldiers as many as thirty at one time who had been wounded during the Tet Offensive.

We had been moving west toward the foothills where the enemy had fled with the platoon from Lima Company walking point. There were scattered clearings among several ridgelines that ran along the foothills. Just before noon, a second platoon Marine spotted an enemy soldier, dressed in white, carrying two grenades. A couple of Marines opened fire, killing the enemy soldier.

As we continued to move toward the foothills, a few times we had to set up while a fire-team or squad moved across an open area. Then we followed or moved forward while they covered for us. We crossed in that manner over open terrain then up a series of ridges, and then southeast along a long ridgeline toward Hotel 2/7's position who had set up as a blocking force at the bottom of the hill near the Song Thu Bon River.

At midmorning with Hill 38 as our objective, First Platoon took point with the rest of the company as well as the platoon from Lima Company bringing up the rear. I could sense the enemies' presence; it would be only a matter of time before contact would be made.

We entered a dense forested area then moved down into a small valley between two ridges. When we reached bottom, we got hit.

The platoon returned fire as best as we could. The enemy had the advantage. James, with Rahm A-gunning, was returning a heavy volume of machine-gun fire at the enemy, but the platoon remained pinned down. Aggie set up the gun near a small rock formation and was returning fire as best as he could, but he had no clear target. The enemy above us was well concealed. While we remained engaged in the firefight, the rest of the company was trying to get around the enemy, using the ridgelines above us.

For thirty minutes the enemy continued to pitch grenades and drop mortars on us. Finally, Second and Third Platoons had moved up a steep side of a hill and were in a position to protect our left flank. Meanwhile, the Lima Company platoon moved up another ridge. Once they got into position, they and the rest of the company engaged the enemy in a cross fire.

The enemy switched from firing down at us in order to defend themselves and a fierce firefight continued as they exchanged rounds with our company on the ridge to the left of us and with Lima Company's platoon above firing at them from their right. The firefight lasted another ten to fifteen minutes before fixed-wing aircraft dropped a heavy load of napalm on the ridge where the main enemy force was located, and all the firing stopped.

Diddy-Bopping In The Boonies
Operation Rock
March 10, 1968, D+4, 1300 hours

The rest of the morning, we kept getting hit from spider holes and spent most of our time crouched down, crawling along the ground searching for individual enemy soldiers who would pop up out of spider holes, snipe at us, then disappear.

At 1300 hours, we reached our objective, Hill 38; it was a key hill at the end of a series of mountain ridges. When we reached the top, we were expecting contact but there was none. It was evident the site had been occupied several times before by both friendly and enemy forces. It was a barren hill with no real significance other than it was our objective for the day.

At the top, we could see a beautiful green valley below; as I sat at the edge of the ridge, Aggie joined me and we sat there silently taking in the beauty of the land all around us while we waited for the rest of the company to catch up to First Platoon.

Then, in the valley below, we couldn't believe what we were seeing. Smack in the middle of it, coming out in formation from a distant tree line was the U.S. Cavalry.

They were marching across open rice paddies in the middle of Arizona Territory, singing with their rifles slung over their shoulders, diddy-bopping as if they were out on a Sunday picnic.

James, Dumont, and Rahm joined us. They too stood at the top of the ridge next to us, not believing what we were seeing. "Don't those guys know that there's a war going on?" James asked as he put down the gun and sat down next to us. Others in the company came up and stood behind us, looking down, watching in disbelief as if the army was passing in review below us.

Trucks, tanks, and armored personal carriers, all of them were making such a racket down in the valley that the ground trembled below us. A number of gunships and medevac helicopters with the Red Cross insignia boldly stamped on their noses flew overhead. A new type of helicopter, slick like the face of a cobra, shot through the valley at breathtaking speed; others followed behind. We stood there in awe at what we were seeing.

C Troop, Third Squadron, Fifth Armored Cavalry and their supporting forces were marching across yesterday's battlefields like they had no idea a real war was going on. "Ice cream soldiers" is what we called them, and now I knew why. We had been fighting and dodging bullets every day since the operation began and had been up to our necks in filth and dirt for days, crawling, searching for hidden enemy soldiers, and they were marching through the area as if nothing was going on.[252]

We moved down the side of the hill and reached the bottom just as the beginning of the army's parade showed up to pass by us.

The soldiers were wearing clean starched colorful tiger fatigues. They began to whoop it up, hollering at us as they passed by. Then one of their track vehicles, a personnel carrier with its tracks caked in mud, slowed down and stopped, waiting for the rest of the formation to move out. An army corporal stood up on the seat of the personnel carrier to view what was holding the army column from moving on. They were waiting for a tank in front of them to pivot and turn.

A Marine called out to them, "Hey, doggie, where you get those pajamas?" The soldier, hearing the Marine's remarks, bowed then took his tiger-striped boonie hat and displayed it for us to see in the manner one would see in a fashion show. He pointed to the different features of his uniform, and you could almost hear the runway host begin to describe each article of clothing the army soldier was wearing:

"The uniform comes in a variety of colors. The one you see here has a golden fade to it with some slight green tones and the famous jet-black tiger stripes. It is preferred by many soldiers fighting the war in Southeast Asia. The fatigue shirt seen here, you will notice, has reinforced elbow pads for low-crawl positions. It comes with four large button-down cargo pockets capable of carrying two to four grenades. In addition, it has two button cuffs with side adjustments for the various tasks a soldier must perform. The pants have a newly designed button-fly feature for quick release while under fire or while on R&R. They have adjustable waist tabs to fit fat sergeants and skinny privates alike. They also have two large leg cargo pockets in front and two wide back pockets. All four pockets button down to secure your property. Special features of these pants are the front slash pockets and the reinforced seat and knees. The trousers have double-stitched seams, and all come with their very own drawstring ankle ties."

The soldier twisted and turned every which way modeling his new tiger uniform. He stood in various positions of attention, parade rest, right face, left face, and then while standing at attention, extended his arms, spreading them wide then spread his fingers apart; and in one quick motion, snapped off his new quick-release haversack and the whole pack and everything attached to it fell off. When he did that, we applauded, clapping our hands, whistling, and calling for more. Then the tank in front of them started moving again, and the soldier bowed to acknowledge the applause then stood at attention and presented arms, saluting us, as they moved out. His presentation was followed by a Cobra helicopter that zoomed by with two others in close formation. Such a parade and timing no one could have arranged, not out in the open fields, not in the Arizona, not in war, or Southeast Asia.

We all stood there looking at each other, amazed by it all laughing and shaking our heads; it was all so unbelievable.

"I should have joined the army," I said to Aggie.

On the other side of the Arizona territory, the rest of Lima Company had uncovered eight freshly dug graves. In them, they found eight dead NVA soldiers all buried in black plastic bags; all were dressed in freshly laundered khaki uniforms.

At 1500 hours, Operation Rock was officially over and by 1530 hours we were chopped out and dropped off at Hill 3/7 Battalion Headquarters.[253]

New Temporary Home
Battalion Headquarters 3/7
March 11, 1968, 0800 hours

On the morning of the eleventh, we were informed to stand by. India Company had been designated as the reactionary force for the battalion, and we could be sent anywhere in our TAOR. Later, I wondered how many times we had gone out and were never told what we were doing or why we were on the operation. Sometimes there may have been the friendlies just a few klicks away, and we never knew it. There may have been operations where I thought it was only us out there when in reality; there were a number of units nearby. Perhaps even while we had been engaged in fierce firefights with the enemy, the U.S. Army may have just been over on the other side of a ridge just a few klicks away or marching in formation and singing their songs, unaware that Marines were fighting and dying close by.

At 0905 hours, a U.S. Army armored personnel carrier (APC) from C Troop, Third Squadron, Fifth Cavalry (Armored), Ninth Infantry Division, the same unit that had been our blocking force during the last days of Operation Rock, was traveling in a squadron movement on Route 4 near Cam Van (3) when a mine was detonated by the enemy under an APC. The APC's gas tank exploded immediately, killing a soldier by the name of Willie Amos Williams and seriously wounding several others. The track commander, Bill Helm, and the driver of the APC, Christopher Delwiche, survived. They were all transported back to Battalion, and as we stood by waiting for them to be medevaced to Da Nang, we couldn't help but think how the day before they were our supporting unit and some of those same soldiers were killed or seriously wounded. As the bodies were loaded on the choppers, we stood silent, equally feeling their unit's grief.

At Da Nang, one of the crew members, Benny Burns, died and the following day so did another crew member by the name of William Edward Lilienthal as did John Doc Mattock, their medic.

Another Typical Marine Corps Day In Vietnam
Battalion Headquarters 3/7 AT 916582
March 12, 1968, 0800 hours

On the morning of the twelfth, we saddled up and got on board six-bys to go to Hill 41. That same morning, a Marine from Kilo Company, operating near Liberty Bridge, was wounded when he set off a booby trap near where Ira Hullihen had been killed. Later, a Hotel platoon at Liberty Bridge spotted thirty-five NVA soldiers moving east to west across rice paddies and called in an Arty Mission. Meanwhile, Mike Company at An Hoa received twenty-five rounds from an unknown number of enemy soldiers. They returned fire and also called in artillery.

Lima Company on Hill 65 spotted ten to fifteen suspicious acting villagers carrying baskets and walking toward the Song Vu Gia River. A squad was dispatched to the area where they detained eighteen women and children whom they took to Lima Company's CP for questioning. A search of the area where they were gathered revealed two M-26 grenades, ten gallons of kerosene, twenty-four 1.5 volt batteries, 300 pounds of rice, three ID cards, $12,115 in piastres, twenty-five pounds of chicken and fish, and numerous battle dressings. The suspects were all from 'No Name' Village; it was just another typical day in Vietnam.

Things were back to normal in our little corner of the world, and this was our way of life. Our job was shooting and killing enemy soldiers. Patrolling and ambushing the enemy before they could kill innocent civilians. Civilians who were indifferent to us and to the world who sat by the roadside sitting and spitting. We went on search and destroy operations to kill the enemy before they could kill us or kill civilians and that was what was important now. Killing was what we were assigned to do; nothing else mattered, so we saddled up and jumped on board the six-by truck and were now off to another adventure and to another battlefield, to another time and another place, to live or die, to write history and to add another chapter to the stories of war; but no one told us where we were going or why this time we were going there.

Hill 41
Delta Co. Combat Base, AT 934664
March 12, 1968, 1300 hours

For the next few days, we were OpCon to First Battalion Seventh Marines, assigned to man Delta Co. Combat Base on Hill 41.[254] We were there to man First Battalion Seventh Marines lines, while they went on Operation Worth.[255] The hill was located four miles north of 3/7 headquarters, just off convoy road or Route 540 according to some maps. The hill was only about two klicks away from where Bro had gotten killed and from where I had first opened fire in combat.

It seemed like years ago that Bro and Stoker had been killed. So many others had died since then, many more wounded. Thousands of bullets had been fired, many gooks had been killed, so many of our Marines were maimed for life, and others were no longer around. Some no longer lived, no longer breathed, and the memories of them made me wonder about life and eternity. I'd seen blood trails and body parts of the enemy and villagers covered with blood. I'd seen the blood of innocent women and children, older men who had been hacked to death by the same Communist soldiers who had promised them a better life. I'd heard the wailing cries of mothers whose children, some as young as twelve years of age, had been kidnapped from their villages and dragged off to war and forced to join the NVA/VC ranks. We'd found Communist propaganda leaflets written in English and dropped on the trails we patrolled, promising Americans safety in Hanoi if we joined the "People's" struggle for independence. The leaflets were signed by the Liberation Army of South Vietnam; however, they were not South Vietnamese but northern soldiers from Hanoi. Some villagers believed those soldiers while others plainly saw the invisible footnote at the bottom of each propaganda leaflet that was never printed but written in blood that called for the death and slavery of the South Vietnamese people if they did not support their cause. Now we were returning to patrol and to hold ambushes in the area where I had first been introduced to war. Nothing much had changed, except now when I held the trigger down, I did so not only for our lives but also for the lives of the South Vietnamese people.

Hill 41, like many others around us, was barren with small chunks of rocks lying on top of the ground and soft red clay just inches below the hard surface. The dirt road leading to and around the hill had a new coat of oil that had recently been sprayed on, and we could still smell the waxy waste oil's presence.

On the east side of Hill 41, a long slope reached all the way to convoy road; on the north side of the hill, just a short distance away, a smaller road went west toward the mountains. The hill had two to three different levels. A large tower was located on the northwest slope that provided a good view of Charlie Ridge located west of the hill.

From the top of the hill, you could see the local peasants walking along the road below; for some reason, they seemed dirtier and poorer in this area of Vietnam.

From the base of the hill were dry patches of earth followed by some cultivated rice paddy fields then thick jungle growth with bushes and trees clustered together. The tree lines were thick barriers with cutouts that led to individual huts or scattered small villages. On the side leading toward Charlie Ridge were thick bushes; some were three to five feet high and broad-leafed. The bushes were scattered like a puzzle that had never been put together. They provided good concealment for Charlie's approach to the hill.

All around the hill's perimeter were sandbag bunkers with flat tops. On top of each bunker were a limited number of sandbags; these were used to stand watch at night and provide quick fighting positions. From inside the bunkers, we could stand up and fire down on the enemy. The bunkers were up close to the wire and had several strands of wire all around them. I couldn't see any trenches, and the living quarters were canvas barracks much like we had on Liberty Bridge, but they were separated from each other, with some distance in between. There were seven or eight of them for the whole company. While most platoons had their own barracks, squads from weapons platoon shared a barrack with other squads.

We were showed around the perimeters by some of the Marines of Delta Company 1/7. Since it was in their barracks where we would be sleeping and their bunkers where we would be standing watch. Before leaving the compound on top of six-bys, one of the Marines on board, as a welcoming gift, popped off a C-S grenade and threw it at us, and we scrambled to get out of the way the smoke was blowing. We did not cuss at him or throw anything back in return because it might be the last chance for that man to play a joke. Deep inside we wished them well and wondered if we would be sleeping on a dead man's cot tonight, a man who didn't know he wasn't coming back.

New Area, New Patrols
Hill 41, AT 934664
March 13-16, 1968, 1300 hours

Over the next few days, we were assigned to go out on patrols day and night; we stood watch on the hill or went out on ambushes in the area. The first night First Platoon stood perimeter watch while one of the other platoons went out on a night ambush. The following night it was our turn, and the platoon went out two klicks, which was unusual for a night ambush and dangerous in an area we were not familiar with. The area was heavily forested, the trails ran along terrain that was difficult to navigate through.

If They Piss In Their Pants, I'll Shoot You
Hill 41, AT 934664
March 15-16, 1968, 1900 hours

On the fifteenth we stood watch, and that evening Aggie and I went out on a night squad-size ambush with Third Squad.

As soon as we saddled up, I knew there was going to be trouble. Not with Charlie, but with Third Squad. Boone had become lax in disciplining his squad. Since his promotion to sergeant he no longer seemed to care about leading a squad; he may have figured he was supposed to have a higher position in the platoon, such as first platoon sergeant. He certainly did not display any concern about the squad he was now leading.

Before we left, there was no squad crosscheck; no one checked each other's gear and clothing to make sure there were no loose things that would shine or make noise at night. No one checked to make sure there were no half-empty canteens or that the trouser legs were bloused and dog tags were tucked in. No one made sure no one was wearing a wedding ring or a watch that shines at night. No team leader made sure things were taped down nor did they make sure no one was wearing a white T-shirt that may be visible at night. I saw all that as we walked out the perimeter's wire and knew that if we made it back, it was going to be a miracle.

There was a full moon overhead, and there was no attempt to hide or use the bushes or stay near the trees' shadows for covering. The squad moved out and did not keep their interval, nor did they keep their mouths shut. The men kept whispering to each other and were not at all on the alert. They weren't watching where they were going nor were they keeping their eyes and ears on alert.

We moved out one klick, then two klicks, and the noise the squad made was noticeable. When we set in, Boone did not bother to change positions. He dropped his gear, put on his soft cover, and called in the checkpoint. The radio cracked with static. It was as if Boone wanted the attention, wanted the contact, but such an encounter would favor the enemy.

The ambush site was out in the open, and no one was quiet or still. Some kept getting up and moving up and down the squad positions. No one was on alert status or expecting the enemy to be nearby.

Aggie knew I was pissed with Boone and his squad. As soon as the squad was set in and the gun was set in place, I crawled over to where Boone was.

I looked him straight in the eye, took out my .45 out, grabbed him by the shirt collar, and as I brought his face next to mine, I shoved my pistol under his chin, then cocked the hammer back. His radioman dropped his handset and backed off.

"If we get hit tonight, I gonna kill you first," I whispered into Boone's ear, and there was real fear in his eyes and I was glad he hadn't lost that. He looked at me, and I saw a dead man. He knew I was serious, that I would do what I had to do.

"You better pass the word down to your squad that if any one of them so much as breathes too hard, if they piss in their pants and I hear it, or if they make any noise whatsoever to bring attention to us, it will be the biggest mistake they will ever make and I'll shoot you first and tell them I said so."

"Okay," was the only response that came from Boone, and he said that with a trembling lip. If Boone feared me, the squad would survive.

With that said, I let go of Boone's collar; and as I walked away, I reached down to turn down the squad's radio. The radioman jumped back, throwing his hands up as if to protect himself.

For the rest of the night, I did not hear a single word or any sound coming from the squad. No one moved from the position they were in and I believe even the mosquitoes were afraid to land or bite any Marine that night. It seemed as if the squad of Marines were too scared and feared that the crazy machine-gunner would shoot them first if we got hit because of any noise they made. Because of fear, they stayed quiet and were on alert with their eyes and ears open, and they maintained their noise discipline all night long. That night the moon didn't move, the shadows remained hidden behind the trees and shrubs. No critter dared to cross anywhere near a Marine, and Tired Aggie, without saying a word, looked at me and chuckled to himself in silence.

In the morning on our way back, just as we were nearing the front gate, I walked up to Boone. "You better square it away with the lieutenant," I said to him, "because my gun team is never going out with you or this squad again."

As we arrived at the entrance to Hill 41, a small boy of about twelve years of age was being paid two hundred piastres for bringing in a found claymore mine with a firing device attached as well as some small arms rounds and a ChiCom grenade.

That afternoon, Third Squad's squad members were called individually before the lieutenant, and one by one they were questioned. In the end it was up to Boone as to what he wanted to do about the incident. The lieutenant never bothered to call me to his CP. I didn't know if he was also afraid of me or figured I had reasons for doing what I did. He didn't push the issue; maybe it had to do with what the squad members told the lieutenant. Marines are like that; they know what is right. You volunteer to be a Marine, and Marine discipline is necessary in war. If they wanted to survive, they needed a squared-away squad leader who would look out for them, one who honored Marine tradition and his responsibilities to his men.

Bruce Alan Cobb
Hill 41 AT 934664
March 17-24, 1968, 1300 hours

For the next few days, our schedule was about the same. We stood perimeter watch during the day, night ambush, perimeter watch, night ambush, perimeter watch, night ambush. Platoon size, day patrol, perimeter watch, night ambush, perimeter watch. On the 25th after having stood perimeter watch we went out on a platoon size patrol.

On the morning of the twenty-fifth, we went out with the lieutenant leading our platoon-size patrol. After a while, it seemed as if we were circling around aimlessly. We had traveled about six klicks when the patrol had called for us to go out only two klicks. Everyone was beginning to wonder if the lieutenant knew where he was or where he was going. We found ourselves on the outer fringes of our assigned area on the other side of Hill 22 between a small lake and the Song Yen River, neither of which we had ever seen before.

We continued our patrol and, on our way back, the lieutenant had Second Squad cut across an open field to a far tree line to follow a trail that led through a village so that we could get back quicker.

As he went to enter the village, Bruce Alan Cobb, a Marine that had only been with the platoon for a few months, pulled back the main village gate.

A huge explosion engulfed the area where he had been standing.

An 81 mortar round had been set up as a booby trap, killing Cobb instantly in the explosion.

As we waited for the medevac choppers to come in, we checked out the village and were unable to find any of the villagers. They were all gone.

One thing I had learned about how the VC/NVA operated in our area was that they were all assigned an area to patrol. They did this as individuals, often without their weapons, to blend in with the locals.

If the one man patrol saw Marines, or a squad of Marines he would alert the others also on patrol by a prearranged signal, run and get his weapon, and they would gather and decide to set in an ambush, or set-up an anti-personal mine, where we would most likely travel through.

We made our way back to the hill in silence. That night, Aggie and I went out with Third Squad on a night ambush, and this time the squad's silence was reflective.

Patrol, Night Ambushes, And Hole Watch
Hill 41
March 23-26, 1968, 0800 hours

The next two days were spent on perimeter watch, running daylight patrols and a night ambushes from Hill 41. On the night of the twenty-sixth, we were told to be ready to move out the next day. We were returning to Hill 37, but only for the day.

Re-Assigned To Regiment Hill 55
Seventh Marines Regiment Headquarters and Dodge City
March 27, 1968, 0800 hours

On the morning of the twenty-seventh, we were informed that the company was reassigned to regiment and would be humping there the following day. Our gear would be transported by six-by trucks, and we were to patrol our way to regiment, joining the other two platoons somewhere along the way. Being at regiment with the hot meals and showers was like being on R&R compared to other places we had been.

There was no building of bunkers, and hole watch was assigned by squads; often, guns was ignored or not counted in those assignments. However, our patrols would be patrolling in Dodge City, and there was a reason why Marines named it that.

Dung Lai, Dung Lai
Dodge City
March 28, 1968, 0900 hours

The platoon was sent out from regiment on trucks to Route 4 where we disembarked and joined the rest of the company on a wide road sweep on convoy road heading back toward regiment.

First Platoon was assigned to sweep northeast along the south edge of the Song La Tho River that ran on the east side of regiment in the area. As we moved out, the lieutenant wanted my gun team walking with Rahm's Second Squad, covering the platoon's right flank. It was not the best way to deploy a gun team, but that's what the lieutenant wanted and with Rahm, leading that squad, I felt we would be able to handle any situation we might run into. We fell in behind Rahm's first fire-team, followed by Rahm, his radioman, and the rest of his squad and we moved out.

By mid-morning, shortly after we had cleared a tree line, the point man saw three villagers that seemed to be working out in an open rice paddy field a short distance away. They looked up and saw us as we moved out of the edge of the tree line, and they started running. The point man yelled for them to stop, but they continued to run. We yelled again, and they ran harder. According to our military rules of engagement at that time, anyone running from us was considered VC. The local civilian population knew this, the NVA knew this, and we knew this. The point man was hesitant to open fire on the running Vietnamese since we hadn't been fired upon.

Rahm, standing next to me, took aim and fired a round at them from his M-16 rifle; by then the villagers were running at a good pace and his round fell short.

I flipped the machine-gun off my shoulders and pulled it up to my right shoulder, opened fire low with a short burst of machine-gun fire.

The tallest of the three individuals fell first as did the one running behind him. Then the third male ran up to them, and with his help, all three disappeared into the jungle behind a small hooch.

When Lieutenant Nowicki and the rest of the platoon joined us at the clearing, he was furious because I had opened up and the villagers were all gone. There was no way we could prove that they were VC, he kept saying. Several of the veteran squad leaders tried to explain to the lieutenant what the battalion's policy was—you shoot at Vietnamese that run away from us, they told him. Still the lieutenant's anger was evident; he wanted evidence that they were enemy soldiers, so he ordered Rahm's squad and my gun team to go look for the persons I had shot.

We moved out along the tree line, found blood trails, and reported this to the lieutenant by radio. He then told us to continue to search for a body. After a while we notified him that we couldn't locate a body but the blood trail led away from the small hooch he could see from where he was. He said for us to continue to follow the blood trails into the jungle. We searched the hooch near the tree line, but decided not to go into the Dodge City jungle with only a squad. Both Rahm and I did not like the spot we were in as there was a sense of immediate danger in the air, and we knew that we were too far from the rest of the platoon as it were. We followed the blood trails that led off into the jungle for a short distance and reported this in. We figured that he would not have us follow the trail into the jungle with only a squad, but that's what the lieutenant wanted. He wanted us to follow the blood trail deeper into the jungle, and this angered Rahm.

"That stupid lieutenant! If we get hit, it'll be a while before he can figure out where we are and a reactionary unit can get to us. If I get killed because of that stupid lieutenant, you make sure you shoot him!" Rahm said.

"Okay," I said and figured I probably would.

Rahm decided not to follow the blood trails into the jungle.

"Ain't no way we're going to look for wounded gooks in that jungle and get ambushed," he told his men. Instead the squad returned to the hooch, and Rahm deployed his squad behind the hooch close to the tree line but out of sight from the rest of the platoon. Since the front door and open window of the hut faced toward the platoon's location, we cut a hole in the back of the grass hut and Rahm and I and his radioman sat there inside the hut watching the platoon and called in checkpoints while the squad remained on alert and we sat and waited.

"The lieutenant's mad because we were supposed to be sweeping toward regiment and we were supposed to meet up with the rest of the company on Ambush Road[256] and then march into regiment together, and now we won't be able to do that because of this," Rahm said. After about a half an hour, Rahm called in to report that we had lost the blood trails and were coming back in. The lieutenant never responded, only the radiomen rogered the transmission. An hour later, we met up with the rest of the platoon, and the lieutenant never bothered to ask for a briefing from Rahm.

It wasn't long before amtracks came out to where we were. The track commander told our lieutenant that the regiment commander had sent out the amtracks to pick us up so that we could join the rest of the company as they entered regiment. As we passed the rest of India Company who were walking on the road toward regiment, they shouted insults at us for getting a ride while they still had another half mile or so to hump before getting there.

Called Into Regiment Because Of The Villagers I Shot
Hill 55, 7th Marine Regiment CP, AT 970620
March 28, 1968, 1500 hours

Late that afternoon, the platoon sergeant came looking for me. "Barela, the major wants to see you at his CP," he said.

When I arrived at Maj. W. W. McIver's headquarters, a group of Vietnamese were huddled around a small table inside his command barracks. Our CO Captain, Reeder was present as was Lieutenant Nowicki. The platoon sergeant was sitting down with a notepad taking down notes for our lieutenant. The major asked me if I had opened up on a civilian during the sweep. I answered, "Yes, sir, I did." He then asked me to tell him about it.

"I was with a squad carrying the M-60 when we came out into a clear area out of the tree line. When they saw us, they took off running. There were three of them running so I opened up. We searched the area and couldn't find anyone," I said.

There was a stir of conversation back and forth between what seemed to be a village official and an interpreter. Their voices were harsh and loud, the village chief was speaking angrily; I noticed that an older woman who had been silent stepped forward and joined in the argument. Her teeth were black from chewing betel nut. Black spittle dripped out the corner of her mouth as she spoke. Her voice was loud, angry, but the Vietnamese always spoke loud and angry so I knew their conversation could mean anything. The interpreter then told the major that the woman whose legs I had shot off was the other woman's sister. The woman wanted us to pay her because she would now have to take care of her sister's house and her sister's unmarried daughter. The major turned to me and asked if I had yelled for her to stop. I answered, "Yes, the squad leader yelled twice for them to stop, and so did I before I opened fire. I yelled for them to stop, from the distance we couldn't tell if they were men or women. There were two other people with the one I shot at," I said to the major. "They looked at us and then took off running as if they were running to hide. We searched the area for them, but they went into hiding. I hit two of them," I mentioned.

Another loud discussion ensued between the older woman, the village official, and the interpreter. Then the interpreter told Major McIver he believed the women

I had shot was VC or VC sympathizers and they hadn't told him before that there were three people out in the field.

With that said the major turned to me and said I was dismissed. "There will be no charges drawn up against you," he said. The lieutenant seemed irritated because of this, and while I felt sorry for the woman I had shot, I did not regret having shot at her. I had shot low on purpose, but perhaps that only frightened her to run faster.

Every villager knew that when we came into the area, they shouldn't run from approaching American troops as they would then be considered Vietcong and would be shot at. Often when we swept through an area, if the villagers did not have anything to hide, they would just stay still where they were, ignoring us while they continued to work in their rice fields or they would silently work their way into the safety of their homes. If we approached them, at most we asked for their ID cards, "Cam-kook."

I left the CP and remembered that I had yelled at them to stop in English. I had not yelled "Dung Lai," which means stop in Vietnamese. It all happened so fast. Everything happens fast in war. I hadn't even thought of yelling for them to stop in Vietnamese. We were not required to learn the Vietnamese language. I did not regret having shot the woman because we knew that certain individuals in some of the villages remained loyal to the Vietcong, and it was their job to warn others of approaching American troops or they would alert the local VC to set up an ambush or a sniper that we were in the area.

The platoon sergeant later told me the major was proud of my machine-gun shooting skills. "That was some shooting," he had told our lieutenant. I had shot at a running VC with the machine-gun from the shoulder and had hit all three of them. The woman's legs had been shot out from under her when she was hit with four of the bullets. Her sister would be compensated a little for the care of her sister, and the village chief confirmed after I left that the other two were enemy soldiers, NVA. Both had died later that day from their wounds and had been buried.

Ambush Row
Dodge City
March 29, 1968, 0700 hours

Lieutenant Nowicki was called away for administrative duties, and Staff Sergeant O'Keefe was left in charge of the platoon. For a few days we were running day patrols along Ambush Road near regiment close to Dodge City. The early morning mine-clearing detail had recently been ambushed, and we were assigned to patrol near the roadway, trying to catch the enemy, from behind.

The NVA/VC were becoming bolder in their mining of the road frequently traveled by military units, especially between Ambush Road and the CAP unit where Liberty Road intersected Route 4.[257] The enemy was now replanting mines in the roadway during the day after the road had been cleared.

We went out light to be able to travel quickly. We were not carrying much water, heavy gear, or packs. During the early afternoons, we would emerge out of the jungle and stop near the road where a supply truck would meet us there or at a CAP unit where we got supplied with C-rats and fresh water, and then we would slip back into the jungle.

Clearing Ambush Row
Dodge City
March 30, 1968, 1300 hours

Early afternoon and we emerged from the tree line at the bend on the road that led from regiment to Highway 4. Many Marines had experienced fierce firefights on this road, and most felt the jungle was a better way of travel than down ambush road. Ahead of us, a Marine fire-team was providing security for a crew of Seabees as they used large Caterpillars to clear brush from the east side of the road. As we came out of the jungle, the supply truck was already waiting for us, and the platoon moved south in that direction. Aggie, James, and I were the gun team assigned to bring up the rear along with Third Squad's last fire-team.

As we neared the supply truck, Aggie spotted 18 VC running across the road about 150 meters behind us. They were the first VC that we had seen; at least the first that I had running together carrying weapons and wearing raggedy black pajamas and straw coolie hats. They actually were dressed like what we had been told the typical VC looked like. Other than catching a glimpse of them here and there, you didn't see the enemy often, not like what we had just seen. They were not wearing military uniforms, like the NVA, but by the way they quickly ran across the road behind us, you could tell they were a well disciplined unit. They were too far for the M-16s, so James pulled the M-60 in tight, against his hips, and opened fire on them just as the last of them disappeared into a thick tree line. A couple of tracers disappeared behind them into the tree line.

Staff Sergeant O'Keefe called the squad leaders together and told them we were going to outflank the column of enemy soldiers we had seen. We quickly grabbed what chow and water we could off the supply truck and moved out. The gooks must have been following us for some time. Now we would be going after them.

It wasn't long before that sixth sense of danger was all around us. We were moving into a deep jungle area with heavy bushes and tall trees on two or three ground levels. We stopped and Sergeant O'Keefe instructed Second Squad to move out toward our right flank and to take a gun team with them. They were to stay about a hundred yards behind us. We quickly moved out and no more than ten minutes later, we walked into an ambush.

It was a U-type ambush, a normal practice of the NVA/VC. They opened up from our front, and as the front of the platoon responded, another more concentrated volley of incoming fire and grenades were launched at us from our right. As the front of the squad responded to the first volley of incoming fire, I opened up with the M-60 at the enemy that was firing at us from our right. All of a sudden, the enemy's right flank was reinforced and a more heavy volume of incoming fire came from our right side where the enemy had an elevated advantage over us. They were no more than fifteen meters from us when they sprang their ambush. They had waited until we were clearly deep into their kill zones and they had the advantage.

The firefight continued for another ten minutes before bullets came slicing through the enemy's entrenched position from their left side. Second Squad and James's machine-gun had moved up and had caught them by surprise, and the enemy immediately broke off contact and disappeared into the jungle just as fast as they opened fire. Fortunately, no one in the platoon was hit.

Retaliation, USMC Style
Dodge City
March 31, 1968, 0700 hours

We went out on another patrol in the Dodge City area near regiment on the thirty-first. Dodge City as we knew it was bordered on the west by the Song Ai Nghia, on the north the Song Lo Tho, on the east by the rail road tracks, and south by Route 4.[258]

As we were crossing an open rice paddy field, a sniper began to pop off some rounds in our direction. They sounded like they were coming from a carbine and at a great distance. Sergeant O'Keefe ignored it, and we didn't bother to stop or even send out a fire-team to outflank the sniper.

It was evident that the rounds were coming from a small village about 300 yards away. If we responded, by the time we got there, the VC sniper would be long gone. We would find the village vacant or we might find a couple of villagers who would deny knowing anything.

Sergeant O'Keefe ignored the sniper but called in for an artillery-spotting round as a precautionary warning. The spot round exploded harmlessly to the left of the village on the opposite side of where the sniper was shooting at us from. The VC sniper didn't get the message and opened up from the village with automatic rifle fire from an AK-47, and one of the rounds struck one of the new men in the legs. As soon as he went down, O'Keefe was on the radio calling in .81 mortars from Hill 55. He called in grid coordinates farther away from the village.

Then O'Keefe switched radio channels and ordered a barrage of artillery rounds from Hill 65. Having done this, he once again changed frequency and called in naval gunfire, giving them all the same grid coordinates and telling all to fire one round for accuracy then stand by for a fire for effect mission.

As soon as the first mortar round struck, he was back on line with mortars adjusting coordinates that would be dead center on the village and right on top of the VC who had opened fire at us. He then did the same thing with artillery and naval gunfire, switching radio frequency each time and telling them all to fire for effect.

As soon as the barrage of explosives rounds began to rain on the village, O'Keefe was back on line with section, screaming at the top of his lungs loud and clear so that he would have witnesses that he tried to stop the village's destruction:

"Cease fire! Cease fire! You're hitting a friendly village! Stop firing!" He then switched channels and did the same thing two more times. But by the time he was back on our regular radio frequency, the village was engulfed in smoke and fire. When the smoke cleared, not a hut was standing. Secondary explosions in the village validated our belief that the village was being used by the enemy. The sniping stopped.

An April First Remembrance
Dodge City
April 1, 1968, 0800 hours

On the first of April, First Platoon was reassigned to Golden Gate Bridge security located south of the hill. Our duty was to guard the south side of the bridge near the village of Cam Van (2), AT 964605. Third Platoon was assigned to guard the north side at the base of Hill 55, and together we were to do saturation patrolling in the Dodge City area during the day and go out on ambushes at night. Second Platoon was assigned security at Seabee Bridge near Hill 37.

The day began with a series of explosions for 3/7 Marines. A squad of Marines from H&S Company assigned to the early morning minesweeping detail found two rock mines on Liberty Road. The first one, in the center of the road, was melted in place by the engineers with the use of an incendiary grenade. As the rock mine melted, it released the triggering wire attached to a secondary mine the enemy had placed below the first mine. Both mines exploded, showering the minesweeping detail with shrapnel, but no one was hurt. A short time later, the detail found another rock mine and that also was melted in place. This time there was no secondary explosion.

Within the hour, Marines with Kilo and Lima Company on separate combat patrols tripped separate antipersonnel booby traps resulting in two WIA Marines from each company. India Company was to suffer the worst fate that morning.

Shortly before noon, Pfc. Cecil L. Jones, nicknamed Jonesy, was walking point for his squad in Third Platoon. They were moving through Dodge City on a routine patrol. David "Tex" Prasifka, from Texas, had just returned from R&R and was behind him followed by John J. Costa and Robert E. Fields. Before they started out on patrol that morning, Prasifka had asked Jonesy if he wanted him to walk point. It was the practice in their squad for each squad member to rotate walking point for a week. The week he left for R&R was Tex's week to walk point. Because he still had two days left from that week, he asked Jonesy if he wanted him to take over walking point. Jones answered by saying, "Forget it," and took point.

At 1400 hours, the first fire-team stepped out of the tree line and began to slowly cross an open field that had been recently plowed. The point man was looking for trip wires in a newly plowed field, but it was difficult for both Jonesy and Prasifka to see anything undisturbed in the wild jagged clumps of dirt clots that covered most of the field. As the four men were halfway across the torn field, Jones tripped a trip wire.

Prasifka heard then felt the blast of the explosion as flying dirt, debris, and shrapnel lifted the point man into the air. The impact of a secondary explosion picked up Prasifka, twisting, turning, and flipping his body every which way twenty feet into the air. As he began his descent, he was thinking, *Oh my God! I have to fall that far!*

On his way down, he heard a third explosion behind him as Costa and Fields were violently hurled backward. It was a daisy chain of three 60mm booby-trapped mortars that had been triggered.[259]

Tex landed hard on his back, and all the air was knocked out of his lungs. As he gasped for air, his ears were ringing, and it was hard for him to hear anything. He landed about eight to ten yards from Jones. Prasifka rolled over and called to Jonesy who was lying on his side facing in his direction but was not moving. It looked as if he was wounded in the chest. The speckled earth where Jones lay was being peppered with puffs of dust from automatic small arms fire, but Prasifka because of the explosion still ringing in his ears, couldn't hear the sound of the incoming rounds.

He called out to Jones again, but there was no answer. He got up to run toward Jones to help and protect him from the incoming rounds, but as he tried to step forward, he fell. In the background he could faintly hear the voices of Marines yelling for him to get down.

"Get down! Get down!" they cried out as they tried to return fire but couldn't with Prasifka in the way. Prasifka's only concern was to run toward Jones to give him aid. He got up again and once again started to run toward Jones, only to fall again; by then, he had gotten close enough to see that Jones' open flak jacket revealed a massive chest wound. It was evident to him that Jonesy was dying.

Tex looked down at his feet to see why he had fallen each time he rose to get to Jones and noticed he was losing blood from his upper legs. Then he saw that his right leg was missing. It was barely being held together by a strip of flesh. His thigh was smoking from several pieces of embedded, sizzling shrapnel that had ripped through his body.

He turned to better hear and see the other members of his squad yelling and motioning for him to stay down.

He lay back down and began to feel the pain. Every time he tried to get up to look around, puffs of dirt appeared nearby as shots were fired at the fire-team from the tree line in front of them.[260]

As bullets tore up the ground close to where he and Jones were, the men in his squad behind were them trying to lay down suppressing fire upon the enemy force who was trying to finish off the wounded fire-team.

With their bait laid out in the open, the enemy began to work their way around the platoon to come up behind them. Twelve enemy soldiers wearing black pj's were spotted running from a tree line north to get around Third Platoon to outflank them.[261]

It wasn't long before the rest of Third Platoon joined up with their pinned-down squad and began to return fire. Setting up his gun to the right of the exposed Marines, Darrel Borgman, one of Third Platoon's machine-gungunners opened fire with the M-60 machine-gun, spraying the enemy's position with relentless machine-gun fire. The sizzling red tracers were striking the enemy position right on target; but the merciless enemy, were fierce in their determination to kill as many Marines as they could, returned fire with renewed violence at the pinned down fire-team and at the rest of the platoon.

Two Marines and a corpsman, while under fire, rushed toward Prasifka, hugging the ground and crawling as fast as they could toward the wounded Marines. Bullets continued to pepper the ground where the wounded Marines were. The two Marines escorting the corpsman then stood on their knees in the open field and returned fire at the enemy hidden in the tree line directly in front of where they were. While Doc Keller tried desperately to stop the bleeding by putting a tourniquet on Prasifka's leg. A new corpsman to the platoon by the name of Waugh came rushing out of the tree line to help the senior corpsman. Neither fierce incoming rounds nor the 110-degree temperature stopped the two corpsman and Marines from trying to save the lives of the two seriously wounded Marines. The Marines provided cover, while the two corpsmen worked on the wounded Marines, trying to keep them alive.

An enemy soldier rushed forward and threw a grenade at the wounded Marines position while the corpsmen were working on them.

"Grenade," cried out Doc Waugh, and everyone hugged the ground. The grenade landed between both Doc Keller and Waugh. It exploded without causing injury to anyone. Out in the open, the corpsman continued to work on the two seriously wounded men while two other Marines at their sides provided cover. Working together, they finally managed to bandage Prasifka's wounds and the bleeding stopped. The corpsman and Marines placed him on a poncho and waited to get a medic chopper in as soon as possible.

Doc Waugh then turned to work on Costa, the platoon's 3.5 rocket launcher, who had over 60 percent of his body riddled with shrapnel and was bleeding heavily from his neck. Fields, the other wounded Marine had also received numerous shrapnel wounds to his body, but with the help of other Marines he had managed to get out of the open field and into the safety of the tree line where the rest of the platoon was located.

That Jones was still alive despite his massive chest injuries was one of the reasons the corpsmen were hesitant to move him; they hoped the medevac helicopter would be able to land close enough so that they wouldn't have to move him far. With the platoon continuing to take incoming fire, the medevac choppers could not come in for the emergency evacuation of the wounded.

A half hour later, the platoon engaged the enemy force that had tried to get around behind them and killed two of the enemy soldiers. The platoon soon after that gained the firepower they needed to force the enemy to withdraw.

More than an hour had passed before the first chopper was able to land. By then, the two corpsmen and Marines who had been at the wounded Marines' side out in the hot sun while under fire were exhausted and were quickly becoming heat exhaustion casualties themselves.

The first medevac chopper landed, and Dennis George Dustin and other Marines helped load Jones, Prasifka, Costa, as well as Doc Keller into the first chopper. As Prasifka was being placed inside the chopper, the enemy opened fire again.

The bullets struck the insides and sides of the chopper. As the smoking medevac chopper lifted off the ground, a bullet struck the pilot's foot, but he managed to continue to operate the chopper and turned it so that its gunner could spray the area with M-60 machine-gun fire. By then, Dustin and Borgman, the two Marines I had gone through boot camp and M-60 school with, were also returning machine-gun fire on the enemy.

An artillery barrage was then called in on the enemy's position before the second chopper was able to come in to medevac the other Marines. A search of the area found two confirmed VCs killed.[262]

Before the first chopper landed in Da Nang at first med, smoke was billowing out of the chopper's door and the aircraft was losing altitude. The pilot, though wounded, managed to keep the helicopter flying long enough to land at the emergency helipad before the chopper caught fire.

Incoming
Golden Gate Bridge AT 964605
April 3, 1968, 0120 hours

The morning of April 3, 1968, we were awakened by the distinct sound of incoming small arms and automatic rifle fire on our side of the bridge.[263] We scrambled outside, and I rushed to the gun's position located at the northeast corner of the bridge. While we were getting hit with automatic small arms fire, behind us, regiment was also being hit with small arms fire, 82mm mortars, and 122mm rockets.[264]

The majority of the incoming fire was directed across the bridge to where the tower was located. I stood by the gun inside the bunker near the opening but didn't open fire as the incoming we were receiving was sporadic. When the incoming fire increased, it was AK-47 automatic fire. The location the enemy was firing at us from was a pre-designated position I had already marked on the machine-gun's tripod. I swung the gun over and tightened down the screw. When the enemy opened up again, the location was perfectly lined up with the gun's front sight. I tightened my hold on the machine-gun's pistol grip, pulled the gun in tight up against my cheek, and opened fire. The red tracers made a beeline toward the enemy's muzzle flashes. It was a short burst, but it was effective. The enemy's gun went silent. I loosened the lock on the tripod, and the gun swung free. I sighted in on the next spot from which the VC had opened up, and once again, they opened fire from that location. I opened fire right on the targeted spot and the enemy stopped firing. The process was repeated three, four times before the enemy stopped firing altogether. A short time later, a series of artillery shells were dropped on the same targets.

That afternoon, a squad patrol from First Platoon observed eight Vietnamese of military age following them. They stopped and the group stopped and hid. They continued their patrol then turned to approach the Vietnamese. All of them took off running, and the squad opened fire, killing a female that had been among the group.[264]

Third Platoon's Missing Man
Golden Gate Bridge, AT964605
April 3, 1968, 1600 hours

Later that afternoon, Third Platoon was again to suffer the loss of one of their men. The platoon was on a routine patrol in an area near regiment. The area was heavy with jungle brush, tall trees, numerous trails, and a number of small villages. Just before returning to regiment from their patrol, they found one of their members missing, a black Marine by the name of James Calven Thomas from Safford, Arizona. The Marine had last been seen at AT 962595 by his fire-team leader near a very small village halfway between Cam Van (1) and Cam Van (2); it wasn't far from Golden Gate Bridge.

The platoon had taken a break, and Thomas was seen talking with two young Vietnamese children that were about eleven years of age. The platoon returned to that area, and found his helmet, backpack, and canteen but the Marine was nowhere to be found. The platoon spread out to search the area but was unable to find him. The rest of India Company joined the platoon and made a sweep throughout the area near where Thomas was last seen at Cam Van (2) AT 964603 with negative results.

During the search, seven adult males were detained to be questioned as were three boys about the same age of the boys the Marine was last seen speaking to. As a squad of Marines from Third Platoon approached a hooch, a male ran out trying to flee, but he was captured and returned to the hut he ran from. There the squad found Thomas's watch with blood on it. Three Marines from Third Platoon—Timothy J. Keaney, Clifford A. Norman, and Frank C. McArthur—took custody of the prisoner but were unable to obtain any information from him before he was turned over to Battalion ITT.[266]

Chapter Twenty Four

Return To Dodge City
Golden Gate Bridge, AT964605
April 4, 1968, 2115 hours

On the evening of the fourth of April, Aggie, Rahm, and I settled up and we moved out with First Squad at a steady pace to set up an ambush along a small trail near Giang La (1). As we neared the area where the trail intersected another trail that ran north, the squad slowed down. Something didn't seem right—that sixth sense of danger was present. As the squad came to a complete stop, the enemy opened fire.

The first rounds ripped through the bushes right in front of where Aggie and I were standing. The enemy force was no more than fifteen meters in front of us. We hit the deck as the first volley of enemy fire ripped apart the ground all around us. We found cover and prepared to return fire, but there was no more incoming fire. Dead silence followed. We got up and moved out quickly. No sooner had we cleared the area than another firefight broke out just a short distance from where we had been. At first we believed the gooks had been ambushed by their own as no other Marines were operating in the area. When we returned to base, we were told ROK Marines (Republic of Korea) were operating in the area and had ambushed the gooks as they fled the site from where they had ambushed us.

The following day at 1015 hours, Third Platoon went on a patrol in the same area we had been ambushed the night before; they also got hit with automatic rifle fire. The platoon returned fire and called in 81mm mortar fire on the enemy position; a search of the area proved no signs of enemy casualties.

At 1920 hours, Second and Third Squad from First Platoon moved out on a night ambush while guns, along with First Squad, stayed behind as bridge security. The squads were going into the area just south of where the daisy-chain mortars were tripped just days before by Third Platoon. A couple of hours later, they observed twelve enemy soldiers carrying weapons and wearing black pj's moving in a westerly direction. The squads opened fire, and five enemy soldiers fell. The rest of the enemy force fled into a tree line but quickly returned small arms and automatic rifle fire. An artillery mission was called, and afterward, five dead enemy soldiers' bodies were found where they had fallen. The following day, a squad went through the area where the artillery had been dropped on and found three separate blood trails, some drag marks, an eyeball, ChiCom grenades, and a ChiCom submachine-gun.

For the next three nights, First Platoon stood perimeter watch at regiment. On the seventh, Third Platoon, patrolling in the same grid coordinates where Thomas had gone missing, received an incoming rifle grenade and small arms fire. Paul Bembry, a Marine that had been with the company since Foster, was wounded in the explosion and medevaced by tank to regiment.[267]

Phone Home
Da Nang, Mamasan's Daughters and a Trade
April 7, 1968, 1300 hours

On the seventh of April, the lieutenant called me into his CP tent.

"Barela, your wife had the Red Cross contact Battalion HQ again because you have not written to her. I can order you to write to her, but I won't. Instead, I want you to go into Da Nang and get to that MARS station and call her yourself. I want that Red Cross off my back."

There were more runs than just the mail run from regiment to Da Nang so that would be easy and I looked forward to the trip into Da Nang, but we had nothing to trade. We hadn't been in a good firefight in a while and hadn't captured any good stuff to trade with the pogues in the rear. The weapons and trophies of war that we had had been obtained on a more personal encounter with the enemy so everyone wanted to keep them. Most of the worn-out clothing we had, including boots, would have to last us for a while. The regular-size boots were not available; new arrivals were being issued, new boots that were odd-sized and double—or triple-wide that were always either too big or too small, so we didn't want to trade our boots because we didn't know what we would end up with.

Then Rahm came up with an idea; with $5 in our pocket, we went to Mamasan at the CAC unit near Dai Loc with a proposal. She took it without any question, and on the morning of the eighth, I was on my way to Da Nang.

A grunt with time in the bush doesn't have to prove himself in the rear. One look at him and everyone can tell the guy has been around for a while and had seen his share of combat. Worn old jungle utilities, scuffed and torn boots and that look of not caring about anything gives the combat veteran away.

After I made my call Stateside, I went trading. I would have preferred to have traded with air force personnel or maybe even a swabbie. I hated to do the trade with Marine air wingers, but what the heck, the two of them were easy targets that day once they started to ask questions.

The two air wingers, mechanics from the look of their hands, were standing near a large hangar. I asked them if they knew where I could go trade some stuff we had gotten during our last operation in the Arizona area. Of course, they wanted to see what I had to trade.

The tallest of the two was a city kid; you could tell as he took charge right away, taking a step forward and arching his head up to look down on what I had in my backpack. The small Marine was chubby, more reserved; he wore glasses and had small round hands, and I wondered how he could be a mechanic with tiny stubby hands.

"I don't know if you guys would be interested," I said as I brought up my knapsack and began to unhook the straps. "Just right after the Tet Offensive, my gun team with a squad set up an ambush across the Song Thu Bon River in the Arizona Territory near Football Island," and they both nodded as if they knew where it was. I wasn't sure if they would know about the river, but more than likely, they would have heard of the Arizona area and pilots often referred to Football Island so they might be somewhat familiar with it. Anywhere in that area was know as a free-fire zone so all movement was a target.

"We set in and about midnight," I continued. "We saw two boats with three NVA soldiers in each of them cross over to where we were. They landed right in front of us. Two of the guys were taller than the others and were wearing black. They each had a red-star belt buckle and were giving orders to the others. That's when we realized they were Chinese advisors. We were going to try and capture them alive, but one of the NVAs got into an argument with one of the advisors and the Chinese guy went to shoot him. The NVA guy took off running, and we opened up. We killed four of them. The first NVA and another one got away. The Chinese were dressed in black and the others in khaki. We searched them for paper, and one of the Chinese had some type of orders on him. Regiment wanted everything: weapons, uniforms, all their equipment, everything. They want everything from now on, so it's hard to get anything to trade unless we don't tell regiment what happened or don't count all the bodies killed. Anyways, Tired Aggie, my A-gunner, couldn't see turning everything in and us not getting anything; after all, it was our firefight, he said. So after we had stripped them, he decided to scalp the two Chinese advisors. That's got to be worth something he said, and that's what I got."

As I pulled out the hair Mamasan had cut off her daughters for which we had paid her five bucks for, I put on a crazed look as if I was reliving the event. The two airmen's eyes opened as wide as their mouths as I showed them the globs of hair tied tight by Mamasan.

"Shit, we'll buy them," the tallest of the air wingers said right away.

"What do you want in trade?" the other asked, his round eyes becoming glossy with delight and a small grin appearing at the sides of his mouth.

Since it was going to be an easy trade, I said, "How about two bottles of Bacardi, a bottle of Johnny Walker Red, and a case of beer? And if you guys can throw in a couple of pairs of sunglasses?"

They didn't argue, and the deal was made. I cautioned them not to say where they got the scalps, and the small one with his fist rolled up showed a thumbs-up, his little thumb barely visible at the top of his ball-shaped hand. I really hated to jive Marine air wingers like that, but what the heck, a lot of what I had said was true; it was just a combination of several incidents rolled into one.

I could have stayed over and spent the night there. The air wingers invited me to do that, and with those four-inch-thick mattresses on their bunks, I was tempted. But I was sort of feeling bad about what I had done. You have to be careful in Nam and not bring any bad luck on yourself by taking advantage of others, you can't afford that in a battle zone. I had taken advantage of them as it was, so I thanked them and hopped a ride back to regiment. However, that guilty feeling only lasted until I was on my way back; we hadn't passed the area known as Dog Patch before I was feeling good about the trade, but wondered what story they would tell about how they got the hair.

Clearing Ambush Row
Dodge City, Seventh Marines Regiment Headquarters
April 9-12, 1968, 1300 hours

For the next few days while Mike, Lima and Kilo Company's participated in Operation Jasper Squad in the Foster area we went out on ambushes at night and during the day provided flank security for the Seabees that were using Caterpillars to clear Ambush Road of bushes and vegetation. During this time we stayed in the bush.

Both sides of the road were being cleared from regiment to Route 4. The NVA/VC had many times ambushed Marines on this stretch of roadway, and with the clearing, it was hoped that it would prevent some of the sniping and ambushes along the road.

For the past four days and nights, we had been living, sleeping, and patrolling throughout the rice paddy fields, villages, and the jungle areas between regiment, Route 4, Hill 37, the CAP units, and the railroad that ran north and south on the east side of the Dodge City area. We passed areas we knew were often heavily booby-trapped, set up ambushes near the road that led to regiment, which the enemy often booby-trapped late at night. We were moving around quickly trying to catch the enemy and we weren't being resupplied with chow or water. During the day, we stood by alongside the roadway or near a tree line sitting and waiting in the hot sun while Navy Seabee Caterpillars cleared both sides of the road. On the evening of the eleventh, the rest of the company joined us for a one-day operation, which would commence the following day.

On the morning of April 12, I awoke with a stiff neck. The platoon settled up to move out early again. I ached from having slept for the last two hours on the hard Vietnamese ground. During my early morning watch, a heavy fog had covered the jungle's floor. The rising sun was now quickly dispersing the fog. An hour later we moved out, and I was walking point. Within minutes, we were all drenched in sweat from the hot, humid air.

We moved out cautiously through thick overhanging vines and heavy underbrush. We were patrolling in Dodge City on a search and destroy mission. The area was known for its many booby traps, ambushes, heavy enemy engagements, and fierce firefights. As we moved out, I was looking for trip wires hooked to booby traps and smelling the air for the odor of the enemy. In the thick underbrush, I knew we would smell them before we could see them. Behind me in a long stretched-out column, the rest of the company followed.

Sweat was flowing steadily from my forehead, neck, and back, soaking my undershirt and waistband with dirt and grime. My soiled trousers were torn from the day before the day we entered the thick jungle. The slits were cut straight across by sharp needlelike leaves that poked and cut with razor-sharp edges. We hadn't been resupplied for days and hadn't eaten for two. We were out on patrol, dirty, hot, hungry, haggard, and miserable. It was the beginning of another day in Vietnam.

My eyes began to sting from the salty sweat that was steadily flowing from my helmet's wide web band. As I reached up to wipe the sweat away, I walked out of the thick underbrush into a small clearing. Over to my right about fifty feet away, an enemy soldier broke into the clearing at about the same time.

I stopped, and the company stopped behind me. The NVA Communist soldier was looking down. He had been carrying his AK-47 rifle parallel to his right leg. The protruding vines had entangled themselves in his rifle's front sight housing and its bayonet attachment. As he jerked it free, he turned and saw me. He froze, and the dead of silence quickly filled the air.

We stood there silently, staring at each other—two, three, five long seconds passed. My mind, wide alert, was taking it all in. His hair wasn't combed. One side stood stiff from having been slept on. Sleep wrinkles were still clearly visible on his light-skinned, unwashed face. His uniform was dirty, tattered, and torn like mine. A thin limp bedroll was draped over his shoulder, and he wore no hat.

His eyes, fixed on me, revealed much pain and sorrow. He was young, but aged by the turmoil of war. His rifle was pointed downward, mine was at port arms, and we both knew I had the advantage. Behind us, others didn't know what was happening.

In the next few seconds, we were going to be engaged in a fierce firefight. There was going to be a spattering of blood, guts, and pain. We would be firing blindly and violently at each other. The bullets, noise, and the clamor of war would soon wreak havoc, death, and destruction. He knew it, and I knew it. Then the NVA soldier took one small step backward and waited for me to react.

Life, death, and eternity flashed before us. I heard his stomach growl, loud and empty. Instead of raising my rifle, I lowered it slightly and also took a small step backward. Life returned between us with its promises of tomorrow. His eyes grew wide, and he released a deep sigh. He took another small step backward, and I followed suit. Our eyes never moved, never blinked. He turned to his left and quickly disappeared into the tall elephant grass. I turned to my right to get out of the clearing, and behind me the company started moving again. Today, no one in our platoon or company was wounded, no one died. We sweated instead, we got hungry, and got tired; but we all went in and at night, we slept and some went on another patrol. Tomorrow would be another day.

On the thirteenth and for the next three nights, we were assigned to perimeter watch at regiment and we knew something was up. On the sixteenth, we were back at Golden Gate Bridge running ambushes at night and by day standing security on Ambush Road while the Seabees continued to clear the area. Second Platoon, meanwhile, was reassigned to Liberty Bridge security.

CHAPTER TWENTY FIVE

The President's Son-in-Law, Capt. Charles Spittal Robb
Regiment Headquarters
April 18, 1968, 1300 hours

On the eighteenth, we were back at regiment with no duties to perform. We were told to stand down to rest and wait. Something was up. That evening, Third Platoon at Golden Gate got mortared with 60mm mortar rounds; on the nineteenth, regiment got hit with small arms fire.

That same day, we were told we had had a new company commander assigned to India Company since the ninth of April: Capt. Charles S. Robb, President Johnson's son-in-law, who was married to Lynda Johnson. At first we felt this was a good thing because we might get a break. Certainly the regiment was not going to take any chances with the son-in-law of the president getting wounded, killed, or captured so we figured our assignments might be more security for regiment or battalion than going out on a major operation. While that sounded great, none of us liked staying in the rear. In the rear, there were too many things you had to care about like haircuts, wearing covers, rank insignias, and clean utilities. Welsh suggested that with Robb as our new company commander we might even have to shine our boots. Aggie raised his boots; they were torn and falling apart, we laughed. "They ain't going to take no chances with Captain Robb," they won't be sending him out in the field with just us," and we all knew what Aggie had said was true.

Captain Reeder for the short time he had been with us had been a good captain. He hadn't completed his six-month field assignment, so something was amiss; things had already been shuffled around for some reason, probably to accommodate the president's son-in-law and we didn't know if that was good.

We found out later that when regiment was deciding what battalion Robb should be assigned to and what company he should command, or if he should even be out in the field at all; Colonel Barnard suggested India Company. Not only did the company have a good number of combat veterans from the battles during Foster and other operations in the Arizona area, but Barnard also argued that if anyone could protect the president's son-in-law, it was a company of field Marines. What we were not prepared for and to play it safe and protect Robb, the company would be split. A Marine officer is supposed to be where the majority of his unit is located, but if the company is split, the CO can be anywhere and nowhere at all.

With Operation Rock, we had learned that the enemy was capable of knowing what we were up to, and it wouldn't take much to know that the president's son-in-law was at regiment, battalion, or any other place in our TAOR.

On the nineteenth, the platoons were reassigned. First Platoon was assigned to saturation patrolling south of regiment in the Dodge City area, Second Platoon to Golden Gate Bridge security at AT 968606, and Third Platoon to 3/7 Battalion Headquarters on Hill 37 at AT916583.

Robb was not the only one of the president's sons-in-law in Vietnam. Pat Nugent, U.S. Air Force, married to Luci Johnson was also serving in Vietnam. Stationed in Da Nang he was assigned to Operation Ranch Hand, the official unit spraying South Vietnam with the chemical Agent Orange. Agent Orange was manufactured by Dow Chemical and Monsanto companies. The chemical agent was sprayed by air and by tank trucks. The spraying killed the vegetation along the sides of the road we patrolled in and as the plants died it helped in preventing Charlie from springing ambushes from bushes or shrubs near roads or tree lines.

Seventh Marines Regiment
Hill 55
April 20-25, 1968, 1300 hours

For the next four days, we stood down at regiment, not doing much of anything, except standing perimeter watch at night. On the twentieth of April, Second Platoon was doing a sweep through Dodge City and suffered two WIA's.

Lima Company conducted a company-size raid in the Foster area, departing during the early morning hours and crossing the Song Vu Gia River, sweeping through O Gia Village, and returning that same afternoon. They encountered an enemy force that was estimated at approximately thirty and killed twelve of them while detaining four possible NVA soldiers.

One-Day Show-and-Tell Sweep For Robb, For The Press
Hill 42
April 26, 1968, 1300 hours

On the twenty-sixth of April, we saddled up and went on a one-day operation from regiment to Hill 42. It was called an "offensive sweep" and was one of those memorable days that would be better not recorded in Marine Corps history. As we left the compound, I couldn't help but to think that we looked like the U.S. Army when they went parading through the Arizona territory during Operation Rock. Here we were going on a similar run through Dodge City. We had amtracks, tanks, jeeps, and the media was all over the place. All we needed was for the company's right guide to step up, take point with the banner "Suicide India" held high, and lead us in the parade. The media got to ride and we walked.

The last time the company was on Hill 42 was seven months before during Operation Patriot or Bombay—I had forgotten which one; it seemed so long ago. That had been the day Stoddard and Berg were wounded, and the following day was the one when Prescott had given us all a wake-up call when he woke up screaming after finding leeches inside his trousers.

I wondered where Stoddard, Berg, and Prescott were. Keenan had been assigned to battalion, after he played dead at the Battle of Finger Lake.

I hadn't seen Prescott since he was medevaced during Operation Foster that day. Lieutenant Mullens from Third Platoon called it to the attention of Lieutenant Wilson that one of his men was in need of medical attention.

It was Prescott and Wilson thought he might have been wounded or suffered from a concussion. But Prescott was just walking around after the last assault at the grave mounds babbling to himself, making no sense what-so-ever. He would scream then cry. Prescott was out of it, he had lost it. He had met his limit in war, and Lt. Wilson evacuated him from the battlefield. Prescott had been one of the Marines that had played dead while gooks stripped him of his gear; I had wondered why Prescott hadn't been medevaced from the field that day.

We moved out of the hill's rear perimeter gate shortly after 0800 and headed northwest along the edge of the hill in a counterclockwise direction. India Company was moving out, reinforced with mortars and other support personnel which flanked the sides and rear of Captain Robb's CP. We passed Duc Ky (2), the Peace village, and reached Chau Son (1) before heading toward Chau Son (2). The Vietnamese in those hamlets were very supportive of the South Vietnamese government and of the Marines on Hill 55. During Tet, the villagers of Duc Key (2) and Bich Bac—another village at the base of Hill 55—had come to the gates of regiment and presented Tet greetings and gifts of food to the Marines on the hill. During that time, regiment had distributed, pursuant to the Vietnamese custom of giving twenty to forty piastres as a Tet gift, two hundred red envelopes stuffed with South Vietnamese currency to the villagers.

The villagers came out to the edge of their villages and stood at their gates and watched as we passed by. Little kids stood on rice paddy dikes and saluted while others waved as we went by. "Aggie," I said, "all we have to do now is start singing a song and we'll be just like the army on Rock!"

"Do you think we ought to do that?" he asked. "I'll bet everyone will do it," he added. I looked at him and saw that he was serious. "Come on, start singing," he urged.

I had to admit it would be comical, given supposedly the "dangerous" sweep we were on, but we didn't know what type of CO Robb was. The parade stopped often for photo opportunities, and Robb played it up for the cameras as they clicked away. Perhaps this time it was Charlie on the edge watching us pass by who shook his head and couldn't believe what he was seeing.

The New Third Squad, Squad Leader
Hill 65
April 27, 1968, 1300 hours

On the twenty-seventh, Lima Company 3/7 was OpCon to 1/7 and was choppered out to occupy Hill 22 while 1/7 went out on Operation Ballard Valley. First Platoon India Company was then assigned to Hill 65 to man Lima Company's lines. We would be running patrols during the day as well as ambushes and standing perimeter watches at night. It felt good to be back on the hill after so many months away, and I was looking forward to moving into our old guns bunker.

That afternoon, Sergeant O'Keefe came by guns' hooch and asked if I would take over Third Squad for a while. With a shortage of corporals and sergeants in the platoon, the platoon had already shifted Marines to fill the gaps, but the platoon was still a squad leader short. First Squad was now being led by L/Cpl. Steven Rogers, a Marine that had joined us during Operation Foster.

"It's only temporary, maybe only a month," O'Keefe added.

It was getting toward the end of my tour of duty in Nam, and I was considered a short-timer. When you first arrive in country, thirteen months is seen as an eternity away. About the midway point, you really don't care one way or another about what the future holds, but as you begin to get closer toward the end of your tour of duty, you once again become more cautious and are less apt to take chances. Some Marines, kept a short-timers calendar, where the days since their arrival were crossed off, until only a few unmarked spaces remained. I hadn't kept one. I didn't want to be counting the days, one way or the other.

To take over a squad was a plus but also a curse because it seemed that squad leaders never left Nam without getting seriously hurt or killed. If you're going to get hit in Nam, it was always better to get hit in the first few months instead of having to go through twelve to thirteen months of suffering and pain and then get hit. The majority of the men in Third Squad had about three months in country, and I wasn't sure I wanted to take on that responsibility, especially since that encounter with Boone at the ambush site. Still, to command a squad of Marines and help them survive could make a difference in their lives it could make a difference if they lived or died. I really did not have a choice. Rahm had been placed in charge of the weapons section and could run guns with no problem.

I said I would and silently vowed to myself to keep all the men under my command alive while I served as their squad leader. Because I was considered a veteran of many firefights and a short-timer, the men in Third Squad immediately accepted me as their squad leader without reservations. The fact that I came from guns and was a machine-gunner helped give them confidence in my combat abilities as well.

When I arrived at the squad's bunkers, I could see they had a noticeable respect for me and seemed willing to do whatever I asked of them. I didn't know if they were concerned about that night out with Boone at the ambush site and, as a result, were afraid to cross me or had just heard of my combat experiences from others. One thing for sure, when a Marine rifle squad gets a new squad leader, they do all they can to find out as much as they can about him before he takes over.

In the following days, I sent the squad out on working parties according to the assignments we received from the CP. At first, I was going to go on the working parties with the squad, but they wouldn't hear of me going with them. One of the fire-team leaders requested I allow them to take their teams out and get the work done themselves. They all seemed genuine in their demeanor and were willing to carry their own load, so I gave in to their request and stayed behind and became acquainted with the process of obtaining information and drawing supplies and other items that would help the squad enjoy what comforts I could obtain for them.

I was able to get the men some poncho liners and rain gear, new canteens, as well as a few of the air mattresses we called rubber ladies. When they returned from their working parties, I had cleaned the squads bunker and had straightened out the place.

I reassigned the men within the squad according to the weapons they desired to carry. Freeman wanted to carry the M-79 grenade launcher and he was appointed to that position as were the automatic riflemen. The fire-team leaders, who had been selected before because of their leadership capabilities and not their time in grade, were left in place. For five days, the squad went on working parties and stood watch at night, figuring out their own schedule for standing watch at night. I knew I could trust them to stay alert, but every once in a while, I would come out and sit with them as they stood watch.

Overturned Truck On Ambush Road
Dodge City
April 27, 1968, 1700 hours

Marines from Third Platoon went out on the afternoon of the twenty-seventh on an early evening squad-size patrol. The squad left regiment's back door, went past Golden Gate Bridge, and then turned east toward the village of Giang La (1). A short time later, they began to take sporadic sniper fire. The sniper was bait; as the squad of Marines moved in to seek out the sniper, a large enemy force lying in wait opened fire on them with automatic AK-47 weapons fire and grenades.

The ambush was launched with high intensity, but the Marines quickly took cover and returned fire with the M-60 machine-gun, M-16 rifles as well as with their

M-79 grenade launchers while the squad's radioman called in 81mm mortars on the site. The mortars were effective, and the enemy broke contact and disappeared into the jungle. L/Cpl. Robert Stanley Croke, from Walnut Creek, California, however, was killed in the initial ambush.[268]

A short time afterward, a truck traveling south on Ambush Road on the last run of the day was rushing to make it to battalion before nightfall. As the speeding driver turned right onto Route 4 from Ambush Road, the M-54 truck became uncontrollable and overturned. Eleven of the Marines riding in the truck were injured in the accident, and a squad of Marines and a medical team from CAP 2-2-2 responded to the site on a tank.

Third Platoon was also dispatched as a reactionary unit from Hill 55. The injured Marines were medevaced to Hill 37 from where five Marines were then evacuated to first med for treatment.[269]

First Platoon that night was reassigned to man Third Platoon's lines on the bridge, and we got hit with a burst of small arms and automatic rifle fire. A tank assigned to the bridge for the night returned fire as did the 60mm mortar squad.[270]

Night Ambush At The Bottom Of The Hill
Hill 65
May 4, 1968, 1300 hours

We began the month of May with the platoons of India Company dispersed in our TAOR: First Platoon at Hill 65 (AT 877574), Second Platoon at 3/7 Battalion Headquarters on Hill 37 (AT 915582), and Third Platoon was OpCon to Seventh Marines, providing security for Golden Gate Bridge at regiment (AT 967606). Two platoons from Lima Company remained OpCon to 1/7; one platoon from Lima Company was at Seabee Bridge at the northwest corner of battalion headquarters near Route 540 (AT 913587).

Late in the morning of the fourth of May, the word was passed for First Platoon squad leaders to meet with the lieutenant in the CO's CP. Captain Robb was there as was Gunny King. Jack King was a tall, handsome no-nonsense Marine that always took care of business. You knew he was hard but cautious. A Korean War veteran, he had already seen plenty of action before getting to Vietnam. Lieutenant Nowicki briefed us on what our mission was and what to expect.

"Hill 65," the lieutenant said, "is supposed to be hit tonight. The NVA/VC is going to cross the river in the early morning hours and attack the hill. They are going to come from the east, move west along Route 4 at the base of the hill." First platoon is going to set up an L-shaped ambush at the bottom of the hill near Route 4 with Hill 65 to our backs. A primary target of the enemy was Captain Robb, we were told. Capturing or killing the president's son-in-law would be a major victory for the enemy, so we could expect a fierce fire fight.

For the past two months, the enemy had been positioning units in and around the area between the Thuong Duc Special Forces Camp to the west of us and the Dai Loc District Headquarters to the east of us. Captured enemy soldiers had indicated that beginning on the fifth of May, the enemy was going to be hitting several of our positions, culminating with a major strike in Da Nang. Hill 65 had for some time been a major targeted area for the NVA, and intelligence indicated that Hill 65 would be hit that night.

That afternoon, Captain Robb left the hill in the middle of a three-jeep convoy. He was the only captain we knew of that traveled that way. The company only rated one jeep; we had three. The jeep in front and behind him each had an M-60 machine-gun mounted on them, and each had a driver and three other Marines in them. Eight Marines total were assigned to him during those travels between Hill 65 and battalion headquarters. In the jeep with Robb was his driver, his radioman Donald Gillette, and Gunny King. We didn't know if Robb was going to spend the night with Second Platoon at battalion or with Third Platoon at regiment. As evening fell, we saddled up for a platoon-size night ambush at the edge of the river where the enemy was supposed to cross over.

I had the squad check each other out to make sure we were all prepared for the night ambush, ready to be out in the dark in Charlie's playground. Two men would have their weapons prepared to respond with full automatic rifle fire. The M-79 grenadier would be next to me. First Squad was walking point followed by the lieutenant and his CP group then Second Squad. Third Squad was bringing up the rear.

Rahm, who had been promoted to corporal in November, was now in charge of weapons and had two new men in guns. He was in front of the CP group, just behind the first fire-team in First Squad.

Pfc. Raymond C. Custer was carrying the gun, and Private Doss was his A-gunner. That gun would be set up next to the abandoned concrete building on the east side of the dirt road where it intersected with Route 4 at the bottom of the hill.

James was carrying the other gun, and he and Aggie were sandwiched in between my last two fire-teams in Third Squad.

The ambush would be set up to the left of Hill 65, with the longer strand of the L-shaped ambush set in along the tree line to the left of the dirt road. We would be facing east with our backs to the road that ran down the hill, and the shorter leg of the ambush was to be set up facing south along the Northern edge of Route 4.

The platoon was shorthanded; all the squads undermanned, still we had more men in First Platoon than normally. There were nine men in Third Squad including myself and it was the biggest of the squads.

Only Keene had been with the squad before Foster and had experienced the first two major firefights of that operation.

Most of the other men in the squad had come to the company at the tail end of Foster: Randy Feight, whom we called "Hippie," James Freeman, Mark Saylor,

Eugenio Guzman, Thomas Paone, Raul Serrato, Samuel Eklofe, Stephen Sellers, Lonnie Mitchell and a brand-new kid by the name of Kenneth Miller.

As we walked out the front gate near midnight, we were sticking close to the left side of the road. Already, I had an uneasy feeling about the night. The quarter moon was shining through scattered clouds, and its light beams seemed to be following the column of Marines moving into history to change lives forever. If the enemy was looking, the moon was helping by making us very visible.

We left the hill from the front gate; from there, I could see the concrete bunker at the bottom of the hill. How many days had I stared at that bunker and the area all around us while standing guard duty at the front gate when I first arrived on Hill 65? A lot had changed since then although the clear rice paddy fields on both sides of the road remained the same.

The moon's light offered clear visibility to a distant tree line east of us where the village of Tam Hoe was and beyond that, the peaceful village of My An (1). The thick tree line on the east side of the road, to our left as we walked down the hill, hid the uninviting village of Dai Phu. There, in concealed and scattered hooches, the enemy had often found shelter and support to snipe at or launch attacks on Hill 65.

We were about halfway down the narrow dirt road when the platoon turned left, going east on top of the broad berm that ran parallel to Route 4. The raised berm which ran east and west was used by farmers to move their water buffaloes and small carts between villages. It now carried our weight as we traveled east toward the dark shadows of the tree line ahead. I expected the enemy to open fire on us at any moment, but nothing but silence surrounded us.

When First Squad reached the tree line, they turned right, going south along a small trail that ran along the tree line toward Route 4. The tree line ran parallel to the dirt roadway that led from Hill 65 to Route 4. When the squad reached the edge of Route 4, the point squad turned right going west and Rahm's gun team followed. At the corner where the squad turned was a thick cluster of tall bamboo plants. The Marines behind them set in facing east along the tree line and First Squad set up along the edge of Route 4 facing south, facing away from Hill 65. Rahm set up the gun inside the concrete bunker. The hooch had no front door and two windows. From there the gun team would be able to fire across the road or using the side window would be able to fire west or east from an elevated position down Route 4. Corporal Kates, his radioman, and a fire-team set in to Rahm's right on the other side of the bunker at the northwest corner where the two roads came together.

Behind the platoon were open rice paddy fields and the dirt roadway that led to Hill 65. The majority of the platoon had set up at the edge of the tree line looking east toward the village of Dai Phu. My squad, Aggie, and James set up at the tail end of the L-shaped ambush.

Once set in, I modified the instructions I had given the squad. Since we were set up closest to the hill and the rest of the platoon fanned out to our right (south facing east) with Hill 65 being to our left rear, I decided, instead of having everyone on 100 percent alert, to set two-man watches in each fire-team with one guy resting for an hour. I figured that if all the men were already straining to see in the dim light, they would be tired and would imagine moving shadows from the changing moonlight and dark clouds overhead while a rested Marine would be clearer headed and be able to recognize what was friend or foe.

Just to the left of where the wide berm ended, Aggie lay down next to me in a prone position. A small dirt mound ran along the edge of the trail that ran along the tree line. The mound was to keep the rice paddy water in the field, but now it served as a support for Aggie's head and he lay down resting his head on the mound while keeping watch east through the trees. James set up the gun facing east in the direction we expected the enemy to come from. It was set up just the other side of the opening where the wide berm and the trail that ran alongside the tree line came together.

It was a perfect spot for the gun as the gun team would be able to lay down and fire from an elevated level.

I lay down and Freeman laid down to my left. James and the rest of the squad were set in, in the same way. The rest of the platoon lay prone on their bellies across the trail facing the villages. Two to three foot tall elephant grass prevented them from seeing much in front of them they would hear the enemy before seeing them. By positioning our backs on the dirt mound as Aggie had done, we would be able to see the enemy before they were on us. On the other side of the berm were the other two fire-teams from the squad, all lying back the same way. While our positions did not offer the best covering as we would have to twist quickly around in a firefight, the advantage was that we would be able to fire the first rounds.

I still had an uneasy feeling about the night although, with my squad being the closest to the hill, chances of us coming into contact if the ambush was set off would be very slim. The enemy would more than likely use Route 4 or try to stay as far away from the hill as possible to avoid detection until they were able to move into position to open fire. Since we were expecting the enemy to come from the east and with Hill 65 behind us and clear, open rice paddy fields to our backs, it seemed we would be relatively safe. Still, that uneasy feeling remained and I told Freeman, the M-79 man, to keep his eyes open.

"Keep watch toward our rear," I said to him, "down the berm we just came from." We used the berm to get across the rice paddy fields, so might the enemy. I told him and that I just didn't feel right about how we were set up. He acknowledged and while the other man to his left kept watch forward, Freeman did both, keeping watch to our rear and in front of us.

Hill 65 Gets Hit
Bottom of Hill 65, near Route 4 AT 880574
May 5, 1968, 0120 hours

At 0120 hours, Hill 55 got hit with fifteen 82mm mortar rounds. At the same time, CAP 2-1-2 got hit with small arms fire as did CAP 2-1-4 with mortar, automatic rifle fire, and M-79 grenades. At 0150 hours, it was battalion's turn, and they got hit with 82mm mortars rounds. Ten minutes later, Third Platoon on Golden Gate Bridge security reported getting hit with small arms and 60mm mortar fire. No sooner had the first rounds of mortar fire begun to strike the bridge than Hill 65 also got hit from five different positions with mortar rounds. Over sixty mortar rounds were fired at the hill from four positions just northwest of the hill and from a fifth position on the hill's right side, which was the southeast corner, only about two hundred yards south of us from the other side of Route 4.

Hill 65 returned mortar fire—81 and 60, dropping them on the different firing positions where the enemy's mortars were coming from.

Fifteen minutes later, another sixteen rounds of mortars were dropped in on the hill. This time they came from near the village of My An (1). It seemed as if the enemy had moved past us on the other side of Route 4. We now had enemy soldiers to the east of us where we expected them to be, but others were also to the west of us and they were dropping mortar rounds on Hill 65.

While we could see the flares being popped into the air by Marines on Hill 65, the impact of the enemy's mortar explosions on the hill from where we were we could not see or hear. We sat waiting, looking, listening for any movement, but everything remained quiet. It was too quiet.

I lay back up against the rice paddy dike with my back toward the open fields. All of the men were now on alert and sitting up, facing east from where we had been told the enemy would be coming from.

At 0250 hours, Cap 2-2-4 at Tam Hoa village AT 867573 just west of Hill 65 got hit from the north and west side of the compound. The enemy had swept through the friendly village of My An (1), killing civilians and burning down the village. Now they were moving east toward us and we didn't know it.

After I finished my watch, I awoke Freeman for his watch, and as I lay back, I mentioned to him to keep his eyes open to our rear as well as something was not right. He acknowledged and checked his weapon then settled back.

At 0300 hours, shortly after the enemy finished firing a last barrage of 60 mortars at Hill 65, they policed up the area then swung around going counterclockwise around Hill 65. A short time later, they teamed up with other NVA soldiers and then the reinforced NVA company swept east from My An and Cap 2-2-4, traveling east along Route 4. A reinforced platoon was assigned to walk their flank north of Route 4, traveling east on the wide berm at the bottom of Hill 65 toward the dark tree line.

"Here comes somebody," Freeman said. I arose on my right elbow, shaking the drowsiness out. "They look like ARVNs," he said, "and they're walking in formation toward us."

I grabbed hold of the M-16 and turned to look to my right just as the point man leading his platoon stepped up from the rice paddy onto the berm. The enemy must have been relieved to have finished their fire mission and to have escaped the 81mm HE-rounds Hill 65 had fired on them in response. The NVA soldier walking point turned left then stopped to await the rest of his squad to join him in the shadows of the tree line. He noticed there was something on the ground and strained hard to try and make out what it was. As he sought recognition, I looked up and saw a Chinese Communist-made red star belt buckle on the fully uniformed NVA soldier standing over me. The enemy soldier had his AK-47 pointed at my chest, trying to figure out what was on the ground; and I thanked the moonbeam that changed the shape of bushes, trees, and shadows into the form of an enemy soldier that night.

Before the enemy soldier figured out what it was, The M-16's safety came off and I fired three rounds of gunfire straight into his belly. As the first round entered him, his eyes opened wide and I could see that he had finally recognized what the dark form on the ground was.

As he started to react to that realization, I fired two more rounds and his eyes acknowledged that he was dead. Two other bullets tore into his chest, and in that split second as he submitted to death and eternity, he uttered his last word on earth—it was loud and clear: "UUUUuuugh!"

The momentum of his backward reactionary movement coupled with the velocity of the bullets that struck him sent his body twisting clockwise and flying backward toward my right. He fell at the feet of Aggie's sleeping body.

Aggie, jarred awake from the world of dreams and peace into the center of hell, death, destruction, with the smell and sounds of gunpowder, fear, and red hot blood in the air, saw the blast of the last two bullets as they exited my rifle's barrel and struck the enemy soldier's chest. He saw in those split seconds the soldier's twisting body fall on the ground next to him. With his rifle already set on full automatic, he opened fire with a twenty-round clip, emptying all of it into the twisting, turning body only a foot or two away from him. By then I had completely turned around and fired at the second NVA soldier that was standing frozen in formation to my right rear. Freeman cut loose with his M-79, and the grenade struck a third NVA soldier. The M-79 round struck the skinny NVA soldier smack in the middle of his chest, and the force of the grenade round knocked him back twenty feet. But because he was too close to us, the round hadn't turned the revolutions needed to arm itself, and the grenade did not explode. As Freeman reloaded to fire more rounds at the squad of fleeing enemy soldiers who were all desperately trying to get away from the tree line, Marines from the squad quickly turned around and opened fire at them as well.

As soon as Aggie expended all the rounds in his magazine, I jumped over him and cut loose with the remainder of the rounds in my magazine shooting straight down the wide berm. Aggie changed clips and also opened fire, shooting straight down the top of the berm where the majority of the enemy was running on. A second later, James opened up with the M-60 and Aggie moved over to hold the belt of ammo as James fired at the enemy soldiers scrambling for cover.

Freeman had counted fifteen enemy soldiers walking in formation and thought them to be allies, ARVNs, because they were in formation, wearing uniforms and helmets. Now those same enemy soldiers were scattered, running for their lives, on both sides of the berm, spreading out into the rice paddy fields trying to get away.

Some of the enemy soldiers ran northwest toward Charlie Ridge; others took off southwest along the dirt road toward Route 4 and the concrete bunker where Rahm was located.[271]

As the enemy fled, they threw grenades and some fired back at us with their weapons on full automatic. The squad did not hesitate to engage them and returned fire. This time we were the ones in the shadows of the tree line, taking advantage of the moon's glow to fire at their outlines as they scrambled for cover in the open rice paddy fields. Several enemy soldiers fell from the fierce response they received from the squad, and the rest of the platoon.

Wait Until You See The Whites Of Their Eyes
Bottom of Hill 65, near Route 4 AT 880574
May 5, 1968, 0300 hours

Seconds before the first rounds were fired, Rahm caught a glimpse of a column of enemy soldiers walking west on Route 4 toward their position. He passed the word to his left to alert the CP and directed Doss to tell Custer to get on the gun. The lieutenant quickly radioed back to wait until the enemy column was in the middle of the ambush site before opening fire.

About the same time, across the roadway, a column of NVA soldiers walking flank on the other side of the road spotted movement near the CP group. Their leader signaled for the squad of NVA soldiers to move up to the edge of the road and engage the Marines.

Neither the lieutenant nor Rahm knew the enemy had flanks walking point on both sides of Route 4. The platoon of NVA soldiers were walking parallel and just ahead of their main column and before Custer had a chance to get on the gun, we had opened fire.

When the first round was fired from our position, Custer quickly grabbed the weapon nearest him. Doss reached for his weapon and in the dark and confusion couldn't find it. Rahm, hearing the sounds of gunfire behind him, gave Doss his M-16, grabbed hold of the M-60, and opened fire at the column of enemy soldiers that were by then only about forty feet away and beginning to run toward them. Custer, using Doss's M-16, also opened up and three of the enemy soldiers in front of the column went down.

Realizing he and the gun team were in a dangerous position with the enemy soldiers to their right and firing going on behind them at our tree line position, Rahm told the gun team to grab their gear and get out of the hooch. Custer gave Rahm Doss's M-16 and picked up the M-60.

The NVA soldiers across the road were just about to open fire at the CP group when they heard firing coming from where we were, which was followed by Rahm opening fire at their main column. They, in return, opened fire across the road at the CP and at Rahm's gun position.

As they began to receive incoming fire, Marines along the long stem of the L-shaped ambush were turning around to engage the enemy soldiers behind them that were by then running out in the open rice paddy fields trying to get away.

Caught In The Cross Fire
Bottom of Hill 65, near Route 4 AT 880574
May 5, 1968, 0305 hours

Rahm and the CP group were soon caught in a cross fire from the NVA running from our ambush site toward them and the enemy firing at them from the other side of the road.

Custer, having grabbed the gun to on his way out of the hooch, saw the intensity of the incoming fire being directed at the CP group, so he got down and opened fire at the squad of enemy soldiers from inside the bunker. He fired over two hundred rounds before he let up on the trigger. Kates' fire-team to his right, meanwhile, had engaged the enemy on the roadway. The engagement gave the CP group the time they needed to fall back into the tree line.

The enemy firepower became concentrated on the gun's position. They began to throw grenades and directed their automatic weapons fire at the gun team's location and at the concrete bunker. It was not a good position to be in with the firefight being so close.

"Get out of here!" Rahm yelled out once more to the gun team, and as they ran out the hooch, grenades exploded all around them followed by the flash of an RPG round as it shot past, went through the hooch's open doorway, and exploded on impact inside the concrete building. The bunker exploded, tearing off what remained of the roof and demolishing the bunker's rear wall. Half of the bunker collapsed inward.[272]

To the right of the hooch, the fire-team from First Squad was desperately trying to get out of the cross fire. They had used the bunker's outer wall to shield themselves from the incoming fire until the RPG rocket exploded inside, showering them with dust and debris. When the dust cleared and the walls collapsed, they could see a large group of enemy soldiers to their right front dropping down to shoot at them. At the same time, NVA soldiers running from our ambush location were rushing toward them.

The Marines had to fall back and they hooked up with Rahm's gun team. They were all now out in the open without cover; some of them were pinned down as they tried to make their way back to the tree line where the rest of First Platoon Marines were located. The enemy force running from us toward Route 4, seeing the Marines retreating, stopped, took aim, and opened fire at them.

Marines along the tree line then engaged the main enemy with extensive firepower, which gave Rahm and the Marines with him the opportunity to leapfrog back to the safety of the tree line.

They were stopped suddenly by the thick clump of bamboo plants that stood between them and the rest of the platoon. The bamboo canes were two to three inches thick, some twelve feet tall and heavily grouped together. To try and go around the cluster of plants would expose them to hostile enemy fire.

The NVA soldiers on the roadway, receiving heavy incoming fire from the Marines, stopped firing and ran to join their main force that had advanced to the corner of the concrete building where both roadways intersected. Now all of the enemy forces were together.

Custer, having first reached the thick grove of bamboo, held the bamboo poles back for Doss and the other Marines to pass through. As Rahm was in the process of going through the thick wall of bamboo, Custer lost his grip on the canes and the canes snapped back, knocking Rahm backward about three or four feet. Twice this happened before Rahm and Custer, working together, were able to hold back the thick bamboo and get through to the safety of the tree line.

Instead of advancing forward, the enemy pulled back to the other side of Route 4 and began to drop 60mm mortar rounds on the platoon at the tip of the tree line.

When the firing began to subside, the word, "Corpsman up, corpsman up," was passed down to the CP. In the initial firefight, the fleeing enemy had thrown grenades at our position and both Stephen M. Sellers and Kenneth A. Miller were wounded with shrapnel.

Rahm, hearing the call coming from our squad, grabbed hold of Budda, the platoon's corpsman, and both ran toward our position. The enemy, seeing movement, fired at them as they made their way along the tree line.

The platoon returned fire, as did Custer and James, with the M-60's and the enemy stopped firing, and soon all incoming fire stopped.

A New Dawn
Bottom of Hill 65, near Route 4 AT 880574
May 5, 1968, 0630 hours

Just before dawn, Lieutenant Nowicki made his way over to our position to find out what happened. He wanted to know why we had given away our ambush position by opening fire before the enemy had a chance to move into the ambush site. He arrived just as the corpsman finished bandaging one of the wounded Marines; Rahm sat nearby listening as the lieutenant criticized our performance. I listened and didn't answer. Rahm waited until the lieutenant had finished his condemnation of my squad's performance then stood up and pointed to the bodies of the dead enemy soldiers lying near where he had been sitting. It was then the lieutenant saw two dead enemy soldiers almost at his feet. Another enemy soldier lay facedown in the rice paddy field a short distance away. It was evident the two dead enemy soldiers at his feet had been killed at an arm's reach from our ambush position.

Nowicki stood silent, looked at me, then at the enemy's weapons we had gathered; he tightened his lips and said, "Don't touch the bodies; intelligence may want to go through their papers." He then turned around and slowly walked away.

Captured Family Documents And A Debt Paid
Bottom of Hill 65, near Route 4 AT 880574
May 5, 1968, 1000 hours

When full daylight came, a thick fog lay on the ground and we stayed in our positions, waiting to see the full aftermath of the night's battle. There were two dead NVA soldiers in front of us and just to our right a few yards away was another one. Next to him, we found a dented M-79 round.[273]

At 1000 hours, a whole group of busybodies showed up, including the press, a Marine Interrogation-Translation Team, a Republic of Korea Marine interpreter, a Kit Carson Scout, Captain Robb, other Marines, and local officials. The ITT Marines decided to come out to the battle scene to examine the bodies for papers after a captured wounded NVA soldier had been interrogated by them earlier that day. When they arrived, they were especially interested in the body of the tall enemy soldier I had killed. The Korean interpreter said the dead soldier was a Chinese lieutenant. The dead man's wallet was passed around; it contained pictures of a wife and family, and on his person there were other military documents. [274]

The interpreter read the documents out loud so everyone present could hear. The papers revealed the dead enemy soldier had received a battlefield commission and was promoted to lieutenant for having killed a Marine Corps corporal and having captured his M-60 machine-gun. The certificates of merit awarded to him stated he had successfully directed others in battle and often took the lead in a firefight with Marines. Several certificates we saw had the North Vietnamese Communist flag printed on them. Some of the color ink had ran or faded. They stated he was an honored soldier that served as an example for others to follow. The papers also identified the dead enemy soldier I had killed as a Chinese officer and advisor.

Afterward, Lieutenant Nowicki mentioned he was going to write both Rahm and I up for a Bronze Star with Valor for our actions that night.

Intelligence was only interested in the paperwork found on the dead enemy soldier's possession. Their gear was the spoils of war that were ours to keep. The soldier I killed had been carrying a brand-new SKS-56 rifle, the standard military rifle issued to Chinese soldiers, and I decided to keep the Soviet-made weapon for myself as well as his backpack. The rest of his gear I handed out to other Marines in the squad and gave the red-star belt buckle to Freeman. Other Marines helped themselves to the weapons and equipment the other dead NVA soldiers had been carrying: belts, knives, war memorabilia, and other gear they could get. All of it made good souvenirs or valuable trading goods.

Later that afternoon, Captain Robb made it clear he was interested in getting the brand-new SKS-56 rifle as a war trophy. Nowicki inquired about it, but I did not want to give it up. The lieutenant then said I had just kissed off the Bronze Star medal.[275] When he saw that depriving me of a medal didn't make a difference, he ordered me to turn in the weapon, "Intelligence has requested it," I was told.

The NVA was to have come from the east traveling west along Route 4. The information we had received was either false or someone had read the map backward so we ended up facing the wrong way. Had the lieutenant not decided to set up where we did, we would have been slaughtered as the enemy would have come from behind us as a reinforced company had we set up where we were originally assigned to set up and we would have had to then defend ourselves with our backs to the river at a spot where they were suspected to cross over. They would have come at us from our rear.

The NVA had intended all along to cross the river two miles west of Hill 65 near the CAP unit then travel east, attacking the CAP unit, firing mortars on Hill 65 then sweeping east into the tree lines and crossing back into Arizona territory close to where we were supposed to have been set up, southeast from Hill 65. It was fortunate that we didn't lose a Marine that night, but that's the way it is in war. Sometimes mistakes or luck grants you another day of life.

After hearing the interpreter read what the captured documents declared, I felt a tremendous peace come over me.

Since my arrival in Vietnam, I had wreaked havoc upon the enemy with the M-60 machine-gun. There was no doubt in my mind that I had personally killed and wounded many enemy soldiers over the past few months. I knew I had caused them much pain, death, and destruction and perhaps in the process had also saved many Marines' lives by exposing myself to the enemy's fire—unknowingly at times or through my own naïveté or ignorance. I had opened fire upon the enemy from locations they would never had expected a Marine to return fire on them from. I don't know if it was being brave as Aggie had once said; or just doing what I had been trained to do to save other Marines' lives.

The killing of that NVA lieutenant released me from an inner confinement I didn't know had entrapped me. I felt no remorse for having killed an enemy soldier, a family man. What stuck in my mind were his awards, the papers he had been awarded, and the document declaring his battlefield commission. I felt a release because I felt that somehow, I had repaid a debt owed. I didn't know if I had killed the enemy soldier who had killed Bro and taken our machine-gun, but I felt vindicated and now I was ready to go home.

Sweep Through The Battlefields
Hill 65 (AT 870580)
May 5, 1968, 1300 hours

Later that day, we swept through the other side of Hill 65, the northeast area from where the hill had gotten mortared from the night before. The village of My An (1) had been completely destroyed. All the hooches had been burned down, livestock had been slaughtered, and AK-47 cartridges were scattered all over. Many civilians had been killed or were missing. The platoon found three VC KIAs and three enemy 83mm mortar rounds near where our 81mm mortar HE rounds had impacted and caused the four secondary explosions our spotters reported seeing. All in all, twelve enemy bodies had been left in the fields of battle around the hill. There were blood and drag marks at other places, showing we had killed others who had been dragged away. It remained unknown how many of the enemy walked away wounded. Hill 65 was not the only hill to have been hit that night. The enemy had launched a successive number of firefights throughout our TAOR and had paid a heavy price for it.

During the regular road sweep earlier that day, Second Platoon received constant sniping between Hill 37 and Hill 55. The enemy was still in the area, and they wanted us to know. I knew they would return to try to even the score. The sweeping detail returned fire when they could and called in gunships then continued on with the minesweeping detail, locating five different mines on the road during the sweep.

That evening, just before nightfall, we received twelve rounds of 82mm mortar fire. The company returned the incoming fire with mortar fire, and Rahm opened up with the M-50 from on top of the tower on Hill 65, firing across the river into the Arizona area at the location the enemy mortar flashes could be seen coming from. It was the same spot where we had landed on the first day of Operation Rock (AT 871553). Rahm, after firing several rounds from the M-50, clamped down the M-3 tripod's traversing slide on that target for future reference.[276]

The day after
Hill 65
May 6, 1968, 1950 hours

On the evening of the sixth, with the quarter moon's brightness shining early in the night, one of the Marines in Third Squad could see a Vietnamese male moving toward the wire at the bottom of the hill. The male moved smoothly in a crunched position, slithering from one bush into the dark shadows of another. He wasn't far below Third Squad's bunker position on the southeast side of the hill. I sighted in on him then opened fire with three M-16 rounds, and the enemy soldier went down. Before we could go down to investigate, the hill was hit with small arms and automatic rifle fire, M-79 grenades, eight 82mm mortar rounds, and a series of RPG rockets.

The first rocket struck the base of the hill; the next one took out the shitter. Marines in Second Squad ran out of their bunker seconds before the third rocket struck it, blowing out a large corner section. Mortars were then dropped on the hill and they had come from across the river not far from where other mortar rounds had been fired at us the night before. Had Rahm been in the tower on the M-50 machine-gun, he would have been able to zoom right in for a kill from the marked reference point.[277]

On the seventh, our squad was assigned to set up at "Charlie's Point" a listening post on the northwest end of the hill. Charlie would at times sneak up near that tip and pop off a few carbine rounds into the compound at night and then disappear.

We set in, well dispersed, everyone on 100 percent alert and listening for any movement. The squad moved slowly, silently, and professionally.

Platoon-Size Patrol At The Base Of Charlie Ridge
Hill 65
May 8, 1968, 0800 hours

On the morning of the eighth, while the rest of the company remained on the hill, we saddled up and went on a two-squad all-day patrol toward Charlie Ridge then around the lake located northwest of us. It seemed like we were wandering around listlessly and after a while we were wondering if the lieutenant knew where he was going as we had never ventured so far out from the hill before with only two squads.

On the ninth, we did it again; wandered around listlessly at the base of Charlie Ridge and we were wondering if we were being used as bait. We would get hit and the captain would respond with the rest of the company. That night the squad once again was assigned the listening post.

On the tenth we patrolled along the river with another squad and a gun team. This time, however, the lieutenant wasn't with us and we welcomed his absence. On the eleventh, the platoon swept along the Song Thu Bon River past the CAP unit, looking for 125 enemies who had been spotted in the area earlier that day. We returned before noon to the hill and the men were sent out on working parties.

Cookies From The White House
Hill 65
May 13, 1968, 1100 hours

On the morning of the thirteenth at 0030 hours, Third Platoon got hit at Golden Gate Bridge with small arms fire and 60mm mortars. Two Marines were wounded but not evacuated: L/Cpl. Darrell L. Borgman and Pfc. Gary L. Poppe.[278]

At 1100 hours, Marines from First Platoon were standing watch in the tower and observed twenty enemy soldiers dressed in black and khakis with weapons and camouflaged packs, moving west in the same area that we had been seeing activity over the past week (AT 866554).

At noon, battalion got mortared; at 1300 hours, Captain Robb landed on Hill 65. With battalion getting mortared almost daily since the fifth, we were seeing more of Robb on Hill 65; however, by nightfall he usually was back at battalion or at regiment, which were places considered safer for him to be at during the night. Ever since India Company returned to Hill 65, it had been getting mortared more often than usual. The hill was supposed to be India Company's CP; at least that's what it showed on paper. We just figured the enemy was hoping to get lucky and get Robb while he was on the hill.

That afternoon, as James boarded a truck into battalion to await a flight date for his R&R, the squads that were going out on patrol that night were being briefed by Robb himself at his bunker on Hill 65.

As they sat around listening to the CO's instructions, we noticed a large white box with the imprint of the White House on it. The box contained White House cookies. We had heard Robb received cookies from his wife Lynda Byrd Johnson at least once a week. Kates asked Robb if his wife baked the cookies and Robb answered by saying that his wife couldn't cook; the White House chef had made the cookies.

The captain didn't offer to share the cookies, but he might have seen that his men felt slighted by him not offering them any, so in a gesture of goodness to the squad leaders, Robb opened a large envelope that contained a stack of eight-and-a-half-by-eleven-inch colored wedding pictures taken at the White House of his marriage to Lynda Byrd Johnson. Robb very proudly gave copies of the photographs to the squad leaders as they exited the hooch. He might have felt it was something his men would treasure and write home about.

The squad leaders smiled and took the pictures. No one bothered to ask him to autograph the picture. When they were outside, they noticed the photographs were already autographed with his signature.

That evening at 1840 hours, Hill 65 got hit with 82mm mortars and 57 recoilless rifle fire from almost that same location as before (AT 865555). The hill responded with 81mm HE mortars and 105mm HE artillery rounds at the target. From the incoming fire, two Marines were wounded: Pvt. Roosevelt Johnson Jr. and Cpl. Jose

Cantu Jr. Both were medevaced, and Cantu, as he was being loaded on board the medevac chopper, asked that his parents not be notified of his wounded status.[279] Other Marines often made similar requests and depending on the seriousness of their inquiry, such requests were almost always acknowledged.

A Suicide Mission
Night Ambush
May 13, 1968, 2330 hours

At 2100 hours, Second Squad with Corporal Kates as their squad leader left Hill 65 on a night ambush. An hour later, they were set up on the south side of Route 4 just east of CAP 2-2-4. Before the squad left the perimeter, the communications sergeant had befriended Kates and asked if he could go along on the patrol. It was not unusual for Marines assigned to rear positions to ask to go along on a patrol or a night ambush. While hesitant to do so, Kates finally agreed; the sergeant, saddled up and armed with an M-16, joined the squad.

The squad settled in silence on a small incline from where the squad had a perfect view of the road leading to the CAP unit. If the enemy chose to probe or attack the CAP unit using that stretch of roadway, there would be a fierce firefight. The discipline in the squad was outstanding; all the Marines kept silent. Overhead, the full moon was shrouded with dark clouds. On the ground, there was an air of solemn gloom. Deep loneliness settled throughout the valley, and dark shadows turned into demons of the night. Eternity's door was opened for a time and half a time and deep fear emerged from the heart of wickedness and death was allowed to step out of that spirit world into our world of life to seek the souls of man whose time had come and there was nothing anyone could do, but wonder why.

An hour after the squad had settled in, shortly before midnight, everyone in the squad heard a weird muffled gunshot; it sounded neither incoming nor outgoing. No one could figure out what had made the strange gunshot sound.

No one moved; everyone remained silent, waiting to see what the muffled shot was all about while maintaining their silence. Off in the distance, Hill 65 fired off an illumination round. When it burst high in the air, its eerie glow revealed the body of the communications sergeant lying on his belly with the top of his head gone.

The sergeant had lain down on his M-16, put the barrel in his mouth, and pulled the trigger. As his body was on top of the gun and the bullet had immediately impacted inside his head, the sound had been muffled. The illumination flare revealed what the night had hidden. Kates' squad abandoned their ambush and assumed the unpleasant duty of carrying the communications sergeant's body back to Hill 65. As they moved through a small village on their way back, the men found a bamboo bed and placed the dead body on it; they carried the burden on their shoulders for a while. The bed and body were heavy and awkward to carry quietly through the night, and they realized they were making too much noise.

They stopped to rest; while Kates considered what to do, Doss picked up the body, slung it over his shoulder, and carried it along with his gear for some time. The weight of the body soon became too much, and since no one wanted to relieve Doss of his bloody burden, they stopped often for him to rest until they found a bomb crater on the left side of the road. It was too dangerous to continue to carry a dead man's body when the presence of the enemy could be very near. The men agreed to leave the body there for retrieval with a larger force at daylight.

At daylight, the squad returned along with other personnel assigned to radio battalion. When they searched the sergeant's body, they found a suicide note stating that if he could not marry his Vietnamese girlfriend and bring her back to America, life was not worth living. The sergeant had fallen in love with a local Vietnamese girl whose father did not approve of the relationship, and there also been a question as to the girl's involvement with the enemy. The sergeant's body was placed on top of an amtrack and taken back to the hill.[280]

No one could believe what the communications sergeant had done or why it had happened, not over a Vietnamese girl that may also have been a VC agent.

The only person I knew who had committed suicide was a classmate of mine when we were in fifth grade. We attended Catholic school together, and for some reason, he was living with his grandparents. One day when they came home, they found him hanging from a tree in their backyard. We lived only a couple of blocks from them, and I remember running over to the northeast corner of Second Street and Coolidge Avenue and standing there with other neighborhood kids seeing the body as it was taken down from the tree. Many believed it had been an accident and that he had been playing Batman and accidentally hanged himself.

The communications sergeant's message was clear; he had found out the Vietnamese girl he loved was a VC, so he placed the gun in his mouth and pulled the trigger. On Hill 65 it was the rear echelon Marines who gathered around to see the body of the sergeant taken down from the amtrack.

While the suicide was a bit unnerving, Marines got some laughter that day when they went to use the piss tubes just down the hill.

Someone had taped one of the glossy eight-and-a-half-by-eleven-inch full-color photographs of Captain Robb and Lynda Byrd Johnson's wedding around one of the piss tubes.

Kenneth Shawver—a short, solid Marine machine-gunner from First Platoon, Mike Company attached to us on Hill 65—said that Mike Marines as well as Marines from different companies enjoyed relieving themselves on the picture.

It was easy for tall Marines to hit it, but short Marines like Shawver had to stand on their tippy toes to get the right aim. The platoon of Mike Company Marines, were attached because of Captain Robb. They were, assigned the far north end of the hill to be held as a reserved platoon, just in case they were needed.

A Monopoly Game For Mamasan
Hill 65
May 14, 1968, 1300 hours

For the next three days, we built up our bunkers and reinforced our fighting positions on the hill. With mail call on the morning of the fourteenth, Aggie received a Monopoly game from home and immediately had an idea. Aggie always complained about how Mamasan's Cokes were priced too high. We paid a dollar for a twelve-ounce bottle of coke, and they were always weak with hardly any fizz in them. Aggie believed Mamasan watered them down, and then recapped them.

"Hey, guys, let's go down to Mamasan's and buy a Coke," he said, holding up a handful of the paper Monopoly money. "We'll tell her it's new MPC," he was serious about it, Rahm and I looked at each other wondering if it would work. We often haggled with Mamasan over the high price we had to pay for simple items like cigarettes, candles, a pen, writing paper, or simple cheap souvenir objects. There weren't many places once you arrived in country to shop around or to look for a good deal on a needed item. Mamasan's stand at the bottom of the hill was all we had and she also controlled the price vendors charged us when they came to the edge of the perimeter to sell us items. She always charged PFs and other customers ten to fifteen cents for a pack of smokes while we paid twenty-five to thirty cents for the pack.

With a note of hesitation in his voice, Aggie said, "Come on, let's go. It'll work." That type of persuasive argument was good enough for us, and off we went down to see Mamasan.

After haggling with her and settling on a price, we went to pay for all the items with the Monopoly money.

Mamasan looked at the money, held it up, and said, "No, this No. 10 (bad) money." We looked shocked.

"No, Mamasan," Aggie said, with a smooth tone in his voice that we figured he might have used to get girls back home to go out with him on a date. "This new MPC, new MPC, Number 1 (good)."

Rahm helped Aggie out by telling Mamasan that it was indeed new military payment certificates and that she should quickly get rid of the other MPC because soon it wouldn't be any good. Mamasan knew this had happened before; as governments changed, black market dealings with military payment certificates had caused a change in the design of our currency once before. She looked worried but wanted to make her sale she finally but reluctantly accepted the money.

"Okay," she said. "You not bullshit me? You give me your name," and she gave Rahm a piece of paper for him to write down our names for her. It was assurance to her that our money was legit. We left her hut with about $35 worth of goodies.

A couple of hours later, we saw her and Lieutenant Nowicki walking around the compound looking for the Marines that had given her the Monopoly play money. When she wasn't able to find the Marines, she said Nowicki was hiding the Marines and she wanted to speak to the captain.

Soon the word was passed around the compound for the Marines involved to fess up, and nothing would be done; they just wanted Mamasan reimbursed. Of course, no one went forward, and after a while, Captain Robb called for everyone on the hill to muster into formation including artillery, mortars, engineers, and anyone else assigned to Hill 65. Everyone fell into formation near the mess hall, on top of the hill.

Rahm, Aggie, and I were hiding by the side of our bunker seeing everything that was going on. Marines standing in formation found it amusing that someone finally got one over on Mamasan.

Mamasan, the captain, and our lieutenant went down the formation looking for the Marines, but she couldn't recognize any of those in formation as the ones that used Monopoly money instead of MPC or Vietnamese currency to buy her goods. To her we all looked the same.

"Sorry, Mamasan, maybe Marines from CAP unit," Nowicki said, hoping she would go away.

"No No," Mamasan answered. "CAP Marines Number 1, not bullshit Marines."

Just about the time when all was lost, she remembered she had the names of the Marines written down on a piece of paper. She gave the list to the lieutenant, but before he could read the names, Captain Robb quickly took it away from him and said loud enough for everyone in formation to hear: "All right, since these Marines did not come forward when they had the chance, I will read the names and I want these Marines to step forward. I will assure you that you will now be held accountable." Robb, with his head held high, began to read the names Rahm had written down for Mamasan.

"William Tell, Butch Cassidy—" Captain Robb never finished reading John Wayne's name before the whole formation had burst out in laughter.

Robb stopped reading, handed the list back to Nowicki and walked off, and the lieutenant escorted Mamasan off the hill while trying to explain to her who the historical American legends on the paper she held were.

Third Platoon One KIA, One WIA
Dodge City (AT 963603)
May 16, 1968, 1300 hours

On the morning of the sixteenth, Third Platoon went on a platoon-size sweep through Dodge City. They picked up a thirty-six-year-old Vietnamese detainee who was turned over to ITT. The platoon then continued south and, at 1500 hours, was hit with M-79 grenades and small arms fire. They returned fire and the enemy immediately broke contact, but not before Pfc. Ernest Perry was killed and another Marine, James R. Semple, was wounded. Both were medevaced to regiment. Captain Robb used the incident to request for regiment to allow him to take India Company on a sweep through the area.

Lima Company was to return to Hill 65 the following day and they would be going out on an operation the morning after, so the captain would have his company relieved of security duties. So on the morning of the seventeenth, we saddled up and were trucked to regiment for a company-size sweep through Dodge City.

Walking Point, Between Two Worlds
Dodge City
May 17, 1968, 1100 hours

As we headed out, Third Platoon took the lead, heading southeast off the bridge. We had gone about a klick when Third Platoon was hit with small arms weapons fire. The company responded with M-16s, M-79s, and the M-60s and the enemy broke contact.

As Third Platoon stood still, First Platoon moved forward to take the lead with Third Squad walking point. I had an uneasy feeling about the area and the direction we were heading so I pulled the point man back and took the point position myself. We moved out going southeast through Dodge City in an area we had patrolled through many times before. I was somewhat familiar with the area as we had encountered fierce firefights in that area before.

With the company following behind, I was in no hurry to get to where we were going. We were traveling counterclockwise, following a small trail toward the river.

In the Marine Corps, you are taught to keep your distance from each other and not to bunch up especially while you are out on patrol because of booby traps and ambushes. In Vietnam's dense forest, the recommended five- to fifteen-feet pace distance was extended to twenty to thirty feet, sometimes fifty to sixty for greater safety.

The area we were traveling through was covered with deep undergrowth, tall elephant grass, banana trees, and long vines that stretched out and crossed the narrow footpath we were following. To my right, waist-high elephant grass was intermixed with several clusters of small palm trees and tall bamboo stalks. We were following a footpath that ran along the side of a small creek. The creek flowed northward toward the Song La Tho River. On the other side of the creek was an area we called Boot Hill; it was a raised area full of graves. Beyond the cemetery was the never-used railroad that ran north toward Da Nang.

As I came around a narrow turn in the trail, there was a clear sense of danger present. The majority of First Platoon remained spread out behind me and I knew the enemy's presence was close, very close.

I slowed down the pace as did my squad and the company behind them. Sweat must have been pouring out of the enemy's sweat glands as the area reeked with the foul smell of unwashed body odor. It was the odor made when nervous sweat flowed over an unwashed, tired body. I couldn't tell if the smell was coming from our side or from an enemy force that had moved through the area just ahead of us. There was no mistaking the smell of sweat over dirty skin, but the smell of *nuoc nam* sauce seeping out of the enemy's skin pores, and the scent of fear they left behind was present in the air. A few seconds later, my mind became entirely alert. Perhaps it was fear or what warriors in the fields of battle call a second sense of danger, but there was this steady escalating sense that something was going to happen and it was going to happen soon.

There are many stories we've all heard of men and war about soldiers returning home from war telling of incidents that occurred that could not be explained by natural means. Some men received a warning in advance like Greg Vandewalle, who told Marty the night before he was killed that he knew he was going to die that night; his mother in Texas, waking from her sleep in the early morning hours that same day and saying that she heard her son call out to her and to his girlfriend and she knew he had been killed. Eight hours later, the Marine Corps officer arrived at her home with the sad news. The Marines in the battle at Finger Lake had felt that same sense of danger from early that morning.

Then there was the strange story of Timothy J. Sanderson, whom everyone called "TJ" because no one knew his real name. Sanderson, while standing watch on top of his bunker in the early morning hours on Hill 65, heard someone call out his full name: "Timothy Andrew John Sanderson, come down here!" TJ looked down from the top of the bunker but saw no one. A few minutes later, he heard his full name called out again, "Timothy Andrew John Sanderson, come down from there!" Still he saw no one, and no one in the Marines ever called him by his full name. He wondered if someone in his squad had gotten a hold of his military records, but he remembered his full name did not appear on them.

"Timothy Andrew John Sanderson, come DOWN HERE!" he heard the voice called out to him with such force that he felt compelled to comply even when he saw no one around. As he stepped down to look inside the bunker to see who was calling him, an RPG rocket struck where he had been sitting only split seconds before. There was no one in the bunker or around its base.

Moments like those are private moments when for some unknown reason—perhaps it's chance or divine intervention or an encounter in this world which we don't understand—the unexplainable occurs, and there is intervention of one source or another so that lives are spared or lost. What occurred to me would erase any doubts lingering in my mind concerning the existence of divine beings intervening in the affairs of men in this world. It not only made me a confirmed believer that there is a supreme being, I realized He does intercede in ways that are unexplainable. I was not a religious man in Vietnam; certainly I was not clean in God's eyes. I had not asked for forgiveness or tried to get myself squared away with Him for months. Only He knew how many of the enemy I had blindly shot at, wounded, or killed. I didn't regret that; The Lord's Prayer continued to be the only prayer I knew, and I didn't say that too often; mostly I recited the words when we jumped out of helicopters or set in for a night ambush. Once, months before, I had spent a lengthy period of time trying to dissect, trying to fully understand what the words in that prayer really meant. I had only gone to religious services twice since I arrived in Vietnam, and certainly I wasn't in the best state of grace as I moved down the trail.

When Time Stands Still
Dodge City
May 17, 1968, 1300 hours

I was about to take a step forward when time stood still. I had been walking forward but was now looking down at my left leg that appeared to be stuck in midair. It wasn't moving forward, and I was thinking to myself, *This is odd. Why isn't my foot moving forward? Why is it taking so long for it to move down?*

I noticed a silence all around me. A unique silence as if I had entered another dimension, a dimension without sound, without smells, without life, without time. Only my mind was functioning and everything else in the world all around me had stopped. My breathing seemed to have stopped. My heart stood still; it wasn't pounding. Time was standing still, but my mind was taking in—all in at once—a panoramic view of the whole area and my awareness of that state of consciousness startled me. I was aware of the situation I was in and was trying to figure it all out while my foot still remained in the air.

I then heard the impossible. On my right, I heard the hammer moving forward and striking the primer of a bullet. As I began to turn my head slowly in that direction, I heard the primer ignite the powder that exploded inside the bullet's casing. I then heard the rifling as the bullet turned inside the barrel and made its way forward. My head then began to turn away from the sound, and I heard the exploding sound the bullet made as it cleared the machine-gun's barrel and began to break through the air. While I was still taking all this in, I felt two powerful hands grab me from behind from the top of my shoulders, and I was yanked backward.

In that millisecond of life, time caught up with me, and I saw both of my feet fly out in front from under me. As I flew backward, twelve rounds of automatic machine-gun fire shattered a palm tree that was in a direct line of where I would have been standing had my foot continued to carry me forward.

I hit the ground so hard the M-16 rifle I had been carrying flew out of my hands and landed on the right side of the trail. I scrambled to get to it as our right flank exploded with carbine, machine-gun, and automatic AK-47 rifle fire. Grenades exploded up and down the trail and out toward our right front. We were in an ambush, and half the squad was smack in the middle of the kill zone with incoming fire coming in from in front of me and from our right front. [281] As I reached out and grabbed hold of the M-16 and released its safety, I turned to my right to see the Marine who had grabbed me from behind, but there was no one there.

The Marine that had been walking behind me was flat on his stomach crawling toward the edge of the trail getting into position to return fire. He was about sixty feet away. He looked my way and then opened fire at the enemy. The enemy's firepower was intense. It was coming in thick and fast: grenades and large explosions were blasting away part of the trail. Bushes and trees all around us and all along the trail for about 100 feet from the turn in the trail to where I was were all getting hit and we're being torn apart by the force of the incoming firepower. I opened up with my M-16 on full automatic and wished I had the M-60.

I slapped another magazine into the flimsy plastic rifle's magazine well and opened up again semiautomatic, but by then the major onslaught was beginning to die down. The NVA, for some reason, just stopped firing and broke contact. Seconds later, only single shots were being fired in our direction. They were the rear security the enemy often left behind to harass and delay us from following after them. Those sniper rounds were being fired at the turn in the trail to keep reinforcement from coming around to help us. That delaying tactic gave the enemy the time they needed for the main NVA unit to disappear into the jungle. A few minutes later, it was all over. It had ended just as quickly as it had started.

I crawled my way over to where the Marine that had been behind me was. He was taking out a new magazine from the cloth bandolier strapped around his chest. He had expended four twenty-round magazines in that short firefight. I had shot three magazines and half of another one. As the rest of the company then moved up, Second Platoon passed us; they were now taking the lead.

"Hey, thanks for pulling me back," I said to the Marine that was looking at me as if he was seeing a ghost.

"I didn't pull you back," he said, denying anything at all connected with what had happened. I realized, as he continued talking, he really wasn't anywhere near me when the firing started. He had been a good distance away. "I saw the bullets hit the tree to your left about the same time I saw you flying backward. I thought you were a goner with that many bullets hitting you.

You're not hit?" he asked in disbelief. The Marine was looking at me as if I was a ghost. He looked at my flak jacket, my chest, looking to see where the blood should be and where the bullets had struck me. "I thought the bullets that struck you had thrown you backward," he continued. "Man, that's weird! I saw the first volley of bullets hit you and throw you backward. Man, you went flying backward. I saw you hit before I heard the sound of the bullets and I hit the deck. I was going to run up to you and call for the corpsman then I saw you return fire." He kept looking at me in disbelief, shaking his head. "Man, you're one lucky guy," he said and wondered why I was still alive.

I realized he wasn't lying; he wasn't near me when the firefight started. I remembered that seconds after the first rounds were fired that he was flat on the ground, a good distance away, and returning fire. I recalled that just before I opened fire, I was wondering how he had gotten so far away from me in such a short time. But if it wasn't him that pulled me back, who did? At first, I didn't want to contemplate or understand what had actually happened. I didn't want to be beholden to anyone, not even God. I filed it away in the back of my mind—what had happened?

Did I now owe God one for saving my life that day? Was a divine being sent there to yank me back? How could I have escaped without getting hit? I didn't want to think about it, but still I wondered. I wondered if one day I would end up in heaven and be held accountable for the life I had lived since then since the day the Lord spared my life. Perhaps one day the Lord himself would meet me at heaven's door and show me how he had taken care of me throughout life; he would then take me over to a side room and there I would find a room full of wounded spiritual beings all bandaged up, mangled, and crippled—angels who had taken hits for me in life. I wondered if that's the way it happens in that other world. We had gone out in search of the enemy, and I had survived and so had the others. We took no casualties that day, and for that I was grateful. I never thought of thanking God for that day.

First Platoon stood down as the rest of the company maneuvered around us. A short time later, a Third Platoon squad on our right flank engaged the enemy in a brief exchange of gunfire.

An hour later, the enemy opened fire again at the point platoon with about 300 rounds of small arms and 60mm mortar fire from across the river, a fire mission was called in from regiment, and the enemy broke contact and fled, and we returned to battalion and I wondered how today's battle would be written in Marine Corp history.[289]

Battalion Mortared During The Day
Hill 37
May 19, 1968, 1525 hours

On the afternoon of the nineteenth, battalion was hit with ten 82mm mortar rounds from three different positions coming from the northeast corner of the Arizona area; at the same time, the army advisors' headquarters in Dai Loc was also hit with six 82mm mortar rounds. At battalion, one Marine was wounded; at the army compound, a PF and a U.S. Army soldier were also wounded. It was Ho Chi Minh's birthday and the enemy was celebrating.

Working Parties
Hill 65
May 22, 1968, 2000 hours

Between the twentieth and the twenty-second, the men from the squad were sent out on working parties on Hill 65. Most of their duties were to repair loose perimeter wire on the east side of the hill.

The night of the twenty second, I took my squad out on a night ambush. We set in at the bottom of Hill 65, there was no contact

Road Sweeps
Route 4 to Hill 52
May 23-24, 1968, 2200 hours

For the next two days, the squad, was assigned to accompany amtracks, on road sweeps to a halfway point where we met Charley 1/7 Marines. They would then take command and escort the minesweeping detail on to Thuong Duc. On the first day as we passed Hill 25, the engineers found a mine which they blew in place.

The following day was another road sweep detail and another hookup with the platoon from Charley Company.

Platoon-Size Night Ambush
Near Song Vu Gia
May 24, 1968, 2200 hours

After running a road sweep on the twenty-fourth, Boone returned and I was relieved of my Third Squad leadership responsibility. That night we saddled up and went out on a platoon-size ambush, traveling south before settling in near the Song Vu Gia River.

Just to the right of us and on the other side of the river was the village of My Hiep (2), the area was a favorite spot for the NVA/VC to cross over from the Arizona territory under the cover of darkness.

The night went without incident until just before daybreak when we got hit with small arms and automatic weapons fire from across the river. Fierce incoming fire was being directed at us from an extensive length of tree line between the villages of My Hiep (2) and My Hiep (4).

Other than the M-60, the distance was too far for the M-16s to be effective. Monte Gennai fired a couple of M72 LAWs (light antitank weapon) into the entrenched enemy's position as did Marines carrying the M-79 grenade launchers. The lieutenant then called in 81mm high explosive and Willie Peter rounds on the enemy target, and the incoming stopped.[283]

Enemy activity was increasing in the area. Squads on patrols were making more and more contact. Not only in our area but all around us, Marines compounds were being hit almost daily.

Successful Ambush
Hill 65 AT 880557,
May 26, 1968, 0350 hours

On the morning of May 26, First Squad set in on an ambush site, just a little east of where the platoon had set up a few nights before. This time the squad purposely set up at the river's edge. For five hours they sat silent and waited. At about 0200 hours, when the enemy knew that most Marine airships were no longer running, the VC decided to cross over the river a short distance from where the ambush site was located. First Squad counted ten enemy soldiers in the water—three in the boat and seven holding on to it—as the boat crossed north from the Arizona territory toward the ambush site.

The Marines could see only one visible weapon, an AK-47; the rest of the weapons were in the boat, and all the soldiers were dressed in black shorts and shirts. The enemy reached the shoreline and pulled the boat from the water. When they were fifteen meters from the ambush site, the Marines opened fire, killing all ten enemy soldiers. When they moved in to search the bodies, they heard movement to their right flank and decided to move out of there as soon as possible and called in a 105mm fire mission.[284] It was one of the most successful ambushes the company had had in a very long time.

First Platoon In Suicide Position
Hill 65, AT 880557
May 26, 1968, 0800 hours

At first light, Lieutenant Nowicki ordered the squad back to the ambush site to retrieve the enemies' weapons that had been left behind. The squad arrived at 0745 hours, and found two bodies still at the ambush site; both were floating in the water along the river's edge. No gear or weapons were found.

At 0800 hours, the rest of the platoon arrived at the ambush site and the lieutenant dispersed the platoon along the river's bank to search for enemy weapons, equipment, or dead bodies. We found some enemy gear, and the lieutenant had us move northwest along the river's bank, following a small trail. When we got to a cleared area, we stopped, but the lieutenant had us move on again out in the open with no cover and out the sandy shoreline that kept getting bigger and bigger as we moved along the river's bank and away from any covering. Before we got to the next batch of tropical covering near the river's bank, the enemy began to fire on us with small arms sniper fire from a carbine in the tree line on the other side of the river.

At first, the incoming was distant and ineffectual. We continued to move along the river's bank without returning fire. Then a pair of AK-47s opened up on us, full automatic, and I dropped and returned fire with the M-60.

Ten seconds later, the first rounds of the enemy's fire were hitting at the water's edge, and we were still out in the open. It was only then that the lieutenant decided to get us out of there. Out of the open sand and back to the tree line. By then, we were receiving more automatic rifle fire, and machine gun fire and the platoon started to scramble for a distant tree line some two hundred meters away.

Seconds later, the distinct sound of a round coming out of a mortar tube was heard and the mortars began to impact at the tree line, which we were running toward.

Third Squad, no longer under my command, was sticking close to my gun team as we ran out from the river's edge. Aggie and I provided cover for them and we all leapfrogged our way back out from the river's bank to the nearest tree line north of us.

The incoming fire continued to increase; Custer and Doss, with one of the other squads, stopped, set up, and opened fire, covering for us as we moved our gun back. We then set up about fifty meters past them and covered for them. We were all running about fifty meters then stopping, turning around, and opening fire to cover for other Marines as they ran and made their way back from the river's edge.

The sand was soft and deep and hard to run on with the gun's weight on my shoulder and about a hundred rounds of ammo connected to it. Third Squad pretty much stayed alongside my gun team as we ran across the open sandy beach. By the time we got halfway across, I was completely out of breath as were the other Marines all around me. Then we stopped, turned around, and covered for the other gun team and the rest of the platoon.

They got up and this time ran past us and made it all the way to the tree line; there they turned and opened fire on the enemy, covering for us.

We were still very much out in the open and a perfect target for Charlie. Bullets were striking the ground close to where we were running, and they were kicking up sand to my immediate right front and rear. I started to think, *Hey, this is just like in the John Wayne movies, running in the sand while bullets kick up sand all around us.*

We continued leapfrogging in this manner until we got tree line, then we stopped and turned right to go through an opening that led up an embankment to Route 4 where the CP had gathered. Third Squad moved up the embankment while Second Squad provided cover. First Squad was to our right, and they also got up to follow my gun team. As I turned, swinging the gun over my right shoulder, another series of sniper rounds struck the ground near me so I stepped back. Then I heard another sniper round fired as I turned to move out.

At that same time, Michael Murphy, a new man in First Squad, stepped in between the sniper and me.

They say you never hear the bullet that gets you; I heard the impact of the round meant for me as it struck Murphy, and he tumbled and fell forward, sliding in the sand as his limp body struck the ground. I dropped down on my knees to see where he was hit and to help get him out of there. It was a head wound, and he wasn't moving. Monty and Rahm ran over, grabbed him, and we all moved into the tree line and onto the edge of Route 4 where amtracks had gathered to pick us up. There was nothing we could do for Murphy. He was our only casualty that day, but it was a heavy loss. He had just showed us a picture of his four-month-old baby girl, a daughter who would never know her father.

Off in the distant tree line, across the river, artillery rounds began to fall at the river's edge from where we had taken fire from; it was no comfort for the pain and sorrow we were all feeling.

Time For Tired Aggie To Go Home
Hill 65
May 27, 1968, 1300 hours

We went out as security for a road sweep to Hill 52 on the twenty-seventh and on ambushes at night around Hill 65 on the twenty-eighth.[285] It was Tired Aggie's last patrol.

The following morning, he was assigned to mess duty and was to await his orders and flight ticket home.

On the night of the twenty-ninth, we sat around and talked about all the things he was going to do when he got home. The food he was going to eat, the movie shows he was going to watch, and the girls he was going to make out with or have sex with without having to pay them five dollars for the pleasures.

CHAPTER TWENTY-SIX

Convoy To Destruction
No Name Village
May 30, 1968, 1300 hours

Word came down for us to saddle up; we would be escorting a twenty-truck convoy halfway to Hill 52. Charley Company 1/7 was going to meet us halfway, and we would be turning over the convoy to them just as we had been doing for the past week during our road sweeps. This time, however, we would be riding on amtracks and only one squad would be going out with the convoy as a platoon of PFs were to join us and they were to continue on to the Thuong Duc Special Forces Camp. With Aggie gone, I was taking the gun, and Rahm was going to A-gun for me.

The amtracks pulled out and assembled on top of the hill. We climbed on board and settled down as the amtracks rattled on. At the bottom of the hill was a twenty-truck convoy with a tank on each end. The platoon of PFs joined us there, getting on board some of the trucks ahead of us. We fell into the tail end of the convoy and traveled west on Route 4.

Because the area had already been cleared of mines up through Hill 25, we rode and there was no need for us to put out Marines walking flank. Once we got past Hill 25, we would disembark and with the PF platoon leading, sweep to the halfway point.

Part of Third Squad was riding on the same amtrack with Rahm and me. As we moved out, the amtrack's treads churned the loose ground, leaving a trail of dust behind us. I was glad that our gun team was on the first amtrack behind the trucks. Already I could see behind us that the second amtrack was being covered with the dirt and filth that we were leaving behind. A couple of Marines wrapped towels over their mouths, and others sat facing backward to avoid the dust.

As we approached a large village, we disembarked to walk on both sides of the road. I couldn't help but discern the noticeable difference between the village we were approaching and the other villages that we had passed along the route. The village ahead was shrouded by a large tree line that hid dark hatred behind

606

bamboo fences and uninviting hooches. The village was more progressive than those around it. Its people were clothed in cleaner, whiter clothing, and most of its huts had aluminum sheet roofs unlike the straw roofing of most hooches alongside of Route 4. A tall barbed wire fence linked thick bamboo poles and shrubs together that outlined and separated the village from the road. The thick long bamboo fence surrounding the village reminded me of the King Kong movie, where the villagers had erected the fence to keep the gorilla out. Only a few openings existed as entrances to the village, and they were not inviting. Inside the village were other fences and barriers designed to be used as defensive fighting positions by the enemy.

It was a secluded village at the edge of the world: a village that straddled the fence between good and evil, between darkness and light, fear and refuge, hope and despair, a village hidden in the shadows of the crossroad that led nowhere. We called it No Name Village.

Mike Company Marines had often told us how snipers as well as a woman sniper would shot at them from the village when they were stationed on Hill 52, knowing the company would not respond with mortars or an air-strike. Each time during the past road sweeps, when we passed the village, some of the villagers looked at us with open disdain while others would count the trucks going by and the troops in them. It was evident the side this village had chosen in the pursuit of life and death and they had sided with the enemy. As I walked along the side of the road nearest the village, I could sense the danger, the anger, and a spirit of open hatred. I saw it in the eyes of the Vietnamese standing by the road or near the entrances to their village.

No Name Village was of limited use to the enemy as it was often patrolled by Marines. A well-known trail led from the village north to Charlie Ridge and south into the Arizona territory.

On the north side of the road, a tree line 100 feet deep with hooches scattered throughout rested at the base of Charlie Ridge. In front of the tree line were rice paddies as well as clear, open fields.

On the south side of the road where the village began was a thick cluster of tall bamboo with a small clearing farther south then thick jungle behind that. Southwest the tree line was also thicker—a tropical jungle made up the heart of the tree line that was some 300 meters in thickness, followed by about two hundred meters of sand in an open area extending to the edge of the Song Vu Gia River. The river had changed courses several times, and gaps in the sand made good hiding places for the enemy to move through the area at night.

As we approached the midpoint of the village where the marketplace sat along the edge of the road, it was surprisingly quiet. Instead of being busy as it had been days before, now there was no one around. No children or old folks lining the road asking for handouts. Something wasn't right: no one was sitting and spitting tobacco juice along the road.

As we passed each of the few openings into the tightly fenced village, only a few old men or some women with babies in their arms stood silently watching and their heads slowly moving up and down, counting as we walked by. I recognized the old woman that Jones had once told us was an enemy sympathizer.

"If you give these people anything, more than likely it'll end up in Charlie's belly," Jones had once said. There was uneasiness in the air and a real sense of danger that could be felt. The VC/NVA used the villagers to move supplies through the area and sometimes they stayed in the village for a period of time while the villagers provided them with food, shelter, labor, and service. It was a Communist-controlled village with no PFs in it nor any friendlies nearby.

Behind me, a Marine stopped at one of the small entrances to the village where a few old women holding babies were standing. All the babies were crying, and the Marine took his rifle and struck one of the women across the face with his rifle's butt. She went flying backward, and the baby fell on the ground.

Doc Keller, who had been walking some distance behind the Marine, saw him hit the woman and ran up to him in a rage, demanding angrily, "Why did you do that?"

"The women are all pinching the babies to make them cry," he told Keller. It's a signal to the enemy that we are in the village. Doc Keller now stared in angry disbelief at the older woman who had gotten up without a word and picked up the fallen infant. The bleeding woman hushed the baby, and the other women at the village entrance did the same. All of a sudden, the absence of the babies' crying was disturbing.

It was not like that in other villages along Route 4. Typically the villagers were more open to Marines and supportive of the South Vietnamese government. Some were genuinely content to see us around, if for nothing else to sell us some merchandise. The difference between the friendly, peaceful villages and No Name Village was noticeable. The villagers there had resisted any government involvement in their lives.

When I first arrived in country—what seemed like a decade ago—a lone jeep could easily travel the area without fear of an enemy encounter. The fact that we now had to escort a large convoy through the area was an indication of how the area had changed, how greatly the enemy had infiltrated into the area.

As we neared the village's edge, the feeling that something was about to happen was present. You knew it was going to happen, and all you could do was just wait for the first bullet to be fired. I dropped the M-60 from my shoulder to my hip, expecting for the firefight to begin.

Just then Charley Company 1/7 Marines met us, and we turned the escort security service over to them. They only had three klicks to go before they would be clear of the tree line and most of the danger zone.

As soon as the convoy continued on, we were loaded back on board the amtracks and started back. The amtracks didn't bother to turn around in the narrow roadway; they just traveled backward or forward—it all depended upon how you looked at things.

We were about halfway back to Hill 65 when the amtracks stopped suddenly and the driver informed us the convoy had gotten ambushed.

Convoy Ambushed
No Name Village AT 810545
May 30, 1968, 1400-1920 hours

At 1400 hours, VMO-2, HMLA-167, piloted by Major Sandson and copilot Major Newton, had departed Hill 55 and were flying over Charlie Ridge when they received a call the truck convoy was under attack, and if they could assist. As they flew overhead, they could see the enemy firing at our forces. When they turned to come in lower, they also began to receive incoming fire and they returned machine-gun and rocket fire at the entrenched enemy soldiers.

The truck convoy was getting hit by hard-core NVA soldiers, and the radio was squeaking loudly about enemy forces advancing toward the trucks. Battalion by then had ordered us back while other Marine units were alerted to also respond to the call for assistance. "Every truck in the convoy has taken hits—they're stopped, unable to move," the amtrack driver told us, reporting what he was hearing over the radio net.

The chatter on the radio wasn't revealing how many were dead or wounded or how large an enemy force they had encountered. The urgent call for additional Marine units could be heard over the radio, as well as the sound of gunfire in the background.

In the back of my mind, I thought of the 125 NVA soldiers we had been searching for in the area just a few days before. If they were the attackers, we were going to be in for a fierce and long firefight.

The amtrack drivers gunned their engines, and the tracks moved on the road at a fast pace. Rahm and I moved the gun forward to be near where the Amtrak driver was seated. The amtrack we were riding on was now the lead track, and we would be the first to arrive at the site.

"Two tanks were hit with RPGs," the driver of the amtracks yelled out, loud enough for us to hear above the uproar and the noise the tracks were making. Tanks from Thuong Duc are also responding, he added.[286] This gave additional information on what to expect.

As we neared the ambush site, it seemed as if the majority of the firefight was going on about two hundred feet in front of the last truck in the column, about six to ten trucks up. The rapid report of the gunfire could be heard being exchanged both ways.

Bullets began to rip through the air over our heads and strike the amtrack's metal body. As soon as the amtracks stopped, we all jumped off to the right side of the road. A concentrated volume of incoming fire was coming at us from the left side of the road.

Protected by the armored body, I moved on the ground toward the front corner of the amtrack. Bullets were flying by in rapid succession. I turned to look to my left: Marines were trying to cross the road to the south side in order to engage the enemy from their left flank, but they were being met by a volley of heavy incoming automatic gunfire, striking the edge of the road where they had found cover. The front amtrack opened up with their .30 caliber gun, and the whole area erupted anew in an explosive discharge of massive destruction. Grenades exploded on the other side of the track, while bullets were striking the gunner's metal plate protection and ricocheting every which way. Marines were dodging as much incoming from the bouncing bullets as the fierce fire the enemy was unleashing at us.

Fiery green tracers were striking the amtracks, and I wanted to get away from the metal giants as quickly as possible. Charlie had figured we would be responding, and we rode right into his plans. I could see Marines up ahead on the right side of the road. They were returning fire at the enemy as best as they could, but their fire zones were limited. They were lower than the entrenched enemy who was firing down on them from across the roadway. I could see no advantageous position for me to return fire from along the road up ahead.

Although most of the incoming was from the left side of the road, we were also getting incoming sniper fire from our right rear. Rahm, as soon as he jumped off the amtrack, was busy giving directions to Marines that were returning fire at the snipers. Unless the snipers were taken out, we would be in a cross fire. Charlie had planned the ambush and had anticipated our response very well. With enemy snipers stationed to engage responding units, it seemed their plan was to keep us pinned down while the rest of the Marines from the convoy continued to be heavily engaged by the main enemy force ahead of us.

Third Squad Marines ran past me along the right side of the road toward the tail end of the convoy. I joined them, running while carrying the gun by its handle. We ran, ignoring for the most part the bullets and the fierce onslaught of explosive discharges occurring all around us. No sooner had I left the secured position behind the amtrack than it was impacted by an RPG round.

Sizzling hot shrapnel flew past us, striking the rear wheels and tailgate of the last truck in the convoy. As we moved in deeper into the kill zone, bullets were ricocheting all over the road, bouncing up and striking the trucks' undercarriages, slamming into the inside rims of the trucks' tires. Every once in a while, you would hear glass break as bullets struck the trucks' windshields or side windows.

Up ahead of us, mortar rounds and grenades were tearing up the road's hard surface on both sides of the trucks. As a high-explosive round struck the cab of one of the trucks, glass was shattered every which way, shards of glass went flying into the air and sharp broken pieces of glass were embedded into the road's hard surface. Bullets and grenades were being thrown at Marines from a wall of enemy soldiers set in on the opposite side of the road.

Besides the visible damage I could see to the trucks, it appeared as if some bodies of dead Marines or PF's were still sitting in the trucks; it was evident both the drivers and shotgun riders had been the target in the initial attack. Some of the trucks in formation seemed to have tried to get off the road, but there was an edge there and they would have overturned had they done so. The truck drivers at least had the presence of mind to hold steady in the face of all that incoming fire, and I wondered how many of them had been killed or wounded. Other than the physical damage, the trucks seemed to be ready to roll except they had no drivers in them.

The NVA soldiers were heavily entrenched on the left side of the road. The majority of Charley Company Marines, I figured, must be on the right side up ahead where most of the fierce firefighting was going on. The embankment on that side of the road was low and steep and useless to return fire from. In order to fire back at the enemy from that position, a Marine would have to have his upper body exposed or lie flat out on the roadway. Neither position was inviting especially since the truck's right side wheels rested close to the road's edge, and that area was being heavily peppered with incoming rounds.

Still, Marines were returning fire as best as they could. Some were using the trucks' wheels as cover; others were just flipping their rifles over the edge of the road and, without having to expose themselves to direct enemy fire were blindly returning fire.

There is something about what can be found in war; duty, pride, honor, courage, commitment and fear. Sometimes these things are very different; sometimes they are the very essence of strength, fortitude, and the willingness to fight and die for others. Fear is very much a part of war; it is often best overcome by ignorance. You ignore the fear by embracing its spirit. You grab a hold of it, wrap yourself in the splendor of its presence, hold on to the power terror holds, and ride the waves of death and destruction with laughter and honor because the fear of death has not gotten hold of your soul.

I did not know the strength of our enemy or the weakness of our side; all I could see in front of me were little green tracers and bright, shiny red ones changing sides in the battle zone on the roadway up ahead; I needed to be there, I craved to be in the center of the turmoil to dance with death and sing my song. Grenades were exploding furiously all around us, yet I was not afraid; adrenaline rushed through my veins, a sense of determination, and painful memories and the experiences gained from fighting in war urged me forward and I ran with speed and unknown strength, while the angel of death at my side, laughed with pride.

I ran along the right side of the trucks at the very edge of the road, running faster between the gaps and space between one truck and another, jumping over Marines huddled like little balls up against wheel wells. I ran until the explosive force of a mortar round, knocked me to the ground.

The enemy continued to unleash a hail of machine-gun fire from the left as well as rocket-propelled grenades, mortars, and automatic rifle fire; and I hadn't yet reached the center of the turmoil.

Most of the firepower was incoming from the left side of the road, and very little was being returned. It had been a half an hour since the enemy first hit the convoy. Had Charley Company Marines been pinned down all that time? How big was the enemy force? I was approaching the midst of the storm and it was time to respond, but from where?

Metal fragments and sharp pieces of burning shrapnel whirred, buzzed, and kicked up dust and dirt in front and to my left side—pieces of metal were being shot off the trucks and from beneath the undercarriage. I was huddled against a truck's wheel looking for cover as shrapnel sailed off in a dozen or so different directions. Twenty feet ahead, I could see Marines trying to fire back, but the incoming was so intense that they could not raise their heads high enough to be able to respond. Some Marines were taking turns flipping their rifles over the embankment and popping off caps in short small bursts. They were firing back against the enemy's powerful AK-47 with M-16's and the comparison was distressing.

Up ahead, I saw a Marine firing his weapon on selective fire, targeting enemy soldier across the road. He was lying prone with little covering out in the open between the trucks. I ran and slid up against the front tire of a truck and slid my back up against the rim and looked at the Marine. He looked up at me, gave me a thumbs-up, and we both chuckled; he knew what I was going to do, so he slipped a full magazine into his weapon and switched to full automatic fire and unleashed a twenty-round burst. As soon as he fired away, I ran by him just as the last of the bullets left his weapon. I was running across the clearing and never looked back, just dove for cover under a truck, picked a target across the road that was returning fire at the Marine, and opened fire. I was using the truck's left rear wheel as covering. One of the Marines from Third Squad was still with me and had found cover behind the truck's wheel well. As soon as he saw my ammo was almost gone, he unhooked one of the 200-round belts he had been carrying and threw it to me. I hooked up the belt, straightened it out, and held the trigger down, ripping the edge of the roadway, where the enemy was looking for targets until some of the enemies' incoming fire subsided a bit.

Reactionary Force From Hill 65
No Name Village AT 810545
May 30, 1968, 1400-1920 hours

By now, the word had been passed for the remaining squads from First Platoon on Hill 65 to saddle up to respond as a reactionary force to where we were. Tired Aggie, assigned to the mess tent, had just gotten off duty and was released for the rest of the day. He already had a flight date and was to leave the next day for battalion and then the following day to Da Nang to catch his flight home when the platoon sergeant came to the mess hall and told him to saddle up.

As Aggie stepped out to go get his gear, the mess hall commander told the platoon sergeant that Aggie was no longer assigned to First Platoon and he was not going to allow him to go.

After a while, the incoming rounds being shot in my direction were growing in intensity. I knew I had to get out of where I was under the truck.

The Third Squad Marine handed me another 100 rounds of machine-gun ammo then slid down the right side of the road and joined forces with Charley Company Marines.

He was now engaged in firing on the enemy's position to my right.

I slid out from under the truck as the incoming continued to increase. The majority of fire being shot at us was machine gun fire coming from my right front, and I would only be able to effectively engage their fire by moving up and to my right. I would then be in the heart of the battle.

As I slid down the right side of the road, I caught a glimpse of a body still seated or slumped over the steering wheel of the truck I had been firing under. A Marine sat bleeding on the side of the road, propped up against the back side of the truck's right front tire. He looked scared; a corpsman lying on the right side of the embankment was trying to urge him to slide down the embankment so he could help him, but the Marine was too scared to move. The incoming fire remained relentless, powerful, and constant bullets were striking the ground all around him. I had never been under such intense incoming fire and extreme danger all at once; it seemed I was in the center of an ever-increasing firefight. It was impossible to distinguish or recognize the different sounds the various weapons made on either side of the road.

I slid down to the bottom of the embankment on our side of the road, grateful for its protection that shielded me from the enemy's fire. Other Marines were there tending to the wounded, reloading or changing their magazines, then inching their way back up to fire again at the enemy.

When I was near the center of where I had seen the fierce incoming fire coming from, I began slowly moving back up the embankment with the M-60 and immediately Marines from Charley 1/7 began passing what M-60 ammo they could find in my direction.

To my right, an M-79 grenadier from Charley Company with his back up against the steep embankment was snapping shut the barrel of his grenade launcher. He lowered the sight slightly, turned, and fired off another round. He then unsnapped the barrel lock, took out the expended round, chambered another round, then slid the slide down farther a couple of clicks, turned, sighted in, and fired again. Twelve empty M-79 casing rounds lay at his feet. The M-79 grenades' impact when they exploded on the other side of the road could not be heard above the roar and clamor of the shards of flying metal and explosive charges violently exploding and shaking the ground underneath us. The hard-pressed ground on the surface of the road was being torn apart by the intensity of the enemy's bullets; I could feel the earth's move below us.

The onslaught of incoming fire demanded a response, and as a Marine provided covering fire, I was able to move up onto the road then crawl my way to a position behind the left front tire of a truck and I prepared to open fire. There was no room for an A-gunner to join me; if he did, he would be exposed to enemy fire. I didn't know where Rahm was or where the other Marines from Third Squad were located. I only hoped that they were all right. I prepared to act as my own A-gunner using the system I had developed over the months in country. Not once while under heavy enemy fire had a Marine acted as my A-gunner in the position the Marine Corps trained the A-gunner to be in during a firefight. To A-gun for a machine-gunner that is firing away at the enemy is too dangerous a position to be in when the enemy targets the gun with intense return fire.

Since the death of Bro, I was the only machine-gunner in our platoon that had a 0331 MOS except for James who was on R&R. I always wondered whatever happened to Eddie Williams; he was assigned to guns for a while. He was with us on Operation Rock and was medevaced because of heat exhaustion, and we hadn't seen or heard from him since. We were undermanned in the machine-gun squad. If we needed an A-gunner, one was sometimes supplied by the squads; normally he would be assigned as an ammo carrier.[287] For the most part, the platoons' regular riflemen, especially those who had seen combat and knew the gun's destructive firepower, willingly carried extra machine-gun ammo for the gun, and some often moved into the A-gunners position if they were needed there.

Right now, we didn't have another gun team in First Platoon. Two days before the two Marines that had been assigned to the gun team with Rahm on the morning of the fifth when I shot and killed the NVA lieutenant had been returned to the squads where they had come from.

I wondered if the rest of Third Squad and Rahm remained pinned down at the edge of the tree line back where the amtracks had stopped, and I wondered how they were doing.

This battle was different; it was vicious, full-blown, intense, and destructive. It was as fierce as if all the battle scenes in all the movies, all the training exercises, and all the combat situations I had seen, heard, felt or been involved in, was all at once rolled into one mean-spirited firefight.

This was a firefight for death and with death. Here, there was no mercy to be showed on either side. I pulled in the gun and opened fire.

When I was about nine years of age, I remember my uncle Manuel visiting his sister, my mother, while all dressed up in his sharp green army uniform. His chest was full of colorful ribbons and silver medals. I was so proud of him and I prayed that when I grew up there would be a war going on somewhere in the world so that I would be able to join the military service and fight. When I came of age, the war in Vietnam was there for me. I could have waited and gotten drafted or joined any one of the armed services, but I had joined the Marine Corps instead of the army because I figured that I would sooner or later end up in Vietnam and in war and I wanted to be among the best trained for war so I would survive.

It wasn't until I was in the corps that I found out that the Marine Corps was always the first military unit called into a hot area. But I had been trained for that and now I was deep in the heat of battle.

As I opened fire, I realized we were playing ping-pong with the death angel, and the foul-smelling demon crossed back and forth as often as he pleased. As the last round was fired through the gun, the incoming fire had grown so intense and so many grenades were exploding all around me that I decided not to reload and instead pulled the gun in and crawled back down the embankment, and welcomed the rest.

Above us, a gunship piloted by Captain Dennison and copilot Captain Barksdale were exchanging fire with the enemy. Their crew chief and gunners had expended over twelve thousand M-60 machine-gun rounds as well as thirty-nine rockets. They had also called in two air strikes on the enemy force; on board with them on this trip was a civilian by the name of Hugh Van Ness, a photographer and correspondent for NBC, and he was clicking away taking pictures of the battle scene.

Returning Fire
No Name Village AT 810545
May 30, 1968, 1400-1920 hours

With the fierce fighting still going on, I knew I had to get back into battle. I needed to get back to finish the job. I reloaded the last 100 rounds of gun ammo I had and asked for more from Charley Company Marines. I had long ago used the 100-round belt gunners carry around their chests. A Marine lance corporal came up with two hundred rounds and said he would look for more. As I began to slowly crawl back to the edge of the road, a Marine crawled over to my left side just a little below the top of the road. I gave him a 100-round belt and buried my head at the edge of the road while the bullets were flying by. The Marine was checking the bullets attached to my gun for long or short rounds. Another Marine handed him another 100-round belt; "That's all I could find," he said. We moved over to our left where we could use some cover provided by the wheel well of one of the trucks.

I did not recognize any of the Marines around me. They must have been Charley Company Marines or Marines from the truck convoy. They were Marines and we were all one unit that day, and that's all that mattered. I wondered where their machine-gunners were. Perhaps the men were all seasoned Marines that had experienced war and knew the power the M-60 could unleash. They didn't know me, but they seemed to know the power of the gun and they needed its firepower to get their dead and wounded out of the gates of hell. The gun was needed in order for us to gain fire superiority. With four-hundred rounds, we could do that.

Aggie, after leaving the mess hall, had ventured over to the Eleventh Marines Battery CP to listen to what was going on with us and the convoy. He couldn't hear anything from our squad coming over the radio net, and as he was about to get up and leave, he heard a squad leader with Charley 1/7 calling for a resupply of M-60 ammo for a machine-gunner from India 3/7.

With the A-gunner and myself protected slightly by a truck's wheel off to our left, I pulled the gun in tight, dropped my cheek up against its side, and flipped my arm to hold the ammo up, sighted in where I could see the green tracers were coming from and with a clear shot at them in between trucks, I opened fire across the road, my bullets striking dead center of where the main enemy firepower was coming from. I was shooting at them from an angle, and it was very effective.

This time the noise the gun made was mute compared to the fierce firefight that was still going on. I could barely hear my own gun because of the explosive fire fight that surrounded us, both incoming and outgoing. Grenades were exploding with rage all around us while recoilless-rifle fire were striking the trucks that remained abandoned on the roadway other rounds were flying past the trucks and exploding in the open fields behind us or embedding themselves in small trees or bushes on our side of the road. The sound of mortars firing or exploding in the open field behind us could be heard, and I could no longer tell if they were incoming or outgoing; it was hard to tell which was which.

The firefight continued to grow in intensity, and soon it was so severe that I could no longer hear the mortars exploding; only the earth shaking under my prone body could be felt when they exploded. The firefight was vicious, and it was all being executed with great bitterness and hatred from both sides.

As my bullets struck the enemy's entrenched position, green and white tracers flew every which way. I held back the trigger and continued to fire at the heart of the enemy's position, sweeping, covering a thirty-yard area. The bullets ripped apart what concealment the enemy had, and seconds later, there was an explosion where my red tracers had been hitting.

I continued to fire and swept the gun's fire back and forth as much as I could before the ground under the truck's carriage exploded into a fiery ball, jerking the gun away from me. Both the Marine from Charley Company and I slid back down the embankment as the area we had been in was now being shattered anew with intense enemy ground fire and incoming grenades being fired from directly across the roadway.

We looked at each other; both of us were okay. We looked at where we had been and were surprised at the intensity of the incoming bullets that were crisscrossing and striking the area we had been just seconds before the explosion. Had we remained where we had been, both of us would have been hit several times.

I removed the short belt of ammo remaining, dropped another 100-round belt, and pulled back the gun's cocking handle and prepared to fire once more. I looked at the Marine that had been there at my side. He looked scared, drained, his eyes filled with uncertainty. I crawled back up the embankment, moving farther to my right and got as close as I could to the edge of the road to get into a good firing position. The Charley Company Marine edged up next to me, and I was glad to see him there; he was risking his life just by being so close to the gun. Two more belts of machine-gun ammo were passed down to us and the Marine draped one over his shoulder as he moved up the embankment next to me.

In Vietnam, I had seen Marines do some pretty heroic deeds while under fire. And while other branches of service rewarded such acts with silver stars and brass-colored medals, it wasn't so in the Corps. In the Corps, courage and fearless actions while under fire were expected. It was common in a Marine rifle squad as we looked out for each other.

The enemy's main firing position had changed; it was now almost directly across from where I was. Like a fan moving back and forth, the enemy was firing their machine-gun back and forth with supporting automatic rifle fire from AK-47s on both sides of their gun.

As I turned to tell the Marine that had been helping me that I was ready to engage the enemy's machine-gun position head-on, I noticed he had already hooked another 100-round belt to the gun. We had a 200-round belt hooked up, and he was prepared to hook up the third belt. With 300 rounds ready, he was as determined as I was to finish the job this time. I knew I would be wiping out the enemy's position in the next few seconds. It was going to be the battle of the guns. I sighted in; and as the Marine lifted the gun's ammo belt for me to commence firing, the belt flew out of his hands as a round struck his left shoulder, spinning him around, and he went flying backward, sliding down the embankment.

I buried my head in the ground as burning-hot red tracers flew by just inches from the top of my helmet. As other Marines cared for the wounded Marine, two other Charley Company Marines showed up on my left side. As one reached out to hold the belt of ammo, the other Marine crawled up to the edge of the road with his M-16 but then he moved forward near the same spot under the truck's carriage where we had been. He looked back at me, motioning me forward; and as I went to warn him that the enemy had that site targeted, I could see the other Marine holding the gun's ammo up, hands starting to shake. Bullets were once again being swept toward us. Just then the Marine under the carriage caught a round in his left cheek and his body spun around like a corkscrew and he tumbled down the embankment. When he stopped falling, his body went limp, at the same time the Marine holding the gun's belt was also hit. He slid silently down the steep embankment.

With my head buried, I could see a corpsman below helping the two wounded Marines that had tried to help me.

I draped the gun's ammo over my left elbow and prepared to open up. A Marine slid up to the edge of the road and opened fire at the enemy that had shot his friends. That was all I needed; as his rounds struck the enemy's position to the left of the truck, their firepower turned to engage him. I dug my feet into the embankment, raised the gun's barrel, and brought the gun's frame in, pressing it solid against my cheek, and pulled the trigger. I held the trigger back hard as red tracers slid steadily across inches above the road's surface.

Being where I was, I had a limited fire zone, so I backed down a bit more and moved to my right, embedding the gun's bipods into the embankment so that the gun's barrel was only about an inch off the ground. The area I was firing gave me the length of the undercarriage of the six-by truck to return fire from. It was a very limited field of fire, but offered me cover from the two AK-47s covering their machine-gun's position.

The rounds I unleashed were well concentrated and centered on what was the heart of where the most intense enemy fire was coming from.

As I opened up, the whole area in front of us all of a sudden exploded with a violent outpouring of enemy machine-gun fire and grenades. You stir up a hornet's nest and the bees come flying after you. Just like the time my sister's husband, Phillip Minjarez, and I stole a watermelon from a field near Eloy, Arizona. We picked up the biggest watermelon we could find, and as we lifted it up, a swarm of bees arose. They had been buzzing near the blossom end of the fruit where the sugar from its ripe end was oozing out. The angry bees shot up then came at us. We took off running. As they attacked, my brother-in-law threw the melon at me and I caught it and ran with it, and he laughed at me as the bees chased me down the field.

Running Out Of Ammo
No Name Village AT 810545
May 30, 1968, 1400-1920 hours

The enemy had been prepared for a counterassault to come from their right side and were entrenched facing in that direction in the tree line in an L shape entrenched position. They were effective in their estimation and military considerations and had pinned down what remained of Third Squad on that other side of the road.

My gun, however, had snuck in and was striking out at them from an area they had not prepared to defend as heavily, but this surprise or thorn in their side didn't last long. In seconds, my firepower was answered by the enemies own M-60 machine-gun shooting back at me. I could see the machine-gun's red tracers coming straight at me. The enemy's tracers first struck the ground in the middle of the roadway then bounced up and struck the truck's undercarriage. The gunner then began to hold the gun steady and use controlled bursts of fire. I was firing back just ten feet further back of where their gun's bullets were hitting. I was glad the NVA gunner hadn't zeroed in, and I was determined not to let him do so.

On Hill 65, First Platoon from Mike Company had saddled up.

Before they left the hill, Aggie had been seen running all over the hill securing machine-gun ammo so that the reactionary unit could bring it out to us. As the amtracks gunned their engines getting ready to move out, Aggie threw the ammo he had gathered onto them and stood still as they turned to get going. As the amtracks moved out, he ran to his hooch; then, before they reached the gate, Marines could see Aggie with his M-16 in hand and a bandoleer of ammo, strapped across his chest, running to join them.

"Come on, Aggie, come on," a couple of our Marines yelled out to him, and he ran harder toward them. But the amtracks were moving out at a good pace. "Come on, Aggie, come on," the Marines from Mike Company also urged him on. Some stood up, motioning for him to come on. "Come on, Aggie, run," they cried out and Aggie ran. He reached the last amtrack as it slowed down to turn to go out the front gate, and Marines reached down and pulled him up. He sat down with tears in his eyes, his lower lip quivering; but he restrained his emotions, wiped the tears away, took in a breath and lock 'n' loaded his rifle.

The M-60's Battle
No Name Village AT 810545
May 30, 1968, 1400-1920 hours

I squeezed harder, and for about two minutes, the two machine-guns were firing almost full throttle in a direct line at each other. The rounds were flying both ways in an area no larger than four to five feet in diameter. The two M-60s were spitting out red tracers at each other with such furious intensity that the bullets crossing each other over the road and under the truck's undercarriage made a fiery red ray of burning hot lead. Red burning strings swung tight across the roadway being pulled into a tighter and tighter point. It was two machine-gunners having their own private little war. I had lost all manner of reasoning and all common sense; I held my head straight, opened my eyes wider, tightened my lips and held the gun in tight, and fired the gun for effect. My priorities became concentrated on a single objective: silencing the machine-gun that was trying to silence mine. The incoming gun's bullets were striking in a solid tight pattern just six inches to my left, and I knew it would only be a matter of time before the enemy would adjust his firepower my way.

The courage of your enemy brings you honor, I had heard someone once say. The NVA machine-gunner was a well-disciplined soldier. He was brave, crazy, or high on drugs. I was fortunate that my A-gunner wasn't with me. The Marine that had snuck up to help was on his back and down about two feet to my left rear. He was holding up the gun's ammo and making sure the belt of ammo went in straight. He was not where the A-gunner should have been and had he been there he would have been dead. With my elbow extended as I always did, the rounds were going in straight into the gun's feedway.

From the pattern made by the rounds that were striking the ground to my left side, I realized that the NVA gunner was fixed, pinpointed, steady, and he was firing while looking through his gunsight. The pattern also told me his gun wasn't sighted in correctly, and I was glad it wasn't.

The realization that I was firing at an M-60 machine-gun, an American-made weapon, in the hands of the enemy irritated me. But at the same time, in the back of all that clamor and outcry of the firefight, there was a distinct and unique echoing sound to the enemy's machine-gun. I found myself listening to the sound the bullets made as they exited the enemy's gun barrel, and I told myself, "Sight in and concentrate!" The rounds were being spit out of my gun's front barrel with a fierce intensity and with a determination that I didn't know my gun or I possessed.

Never had I fired the gun in this manner and with such anger, and I didn't know if the anger was mine or my guns. Hatred controlled me, and little red and green demons were dancing on the enemy's tracers laughing at me as they went by. I buried my cheek into the gun's stock, pulled the gun in tighter, and the strength we drew from each other's beating hearts was vicious and determined. I lined the gun's sights, controlling the direction where the gunfire power was being directed by sighting in inch by inch toward the origin of the enemy's red tracers.

For some reason, in the back of my mind, the reverberation and echoing sound the enemy's gun made as it was fired sounded familiar. From the pattern it was shooting, I knew those bullets were not going to hit me. Then our tracers were missing each other by centimeters until the enemy's gun finally went silent.

There was no time for a pause; the enemy knew its worth and the worth of a good machine-gunner, and they immediately opened up in my direction with two or three AK-47s in full automatic. Their green tracers fired in my direction and at my gun's position, were wild shots and they skipped and bounced off the truck's body and struck the trucks flattened tires. I saw some of the enemy soldiers then move out to my left. At first, I thought they were getting ready to advance across the road, and my field of fire was still very limited: the truck's right and left tires hindered me, and I could not shoot back at them as I wanted to if they attacked.

I squeezed back a new volley of rounds at a new target to my right and began to sweep the width of the undercarriage as far as I could. Their machine-gunner was now gone. They had lost the M-60's firepower. I was still receiving incoming fire, but other Marines were now beginning to more effectively return fire at the enemy's main force from the edge of the road where they now could fire from. I concentrated my fire on a team of NVA soldiers firing at a Marine to my right.

Payback Response
No Name Village AT 810545
May 30, 1968, 1400-1920 hours

When the reactionary platoon reached the ambush site, the enemy waited until they un-mounted and got on line to sweep on the north side of the road toward us. As they moved out, a Marine on the roadway saw movement in the tree line and opened fire, shooting two enemy soldiers. A turret gunner on one of the responding tanks reached out to fire their .30 caliber at the same enemy soldiers when all of a sudden the whole area exploded with incoming fire being shot at them.

First Platoon India Company Marines responded quickly, rushing toward them and moving in toward the tree line, and the enemy soldiers pulled back. The twelve-man squad from Mike Company had also moved to the left on the south side of the road and had also engaged the enemy. At the same time, Marines on the road rushed forward and engaged the enemy soldiers that were providing cover for their retreating troops. In a matter of minutes the battle had turned against them.

To the left of the road, near a good-sized clearing past the cluster of bamboo trees, Ken Shawver, from Mike Company, had moved into the clearing to engage an enemy's machine-gun firing on them. Shawver fired his M-60 from the hip at the enemy's machine-gun position.

The engagement continued as the enemy force fought back, but as the platoon moved into the thick foliage, the enemy stopped firing and they quickly withdrew. Two enemy soldiers lay where the Marines from First Squad had shot them. That their bodies hadn't been removed by the retreating enemy force showed they were now desperately trying to get out of the area.

A Reunion In Time
No Name Village AT 810545
May 30, 1968, 1400-1920 hours

With the reactionary force moving in along the south side of the road, the NVAs firepower began to quiet down. Yet the overall intensity of the outgoing and the incoming rounds being fired each way continued to be fierce, violent, hideous, and terrifying but not as thick as before; this time, we seemed to have gained the advantage.

Moments later, it seemed that my gun was the only one still firing; unconsciously I kept the trigger pulled back hard and soon the bullets that I could see that were striking the ground in front of me were no longer the enemy's; they were not incoming rounds.

My guns rounds were falling down in slow motion directly in front of me, they had no power left in them as they exited the gun's barrel. Everything seemed to be happening in slow motion. It was then I realized the power that was being zapped out of each bullet happened when they exited the barrel and the rounds were falling slowly going out the front of my gun.

The last of my bullets barely had the strength to strike the dirt under the truck's undercarriage in front of me. The gun's barrel was glowing bright white, and you could see the bullet's shadow inside the barrel as it slowly made its way out. The gun's front sight suppressor was glowing a fiery red.

I had run out of ammo and had melted the gun's barrel.

When the reactionary force reached our position, all the firing suddenly stopped. As Rahm approached, he saw the last of my bullets hitting under the truck in front of me. He saw me with a cold glazed look, unmoving behind the gun, and feared I had been hit. A dead Marine was between us. Rahm moved around him and knelt down. The gun's barrel was now solidifying in a down-crescent position.

"I couldn't get here until now," Rahm said with a cry of despair in his trembling voice as he looked at me and saw I wasn't moving.

"Cookie, are you all right, Cookie?" He asked; he couldn't see if I was breathing. I hadn't moved, and he thought I was dead. My right hand was still gripped tight around the trigger holding it back. My hand was as pale as the gun's white glow. When he saw I was breathing, Rahm reached down with his bare hand to unlock the gun's barrel locking lever to change the barrel.

"Get the asbestos glove to change the barrel," I said without moving, my voice soft, almost silent coming from the back of my mind, the words spoken as if behind a dense fog coming from another world, a world without time or space. My right hand wrapped firmly gripping the gun's trigger guard was still holding the trigger back; and in my soul and with my spirit, I was still firing at the enemy. All the ammo attached to the gun had been expended, but my hand had become part of the gun—I was part of the gun. I was in a daze trying to comprehend the world around me. I wanted to continue to fire so things would be set right. This was war, and it was part of me. I slowly looked up at Rahm, and for the first time in four months, I saw my friend as he now was.

I remembered the youngster I had picked up in Da Nang, the innocent kid whom I once knew, but that side of him was now gone. I was looking into the eyes of a Marine warrior. *He's a killer,* I was thinking, amazed at how Rahm had changed. I let go of the gun's trigger, my hand releasing its death grip on the handle.

I took in an involuntary broken, lamented, deep sigh, recalling the cheerful Rahm I had known, the inquisitive kid who was always laughing, joking, and smiling. His innocence was now gone, filled by a blank, sullen stare revealing what he had just witnessed, what he had seen and done in war. He was no longer young and innocent. He had aged years, it seemed, in just the two hours that had elapsed from the time we responded and our present place and time. He had lost a lot in that time, minutes, days, weeks, or months had passed; what had happened to him? I had last seen him just before Operation Foster. Where had he been all these months? Where did the real Rahm go?

He stood, looking at me strangely, then reached down and turned the knob on the top of the gun that held the cover close. When the spring released the gun's cover plate, I finally fully released the gun's trigger.

Rahm unzipped the gun's supply bag and took out the asbestos glove and reached down to remove the barrel. There was a sizzling sound, and he quickly dropped the barrel because it was still too hot to handle even with the asbestos glove. He reached down and picked up a new barrel.

We began again to get some small arms incoming sniper rounds and Marines walking or standing on the road quickly responded. Over to my right, I could see wide-eyed Marines looking at Rahm and me. Some PFs on the road in front of us were dead; others lay wounded. A group of ARVNs could be seen crying over their dead and wounded; they had taken a beating and had lost many of their friends, but they had fought courageously along our side during the battle. One of our corpsmen was tending to their needs. Some Marines below us were covered with mud or blood or both. I took in another deep sigh and exhaled slowly.

Rahm locked the barrel in place and I subconsciously wiped clean the gun's chamber, pulled back the cocking handle, slapped in a 100-round belt, and closed the cover. My body was catching up with my mind; all the firing had stopped.

After a while, other Marines appeared to my right front, standing or kneeling on the roadway, some were looking into the field of fire I had been firing into. There was no longer any incoming fire, just dead enemy soldiers.

A couple of shots rang out. "Outgoing, Outgoing," someone called out, and while standing at the edge of the road, I fired a burst of machine-gun rounds from the hip in the general direction the Marine to my right had fired into.

Tired Aggie, My Old Friend
No Name Village AT 810545
May 30, 1968, 1400-1920 hours

The rest of First Platoon had moved up and were now standing on the side of the road to my left; they seemed relieved to see Rahm and me standing there. Among them was Aggie. He had 300 rounds of machine-gun ammo strapped across his chest. His trousers were unbloused, his boot laces untied. He held in his right hand his M-16 and in his left another hundred rounds of machine-gun ammo.

"Here," he said. "I thought you guys might need this." He smiled and gave me the ammo he was carrying.

"Aggie, what are you doing here," Rahm asked, almost angry at Aggie being there since he had already been relieved of combat duty.

"Well, I heard you guys needed ammo," he replied. That day tired Aggie deserved all the medals in the world in my eyes.

Someone from Charley 1/7 came running up to our location. Charlie is running out across the open sand toward the river, he said. Overhead, Huey gunships could be seen strafing the area and shooting off rockets at the fleeing enemy soldiers. The battle had moved into the open, and the NVA were running for their lives. The platoon, along with Charley Company Marines and the platoon from Mike Company got on line to sweep straight across the jungle to the other side where the tree line ended and the sandy beach area began.

With Rahm and Aggie at my side, we swept through. We were supposed to be sweeping on line, but because of the thick bushes and trees, it was impossible to stay on line so some gaps remained unchecked. When we entered the area where the enemy had been concentrated, blood was spattered all over the place. Dead enemy soldiers could be seen where they fell where they were shot. We started to count the amount of bullets in each of the dead NVAs.

Collect The Spoils Of War and Count The Bullet Holes
No Name Village AT 810545
May 30, 1968, 1400-1920 hours

One NVA had at least nine 5.56mm bullet holes in him before a round may have finally hit one of his vital organs. The entrance the rounds made left little holes in the front and side of each soldier with little holes out the back. That was one of the reasons the enemy kept firing after they had been hit so often: the bullet—unless you got lucky and hit a bone or vital organ—did not have the stopping effect the enemy's AK-47 or the M-60 bullets had.

The enemy bodies we found dead near where the machine-gun had torn into them had larger holes going in, and where the rounds exited, flesh and bone had been viciously torn apart and large chunks of body mass had been ripped off their bodies.

In one dead NVA soldier, it was evident that machine-gun bullets had torn through his chest, struck a bone, and had blown out most of his back. Each NVA body we found had from two to six bullet holes in them. We counted sixty dead enemy soldiers, all confirmed kills by both Charley Company [288] and India Company Marines. First Platoon was credited with killing nineteen of the enemy soldiers that day; the majority of those found dead were near the impact area across from my machine-gun's position.[289]

Drag marks on the ground and broken foliage showed that others had been dragged away. We found large caliber weapons that would be sent to the rear; other weapons were kept as the spoils of war by the Marines that had done battle that day. Many of the weapons we captured we noticed were brand-new AK-47s and SKS-56 rifles.

What was most disturbing in going through the battlefield afterward was not the disfigured and torn bodies of the enemy, not even the wounds and expressionless faces of the dead. What stayed embossed in our minds was that they were all clean-shaven. They all had fresh haircuts. Wore clean, pressed—if not starched—utilities with sharp ironed creases on their trousers. Some of the backpacks we found were well packed with extra clothing and food. In some packs we found black pajama bottoms or a new khaki uniform; all had a rolled-up black plastic body bag. The enemy was supposed to have been out in the jungle for months, but now they looked as if they were dressed for a spit-shine parade. They even smelled clean and seemed to have showered and shaved before the battle.

The NVA always carried away their dead and buried them hastily. *How gloomy,* I thought, *to have to carry your own body bag into battle just in case you were killed!* We had been told by ARVNs that the NVA soldiers often were high on opium when they went into battle. The drug would give them courage for the battle to combat any fear they might have and strength if they were shot so that they would not feel the pain and would continue to fight. That was part of the reason many of them had so many bullet holes in them. They kept fighting and firing at us even though they were already dead, and because of the drug, they didn't know they were fatally wounded. Being high on opiates, they couldn't feel the pain. A few of the bodies seemed to be sixteen- and seventeen-year-old kids; others were mature twenty- to twenty-seven-year old men. All were NVA, not a Cong among them.

The clean, pressed, and starched clothing each dead NVA soldier had on caused me to wonder. Here we were, America's finest, the best fighting force in the world; yet often when we engaged the enemy in battle, we did so while we were hungry, unshaven, dirty, and miserable. But here, the enemy that had traveled hundreds of miles and had spent countless nights in the jungle before today's battle was clean-shaven, had on a clean, pressed uniform, was carrying a food bag and was better equipped for jungle fighting than we were. They certainly had a superior weapon in the AK-47 compared to our M-16s. It just didn't seem right. However, now they were dead and soiled in their own waste and blood and we were alive. The NVA was getting help locally; otherwise, they wouldn't have been so well dressed, so clean, and so determined to fight against such overwhelming odds. Approximately 150 NVA regulars and a reinforced company had ambushed the convoy. Every truck had been torn apart with bullets, drivers and shotgun riders killed or wounded. Many of the ARVNs assigned to truck convoy security had received the brunt of the brutal assault and many of them were killed.

The Beauty Of The Battle Scene
No Name Village AT 810545
May 30, 1968, 1400-1920 hours

Beyond the smell of battle that still lingered in the air, the tropical jungle we were in was beautiful and rich with its own colors and smells. All around us, beautiful broad-leaf bushes and evergreen trees grew with rare strength and beauty. If this wasn't in Vietnam, it would be a beautiful place to live in. There were trees with small branches, trees with too many branches that resembled overgrown bushes more than trees. There were numerous sizes and shapes of ferns, shrubs, and plants that were dark green in color and some had a rich soft gray texture to them.

Here we were sweeping through an area of battle and I was mesmerized by the beauty of the tropical jungle that we were walking through. I welcomed the difference and got lost in my own wonderland of rare beauty in the midst of deep pain. There were short trees, fat trees, round trees, long trees, wide trees, and bushes with skinny fingerlike branches. There was a tree with red flame leaves and brown pods, similar to one my family had in our front yard in Arizona; but here the tree grew darker, greener, stronger, and sparkled with beauty. Banana and betel nut palm trees stood out as proud displays of grace and elegance in the midst of a land torn apart by war. I looked closer at the trees and felt bad for those that had bullet holes through them or slivers of shrapnel embedded in their trunks, but they would survive and grow and add to the beauty the land deserved.

The flame tree's red blossoms and the tamarind tree's brownish-colored pods helped conceal the crimson trails of blood and torn flesh that had been splattered on them. We walked past those trees, moved on, and found other bodies; some were hurriedly half buried. When we reached the outer edge of the tree line, we stood and looked across the sand—the area once again smelled fresh and clean.

The Smell Of Death And Destruction
No Name Village AT 810545
May 30, 1968, 1400-1920 hours

We turned back, and it wasn't long before the smell of death and destruction was back in the air and in our nose and sticking to our clothing as Marines brushed up against bushes that released the odor made by a mixture of sweat, filth, blood, and guts. The smell was mixed in with the smell of decaying plants spent ordinance; it was a smell one never forgets.

I went over to look at the area where the enemy's machine-gun had been. It was the portal where hell's back door had been opened by the spirits of war.

The area was splattered with blood and pieces of torn flesh. Hundreds of shell casing littered the ground. The smell of sweat and fear was still present, and I didn't know if it was mine. Blood trails led south then toward the river, and other blood trails into the deep underbrush. Marine squads regrouped and swept through the area again; this time they walked slowly along where the enemy had been entrenched.

Marines recovered more weapons and equipment the enemy had left behind. I had hoped to have found the M-60 I had engaged, we searched for it but were unsuccessful.

After the final search of the area, we were called back to the road where the bodies of Marines and PFs were laid out. They would be picked up that evening by helicopters and flown into Da Nang. Charley Company stayed behind to provide security for the damaged tanks and trucks that night, and we were loaded on board amtracks for our return to base.

Anger And Justice In Conflict
No Name Village AT 810545
May 30, 1968, 1400-1920 hours

As we rode back, the word was passed that a total of twenty-two Marines had been wounded and six killed.[290] We in turn had inflicted heavy casualties on the reinforced NVA company that had attacked us, but there was no consolation as we rode back in sullen silence on top of the amtracks.

A battle-worn Marine, whom I did not recognize sat next to me, his right hand resting on top of the amtrack's .30 caliber gun. Four or five other battle-weary Marines were sitting to his right and behind him. As we cleared the tree line, an elderly woman with a young man, about fourteen years of age, emerged from one of the side gates of No Name Village. She stood on the side of the road with the boy and both yelled at us. She had been one of the old ladies watching as we had gone by earlier that day, and I remembered that months ago, she was the woman Jones had pointed out and said we should not give any canned goods to her because her sons had gone north to become NVA officers.

She knew, she knew about the ambush, I was thinking. She was standing by the roadway yelling at us, and hatred exploded in my mind. I kept thinking, *She knew! All of them in that village knew what was going to happen to us, and now, they knew what had happened to their sons!*

Now that the battle was over, the villagers were emerging to continue on with their life and to support the enemy at the cost of their fellow men and U.S. Marines.

I turned to see if anyone else on the amtrack was thinking what I was. The Marines' solemn faces registered only a stare into the past.

The battle-worn Marine sitting next to the amtrack driver, next to the .30 caliber gun took in a long sigh then silently took his hand off the top, brought it back around and under to the trigger guard, and pulled the trigger—the rest of his body never moved.

His head didn't move, his breathing never changed, nothing else moved.

He simply squeezed off a ten-round burst as we rode past the villagers and the old woman and the boy fell alongside of the road.

The Marine withdrew his hand and placed it back on top of the gun.

No one said a word, no one moved. An officer with a thousand-yard stare on his face was sitting beside the Marine; the Officer never moved, never heard the bullets.

We were all lost in the battle of life, time, and memories. I still wonder if that was a vision, a dream, or the desires of my heart being played out in my mind.

The Marine did what all of us at that point in time desired to do, to stop the war, but we don't honor warriors like that. No, we judge them with eyes and ears and hearts that have never tasted fear or danced with death. Ironically, it's the reverence for life that a warrior takes a life so that others may live.

Among the Charley Company Marines, killed were;

Pfc Rodriguez, Pedro Angel, Gary, IN, Cpl Rouse, John William, Pittsburg, PA

Cpl Wilbur, William Jr., Lake Ariel, PA, and from the Thuong Duc Special Forces Camp, Sgt Joseph, Michael Arnold USAV, 5th SF Group Det A-109 (1 Mike Force), from Sacramento, Ca.

Return To No Name Village
No Name Village AT 810545
May 31, 1968, 0900 hours

The following morning, we were sent back to bring in the disabled trucks and tanks from the convoy that had been ambushed.

All day we stayed near the road until they were hooked up and towed to Da Nang. Whatever supplies had been on the trucks that could be salvaged were transported to the Green Berets' Camp at Thuong Duc.

By nightfall, not all of the trucks had been removed, so the platoon stayed the night as security while Charley 1/7 returned to Hill 52.

During the night, with only a sliver of a moon for light, the dark shadows of plants and trees remained as black as the jungle floor we sat on. A Marine on watch reported hearing movement in the area where the enemy had been entrenched during the battle, but could see no one. Illumination rounds were called in, and the sounds of movement ceased. It may have been Charlie, searching for their dead or wounded.

An NVA Coward's Weapon
No Name Village AT 810545
June 1, 1968, 0800 hours

The following morning, we got on line to search through the May 30, battle area once more. Battalion wanted a thorough body count as well as weapons or documents we might have missed in our prior sweeps.

We crossed over the road and began our sweep, going west toward the front end of where the convoy had been heading. I wanted to go back through the area where the enemy's machine-gun nest had been and check it out more thoroughly. I placed myself on line as close to the road's edge and with Rahm at my side, the platoon moved out to begin our sweep.

We moved out and Rahm was walking a few feet in front and to the left of me; as we passed a cluster of tall bushes, the reddish-colored bright green leaves of a large fern caught the corner of my left eye. I turned to look back, thinking it was blood that had splashed on the plant. Rahm sensed the hesitation in my gait and he stopped, turned to look at what I was looking at.

We had just passed an NVA soldier that was sitting upright up against a tree, hidden in the bushes. The shrub he was sitting on, had been flattened down.

The enemy soldier, dressed in a green-colored military uniform was alive and staring at us wide-eyed. An AK-47 was lying across his lap.

He was about thirty feet away from both of us, and could have easily picked up his weapon and shot us both. I looked at his eyes, they were distant, he was scared. I kept my eyes on him and his hands as I turned fully to walk toward him

The M-60 was at my side swinging free, my hand on the trigger, the sling holding it tight against my body.

I didn't bother to raise the gun, just walked up to the NVA soldier, reached down, and took the AK off his lap.

Rahm by then, had drawn down on him, ready to blast him away if he moved. He motioned for the enemy soldier to stand up, and he willingly obeyed. As he did, a ChiCom grenade fell from his lap, and we saw that he had a bullet wound in his calf. I grabbed hold of the prisoner, and searched him as Rahm picked up the ChiCom grenade.

Rahm handed me the enemy's AK-47 rifle. I checked it out, smelled it, it was brand-new and had never been fired. The enemy soldier had not fired his weapon, and that may have been the reason why he had been left behind. The soldier's uniform was clean and freshly laundered like the others, we had seen, there was even a visible crease line along the front of the uniform as if he had just picked it up at the local Laundromat. Other than the dirt and debris from where he had lain for two days, his utilities were clean and pressed. He wasn't wearing a hat, but was wearing an NVA belt buckle and uniform. He was in a state of shock and visibly frightened.

In light of the firefight we had experienced two days before I envied his cowardice. The NVA soldier had maintained his innocence. He had not experienced the task of shooting at or killing another human being; he remained undefiled by the blood of war. The scared soldier followed me with his eyes, as if he feared me or the gun and the destructive firepower we had wreaked together. I wished I could have spoken to him and find out what he had seen and witnessed.

Had I shot him? Had he witnessed the gun's destructive power and the impact of its rounds on his comrades? What had he seen?

The lieutenant came over to where we were standing with the captured prisoner and got on the radio with Battalion HQ. This time, the AK-47 was mine to keep if I wanted it, and I decided to do that. After the soldier was helilifted out, we probed our way back to Hill 65 in case there were other NVA stragglers left over from the firefight two days before. We moved out and shortly afterward found a dead NVA body with his weapon, but nothing else.[291]

Sgt. Richard Frank Triske, Ambush Mine Explosion
Route 4
June 2, 1968

Just before midnight, on the Second of June a squad of Marines from Third Platoon set in on a night ambush near a trail in the Dodge City area close to Route 4.

The squad, being led by Sgt. Richard F. Triske, was setting up an ambush on the east side of the road that led from Hill 55 to Route 4, when a twenty-pound box mine exploded, killing Sergeant Triske and wounding Pfc. Manuel P. Guzman and Pfc. Joseph A. Terzo; both Guzman and Terzo received minor wounds and were not evacuated.[292]

Just a Dirty Old Barking Dog
An Hoa
June 7, 1968, 1300 hours

Over the past month, there had been an increase in mines being planted on Route 4 between Hill 55, Hill 37 and An Hoa.[293]

On the morning of June 7th we saddled up for a mine sweeping detail to An Hoa. We swept from hill 65 past Liberty Bridge, and on to An Hoa. By late afternoon we neared the front gate at An Hoa and a skinny white dirty dog with half of his right foot missing ran out in front of us from our right side of the road and started yelping, and barking at the patrol. The dog kept his distance of about 10-20 feet from us, so that none of the men could kick him.

The dog was not old, but he was partly blind you could tell because his left eye was swollen shut and he cocked his head down and to the left to see upward with his good eye. About fifty meters from the compound the dog circled to our right and as there was a gap between the squads he raced toward the left side of the road from where he growled at the first men in Second Squad. We all pretty much, ignored the dog but he became more aggressive and started to bark at Marines back on the right side of the road, while standing out in the middle of the road.

About this time the mine sweeping detail ahead pulled off the road, as the road before them was now clear.

A large six-by truck behind us, accelerated and picked up speed to by-pass us and enter the compound.

The dog to avoid the truck was about to run to the safe right edge of the road but the Marines he had been barking at, were walking on that side.

He looked for a gap in between the Marines, as the truck rapidly approached. He turned and quickly darted across to get away from the truck but it was too late.

The trucks right front tire clipped his rear end and he was tossed under the undercarriage of the truck, then flipped flopped underneath it when the duel rear wheels ran over him from his tail end forward.

He yelped again once more, loud but with a demonized voice, that was almost human and the cry startled all of us.

The trucks tires had flatted him from behind forcing his intestines and guts out through a tear in his throat. His heart came out his mouth, completely separated from the rest of his body and bounced out into the middle of the road.

The heart was still beating, and kept beating for a couple of minutes as we gathered around to see it twitching and beating rapidly in the middle of the road.

It was a heart without a soul beating against the hard Vietnamese ground. Just another strange and abnormal event amidst the turmoil and chaotic acts of war.

Golden Gate B-40 Rocket Attack
Hill 55, Regiment Headquarters
June 10, 1968, 0015 hours

Early morning on the tenth of June, Golden Gate Bridge was awakened by the sounds of small arms fire and a B-40 rocket exploding near the 60mm crew's gun pit. Five Marines were wounded, but only one had to be medevaced to regimental aid station by vehicle. The other four Marines were treated for shrapnel wounds, but not before the mortar crew had responded with 81mm, 60mm, and small arms fire. Among those wounded were First Lieutenant Joel S. Brummel, Cpl. Samuel Muszel, Pfc. Irvin E. Seward, and Pfc. Barry B. Steinberg. Only L/Cpl. Michael P. Skelly was evacuated.

On the thirteenth, we went out on another convoy security escort detail. Halfway to Hill 52, one of the wheels of the bulldozers detonated a forty-pound antipersonnel mine, damaging one wheel and the engine. We waited and provided security for the bulldozer until another squad came out from Hill 65 to escort the bulldozer to that hill. Two hours later, we found the first of three mines. All were destroyed by the engineers.[294]

At 1300 hours, the lead tank coming out to meet the convoy from the Special Forces Camp detonated a mine and that detail then came under enemy fire. When a 57mm recoilless rifle disabled a second tank, we were ordered to continue on to escort the tanks to Hill 65 for repairs.[295] During the month of June, tanks from the First Tank Battalion detonated thirteen mines and five of their tanks were hit by RPGs. There were numerous instances of tanks receiving small arms fire, normal long-range fire designed primarily as harassing fire.[296] That night Hill 65 got mortared; there were no casualties.

Sent To The Rear
Battalion Headquarters
June 14, 1968, 1000 hours

On the morning of the fourteenth, the lieutenant passed the word for me to gather my gear. I was being sent to the rear to await my flight date at Battalion.

This was a surprise; when I first arrived in Vietnam, it was common practice to send those with less than a month to go on their tour of duty to the rear for mess duty or security while they waited for their flight date. But that hadn't happened for months; now it seemed as if I was being given a break.[297]

A few days later, Rahm joined me and for the next few days, we were assigned to stand perimeter watch during the day at battalion, but nothing more. We were going home.

Two times, while at battalion, both of us were sniped at and three times battalion was mortared.

Patrol Disaster
Dodge City
June 16, 1968, 0700 hours

On the morning of the sixteenth, the company was out on an early morning patrol in the Dodge City area. Captain Robb had volunteered the company for the sweep; we didn't know if the company was supposed to be sweeping or setting up as a blocking force for another company.

Third Platoon leader Sergeant Tully was leading his troops through heavy vegetation, when the company suddenly changed directions to sweep toward a tree line. As squad leader Amos O. Moore was telling his men to spread out, Sergeant Tully, moving out to Moore's left, turned to cut across a small patch of knee-deep elephant grass to catch up with the rest of the company, his troops were right behind him.

As he turned, he tripped a wire connected to a 155-artillery round tied to a high branch. The explosion was devastating. Three Marines were killed and eight others wounded.

The KIAs were the following: Robert E. Tully, David W. Gaskin, and Charles M. Hannah.

The WIAs were: Erbie R. Elliott, Bobby R. Epps, Amos O. Moore III, Daniel K. Reghard, Angel L. Soto, Franklin R. White, Thomas A. Whaley, and Jesus P. Zapata.

A Heavy Lost, We All Felt
3/7 Battalion Headquarters
June 16, 1968, 1800 hours

That evening, we were all walking around battalion in sober silence. The loss of so many Marines in a place we knew was heavily booby-trapped was too heavy for us to accept without blaming someone. Captain Robb was looked at more unfavorably by his men from then on, especially since shortly after the blast his radio message directed at battalion was simply, "Send me more bodies." All they seemed to be to him was numbers. [298]

That night and on the twenty-first, CAP 2-2-2, a short distance from Hill 37, got hit between the hours 2200 to 2400. That night, while Rahm and I stood watch at the southeast section of the perimeter, we received sniper fire and a bunker next to ours took one casualty. The following day, we got sniped at again while standing perimeter security.[299] It seemed to us, that we were getting sniped at more in the rear then when we were out with the platoon.

One Last Chance, Before Coming Home
Da Nang Air Base
June 25, 1968, 1300 hours

On the twenty-fifth of June, I was sent to Da Nang to await a flight ticket home. Before I would be allowed to board the plane, I was told I needed to have the captured AK-47 rifle's barrel stuffed with lead.

That meant that I would have to spend an additional three days in Vietnam. I handed the supply sergeant the weapon and took my plane ticket.

On the morning of June 26, I threw my seabag on the cart that was going out to the plane that was to take us home. As the cart pulled away, I looked at my seabag: the canvas was thin, faded, dirty, and torn.

As we were boarding the plane, a Marine Skyhawk was coming in from a bomb run over North Vietnam. He was about to land when a five-hundred-pound bomb became disengaged from under his wing and fell to the ground.

I was standing on the stepladder about three steps from our plane's entrance. I looked at the eyes of the stewardess standing at the doorway, her eyes were opened wide and she had a horrified look on her face.

Others behind me were frozen. The Skyhawk's pilot, either realizing what had happened or having been told by the airport tower, quickly accelerated and pulled out at the last moment. Otherwise, he would have landed right on top of his own bomb.

The bomb struck the ground then began to bounce head over tail; spinning and twisting every which way down the tarmac. It passed by us no farther than 100 feet away. Had it gone off, we would have been blown to bits.

At 1300 hours, the plane took off and all on board felt a tremendous release.

Classmate Reunion
Okinawa
June 26, 1968, 1300 hours

Shortly after arriving in Okinawa, I ran into Benevedo and Bennett at transit barracks. They were also on their way home. I hadn't seen them in over twelve months. They had served their tour of duty with the Third Marine Division near the DMZ, but that's another story, another diary that for now remains written only in their hearts and minds. Perhaps one day they will share their Dreams of Glory and Fields of Fire.

I could find no one else from the old 101 series that went through boot camp together. Did they make it back in one piece? Where were they, wounded or killed?

We were the fortunate ones, the survivors, the ones going home. We had faced death and destruction, knew hunger and pain, war, love and friendship, courage, honor and fear. We were coming home to America, the land of the brave and the free; we had done our duty to keep it that way and were coming home.

CHAPTER TWENTY SEVEN

Return To The Real World
June 28, 1968
Time: 1300 hours

The plane began its descent over the Pacific Ocean, and already a sense of anticipation was in the air. We descended slowly, and when the tires touched ground, a strong feeling of relief came over me. A deep sigh echoed throughout the plane. The eyes of those on board said it all. None of us said a word until the pilot announced, "Welcome to Travis Air Force Base, United States of America."

It was then that the plane erupted into loud shouts of joy. We were back in America.

We were home; this was our country. We had fought our country's battles on a foreign shore, and we had made it home. We were the lucky ones, the ones that lived. The heroes that had died at our side were with us in our memories, in our hearts, and in our thoughts. They did not make it home. We had much to be grateful for, much to live for, to live for them as well.

As the plane's doors opened, this time I was among the first ones to disembark. The air was clean and sweet, and it smelled like America. The birds in the sky were American birds, and the signs all around us were in English. Some Marines were slapping each other on the back others were thanking the stewardess and the pilot. All were sharing their joy with each other. A lone Marine knelt, blessed himself and kissed the ground. I was glad to be home, and I strained to look for a familiar face among the crowd of relatives awaiting our plane's arrival.

Some were already waving hysterically to their loved ones exiting the plane. Others were calling out names: "Bill!" "Honey!" "Roger!" All were straining to see their Marine, their warrior, returning home.

For ages it has always been that way. Countries have always sent their men to battle, and when they returned, they were always given a hero's welcome by their loved ones and by a grateful country whose battles they had fought. Win or lose in the battlefield, at home, they were heroes. At home they were honored for the price they had paid.

Some were running to each other, hugging and kissing, embracing and reaching out across a year's time to restore time that was lost. I looked for my wife among the crowd, but she was not there. Soon everyone that had arrived had gone off with relatives, spouses, cousins, brothers, sisters, fathers, or mothers that had come for them.

"If you need a ride to San Francisco to catch a flight out or a bus, the bus will be leaving in ten minutes," a Marine said.

I called Dorothy's parent's home to see what had happened to my wife. She knew that I was coming home, and we had made plans for her to meet me at Travis Air Force Base. I had been expecting to see her there. Other military wives, friends, and children were there meeting their returning Marine. But my wife, I was told by my mother-in-law, had decided to stay in Fresno. She decided to go to work that day. I could take the bus, and she would meet me at the Greyhound bus depot in Fresno. I could call her when I arrived, and she would come out to pick me up.

The military bus took us from Travis to the San Francisco bus depot from where I could catch the bus going home. People there were looking at us funny, and I didn't understand this. I was not prepared for the animosity I was sensing—not from American people. I felt as if I didn't belong. I had a new uniform on. Fresh new ribbons and medals decorated my chest, and there were new corporal stripes on both arms.

But something was wrong. Things were not the same. People stared at me with the same indifference I had first seen in the Vietnamese people when I first arrived in Vietnam. Some seemed angry; others near the bus station held signs up high, demonstrating against the war. Others looked at me with hatred and hostility as if I had done something wrong.

I wore my uniform proudly. I knew that I had served my country honorably, but for some reason, they seemed to hate me for it. The signs, the signs—I didn't want to read what they said. I didn't read what they said. I looked for others in uniform and moved toward them, and we got on the bus early at the Greyhound bus depot as soon as we were allowed to board.

What was bothering me, the most was the silent majority of Americans, those that saw me and did not or would not acknowledge my presence.

They turned and looked away, not wanting to get involved or labeled as supporting us. That was very hard to understand. But this was America; this was home. This is what we had dreamed about, what we had fought for all those months. America was home where we were supposed to be safe.

When I arrived in Fresno, my wife was not there; she was not home. She wasn't expecting me so soon, so I decided to take the taxi to my mother's home. There my mom cried and hugged me for the longest time. My brothers that were home were glad to see me. They were proud of me as were my sisters. No one asked me about the war or about the medals on my chest. Only my little nephew John-boy did.

"Uncle," he said, "when I grow up, I'm going into the military just like you so I can fight for my country and get medals just like you."

My wife didn't arrive till late that night. She never asked me about Vietnam, about my ribbons or medals, or if I had been wounded. We drove home in silence, a silence that would last to this day.

THE END

EPILOGUE

Concord Naval Weapons Station
Concord, California
1300 hours, January 15, 1970

As I drove out the front gate of the Concord Naval Weapons Station on January 15, 1970, into civilian life, demonstrators and antiwar protestors lined both sides of the highway that led into the naval base. I had spent my last year in the Marine Corps as an MP sergeant with a Top Secret Military Clearance assigned the responsibility of base security and special clearance to assume certain responsibilities relating to our country's national defense in case of nuclear war.

A month before, as the war in Vietnam was de-escalating, and the Marine Corps was allowing early outs. With my background and military clearance, if I chose to re-enlist I would be promoted to staff sergeant and reassigned to embassy duty or 8th & I.

If, however, for some reason I would be sent back to Vietnam, I would again be promoted and receive a bonus. I knew, however, that if I returned to Nam, even as a gunny sergeant, a rank I desired, I would not be coming home.

Other Marines I served with in Nam returned for another tour; some did not make it home. While I was in Vietnam I realized that I had made a difference in many ways.[300] Our artillery and fixed wing air strikes were not selective in what they hit, neither was a bullet once fired. Civilian casualties were regrettable consequences to the fire fights and enemy engagements we encountered. Where we failed in the Vietnam war, was not in our battles, we the American fighting man, did our job. If we failed it was because those who have not witnessed death and destruction at the hands of a merciless enemy would not authorize us to do what needed to be done.

Instead of barricading the seas to prevent China and Russia from arming and re-supplying Hanoi, we allowed it. Instead of going out, finding the enemy, and allowing us to destroy them, we waited for them to pick the date, time and place of confrontation.

But, the most troubling of all, was that the moral well being of the majority of American people was compromised when we allowed those who advocated peace at any cost, to abuse and label our sons and daughters who fought for our freedom.

History reveals that the majority of Americans supported the Vietnam War but stood idle or silent while a small minority made decisions in the newsrooms and in public discourse that cost us American lives. We must never again allow this to happen.

There are Marines alive today that wouldn't be if I hadn't volunteered for duty, if I hadn't believed in my country. Bro gave his life when he volunteered in my place, and today his name is etched on a black marble reflective wall in Washington, DC. If this book hadn't been written his name would have been just that, a name like the more then 58,000 thousand inscribed on that wall, but each one of those man have a story to tell, and that can only be told by those who were there. I pray that this book helps end that silence. I visited that wall a few years back, and it had a profound effect on me.

The tears, I never shed in war, the love I never gave, the moments lost, pains and sorrows warriors once shared were all bottled up and released that day. All Vietnam veterans should experience such a healing to make peace with the past and move on toward the future. *Semper Fi, Cook Barela*

Where are they now?

Steven Paul Aguilar. Aggie lives in Sacramento, California, married with children. He has worked for a school district in Highland for over twenty years. He made the second First Platoon reunion, and we remain close friends till today.

R.M. Cook Barela, divorced his wife, became a Los Angeles police officer, police chaplain, remarried has five daughters, has been twice elected to public office. Following our first reunion, Marines of First Platoon that were there when I was wounded, wrote a letter to the Commandant USMC Headquarters, requesting that I be awarded the Purple Heart Medal and within a month the Commandant wrote the citation and ordered the local military unit at March Air force Base to award me the medal and they did.

James (Jim) Boone changed his name. No correspondence.

Captain Jack Baggette, left the Marine Corps as a Colonel, lives in Port Royal, SC

Jonathan Boyd lives in Muncie, Indiana, works for General Motors as a toolmaker and is married. He received a 10 percent military disability for the injuries, he received in Vietnam.

Leonard Calderon, ran a series of Mexican restaurants and lives in Monterey, Ca.

Capt. Read McFadyen Clark, from Lewisville, North Carolina, remained honored and loved by his troops. He made several First Marine Division reunions with his men. He died in May 1998.

Doc Bernard McNallen, has attended a couple of our reunions, still troubled by his Vietnam experience, he is a successful attorney, practicing law in the state of Washington.

Newman Cuch, "Chief" returned to Vietnam for a second tour; a day before his tour was to end, Hill 65 got overrun by a regiment of NVA soldiers. They fought hand to hand. The next day, with Marine bodies all over, he was placed on a chopper, taken to Da Nang, and flown home. Two days after being involved in that massive battle, with his enlistment over, he was discharged from the Marine Corps at Camp Pendleton, California. He walked out the front gate, put on civilian clothes, and left his uniform, seabag, and everything else there at the gate and walked away. He lives in Wyoming, and drills oil wells for a large company.

Jerry Dumont is a disabled veteran living in Massachusetts.

Felix Duran is still grumpy, married several times, and lives in Florida.

Larry Gibbs (Doc) retired as a deputy chief with the Sacramento Police Department. He became the major source for locating other Marines in India Company.

Monte Gennai, lives in Brookings, Oragon

Al Homan lives in Pierce, Nebraska. When I saw him again after thirty-seven years at one of our India Company's reunion, I paid him the $3.00 he had loaned me at the fence.

Larry Isaacs, Retired after 30 years, from the Marine Corps as a Sergeant Major (E-9). Married has three sons, lives in Lakewood, Oh.

James Keene, successfully married lives as a Chandler, Ok

Ward Keeton, M-60 machine-gunner. Recovered from his wounds, is married, has two boys, and used his VA benefits to obtain his advance airmen certificates and has been flying professionally a commercial jet for a private company.

Quotable quotes:

> I hardly ever talked with anyone about Vietnam to any degree because most did not understand the intensity of our feelings and could not fathom the underlying emotion that we all had. I certainly never expected to contact anyone from India Company but was pleased when you called and totally overcome with the memories and the pride that we all feel.

Herman, "Izzie" LaJeunesse, When he was in the hospital recovering from his wounds, he kept in mind what he had been taught as a Ute Indian. His father had told him, "Son, if you get hurt, think of these hills and valleys and running through them." With all the pain and suffering he was enduring and hearing those around him cries of pain, his mind while at the hospital returned to the Wyoming hills and his youth. When his father came to visit him in the hospital, they both broke down and cried. But Izzie told his father, "Dad, when I see you again, I will be walking." Too proud to have others help or see him fall, Izzie would wait until the late night then struggle night after night to walk. When his father returned to see him in the hospital months later, Izzie walked into his arms. Today, Izzie races horses and lives in Wyoming.

Lergner, Earl, successfully married, lives in Rochester, NY,

Michael Jones. I never saw him again. I heard, he died in a car accident.

Jerry Lucero (TJ) still lives in Lubbock, Texas. He is 100 percent disabled and has not been able to find or hold a steady job due to his war injuries. His sister lives in Oregon, is married, and has three children.

Marty Martinez. When Marty returned home, he didn't tell his folks he was coming home; he spent some time with Toy "TeTe" and finally went home to Sacramento. He now lives in Burbank, California. He has his own construction company, has a family, and three children. He went back to Vietnam twice and started to construct a maternity clinic in Dai Loc near the village by the CAC unit where he once helped a young girl who had just given birth.

Russell Moses, successfully married, lives in Tampa Florida

John Niedringhaus, successfully married, worked as an engineer lives in Enderline, ND

Arthur O'Farrel, lives in Grand Junction, Colorado

Ronald Patrick lived in San Diego, California, worked as a teacher and reunion organizer. He died in 2007, of cancer and is buried at the Arlington National Cemetery in Arlington, VA.

James Perry went back to Vietnam, served with a different unit, is disabled, and lives in Texas.

Glen Prescott, lived in Seneca, Missouri, was married and had two boys and an adopted daughter. He served eighteen years as a postman, retired, suffered greatly from PTSD. Made the first reunion and died shortly afterward.

Keith Pridemore, never married, found him through the Internet just before going to print. He has a great recollection of events of those days looking forward to seeing him.

Steven Puder stayed in the Marine Corps, making it his career; he lived near Quantico, died in 2005.

Bruce Ira Rahm, The Rabbit, aka Combat, is married, went back for a second tour, was seriously wounded, is a disabled veteran living in Popular Bluff, Missouri. He was at our first First Platoon reunion.

Quotable quotes:

> I believe that if I couldn't remember the good times and closeness we all shared together, I wouldn't have made it. I haven't felt like that since Nam and I thank God that we had the opportunity to experience that union again.

Johnny T. Reysack, Reysack, graduated with the platoon. When he was about to leave for his combat duty assignment he visited a friend of his in a Los Angeles hospital who had been severely shot and wounded in Vietnam. His friend urged Reysack not to go and Reysack went AWOL. He was Court-marshaled and dishonorably discharged, but went on to live a successful life, raising several children.

James Jr. Taylor wounded in action with Bro, unknown unable to locate.

Captain Charles S. Robb, was elected a U.S. Senator, from Virginia. He lost re-election, when questions arose about his claim that two Marines had died in his arms in Vietnam.

Arthur Toy, successfully married and lives in Arizona

Edward Welsh made our first reunion has had successful career, lives in New York.

Jackie Williams is married, has a son which made him a grandpa, retired from the state fire services. He lives in Waxhaw, NC, and helps organize our reunions.

Larry Wilson was promoted to Captain, retired from the FBI, lives in Malibu, California.

Timothy Andrew John Sanderson, not his real name, but whenever he hears his name in any variation he listens and responds to God's voice immediately.

Our Dead and Wounded

First Marine Division
Third Battalion Seventh Marines
India Company
Unit Diary Location—Dai Loc
Marines Wounded or Killed in Action

June 20, 1967
Philemon, Henry A. Jr., L/Cpl. WIA

July 19, 1967 Group Entry
Moore, Ronald A., L/Cpl. KIA
Stoker, Kenneth G., Pvt. KIA
McIntosh, John J. Jr., Pfc., WIA
Turner, James Jr., Pfc. WIA

August 7, 1967
Grewelding, Wallace D., L/Cpl. WIANE

August 14, 1967
Williams, Jackie G., L/Cpl. WIANE

August 20, 1967
Patrick, Ronald S., Cpl. WIANE

-September 4, 1967
Bouchart, Ronald R., Pfc. WIA

September 12, 1967
Reid, Harold Erich, Pvt. MIA
Remains Recovered and returned 1998

September 15, 1967 Group Entry
Cortaze, Joseph D. Jr., First Lieutenant
WIA
O'Farrell, Arthur S. Jr., L/Cpl. WIA

September 15, 1967
Perez, Louis P., L/Cpl. WIA

September 21, 1967
Stiteler, Edgar, Cpl. WIA

September 23, 1967 Group Entry
Berg, David W., Pfc. WIA
Stoddard, Billy R., L/Cpl. WIA

October 10, 1967
Erie, Carl E., L/Cpl. WIA
Wilcox, Everett J., Sgt. WIANE

October 11, 1967
Isleb, Douglas G., Sgt. WIA

October 12, 1967
Tucker, Thomas T. Jr., Pvt. WIA

October 18, 1967
Dixon, Terry J., L/Cpl. WIA

October 25, 1967
Sotzen, Harold J., L/Cpl. KIA

November 08, 1967 Group Entry
Dixon, Terry J., Cpl. WIA
McAndrews, Edward A., Pvt. WIA
O'Mearns, Jimmy D., Sgt. WIA

November 08, 1967
Vancleef, Darrel W., L/Cpl. WIA

November 08, 1967
Thomassen, Bruce E., S.Sgt. WIANE

November 09, 1967
Peterson, Bruce E., Pfc. WIANE

November 11, 1967
Vancleef, Darrel W., L/Cpl. WIANE

November 14, 1967
Sessions, Robert S., Cpl. WIANE

November 19, 1967 Group Entry
HC3 Doc Robertson, Charles Edward KIA
Wilson, Robert B., L/Cpl. KIA
Williamson, Joel S., Sgt. KIA
Petersen, Mark C., Cpl. KIA
Virgil, Anthony L/Cpl KIA

November 19, 1967 Group Entry
Faithful, Boyd L. Jr., Second Lieutenant WIA
Nelson, Jon Q., L/Cpl. WIA
Tully, Robert E., S.Sgt. WIA

November 19, 1967 Group Entry
Boyd, Jonathan H., Cpl. WIA
Cole, Thomas J., L/Cpl. WIA
Duran, Felix L., Pfc. WIA
Isaacs, Lawrence M., Sgt. WIA
Keenan, Ralph P., Cpl. WIA
Keeton, Ward S. Jr., L/Cpl. WIA
Lucero, Lionel G., L/Cpl. WIA
McCullough, Lee H., L/Cpl. WIA

Patrick, Ronald, Cpl. WIA
Saunders, Charles R. Jr. WIA
White, Robert Jr., Cpl. WIA

November 20, 1967 Group Entry
Dumont, Gerard, Cpl. WIA,
Howard, Robert W., Cpl. WIA
Hullihen, Ira H., Cpl. WIA

November 21, 1967 Group Entry
Aguilar, Steven P., L/Cpl. WIA
Barela, Refugio M., L/Cpl. WIA
Cuch, Herman R., Cpl. WIA
Jones, Michael J., Cpl. WIA
Stanford, Zaryl F., Sgt. WIA
Whiteside, Calvin J., Sgt. WIA

November 21, 1967 Group Entry
O'Neil, Vaughn T., Pfc. KIA
Taylor, Charles N. III, Pfc. KIA

November 21, 1967 Group Entry
LaJeunesse, Herman Jr., Cpl. WIA
Chambers, Leroy C. Jr., Cpl. WIA
Keenan, James J., Cpl. WIA
Perry, James E., L/Cpl. WIA
Pridemore, Keith G., L/Cpl. WIA

November 21, 1967
Ezell, Jerry D., Pfc. WIANE

November 21, 1967
Imperial, Dennis S., Pfc. WIA

November 21, 1967 Group Entry
Parish, William L., L/Cpl. WIA
Whitaker, Herbert E., L/Cpl. WIA

November 23, 1967
Soule, Joseph D., Cpl. WIA

November 24, 1967 Group Entry
Burdge, William C., Cpl. WIA
Joslin, Frank L., Sgt. WIA

November 26, 1967
DeMunda, Gerard A., L/Cpl. KIA

November 26, 1967 Group Entry No. 1
Brown, Gary D., Cpl. WIANE,
Delarino, Victor R., Sgt. WIANE
Dumont, Gerard N., Cpl. WIANE
Dustin, Dennis, L/Cpl. WIANE
Olson, Richard, Pfc. WIANE
Rahm, Ira B., L/Cpl. WIANE

November 26, 1967 Group Entry No. 2
Henderson, Donald R., Pfc. WIA
Souble, Jerome V., L/Cpl. WIA

November 26, 1967 Group Entry No. 3
Dolison, Leroy, Pfc. WIA
Gonzalez, Harry, Pfc. WIA
Morales, Evaristo, Cpl. WIA
Morris, Roger D., Pfc. WIA
Prescott, Glenn S., Pfc. WIA

November 26, 1967
Gonzalez, Leonard E., Pfc. WIA

November 27, 1967
Coleman, Jerry R., Pfc. WIA

November 27, 1967 Group Entry
Saylor, Mark S., Pfc. WIA
Welsh, Edward J., L/Cpl. WIA

December 21, 1967
Rodriguez, Richard, Pvt. WIA

December 26, 1967
McKenney, George J., Cpl. WIA

December 31, 1967
Hullihen, Ira H., Cpl. KIA

January 05, 1968 Group Entry No. 1
Burke, James J., Pfc. WIA
Gilchrist, Kenneth B., Cpl. WIA

January 27, 1968 Group Entry No. 1
Perez, Roberto, Pfc. WIA
Pridemore, Keith O., L/Cpl. WIA

February 06, 1968
Seguin, Charles M., Pfc. WIANE

February 22, 1968 Group Entry No. 2
Cole, Thomas J., Cpl. WIA
Kidd, Robert L., Sgt. WIA
Thomas, William D., L/Cpl. WIA

March 06, 1968
Capezio, Francis J., Pfc. KIA

March 14, 1968
Chandler, Paul Jr., L/Cpl. WIA

April 01, 1968
Jones, Cecil L., Pfc. KIA

April 01, 1968 Group Entry
Costa, John J., Pfc. WIA
Fields, Robert E., L/Cpl. WIA
Prasifka, Frank D., Pfc. WIA

April 04, 1968
Thomas, James Calven MIA

April 07, 1968
Bembry, Paul, Pfc. WIA

April 13, 1968
Ryan, Richard G., Pvt. WIA

April 27, 1968
Croke, Robert S., L/Cpl. KIA

May 05, 1968 Group Entry
Miller, Kenneth A., Pfc. WIA
Sellers, Stephen M., Pfc. WIA

May 13, 1968 Group Entry No. 1
Cantu, Jose Jr., Cpl. WIA
Johnson, Rossevelt Jr., Pvt. WIA

May 13, 1968 Group Entry No. 2
Borgman, Darrell L., L/Cpl. WIANE
Poppe, Gary L., Pfc. WIANE

May 14, 1968
Been, Robert S., L/Cpl. WIA

May 14, 1968 Group Entry No. 1
Bybee, Joe R., L/Cpl. WIANE
Morales, Evaristo, Sgt. WIANE
Reighard, Daniel K., Pfc. WIANE

May 15, 1968 Group Entry No. 2
Adduci, Dennis R., Pfc. WIA
Aragon, Chester L., L/Cpl. WIA
Beebe, Thomas W., Cpl. WIA

May 16, 1968
Perry, Ernest, Pfc. KIA

May 16, 1968
Semple, James R., Pfc. WIA

May 22, 1968
Hart, Sidney W., Cpl. WIA

May 26, 1968
Murphy, Michael, L/Cpl. KIA

June 02, 1968
Triske, Richard F., Sgt. KIA

June 02, 1968, Group Entry No. 2
Guzman, Manuel P., Pfc. WIANE
Terzo, Joseph A., Pfc. WIANE

June 10, 1968
Skelly, Michael P., L/Cpl. WIA

June 10, 1968, Group Entry No. 2
Brummel, Joel S., First Lieutenant
WIANE
Muszel, Samuel, Cpl. WIANE
Seward, Irvin E., Pfc. WIANE
Steinberg, Barry B., Pfc. WIANE

June 16, 1968, Group Entry No. 3
Tully, Robert E., S.Sgt, KIA
Gaskin, David W., L/Cpl. KIA
Hannan, Charles M., Cpl. KIA

June 16, 1968, Group Entry No. 4
Elliott, Erbie R., Pfc. WIA
Epps, Bobby R., L/Cpl. WIA
Moore, Amos O. III, L/Cpl. WIA
Reghard, Daniel K., Pfc. WIA
Soto, Angel L., L/Cpl. WIA
White, Franklin R., Pfc. WIA
Whaley, Thomas A., L/Cpl. WIA
Zapata, Jesus P., Pfc. WIA

July 02, 1968
Dunn, Harold L., Pfc. WIA

July 08, 1968 Group Entry
Hren, Timothy L., L/Cpl. KIA
Wilson, Thomas L., Pfc. KIA

July 08, 1968
Gennai, Monte J., L/Cpl. WIA

July 19, 1968
Keefe, Dennis W., L/Cpl. KIA

July 22, 1968
Stephenson, Frederick D.

August 05, 1968
Knight, Gerard L. WIA
Bybee, Joe R. WIA
Cooper, Rufus J. WIA
Hoke, Christian E. WIA
Mantei, Mark J. WIA
Lancara, Humberto P. WIA
Aragon, Chester L. WIA

August 05, 1968, Group Entry No. 2
Blagg, William WIA
Bell, Charles B. WIA
Lyons, James A. WIA
Little, Ronnie WIA
Harris, Benwood L. WIA
Hall, Richard L. WIA
Delgado, Leonard W. WIA
Allen, Arthur D. WIA
Musta, Phillip P. WIA

August 05, 1968, Group Entry No. 3
Bayless, Terry D. WIA
Kaleikini, Clement R. WIA
Imperial, Dennis J. WIA
Hennen, Gilsbert N. WIA
Magruder, Allan D. WIA
Dean, Larry W. WIA
Raymond, Stephen F. WIA
Harlan, Joseph R. Jr. WIA
Jones, James E. WIA
Gattis, David N. WIA
Dunn, Charles WIA
Epps, Bobby R. WIA

August 08, 1968
Hale, Terrell W. KIA
Moore, Stephen C., Second Lieutenant
WIA
Lyons, James Andrew
Hall, Richard Le Roy

ENDNOTES

1 The forward to *"U.S. Marines in Vietnam, Fighting the North Vietnamese 1967,"* states, "The uneven quality of the official reports submitted by combat units played a role in what was selected in the material presented," in that publication. Likewise, combat spot situation reports, and actions undertaken by Marine Corps ground units in the field I, found was often under reported, and at times what was reported was never officially recorded, it often depended on who was on duty, and who reported what and when.

2 Marine Air Operations in Vietnam. "At the start of 1967, First Marine Aircraft Wing consisted of three fixed-wing groups: MAGs -11, -12, -13 and two helicopter groups, MAG-16-36 and MAG-11, operated from Da Nang, while the other two were at Chu Lai. The two helicopter groups operated from different bases also; MAG-36 was at Ky Ha, and MAG-16 split between Marble Mountain and Phu Bai." Maj. Gary L. Telfer; Lieutenant Col. Lane Rogers, USMC; and V. Keith Fleming Jr., *U.S. Marines in Viet Nam, Fighting the North Vietnamese 1967,* History and Museums Division, Headquarters, U.S. Marine Corps, Washington, D.C., 1984, p.199.

  *Much of the information I have included in these endnotes, I was unaware of at that time in history. Some of these notes will disclose locations, situations, and events that would later impact our Company or Platoon. They are taken from the Marine Corps' command chronologies, after-action reports, or other military documents, including the newspaper stories of that time. They are included here as a historical note for reference and to help the reader better understand the Vietnam War and our time in history.

3 Private airlines contracted with the federal government to transport U.S. troops to Vietnam and back. These included Continental Airlines, TWA, United, World Airways, National, Air Canada, and Flying Tigers. Most of the planes were stripped of all amenities and filled to capacity. They carried 165 or more men on each flight. James R. Ebert's, *A Life in a Year, The American Infantryman in Viet Nam, 1965-1972,* Novato, CA, Presidio, 1993, P.78 Jaclyn LaPlaca *"Women to Share Stories of Viet Nam," THE WASHINGTON TIMES,* November 11, 1997.

4 In August of 1965, the First Marine Division Headquarters was transferred from Camp Pendleton to Camp Courtney, Okinawa. By then, part of the division's First Battalion Seventh Marines had sailed from Okinawa to Vietnam. The Second Battalion had also been inserted at Qui Nhon in II Corps, and the Third Battalion had become the Seventh Fleet's Special Landing Force (SLF) Battalion. By the end of the year, all three Seventh Marine Battalions and a supporting artillery battalion from the Eleventh Marines were

at Chu Lai. By November of 1966, the First Marine Division Headquarters had been transferred to Hill 327 near Da Nang, South Vietnam. *U.S. Marines in Viet Nam, An Expanding War, 1966*, Washington, D.C., History and Museums Division, Headquarters, U.S. Marine Corps, 1982, p. 9

[5] *Gook* was a term used to describe the Vietcong but used in a derogatory manner to mean any Vietnamese. Other words used were *Charlie, dink, Luke the Gook, Gooner, zipperhead,* and *slanteye.*

[6] Some Marines carried the small Bibles on the outside left breast pocket of their flak jackets. "Bullet stoppers" was what we called them and some did indeed stop a bullet or shrapnel and thereby save a Marine's life, but that was not the reason most carried them or why they had been given to us. Some carried it as a good luck piece, others as a means of identification of belief in God. Rarely did I see anyone reading them.

[7] As our plane was *en route* to Vietnam, six miles south of Da Nang, the following spot reports were being recorded in the unit journal about events occurring in the area, I was to be assigned to: June 14, 1967, at 0700 hours, a squad-sized combat patrol from India Company, Third Battalion, First Marines (Op Con 3/7) went in pursuit of an enemy soldier near the village of Duong Lam (2), AT grid coordinates AT 962693. The VC disappeared into thick undergrowth, and the squad began to cautiously search for him. When a Marine located the enemy soldier hiding in a small tunnel, the NVA/VC soldier threw a grenade at the patrol of Marines, wounding one Marine. The Marines took cover and returned fire with twenty rounds from their M-16 rifles, killing the NVA/VC soldier. The squad recovered an AK-50 rifle, two M26 grenades, a cartridge belt containing two magazine clips, and a large map of the Da Nang area. As the Marines examined the map and other documents taken from the dead soldier just a few miles south of them, a number of helicopters rose into the air from Hill 37, Third Battalion, Seventh Marines headquarters. The helicopters circled overhead, then turned southeast and began to descend into an area located between the Song Vu Gia and the Song Thu Bon rivers. The area was known as the independence area. Operation Arizona, a regiment-size Search and Destroy Mission had just commenced. Seventh Marines, Command Chronologies, Third Battalion, Seventh Marines, First Marine Division, June 1967.

[8] At 1430 hours, a Lima Company platoon-size patrol engaged an estimated force of ten NVA/VC during Operation Arizona near Mai Dong village, AT 845543. One enemy was confirmed killed and another listed as probable KIA due to the large pools of blood and pieces of flesh discovered when the patrol searched the area. Six detainees were apprehended running away from the patrol at grid coordinates 832545.

[9] Also called a duffel bag, a large green military-issued, cylindrical-shaped canvas bag used to transport military uniforms, clothing, and other personal items.

[10] Each kamikaze Japanese fighter pilot had flown an obsolete plane loaded with a 550-pound bomb, and in one suicidal mission after another, dropped their planes straight onto naval vessels and other military targets killing themselves and many American military men.

[11] "Dying in defense of the Vietnamese homeland was an honored death," Paul Berman, *Revolutionary Organization, Institution-Building Within the People's Liberation Armed Forces*, Lexington, MA; Lexington Books, 1974, p. 38.

[12] During the battle of Dien Bien Phu, about 800 dead and dying communist soldiers had been cut down in the final assault before the Algerian soldiers holding on to the top of Strongpoint where Gabrielle surrendered. A Viet Minh officer then ordered the prisoners to the rear, and an Algerian sergeant asked the officer how were they to get across the barbed wire and minefields. The officer replied, "Just walk across the bodies of our men." A dying communist soldier looked up at the prisoners; they saw his lips moving, and they hesitated to use him as a stepping-stone. "Get going," the Viet Minh officer said. "You can step on him. He has done his duty for the Democratic Republic of Viet Nam." Michael Lee Lanning, *Inside The VC and the NVA*, New York, Fawcett Columbine, 1992, p. 22.

[13] The NVA/VC used terrorism and assassination assaults on single individuals or whole villages to force cooperation; obtain laborers; and collect taxes, food, and other supplies. Resistance meant execution. Michael Lee Lanning and Dan Cragg, *Inside the VC and the NVA, The Real Story of North Viet Nam's Armed Forces*, New York, Fawcett Columbine, 1992, p.186.

[14] North Vietnam consistently maintained, to the end of the war, that it had no troops in the south states. Michael Lee Lanning, *Inside the VC and the NVA*, New York, Fawcett Columbine, 1992, p. 163.

[15] Hanoi's communist government had complete control of the Pathet Lao terrorist organization, and the main reason for this connection was to use Laos as the supply route to funnel men and equipment down the Ho Chi Minh trail from North Vietnam to the battlefields of South Vietnam. Larry Henderson, *Viet Nam and the Countries of the Mekong*, Camden, N.J. Thomas Nelson & Sons, 1967, p. 132-33.

[16] "The Soviet Union and the People's Republic of China supported North Vietnam with supplies, arms and food," states Lee Lanning *Inside the VC and the NVA*, New York, Fawcett Columbine, 1992, p. 72.

[17] Operation Arizona, on June 14, 1967, at 2330 hours; Mike Company set in a blocking position near the village of Phu Huong (3) AT 834550, using infrared night-vision devices, observed ten to fifteen NVA/VC attempting to cross the Song Vu Gia River vicinity of AT 845543. The enemy, fleeing the presence of Marines in their area, were using reeds as breathing devices as they crossed the river. As a fire-team maneuvered to the crossing point, tanks from Company B First Tank Battalion (rein) attached to Mike Company in their blocking position opened fire on the main force of enemy soldiers and effectively prevented them from crossing. Meanwhile, the Marine fire-team engaged five NVA/VC fleeing the scene. Seventh Marines, *Command Chronology*, June 1967.

[18] Personal USMC Military Records

[19] The life expectancy of a machine-gunner in Vietnam, once the first round was fired in combat, was three to seven seconds.

[20] Pilots stayed high in the air, then dropped suddenly to avoid getting hit by enemy ground fire while landing at the Da Nang airfield.

[21] A popular commercial of that time was "Coca-Cola, it's the real thing."

[22] A large round metal container used for the storage of water.

[23] The South Vietnamese currency was the piastre, and the official exchange rate was 118 piastres to each U.S. dollar.

[24] The Third Marine Division command post was located at Phu Bai, outside of Hue, north of the picturesque sharp-backed ridge of the Hai Van Mountains that divided the northern two provinces from the rest of South Vietnam. Four of its battalions were in Quang Tri Province at the DMZ; three were in Thua Thien Province. Brig. Gen. Edwin H. Simmons, Marine Corps Operations in Vietnam, 1967, *The Marines in Viet Nam, 1954-1973, An Anthology and Annotated Bibliography*, History and Museums Division Headquarters, U.S. Marine Corps, Washington, D.C., reprinted 1985 p. 71.

[25] In 1954, a force of forty thousand heavily armed North Viet Minh soldiers lay siege to the French garrison at Dien Bien Phu. Using Chinese artillery to shell the airstrip, the Viet Minh made it impossible for French supplies to arrive by air, and the French were defeated. Delegates from nine nations then convened in Geneva and negotiations led to the end of hostilities in Indochina, and the idea of partitioning Vietnam into North and South Vietnam was agreed to. Viet Minh general Ta Quang Buu and French general Henri Delteil signed the agreement on the cessation of hostilities in Vietnam, and as part of the agreement, a provisional demarcation line was drawn at the seventeenth parallel. This became the demilitarized zone (DMZ).

The United States did not accept the agreement; neither did the government of Bao Dai, the president of the Republic of Vietnam. *PBS Viet Nam on line,* Time line 1945-1963, The Public Broadcasting Service, The American Experience.

[26] The First Marine Division's command post was located on the reverse slope of Hill 327, three kilometers west of Da Nang. Seven of its battalions were in Quang Nam Province. At Chu Lai, Task Force X-Ray, a brigade-size force was located with two of its battalions in Quang Tin and two in Quand Ngai Province. Brig. Gen. Edwin H. Simmons, Marine Corps Operations in Viet Nam, 1967, *The Marines in Viet Nam, 1954-1973, An Anthology and Annotated Bibliography*, History and Museums Division Headquarters, U.S. Marine Corps, Washington, D.C., reprinted 1985, p. 71.

[27] *Command Chronologies*, Operation Arizona, June 17, 1967, 1150 hours: A squad-size patrol from Kilo Company 3/1 (Op Con 3/7) apprehended two detainees attempting to elude the squad patrol near the village of Bo Ban (2) at AT 964699 by jumping into the Song Yen river. A third enemy soldier escaped in the river. All three wore NVA khaki uniforms.

[28] Naval Support Activity, Da Nang (NSAD), was located in what was known as the white elephant section of downtown Da Nang. Its Naval Construction Forces, the Seabees, provided construction support to Navy and Marine Corps forces in the combat areas of South Vietnam. Twelve Mobile Construction Battalions under the control of the commander of Third Naval Construction Brigade operated out of Da Nang, Chu Lai, Hue and Phu Bai. Captain Pickett Lumpkin, USN, *The Navy in Viet Nam,* A Navy publication printed in June 1968 to give a brief overview of the various naval activities in the Vietnam War.

[29] One of the benefits of the Vietnam War was that every American fighting man assigned a tour of duty in Vietnam was guaranteed a week off from war. The one-week vacation could be taken either in country or in any one of seven different cities in the Orient, including Australia, Singapore, Bangkok, Hong Kong, or Honolulu. Air transportation was provided free of charge by the government via U.S. commercial airlines. In Hong Kong, arrangements could be made for us for a woman to spend the whole week with you in a private room or several women during your stay. It wasn't unusual for young Marines to fall seriously in love with some of them. Many Asian women sought out naïve young Marines to marry so they could become U.S. citizens, come to the United States, and eventually bring their families over.

[30] In comparison, the North Vietnamese soldier's training lasted three months with additional special training provided for specialized sections that could last from seven to nine months or more. After selection for infiltration, south training intensified and included political indoctrination, physical conditioning, instruction in enemy weapons and mines, and additional proficiency training with their own weapons that included shooting at moving targets and night shooting. What was a plus to the Vietnamese soldier both from the north and from the south was that he learned from birth, to face hardships and had the endurance needed to fight in the jungles and the mountain conditions of Vietnam.

[31] It was not unusual for Marines to write home and ask for parents and others to send gun-cleaning equipment as well as other needed items such as rain gear, T-shirts, socks, or other clothing.

[32] Operation Arizona on June 18, 1967, at 0800 hours; A mechanized column from Lima Company engaged twenty to twenty-five NVA with packs, weapons, and extensive camouflage in a trench line on the eastern edge of the Phu An (1) hamlet at 872520 (villages were numbered in order to be able to identify the different hamlets within a general area that used the same name). The unit pursued the enemy into the Phu An (1) hamlet; the unit received heavy S/A and A/W fire, including twenty-rounds 60mm mortar and five RPG-2 rockets. The NVA continued to fall back, attempting to draw the Marine units into a U-shaped ambush. The Marine platoon held its ground; however, and requested artillery and fixed-wing missions. Amtracks with infantry reinforcements killed ten NVA in spider holes as they fought to take Hill 11, at AT 877517. A sweep of the area uncovered large pools of blood, packs, and weapons. Captured were one M-14 with magazines, one M-16 with magazines, one AK-47 with magazines, one BAR, and one ChiCom K-44 rifle. A total of four VC KIA (C) and fourteen VC KIA (P) were recorded. C = Confirmed, P = Possible.

[33] It was well known in Hanoi that U.S. policy prohibited the pursuit of communists into the DMZ. The enemy's two major thrusts in the south during the summer and fall of 1966 had resulted in the Third Marines Division's shifting ten thousand Marines north to meet those threats. Marines there faced a hierarchy of enemy units ranging from local, part-time guerrillas to conventional North Vietnamese Army divisions. Just north of the DMZ, four NVA divisions were located: the 304, the 320, the 324B, and

the 325C. All were under the command of North Vietnam's Military Region 4. The 324B had suffered heavy casualties in combat with the Third Marine Division in July and August 1966 and had withdrawn back across the DMZ to refit. The 325C served as the strategic reserve for MR-4. Maj. Gary L. Telfer; Lieutenant Col. Lane Rogers; and V. Keith Fleming Jr., USMC, *U.S. Marines in Viet Nam, Fighting the North Vietnamese, 1967*, History and Museums Division, Headquarters, U.S. Marine Corps, Washington, D.C. 1984, p. 6-8.

[34] A boot band is made up of two twisted small round elastic strips, usually quarter inch in size that are covered in green-colored cloth. They are used to blouse the bottom of utility trousers, which also keeps small insects and leeches out of one's boots and trousers. Boot bands were among the most prized possessions in Vietnam.

[35] A six-by, six-wheel flatbed or dropside two-and-a-half-ton GMC truck used for troop and supply transportation.

[36] Actually an equal number of regular NVA enemy soldiers were known to be operating in the First and Third Marine Divisions' area of responsibility. Hanoi called our assigned area Military Region 5 (MR-5), which was located in Southern I Corps and commanded by a North Vietnamese general; two North Vietnam infantry divisions were assigned there. One of those divisions, the Third NVA Division, was made up of two NVA and one VC regiment. In the Third Marine Division's area of responsibility, located north of Da Nang, the Second NVA Division, also known as the 620th operated. It also was composed of two NVA regiments and one First Vietcong Regiment. Maj. Gary L. Telfer; Lieutenant Col. Lane Rogers; and V. Keith Fleming Jr., USMC, *U.S. Marines in Viet Nam, Fighting the North Vietnamese, 1967*, History and Museums Division, Headquarters, U.S. Marine Corps, Washington, D.C. 1984, p. 6-8.

[37] These geographical fears did not have truth behind them. Historian Guenter Lewy, *America in Viet Nam*, pointed out that Quang Nam Province, located southwest of Da Nang, exacted the most Marine casualties. Between 1965 and 1969, the First Marine Division responsible for operations in this province, suffered more than six thousand combat-related deaths, which accounted for nearly half of all Marine fatalities during the war. James R. Ebert, "*A Life In a Year, The American Infantryman in Viet Nam, 1965-1972*, Presidio Press, Novato, CA, paperback, 1995, p. 95.

[38] Cobb Bridge was located at AT 946699 Dai Loc Map Sheet 6640 IV, Series L7014

[39] The terrain of the Third Battalion, Seventh Marines TAOR is primarily flat, laced with open rice paddies throughout the eastern, central, and southern sectors. The northern and southern limits of the TAOR are mountainous with heavy secondary vegetation and steep foothills. Two main rivers flow through the central and southern sectors, the Song Vu Gia and the Song Thu Bon respectively. The principal terrain features of the TAOR are Hills 55, 37, 65, 52. Third Battalion, Seventh Marines, *Command Chronology*, January 1968.

[40] South Vietnamese Popular Force, local militia.

[41] A Combined Action Company (CAC) unit or Combined Action Platoon (CAP) was made up of a squad of U.S. Marines and usually a platoon of PF's (Vietnamese Popular

Force) that lived in or near a protected village to provide security against Vietcong aggression.

[42] The Seventh Marines operated twenty-five CAC Combined Action Company in its TAOR. The name was later changed to CAP, Combined Action Program.

[43] London Bridge located at AT 914587

[44] Ontos were a powerful but ugly looking light-armored, anti-tank tracked vehicle loaded with six 106mm recoilless rifles. Amtracks looked much like a slow-moving oversized rectangular-shaped armored green beetles. Some had a .30 caliber or two M-60 machine-guns mounted on top. They were watertight and inside were two benches capable of seating up to ten soldiers, but no one ever rode inside because it was too hot and many considered the amtracks as death traps if it hit a mine.

[45] The mechanical mule resembled a miniature flatbed truck without a cab. It was a highly mobile vehicle able to transport supplies between points. The mule (M-274) was fitted with a steering wheel and one seat that rested on top of a four-by-eight-feet metal and wooden flatbed. It was a highly mobile vehicle used to transport supplies between points. Some of the mules were fitted with 6.05 rocket launchers, and in this capacity they became very dangerous quick-moving mobile vehicles. When other vehicles were not available, the mules were used as minicabs to run to battalion headquarters or Hill 65. At Battalion HQ, Marines often raced them for sport.

[46] The heavily populated village of Dai Loc, aka Ai Nghia, with its 600 to 800 homes was located at the base of Hill 37's south side.

[47] Headquarters and Service Company (H&S) is designed primarily to assist the battalion commander. They are the supporting element needed to properly train, feed, clothe, and supply the needs of all the Marines assigned to the battalion.

[48] In general, one does not salute an officer under battle conditions, *Guidebook for Marines*, May 1, 1966, The Leatherneck Association, Washington, D.C. p.20

[49] Mess kit, a flat-oval shaped skillet and a two-compartment food tray constructed of lightweight aluminum lids that contain a fork, spoon, and knife. The two trays close tight as covers for each other and are held together by a folding handle for storage. The companion canteen fits inside a separate aluminum cup with a similar folding handle. All can be hooked together for easy cleaning.

[50] Every morning, a Marine rifle squad from a platoon on the hill would accompany a team of Marines from the Seventh Engineers as they made their way out of the compound toward Da Nang. At the perimeter wire, the engineers would begin to sweep for mines; the enemy might have planted the night before. Somewhere about halfway to Da Nang, they would meet another team of engineers that had cleared the road toward Battalion HQs from Da Nang. The routine was repeated daily.

[51] The M-16 rifle was lightweight, only 7.6 pounds compared to the 10.1 pounds of the M-14 rifle. The M-16's smaller 5.56mm ammunition; however, was only accurate to 300 yards while the M-14's 7.62 ammunition had a maximum effective range of 700 meters. In close firefight engagements like those experienced in Vietnam, the M-16's rapid firing power was much appreciated. The M-14 rifle's long-range accuracy for sniping at distant

targets made it a valuable weapon to have in a platoon, especially when used by snipers and others confident in shooting the weapon. Some old-timer Marines requested and were allowed to continue to carry the M-14 in combat instead of the M-16. The M-14 ammo was also the same size round the M-60 machine-gun fired, so a Marine carrying the M-14 rifle was not only assured of carrying an effective and proven weapon but also knew that there was always a ready supply of ammo nearby.

[52]   The boots were made of cloth with rubber soles and a large green elastic band that allowed the foot to breathe.

[53]   According to the books, each weapons platoon company is supposed to have an M-60 machine-gun section. The section was supposed to be commanded by a sergeant and consist of three machine-gun squads with two M-60 machine-guns per squad. Each squad was supposed to have two machine-gun teams; each fire-team within that squad was supposed to be commanded by a corporal and the MG teams made up of a gunner, an assistant gunner (a-gunner), and an ammo carrier.

[54]   Famfire is the acronym for familiarization firing.

[55]   Kilometer, a metric unit of length is equal to one thousand meters (0.62 mile).

[56]   Operation Arizona, Search and Destroy Operation, June 14-22, 1967.

[57]   Operation DeSoto, Search and Destroy Operation in the Duc Pho, Quang Ngai province area, was launched on the twenty-sixth of January and terminated on the seventh of April '67. Corporal Moses was wounded on January 31, the day India Company suffered many casualties. Enemy killed during the entire operation was 383 confirmed, 716 probable, 117 WIA, and nine POWs. USMC killed was listed as seventy-two, with 573 WIA.

[58]   For his actions that day, S/Sgt. Spahn was awarded the Silver Star.

[59]   For his leadership role and actions that day, Captain Clark was awarded the Silver Star.

[60]   For his actions that night, Garcia was awarded posthumously the Silver Star. Garcia was from Galveston, Texas, and is buried at Galveston Memorial Cemetery, Hitchcock, TX

[61]   Just before the United States intervened, the VC had free reign over most of the countryside we now occupied.

[62]   Getting to know and work with the locals was called a pacification program. A Marine could volunteer for CAP unit duty and live among the villagers. In turn for providing close security, villagers often provided valuable information on enemy activity. This type of program had worked in Nicaragua, and it seemed to be working in Vietnam.

[63]   The Marine had stepped on a Bouncing Betty bomb, which was an antipersonnel mine designed to explode at waist level. The enemy liked to use the "Bouncing Betty" mine. The bomb resembled a twelve-ounce can of tomatoes and had three small antenna wires protruding from the top. The mines were usually covered over with light dirt, hidden in grass, or they were simply laid underwater near a rice paddy dike. When you stepped on it, you'd hear a loud click. If you removed your foot, the released pressure would ignite the explosive charge and shoot a small deadly canister about four feet into the air. When the bomb explodes, it disembowels or cuts its intended victims in half.

[64] The black syphilis wandering ship had been drilled into us from MCRD days. The mysterious black ship supposedly carried on board, hundreds of Marines and sailors who had come down with what were called black syphilis. It was the worst form of clap, among a group the corpsman called the Heinz 57 variety. It was incurable and caused an endless drip that was so contagious Uncle Sam made sure that anyone contracting the disease was sent to the ship and stayed there until he died. None of this was true, of course, but many guys believed this.

[65] For AT grid coordinates references used in this book, Dai Loc Map Sheet 6640 IV series L7014 is used.

[66] For his actions that day, Ringer was awarded the Silver Star

[67] Song is Vietnamese for river. I have chosen to keep the Vietnamese word in front as well as in its description. Song Vu Gia, Song Thu Bon River.

[68] The Popular Force, or Dan De as they were called by the Vietnamese, were a paramilitary unit made up of local villagers much like our military reserve forces, except they had very little or no military training. It was also questionable whether they would fire the small arms weapons they had been issued in defense or if they even knew how to use them. In what direction they would fire, if they did, was another question Marines worried about.

[69] Dog Patch was a dingy little village near Da Nang where you could get just about anything your heart desired. If it was available on the black market, it could be bought in Dog Patch.

[70] No Name Village was a heavily forested village near Hill 52 that was known to provide food, shelter and supplies to the enemy.

[71] A few months later, the camp was overrun by VC and North Vietnamese soldiers. We heard that somehow over thirty percent of the ARVNs stationed there turned out to be North Vietnamese sympathizers.

[72] I had forgotten the words to this song, but Leatherneck Magazine published at my request a shout out for the words, and I received a number of calls and letters from Marines that had a copy of the words or remembered them.

[73] Kit Carson Scouts were former Vietcong or NVA soldiers who had defected and now served the South Vietnamese government. After defecting, the Hoi Chanhs was retained for two months at a Chieu Hoi center, some entered the Kit Carson program initiated by Marines and soon adopted by other military services.

[74] It was Marine Corps policy and taught in basic officer's school that a small unit officer should always remain with the main body of Marines under his command.

[75] Hill 25, was also known as Dineen Hill, named after Second Platoon, Second Lieutenant Thomas G. Dineen killed on August 10, 1967, when leading a squad of Marines in response to incoming fire on Hill 25; tripped an AP mine made up of three blocks of C-4, resulting in his death and the wounding of another Marine.

[76] Not his real name, or a known Marine, a name and image given to an American serviceman who endured and was changed by war.

[77] Ninety-day wonders were officers that were commissioned after only a few months of training. The only experience they obtained was at OCS (Officers Candidate School)

before they were sent to a command position in a combat zone. Most of the new officers in Vietnam had only thirty or sixty more days of military training than what a grunt went through. That was the only difference, we were told, between their boot camp and the one we had gone through and that made it easier for us to accept an officer as a Marine, knowing that they had gone through the same type of basic boot camp as we had. A ninety-day wonder did not come up the ranks nor was he a West Point graduate. The term was meant to be derogatory or humorous because second looeys usually messed things up. A ninety-day wonder just happened to have scored higher on his entrance exam or had graduated from college, so he was sent to Officers Candidate School.

[78] Within minutes of the heavy rocket attack, an Air Force C-47 "Dragon" on air alert had the launching sites under fire. Two minutes later, he called down a series of artillery counter battery fire, but the enemy rocket launchers had by then caused great damage to the airfield at Da Nang. Within five minutes, from six different sites, the enemy had fired over fifty projectiles that struck the airbase. Most of the rockets had been launched from Hoa Hung Village, a small Vietnamese village six miles southwest of Da Nang. There had been six firing sites, each with two clusters positions of three positions each. Eight airmen were killed, and another 138 wounded; thirty-seven Marines had also been wounded. Ten planes had been totally destroyed, and many others were severely damaged. That had also been the first time that Russian-made 122mm rockets had been used in South Vietnam. In early February of that same year, military intelligence had identified 134 such firing points within five miles of Da Nang. The day the NVA elected to bombard Da Nang with rockets was near the anniversary date of the Marine Corps' first charges of atrocities in Vietnam. In August of 1966, men of the First Battalion Ninth Marines torched the village of Cam Ne near Hoa Hung village. The American press had chosen to run pictures of the dozen or so burning hooches in 1966 while failing to mention that it was a village that was heavily held by the NVA. By launching rocket attacks against Da Nang on the anniversary date of those former conflicts, the Communist-propaganda machine had hoped to sensationalize once again that incident, but they didn't know that war correspondence reporters had limited perceptions of the way insurgents operated and even less knowledge of Communist strategy. They hadn't figured out how important anniversary days of historical war incidents were to the North Vietnamese people. It was an important consideration that many of our military officers seemed to have also overlooked in Vietnam. One thing I had already learned about our enemy was that they always repeated themselves in how they operated and planned.

[79] For his actions that Day, Ronald Allen Moore was awarded posthumously the Navy Cross.

[80] There are several accounts of what happened that day. What I have written of the events is from my diary, my personal recollections, and from what others who were there recall. Some of it was verified, some not. The Marine Corps spot and situation reports give different times and accounts of what happened that day. I don't recall fixed wing air strike, or a 1/7 unit responding as a blocking force.

"On July 19, a fire-team patrol from Co I was ambushed at noon at AT 946643 by an estimated VC squad. Two Marines were killed and two others wounded. The wounded estimated that they had killed two VCs and four wounded. Later in that same general area, a VC unit commander was killed by a Co K patrol. The VC unit commander's journal recorded the July 19 ambush and verified that two VCs were killed and others wounded in the action" (Narrative, Third Battalion, Seventh Marines, First Marine Division, *Command Chronology*, July 1967).

"On 19122OH the flank security fire-team of a Co I squad on patrol was ambushed by an estimated VC squad. Enemy fire was returned and reaction force from Co I was dispatched to the area arriving at 191240, but the VC had already broken contact and fled. The ambush resulted in two USMC KIA and two USMC WIA (Medevac) and loss of one PRC-25-radio, two M-16 rifles and assorted individual equipment. A search of the area revealed blood trails indicating four VC WIA. (Later intelligence reports revealed that there were two VC KIA and two VC WIA in the said action). Additionally, [*sic*] a fixed wing air strike was called" (Third Battalion, Seventh Marines, First Marine Division, *Command Chronology*, July 1967).

From the Seventh Marines, *Command Chronology*; (entry #273) Spot Report 7I4 Squad security 1120H, AT 951643 Ftm flank security from 7I4 squad patrol encountered heavy automatic weapons fire and incoming grenades from est VC Squad in tree line. Returned fire and requested reaction force from First Plt Co I. 1 squad dispatched to sweep area to north and another squad to sweep area to south. Both arrived at 1140 hours. Nearby units alerted. Air Observer requested an on station. Operating area and free fire zone cleared with 1/7 and First Mar and blocking forces inserted by those units. Fixed wing on station. Sweep continued south. Will follow up. One USMC WIA medevac completed at 1150 hours. Two USMC KIA, two USMC WIA (One EVAC), two M-16 rifles, one PRC-25-radio and assorted individual equipment all lost to enemy. [Authors Note; the M-60 not listed as missing]

Follow-up Spot Report to 191120H, (entry #276), Plt + H&S Co 3/7 1300-1600 hours At 950620 to 953655. Search of area revealed pools of blood resulting four VC WIA. Found two ChiCom grenades and one Punji pit (AT 948630) which were all destroyed. Located two houses (AT 948630), which had signs saying the houses were mined. Search of houses revealed no mines of any type.

[81] On June 29, 1967, Pvt. Le Thanh Hung, age twenty, was captured, he said, in the NVA battalion; he belonged to operating in southern Quang Nam Province. There are three corpsmen/nurses per platoon and one doctor in the battalion. First Marine Division, *Command Chronology*, July 1968. "The difference between a medical corpsman and a first aid man (nurse) was the amount of training received. A Corpsman had formal classroom training while the aid man likely got his in the field." Inside the NVA, p.134.

[82] An example of the complex tunnel networks that could be found in this area was the discovery of a 1,000 meter long tunnel discovered on the July 8, by Charley 1/5 Marines. The tunnel network was large enough for an average sized man to walk through. The tunnel was discovered in the very same area where the Fifth Marines were engaged

in a day-long battle against a dug-in-force on June 2. First Marine Division, *Command Chronology*, June 1967.

[83] My hometown newspaper, the *Casa Grande Dispatch* newspaper, in mid-1967, published drawings of both the tunnels and types of booby traps, the Vietcong used in South Vietnam.

[84] The Marine Corps Command Chronologies shows this as occurring on the twenty-third of July. My diary records it as occurring on the twenty-second of July. There are only a few times when my dairy entries and the Marine Corps journal are off by one or two days. I found if I tried to change my entries to match the Marine Corps account, other historical events recorded by other units entered in Marine Corps records did not match up.

Since this book is based on my recollection of events according to how I viewed them at that time, I have decided to keep my diary date entries, the majority of which are correct as verified by other witnesses of those events.

On 231255, three VCs dressed in black, fired approximately forty rounds S/A at a Co I squad at AT 950635. The squad responded with thirty rounds M-16. A search of the area revealed one open medical kit with medical supplies indicating one VC KIA (prob).

231124H, I squad security AT 945653 received one round small arms fire from AT 947653, Returned five rounds small arms fire and one round M-79. Searched area neg results. Third Battalion, Seventh Marines, *Command Chronology*, July 1967.

231255H, Co I Sqd Sec AT 950635, recorded three to four rounds S/A fire from three VCs dressed in black. Returned thirty rounds S/A fire. Searched area & found one VC med kit containing needles, antibiotics, & personal effects; med kit had three bullet holes in it. Gear forward to BN S-2. Seventh Marines, *Command Chronology*, July 1967.

[85] 3/7 July 1967, *Command Chronology*.

[86] CAC, or CAP-C1, CAP 2-2-1 was located at grid coordinates AT 923567/922562, at times this CAC unit has also been referred to as CAP 2-2-2, in some of the Command Chronologies. My diary records it as being CAC 2-2-1, as does other *Command Chronology* reports.

[87] July 29, 1967, 2220 hours, AT 860573, CAP 22 CAP LZ post received fifty rounds S/A fire from unknown number of VC. CAP returned forty rounds 30 cal. forty rounds M-60, and 120 rounds carbine and ten rounds 81 illum.

[88] Phan Van Tin, a fourteen-year-old NVA who surrendered under the Chieu Hoi in July, stated that he received orders to report for induction at age thirteen. All of the men of his village between the ages of twenty to thirty had already been drafted, and all boys who were fourteen or near fourteen were drafted with them. Hoang Van Minh, a fourteen-year-old squad leader with the Seventy-Second VC Battalion who rallied at Que Son, stated morale in his unit was low as most personnel were forcibly inducted.

[89] July 30, 1967, at 1305 hours, CAP 22 CP, AT 865565, received four rounds sniper fire. Returned fire of twenty-five rounds 50 cal. A/W. No search of area due to river barrier.

[90] July 31, 1967, at 1420 hours, received five rounds small arms fire. Refugee village recorded S/A fire also. Returned fifteen rounds 50 cal MG, one USN taken to BAS. In

position; fourteen USMC's, two PF's, one USN; On rolls—fourteen USMC's, 10 PF's, and one USN.

[91] Hoa Tay was where a fourteen-man (Lost patrol) from Bravo Company 1/9 became engaged on May 12, 1966, in three days of heavy fighting, against the R20 Doc Lap VC Battalion. In the end, only two Marines survived.

[92] U.S. Army map depicting where Agent Orange was sprayed during this time.

[93] Every fifth round fired from the low-flying plane was a red-burning tracer. A steady burst of fire produced a ray of red tracers streaking toward the ground. The red fiery glow struck terror in the hearts of those under its shower of death. It was a very powerful and destructive weapon; the enemy feared it. "The plane could also drop two-million-candlepower, slow-burning parachute flares that turned the night into day" (U.S. Marines in Viet Nam, *Fighting the North Vietnamese* 1967, p. 43).

[94] FAO, Forward Air Observer, used to call in artillery or air strikes.

[95] The claymore mine was housed in a hard green rectangular plastic shell about five inches in height and eight inches wide. While only a couple of inches thick, the claymore mine housed a pound and a half of high explosive C-4. The plastic explosive charge, once detonated, was powerful enough to release over seven hundred steel pellets in a sixty-degree fan-shaped pattern over fifty yards. The claymore mine was often used in night ambush positions by both sides.

[96] The rocket-propelled grenade launcher (RPG) is a muzzle-loaded, shoulder-fired, smooth-bore, recoilless launcher; it fires a 40mm explosive round.

[97] On 071230H Co I CP (AT 924536) observed 8 VC in two boats moving southeast vicinity AT 902525. Fired two rounds M-16. Boats continued moving. Fired two rounds 06mm. VC deserted boats and fled into tree line. three VC KIA (P) and two boats destroyed. *Command Chronology*; Month of August 1967; Third Battalion, Seventh Marines, First Marine Division.

[98] It was common for the Vietnamese to live in the same village for generations. Their religious beliefs called for ancestral worship in the villages where they were born. Vietnamese peasants stayed rooted to the same land for many generations. They believed the spirits of their ancestors inhabited the villages in which they lived. To dwell where their ancestors had lived before them, they believed, brought the ancestors honor. The ancestral spirits were considered to be part of the wealth attributed to the property owned by the peasant. They believed that such observance was the cause of their prosperity. Getting the Vietnamese to leave the area in the presence of imminent danger was not an easy task. No matter how carefully we cleared an area, someone almost always stayed behind. They usually came out of hiding shortly after we moved out of an area.

[99] CAC 2-2-2 AT 865574 b22 (Tam Hoa) is also known as CAC 22, CAP C4, and CAC B2-2, First Marine Division, Seventh Marines and Third Battalion, Seventh Marines, Command Chronologies: Month of May 1967.

[100] The city of San Antonio, Texas named a park in honor of Gregory Van De Walle, the park is located at 1925 Herbert St. in San Antonio, Texas.

[101] The Marine Corps, under the Department of the Navy, did not have Marine medics that served with us in the field; instead the navy provided navy corpsmen.

[102] "On 071315H Co I squad security (AT 938555) tripped a trip wire attached to M-26 grenade. Grenade was rigged in tree as an A/P mine with trip wire across trail resulting in one USMC WIA (minor) (non-evac)" (Third Battalion, Seventh Marines, *Command Chronology*).

[103] First Marine Division *Command Chronology*, August 1967.

[104] "On 101145H Co I platoon CP (AT 924536) observed two VCs in boat land on bank. Observed eight VC load supplies in boat. Fired nine rounds 06mm HE [high explosive or heat rounds] resulting in boat being destroyed and killing of VC. Observed six additional VC pull bodies from river. Fired two rounds 106mm HE, direct hit. Total VC casualties: 15 VC KIA (P)

On 101300H Co I platoon CP (AT 924536) observed three VCs in small boat moving toward two VCs on north bank. Fired three rounds 06mm HE sinking boat. five VC KIA (P)" (Third Battalion, Seventh Marines, *Command Chronology*, p. 9).

[105] On April 10, 1967, Wheat was wounded the first time when a fragment of shrapnel from a mortar round tore a hole in his helmet and grazed his head. His second Purple Heart was received on July 30, 1967, when a hand grenade thrown by a Vietcong exploded near him. The oldest of four sons, Wheat, already wounded twice, volunteered to return to his unit. On August 11, 1967, L/Cpl. Roy M. Wheat from K Company, Third Battalion Seventh Marines, with shrapnel still embedded in his right thigh, from his prior wounds, triggered a bouncing Betty mine. Wheat and other K Company Marines were on Route 4 providing security for a Navy construction battalion crane. Yelling a warning to other nearby Marines, Wheat hurled himself on the mine absorbing the full impact of the explosion with his own body. He was killed and the other two Marines near him were seriously wounded. For his actions, in saving the lives of his fellow Marines, Wheat was awarded the Medal of Honor. He was—the first for members of the Seventh Marines in the Vietnam War.

[106] "Mike Force" from Fifth SFGA with 3D LVT was providing the river boat transportation. Mike Company 3/5 may have been involved in Operation Cochise in this area chasing after the Third NVA Regiment and the First VC Regiment out of the Que Son Valley.

[107] *Command Chronology*, Month of August 1967.

[108] Second Platoon, out on a short patrol traveling northwest along the east side of the river, received twenty-four rounds small arms fire at 1130 hours. The squad returned 240 rounds M-16 fire, resulting in one VC KIA (C). They searched the area with no other signs of VC casualties. Third Battalion, Seventh Marines, First Marine Division, *Command Chronology*, Month of August 1967.

[109] Lieutenant Rathbun, India Company's supply lieutenant had seen twelve Starlight scopes that were brand-new and available at regiment and signed for all twelve of them. A few days later, we had to give ten of them back.

[110] Sappers sometimes probed in preparation for assaulting our positions. They would probe a little at a time, looking for weak spots in the perimeter wire, then coming back

the following night to probe again, going a little farther each time. Sappers were always the primary lead in an assault wave prepared to overrun a compound. One thing we would learn about the NVA/VCs military tactics was that they were patient. They would sit and watch and plan and plan until the most opportune time and then they would launch their all-out offensive.

[111] Vietnamese slang for "real crazy."

[112] First Marine Division, *Command Chronology*, August 1967.

[113] The NVA were known to have women accompany them into battle. Many served in communist military supporting units as ammo bearers or medical assistants and others as hard-core fighting women who lived and fought alongside the NVA soldiers. Often they were very pretty and were known to service NVA officers' sexual needs even though the local communist cadre leader assigned to each NVA unit heavily condemned such actions.

[114] 3/7 Sport Report, Co I Plt, combat 0730 hours observed two VCs wearing black pj's with one weapon moving west. Fired three rounds M-16, one VC fell and appeared to crawl away. Other VCs ran toward the roads and disappeared. Plt leader and one man crossed river and captured one VCS (At 914538). Seventh Marines, *Command Chronology*, August 1967. On 270730H Co I platoon combat base (AT 906540) observed two VCs with one weapon vicinity AT 903539. Fired three rounds M-16 and observed one VC fall indicating one VC KIA (P). Searched area and detained one VCS (914537) with no ID card, aged sixty-two. Forwarded detainee to Battalion S-2. Third Battalion, Seventh Marines, First Marine Division, *Command Chronology*, August 1967.

[115] At 060200H, a thirty meter section of Liberty bridge AT 927533 was destroyed by unknown explosive devices. The Explosion appeared to have occurred either at ground level or below. No enemy fire or movement was observed and indications are that the VC employed divers to plant the device. 3/7 command chronologies.

[116] Jody was the guy back home that every serviceman believed might be busy with his girlfriend or wife while he humped the hills of Vietnam or died in the rice paddies.

[117] The Second NVA Division moved into the Que Son Valley and engaged elements of the Fifth Marines. The Operation lasted from 4-15 September with over 100 Marines killed in action and over 500 enemy soldiers killed during that time. Prisoners stated that elements of the First VC and Third NVA Regiments were engaged in the various battles. First Marine Division, *Command Chronology*, September 1967.

[118] When Harold Reid walked off Liberty Bridge, no one in India Company saw or heard from him again. Over the years, Reid remained listed as MIA. On December 3, 1974, with no further information on Reid, the secretary of the navy declared Reid officially dead. The story above was obtained from interviews and statements of the now-deceased Vietnamese citizens from the village and the VC soldiers involved in the firefight. Those interviews were made in 1993, 1995, and 1996 when Reid's remains were finally located. On Saturday, March 27, 1999, Reid's remains were sent home for burial.

[119] Blackcoat was also the First Marine Division—AO unit's call sign. In November, it was changed to Benchmark.

[120] On 211700H Co I squad security at (AT 896520) received fifty rounds S/A fire from 895514 resulting in one USMC WIA (non-evac). Fired two hundred rounds M-16, Blackcoat fired rockets, two 90mm HE rounds. Searched area with negative results. Third Battalion, Seventh Marines, First Marine Division, *Command Chronology*, Month of September.

[121] The Asian tropical black leech is a slimy, slow-moving, carnivorous, bloodsucking worm that can grow up to eighteen inches in length. They're parasites that suck blood through a front or rear sucking disk and can grow to about three times their weight and length in just one feeding. Once swollen with all the blood they can consume, they fall off by themselves. If you try to pull them off, the sucking head stays embedded under the skin and the area becomes infected. Burning and bug spray were the best ways to remove them safely.

[122] The 3.5 rocket launcher was used in World War II as an antitank weapon capable of penetrating as much as five inches of armor plate. It was named bazooka after the unique, homemade musical instrument invented by the ruddy-faced radio comedian Bob "Bazooka" Burns. Burns became famous during the 1930s and '40s as the strapping guy who had radio audiences from coast-to-coast belly laughing at fanciful yarns about his kinfolk and old pals back in Arkansas. Because the strange horn was so well-known, World War II combat soldiers nicknamed the army's new shoulder-held rocket launcher the "bazooka" because of its blunderbuss appearance—just like Burns's popular horn.

[123] A company "B" tank spotted a sampan at (AT 941541). The Tank fired one round of 90mm HE, sinking the sampan. Enemy casualties are unknown. Ref: S-3 Journal, October 6, 1967, Entry 4. Company B, First Tank Battalion, *Command Chronologies*, October 1967.

[124] The area experienced tropical rainstorms with peak rainfall on the morning of October 9 with 5.52 inches of rain. Severe flooding was experienced; five bridges were washed out. Seventh Marines, *Command Chronology*, p. 9,12.

[125] "'Rough Rider' movements, consisting of as few as fifteen to as many as 106 trucks and escort vehicles, were offensive operations. With preplanned air and artillery support, including truck-mounted infantry (for Close in security); engineer detachments capable of mine clearance, explosive ordnance disposal, and bridge or road repair tasks, and communication augmentation. Armored elements often accompany the convoys and naval gunfire support ships are normally available, should additional fire support be required" (Operations of U.S. Marine Forces Vietnam, November 1967, p.45).

[126] A Marine company-size helicopter response to a unit's call for assistance.

[127] CH-46 *Sea Knight* helicopter is an all-weather, day-or-night Marine assault transport helicopter, capable of transporting twenty-two combat troops, their supplies, and equipment. Additional tasks may be assigned, such as combat support, search and rescue, support for forward refueling and rearming points, aeromedic evacuation of casualties from the field, and recovery of aircraft and personnel. US Navy Aircraft Fact File, Updated: February 12, 2002.

[128] First Marine Division, *Command Chronology* in the month of October 1967.

[129] For his actions that day, Lieutenant Klaus Schreiber received the Navy Cross.

[130] The Bald Eagle information was obtained from the Seventh Marines, Command Chronologies of the month of October as well as firsthand accounts of those incidents from Marines in Second and Third Platoons.

[131] Rick Oglesby, a FO with the platoon, and other First Platoon Marines related this information to me.

[132] Within 2/7's TAOR, increase in enemy activity substantiated earlier reports of enemy movement in the area. Two reports of regimental size units had been received. A large number of reports had also been received concerning platoon and company size units located in the KIM LIEN area vicinity of 8986 and along route #1 and increased enemy activity in the mountains near An Hoa. Seventh Marines *Command Chronology* for October 1967, p. 5.

[133] AT 875877.

[134] The actual Seventh Marines, *Command Chronology* reported four NVA uniforms found, but only specified the color of three of them. Often, the color of an enemy's uniform designated the type of unit they belonged to.

[135] at ZC 175975

[136] Howard Ogden's family received a posthumous Silver Star for his actions during the rescue of Recon Team PETRIFY - but his body could not be recovered, and he remains missing. Source 3/7 and Recon unit, command chronologies, and Virtual wall documentation at www.virtualwall.org

[137] 3/7 CP Benchmark (bird-dog plane) called in an air strike on newly dug bunkers at grid coordinates 815474. A Marine jet by the call sign of "Black Ace" dropped six 250lbs. bombs, but they all failed to go off, so Benchmark called in an artillery, a 155mm howitzer-fire mission on the duds. Seventh Marines, *Spot Reports* Month of October 1967.

[138] A Puff or Spooky was any plane—such as a C-130, C-47, AC-47D, AC-130—that would fire mini-machine-guns or gattling guns downward in a tight circle.

[139] The road had been blown by a charge that had been placed inside the culvert. The explosion during the night had been noted by the Marines on watch, but they thought it was artillery being dropped in the area. The hole the explosion made was 5' deep, 6' wide, and 15' long. 3/7 *Spot Report*, Month of October, 1967.

[140] Operation Knox was a Search and Destroy Operation conducted by 2/7 & 3/7 (rein) with BLT 2/3, and Co C, First Recon Bn, Marines, in Phu Loc District, Thua Thien. Prior to the operation reconnaissance elements had made several fierce contacts with enemy forces in the area.

[141] Operation Knox, in the Phu Loc-Hai Van Mountains, Hill 1192, 24 October-November 4, 1967.

[142] Prior to the airstrikes, the area had been prepped with Naval Gunfire, USS New & USS Lynde McCormick.

[143] Harold James Sotzen was from Clawson, Michigan.

[144] Flammable tablet used to heat C-rations. It took a long time to heat the food and gave off harsh fumes.

[145] The enemy force Meaney's squad encountered estimated at over 100 NVA soldiers were there to overrun Hill 52 (AT 798552). The enemy wanted Mike Company to make it pass them all the way to Route 4, where they had dug fifty-two fighting positions, on both sides of the road to engage the Mike Company's reactionary force there. A larger battalion-size force was ready to hit Hill 52 from several positions, including the footbridge location. Hill 25 was the bait. At the start of that engagement, the enemy dropped twenty well positioned 82mm mortar rounds on the Marine compound, while their sapper units, used Bangalore torpedoes and wire cutters to breach that hill from four different positions. Another well coordinated attack had started an half hour earlier when fifty NVA soldiers mortared, then attacked the Dai Loc Bridge. This tactics was designed to keep both Hill 65 and Battalion on Hill 37 occupied while the NVA devastated two remote hills occupied by Mike Company Marines. A mistake by artillery from Hill 65 firing first on the wrong hill (Hill 25 AT 806553) near Hill 52 caused the enemy soldiers gathered there to disperse, carrying away their dead and wounded. S/Sgt. Bolton's call in of an artillery airburst barrage over the Marine occupied Hill 25 (AT839568) ended the enemy's plans, to annihilate both hills.

[146] For his leadership and courage that night, S/Sgt. Gilbert Bolton was awarded the Silver Star.

[147] Information on the Hill 25 battle was obtained from government sources as well as through interviews of Marines that were there, by the author and by Vic Villionis that has documented much of the Seventh Marines historical accounts of our time in Vietnam.

[148] Est seventy NVA/VC with AK-47's, wearing black shorts and red head-bands, attacked Cac C-1, AT 922562 with mortars, 57 recoilless rifle fire, B-40 rockets, satchel charges, bangalor torpedoes, and grenades.

[149] Dai Loc (Al Nghia) and Phu Loc (2) just south of Route 4 were also being hit by an some seventy VC/NVA soldiers.

[150] Hill 37 was impacted with thirty to forty 82mm mortar rounds, the Dai Loc Army compound as well as the Dai Loc Bridge was also hit with s/a, automatic fire and mortars. H&S platoon from 3/7 responded to reinforce the bridge.

[151] We were now receiving the M-16 ammos in small cardboard boxes stuffed in cloth bandoliers. We learned to take the clips out, remove the ammo, place the ammo in magazines, and then carry the fully loaded magazines in the seven-pouch cloth bandolier in which the ammo had come.

[152] A flareship by the call sign of Basketball had dropped high illumination flares to light up the area Spooky twelve and thirteen, were working out with their guns on both sides of the river and around the CAC unit.

[153] For his leadership and courage while under fire Sgt. Everett James Wilcox was awarded the Navy Commendation Medal with Combat "V".

[154] The Starlight scope enhanced the light from the stars and moon, enabling the user to see clearly in outline form or the images of the night. But there was no real way of telling from a distance if the image was that of the enemy or a friendly force.

[155] A number of small refugee hamlets were attacked: Al Nghia, Hoan My, and Giao Dong, along with the refugees camps at Ky Tan, Hoa Phu, Loc My, and Doc Hung. Three other hamlets and a Peace village had also been attacked. All of these camps and villages were in the Dai Loc District and had been burned down and many civilians killed or taken hostage

[156] For his actions that night, Staff Sergeant Robert Edward Tully was presented with the Bronze Star medal with Combat "V."

[157] Hmm361 Door gunner, Gy/Sgt Stofl, expended 200 M-60 rounds, VMO-2 After-action Report, November 1967

[158] For his actions that day, Doc Keller received the Navy Commendation Medal with combat "V".

[159] An NVA battalion usually consisted of three-hundred to six-hundred or more men. A battalion with over three-hundred men was considered to be a reinforced battalion with possibly a sapper and/or a reconnaissance platoon attached. The first two prisoners captured by Second Platoon, Pham Sau and Nguyen Hieu, as well as another prisoner had quickly indicated that the attached unit was the R-20 Battalion, a force of normally four-hundred men which had almost been entirely wiped out during the night. Sweeps of the area—uncovered areas that were completely covered with blood. Many of the dead enemy bodies had also been dragged and buried in prepared positions in the Arizona area and local villagers were also forced to bury the dead in individual graves to reduce detection of the total casualties the enemy had suffered. Seventh Marines, *Command Chronologies* and *Spot Reports*, November 1967, p. 6.

[160] A liquid fire of hot burning drops of melting acid that burns and melts skin and bone together.

[161] 3/7 November, Command Chronologies.

[162] A D Platoon MCB-9 Seabee using a torch welder accidentally set the bridge on fire. The entire northern section of the bridge was burned.

[163] Casualties on Hill 37, one KIA, twelve WIA's, twelve Regional Force ARVN'S KIAs, The CAC unit sustained nine PF's KIA, USMC two KIAs and five WIA's.

[164] The Chieu Hoi (appeal return), program offered amnesty to persons who had previously supported the activities of the Viet Cong or NVA, and who decided to return to the side of the South Vietnamese government.

[165] Cam Ranh Bay was very much like a miniature American city. Located about three-hundred miles south of Da Nang, it had its own electrical power plant, lights, traffic, music, and round eyes. It had a large recreation area, and just about everything you could get in the real world was available there. You got to sleep on real beds and firm mattresses. You could go to the beach, the local bars, nightclubs, or to one of the many outside movie theaters. The city had pizza restaurants and French cafés. The barracks were air-conditioned, and it had the largest PX in Vietnam.

[166] Spider holes were individual fighting positions from where the enemy could pop up, fire at us, then slip back into a concealed hole in the ground that was hard to see.

[167] Less than a klick away, Air Observers called in fixed wing air strikes on an estimated thirty-five NVA soldiers running Southwest along the northern bank of the Song Thu Bon River, from Phu Long (2).

[168] The footnotes inserted here, for this operation, depict the activities of other units as well as enemy activity occurring around us, that for the most part we were not aware of, at that time.

Light sniper fire characterized enemy activity throughout the day. Air observers conducted fixed wing strikes on an estimated thirty-five fleeing enemies (AT 8751), resulting in twenty VC KIA (Prob). Unclassified After-action Report, Operation Foster 3/7.

[169] The enemy continues to harass maneuver elements in their respective zones of action with long-range, sporadic sniper fire. Refugees seeking evacuation continued to increase. after-action report 3/7.

[170] Elements of BLT 2/3 discovered twenty tons of rice in scattered caches. At 1955 hours Co G received twelve rounds 60 mm mortars from vicinity (AT 822513), counter fire cause incoming to cease. after-action report 3/7.

[171] BLT Co F & G had moderate contact for brief periods of time with squad size groups of enemy. Air strikes and artillery called on twenty-five enemy in uniform (AT 885505). Enemy broke contact when attempts to close in were made. Co H helilifted vicinity (AT 808492) to increase pressure on enemy forces. after-action report 3/7.

3/7, Co F 2/7 op-con 3/7 helilifted vicinity (8755) at 1535 hours to exploit intelligence report of enemy force hiding in tunnels in that area. A Major rice cache of forty-five tons unearthed at (876522) by Co. I, First Platoon. After-action Report 3/7.

[172] BLT 2/3 began sweeping east where intelligence source indicated, a main force Battalion was setting up an ambush, contact however was limited to light sniper fire. 3/7 found rice moved to Dai Loc via LCM-8. Refugees now totaled 4,200 from both zones of action. Reconnaissance inserts in the mountains to the west of the operation area reported a total of eighty-one uniformed enemy soldiers in three separate sightings and they were engaged with artillery resulting in thirteen KIA (prob). after-action report 3/7.

[173] Recon Inserts "Gold lemon" and "Pony Boy," called in artillery and air strike mission on approximately 175 enemy soldiers moving east in trace of 2/3. after-action report 3/7.

[174] Enemy forces were hidden in tunnels directly under us, relaying information to the unit that had engaged Second Platoon in the firefight a short distance away, and we didn't know it. The extensive network of tunnels running along or near the trails we were on would be discovered the following year by Mike 1/7.

[175] By the end of the day, mortars, artillery and four fixed-wing close air support sorties had been dropped on the entrenched enemy.

[176] Lieutenant Mullens was awarded the Silver Star for his actions this day.

[177] The Command Chronologies report four close air support sorties were flown in, in our support that day. I don't recall that many nor who the sixth Marine was that was killed. That report also estimated the enemy force at approximately twenty since twenty fighting positions were reportedly found with large pools of blood.

[178] We would later learn that while at the hospital in Da Nang, the doctors there had decided that Lieutenant Faithful was too far gone to save, as a flood of other wounded Marines were arriving and needed the hospital staff's attention. Sergeant Tully, lying on a stretcher nearby, overheard the doctors tell the stretcher bearer to move Lieutenant Faithful out

of the way and to bring up the next wounded Marine. Tully, we were told, then got off his stretcher, drew his pistol, and demanded the doctors to work on Lieutenant Faithful. Without hesitation, they complied and were successful and Faithful lived.

[179] George of the Jungle was an animated television series that ran every Saturday morning stateside.

[180] At 1615 hours forty enemy soldiers in prepared position attacked a Company I reconnaissance squad in vicinity (AT 872519). Plt reactionary force to assist was also taken under heavy small arms and automatic weapons fire, sustained six KIAs and twelve WIA's. The remainder of Co I was committed within thirty minutes of the initial contact. Artillery and four air support sorties were directed on the entrenched enemy who defiantly fired upon the aircrafts. Contact continued until dark and delayed a search of the area until the following morning. Recon inserts continue to make frequent sightings of enemy force (totaling approximately 130), moving in the western portion of the operational area. After-action Report, 3/7.

[181] The command chronologies show two separate individuals calling in air strikes, with a comment inserted in H&MS-16 *Command Chronology*: "Ran air strike AT867524, three huts destroyed but took .30 calfires. No damage to aircraft."

[182] From captured documents and prisoners captured during the operation, we found out that Aggie had opened fire against one of the NVAs lead platoons who were coming into the French village to pick up rice supplies for the Thirty-first NVA Regiment. In our firefight on the berm, we had engaged a reinforced NVA company-size enemy force.

[183] The Hanoi government revealed that Military casualties during the Vietnam war were 1.1 million killed and 600,000 wounded. The NVA casualty data was provided by North Vietnam in a press release to Agence France Presse (AFP) on April 3, 1995, on the 20th anniversary of the end of the Vietnam War.

[184] 3/7 Co I swept the area of the contact on November 19, finding a pack, khaki uniform, documents, twenty fighting positions, blood pools and expended AK-47 and .30 cal cartridges in the vicinity of (AT 872524). Ground activity characterized by light to moderate contract with Co I encountering an estimated twenty VC soldiers in the vicinity of (AT870520).

[185] The M-16 magazine bandoleer was made of soft cloth and had seven pockets that held a magazine loaded with eighteen to nineteen 5.56mm rounds. So, each Marine carried close to 240 rounds ammo each.

[186] On November 9, 1861, soldiers of the Illinois Eleventh, Eighteenth, and Twenty-ninth Regiments, after forcing the Confederates South, set up camp in Bloomfield, Missouri. Upon finding the newspaper office empty, they decided to print a newspaper for their expedition, relating the troop's activities. They called it the *Stars and Stripes*. This was the beginning of the "soldier's newspaper" that serves as a medium between soldiers and their families as well as a reporter of news.

[187] Reconnaissance sightings of large groups of uniform enemy soldiers during the operation supported low level reports before the operation of a newly infiltrated NVA battalion in the area. Foster After-action Report, p. 4

[188] Combat Action Report for Operation Foster p. 9.

[189] Pilot Shinnick, Co-Pilot Barr, Crew-Chief Day, Gunner White, remained over the area off and on in between refueling and rearming, for four hours, expanded over 3000 machine-gun rounds, and forty-eight rockets.

[190] Personal conversation about this event with Sergeant Gus at a reunion thirty-six years after this battle.

[191] Beehive rounds were artillery-fired antipersonnel shells that when they exploded fired off over eight-thousand-inch long shaved flechettes (miniature steel arrow shaped darts). They were called beehive rounds because of the sound the flying arrows made as they traveled toward their target.

[192] The NVA operated in cell groups of three, and if a member was wounded or killed in battle, the other two members would remove him and another three-man cell group would take their place in battle often in the very same spot.

[193] The bird-dog pilot, Capt. Rob Whitlow, was Benchmark 3 assigned as an AO to the First Marine Division. the Aerial Observation (AO) Unit, flew out of Marble Mountain Air Facility which was about six miles south of Da Nang. Flew in Marine, Army and Air Force Bird-Dogs because the Marines did not have enough planes to support operations for the First and Third Marine Divisions.

[194] Whitlow's personal recollection of that day, as well as entry in his log book, indicated; A Marine infantry company was operating along the finger lake that ran diagonally through the Arizona area, and was taking serious automatic weapons and machine-gun fire from a pretty good sized Viet Cong force. (from Rob Whitlow's E-mail correspondence 38 years later).

[195] Snake-eyes were 250 pound high-drag bombs. The A-4 was a reliable attack bomber and the ordnance package they were carrying was perfectly suited for close air support of troops on the ground. The AO was pretty comfortable with the situation, even though the target was only a couple of hundred meters from the Marine positions.

[196] "There were never sufficient Marine gunships in RVN to fulfill all the missions requested of them. Medevac escort, Recon-team-inserts and extractions, assault operations, direct fire support of engaged Marine ground units, TACA duties, and convoy escort, as well as other missions flying Huey "slicks" had VMO aircrews overcommitted throughout their entire tours. If ever the Marine Corps got its money's worth out of any aircraft and aircrews, it was these. (source; Popasmoke.com)

[197] This scene would play in my mind for years as no one else remembered this until a Marine from Lima Company at a First Marine reunion in Florida recalled the event as he was on the other side of the lake at that time. The Bird-Dog pilot over us at that time, also attending that same reunion, recalled the bodies in the water and in the tree line in front of our positions. He stayed with us for hours that day, he said.

[198] Operation Foster, after-action report, p. 4.

[199] The Second Battalion, Third Marines, under the command of Lieutenant Col. Henry English, served as a Special Landing Force (SLF) from April 13 until November 30, 1967. Red Dancer was also 2/3 Battalion's call sign.

[200] At 1720 hours, 3/7 assumed operational control of F 2/3. after-action report, Operation Foster, p. 9.

[201] Two Marines from Third Platoon were wounded; Lima Company also took casualties and were requesting an emergency medevac.

[202] VMO-2 after-action report, November 21, 1967, pilot Leach O'Neil, copilot Dunn, his Crew Chief King, and gunner Jefferies M. Roberts. By 1700 hours, Marines from Foxtrot 2/3 on six UH-34 HMM 364 (US Marines Medium Helicopter Squadron 364) provided escort service, while two UH-IE Gunships provided escort service for the Sparrow hawk inserted into AT 855534.

[203] First Platoon Foxtrot 2/3 under the command of Lieutenant Charles Woodard, had been given the assignment to clear the top section of the area to the left of the main landing force. They encountered fierce resistance, but soon cleared the area, killing several NVA soldiers.

[204] The following aircrafts were hit by enemy fire when they came in to medevac our wounded. A bird-dog single engine plane; 01-C belonging to the 01, Detachment H&MS-16. Two HMM-363 UH-34D VMO-2 Command Chronologies.

[205] Lieutenant Woodard also kept a dairy during his tour of duty, his entry for that day read; "Received emergency word. 3/7 in trouble, Fox to be lifted in to help; Platoon surrounded with no comm. No enemy position or strength info. We went in before dark and rescued the platoon. First Plt. swept the enemy ville in the dark, throwing grenades in bunkers and then set in an ambush in the danger area."

The entry for the next day notes that we found dead NVA in the ville, and then assaulted another fortified ville beyond it.

[206] In an email message to me, from Charles Woodard, a day before the book went to the publisher, he noted; "The way I remember it, the situation when we got there was pretty surreal, and some of your Marines seemed kind of dazed by all that had happened. I also remember getting some of my troops together in a hurry and sweeping a tree line adjacent to where you were before it got dark. I don't remember sweeping the ville in the dark, as is noted in my diary entry."

[207] At 0630 hours, Co I ambushed four VC soldiers killing one and capturing one K-44. At 1145 hours while pursuing enemy snipers, Co I encountered an entrenched, unknown size enemy force at (AT 865535) and (AT 867535). The contact gradually increased in intensity with Co L being committed at mid-afternoon. At 1720 hours, 3/7 assumed operational control of Co F 2/3 which was helilifted to vicinity (AT 856530) to provide blocking forces. Total friendly casualties were two KIA and six WIA (medevaced). After-action Report 3/7.

[208] For his actions during Operation Foster, Lieutenant Wilson was awarded the Bronze Star Medal and later for his overall combat and leadership skills, the Navy Commendation Medal.

[209] BLT 2/3 At 1045 hours Co E was helilifted to vicinity (AT 840519) and established blocking positions for 3/7 Marine elements sweeping northwest. However, sightings by aerial observers of large numbers of enemy in the western portion of the AO caused a

change of plans. BLT 2/3 resumed Operational Control of Co F 2/3, which was helilifted at 1435 hours to (AT 823538).

3/7 Elements swept the area of enemy contact on November 21 receiving only light sniper fire and finding one enemy KIA from shrapnel. Refugees now total over 7,000. After-action Report 3/7.

[210] 3/7, a detailed search of the lake vicinity (AT8653) for underwater caves was conducted by First Reconnaissance Battalion divers, but no significant findings were uncovered. After-action Report 3/7.

[211] 3/7 scattered light contact. An aerial observer directed Co F 2/7 who engaged and killed tow VC. A third enemy soldier hiding in a bunker was captured. after-action report 3/7.

[212] Hill 11 (AT 873513)

[213] Hill 10 (AT 873522)

[214] WP (white phosphorus) incendiary rockets were often used to mark or destroy a target.

[215] Tactical area of responsibility.

[216] From an interview with Leatherneck Magazine.

[217] VMO-2 after-action report (AAR), Pilot Robbins

[218] A cook-off occurred when the barrel became so hot; it caused the bullet stuck in the chamber to explode.

[219] I recall counting eighteen dead Marines for the twenty-sixth; USMC records do not reflect that number until the full count included the following day's battle. It may be that I walked by them again the following day.

[220] Contact with an entrenched and bunkered unknown size force began at 1120 hours when Co F 2/7 pursued three enemy snipers at (AT 873525). Co L then made contact with twelve enemy soldiers at 1130 hours in vicinity (AT 872522). By 1330 hours Co F 2/7 and Co L were receiving heavy small arms, automatic weapons, machine-gun and mortar fire from vic (AT 872518). Co I was committed to the attack by midafternoon. Three assaults on the well-concealed enemy positions made little headway. Casualties continued to mount from mortars and accurate small arms fire from an enemy who stubbornly resisted constant artillery barrages and air strikes. The fierce battle lasted until approximately 2030 hours. Co I and Co L linked up for the night. after-action report 3/7.

[221] From this time forward, except for some minor and a couple of some major encounters, my independent recollection of events that occurred becomes vague. My diary notes no longer triggered a fresh recollection of what occurred on those days. Others filled in many of the events I describe, or with their help, I later recalled them more clearly. During this assault, I don't recall ever firing the gun; others recall seeing me firing it from the hip during the assault.

[222] HMM-363, 265, 262 By the gunship after the troop lift, received and returned fire in the area and later flew 3/7's Regiment and Battalion commanders as well as the SLF Commander in an over flight of the Foster area. VMO-2; after-action report.

[223] The total Marines killed and wounded this day according to command chronologies was six KIA and twenty WIA. It's unknown if the other companies helilifted that morning were counted in those casualties.

[224] Hill 12 AT 872538

[225] A day before Operation Foster commenced, Boone had either accidently shot himself in the foot with a small caliber gun, or stepped on a large nail poking out of a wooden plank, near Liberty Bridge. Both accounts have been repeatedly shared at reunions. I don't have an independent recollection of this.

[226] 3/7 contact resumed at 0655 hours when Co F 2/7 (AT 873521) received heavy small arms and mortar fire. Co I moved north and linked up with Co F at 0945 hours. Both units continued to receive heavy fire but determined sweeps of the battle area resulted in twenty VC Kill (confirmed) and capture of two individuals and two crew served weapons. Villagers detained in the area reported that they were forced to bury thirty-six other enemy soldiers killed. A tunnel complex was suspected of harboring the enemy in the battle area Vic Phu Long (1) (AT 870518). Diligent searches failed to uncover the complex. Total friendly casualties of the two days of battle were twelve KIA and eighty WIA.

   BLT 2/3 chopped to vicinity (At 874518) at 1300 hours, no real contact incurred. after-action report 3/7.

[227] 3/7 enemy contact was not established. Four detainees who claimed to have escaped from the VC were detained by 3/7 vicinity (AT 848498)

[228] At 1200 hours, Operation Foster was terminated with the extraction of 3/7 Marines from the Operational area by LSCM-8.

[229] Unless an officer chose to stay in the field, he was routinely rotated out of a combat zone in six months. The reason for this was that the corps wanted as many of its officers to have the opportunity of serving in a combat zone as possible. That experience was valuable for promotion, medals, and a string of battle ribbons on an officer's chest that he might not otherwise receive.

[230] Ira Rahm was called Timber Wolf by members of the platoon because of his keen awareness of the area we patrolled in. He received the nickname Rabbit because of the hole he fell in during the assault on Foster, and "Combat" was a name given to him by Sergeant Whitesides because he carried so much equipment and ammo with him; he was always loaded with weapons and ammo.

[231] At this same time, northeast of us, Third Platoon, standing bridge security, got hit by ten incoming carbine rounds; they returned 50-caliber and M-16 fire. First Marine Division, *Command Chronologies, Spot Report.*

[232] D-1-B Seventh Eng road sweep

[233] At the time, Boone was the only black squad leader of the three squads in First Platoon.

[234] Mike boat, **a** converted LCM-6 landing craft. Armed with various weapons, some with a 40mm Bofars gun, .50 cal or .30 cal machine-guns, a 20mm gun, and some even had a 81mm mortar in the well deck midships. The sailors assigned to this type of duty often referred to themselves as serving in the Brown Water Navy.

235 Fifteen tons of rice (according to my diary), 260600-260710H Co I (AT 893515) search of Plt ambush site found 582 bags of rice of approximately 100 lbs each, three cartridge belts, two flashlights, thirty-eight pistols (Russian made), holster, magazine pouch two mags, ten rounds ammo, poncho, two Chicom grenades, four entrenching tools, rain gear, two pairs of Ho Chi Minh shoes. Seventh Marines, *Command Chronology*, December 1967.

236 The following two incidents are recorded in Marine Corps records; I don't mention them in my diary nor can I truly remember all the details on how they happened. If they occurred as recorded in the CC report, the time and location is wrong as the distance and time would not correspond to where I knew we were. I remember the area however quite clearly.

237 Enemy activity in our TAOR increased noticeably from a reported 336 incidents in December to 610 in January with a fierce free-for-all on January 31. On January 2, Regiment (Hill 55) got hit with automatic weapons fire and B-40 rockets. The following morning, MACK-V Hieu Duc District Headquarters near Da Nang also received incoming rockets. Shortly after that, Hill 10 1/7's CP came under mortar attack and the tower on Hill 41 observed mortar flashes streaking toward that hill and Hill 10 firing counter mortar fire at the sites. At 0100 hours, sappers were reported in the Hieu Duc compound and a reactionary force from 1/7 CP was sent. The reactionary force consisted of two tanks and some Marines riding along as security for the tanks. At 0105 hours, they were hit with nine RPG rockets (AT 931689), the tanks returned 90mm and .30 caliber machine-gun fire. Both tanks while still mobile could no longer fire their major weapons. The tanks and the reactionary force returned to the 1/7 CP base with their wounded. At 0116 hours, a third tank moved out to help MACK V and it was also hit with RPG rockets, but the tank continued to fire its 90 mm and machine-guns. It broke through the enemy's ambush site and reached MACV. Another reactionary force of Marines on foot followed and at 0125 hours, the enemy began to break contact. Under mortar fire the Marines suffered seven WIA and one KIA. Five VCs were KIA (confirmed). That same morning, a highly coordinated rocket attack was launched on the Da Nang Airbase. On January 4, CAP Q-2 (AT 903791) was assaulted by a large enemy force that hit the compound with twelve B-40 rockets, five satchel charges, one LAAW, and hundreds of automatic weapons fire. Seventh Marines, *Command Chronology*, January 1968.

238 On the morning of January 7, 3/7 assumed control of an additional TAOR when Second Battalion Fifth Marines were displaced to Phu Bai. India Company was moved from Liberty Bridge to the An Hoa industrial complex for defense of that area and assumed responsibility of that TAOR. This new responsibility not only included providing base security at An Hoa, but to run patrols in the area and road sweeps on the An Hoa road leading to Liberty Bridge, Liberty Road, Route 4, as well as Convoy Road. Hotel Company, Second Battalion, Seventh Marines, meanwhile, became OpCon to 3/7 and were moved to provide security at Liberty Bridge. Lima Company 3/5 took over Kilo Company's lines, and this freed up Kilo Company to conduct saturation patrolling and setting up ambushes within the southeastern portion of 3/7's TAOR in the area where Ira Hullihen was killed.

[239] Co I 3/7 Combat base, 1400 hours AT 873475, C-130 rec'd four rounds 30 cal fire while approaching from the East. Two rounds hit gas tank, one round hit engine, one round hit tail. 1 engine lost all oil. Aircraft landed w/o difficulty at An Hoa. Repairs being made, unknown when aircraft will be ready to fly. Seventh Marines, *Command Chronology*, January 1968.

[240] Significant activity occurred throughout the battalion TAOR, particularly in the Company M and Company H (OpCon at Liberty Bridge) areas. Enemy activity and movement increased and the Battalion inflicted a record number of enemy casualties. Mining activity increased to a high level within the TAOR, with the most serious and frequent incidents occurring along the An Hoa Road. Narrative Summery, 3/7 *Command Chronology*, January 1968.

[241] 3/7 to Seventh Marine *Spot Report* I 3/7 reporting for thirty-ninth ARVN Ranger Bn PLT AT 909491 AT 905493 Rangers observed three enemy soldiers wearing black uniforms, carrying three to four small arms weapons heading south. Tank fired 90mm one round that had secondary explosion. The enemy changed direction and headed north. Seventh Marines, *Command Chronology*, January 1968.

[242] 3/7 to Seventh *Marine Spot Report* Co I Squad Sec 1300 hours, AT 910487, Tank hit 40 lb command detonated mine. Command Detonator was found in the area. Tread and fender blown off and four WIA minor resulted from mine. Fired s/a into tree line tank was towed to An Hoa. Search of area with no signs of enemy casualties. Seventh Marines, *Command Chronology*, January 1968.

[243] The Vietnamese Lunar New Year Tet Offensive attacks for some reason came on two separate nights. Farther north of us on the night of the twenty-ninth, morning of the thirtieth. In our area on the night of the thirtieth, the morning of the thirty-first.

[244] Seventh Marines, *Command Chronology*, January 1968.

[245] 3/7 to Seventh Marines' Spot Rep Co I CP, received reports from industrial complex and dist that enemy platoon in vicinity of AT894473, Plt sent to ambush area. Seventh Marines, *Command Chronology*, January 1968.

[246] *Command Chronology*, Seventh Marines, First Marine Division, March 1968.

[247] Prior to the operation, low-level intelligent reports, indicated the Q-14 (local force) Co, Third/Thirty-First NVA Regiment, two-third NVA Division and local guerrillas, with a combined strength of 400-500 were operating in the area.

[248] At 0945 hours, fixed wing prep LZ Bluejay, vicinity AT 870566.

[249] Both prisoners, Ngo Lanh and Ngo Hong claimed they had been recruited by the NVA to carry rice, but could not identify the unit. They further said that between twenty-sixth February and fourth of March, sixty-five NVA carrying individual weapons had traveled north through Phuoc Loc toward Charlie Company. Seventh Marines, *Command Chronology*, March 1968.

[250] Lima 3/7 received forty-one 81mm mortar rounds, small arms and automatic rifle fire, resulting in one KIA, and four WIA's.

[251] Combat Operations, After-action Report (Operation Rock).

[252] C Troop, Third Squadron, Fifth Armored Cavalry was OpCon to 3/7 for the operation after our tracks left the Foster area and they had crossed the river at AT862564 on the ninth.

[253] Operation Rock, ended with the lost three KIAs, and twenty-seven WIA's. Enemy killed were thirty-five and thirty-three suspected enemy soldiers detained.

[254] The Thirty-First NVA Regiment and the Sapper Battalion No.402 were reported operating on "Charlie" Ridge, near Hill 41.

[255] "Operation Worth," March 12-21, 1968 1/7, 2/7th Marines, and Third/Fifth Cavalry OPCON to 1/7. Approximately fifteen to twenty miles from Da Nang.

[256] We called the road that led north from Route 4 through Dodge City toward Hill 55, Ambush Road.

[257] Seventh Marines, *Command Chronology*, March 1968.

[258] Others described the Dodge City as being from Hill 55 on the north to the RR tracks on the east, to the Song Thu Bon River on the south and on the west bordered by Convoy Road (Route 5).

[259] Spot Report; Co I 3/7 Plt Combat at 1145 hours, AT 975595 Platoon detonated three 60mm rounds rigged as A/p mines. Immediately after, rec'd one incoming grenade, resulting in three WIA. Observed one enemy in black shorts across the river; Called medevac; completed at 1210 hours fired s/a on enemy. Enemy ret'd 100 rounds s/a, observed one enemy fall and his body was observed for ten minutes. Unable to search area due to river barrier. Seventh Marines *Command Chronology*, April 1968.

[260] For his efforts that day while severely wounded and still attempting to help another Marine and his duties as a rifleman during his tour of duty where he displayed leadership and professionalism, Private First Class Prasifka was awarded the Navy Commendation Medal with combat "V" for valor.

[261] Seventh Marines *Command Chronology*, April 1968.

[262] Seventh Marines *Command Chronology*, April 1968.

[263] I 3/7 received 100-rounds small arms, Seventh Marines, *Command Chronology*, April 1968.

[264] Hill 55 received 200 rounds of small arms fire, ten rounds 82mm mortars, (4) 122mm rockets, and one US 2.75 aircraft rocket that damage the power generator. Seventh Marines, *Command Chronology*, April 1968.

[265] Seventh Marines, *Command Chronology*, April 1968.

[266] The Marines were held responsible for having mistreated the prisoner. One was allowed to return to the company, the other two were transferred to another unit. Thomas was never found and is still listed as missing in action.

[267] Seventh Marines, *Command Chronology*, April 1968.

[268] I 3/7 sqd combat patrol at 1700 hours AT 974607 received twenty rounds sniper fire, followed by 500 automatic rounds and ten rounds M-79 from 8-10 enemy, resulting in one USMC KIA. Ret'd fire with M-79, and M-60 at 0556 hours called in 81HE fire mission destroying two hooches. Seventh Marines *Command Chronology*, April 1968.

269 I 3/7 1830 hours, AT 969584 while negotiating a turn traveling South from Hill 55 an M-54 went out of control and overturned resulting in eleven USMC NBC. Squad reaction force from Cap 2-2-2 and I Co sqd on tank and medical tram were dispatched from Hill 55. Five persons were medevaced from Hill 37. Seventh Marines, *Command Chronology*, April 1968.

270 I 3/7 Spot Report of bridge sec at 2030 hours, tank rec'd twenty rounds s/a fire, Ret'd 60mm w/excellent coverage. Seventh Marines *Command Chronology*, April 1968.

271 (Late Entry) Observed fifteen to twenty enemy with weapons approaching ambush site from the west. Opened fire s/a checked area and found two enemy KIA, rest of the enemy believed to have headed northwest. Daily Sit-Rep Seventh Marines, *Command Chronology*, May 1968.

272 Co I 3/7 Platoon ambush at 0300 hours at AT 885572 -884579 ambush site received six 60mm rounds and 100 rounds s/a fire. Returned s/a fire killing 2 enemies, Seventh Marines, *Command Chronology*, May 1968.

273 0600-0730 hours, AT 884579 searched area and found three enemies KIA and 1 WIA. Brought WIA to army district advisors where he was picked up by ITT personnel for interrogation. Captured one M-1 carbine, one AK-47, two magazines, three ChiCom grenades, assorted documents, and ammo.

274 The People's Republic of China sent 320,000 troops to North Vietnam that were integrated into the North Vietnamese Army, states a report from the China News Service, May 1989.

275 For his actions on the morning of May 5, 1968, Ira Rahm was awarded the Bronze Star Medal with Combat "V".

276 Seventh Marines, *Command Chronology*, May 1968.

277 AT 866553 received 6-8 possible 82mm mortar rounds. Returned WP/HE 105mm. Enemy fire ceased. Seventh Marines, *Command Chronology*, May 1968.

278 Co I 3/7 Plt bridge sec (Golden Gate) 0030 hours; AT 966605, rec 25 rounds s/a and eight rounds 60mm mortar fire. No damage to bridge. Ret'd s/a and 60mm and 81mm fire AT 963603, 970603, enemy fire ceased. 1 USMC WIA. Seventh Marines, *Command Chronology*, May 1968.

279 Co I CP 1840 hours, received nine rounds 82mm mortars resulting in one USMC WIA; returned 81mm HE and called 105 Arty Missions. One USMC Medevac Priority Jr Doesn't want next to kin notified. Seventh Marines, *Command Chronology*, May 1968.

280 3/7 to Seventh Marines' Spot rep Co I squad ambush at 2330 hours, AT 867574, after approximately one hour of sitting in ambush site, one shot was heard by all members of Plt. Examination revealed one Marine with Gunshot wound in head. Reason was Marine was lying next to rifle and rifle discharged. One NBC from Radio Bn. Seventh Marines, *Command Chronology*, May 1968.

281 Co I combat sweep at 0130 hours, AT 982602 AT 985606, rec'd fifty rounds semi-auto weapons; fire, returned M-79, s/a fire. Seventh Marines *Command Chronology*, May 1968.

282 Co I 3/7 Plt Swp AT 976576 (sic), rec'd 300 s/a auto rounds, and 5.60mm, rounds. Ret'd s/a. M-79. Called in fire mission with 4.2 mortars HE. Unable to search area due to river barrier. Seventh Marines, *Command Chronology*, May 1968.

283 Co I Plt, at 0600 hours, AT 879558, AT 878555, rec'd approximately 500 rounds s/a and a/w fire. Returned 81mm HE/WP mission and M-72 on enemy position. Unable to search due to river barrier. Follow Up at 0750 hours, AT 879558 detained two VCS carrying rice, in baskets on advice of KC Scout. Seventh Marines, *Command Chronology*, May 1968.

284 Co I Plt combat at 0200 hours, AT 880557, observed ten enemy soldiers in river (seven in water, three in boat), 1 was armed with AK-47. All dressed in black shirts and shorts. Enemy approximately fifteen meters from the ambush engaged enemy with SA. Searched area and found ten VC KIA. Observed enemy movement on flank; Plt withdrew and conducted 105mm fire mission.

285 Unknown to us, that morning, a recon insert by the name of Lucky Lark, at 0620 hours, observed twenty NVA/VC moving north across Song Vu Gia River vicinity (AT 838548). They were wearing black pajamas; with packs and rifles, artillery fire resulted in six VC KIAs. The area they were spotted was east of No Name Village, located near Phuong Trung (1) and Phu Huong (1), First Marine Division, *Command Chronology*, May 1968, p. 39.

286 At 1400 hours, a convoy traveling on Route 4 from Hill 52 to Hill 65 was ambushed and a Company B tank which was escorting the convoy received five RPG hits resulting in one (1) USMC WIA (medevac). The tanks returned fire with unknown results. (Ref: S-3 Journal, May 30, 1968, Entry 11) B-13 USMC # assigned to Hill 55 took the five RPG rounds. One Marine DME 1648, received gun shot wound on jaw. Tank B-31 # 202015 assigned Thoung Duc, and Y34 reacted to ambush from Pennywise CP, Y15 and B32 reacted from Hill 65.

287 MOS shortages as of April 30, 1968 in the thirty-second Battalion: 0331, machine-gunners. Third Battalion, Seventh Marines, *Command Chronology*, April 1968.

288 At 1445 hours, Seventh Marines convoy of twenty trucks and two tanks, with C/1/7 as security was hit by two enemy platoons at AT 826556. Gunship and fixed wing were called for, resulting in thirty-nine NVA KIA. Enemy Activity, First Marine Division, *Command Chronology*, May 1968.

289 On May 30, a convoy was ambushed between CAP 2-2-4 and Hill 52. A platoon from Company; I reacted to the ambush, killing nineteen NVA and capturing several weapons. Narrative Summary; Third Battalion Seventh Marines, *Command Chronology*, May 1-31, 1968.

290 Of the Marines listed as being killed this day, only one PFC Pedro Angel Rodriguez is listed as having served with Charley 1/7 and killed on this day. Neither the Mike Company Platoon nor our platoon suffered any KIAs, unknown how many were wounded. Of the Marines, I saw wounded or killed that day I couldn't find them listed nor ascertain what units were there. Perhaps they were transportation engineers, or other support personnel. I have only found two Charley Company Marines that were

there that day, while they also remember it as a fierce day of battle with heavy casualties suffered; both recalled their Platoon commander after that day, being removed from the field because he didn't put our flanks that day.

[291] Co I 3/7 Plt combat sweep 0800 hrs, AT 815548, while conducting search of area, found one detainee with ChiCom grenade and one KIA armed with an AK-47. Detainee will be forward to 3/7 CP along with captured gear. 3/7, *Command Chronology*, June 1968.

[292] I Co squad ambush at 2230 hrs, AT 964585, while moving into ambush position, squad leader det a 20 lb box mine located fifteen to twenty meters on east side of the road resulting in one USMC KIA and two WIA; crater was four feet in diameter and three feet deep. Squad reactionary force was dispatched from Golden Gate Bridge to assist in the evacuation of casualties. Seventh Marines, *Command Chronology*, June 1968.

[293] Third Battalion, Seventh Marines, *Command Chronology*, May 1968.

[294] Co I 3/7 convoy sec. 0845 hours, AT 837561 Bulldozer detonated 40 lb AT mine damaging 1 wheel and engine. Will retrieve bulldozer to Hill 65 with sec. force at 1100 hours, AT 818550, found one 5 lb AP Mine, Eng. blew in place. 1120 hours, AT 815548 5 lb AP mine, and one 50 lb box mine, Eng blown in place, 1200 hours, AT 814547 found one 55 lb AP mine with pressure release detonator, Eng. destroyed. Seventh Marines, *Command Chronology*, June 1968.

[295] AT 131155H, two First Tank Battalion headquarters' tanks were in support of a convoy when they came under heavy fire at (ZC192559). One tank struck a mine and the other was hit by 57mm recoilless rifle fire. An air strike was called with unknown enemy casualties. There were no friendly casualties. First Tank Battalion, First Marine Division, *Command Chronology*, June 1, 1968 to June 30, 1968 (Ref: S-3 Journal, June 13, 1968, Entry 8).

[296] First Tank Battalion, First Marine Division, *Command Chronology*, June 1, 1968 to June 30, 1968.

[297] Actually instead of a thirteen-month tour of duty, the Corps had implemented a new twelve-month and twenty-day in-county rotation policy.

[298] From the fifteenth until the twenty-third, of June, 1968, I was unable to find the activities of India Company mentioned in any of the command chronologies, after-action reports, unit diaries or daily journals.

[299] Seventh Marines, *Command Chronology*, June 1968.

[300] I had heard that a number of Second Platoon Marines, had been wounded shortly after I left.

Years later, I found out that Captain Robb in a dispute with the Amtrack commander, had all of Second Platoon Marines get on an amtrack, following a road sweep. A short time later, the enemy detonated a command explosive mine, wounding 28 Marines on that amtrack. Robb, never completed his six months tour of duty as a CO for India Company, he was transferred shortly after that incident of August 5, 1968.

INDEX

PHOTO SECTION

Me lower left and Perez, on mail run detail

Vietnamese refugee Kids at dump site

Rice paddies, dike with an agricultural ditch alongside dike

Ron Moore

Boone left and Jones

Goofing around Hill 65

Gun team, Jones myself and Marty on Patrol

Getting ready to assault Hill 42

Back on Hill 65 after Patrol

Operation Knox Dumont, Jones and myself

Ira Rahm and Boyd Operation Knox

Jones, Dumont, tired Aggie and myself Operation Knox

One of several villages destroyed by the NVA

Arizona Territory

Some of our KIA's during Operation Foster

Killed on Foster, 2nd platoon Marines Peterson, left and Williamson right. Doc Avery stands in between the two.

Sgt. Gus, after having to take over 2nd Platoon

Doc Gibbs after the November 19th battle

Myself after combat operation

Aggie (left) and myself a week before he was to leave Vietnam

weapons of our times, M-14, M-16, M-60

Marine Sign on ambush Row

MAPS

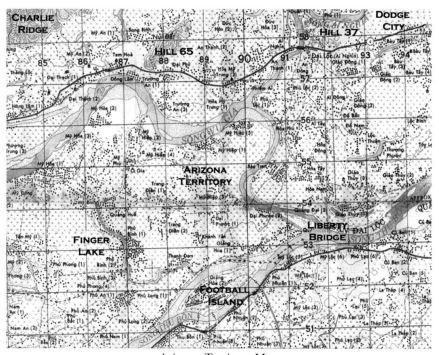

Arizona Territory Map

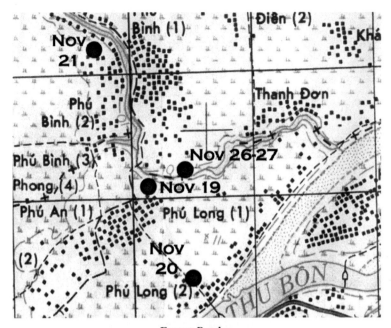

Foster Battles

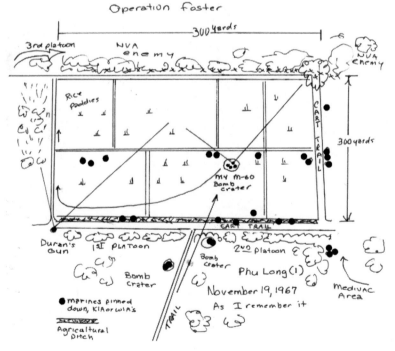

November 19, 1967 Battle

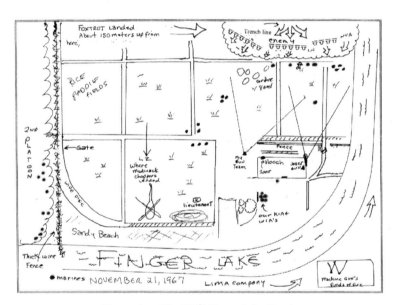

November 21, 1967 Fingerlake Battle